ON THE AGENDA

CURRENT ISSUES AND CONFLICTS IN U.S. FOREIGN POLICY

Howard J. Wiarda

UNIVERSITY OF MASSACHUSETTS, AMHERST

SCOTT, FORESMAN/LITTLE, BROWN HIGHER EDUCATION
A Division of Scott, Foresman and Company

Glenview, Illinois   London, England

Library of Congress Cataloging-in-Publication Data

On the agenda : current issues and conflicts in U.S. foreign policy /
   [edited] by Howard J. Wiarda.
      p.   cm.
   Includes bibliographical references.
   ISBN 0–673–39763–7
   1. United States—Foreign relations—1989– 2. United States—
Foreign relations—1981–1989.   I. Wiarda, Howard J.
E881.05 1990   89–70228
327.73—dc20   CIP

1 2 3 4 5 6–MVN–94 93 92 91 90 89

Preface

American foreign policy and the main issues of American foreign policy are changing so rapidly that it is difficult to keep up with them all. Although we have thought of the Soviet Union as the primary international threat to the United States since World War II, the Soviet social and political system and its empire are undergoing such far-reaching changes that we are no longer certain what our foreign policy response to them ought to be. Even relations between the United States and its traditional allies and with the developing countries of the Third World are undergoing fundamental transformations.

At the same time, a host of new foreign policy issues have come to the fore. We have only begun to figure out the way to grapple with such issues as immigration, hunger, disarmament, drugs, over-population, the environment, terrorism, unpaid (and unpayable) Third World debt, trade imbalances, human rights, and democracy.

On the Agenda: Current Issues and Conflicts in U.S. Foreign Policy focuses on both these new, "hot" issues and the new aspects of some of our more traditional foreign policy concerns. It is not so much concerned with the historic questions of the past as with the exciting and controversial issues that, as one of my foreign policy colleagues put it, are "On the Front Burner"[1] of our current foreign policy debate.

Several criteria were used in deciding what to include in this reader. The book concentrates on the issues that are ready to boil or boiling already on the front burner. It includes good, solid, readable statements from a range of sources, some scholarly and others more popular and journalistic. I have tried to include balanced and sensible points of view and at the same time have tried to provide a variety of perspectives.

A reader such as this one, dealing with current, volatile issues that are affected by ever-changing world events, will always have the potential to be dated almost by the time it is published. For that reason, I have attempted to select articles presenting information that will provide a strong base from which to launch further investigation and serve as a guide to thinking on these issues. The readings here are meant only to introduce a new subject area and not provide final conclusions about it. The list of additional suggested readings included in each chapter encourages readers to explore other materials on these subjects.

On the Agenda was developed to accompany my *Foreign Policy Without Illusion,* also published by Scott, Foresman/Little, Brown (1990),

---

[1]Seyom Brown, *On the Front Burner: Issues in U.S. Foreign Policy* (Boston: Little Brown, 1984).

but it can easily complement any general foreign policy text. As an issue-oriented companion to *Foreign Policy Without Illusion,* a text which analyzes the political processes involved in foreign policy decision-making, *On the Agenda* may be used in either one-term or two-term foreign policy courses. The reader can be used either alongside the main text in a single-term course, or as the main text in the second term of a two-term sequence in which the first term explores the processes of policymaking and the second term focuses on the issues addressed by the processes.

Numerous friends and colleagues have assisted me in the preparation of this book by suggesting essays and readings for inclusion that they consider the best available in their particular areas of expertise. I am particularly indebted to Pauline Baker of the Carnegie Endowment for International Peace, and Eric Einhorn, Peter Haas, Franklin Houn, and Karl Ryavec of the University of Massachusetts/Amherst.

Nevertheless, the final choice of which materials to include was mine alone.

Howard J. Wiarda

Contents

This is an era of considerable ferment in American foreign policy. Not only are our foreign policy-making processes and decision making undergoing major transformations,[1] but the issues that we have to deal with are changing rapidly as well. Many of the old issues are either fading away or undergoing transformation; in the meantime, a host of new issues has come to the fore and become part of our foreign policy agenda.

It used to be that American foreign policy was relatively simple. The Soviet Union was our principal antagonist in the world, the only country that had the capacity to destroy us, and therefore it was our obligation to contain Soviet expansionism. For this purpose we relied on our allies, principally those European countries associated with us in NATO (the North Atlantic Treaty Organization). To prevent Soviet expansionism in Asia, we helped restore the economies of Japan and the other smaller countries, and we eventually learned to play the "China card"—that is, to play China, the other great communist country in the world, against the Soviet Union. In the Third World we formed regional defense blocs, provided economic aid, and sought to prevent any other countries from going communist.

But recently the world that we have known since World War II has turned topsy-turvy and become far more complex. The Soviet Union may be in the process of reducing its commitments abroad. Its Eastern European empire is in considerable turmoil, and the Soviet Union itself may be concentrating on domestic restructuring rather than new foreign policy adventurism. In the process, while the Soviet military arsenal is still formidable and continues to constitute a threat to us, Soviet society and its political system are undergoing considerable change. We are not certain whether we should help that process along or try to prevent it.

Meanwhile, as the Soviet threat has appeared to diminish, our allies in both Asia and Europe have become stronger and increasingly want to go their own way. Both Japan and the countries of the European Economic Community now compete with us globally on the economic front, and more and more they are pursuing independent foreign policies as well. China is also going its own way, even toward a new *rapprochement* with the Soviet Union. And Third World countries are similarly pursuing more independent foreign policies, trying to break out of the American orbit of influence but in the meantime heading toward future eco-

---

[1] Howard J. Wiarda, *Foreign Policy Without Illusion: How Foreign Policy Works and Fails to Work in the United States* (Glenview, IL: Scott, Foresman/Little, Brown, 1989).

nomic and political calamity because of the debt issue and other problems.

While these older, more traditional issues in U.S. foreign policy are undergoing transformation, a large number of new issues are becoming more prominent. While these have not often received much attention in the past, they are now "hot" and controversial. The new issues include world hunger, democracy and human rights, the environment, population control, immigration, drugs, terrorism, Third World debt, trade, North-South relations, and disarmament. These issues have acquired a new-found importance; moreover, they have begun to shove aside some of the old issues—such as containing the Soviet Union—that used to be our main foreign policy preoccupations.

That is why we may be entering a new era in American foreign policy. All the old alliance systems are now being severely questioned, the Soviet Union may be on the verge of fundamental restructuring (or unraveling), and the *whole agenda* of foreign policy issues seems now to be changing. That is in essence the focus of this book.

CAUSES AND AREAS OF CHANGE

Why have all these changes in our foreign policy agenda taken place? What causes one issue to fade away or to become, over time, less important on our list of priorities, while others rise in importance? Are there any patterns to these changes to help us sort them out and understand them better?

There are, in fact, patterns and broad, sweeping trends at work that help us understand this changing foreign policy agenda. Here we identify six such changes: changes in communist regimes; greater affluence, independence, and assertiveness on the part of our allies; changed international economic relationships; the rise of new global issues; the greater independence and assertiveness of the Third World; and changed foreign policy preoccupations and concerns. Each of these areas of change is discussed in the following paragraphs.

The Soviet Union has long been our chief adversary in the world and the main potential threat to our security. But profound changes are now sweeping through both the Soviet Union and the Soviet international system. The Soviet Union is undergoing a major transformation and is facing serious crises. The crises include (1) a crisis of ideology (few people believe the Marxist-Leninist ideology anymore); (2) a crisis of the economy, which has proved to be enormously inefficient and even backward; (3) a crisis of leadership (a rapid succession of premiers, uncertainty about Chairman Gorbachev's tenure); (4) a crisis of society (severe generation gaps, ethnic and nationality discontents); (5) a crisis of institutions, including an inefficient bureaucracy and challenges to the Communist Party's monopoly of power; and (6) a crisis of morale—in the sense of widespread discontent with, disillusionment with, and cynicism about the regime. The communist system is not yet threatened internally, but there certainly is a great deal of discontent and even some fragmentation within the Soviet regime.

All these changes in the Soviet Union have immense implications for foreign policy. Has the Soviet Union been weakened? Can it no longer control its restive East European allies? Are the Soviets no longer a threat to us? Is the Cold War over? Did we win? Can we now look forward to an easing of tensions between the superpowers or, alternatively, would a weakened and insecure Soviet Union constitute an even greater danger to us? These are among the major *new issues* in U.S.-Soviet relations, issues that may have rendered a great deal of our earlier strategic thinking obsolete. A large number of very important foreign policy decisions depend on the proper response to these critical questions by U.S. government officials, as well as by the general public.

The second area of change concerns our allies. It used to be that our allies, in Europe and elsewhere, were economically weak and absolutely dependent on the United States for their defense. Hence they generally followed the U.S. lead on foreign policy matters. But now our allies have become increasingly affluent, their economies are robust (thinking particularly of Japan, West Germany, and France), and they are no longer quite so inclined to follow the U.S. lead. These countries have developed strong and often more independent foreign policies of their own; they have not fully trusted recent American leadership (either Carter or Reagan); and they do not always see the issues in quite the same way that we do. For example, Western European leaders want to trade more extensively with the Soviet Union and Eastern Europe. They no longer see the Soviet Union as constituting a major threat, and they are strongly opposed to even the mention of war with the Soviet Union—since it would very likely be fought on their territory—and to U.S. rhetoric and saber-rattling on these issues.

Hence, in terms of our relations with our allies, as well as with the Soviet Union, we are in a new era. Our relations with our allies are sometimes testy. NATO is in crisis as the reason for its existence (the Soviet threat) seems to be diminishing. In southern Europe (Portugal, Spain, Italy, Greece, and Turkey) there are a number of socialist governments that are not always in sympathy with American perceptions. Their foreign policies are often more oriented toward the Mediterranean than toward the Soviet threat. Long-festering hatreds exist between two countries, Greece and Turkey, that are ostensibly part of the Western Alliance but are more interested in fighting each other. There is also the problem of German nationalism and the desire for reunification, which might well result in the neutralization of Europe's strategic central area. Europeans also want to be free to trade with the East, with the Soviet Union and Eastern Europe; such trade is leading to rising demands for change in the East, the blurring of the Iron Curtain separating the Western from the communist countries, and a growing trend toward a pulling-apart of both NATO and the Warsaw Pact.

The third major area of change affecting our foreign policy is in the economic realm. The United States still has the world's most powerful economy, which continues to grow and expand—but not relative to some other economies that have also grown. For one thing, the United States can no longer afford to be the policeman of the world, to get involved in every small skirmish everywhere, and there are immense pressures to reduce our defense budget. For another, economic issues—trade, debt, interdependence—have begun to have an importance that rivals the strategic issues. If the Cold War begins to wind down, these economic issues will acquire even greater importance. The increased importance of economic issues has also brought to the fore agencies of the United States government (the Treasury and Commerce departments, the office of the U.S. Trade Representative) that never played important foreign policy roles before but now have an importance rivaling that of the State or Defense departments. For students, there are two lessons to be drawn from these trends: (1) study economics and political economy as well as international politics and (2) apply for jobs in Treasury, Commerce, or the Trade Representative's office and not just in the traditional foreign service.

The fourth area of change is in the rise of new global issues that had not been of major international concern before. The rise of these new issues results in part from the fact that the Cold War no longer seems so threatening; therefore, we can now afford to pay greater attention to other matters. These include such issues as world hunger, immigration, population, drug trafficking, and the environment. Historically, our major foreign policy concerns have been primarily political, military, and strategic; but now these "new issues" command at least as much attention as the more traditional ones. And, like the economic issues previously discussed, these new issues have brought to prominence agencies of the U.S. government that have not had very much foreign policy experience or expertise in the past: the Drug Enforcement Agency, the Immigration and Naturalization Service, the Justice Department, and others. Not only are there a host of new issues to deal with, but there are now a large number of agencies that have gotten into the foreign policy "act," with enormous consequences for the conduct of American foreign policy.

The fifth major area of change is in the Third World. At one time, the countries of the Third World were mere pawns in the Cold War, clients of the two superpowers. Now that has changed as well: nationalism is rising, and the clients are no longer content to be treated as clients. Many Third World nations have become more assertive and independent—even from the super-powers. Quite a number of them—Egypt, Iran, India, Pakistan, Indonesia, Nigeria, Brazil, Mexico, Venezuela, Argentina—have made it into the ranks of what the World Bank calls Newly Industrialized Countries, or NICs. They have become not only economic but also political and military powers within their respective regions, with aspirations to play larger roles. Few of them are willing simply to follow the U.S. lead on foreign policy matters anymore, and quite a number—like Brazil or India—have the resources to strike off on their own.

Once again, these changes imply major adjustments in U.S. foreign policy, and we know that the Soviet Union is having similar problems with its client states. It will no longer do for the U.S. to treat these aspiring, ambitious Third World countries with disdain and condescension or to expect that they will simply follow our lead. In the past, our policy toward them has often alternated between benign neglect and indifference on the one hand and dramatic interventions on the other. But now we need a policy toward the Third World based on maturity and a sustained interest—as we have long maintained with Western Europe—and on the recognition that we are in many ways interdependent with them in terms of trade and political interests, just as we are with Japan and other countries. Hence, we will need to reexamine and likely reformulate our policies regarding Third World debt, the North-South dialogue (involving conflicts between the developed, wealthy, industrialized countries of the northern hemisphere and the developing, poorer countries of the southern hemisphere), and numerous other issues.

The sixth area of change is in terms of new foreign policy concerns and preoccupations. In addition to those already listed (hunger, population, and the like), a variety of moral and ethical concerns have also become prominent. These include disarmament issues, as well as democracy and human rights concerns. These new ethical concerns have taken their place alongside, and in some cases supersede, the historic concern for defending the national interest. In a sense, they have forced us to *redefine*

the national interest, no longer in purely military-strategic terms, but in terms that also incorporate human rights and democracy. Even the hardest-nosed practicioners of *realpolitik,* such as Henry Kissinger, have concluded that in this era and in this country, we cannot have a successful foreign policy without incorporating into it a strong democracy/human rights component. So any calculus of U.S. national interest and of a successful foreign policy must now include these concerns.

These are among the major new driving forces and issues in foreign policy. They force us to rethink many of our foreign policy assumptions of the past. For in many respects we are in a completely new era in foreign policy making. New areas of tension as well as a whole slate of new foreign policy issues have come to dominate the agenda. Policy-makers in the U.S. government usually have access to more raw information about many of these issues than the rest of us do, but quite frankly they are often as mystified by what all these changes *mean*—and what the U.S. policy *response* should be—as is the general American population. One thing is certain, however: unless we as citizens, as well as policy-makers, begin understanding these issues soon and devising appropriate responses to them, American foreign policy could quickly be in deep trouble: outdated, irrelevant, and by-passed by the great issues that are stirring the world. Hence it is critically important that we begin examining these issues, coming to grips with them, and formulating a sensible, coherent, long-term foreign policy in response to them.

THE BOOK: A LOOK AHEAD

This book is divided into two parts. In the first part, called "Regions of Conflict," we examine changing American relations with the Soviet Union and the Eastern bloc, with NATO, Asia, the Middle East, Latin America, and southern Africa. These are the main crisis areas for U.S. foreign policy. In the second part, entitled, "Issues in Contention," we look at the new issues in American foreign policy: drugs, immigration, hunger, population, the environment, terrorism, Third World debt, disarmament, trade, North-South relations, and human rights and democracy.

Each section is preceded by a short introduction to the subject matter that follows. And since in a comprehensive issues volume such as this we cannot possibly provide *all* the diverse points of view and background necessary for a full understanding, each section concludes with a list of suggested additional readings.

PART ONE

Regions of Conflict

*
*

CHAPTER ONE

The Soviet Union and Eastern Europe

✳
✳

The Soviet Union has been, since World War II, the United States' foremost rival and antagonist, and it is the only country that has the power to destroy us. Now, however, we seem to be in a new era. Or are we? The reforms opened up by Chairman Gorbachev have been significant, but how much has really changed in the U.S.-Soviet relationship?

The Soviet Union is experiencing severe tensions. Essentially, these are the tensions faced by a former Third World nation, which is still underdeveloped in many respects (except for its modern military and nuclear capacity) as it makes the transition to modernity. The question is, can a rigid, sometimes ossified, bureaucratic authoritarian or totalitarian regime adjust itself to the requirements of modern pluralism, technological change, a modern economy, and the desire for greater freedom, *glasnost* ("openness"), and *perestroika* ("restructuring")? These tensions have become especially severe in recent years, leading some analysts to conclude that the Soviet Union might unravel, that the "great and glorious" experiment that is communism is dead and finished. Others are not so sure that the Soviet Union is about to fall apart and suggest that it remains a dangerous adversary. Still others would have us go so far as to assist Gorbachev against his domestic foes and aid the Soviet Union as it embarks on this quest for liberalization.

The foreign policy implications of these domestic changes in the Soviet Union are enormous. But because our experts disagree about the nature of these domestic changes and what our response to them should be, we are not entirely sure what the foreign policy implications will be either. Will the Soviet Union's efforts to reform and restructure its domestic economy result in its devoting less attention to foreign affairs? Is the Soviet Union beginning a process of retreating from its global superpower role, or will it find a way to hang on to its empire? Do the failures of the Soviet system mean that Marxism-Leninism will no longer constitute an attractive alternative model? Is it really true that we won the Cold War, that the Soviet Union cannot keep up with the United States economically and technologically? If it is true, should we put added pressures on their system (through the building of SDI, the Strategic Defense Initiative, for example), or should we ease up in the Cold War as they ease up? Will a reformed and restructured Soviet Union be a more dangerous antagonist or a less dangerous one? And based on our answer to that question, should we help Gorbachev along with his reforms or try to frustrate them?

If the Soviet Union is going to be preoccupied with its domestic reforms for the next few years, does that mean its hold on Eastern Europe will lessen and that we should therefore seize that opportunity to woo Eastern Europe closer to the West? Or, alternatively, will the whole Soviet empire begin to crumble, and if it does, should we see that as a strategic opportunity to take advantage of, or a potentially destabilizing situation that we should seek to avoid? What about regional conflicts in the Third World? Do the Soviets' new domestic preoccupations mean they will try to reduce their Third World commitments, and does that mean that in such far-flung areas as Southeast Asia, southern Africa, and Central America that the U.S. will be in a better bargaining position and the Soviets a weaker one—even to the point that they will try to extricate themselves from some of these Third World conflicts and no longer be willing to support such Third World "basket cases" as Ethiopia and Nicaragua?

These are among the questions raised by recent changes in the Soviet Union. The readings that follow begin to grapple with many of these issues, but they by no means resolve them all.

Our readings on the Soviet Union begin with a balanced overview of recent changes there by the New York-based Foreign Policy Association. Then, in a provocative commentary, Robert Kaiser analyzes Prime Minister Gorbachev's foreign policy "new thinking"; he also suggests the Soviet Union may be beginning a process of unraveling. Finally, in a brief statement, Secretary of State James Baker suggests the continuance of a prudent and gradualist policy toward the Soviet Union.

The Soviet Union   *Gorbachev's Reforms*

Early in June 1987, Soviet citizens in 5% of the U.S.S.R.'s more than 50,000 districts went to the polls, not to vote approval for the usual single candidate on the ballot, but to choose among several candidates for local office approved by the party. In March, Moscow announced that Boris Pasternak's *Doctor Zhivago,* formerly banned in the Soviet Union and its author denounced as a "pig rooting in our Soviet garden," would be released in the U.S.S.R. In early August 1987, a Soviet comedian complained to a *New York Times* reporter that he no longer had any material; since today "we can say anything we want ... nobody is very interested. The newspapers are already saying it." In October 1987, Moscow announced it would pay all its outstanding debts to the United Nations, including $197 million for peace-keeping forces, which it has refused to finance in the past on the grounds that they are illegal. And within two months of being released from internal exile in the city of Gorky, noted physicist, dissident, and human rights activist Andrei Sakharov made a speech in which he expressed his approval of the Soviet Union's new leader, Mikhail S. Gorbachev, under whose rule all of these things have occurred.

Gorbachev has been surprising people since he succeeded Konstantin Chernenko as general secretary of the Communist party on March 11, 1985. He has impressed Western diplomats and leaders with his intelligence, his outgoing manner and his imaginative approach to a variety of issues. At home, he has shaken up the party bureaucracy, cracked down on alcoholism and absenteeism among Soviet workers, permitted some dissidents and Soviet Jews to emigrate and loosened restraints in the arts and the press. At a plenary meeting of the Central Committee of the Communist party in June 1987, Gorbachev announced a range of economic reforms that included legalizing some small-scale private enterprise and allowing those running state-owned businesses to decide how to spend some of their profits.

In the West, Gorbachev has prompted questions, at first, about whether his actions were any more than window dressing and, more recently, about whether the reforms he is pursuing will be drastic enough to produce the results he wants. Above all, observers wonder whether a reformed Soviet Union would be good or bad for the U.S.

What is Gorbachev up to? What are his intentions? How significant are the changes he is implementing, and what are the implications of his reform program for the U.S.?

A Country in Crisis?

Gorbachev's accession to power in March 1985 ended a protracted succession crisis. Leonid I. Brezhnev, who died in November 1982, had ruled the Soviet Union for 18 years of unprecedented political stability. His tenure was characterized by such low turnover in the upper echelons of the government and Communist party apparatus that the people available to take over when he died were almost as old and as ill as he had been.

The election of Yuri Andropov, 68, as general secretary to succeed Brezhnev seemed to reflect a recognition by some in the Kremlin that the Soviet Union needed to be shaken out of the torpor of the later Brezhnev years. Although Andropov was a reformer, he ruled for only 15 months before dying in February 1984. His successor was Konstantin Chernenko, 73, a Brezhnev protégé. The Chernenko regime abandoned Andropov's reform program in all but name and undertook no major initiatives, either on the domestic or the foreign policy front. Thirteen months after his election, much of which he spent out of sight because of poor health, Chernenko died.

Soviet fortunes in 1985, both domestic and international, were in a state of decline. Although Brezhnev had achieved some economic successes and had presided over the Soviet Union's emergence as a military superpower, economic growth had slowed dramatically since the 1960s. Labor productivity fell as the ready availability of energy and other needed raw materials declined and as industrial machinery and equipment aged. In agriculture, the Soviet Union, which had been a net exporter of grain in 1963, was heavily reliant on imports by the early 1980s. Despite heavy investment throughout the Brezhnev era, agricultural productivity fell drastically after the mid-1970s. When poor weather caused four straight disastrous harvests beginning in 1979, food shortages became so severe that rationing had to be adopted in major Soviet cities in 1981–82—

Source: From *Great Decisions 1988,* Foreign Policy Association, New York, 1989. Reprinted by permission.

despite the importation of some 40 million tons of grain. Average citizens have experienced Soviet economic woes daily in the form of shoddy manufactured goods and long lines for staples that may well run out by the time they get to the counter.

As economic troubles multiplied, so did social problems. Corruption in government and industry flourished, as did alcoholism and absenteeism in the workplace. The divorce rate rose, life expectancy dropped and infant mortality climbed to levels more on the order of a developing country than of one of the world's largest economies. These statistics did not bode well for the Soviet Union at a time of labor shortages and low worker productivity.

Internationally, after reaching a pinnacle of military and diplomatic power and prestige in the mid-1970s, Moscow suffered reversals in countries where it had invested heavily. In December 1979, the Soviet Union invaded Afghanistan to prop up the pro-Soviet government there, which was under attack by Muslim resistance groups. That war cost Moscow over $5 billion and claimed an estimated 12,000 Soviet lives. Unrest in Poland, geographically the most important of the Soviet Union's East European allies, became so severe in 1980–81 that the Polish government imposed martial law.

Many of the Communist party elite feared these problems were gradually undermining the viability of Communist party rule. Arkady N. Shevchenko, a Soviet diplomat who defected and is now a U.S. citizen, has written that they "became increasingly concerned that social and economic stagnation, complemented by the population's

inertia, apathy, and cynicism, would undermine the foundation of the Soviet system … and, along with it, their own positions and privileges. For the powerful, an urgent need to keep the regime viable dictated national renovation."

Reform in the Soviet Union

Gorbachev's rise to the top, Shevchenko concludes, "was no accident." But even if Gorbachev was brought in as general secretary with a mandate from a significant portion of the Soviet political elite for reform, he still has to tread very carefully: alienating his chief constituencies could result in his removal from office.

There have been reform movements in the U.S.S.R. before. In 1921, V. I. Lenin introduced his New Economic Policy (NEP) in an attempt to win the support of the Soviet peasantry, which had suffered greatly during the civil war of 1917–21. NEP policies permitted some of the economy to be regulated by market mechanisms, although heavy industry remained under state control. But the NEP did not outlive Lenin; his successor Joseph Stalin abolished it by 1929 as part of his industrialization drive.

It was Stalin who created the present centralized Soviet economic system to help him direct all available resources into heavy industry as the first step of a crash modernization program. The plan worked: during the 1930s, while Western economies were mired in the Great Depression, Soviet gross national product (GNP) grew 8–9% a year, and industrial production grew by nearly 15% annually. Economic growth continued at impressive rates well into the 1950s.

But Stalin's accomplishment was achieved through extreme

measures and at tremendous cost. In order to extract as much production from Soviet agriculture as cheaply as possible to feed industrial workers, Stalin confiscated the farms and goods of the Soviet peasantry, forcing them onto collective farms between 1929 and 1931. When the wealthy peasants, or kulaks, resisted, Stalin announced that they were to be "liquidated as a class" and their property expropriated. Millions lost their lives during collectivization and the 1931–32 famine that it led to.

Stalin also cemented his political power by unleashing his secret police to sow fear, insecurity and suspicion among the Soviet populace and ruling class. During the 1930s, Stalin rid himself of real and imagined political enemies in the "great purge," which resulted in tens of thousands of deaths—some estimate many times that number.

Nikita S. Khrushchev led the Soviet Union first as one of three top leaders after Stalin's death in 1953 and then alone from 1957 to 1964. His main and lasting achievement was to eliminate the use of terror as a political instrument. He also ended the Soviet Union's extreme isolation in the world and lifted many of the stifling restrictions on the arts that Stalin had imposed. Khrushchev's brief cultural "thaw" included publication of books like Alexander Solzhenitsyn's novel of life in a Stalinist labor camp, *One Day in the Life of Ivan Denisovich.* Khrushchev was ousted largely because some of his later ideas on organizational reforms threatened to undercut the position of a large portion of the party bureaucracy.

Brezhnev, who succeeded Khrushchev, restored the stability and predictability that the Khrushchev years had upset. Central party bureaucrats gained both power and job security. Stability was also assured by a return of repression: an extensive secret police network was revived, although not the use of terror. Brezhnev's economic policies, which focused on investment in consumer goods, also provided stability through a sizable rise in the standard of living for Soviet citizens, especially the poorest. Some structural reforms aimed at checking the continued decline in economic growth were attempted during the early Brezhnev years, but they did not work well and were quickly abandoned.

Andropov, during his brief tenure, concentrated on a discipline campaign aimed at improving the productivity of Soviet managers and workers. Following the Chernenko interlude, this is where Gorbachev picked up upon taking office in March 1985.

Gorbachev: Power and Limits

Gorbachev was born to a peasant family near Stavropol in 1931. Trained as a lawyer and as an agronomist, he is better educated than most of his predecessors and has enjoyed an unusually rapid political ascent.

Gorbachev's power derives from his position as the head of the Communist party, the source of all power in the U.S.S.R. The party controls the nation's economy and all aspects of daily life. As general secretary, Gorbachev heads the party bureaucracy and chairs the meetings of the Politburo, its chief decision-making body. He is also head of the Secretariat, the permanent staff for the Politburo, which gives him additional control over scheduling and the agenda for Po-

litburo meetings. The general secretary also has considerable influence over appointments and dismissals in all the bureaucracies. His position therefore gives him a high degree of control over the entire process of making and implementing policy.

Gorbachev's first order of business was to replace as many ineffectual holdovers from the Brezhnev era as he could with people loyal to him. By mid-1987, 40% of the Central Committee's 307 seats had changed hands. He also expanded the 11-member Politburo by adding three supporters and installed several more as nonvoting members. Most Western experts think that his political position today is fairly strong. But Gorbachev is out to make radical changes, a potentially risky course because it involves upsetting vested interests. Change can also get out of hand, producing unintended results. For these reasons, experts are divided as to how long they think Gorbachev can last.

The New Buzzwords

By the end of Gorbachev's second year in office, Westerners and Soviets alike had heard a lot about *glasnost,* meaning "openness" or "public airing." In today's press, Soviet citizens can read about their country's problems as well as criticisms of high—though not top-level—Communist party officials. Books, films, and plays banned for years have been released, and internationally renowned human rights activists like Anatoly Scharansky have been permitted to emigrate to Israel and elsewhere.

The significance of these moves is the subject of considerable debate in the West. Figures compiled by Helsinki Watch reveal that some

200 out of 500 known political prisoners have been released since January 1987. Although Jewish emigration figures are up significantly (over 5,000 for the first three quarters of 1987), they are still well below the 1979 peak of 51,000. Press attacks on public officials have, with one or two exceptions, not extended to the Soviet secret police, the KGB. And court procedures for those convicted of political crimes have not been reformed, although new legislation is reportedly under consideration.

Is glasnost, then, designed primarily for Western consumption? Many believe so; one former Soviet journalist, for example, argues that the U.S.S.R today is like a giant gate, cracked open just far enough for those outside it to see what the Soviet leaders want them to.

Others see glasnost as a shrewd political tactic calculated to get the Soviet intelligentsia to help Gorbachev expose the weaknesses in Soviet society to the public, and to generate support for reform. A *New York Times* editorial described it as a "club handed by Mr. Gorbachev to Russian intellectuals to beat economic inefficiency out of the bureaucracy." One U.S. government expert suggests that glasnost may encourage a broader debate on the system, which will then give Gorbachev a wider menu of acceptable options to choose from as he seeks to reform it. What it is not, most Western experts emphasize, is any indication that Gorbachev is moving toward a Western concept of openness or democracy.

THE SOVIET ECONOMY

Gorbachev has emphasized repeatedly that reviving the economy is his top priority. He set the tone for his program at the 27th Communist party congress in late February 1986 with a speech that was highly critical of the system. Gorbachev spoke of the damaging "inertia and rigidity of the forms and methods of administration, the decline of dynamism in our work, and the growth of bureaucracy." He criticized his predecessors' tendency to try "to improve things without changing anything," and he promised that Soviet industrial output and GNP would double by the end of the century.

Accomplishing this will require the Soviet economy to expand at twice its current annual rate—no mean feat for an economy best described by the old joke, "They pretend to pay us and we pretend to work." Soviet economic growth has fallen each decade since the 1950s, crawling along at 2–3% a year—a rate lower than any industrialized country other than Britain.

There is nothing disgraceful about a 2–3% economic growth rate—unless you are a Marxist-Leninist. Marx predicted that communism, lacking the injustices and inequalities present in a system based on private property, would solve economic problems better than capitalism could. It has been the goal of every Soviet leader since Lenin to overtake and surpass the economies of the leading capitalist nations. Economic expert Joseph Berliner compares Gorbachev's problem to that of an American mayor whose city can claim the best baseball player—in the minor leagues. With less output per person than capitalist countries, the Soviet Union will not be able to move into the major leagues unless it can raise its low rate of growth.

Doing so, Western economists agree, will be extraordinarily diffi-

cult. The Soviet economy is owned by the state, planned by the Communist party leadership and managed through a huge, unwieldy bureaucracy. The central planning agency, Gosplan, passes party directives on to scores of different economic ministries, which tell the 37,000 or so local enterprises what and how much to produce. Economic plans are rigid, with quotas set equal to or higher than the target for the previous year, and managers are rewarded for making their quotas on time. There are few incentives for attention to quality, which might make a manager miss his production deadline and therefore his bonus. Quality is also not reflected in a product's price. Because of the lack of a rational price system, there are also few incentives to keep down the costs of materials or to use them efficiently. *The Economist* magazine noted in 1985 that the U.S.S.R. uses roughly two to four times the amount of coal and steel that Western countries do to produce an equivalent amount of revenue from finished goods.

In spite of the fact that it employs more than a quarter of the population (compared with about 3% in the U.S.), Soviet agriculture is so inefficient that Moscow must rely heavily on grain imports. (Approximately 20% of the annual Soviet harvest is left to rot in the fields because of inadequate storage and transportation facilities.) Roughly one third of total annual Soviet investments in the economy go to agriculture, much of it in the form of subsidies which keep food prices artificially low. With demand for cheap foodstuffs consistently higher than the supply, chronic shortages occur. Corruption thrives in this environment, as peo-

ple who can provide goods or services that are in short supply are eager for the cash they can earn by doing so.

The one sector of the economy that does not suffer from these chronic problems is defense. The military has always had first claim on the country's best brains and resources, and the interminable delays that characterize most economic activity are usually absent in defense projects. Pay is higher and benefits are better. The military also uses resources more lavishly than other sectors of the economy and has higher standards for quality control.

Brezhnev built up the military through a steady 4% annual growth in defense expenditures from the mid-1960s to the mid-1970s. As a result, the Soviet Union emerged as a military superpower, on a par with its major adversary, the U.S. The dichotomy between the Soviet Union's military strength and the weakness of the rest of its economy is what Sovietologist Seweryn Bialer refers to as "the Soviet paradox": "internal decline coupled with awesome military power."

Gorbachev's Agenda

"Acceleration of the socioeconomic development of the country is the key to all our problems," Gorbachev told the delegates to the 27th party congress in early 1986. Over the next year and a half he hammered out the specifics of a program that he hopes will not only increase the efficiency of the existing system but actually equip the economy better for greater scientific and technological progress.

During his first two years as general secretary, Gorbachev attacked laziness and inefficiency and waged a harsh law-and-order campaign aimed at increasing discipline and productivity in the workplace. Penalties for absenteeism and drinking on the job were stiffened. Gorbachev also made it illegal to buy vodka before 2:00 in the afternoon, raised its price and reduced its supply.

Gorbachev replaced scores of officials at all levels. Many local authorities, who had basically been allowed to operate as a law unto themselves during the Brezhnev years, have been made accountable to the central authorities.

'To Each According to His Work'

Although he talked a great deal about the need for *perestroika* (restructuring) and *demokratizatsiya* (democratization) as well as *glasnost* Gorbachev did not lay out specific steps for overhauling the creaky Soviet economic machinery until early in his third year in office. At that point even those most skeptical about Gorbachev's intention to implement truly radical reforms were impressed by the far-reaching nature of the proposals he presented at a plenary meeting of the Central Committee in June 1987.

The new Law on the Socialist Enterprise has made profitability, rather than plan fulfillment, the main criterion of economic performance. As of January 1988, employees of the Soviet Union's 37,000 largest enterprises will not be eligible for raises or bonuses if their plants do not show a profit. The law will apply to all Soviet enterprises by 1991. Such a policy means that a higher degree of income disparity will have to be tolerated. This poses some interesting questions for a socialist society,

where such inequalities are not supposed to exist. But Gorbachev and his economic advisers seem to have recognized that greater income differentials are necessary if individuals are to have an incentive to work harder. "Work, and work alone, should be the criterion for determining a person's value, his social prestige and his material status," Gorbachev said in February 1987. "Some will come off badly—the slacker, the drunkard, the slovenly. Let them not take offense—they are getting what they deserve."

The law also gives individual enterprises more autonomy. Farm and factory managers will no longer be able to count on receiving funds from the government but will be expected to run their operations with the revenues their activities bring in. Managers will also be able to decide for themselves how to spend some of their profits—whether to reinvest in plant and equipment or to raise salaries, for example. By 1991, Gorbachev wants all central planning agencies out of the day-to-day management of individual enterprises altogether.

Gorbachev also won ratification for part of his plan to have local managers elected, rather than appointed, possibly on the theory that popular managers can get more out of their workers. The state quality control system has also been overhauled. Since early 1987, quality inspectors have been employed by an independent state agency instead of by the factories they are charged with inspecting as was formerly the case. The new system has met considerable resistance, not only from plant managers whose authority is imperiled by the new plan but also from workers whose bonuses have been

reduced because of the poor quality of their output.

Consideration is also being given to forcing plants that consistently lose money into bankruptcy. Such a policy would mean that significant unemployment will become a possibility for the first time since 1931, when it was officially declared nonexistent in the Soviet Union. Gorbachev has recommended the creation of retraining programs for workers whose factories are closed.

Unemployment will become an even touchier issue if Gorbachev overhauls the price system by making prices more accurately reflect costs. In most cases this would result in prices rising as state subsidies are cut back. Gorbachev did not try to get this move ratified at the recent plenum, possibly because he lacked adequate political support in the Central Committee.

Gorbachev is also encouraging the private sector of the economy, which until now has flourished outside the law. Today it is no longer illegal for a Soviet citizen to run a taxi service with his car during his off hours. He may not, however, quit his state job to drive his cab full time, so it is hard to tell how much additional individual enterprise will take place. Taxes are also a question: will people who ran their own businesses off the books before now register them legally if it means their income will be heavily taxed?

Trade and the Economy

Soviet exports beyond Eastern Europe are very weak, consisting largely of raw materials, especially oil and gas. The fall in oil prices in recent years has hurt Soviet hard-currency earnings. To remedy this situation, Gorbachev has removed some of the many administrative blocks to foreign trade. Soviet firms can now arrange deals directly with companies outside the country instead of having to go through state organizations. Joint ventures—formerly a doctrinally unacceptable option—have also been legalized, making it possible for foreigners to own up to 49% of a Soviet enterprise. Moscow hopes that such ventures will open new markets for the goods they produce, as well as provide greater access to Western expertise and technology.

Gorbachev's discipline campaign and administrative reshuffling produced noticeable effects almost immediately, and economic indicators improved after his first year in office. But will the program be enough to double the Soviet GNP and standard of living by the end of the century?

Unlike Stalin, Gorbachev does not have the option of increasing output by pouring increasing quantities of people and resources into priority sectors of the economy, a strategy known as "extensive" growth, because resources and manpower are no longer as cheap or readily available as they were in Stalin's day. Even if they were, they could only help Gorbachev build more factories and more machines—not necessarily better machinery. What Gorbachev needs now is "intensive" growth, which requires technological innovation. At the 27th party congress, Gorbachev made this point when he said he was after "a new quality of growth: an all-out intensification of production on the basis of scientific-technical   progress...." He wants the Soviet Union to become competitive internationally even in high-technology fields like electronics and computers.

Outside of the military sector, however, the Soviets have not done well at technological innovation. High-technology fields change rapidly, which puts a premium on quick decisionmaking. "The more quickly technology moves," notes the American Soviet economic expert Marshall Goldman, "the harder it is for large bureaucratic units to keep up...."

Another problem is that the Soviet leadership has always maintained tight control over access to information and communications. As one observer has noted, "a society that treats the telephone as a suspicious instrument, [and] classifies and locks up mimeograph and xerox machines ... obviously handcuffs itself." A computer system works best if individual terminals are linked together by a reliable phone system, something the U.S.S.R. lacks. Moreover, any computer connected to a printer is a potential printing press, and private ownership of presses is prohibited. Although Gorbachev has called for computer literacy of the entire generation of young Soviets now in school, it will take some doing. As of early 1986, the best personal computer the Soviet Union had manufactured weighed 110 pounds and had one tenth the capacity of its 28-pound IBM equivalent.

There are some who dispute this assessment of Soviet computer technology. Seymour Goodman, management and information systems expert at the University of Arizona, says that despite failures the Soviets "are doing better than all but the U.S. and Japan. They are not in the dark ages." In addition, barred by the U.S. and other countries from importing computer technology legally, the Soviet Union has long engaged in a suc-

cessful espionage effort to obtain the technologies it wants for its defense and other industries.

A more pervasive obstacle to innovation has been what *New York Times* economic columnist Leonard Silk calls the "gridlock dilemma." Where is the incentive for a Soviet worker to produce more and better goods in order to make more money, until there are quality goods on which to spend that money? And how can Gorbachev provide those high-quality goods unless he solves this problem first?

Prospects

"We intend to make socialism stronger, not replace it with another system," Gorbachev reminded an audience in July 1987. But many Western economists believe that the contradictions inherent in trying to impose market-style reforms on a centrally planned economy will ultimately doom Gorbachev's efforts. "The Soviet economy needs its inefficiencies to remain Soviet," in Silk's words; making it work better would require weakening party control over the economy, which is not a viable option. Some think Gorbachev may already have gone further than is politically safe.

Liberalization can cause tremors both outside and inside Soviet borders. Khrushchev's "secret speech" denouncing Stalin at the 20th party congress in 1956 produced a wave of unrest in Eastern Europe that necessitated Soviet military intervention in Hungary. When the Khrushchev regime raised meat, milk and butter prices in 1962, there was rioting in the city of Novocherkassk. Gorbachev will also have to keep his eye on the 130 nationalities and ethnic groups within Soviet borders, which are already proving difficult to rule. Whether economic decentralization will make it more difficult to maintain control of a country as geographically large and ethnically diverse as the Soviet Union remains to be seen. How will Soviet citizens adjust to the changes Gorbachev is implementing? Used to taking orders, can they be educated to become independent-minded, aggressive managers? *Washington Post* editor Robert G. Kaiser doubts whether Gorbachev can keep criticizing Soviet society for long unless visible improvements appear quickly. Otherwise, he says, "In a few years, Gorbachev could face an unhappy choice between resorting to the old Big Lie, bragging how well things are going in the face of blatantly contradictory evidence, or acknowledging that the system itself is to blame . . . for the country's persistent shortcomings."

The changes Gorbachev is instituting are more radical than many Western scholars expected him to attempt, and most expect to see some improvements in Soviet economic health. The consensus so far, however, is that because of the political dangers inherent in radical reforms, Gorbachev will stick to changes of a limited nature. Their impact will therefore be limited as well.

THE SOVIET UNION AND THE WORLD

"Before my people, before you and before the world, I state with full responsibility that our international policy is more than ever determined by domestic policy, by our interest in concentrating on constructive endeavors to improve our country. This is why we need lasting peace, predictability and constructiveness in international relations."

In contrast to the bluster and threats of his predecessors, Gorbachev has launched a "charm offensive." Is Gorbachev's foreign policy qualitatively different from that of his predecessors, or is it just the public-relations skills of the new leaders in the Kremlin that have improved?

Most Soviet scholars agree that neither Gorbachev nor his successors are likely to abandon certain constants. These include a belief in the inherent superiority of Marxist-Leninist ideology, the need to preserve the Soviet Union's superpower status, and maintenance of Soviet control of Eastern Europe.

At the same time Soviet foreign policy has changed noticeably in both style and substance. Gorbachev's public pronouncements show greater appreciation of international realities than those of his predecessors. The Soviet Union has abandoned the belief that socialism is about to become a worldwide phenomenon. It no longer believes that Third World nations will automatically become allies of communism and enemies of capitalism. And it no longer thinks, as Brezhnev still professed to do in his report to the 26th party congress in 1981, that the international "correlation of forces" is shifting against the capitalist world.

'New Political Thinking'

The Soviet diplomatic style has changed markedly, too. This many observers credit in part to the influence of longtime ambassador to Washington Anatoly F. Dobrynin, now head of the Central Committee's International Department and one of Gorbachev's chief foreign policy advisers. Today's envoys from Moscow are better informed, less dogmatic, more flexible and more sophisticated in their dealings with Western officials and the press. Gorbachev has asked that the U.S.S.R. be considered for membership in the General Agreement on Tariffs and Trade (GATT), once denounced as "an imperialist conspiracy." He has made new diplomatic approaches to China, Japan, Israel, conservative Arab states and a wider variety of Third World countries than Moscow has dealt with in the past. He has also supported a strengthening of the role of the United Nations and backed up his rhetoric by paying the $225 million debt owed to the UN since the early 1960s.

Robert Legvold, director of the Harriman Institute for Advanced Study of the Soviet Union at Columbia University, believes these actions reflect a new and sophisticated Soviet view of national security in the modern world. Under Brezhnev, Moscow considered military power its most important foreign policy instrument. By intervening with its troops and supplying Third World allies with weapons, advice and cash, the Soviet Union saw its influence expand on every continent.

Moscow has learned in the years since then that, in the words of an *Economist* editorial, "a lot of good money can be poured after bad down faraway drains," as Third World friends bought with arms and money during the 1970s have "refused to stay bought, or squandered the help given." By 1980, Moscow's Third World clients were costing somewhere between $36 and $45 billion annually.

Gorbachev's words and actions indicate that he believes military power has limitations as a diplomatic instrument in today's interdependent world. "Security," Gorbachev declared at the 27th party congress, "is increasingly a political function that can be accomplished only by political means." He is the first Soviet leader to talk about the relationship of national security to "mutual security": "Less security for the U.S. compared to the Soviet Union," he said, "would not be in our interest since it could lead to mistrust and produce instability." This is diametrically opposed to the traditional Marxist-Leninist view of international relations as a matter of *"kto-kogo,"* meaning "who will prevail over whom."

Gorbachev has by no means abandoned the military. Soviet defense spending has picked up slightly since Gorbachev took power, growing at roughly 3% in 1986 compared with 2% per year between 1975 and 1985. Aid to most Soviet allies has remained constant or increased. But, in the words of University of Michigan Soviet expert Matthew Evangelista, "Soviet support for national liberation movements has changed from promises of economic and military assistance to expressions of 'profound sympathy.'" Gorbachev is directing today's diplomatic overtures to large and economically important Third World nations like Mexico and Brazil—countries with whom it hopes to have a profitable diplomatic and economic relationship in the future.

Pacific Overtures

East Asia has become a focus of Soviet attention since Gorbachev's Vladivostok speech of July 28, 1986, in which he reminded the world that "the Soviet Union is also an Asian and Pacific country." Gorbachev has built up Soviet forces in the Far East. In 1986–87, Moscow nearly doubled its aid to economically troubled Vietnam, where it has access to important naval facilities at Cam Ranh Bay (originally built by the U.S. during the Vietnam War). U.S. intelligence sources indicate that those facilities have quadrupled in size, although Moscow denies it even has a base there.

Gorbachev has also made a concerted attempt to improve relations with the People's Republic of China, with whom it has been at odds since the early 1960s. Beijing has identified three "obstacles" to normalization of relations with Moscow: the presence of Soviet ally Vietnam in Cambodia, a number of long-standing Soviet-Chinese border issues, and the Soviet occupation of Afghanistan. Although there has been little movement so far, there has been more conversation and trade between Beijing and Moscow than at any time since the early 1960s.

Moscow has also been paying increased diplomatic attention to Japan but has been rebuffed because it refuses to consider returning four Soviet-occupied islands over which Japan claims sovereignty. The new emphasis of Soviet foreign policy on East Asia seems to reflect Gorbachev's determination that the U.S.S.R. not be left out of this dynamic region's economic growth.

Probes and Priorities

The U.S.S.R. has become more active in Middle East diplomacy since Gorbachev took power. Moscow has made overtures to Israel, with whom it broke relations in 1967, and has been permitting greater numbers of Russian Jews to emigrate. Moscow has also maintained its traditional friendship with Syria and remains its chief arms supplier. The Soviets have urged a resumption of the Arab-Israeli peace process in the form of an international conference at which it would be represented. They have also become diplomatically active in the Persian Gulf, especially in the wake of the scandal involving U.S. arms sales to Iran, and have offered to act as mediators between Iran and Iraq.

Experts agree that Gorbachev's top foreign policy priority is stability in Eastern Europe. But Gorbachev would like to maintain Soviet hegemony in the region at less cost, and is encouraging Eastern Europe's leaders to be innovative in getting their countries onto firmer financial ground. On his trip to Czechoslovakia and Hungary in early 1987, Gorbachev barely veiled his criticism of the aging Czech leadership, much to the delight of the Czech public. One onlooker joked to a *Christian Science Monitor* reporter, "How do Czechoslovaks express dissent? We applaud Gorbachev." But observers warn that Gorbachev must proceed with caution: the unintended result of his liberalization could be an explosion in Eastern Europe, as happened in Hungary in 1956 and Czechoslovakia in 1968.

Gorbachev and the West

Traditionally, Moscow's approach toward the Atlantic alliance has been to try to drive a wedge between Western Europe and the U.S. It has cajoled and threatened Western Europe in an effort to limit the military power facing the Soviet Union from the West, to gain European recognition of the postwar status quo in Eastern Europe, and to acquire access to Western Europe's technology and financial credits.

Gorbachev's objectives appear no different, although he has shifted tactics. He has dropped threats—especially toward West Germany—in favor of charm, telling West Europeans in a 1986 speech in East Berlin: "Do not believe allegations about the aggressiveness of the Soviet Union. Our country will never, under any circumstances, begin armed operations against Western Europe unless we or our allies become targets of a NATO attack! I repeat, never!" Gorbachev has also approved—and probably encouraged—the recent increased diplomatic contact between East and West Germany.

Gorbachev's approach has paid off at least in terms of an improved Soviet image in Western Europe. Several polls conducted during 1987 indicated that West Europeans, particularly in Britain and West Germany, see Moscow as more deserving of credit for progress in arms control than Washington.

The U.S.S.R and the U.S.

The enormous size, resources and military strength of the two superpowers, combined with their ideological differences, make each the other's most serious security threat and most significant competitor for influence throughout the world. Each of the U.S.S.R.'s leaders has left his mark on the relationship. Stalin built the Iron Curtain and retreated into hostile isolation behind it. Khrushchev became active in world affairs, involving the Soviet Union in Third World political struggles and bringing the superpowers to the brink of nuclear war over Berlin and Cuba. Brezhnev transformed the country into a nuclear superpower and worked

with the U.S. to forge détente from the competitive relationship. Détente foundered on the divergent views of Washington and Moscow on the arms race, Soviet involvement in the Third World and Soviet human rights policy at home. From Washington's viewpoint, these remain the major stumbling blocks to better relations today.

Polemics between the superpowers were more strident during the first four years of Ronald Reagan's presidency than they had been since the Cuban missile crisis of 1962, as the U.S. engaged in a major military buildup and progress on arms control stalled. After Gorbachev's accession and Reagan's reelection, the atmosphere improved. How has the new man at the helm in the Kremlin affected the relationship?

The most visible area so far is arms control. Although Western experts differ as to what his long-term motives are, most believe that Gorbachev sees more to be gained from arms control than just the propaganda points he has earned with Western Europe. Gorbachev has talked about the need for a "breathing space." Reaching an agreement with the U.S. on limiting nuclear weapons could permit him to spend more money on butter instead of guns—at least until his economic reforms have begun to pay off. Gorbachev may also be hoping to use arms control to hold back American military technology. The Soviet Union is especially concerned about the U.S. Strategic Defense Initiative (SDI), the program created to research and develop defenses against nuclear weapons. Without an agreement to restrain SDI, the Soviet Union would be forced into an all-out high-technology competition with the

U.S. before Gorbachev's reform program has a chance to work.

The focus of future Soviet military research and development, a growing number of military analysts believe, will probably be on advanced *nonnuclear* weapons. This is not a sudden new development, they emphasize, but an evolution in military thinking that began in the mid-1960s. Former Soviet Chief of Staff Nikolai Ogarkov, who now heads the U.S.S.R.'s Western forces, has argued that "you do not have to be a military genius to see that stockpiling nuclear weapons is senseless. Now in contemporary conditions . . . there are weapons based on new physical principles which can achieve yields close to those of smaller nuclear weapons."

Some experts are convinced that Gorbachev's goal in the nuclear arms control negotiations is a breathing space now to ensure Soviet military superiority later. An editorial in the conservative *National Review* interprets Soviet objectives as "total Soviet superiority in biological and chemical weapons; overwhelming superiority in conventional forces; almost certainly, the decoupling of Europe from America. . . ." Many conservatives warn that the Soviets can afford to reduce the levels of nuclear arms because of their superiority in conventional weapons. It remains to be seen whether the Soviet concept of mutual security will lead them to reductions in nonnuclear weapons, especially in Europe.

So far, the Soviet Union and the U.S. have agreed "in principle" to eliminate intermediate-range nuclear weapons (known as INF, for intermediate nuclear forces). Both sides have also agreed to permit on-site inspections of military installations for the purpose of verifying compliance with the agreement. This represents a substantial change in the Soviet position. In September 1987, Moscow even permitted a U.S. congressional delegation to tour the Soviet radar installation at Krasnoyarsk in Siberia. The Reagan Administration claimed Krasnoyarsk is a violation of the 1972 Antiballistic Missile Treaty because it is not on the Soviet Union's periphery. Although the visit did not completely end the violation debate, it was a propaganda coup for the Soviet Union.

The superpowers have also agreed to establish "nuclear risk reduction centers" and improve communications between the two capitals, and to begin talks on improving verification of current nuclear testing limits as a first step toward negotiating new limits.

There has also been progress in a number of other areas. Academic, cultural and people-to-people contacts have expanded under a new exchange agreement.

On the subject of bilateral trade, which the Soviet Union would like to see expanded, the picture has been mixed. American trade with the Soviet Union has never been large—the U.S. imported some $555 million in Soviet goods in 1986, and exported $1.2 billion. In early 1987, Soviet exports of untreated cotton fabric ("gray goods") to the U.S. increased so dramatically that they were restricted by legislation in July in response to an outcry by American textile firms. Some legal obstacles to the export of basic U.S. personal computers to the U.S.S.R. were lifted in September 1987, but not on state-of-the-art technology. Overall, trade between the two countries is still restricted by the Jackson-Vanik and Stevenson amendments to the 1974 Trade Act, which impose high tariffs on Soviet exports and limit Export-Import Bank credits to finance Soviet purchases of U.S. goods because of restrictive Soviet policies on Jewish emigration. So far there has been no move to waive these provisions, despite critics' protests that they hamper the U.S. ability to compete.

Looking Ahead

If it is too early to judge whether Gorbachev can succeed in reforming the Soviet Union, it is not too early for outside observers to have begun wondering what it would mean for the U.S. if he did. Would a reformed Soviet Union be a greater or lesser threat to the U.S.? Would it be more or less prone to raise tensions? If, as they suspect, Gorbachev's reforms are aimed at making the Soviet Union a more assertive international actor, many conservatives see no reason why the U.S. should help or applaud his efforts. They believe that Washington should continue to criticize the Soviet policies it disapproves of and refrain from signing agreements that would help Moscow achieve its aims. A creaking, inefficient Soviet state is vastly preferable, from this point of view, to a rejuvenated and stronger— and still Communist—U.S.S.R.

Many liberals, on the other hand, think that Gorbachev should be encouraged, first because liberalization and democratization are intrinsically good for their own sake; and second, because in the words of French Kremlinologist Michel Tatu, "If a totalitarian system opens itself up even partially and chooses economic reforms, it tends to moderate its foreign policy. Domestic change needs a peaceful environment and is hardly compatible with militarism or expansionism."

The vast majority of analysts believe that Gorbachev is preoccupied with internal problems and that he does want at least a breathing space in foreign relations to get his domestic reforms off the ground. Many, including former U.S. Ambassador to Moscow Arthur Hartman, stress that outsiders can do little to affect Soviet policy: the decisions that need to be made are in Moscow, not Washington.

Others, including participants in a recent study on new Soviet thinking convened under the auspices of the Institute for East-West Security Studies, do not believe that "a purely reactive Western approach" to new Soviet policies is enough. But even those who favor a significant warming in Soviet-American relations warn that the U.S. and other countries should remain conscious that the Soviet Union has no intention of giving up its active role in world affairs. The means it chooses to compete may or may not be different from those it has chosen in the past, but it will remain a competitor.

How should the U.S. deal with Moscow in the years ahead? Some options currently under discussion follow.

U.S. Policy Options

☐ In economic relations with the Soviet Union, the U.S. should:

1. Welcome Soviet efforts to become more a part of the world economy. Washington should loosen barriers to the transfer of high technology, since Moscow is able to obtain much of what it seeks through purchase or theft or from other sources. It should consider repeal of the Jackson-Vanik and Stevenson amendments in return for Soviet improvements in the recognition of human rights. And, when the Soviet Union is able to meet the criteria for membership, the U.S. should approve Moscow's application to GATT. If Gorbachev succeeds in reforming the Soviet economy, the process may in the long run have a liberalizing effect on Soviet domestic politics and may make it a less dangerous player in the world, with an increasingly large stake in global stability. The U.S. should not try to prevent that happening.

2. Seek to block Soviet efforts to integrate the U.S.S.R.'s economy with the rest of the world's. Don't feed the bear: a more economically healthy and efficient Soviet Union is likely to be a more aggressive one. Making advanced technology more accessible will make it that much easier for Moscow to build a stronger military machine for the 21st century. Concluding trade agreements that provide needed commodities or hard currency under conditions favorable to Moscow likewise permits the Soviet Union to direct funds into the Soviet military. ☐ On security issues, the U.S. should:

1. Take advantage of Gorbachev's eagerness for arms agreements to intensify talks on a range of arms issues, particularly on offensive nuclear and conventional forces. Now is the time to explore the extent of Gorbachev's flexibility, to reach agreements that will benefit not only the Soviet Union but both the superpowers by increasing stability and predictability in the bilateral relationship.

2. Resist signing arms control agreements, which will permit Gorbachev a breathing space to make the Soviet Union a stronger military power later. If this is a moment of weakness for the Soviet economy, then it is in the U.S. interest to exploit that weakness, not give it time to recover and menace the West again when it is stronger. ■

The U.S.S.R. in Decline

By Robert G. Kaiser

The news from the Soviet Union is enthralling—nothing so interesting or exciting as Mikhail Gorbachev's reforms has happened in Russia in modern times. The world is rightly transfixed by the spectacle of Russians telling the truth about their past and their present, encouraging private enterprise, urging a diminished role for the Communist Party and generally committing mayhem against Marxism-Leninism.

But there is a paradoxical aspect to perestroika that deserves more attention. The rhetoric of Soviet reform emphasizes renewal and progress, but the facts that made reform necessary describe failure—the failure of the Soviet system. For the foreseeable future, the fact of that failure is likely to be more important for the world than Gorbachev's efforts to overcome it.

That is because the failure is a fact, while the reforms—at least the practical ones affecting the economic life of the country—remain just a hope. It is likely to remain a forlorn hope for years to come.

The failure of the Soviet system—Joseph Stalin's system, which organized Soviet life for more than half a century—is a larger event than many have yet acknowledged. It signals more than the collapse of Stalin's dream of a centrally planned economic powerhouse that might someday dominate the world. We are also witnessing the beginning of the end of the Soviet empire. The fear of Soviet conquest and hegemony that dominated world politics for more than a generation should

Robert G. Kaiser, assistant managing editor of *The Washington Post* and the newspaper's Moscow correspondent from 1971 to 1974, is the author of *Russia: The People and the Power,* Copyright © 1988 by Robert G. Kaiser.

Source: From *Foreign Affairs,* Vol. 67, No. 2 (Winter, 1988–89), pp. 97–113. Reprinted by permission of *Foreign Affairs,* Winter 1988/89. Copyright 1988 by The Council on Foreign Relations, Inc.

now dissipate. We have passed the high-water mark of Soviet power and influence in the world.

II

The crisis in the communist world has provoked radical changes from Beijing to Warsaw, and all of them contain a common ingredient: liberalization. Milovan Djilas describes what is going on as the inevitable consequence of the realization that the Stalinist model does not work in the present age. Its rigid, centralized institutions have proven incapable of producing modern, efficient economies; to fight their rigidity, communist regimes must turn to decentralization and liberalization.[1]

Djilas is convinced that liberalization in the communist world will continue—probably in fits and starts—because the crisis of the old order will continue. "Liberalization, crisis, they are the same thing," Djilas has said. In other words, the only available antidote to the backwardness and stagnation that afflict communist countries is decentralization, loosening of controls—liberalization. It is a shrewd argument, not easy to dispute in light of the evidence from so many different communist countries.

Gorbachev clearly sees the world in similar terms. He speaks repeatedly of the need to democratize his country to make it work better. Economic reform, he has concluded, is impossible without political reform, so he has proposed astounding changes to remove the Communist Party apparat from day-to-day administration of the economy and society, to replace it with new, elected bodies. He proposes to make the Soviet Union into a society ruled by law,

not party, and to assure personal freedoms and the right to privacy. All of this is deliberate—to improve the economy, raise the standard of living and restore the Soviet Union to the front rank of nations.

Similar tactics to achieve similar objectives have been adopted in China, Poland, Yugoslavia and Hungary, and they are surely to come throughout the communist world. Even Vietnam is toying with such changes to modernize its failing economy.

Declaring or even initiating a plan to reform is a far cry from achieving its objectives, however. The Chinese have made great but uneven progress; the Poles have made negative progress; the Soviets have made none. In the years ahead, Gorbachev and his allies—or their successors—will discover just how difficult a task they have undertaken.

The Stalinist system has done profound damage to Russia—so much damage that a decade or two of reform is most unlikely to put things right. Of all the communist countries, Russia will have the most difficulty finding a new path to real progress, because the foundation on which the Soviet leaders must build is so rotten. No other communist system is even half a century old; the Soviet model has had three or four generations to reach its present, dismal condition. The new openness of the Gorbachev era has illuminated that condition—made it painfully vivid and undeniable.

That is the most significant contribution of glasnost. In the West we are fascinated by Soviet truth-telling about historical figures like Bukharin and Trotsky, or revelations about Stalin's crimes in the

1930s and 1940s, but the truly devastating revelations are about contemporary reality. If Gorbachev were ousted by more conservative comrades tomorrow, and they moved at once to shut off glasnost and restore Brezhnevite orthodoxy (something like that could happen—the road to liberalization will not be a straight one), the new leaders could not remove the damning facts that have now been spread across the official record.

Admissions of the failure of the system are now published so often that they are routine. And they are found in much more august forums than the pages of newspapers. Last summer's Communist Party conference, convened as a solemn event of great national significance, was filled with vivid confessions of past sins. Until Gorbachev came to power, such events were usually devoted to rosy propaganda.

The new tone was set in Gorbachev's own report to the conference: "It must be said frankly, comrades—we underestimated the depth and gravity of the distortions and stagnation of the past. There was a lot we just didn't know, and are seeing only now. It turned out that neglect was more serious than we thought."

In speeches that followed, others spelled out many particulars. For example:

Evgeny Chazov, the minister of health, spoke bluntly on subjects once considered taboo in public discourse: "In the past . . . we kept quiet about the fact that we were in 50th place in the world for infant mortality, after Mauritius and Barbados. . . . We kept quiet about the fact that our life expectancy ranks 32nd in the world." And he revealed one reason for this situation, listing the per capita expenditure on health care in a number of Soviet republics—from 70 rubles a year in Latvia down to 42 in Tadzhikistan. (A ruble is worth about $1.50 at the official rate, or about $.35 when freely traded. So the government is paying somewhere between $25 and $105 per year for health care in Latvia, apparently the highest amount for any republic in the country. In the United States per capita health care expenditure last year was just under $2,000.) "The malaise, after all, is not in medicine alone," Chazov told the conference. "It is a malaise of our whole society, and we have to acknowledge this."

G. A. Yagodin, chairman of the state committee on public education, told the conference that *half* the schools in the Soviet Union "do not have central heating, running water or a sewerage system." He said a quarter of all students attend school in split shifts. He quoted statistics from the Ministry of Health showing that 53 percent of all schoolchildren are not in good health, and "during their education, the number of healthy children drops by a factor of three or four. This is a calamity."

D. K. Motorniy, chairman of a collective farm in Kherson Oblast, acknowledged that in his rural area, the authorities had failed "to resolve the three most important tasks: providing heat, constructing roads and providing running water and sewerage." As a result, he said, "people are simply leaving for the cities."

One of the most interesting speeches to the conference was delivered by A. A. Logunov, rector of Moscow State University and a man not considered a particularly enthusiastic Gorbachev ally. Lo-

gunov must have startled many in the hall with his blunt evaluation of Soviet science. "The situation," he said, "is altogether unfavorable. . . . Essentially, science has been a hollow word in our country. We have talked about it a great deal, we have allegedly done everything scientifically, but we have done very little for its development. . . . It is simply amazing that in a number of fields, especially theoretical fields, we can still keep up." This of the society that launched Sputnik!

Lest the conference delegates got the impression that these shortcomings had some external or easily curable cause, the editor of *Izvestia,* Ivan D. Laptev, put the blame squarely on the people in the hall—the Communist Party of the Soviet Union. The Soviet system, he said, "created an astonishing, unique situation: the person who makes the decisions [i.e., an official of the Communist Party] bears no legal or material responsibility for its consequences, and the person who bears that responsibility [e.g., a factory director, a school administrator or the like] does not make the decisions."

Perestroika—economic restructuring and reform—is the only way out, the delegates were told. "Either the country is doomed to further stagnation, or we gain strength and forge ahead to progress. That is how the question stands. We have no third course." Those were not Gorbachev's words; they were spoken by Yegor Ligachev, the leading Politburo conservative and Gorbachev rival, whom Gorbachev bumped from the ideology portfolio into new responsibilities for agriculture in his dramatic personnel reshuffle in early October 1988.

III

We in the West have little first-hand experience with societies that are structurally unsound. We tend to take for granted the remarkable adaptability of democratic, capitalist nations. Much of the current Western commentary on Gorbachev's prospects implicitly presumes that Soviet society is similarly adaptable—so that, for example, Gorbachev may pull off a successful reform that actually makes the Soviet Union a more formidable adversary in just a few years. But Soviet society is not flexible or adaptable, and the chances of a truly effective reform in Gorbachev's lifetime are negligible.

The Russians themselves understand their own inflexibility. The most-discussed shortcoming in the Soviet Union today is the failure of officials at all levels to adapt to the first, easiest steps of perestroika. The very idea of change is a threat to millions of citizens in that most conservative of countries. Yet Gorbachev is pressing for profound, sweeping changes—so sweeping that they would alter every important facet of Soviet life outside the family. As his initial experience has shown, he will meet resistance every step of the way.

Gorbachev is struggling against the consequences of five decades of misrule—and in some of his ambitions, against all of Russian history as well. "Our model failed," one official in Moscow told me last spring. "It took us nowhere." Another prominent intellectual—a well-known member of the avant-garde of glasnost who was a delegate to the party conference—offered an ironic elaboration of that judgment. "We have made one important contribution," he said.

"We have taught the world what *not* to do."

The model failed, but it also distorted the life of a huge nation, creating an inefficient, backward society riddled with bad habits, many of them now ingrained over two generations or more. Glasnost has finally allowed thoughtful Soviet analysts to address the distortions of Soviet life directly. Nikolai Shmelyev, an economist, took advantage of the new opportunity to speak bluntly in an article published last spring in *Novy Mir*.

"It is important that we all recognize the degree to which we have gotten out of the habit of doing everything that is economically normal and healthy, and into the habit of doing everything that is economically abnormal and unhealthy," Shmelyev wrote. "We are now like a seriously ill man who, after a long time in bed, takes his first step with the greatest difficulty and finds, to his horror, that he has almost forgotten how to walk."

This notion of forgotten skills runs through much Soviet discussion of the obstacles to reform, as well it should. Millions of Soviet workers have no idea of the difference between careful, high- quality work and what has traditionally been acceptable in their country. Soviet citizens now have an utterly contemptuous view of Soviet workmanship. "It's ours, it's bad," a working man in Moscow told me, as though the two adjectives were synonyms.

This is more than a generalized complaint; it has real consequences. Machinery that can only be produced under conditions of stringent quality control is simply not made. Thus, there are no mass-produced Soviet personal computers and no mass-produced copying machines. Sixty percent of all apartment fires in Moscow are caused by mass-produced Soviet television sets, which have a tendency to explode. What might be called the Soviet industrial culture has no tradition of quality control, cleanliness, attention to detail and the like. Only in special military plants have the Soviets regularly been able to produce high-quality, complicated machinery—and the costs of production in those enterprises are apparently enormous, because the principal method of assuring quality is simply to reject a large percentage of what is made.

In industry, the traditional solution to all problems is forced production to meet arbitrary plan targets. This means wild days and nights of around-the-clock production (Russians call this the *shturm,* or storm) to meet monthly, quarterly and annual targets, followed by long periods of lackadaisical production to recover from the extra effort expended in the *shturm.* Quality inevitably loses all significance in a system built around mandatory, quantitative deliveries. And because all production targets—and all plans for the delivery of raw materials and machinery—are set by bureaucrats outside the factory, there is no real opportunity for significant innovation in product design, production methodology, etc. This is what Shmelyev meant when he accused his countrymen of doing "everything that is economically abnormal and unhealthy." Sweeping though that accusation is, it is fully justified.

Soviet economists make no attempt to disguise the severity of the problems the country faces. One could scour the institutes in Moscow and not find an economist who thinks that perestroika or any other imaginable reform will give the Soviet Union a world-class industrial capability in this century, or in the next generation. Structural shortcomings are compounded by technological ones. The Soviet Union did not keep up with the rapid technological change of the last generation—it has missed out almost entirely on the computer revolution—and has no infrastructure to enable it to catch up now. For example, the primitive telephone system, which still only reaches a fraction of the population, is incapable of transmitting computer data. There is no reason to expect that at any time in the foreseeable future the Russians will be able to match the industrial culture of the Taiwanese, let alone the Japanese or the Germans.

IV

Agriculture is often cited—by Soviets and outsiders—as a sector in which speedy improvements could be made with reforms that could be relatively easily put into effect. Gorbachev has apparently adopted this hope himself, and recently has emphasized solution of the national food problem as his first priority.

At first blush there seems a certain logic here; farmers have been tied to a hopelessly inefficient structure of state and collective farms, forced to fulfill orders from far-off bureaucrats who know nothing of farming, while managing, almost as a hobby, to produce more than a quarter of the nation's food on their tiny, legal private plots. Give that private initiative freer reign, it is argued, and the food problem can be solved.

We will see soon enough if this optimism is justified. The available evidence challenges it. Again, the ineradicable consequences of a half-century of misrule have created obstacles to rational progress that may be insurmountable.

The biggest of those is the absence of rural residents with the inclination or the ability to manage a big piece of land for an extended period of time. The official policy now encourages long-term rental agreements with families or other small units—edging toward a new form of individual enterprise. But the official policy has changed so often, and so dramatically, in the half-century of collectivized agriculture that by many accounts farmers have no confidence that this latest change will last. Others complain that renters are a far cry from owners, and cannot be expected to act like owners.

Even more important, there is no tradition of entrepreneurial farming in the Soviet countryside, and no living farmers who ever practiced it. The successful entrepreneurs of old, who made pre-revolutionary Russia an exporter of grain, were wiped out as unwanted kulaks in the ugly first stages of collectivization. A new rural elite then arose—tractor drivers, who had the best jobs and the highest status. The mechanics who cared for the machinery were also better off than the ordinary farm workers. In many areas the bulk of the manual labor on the land is performed by women who fall at the very bottom of the rural pecking order.

But tractor drivers and mechanics know little if anything about managing farm acreage, protecting its vitality from season to season, planting and harvesting to get the most out of it. Even if new regulations make it genuinely attractive

to go into business on one's own, there may be few takers. The traditions that would enable farmers in some areas—for example, in the Baltic states, which were not absorbed into the Soviet Union until 1940—to take advantage of new opportunities for entrepreneurship are so long forgotten in Russia and the Ukraine that they have simply been obliterated.

For many decades the Soviet countryside has been dreary and backward, lacking in the most basic amenities. Roswell Garst, the Iowa corn farmer who befriended Nikita Khrushchev, used to note that there were more miles of paved roads in his county in Iowa than in the entire Ukraine, an area thousands of times larger. Every oblast and republic—indeed, every collective and state farm—is burdened with a bureaucratic class that purports to manage, but actually frustrates, agricultural production. By closing the countryside to foreigners, the Soviets for years hid the truth about it, but Gorbachev, as the product of a successful farm area around Stavropol, knows the truth. That may explain why he has put his rival, Ligachev, at least nominally in charge of agriculture.

V

When a particular enterprise is unusually successful in producing good-quality products or overfulfilling the targets of the plan, that success is often tied to a single individual—a boss who can make things work. A number of such figures have national reputations in the country—Soviet versions of Lee Iacocca or H. Ross Perot. One of them, V. P. Kabaidze, general director of the Ivanova Machine-Tool Building Association, caused a stir

at the party conference last summer by declaring from the podium that he had no need for the Ministry of Machine Building that supervises his plant. "What can the minister give us? Nothing at all!" He ended his address on a gloomy note: "The devil knows what sort of habit we have got into: everybody keeps waiting for some instructions or other . . . [but] now it really depends on us. We must do our thing."

It is that nearly universal tendency in the Soviet Union to wait for instructions that makes an outspoken individualist like Kabaidze so rare. Gorbachev constantly demands more Kabaidzes—more comrades who will take initiative and responsibility for remaking the country—but I found no optimism anywhere in Moscow during a three-week visit last spring that such people will soon be found. Instead, one hears expressions of concern that the reformers in Moscow will summon too many of the good factory directors to the capital to work with them. "If you have to lose a good factory director to get a good minister, that may be a bad trade," one official observed.

The smothering of initiative and responsibility is one of the most discouraging but also most palpable consequences of the Stalinist epoch. Soviet citizens at every level instinctively look upward for guidance and instructions.

Kabaidze's suggestion that citizens do their own thing is as un-Soviet as cherry pie. Russia's great writers have bemoaned the sheeplike qualities of their countrymen for centuries. ("Graze on, you peaceful sheep and cattle," Pushkin wrote angrily early in the last century.) Stalin exacerbated these qualities with a vengeance, literally, by imposing horrific penalties on those who defied instruction—and, even more horrifically, on many who did not, chosen almost at random. The result is what a friend in Moscow called "characteristic Soviet fear"—a reflexive instinct to stay out of trouble by staying low to the ground, never speaking up or taking an initiative. Now Gorbachev insists he wants people to speak out, argue with authority and the like, but this doesn't come easily. "We are trying," said one Moscow scholar, "to squeeze the slave out of us."

The Stalinist system created a presumption of equality among workers that Gorbachev has now discovered is another impediment to rational progress. He assails this as a "leveling mentality"—the idea that everyone should receive about the same rewards, no matter what their contribution. But this instinct, too, runs deep in the national character, in part because it grows from a peasant reflex much older than Bolshevism. Georgi Arbatov, the survivor who is director of the Institute of the United States and Canada, described this peasant outlook: "Okay, maybe I'll have to go hungry, but just don't let my neighbor prosper!" Envy of one's neighbor's success, still widespread, can frustrate efforts to create a successful class of entrepreneurs, which is the unpopular goal of the new cooperative movement. Socialism, after all, was meant to eliminate the exploiting class, so why should some comrades be dramatically richer than others?

It would be easier to instill new attitudes in a population less cynical and demoralized than today's Soviet citizenry. I asked an old friend who works in a well-known factory in Moscow what the men on the shop floor thought of Gorbachev's reforms. "They don't believe in anything," he replied, "and they especially don't believe that things will get better." Even the rare optimist among the workers would only argue that in forty years or so, things might improve as a result of reform. The Soviets' incredible drinking problems are vivid evidence of that demoralization. It is revealing that Gorbachev's one clear failure has been his anti-drinking campaign. It has angered the population by making it so difficult to buy legal vodka, but it has also done little to reduce drunkenness, because bootlegging is now so widespread and so profitable. In late October the Central Committee announced that steps would be taken to make available more alcoholic beverages.

Another sign of demoralization is the fact that Gorbachev's reforms have no ardent support from the young. Logic would suggest otherwise—a modernizer who is obliterating the taboos of a strait-laced dictatorship, opening the country to the outside world and making room for the evolution of a genuinely Soviet youth culture ought to be a hero to young people. But no one in Moscow makes that claim. Teachers and parents both agree that the young people who came of age in the 1970s and early 1980s generally have no interest in politics, and are deeply suspicious of politicians' claims. One senior figure in Moscow called this "a lost generation." It is another symptom of a society that is not well.

VI

Just as Gorbachev must work with the Soviet society and economy that exist, he must also deal with an existing political system and Communist Party apparatus that are resistant to—and ill suited for—the changes he seeks.

Perhaps his single greatest practical problem today is a shortage of like-minded allies within the party on whom he can rely to carry out his reforms. Many comrades simply cannot make the leap to the "new thinking," as Gorbachev calls it; obviously, numerous party officials cannot abandon the prejudices and reflexes of a lifetime. It is doubtful that even a substantial minority of party members personally accept Gorbachev's indictment of the Soviet past, or can embrace his glum assessment of the present. And even those who may privately agree with him can be reluctant to say so openly. "People are still afraid to reveal themselves" as ardent allies of reform, according to one prominent editor, for fear that the party line will change again next week or next year, leaving them exposed.

This caution is understandable. Since Stalin forcibly purged all the individualists from the Communist Party, it has hardly been a breeding ground for resourceful leaders. One of the miraculous aspects of the present situation is the fact that this scared, bureaucratized political organization produced the likes of Gorbachev, his principal associate Aleksander Yakovlev, and the other leading figures of reform. Much more predictable are the gray men we have come to know only in formal photographs who have filled the Politburo throughout the modern era.

Gorbachev has not found a route around those gray figures. He has them in his Politburo; his prime minister, Nikolai Ryzhkov, theoretically responsible for running the economy, is one of them. When Gorbachev had the idea of a special party conference to be held in 1988, midway between traditional party congresses, he was obviously hoping for a gathering that would support sweeping personnel changes. Sometime last spring that ambition evaporated. After a controversial selection process, delegates were chosen for the conference who—according to numerous senior officials—were more conservative than progressive.

Several delegates to the conference told me that the majority there were at least very nervous about what Gorbachev was up to. This was evident in a number of the speeches, some of them blatantly reactionary and anti-Gorbachev. The most striking was made by Yuri Bondarev, deputy chairman of the writers' union of the Russian Republic, who asked from the podium of the conference: "Could our perestroika be compared to an airplane that has taken off without knowing if there is a landing strip at its destination?"

In the end the party conference was a chaotic event; no line emerged from its speeches, only a sense of political ferment and uncertainty. The resolutions adopted (but never specifically debated) by the conference gave staunch support to all Gorbachev's policies, but they were obviously produced in advance and blessed in the traditional Soviet manner—unanimously.

Gorbachev's continuing reliance on traditional—that is, Stalinist—methods of control is revealing. His enunciated platform is decentralization, democracy and the rule of law, but his actual performance is still dictatorial. This was most vividly evident last October when he strengthened his po-

sition in the Politburo with several sudden personnel changes at the top of the party apparatus, including his own installation as titular president of the country. These changes were ratified by meetings of the party Central Committee and the legislative Supreme Soviet on September 30 and October 1; both meetings were over in less than an hour, no debate was heard at either, and the vote was unanimous at both.

Even if we credit Gorbachev with honest intentions someday to fulfill his democratic platform—and many Soviets still do—for now he must rely on traditional centralized control to impose democracy. On its face this seems a problematic undertaking. It is more uncertain in light of the nature of the people on whom he must impose it.

Soviet bureaucrats and party factotums have no experience and no evident interest in a truly democratic system in which popular will is stronger than they are. The local party secretary is used to being the local regent; his word has traditionally had the force of law—in fact, it has exceeded the force of law, since one of his prerogatives has been to tell the courts in his jurisdiction how to behave. The party secretary and a handful of other bureaucrats have had no challengers for power and influence for sixty or seventy years. Now Gorbachev says they must be elected in multi-candidate elections. He says the party organizations must give way to democratic councils or soviets, local legislatures also chosen by the people in multi-candidate elections.

Are such changes really in the cards? There is room for doubt. One compromise introduced on the eve of the party conference to

make the idea of "all power to the soviets" more palatable was to install as leader of every soviet the existing party secretary in that region. This was a sop to the party, but it scarcely looks like a contribution to real democracy.

Critical to Gorbachev's vision of a better future is the idea that a new popular will can be formulated and expressed from below. It appears that Gorbachev is banking on this as the ultimate solution to the problem of the reluctant bureaucracy. If he can overwhelm the bureaucrats from above and from below, they will have to go along, or move out of the way.

This beguiling idea can only work if the mass of Soviet citizens makes it work. But can a people with no democratic traditions whatsoever, who by habit or even instinct look to higher authority to organize society and their lives, suddenly become fervid democrats eager to challenge old ways and established leaders? "I am not an optimist," answered a Moscow intellectual now regarded as one of Gorbachev's key allies. "Processes that took four hundred years, sometimes six hundred years, to develop in West European societies never even began here. . . . The organization of our society is very poor."

VII

Success will not be easy. But without any guarantees of success, dramatic *change* in Soviet society is continuing—the distinction is an important one. Already in three and a half years, Gorbachev has brought changes to his country that can never be fully undone. The pre-Gorbachev Soviet Union —the Soviet Union of what is now officially called the "era of stagnation"—will not be restored.

What has happened in the past three and a half years was not predicted—could not have been predicted—by anyone. Gorbachev has gone much farther, much faster than his countrymen or outsiders ever dreamed possible. He has gone very far toward completing the demythologizing of Stalin, a process that was begun by Nikita Khrushchev thirty years ago but abandoned in the mid-1960s. He has introduced a degree of freedom of expression in newspapers and journals that has no precedent in the Soviet period. He has shattered taboos that prevailed in his country for generations, permitting debate—and doubt—about some of the most cherished myths of Soviet history. Not even Lenin himself, the icon of the Soviet system, has been spared.

Gorbachev has made change a value in itself. "Our society will change," he promises. He has taken much of the fear out of everyday life for the people who used to feel it most—members of the intelligentsia, who felt most victimized by censorship, controls on travel and the close attention of the KGB. For veterans of earlier periods, the new mood in Moscow is quite incredible. Soviet officials openly make appointments by telephone to see Westerners; journalists brag of the scandals they have caused by exposing official misconduct; editors boast of the historical taboos they have broken in their journals. Soviet television has broadcast suggestions that the country needs a new, multiparty political system. Television has also

made room for rock music and Soviet-made rock videos. Citizens gather signatures on petitions to protest the decisions of Communist Party organs. Interest groups form to defend nature against industrial pollution, or to promote anti-Semitic views of Russian history, or to lobby for preservation of historic buildings threatened by official notions of progress.

Travel has suddenly become much easier, so Soviet citizens who never dreamed it would be possible can readily travel to the West. And Soviet emigrés of the last generation, people who left as Jews or political dissidents expecting never to see their homeland again, are now returning for visits in large numbers. All these things are signs of what is clearly most important to many Russians—the creation of a "normal" Soviet Union. The adjective normal, used to describe both what is beginning to happen and what is most sought after, is often heard in Moscow conversations today.

Most amazing for many non-Russian Soviet citizens, the various nationalities have been given extraordinary freedom to organize, to demonstrate and protest. For the multinational Soviet state, nothing could be more exciting (or potentially more threatening) than the manifestations of nationalism seen recently in the Baltic states, in Azerbaijan and Armenia, and elsewhere. The CIA reported in October that it had counted nearly three hundred public disturbances provoked by ethnic issues between early 1987 and late 1988. For de-

cades scholars in the West speculated on what would happen when the ethnic genie got out of its bottle. Now it is out.

One of the most intriguing aspects of Gorbachev's rule has been the way a little change has thus far invariably produced in him an appetite for more change. A clear trend of increasing radicalism is obvious in Gorbachev's speeches and interviews. The truly radical political reforms approved at the party conference this June were never even hinted at in Gorbachev's first years, just as the virulent anti-Stalinism evident during 1988 was avoided by Gorbachev himself as recently as his speech in November 1987. As Gorbachev told the party conference, "there was a lot we just didn't know" when he took power in March 1985 and launched his reforms. In the first stages Gorbachev declared that conditions were bad; now he and many others show, in painful detail, just how bad they are. And he has placed much of the blame on the past shortcomings of the Communist Party itself.

The Gorbachev period has changed the thoughts in Soviet citizens' heads. Gorbachev has not yet reformed the economy effectively, but he has enshrined an entirely new set of principles for his countrymen. His most important contribution in this regard may be the destruction of old definitions of "impossible." So much that was once considered impossible is now routine that many thoughtful Soviet citizens have ceased being intimidated by the old taboos. By speaking out with some candor during this period, Gorbachev has accomplished something comparable to the feat of the little boy who shouted out what everyone else knew—that the emperor was naked. It will not be possible for any future, more reactionary Soviet leader simply to announce—as Soviet leaders did for so long—that everything is rosy and wonderful. Gorbachev has eliminated that argument from the usable political vocabulary.

Nor does there appear to be an option of abandoning economic reform and returning to Brezhnevite central controls. Ligachev and his allies have long since acknowledged that the old ways were corrupt and ineffective. Vitaliy Korotich, the editor of *Ogonyek,* one of the loudest trumpets of glasnost, told me: "Without liberalization, the country would just grind to a halt."

His sentiment is widely shared—so widely that no voice can be heard making the traditional, contrary argument. This is Gorbachev's biggest advantage: no element in the party has come forward with a plausible solution for the country's problems that differs from his. Even the traditional bureaucrats most discomfited by what is going on cannot offer a hopeful alternative. So it seems most likely now that Gorbachev's colleagues will give him more time to try to find successful antidotes to economic stagnation.

VIII

Russians are coming to terms with the failure of their system, and so should we. Of course they are eager to put it right; many of them would like to return to the days when both they and the outside world saw the Soviet Union as the only genuine rival to the United States for international preeminence. But the return of that day is at best a long way off. In truth, it is unlikely ever to come again.

Stalin's goal was to create an empire tied together by communist ideology, fueled by communist efficiency and dominated by Great Russian ambitions. But the ideology has failed, the efficiency has proven illusory, and the ambitions are anachronistic in the modern world. What is left is a brontosaurus empire, one unfit for survival in a new environment—today's world.

This metaphor was suggested by Lev Kopelev, an extraordinary Russian who was born in Kiev five years before the Bolshevik Revolution, personally participated in many of the most exciting phases of the Soviet experiment, and was driven from his homeland in 1981 because of his own brand of glasnost, then not in favor. He now lives in Cologne, West Germany. In his own lifetime Kopelev has seen the demise of the German, French, British, Austro-Hungarian, Portuguese, Dutch, Italian and Japanese empires—the twentieth century has not been hospitable to such enterprises. This century has been marked by the rise of science, technology and self-knowledge, all of which work against the kind of centralized power needed to maintain an empire or an authoritarian society.

The Russians fought against the times despite setbacks that began long ago, with the defections of Yugoslavia and China, and the rebellions in East Germany, Hungary, Czechoslovakia and Poland. But the fight cannot be waged much longer, because there is no more adhesive to hold the empire together. Even within the borders of the Soviet Union there are signs of grave strain.

Most of the twentieth-century empires collapsed peacefully, but some only fell under the pressure of violence. The French held on too long at too great a cost; the Russians may do the same. It is hard now to imagine how Gorbachev or any future Soviet leader could gracefully yield to the Poles or the Hungarians—not to mention the Armenians or the Estonians—their independence.

But the entire Gorbachev phenomenon was hard to imagine before it happened. These are amazing times. The most dramatic political experiment of the century is collapsing before our eyes— slowly, but certainly. ∎

Notes

1. Djilas expressed this opinion in a seminar conducted at the School of Advanced International Studies in Washington on March 4, 1988. For more of his views, see "Djilas on Gorbachev," an interview with George Urban, *Encounter,* September/October 1988, pp. 3–19.

The Soviet Union: Realism Requires Prudence

James A. Baker III

There are good reasons for both optimistic and pessimistic views of today's Soviet Union. No one can doubt that there are very real changes. Many were unthinkable just a few years ago. The SS-20s are being destroyed. Soviet troops are leaving Afghanistan. Some political prisoners have been released. American doctors will soon visit psychiatric hospitals where prisoners of conscience have been sent. Soviet history itself is sometimes subject to harsh scrutiny. In other words, the slogans of *glasnost* and *perestroika* are being given content.

These are reasons to be hopeful. But realism requires us to be prudent. However fascinating the twists and turns of *perestroika* may be, and however riveting the details of Soviet decline as reported in Soviet newspapers, the Soviet Union remains a heavily armed superpower. The talk is different but the force structure and policies that support far-reaching interests and clients have not changed commensurately. Many of those policies and those clients are hostile to American values and threaten our interests and our allies. That's a reality.

In light of both the change and continuity in the Soviet Union, realistic American policy should be guided by these principles:

First, we should continue to welcome reform and changes in the Soviet Union that promise more freedom at home, in the workplace, or in public institutions. But we should never measure the progress of Mr. Gorbachev's reforms by how many credits, concessions or accommodations we might make ostensibly to help him succeed with his domestic plans. Ultimately, as the Soviets themselves acknowledge, *perestroika* depends not on help from outside, but on political, bureaucratic, and sociological changes in the Soviet Union.

Second, while recognizing that Moscow's policies are informed by a new sense of realism, we should also understand that our policies have contributed to that sense of realism. Our willingness to support the *mujahidin*—not only economic dilemmas in the Soviet Union—helped bring about the Soviet withdrawal from Afghanistan. Our willingness, with NATO, to deploy the Pershing and cruise missiles—not only food shortages—helped bring about the INF Treaty. Where we have not raised the cost of adventure or aggression, we see little evidence of change. Can it be a coincidence that the only regional conflict where we have failed to bring consistent, effective pressure—in Central America—we see little trace of new thinking in Soviet foreign policy?

Third, we must continue to probe Moscow along every aspect of our agenda—arms control, human rights, regional conflicts, bilateral relations. We are interested in cooperating and negotiating to make progress wherever it can be made. Arms control should encompass conventional weapons and chemical and ballistic missile proliferation, going beyond expressions of general principles to practical details. And human rights means full compliance with the Helsinki Accords. There can be no relaxation of our standards on this issue.

Fourth, we need additional focus on the regional conflicts, whether in Central America, South Asia, Southern Africa, the Persian Gulf or the Arab-Israeli conflict. Does the Soviet Union truly see a lowering of tension, and negotiations to be in its own interests? We should not allow the rhetoric of restraint to become a substitute for restraint itself; nor should we permit interest in diplomatic processes to be sufficient in the absence of a commitment to making actual progress.

Fifth, we may need a new category in our relations, to deal with global problems such as terrorism, drugs and the environment. We ought to find out whether Moscow can be helpful on these issues and if not, why not.

I am convinced that Western strength and Soviet domestic weakness have set the stage for the remarkable realism that has distinguished Mr. Gorbachev's tenure so far. Our task is to arrange affairs so that whatever the outcome of *perestroika,* a more responsible, constructive Soviet foreign policy will remain in Moscow's interest. ∎

James A. Baker III is U.S. Secretary of State. This article is drawn from prepared testimony given at his confirmation hearings before the Senate Foreign Relations Committee.

Source: From U.S. Arms Control and Disarmament Agency, *Arms Control Update,* No. 11, February 1989.

Suggested Additional Readings

Brzezinski, Zbigniew. *Game Plan: A Geostrategic Framework for the Conduct of the U.S.-Soviet Contest* (Boston: Atlantic Monthly Press, 1986).

Cohen, Stephen. *Sovieticus: American Perceptions and Soviet Realities* (New York: Norton, 1986).

Gaddis, John Lewis. *The Long Peace: Inquiries into the History of the Cold War* (New York: Oxford University Press, 1987).

Hough, Jerry. *Russia and the West: Gorbachev and the Politics of Reform* (New York: Simon & Schuster, 1988).

Hyland, William G. *Mortal Rivals: Superpower Relations from Nixon to Reagan* (New York: Random House, 1987).

Korbonski, Andrzej, and Francis Fukuyama. *The Soviet Union and the Third World* (Ithaca, NY: Cornell University Press, 1987).

Nye, Joseph S. (ed.). *The Making of America's Soviet Policy* (New Haven, CT: Yale University Press, 1984).

Ràanan, Uri. *et al. Third World Marxist-Leninist Regimes: Strengths, Vulnerabilities, and U.S. Policy* (Washington: Pergamon-Brassey, 1985).

Rowen, Henry, and Charles Wolf, Jr. (eds.). *The Future of the Soviet Empire* (New York: St. Martin's Press, 1987).

Rubinstein, Alvin Z. *Soviet Foreign Policy Since World War II* (Glenview, IL: Scott, Foresman, 1989).

Ryavec, Karl W. *United States-Soviet Relations* (London: Longman, 1989).

Saivetz, Carol R., and Sylvia Woodby. *Soviet-Third World Relations* (Boulder, CO: Westview Press, 1985).

Tismaneanu, Vladimir. *The Crisis of Marxist Ideology in Eastern Europe* (London: Routledge, 1988).

Wildavsky, Aaron. *Beyond Containment: Alternative American Policies Toward the Soviet Union* (San Francisco: ICS Press, 1983).

CHAPTER TWO

Western Europe

*
*

As Western Europe has recovered from the devastation of World War II, become more affluent, and regained its self-confidence, it has begun staking out positions of increasing independence from the United States. Also involved in this new independence are distrust of United States foreign policy, which Western Europe sees as erratic and inconsistent; a desire to trade with the East (Eastern Europe and the Soviet Union); and a stronger belief than most Americans have that the Cold War is basically over and that Western Europe can therefore afford to go its separate way.

The foreign policy issues that these changes give rise to are many, complex, and difficult. Some have argued that, because of Europe's greater independence, NATO is no longer serving a useful purpose and that we should therefore disband it and also go our separate ways. Others argue for the permanence of the Western Alliance of democratic nations and that NATO need only be reformed. We also need to ask what it will mean when Europe unifies in 1992—both economically to some extent politically—and thus forms a gigantic economic bloc that rivals the power of the United States and Japan. A related issue is what to do with all the U.S. troops in Europe: if Europe doesn't want them there any longer, if the Cold War is essentially over—and since we in the U.S. need to reduce our military budget—then the pressures are sure to mount to bring the troops home—or at least a goodly share of them.

The NATO alliance is riven with present and future difficulties. Each of the individual countries wishes to pursue its own independent foreign policy as well as an alliance policy. Great Britain wishes to play a special role in the Alliance; but one of these years, however, the Labour Party will doubtless come to power with its more independent foreign policy, and that will cause major problems. France has a special role in Africa and sometimes wishes to pursue its own foreign and even military policy. West Germany wishes to expand its commerce with the East and may one day reunify with East Germany, but the cost of that will likely be the neutralization of Germany. Spain is more concerned about its interests in the Mediterranean than about any presumed Soviet threat; Italy simultaneously pursues both a Mediterranean and a European policy; and Portugal also pursues both a European and an "Atlanticist" (Azores, Brazil, and former Portuguese Africa) policy.

In addition to the individual countries, the several distinct regions of Europe have their own preoccupations. On the northern flank, the Scandinavian countries lie very close to the Soviet Union and many of its main military bases. They often wish to distance themselves from the United States and to pursue a more neutralist stance, which may result in the "Finlandization" of Northern Europe—that is, a neutralist and independent foreign policy in return for Soviet promises not to attack and overrun them. Southern Europe is at present pursuing both a North-South (across the Mediterranean) and an East-West foreign policy; it also runs the risk of getting caught up in the violence and terrorism of the Middle East conflict. Central Europe (Germany and its neighbors) may also undergo fundamental transformations in the next decade as East and West are increasingly linked together on a host of trade, cultural, diplomatic, and foreign policy issues.

The most volatile area is Eastern Europe. Yugoslavia is deeply divided and may well unravel. The discontent with the dismal economic performance and poor living standards in several countries is rising. Eastern European young people, especially, want the same freedom, culture, and opportunities to travel as young people in the West. Eastern Europe is impatient with its stifling bureaucracies, the political monopolies of the local Communist regimes, and the continuing presence of Soviet occupation armies. We should not be too surprised if these simmering discontents produce some violent anti-Soviet explosions in future years. Since the Soviets are now preoccupied with their domestic reforms and are beginning to pull some of their troops out of Eastern Europe—thus increasing the odds

of such rebellions succeeding—the question is surely going to arise as to what the U.S. response should be. Should we aid these freedom fighters, which we failed to do the last time (1956) Eastern Europe rose up in rebellion against its Soviet overlords. Should we stand by neutrally and let the protagonists fight it out? Or, for the sake of preserving stability in Eastern Europe, should we aid the Soviets and the Eastern Europe communist regimes in discouraging these potentially dangerous and destabilizing rebellions?

Overall, with conflicts in the Third World (Afghanistan, Southeast Asia, southern Africa, Central America) now winding down, it may well be that in the next decade these and other changes in Europe will once again make that area no longer the periphery but the main focus of foreign policy.

Our readings in this section begin with a balanced statement prepared by the Foreign Policy Association on Western Europe between the two superpowers. Next comes a background piece on the history of NATO written by James Miller of the Department of State. Melvyn Krauss and Jack Forrest then engage in a spirited debate about whether we should pull out of or stay in NATO. Several brief journalistic pieces follow, focused on Europe, our European alliances, the conflicts within NATO, and the future of the area.

Western Europe   *Between the Superpowers*

In October 1986, President Ronald Reagan and Soviet General Secretary Mikhail S. Gorbachev met in Reykjavik, Iceland, to discuss nuclear arms control issues in preparation for a possible summit meeting in the U.S. During the course of the talks, the two leaders ventured into uncharted territory. Gorbachev called for the elimination of all long-range nuclear weapons by the year 2000; Reagan countered with a proposal to eliminate all nuclear ballistic missiles within 10 years. Although Reykjavik ended without agreement, many observers concluded that the meeting represented a watershed both in the arms control negotiations and in U.S.-European relations.

Moreover, many who thought so were not happy about it. In the U.S., experienced military and arms control analysts charged the Reagan Administration with not having thought through the implications of its proposals. "Reykjavik," wrote former Secretary of Defense James R. Schlesinger, "represented a near disaster from which we were fortunate to escape. . . . Perhaps the summit's only useful result is that it has changed what had been the universal European clamor for an arms control agreement into a keen European awareness that such agreements might seriously damage their security interests."

At Reykjavik, the U.S. discussed —without consulting its West European allies—eliminating the nuclear weapons that Western Europe has relied on to deter a Soviet attack for the past four decades. This raised anew questions in

many West European minds about the future of the North Atlantic Treaty Organization (NATO) that links the U.S. and Western Europe, and about the extent to which West Europeans can continue to depend on the U.S. for their security.

Indeed, West European—especially West German—reservations complicated prospects for a more modest agreement between the U.S. and U.S.S.R. limiting intermediate-range nuclear forces (INF) for nearly a year after Reykjavik. But in September 1987, Soviet Foreign Minister Eduard A. Shevardnadze and U.S. Secretary of State George P. Shultz met in Washington and agreed "in principle" to eliminate all longer- and shorter-range INF. Critics of the agreement, like former Secretary of State Henry A. Kissinger, think it spells a serious crisis for the alliance.

Concerns about NATO's future have been raised on numerous occasions before, as the alliance has gone through crises of confidence over nuclear strategy, East-West relations, Third World policies and economic issues. The very real differences of interest and outlook on various issues between the U.S. and some West European countries have led people on both sides of the Atlantic to question whether each would be better served by at least a lessened dependence on the alliance.

What do West Europeans, wedged as they are between the Soviet Union, whose motives they distrust, on one side, and the U.S., whose values they share, on the other, find most threatening? What reassures them? Can they continue

to rely on the U.S. for security? Or would they be better advised to become more self-sufficient? Should they move toward a more neutral position between the superpowers rather than putting so much emphasis on their military alliance with the U.S.? And what about U.S. interests? Are Americans well served by their defense tie with Western Europe, or would they be better off without it?

Two Europes

In February 1945, on the eve of victory for the U.S. and its World War II allies, Britain, France and the Soviet Union, over Nazi Germany, U.S. President Franklin D. Roosevelt, British Prime Minister Winston Churchill and Soviet leader Joseph Stalin met at Yalta, a resort in the Soviet Crimea. They discussed, among other things, how to prevent German power from ever again threatening the peace in Europe. The agreement they reached in effect gave political permanence to the military division of Europe in existence at the end of the war, with Soviet troops in control of Eastern Europe and with U.S., British and French forces predominant in most of the rest. In return, the U.S.S.R. promised to adhere to basic standards of freedom and human rights, including "the right of all people to choose the form of government under which they will live" and to hold democratic elections at the earliest possible time.

Critics have blamed Roosevelt and Churchill ever since for permitting the creation of a Soviet satellite system in Eastern Europe.

Source: From *Great Decisions 1988,* Foreign Policy Association, New York, 1989. Reprinted by permission.

But neither believed at the time that he had sanctioned such a degree of Soviet control, and no one, in the West at least, realized how permanent the division would become—or how quickly and thoroughly the rivalry between the U.S. and U.S.S.R. would come to dominate the postwar world order.

However, subsequent events hardened the division. While the U.S. demobilized as rapidly as it could, the war-devastated countries of Western Europe tottered toward economic and political collapse. This was fertile ground for European Communist parties and their allies in the Kremlin. When the British announced in March 1947 that they could no longer maintain their presence in the eastern Mediterranean, Greece was in the throes of a civil war between the royal government and Communist-led guerrillas, and the Soviet Union was threatening Turkey, which controlled the only Soviet access to the Black Sea. Recognizing that the U.S. was the only country in a position to counterbalance the growing strength of the Communists in Europe, President Harry S. Truman pledged to help any country faced with the threat of Communist invasion or subversion. To back up this commitment, the U.S. sent aid to Greece and Turkey in 1947 and provided over $13 billion in Marshall Plan aid to 16 European countries between 1948 and 1951.

In the meantime, the Soviet Union was consolidating its hold over Eastern Europe, in violation of the Western understanding of the Yalta terms. In 1946, Churchill made his famous speech warning that Moscow was building an Iron Curtain across Europe. Between 1945 and 1948, Bulgaria, Hungary, Poland and Romania were all converted to "people's democratic republics" under tight Soviet control.

By 1948, when democracy in Czechoslovakia came to an abrupt end, congressional alarm in the U.S. was strong enough to overcome the traditional American fear of "entangling alliances." A bipartisan majority in June approved the Vandenberg Resolution calling for the association of the U.S. with a regional "collective security arrangement" in Europe, paving the way for the signing of the North Atlantic Treaty on April 4, 1949, and the creation of NATO. In 1955, the Soviet Union set up the East European equivalent of NATO, the Warsaw Pact. Where the allied Soviet and Western troops had met at the time of Germany's surrender in 1945 was now the front line of the cold war.

Europe Between the Superpowers

The division of Europe has, in the words of one observer, turned out to be "the first set of stable relationships Europe has known since the rise of German power [in the late 19th century]." There has not been a war in Europe—or between the superpowers—since the end of World War II.

But the postwar situation created new problems for West Europeans. The era when West European nations were colonial powers dominating the global political order ended with World War II. Smaller and weaker than the two superpowers, West European governments chose a military alliance and a close economic and political relationship with the U.S., an ocean away, to protect themselves from their Communist neighbors.

When NATO was first formed, West European dependence on the U.S. for its defense was unavoidable, and U.S. willingness to provide assistance and protection served both Europeans and Americans well. West European governments could concentrate on rebuilding their economies. and the U.S. could count on West European support for its foreign policy objectives. But, as Kissinger once wrote, "while generosity makes hegemony bearable it does not render it acceptable." The transatlantic relationship at its smoothest has never been totally calm.

The Legacy of Yalta

Most European-American quarrels can be traced to a difference of opinion over security. Although there is general agreement that the Atlantic alliance exists to guard against "the Soviet threat," Europeans and Americans frequently disagree over the exact nature of that threat and the best strategy for countering it.

At the root of the problem lies the geographic fact that "we [the U.S.] are here and they are there." Europeans know that should a war break out, it would probably be fought on European territory.

Europeans are not unfamiliar with war: two devastating world wars have been fought in Europe in this century. Americans have been more fortunate: except for the Japanese attacks on Pearl Harbor and the Aleutian Islands during World War II, there has not been a war on U.S. territory since the Civil War. Of the 50 million lives lost during World War II, fewer than 1% were American. The Europeans' fear of war and their proximity to the Soviet Union make them acutely conscious of the fine line between guarding against hostile

Soviet actions and provoking them—a line which they think Americans, from their different vantage point, sometimes overlook.

EUROPEAN SECURITY: WEST GERMANY

The fault line through Central Europe cuts through the middle of what was a united Germany before World War II. Until recently it was one of the most heavily armed stretches of ground anywhere on earth. Of all the NATO allies, West Germans feel the division of Europe most acutely: with access to family and friends in East Germany controlled by one superpower while their defense rests with the other, West Germans are uniquely exposed to the complexities and dangers of life in a divided Europe.

Flashpoint: Berlin

At the close of the war, the occupation forces of the U.S., Britain, France and the U.S.S.R. divided the defeated country into four administrative zones, as had been agreed at Yalta. Berlin, the former capital, 100 miles inside the Soviet zone, was similarly divided into four parts. The division was to be temporary, but the occupying countries never reached agreement on how Germany was to be governed. With the onset of the cold war, the temporary lines between the western and eastern zones hardened into political partition.

The U.S. and the Soviet Union took steps that eventually bound their German zones to their own political blocs. The U.S., French and British zones were merged in 1948. The three powers then decided to ensure the political stability and economic viability of their

part of Germany by organizing it into a new entity, eventually the Federal Republic of Germany (FRG). The Soviet Union tried to force the West to drop its plans for the new state by cutting off Western access to Berlin. The blockade failed because of the successful year-long airlift of vital supplies mounted by the U.S. and its allies, and the FRG came into being with the proclamation of its Basic Law in September 1949. The Soviet Union announced the birth of the German Democratic Republic (GDR) the following month. Berlin's vulnerable location inside the Soviet bloc underscored West Germany's precarious position and made the city a focus of East-West tensions for two decades.

The 1950 invasion of South Korea by Communist North Korea, apparently with the knowledge of the Soviet Union, heightened European and American fears that the U.S.S.R. might be planning to attack Western Europe. NATO leaders decided that in order to strengthen Western defenses, West Germany should be rearmed, but only on condition that it renounce the manufacture of nuclear weapons and that its armed forces be integrated into the alliance—and therefore under U.S. command. West Germany rearmed and was accepted as a full member of NATO in 1955. Immediately thereafter, the Soviet Union established the Warsaw Pact and allowed East Germany to create its own armed forces.

The German Question

Following both world wars, "the German question" concerned how to find a way to prevent Germany, the most populous and powerful country in Europe aside from

Russia, from starting another conflict. Since 1945, Germany's European neighbors—both east and west—have felt more secure because the country is divided, and because the military power of the larger, stronger Federal Republic is constrained by its participation in NATO.

Although most West Germans continue to feel, as they have since they joined NATO, that their participation in the alliance is essential to their security, at the same time they have a strong interest in expanding ties with East Germany. To West Germans today, the German question has to do with how they can overcome the worst effects of the division without alarming their neighbors.

West Germany's Basic Law kept the possibility of reunification open. The preamble closes by calling upon "the entire German people... to achieve in free self-determination the unity and freedom of Germany." Until 1969, reunification remained a formal goal of the West German government in Bonn. It refused to recognize East Germany—or to deal with any government that did recognize it (except the Soviet Union)—claiming to be the sole representative of all of the German people. During this period, the policies of the ruling conservative Christian Democratic and Christian Social Union parties served to weld West Germany more firmly to the Western alliance. The Federal Republic and the U.S. developed a close relationship, which strengthened as the "German miracle" of economic revival turned West Germany into a major economic power.

The opposition Social Democratic party (SPD) argued during the 1950s that increasing military cooperation with the West would make reunification impossible. But under the leadership of West Berlin Mayor Willy Brandt in the early 1960s, SPD thinking gradually changed. Brandt emphasized the need for a close defense and economic relationship with the West as well as diplomatic ties with the East aimed at overcoming the worst effects of the division—the separation of families, the restrictions on travel, the severed economic ties, and the vulnerability of West Berlin.

Several events helped swing a majority of West Germans over to the SPD way of thinking. One was the construction of the Berlin Wall, which was built in 1961 to stop a mass migration of East Germans to West Berlin. To the dismay of West Germans, NATO's response to construction of the wall was limited to a verbal protest.

The following year, Moscow attempted to base nuclear weapons in Cuba, within striking distance of U.S. territory. The crisis, which brought the superpowers to the brink of nuclear war, alarmed Europeans, who feared they would be drawn in, even though the issue was not a European one, and without being consulted. Europeans welcomed the lessening of tensions between the superpowers in the wake of the crisis, although they were also fearful of U.S.-Soviet dealings from which they were excluded. But the easing of tensions between the superpowers also cleared the way for West Germany to pursue its own diplomatic overtures to the East.

When Brandt became chancellor in 1969, *Ostpolitik,* or "eastern policy," became the guiding philosophy of the West German government. In the future, West Germany would seek security through diplomatic initiatives to the East as well as through its ties to NATO. Over the next three years, West Germany signed a series of treaties which served to defuse some of the major sources of conflict in Central Europe, including Berlin. These were:

• the 1970 renunciation of force treaty with the U.S.S.R. that declared the postwar boundaries of Germany inviolable;
• the 1970 treaty with Poland that recognized the Oder and Neisse rivers as the boundary; West Germany renounced all claims to Polish territory;
• the 1972 "basic treaty" with East Germany that recognized the status quo between the two countries and adopted the formula of "two states in one nation."

Critically important, the four occupying powers of Berlin negotiated the Quadripartite Agreement, signed in 1971, that recognized the rights of both East and West in Berlin. The U.S.S.R. assured unimpeded access to West Berlin from West Germany and recognized West Berlin's right to maintain and develop contacts with West Germany, but Berlin was declared "not to be a constituent part of West Germany."

Contrary to earlier West German policy, Brandt's "*Deutschland-politik*" —that aspect of Ostpolitik dealing with relations between the two Germanys—accepted the division of Germany as a fact of life, and focused on softening its effects. Unlike the Christian Democratic government's approach, Brandt's idea was to establish diplomatic contacts with the East *first,* rather than insisting on reunification as a precondition. In this way, he hoped to reduce tensions between the Germanys and to allay East European suspicions of the FRG. In a calmer, more predictable atmosphere, human, cultural and economic ties across the Iron Curtain could be multiplied to the benefit of both East and West Germans, perhaps making the long-term goal of reunification more likely.

Future West German Policy

Ostpolitik has remained central to West German foreign policy even though the SPD lost power in 1982 to a coalition led by the Christian Democrats, who had opposed the policy. The improvement of inter-German trade and political relations has produced tangible benefits for West Germans: normalization of what had been a volatile situation in Berlin, increased personal contacts with East Germans, and a profitable strengthening of economic ties between East and West Germany provided a major boost to the already thriving West German economy.

As tensions with the East have lessened, "the Soviet threat" seems a less immediate menace to many West Germans. At the same time, public concern about nuclear weapons has risen. Today, a greater percentage of the population than ever before is actively interested in the country's defense policies, a chronically touchy subject. A majority of West Germans have shown conclusively that they continue to support the government's policies by returning Chancellor Helmut Kohl's strongly pro-NATO government to power in 1983 and again in 1987. The opposition SPD, meanwhile, has moved to the left, and today supports some policies that, if adopted, would have a significant impact on NATO strategy, such as calling for a nuclear-free zone in Central Europe and the creation of West German armed forces that are "structurally incapable of aggression." Whether the SPD would actually hold to this line if returned to office is unclear.

THE NUCLEAR DILEMMA

The NATO treaty provides that "an armed attack on one . . . shall be considered an attack against . . . all." When the treaty was first signed, it was mainly a symbol of the American political commitment to Western Europe, resting on a unilateral pledge by the U.S. that it might respond to any conventional attack on Western Europe with nuclear strikes on the Soviet Union—a strategy that became known in the 1950s as massive retaliation.

The idea behind the guarantee was to *deter* the Soviet Union from attacking by convincing Moscow that the U.S. response would be so devastating as to outweigh any conceivable gain. Nuclear deterrence depends both on military capabilities and on credibility: the other side has to believe that you can and will inflict unacceptable damage on it if provoked.

The defense of NATO's European members depends on "extended deterrence"—effectively "coupling" the nuclear arsenal of the U.S. to the defense of Europe in a highly visible way, so that both the Soviet Union and West Europeans feel sure that the U.S. will quickly become involved if war breaks out in Europe. Since the 1950s, coupling has also been assured by a large U.S. military presence in Europe (over 325,000

ground troops today) and an American commander in chief of NATO forces. But because of the Soviet strength in ground forces, the nuclear component of deterrence has always been considered crucial.

When the U.S. possessed clear nuclear superiority, its threat to respond with nuclear weapons to a conventional attack on Western Europe was believable. But by the time massive retaliation became official NATO policy in 1954, Soviet advances in nuclear weapons had already begun to undermine the credibility of the strategy. In 1957, the Soviet Union successfully tested its first intercontinental ballistic missiles (ICBMs), which gave it the means to strike back. (With a range of 4,000 miles or more, ICBMs can hit the territory of one superpower from the territory of the other. The U.S. also calls weapons with such a range "strategic.") Once Moscow could strike back, some West European observers began to doubt that the U.S. would necessarily treat an attack on Europe as an attack on itself. French President Charles de Gaulle made this argument most forcefully to justify pulling his country out of NATO's integrated military structure in 1966.

Flexible Response

Seeking to put European doubts to rest and to bolster the credibility of its nuclear deterrent, the U.S. developed the policy of flexible response. Under this doctrine, NATO would respond to a limited attack with limited means, rather than being forced to make the dubious claim that it would risk an all-out nuclear war and the devastation of American territory in response to, say, an isolated

Soviet attack on a West German military base. The strategy calls for a "ladder of escalation options," from conventional through intercontinental-range nuclear, which would permit NATO to match or prevail over the Soviet Union at any level of conflict.

Although NATO officially adopted flexible response in 1967, it did so only after a lengthy debate. Flexible response, to many Europeans, implied the possibility of a "limited war," which sounded to them as if it might mean "war limited to Europe." As historian Theodore Draper put it, the principle that a limited war is preferable to a full-scale conflict "is reasonable enough—so long as no one asks where the level is . . . located or where that limited war is going to take place." Americans, on the other hand, were interested in avoiding an all-out strategic nuclear exchange that would put American territory at risk over a European issue. This has made coming up with a common NATO defense policy that is agreeable to all an extremely difficult and always politically charged proposition. Flexible response was designed to circumvent this problem by being intentionally ambiguous: as one study put it, the doctrine calls for the use of nuclear weapons in defense of Europe "as soon as necessary but as late as possible."

Defense and Détente

The same year that flexible response became official NATO doctrine, NATO released the Harmel Report, which established defense and détente—a lessening of tensions —as the "twin pillars" of the approach to be taken by the alliance toward the Soviet Union. The Harmel Report was an answer to critics of NATO like de Gaulle and the political left in some countries who charged that defense was being pursued at the expense of political solutions, making life in Europe more, not less, dangerous. The inclusion of détente as a component of Western strategy toward the Soviet Union helped build a consensus in Western Europe on security matters that lasted for over a decade.

European détente also linked West European efforts to those of the U.S., which had been pursuing arms control and other negotiations with the U.S.S.R. since the Cuban missile crisis. The U.S. was not without reservations about some European thinking: it feared that too much friendliness between Western Europe and the Communist East might weaken NATO, or even encourage the rise of neutralism—especially in West Germany. But the Administration of Richard M. Nixon (1969–74) hoped that the alliance could agree on overall guidelines that would keep Europe from lowering its guard.

The American concept of détente was to use the common U.S. and Soviet interest in avoiding nuclear war as "a springboard for building a network of mutually advantageous relationships." As conceived by Nixon and his chief foreign policy adviser Kissinger, détente was to work primarily through "linkage": offering the Soviets the possibility of agreements in areas of special concern to them—for example trade, which would give them access to more Western capital and technology. The idea was to discourage Moscow from seeking to upset the status quo by giving it a greater stake in the existing world order.

The crowning achievements of U.S.-Soviet détente came in 1972. At a summit meeting in Moscow between Nixon and Soviet leader Leonid I. Brezhnev, the SALT I (strategic arms limitation talks) agreements—the Interim Agreement on strategic offensive weapons and the Antiballistic Missile (ABM) Treaty—plus a number of other treaties and a statement on basic principles of coexistence were signed.

The U.S. reaffirmed its support for détente in Europe by participating in the European negotiations on reducing nonnuclear forces (the mutual and balanced force reductions, or MBFR talks) that got under way in 1973 and are still continuing, and in the 35-nation Helsinki Conference on Security and Cooperation in Europe, for which preparations began the same year. Under the Helsinki accords signed in 1975, the West agreed to accept Europe's existing boundaries in return for Soviet promises to respect human rights and fundamental freedoms.

Détente Unravels

Improved superpower relations began to unravel in less than two years when it became clear that Washington and Moscow understood détente and the signed statement on basic principles to mean different things. Moscow did not gain the "mutually advantageous" trade it sought, mainly because of the Jackson-Vanik and Stevenson amendments to the 1974 Trade Act that made U.S. trading privileges contingent upon an improved Soviet human rights policy. Washington also failed to win a Soviet commitment to stay out of Third World political and military struggles. Although Moscow main-

tained that it had never promised to stop providing military and economic support to "revolutionary" regimes, Americans felt betrayed: it seemed to them that Moscow had taken advantage of a more relaxed international climate to gain unilateral advantage.

Although the superpowers did sign a second arms limitation agreement (SALT II) in 1979 during the Administration of Jimmy Carter (1977–81), Senate ratification of the treaty became a casualty of deteriorating relations. (The U.S. nevertheless agreed to honor its terms.) Détente gradually developed into a dirty word in the American political vocabulary as the atmosphere between the superpowers soured. This posed a knotty problem for West Europeans—especially the West Germans—who could point to a number of tangible benefits from European détente and who did not want these gains jeopardized by Soviet-American quarrels.

In retaliation for the December 1979 Soviet invasion of Afghanistan, the Carter Administration embargoed grain and high-technology exports to the Soviet Union and boycotted the 1980 Moscow Olympics. Washington urged its allies to join it in these sanctions. But although Western Europe supported the embargo of militarily relevant technology, it declined to support the rest of the sanctions. (West Germany was the only European country to boycott the Olympics.) Europeans did not feel they should have to go along with American political and economic policies on issues that fell outside of the Atlantic defense area. In addition, past experience with economic sanctions had taught them that Europeans would suffer from them more than Moscow. But to Americans, this lack of support from allies dependent upon U.S. military protection smacked of ingratitude or worse—blindness to a growing Soviet threat.

The Pipeline and Poland

A more serious crisis in the alliance was precipitated by the Soviet-West European pipeline deal negotiated in 1978. In return for supplying the Soviet Union with capital, equipment, materials and technology to construct a natural gas pipeline from Siberia to Western Europe, six West European countries were guaranteed delivery of approximately 5% of their total energy needs over 25 years. Both the Carter and Reagan Administrations opposed the deal. They argued that depending on the Soviet Union for energy would make Western Europe more vulnerable to political blackmail, and that providing technology and some $8 billion to $10 billion in hard currency to Moscow was tantamount to a direct contribution to the Soviet military. Europeans responded that they needed an alternative source of oil to the volatile Middle East and that the amount of oil and gas they would receive through the pipeline did not constitute dependence.

In December 1981, the Polish government, under pressure from Moscow to clamp down on the independent labor movement Solidarity, declared martial law. Washington retaliated against Moscow by forbidding U.S. firms to export oil and gas technology or equipment to the Soviet Union, and urged West European countries participating in the pipeline project to follow suit. When they

refused, the U.S. extended its trade sanctions to include overseas subsidiaries and licensees of U.S. firms. Washington in effect was asserting the right to tell West European firms that they could not fulfill their contract obligations. This did not sit well with West European governments, who resented Washington's challenge to their sovereignty.

In the U.S., the conclusion many drew was that West Europeans had become so addicted to détente that they were prepared to tolerate Soviet behavior—including aggression in Afghanistan and repression in Poland—in order to preserve it. But to most West Europeans, the pipeline deal was a straightforward, good-sense economic deal, without the menacing strategic implications the U.S. saw in it. West Europeans were also incensed because Washington was asking economic sacrifices of them while at the same time lifting its own embargo on grain sales to the Soviet Union in order to appease U.S. farmers.

Apparently persuaded that this acrimonious marital dispute was more injurious to the health of the alliance than the pipeline, the Reagan Administration eventually backed down, settling for an agreement to reexamine East-West trade guidelines.

EUROMISSILES AND THE FUTURE

U.S.-European differences over Afghanistan and Poland were indications of how much the relationship between the U.S. and its Atlantic allies had changed since the late 1940s. Western Europe had developed into an economic power, helped by the formation in 1957 of

the European Economic Community (EEC), a free-trade zone with a common agricultural policy and external tariff. The Community had more weight than its six members would have had on their own and had become both an important economic partner—and rival—of the U.S.

Moreover, the image of the U.S. as a powerful global actor had been tarnished by its long, unpopular and ultimately unsuccessful involvement in the Vietnam War (1965–75), by the Watergate scandal (1972–74) and by the inability of the Carter Administration to end the 444-day Iran hostage crisis (1979–81). On top of this was the fact that the Soviet Union had caught up with the U.S. in the arms race by the 1970s, casting further doubt on the effectiveness of the U.S. nuclear umbrella.

The Peace Movement

By the end of the 1970s, too, the consensus over the Harmel formula of détente and defense was in trouble. Europeans were shocked when Defense Secretary Caspar W. Weinberger told a group of NATO defense ministers in 1981 that "If the movement from cold war to détente is progress, then let me say we cannot afford much more progress."

And there was trouble on the defense front. During the mid-1970s, while Moscow and Washington engaged in the SALT II negotiations to limit their intercontinental nuclear arsenals, the Soviet Union began deploying a new generation of intermediate-range nuclear weapons—the Backfire bomber and the SS-20 missile—aimed at Western Europe. (These weapons are usually referred to as INF. Longer-range INF, like the Backfire and the SS-20, can

Table 1   The INF deal: What will be Eliminated

U.S. Longer-range	U.S.S.R. (600–3,400 miles)
Pershing II	*SS-20*
108 launchers	441 launchers
108 warheads	1,323 warheads
Cruise	SS-4
116 launchers[1]	112 launchers
464 warheads	112 warheads
Shorter-range	**(300–600 miles)**
Pershing IA[2]	*SS–12/22*
72 launchers	110–20 launchers[3]
72 warheads	110–20 warheads
	SS–23
	20 launchers[3]
	20 warheads

[1]Due to be deployed by late 1988, number currently deployed is classified.
[2]Not specifically mentioned in agreement.
[3]U.S. Government estimates; the U.S.S.R. does not release these figures.
Sources: U.S. Government. International Institute for Strategic Studies. Jane's Weapons Systems. The Associated Press.

travel between 600 and 3,400 miles; shorter-range INF can travel between 300 and 600 miles. There are also nuclear weapons with still shorter ranges, known as tactical or battlefield nuclear weapons, with ranges of 0 to 300 miles.)

In an influential speech in October 1977, West German Chancellor Helmut Schmidt warned that European interests were being ignored in the SALT II talks: if the U.S. and Soviet Union agreed to reduce their strategic nuclear weapons to equal levels, they would in effect cancel each other out, leaving Europe decoupled from the U.S. and vulnerable to the growing Soviet superiority in INF weapons in Europe.

West European concern led NATO to undertake two major studies that resulted in the dual-track decision of December 1979.

One track called for the development and deployment in Europe of new U.S. INF weapons—Pershing II ballistic missiles and cruise missiles. The second track called for arms control negotiations with the Soviets aimed at removing all INF from Europe. The call for arms control negotiations was included primarily to make the new weapons more palatable to that part of the European public—especially in West Germany—that viewed the addition of more nuclear weapons to the Western arsenal, even in response to a Soviet buildup, as adding to the risks of a nuclear conflict in Europe.

When there was no movement at all on arms control during Reagan's first months in office, West European opposition to the missiles gained momentum. Several weeks after some 250,000 demonstrators turned out in Bonn to protest the stationing of the missiles—and after full consultations with NATO—the Reagan Administration presented Moscow with the proposal foreshadowed by the dual-track decision. This was the "zero option" proposal of November 1981. The U.S. offered to cancel the deployment of American Pershing II and cruise missiles if the Soviet Union would eliminate all of its INF weapons. Because the U.S. missiles were not scheduled to be installed for another two years, the proposal asked Moscow to trade something for nothing. The European governments welcomed the offer, which they did not expect Moscow to accept, since it enabled them to tell their publics that the ball was now in the Soviet court. "The purpose of this whole exercise," one then State Department official put it, "is maximum political advantage. It's not arms control

we're engaged in, it's alliance management."

The first of the missiles were installed in West Germany and Britain in November 1983. In the face of the peace movement's campaign against the missiles and Moscow's attempts to prevent their emplacement, the deployment was widely hailed as a triumph for NATO. But the INF crisis had raised once again—this time with an unprecedented level of public debate—alliance disagreements over nuclear weapons issues.

Reykjavik and Washington

The storm temporarily died down once deployment began. But three years later, at Reykjavik in October 1986, Gorbachev offered the West the very deal the U.S. had offered Moscow back in 1981: the zero option, with the exception that each side would be able to retain 100 INF missiles on its own soil. Reagan agreed in principle—without consulting the allies—to remove the very missiles that had been so politically costly to put in.

This placed West European leaders in a quandary: how could they now reject a proposal they had previously endorsed? West European publics by and large supported the proposal, which put added pressure on their governments. On the other hand, some experts feared that flexible response would be weakened if all NATO's longer-range INF were removed—even if Soviet INF were eliminated as well—because of Soviet superiority in nonnuclear weapons. West Germany was also concerned that the zero option did not address shorter-range INF missiles, a category in which the Soviet Union has a near monopoly. (The U.S. has none, although West Germany has 72 Pershing 1A missiles, whose warheads are under American control.)

Following the Rekyjavik meeting, an INF agreement was hammered out that Soviet Foreign Minister Shevardnadze and U.S. Secretary of State Shultz agreed to "in principle" in September 1987. All longer-range and shorter-range INF missiles on both sides will be eliminated, under what has been dubbed the double-zero approach. Bonn removed what appeared to be the last major hitch to the agreement in August 1987 when it offered to scrap its Pershing 1A missiles once U.S. and Soviet INF were eliminated, as the Soviets had demanded. (Both the U.S. and West Germany had maintained that these missiles could not be a subject for U.S.-Soviet talks, since they are German, not American missiles.)

The agreement received a mixed reception on both sides of the Atlantic. Former NATO commander General Bernard W. Rogers, for example, has argued repeatedly that removal of the missiles would eliminate NATO's ability to strike targets inside the Soviet Union from Western Europe. "We can't have just disadvantaged conventional forces on one hand and strategic nuclear forces on the other and no coupling in between. . . . You have to have nuclear weapons in there someplace. That's what makes our deterrent credible. . . ." Former President Nixon and former Secretary of State Kissinger argued in a *Los Angeles Times* op-ed piece that "removing medium- and short-range nuclear weapons would simply make Europe safe for conventional war."

Others disagree that INF are that crucial: nuclear deterrence is effective so long as an adversary cannot rule out your nuclear response to his aggression, according to this point of view. This requirement is more than met by the presence of over 325,000 American troops in Europe in addition to the rest of the roughly 50,000 nuclear weapons in the U.S. arsenal that can reach Soviet territory. Supporters also point out that the plan will require the Soviet Union to remove over three times as many missiles as NATO. The agreement

will also not affect the independent French and British nuclear forces, or the bombers and battlefield nuclear weapons in Europe.

Strategic Rethinking

Another issue on the U.S.-Soviet agenda, outside of the INF agreement, is the elimination or reduction of all nuclear ballistic weapons—including the ICBMs that form the backbone of the U.S. nuclear deterrent, a prospect that has refocused European attention on the inadequacy of NATO's conventional forces and on the question of how much longer Europe's dependence on the U.S. for its defense could last.

These concerns were reinforced by other developments in strategic thinking. Some critics of Reagan Administration policies, among them former Secretary of Defense Robert S. McNamara, have suggested that the U.S. adopt a "no-first-use" nuclear weapons policy—that is, abandoning the threat to respond to a conventional attack on Western Europe by using nuclear weapons.

Nuclear weapons, to McNamara, "serve no military purpose whatsoever. They are totally useless—except . . . to deter one's opponent from using them." Moreover, supporters of no-first-use worry that basing military plans on the assumption that NATO would use nuclear weapons first—however incredible the assumption—may actually increase the risk of nuclear war through accident or miscalculation.

The implications of no-first-use worry most European leaders. In a 1983 *Foreign Affairs* article, four West Germans argued that a no-first-use declaration would actually *increase* the probability of war by

Table 2   The East-West Conventional Balance in Europe

	NATO	Warsaw Pact
Aircraft	2,672	4,586
Main battle tanks	20,314	46,610
Artillery	8,974	24,035
Antitank guns and missile launchers	2,091	5,075
Antiaircraft guns	3,379	3,525
Surface-to-surface missile launchers	387	1,235
Surface-to-air missiles	786	5,365
Division equivalents[1]	38⅓	90
Total ground forces deployed in Europe[2]	1,858,000	2,704,000

[1]NATO divisions normally have more people; Warsaw Pact divisions have more tanks and artillery.
[2]Does not include Spanish troops, which are not yet part of NATO's integrated military structure.
Source: International Institute for Strategic Studies, *The Military Balance* 1986–1987.

freeing Moscow from the "decisive nuclear risk" it knows it runs if it attacks Western Europe under current NATO policy. A no-first-use declaration would undermine NATO solidarity by destroying the "confidence of Europeans and especially of Germans in the European-American alliance as a community of risk. . . ."

Although the U.S. government has emphasized repeatedly that it will not adopt a no-first-use policy, its commitment to the Strategic Defense Initiative (SDI, popularly known as Star Wars) has shaken European faith in the continued American commitment to such a community of risk. The goal of SDI is to develop and build a defensive shield against ballistic missiles. The Administration embarked on a concomitant effort to redefine the terms of the 1972 ABM Treaty to permit research, testing and development of SDI systems that Administration critics believe are forbidden by the treaty. Although Reagan promised that any defense system would protect Western Europe as well, Europeans are skeptical that SDI could work and concerned that it may be blocking agreement on a new strategic nuclear arms control accord. Above all, in the words of Christoph Bertram, chief political editor of the West Germany weekly, *Die Zeit,* Europeans fear that "the U.S. will remain vitally concerned about Europe only if its own survival is at stake." Despite their eagerness to take advantage of any technological and economic benefits SDI research may bring (many European firms have signed contracts with U.S. firms on SDI projects), what underlies West European worries is the prospect of having to face Soviet conventional might alone.

A Nonnuclear Deterrent?

The reigning conventional wisdom in NATO has been that the Warsaw Pact so outnumbers NATO in nonnuclear weapons and troops in Europe that Western Europe could not withstand a full-scale Soviet attack without the U.S. nuclear deterrent to back it up. In order to reduce reliance on nuclear weapons, NATO in recent years has developed new weapons technologies and strategies to help counter the Warsaw Pact's numerical superiority. Former NATO commander Rogers has urged that NATO members raise defense spending by 4% annually in order to pay for the expensive new technologies. However, given the failure of most West European governments to meet a 1978 goal of 3% real annual increases and the fact that most face a serious budget crunch, substantial defense increases seem unlikely. Manpower is also becoming more of a problem as West European population growth rates decline and fewer young people are available for military duty.

There are growing numbers of analysts, European and American, who are challenging the longstanding assumption of NATO's conventional inferiority. French weapons and troops are not counted in NATO totals; if they were, these critics say, the numbers would be much more favorable to NATO. And since the French, without formally rejoining the alliance's military structure, are increasing their cooperation with European defense efforts—especially with West Germany—it is probably wrong to assume that they would not fight were Germany attacked. French President François Mitterrand has declared on more than one occasion that "If France's survival depends on what happens on our borders, its security depends on what happens on our neighbors' borders."

Analysts also point out that despite the Warsaw Pact's greater numbers of tanks and antitank weapons, NATO has superior air power. NATO also has only one well-armed adversary to contend with; the Soviet Union has the People's Republic of China on its eastern flank as well as NATO to its west. Above all, NATO is more politically cohesive than the Warsaw Pact.

Those who favor developing a stronger conventional deterrent, among them British military historian Michael Howard, argue that building up conventional forces might meet less popular resistance than expenditures on nuclear weapons, making raising defense budgets an easier task. Those opposed to decreasing reliance on nuclear weapons stress that conventional weapons will never have the deterrent effect of the nuclear threat. "Europeans fear a large-scale conventional war on their territory almost as much, in some moods, as a nuclear conflict," notes long-time State Department official A. W. DePorte.

However, military historian Edward N. Luttwak observes that, like it or not, "the *effect* of nuclear weapons on the military balance has continued to diminish," moving the world toward a 'postnuclear age' in which the nonnuclear invasion potential of the Soviet Union will have to be matched by nonnuclear defenses of comparable strength." To prepare for the coming era, Luttwak warns, "Washington must either reorganize its military strength ... by increasing its forces for defense of the Continent, or it must give up its great power role in Europe."

NATO'S FUTURE: EUROPEAN AND U.S. CHOICES

The renewed debate over nuclear strategy, combined with the continuing (some would say increasing) transatlantic differences in perspective over issues like East-West trade and how to deal with out-of-area challenges to NATO, have made the 1980s a trying time for the alliance. Some, like congressional NATO analyst Stanley R. Sloan, think that the summit at Reykjavik may have marked the beginning of the end for NATO. Others, like DePorte, doubt that this "terminal crisis" is any more serious than the many others the alliance has weathered. French foreign policy analyst Pierre Hassner recalls historian Edward Gibbon's remark about the decline of the Roman Empire: "this intolerable situation lasted for about 300 years."

What kind of alliance would best serve European and American security needs in the coming years? Some ideas currently in circulation follow.

Policy Choices for Western Europe
☐ **Support present NATO structure.** The countries of Western Europe cannot afford to counter Soviet military might alone in an era of tight budgets and shrinking population growth. Should Western Europe attempt to replace the

American nuclear deterrent with one of its own, its "national rivalries would be at their most disruptive," *The Economist* magazine warned in a March 1987 editorial. France and Britain, Europe's current nuclear powers, are unlikely to share control over their national nuclear arsenals, and their neighbors would have no reason to place more confidence in a French or British nuclear umbrella than they do in a much stronger American one. Most West Europeans would probably reject any suggestion that West Germany, the one nonnuclear member of NATO most able to pay for a nuclear arsenal, should acquire one. West Germany might refuse under any circumstances, since doing so would violate the 1954 agreement that led to its statehood (as well as the nuclear nonproliferation treaty which it has signed), antagonize its neighbors on both sides and jeopardize the gains of two decades of Ostpolitik.

While preserving the current NATO structure, Western Europe should make every effort to become a more equal partner with the U.S. Europeans should increase their share of NATO's costs to underscore to U.S. skeptics that they are not getting a free ride.
☐ **Move toward a lessened dependence on U.S. nuclear deterrent.** Western Europe should take steps to shore up its conventional defenses to prepare for—and to forestall—the day the U.S. decides it no longer wishes to provide for European security with its nuclear weapons and its troops in Europe. European publics—no matter what policymakers and other experts tell them—tend to see efforts to bolster nuclear deterrence as actually serving to make nuclear war

more likely. Given the continuing decline of nuclear weapons as a credible deterrent anyway, increasing reliance on conventional forces is preferable and would do much to restore alliance political cohesion.
☐ **Move toward a position of neutrality between the U.S. and the Soviet Union.** Some on the political left in Western Europe believe that Western Europe's alliance with the U.S. is contrary to European interests. British peace activist E. P. Thompson believes that Europe should become neutral in the sense of "acting as a Third Negotiator, between both superpowers, with the ultimate objective of reunifying European societies and culture." West German journalist Peter Bender writes that what Western Europe needs "is not simple protection from Moscow, but rather security against complications that arise in the interaction between Washington and Moscow." Most who hold these views (and they remain a minority in all West European countries) hope to rid Western Europe not only of all nuclear weapons, but of any conventional weapons or strategies that would look threatening to the Soviet Union.

Policy Choices for the U.S.
☐ **Continue participation in NATO.** Every Administration since Truman's has believed firmly, in Vice President George Bush's words, that NATO "is the best investment in peace we have ever made." No matter what the expense, it pales compared with the cost of another world war. It is cheaper to preserve the balance of power than to restore it once lost, and the U.S. is the only country powerful enough to counterbalance the Soviet Union. Failure to

agree on every issue is not grounds for terminating the U.S. commitment to Western Europe. Claims that West Europeans do not pick up enough of the tab for their own defense ignore substantial European contributions to the alliance: 90% of allied forces in Europe, contributions to weapons stocks, the real estate on which U.S. bases are located and the political costs of conscription that enable Europeans to pay less for military salaries, for example. What the U.S. should try to do is to obtain the "maximum of means and commitments" from its allies, rather than stressing the differences.

☐ **Encourage greater European autonomy in defense.** In 1984, Senator Sam Nunn (D-Ga.), now chairman of the Senate Armed Services Committee and a staunch supporter of NATO, proposed an amendment that would have mandated the withdrawal of one third of U.S troops in Europe if the allies did not live up to their pledge to increase defense expenditures by

3% annually or make a variety of improvements in their conventional forces. Nunn did not mean the measure to pass (it did not), but rather to make Europeans aware of a growing anti-NATO sentiment in the U.S. It worked: there has been increased defense collaboration among NATO's European members since then, especially on issues such as joint weapons research and standardization. A more recent Nunn amendment sought to encourage this trend by offering a $200 million incentive for joint U.S.-European weapons projects. One rocket system being produced under this arrangement will give the U.S. a new rocket for only 40% of its cost; Western Europe is footing the rest of the bill. Former U.S. ambassadors to NATO David Abshire and W. Tapley Bennett, Jr., believe that these kinds of positive incentives, including extensive consultations and a "resource strategy" designed to make the most efficient possible use of NATO's $340 billion annual budget, are the

best ways to encourage an increased European contribution to NATO.

☐ **Withdraw from the alliance.** Irving Kristol, editor of the neoconservative journal *The National Interest,* argues that, because of the weakness of NATO's conventional forces, membership in NATO increases the risk of U.S. involvement in a nuclear war. For this privilege, the U.S. is paying enormous sums of money—some $134 billion in 1986—at a time of mammoth U.S. budget deficits. This level of economic commitment not only "subverts Western Europe's will to resist" by encouraging an unhealthy level of dependence, says Kristol, it "interferes with America's responsibilities as a global power." It limits American funds available for military commitments in other areas of the world like the Persian Gulf or the Pacific rim, regions which some believe have become more important to U.S. national security than Western Europe. ■

The North Atlantic Treaty Organization

By James E. Miller

The North Atlantic Treaty Organization (NATO) was born in an era of rising East-West tensions. Its member states joined together to safeguard their national security and political democracy from the challenge posed by Soviet expansionism. In spite of frequent, well-publicized disagreements, the Alliance has been durable, responding

to changing international conditions and expanding from its original 12 member states to 16. NATO's strengths remain the military security that membership provides individual states, its ability to facilitate consultations among its member states, and the underlying U.S. commitment to come to the defense of Europe.

THE ORIGINS OF NATO, 1947–1949

The decision of the United States, Canada, and 10 European states to enter into a peacetime defensive alliance was one of the most significant developments of the post-World War II era. For the United States in particular, mem-

This paper, by James E. Miller of the Office of the Historian, is one of a series that provides historical background information on selected foreign policy issues.

Source: From U.S. Department of State, Bureau of Public Affairs, *Department of State Publication 9511,* September 1987, pp. 1–5.

bership in NATO represented a fundamental change in its more than century-old foreign policy of refraining from involvement with "entangling alliances." The emerging East-West conflict provided the context for the development of NATO. By 1947, the United States and Soviet Union had clashed over nuclear disarmament, the nature of the postwar economic and political settlement in Central and Eastern Europe, Iran, and the shape of peace treaties with the defeated Axis nations. The pace of Western European economic recovery was agonizingly slow. Severe shortages in food, fuel, and the basic necessities of life stimulated popular discontent. Concern grew over the establishment of Communist regimes in Eastern Europe. The U.S. Government responded with a series of highly creative economic and political initiatives that stabilized both European democracy and a free trading system.

The European Recovery Program (Marshall Plan) of 1948–1952 was a key element in the U.S. program of European stabilization. It rebuilt the sinews of Europe's economy, committed the United States to a long-term role in Europe, and created mechanisms for political consultation between the two sides of the Atlantic. Simultaneously, the European states, with the encouragement of the United States, took the first steps toward economic and political integration by creating in 1947 the Organization for European Economic Cooperation and in 1948 a security arrangement, the Brussels Pact (known after 1955 as the Western European Union). Economic weakness, however, limited Europe's ability to provide for its defense.

After considerable debate within the United States, the leaders of the executive and legislative branches agreed on two immediate U.S. responses to Europe's crisis: participation in a defensive peacetime alliance, and provision of military equipment and technical assistance. Negotiations for the alliance began quietly in March 1948 among the United States, Canada, and Great Britain. On June 11, 1948, the U.S. Senate adopted the Vandenberg Resolution, encouraging U.S. participation in a collective defense arrangement. The Benelux states and France joined the talks in July. Initial discussions focused on the text of a treaty and the definition of the alliance's geographical extension and membership.

CREATING AN ALLIANCE STRUCTURE, 1949–1955

On April 4, 1949, the Foreign Ministers of the United States, the United Kingdom, France, Italy, Belgium, Canada, Denmark, Iceland, Luxembourg, the Netherlands, Norway, and Portugal signed the North Atlantic Treaty in a ceremony held in Washington, D.C. The NATO Treaty came into force on August 24, 1949, when the 12 participating nations formally deposited their instruments of ratification.

The state of East-West relations did not permit a leisurely approach to building the military and political structures of alliance. During the summer of 1949, the Soviet Union exploded its first atomic weapon. China fell to a Communist revolution during the autumn of 1949. Then, in June 1950, North Korean forces invaded South Korea. U.S. and Western European leaders concluded that the attack

on Korea might be the prelude to a military move against Europe.

These external stimuli quickened the pace of NATO's transformation into an active defense structure. Immediately after the Senate approved the NATO Treaty in July 1949, the Truman administration presented Congress with legislation authorizing a Military Defense Assistance Program (MDAP) to provide equipment and training for the armies of the NATO Allies. In October 1949, Congress approved a $1.3 billion MDAP appropriation. After the outbreak of the Korean war in June 1950, the size of U.S. military assistance grants rose rapidly. The Offshore Procurement Program, which encouraged the creation of defense industries in Europe, supplemented MDAP.

The North Atlantic Council, composed of the Foreign Ministers of the NATO states, met in Washington on July 17, 1949. The Foreign Ministers created committees to handle military planning, established regional planning groups to look at specific local issues, and took the first steps toward building standing mechanisms for economic and political cooperation. A December 1949 agreement provided for an initial division of responsibility among the Allies: the United States would provide the Alliance's strategic bombing capability, while the European states contributed the bulk of its ground troops and tactical air defense. The United States and Great Britain would defend NATO's Atlantic lines of communication, while the United States would increase its military presence in Europe.

The Allies agreed to speedily build a permanent military command structure. President Truman, at the request of the NATO Ministers, appointed General Dwight D. Eisenhower as Supreme Allied Commander in Europe in December 1950. Eisenhower quickly built a military chain of command and in 1952 put the NATO armies through their first major combined exercises. The North Atlantic Council's February 1952 Lisbon meeting established force goals for each NATO member state. Although these goals were not completely met, the Allied states increased their military preparedness and allocated more of their resources to the common defense. In September 1951, the NATO member states agreed to invite Greece and Turkey to join the Alliance.

By 1954, the NATO states had created a permanent defense mechanism. The North Atlantic Council became the executive, and its standing council of representatives, made up of ambassadors from the member states, provided policy coordination. NATO's permanent planning groups and secretariat were located in Paris. The Supreme Headquarters Allied Powers Europe (SHAPE) coordinated defense preparations.

NATO then focused on the role West Germany would play in the defense of the West. Meetings of NATO Ministers in September and October 1950 produced general agreement that West Germany must be part of NATO. The Allied strategy of forward defense along the borders of Communist states required West German participation. France and other continental European Allies were deeply concerned about the effects of rearming the Germans so soon after the defeat of nazism. On October 24, 1950, French Premier René Pleven unveiled a plan for a European Defense Community (EDC), consisting of a standing European army under the control of a European Defense Minister. The plan would commit German manpower to the common defense but without forming a separate German army or general staff. Although the United States actively supported the plan, the United Kingdom declined to join, citing its imperial commitments. The absence of a postwar German peace settlement and the creation of East and West German states made European states wary of the concept of an integrated defense force. The French and Italian Governments delayed parliamentary action on the European Defense Community in the face of combined Communist and nationalist opposition. Finally, in August 1954, the French Government presented the EDC measure to the National Assembly, which rejected it.

The defeat of the EDC was followed by West German rearmament. A September-October 1954 meeting of the Foreign Ministers of nine NATO powers agreed to terminate the military occupation of the Federal Republic of Germany and invite the West German Government to join NATO. Italy and the Federal Republic at this time acceded to the Western European Union. The Government of the Federal Republic voluntarily agreed to limit its arms buildup and undertook not to construct nuclear weapons and certain other types of armaments. In May 1955, the Federal Republic joined NATO.

THE NUCLEAR CONTROL ISSUE, 1958–1964

In 1958, France's President Charles de Gaulle brought to the surface two of the underlying tensions within the Alliance: concern over nuclear strategy and France's claim to a special leadership role within NATO. Although Great Britain also maintained a nuclear capability within the Western Alliance, the United States possessed an overwhelming predominance in nuclear weapons stockpile and delivery systems. At their December 1954 meeting, the NATO Foreign and Defense Ministers adopted a policy of nuclear response to a Soviet attack on Europe, commonly referred to as "massive retaliation." The policy reflected a U.S. desire to maintain a credible deterrent at the lowest possible cost. By 1958, however, the Soviet Union had made major strides in both long-range bomber and missile technology, and it was capable of striking the United States. Increasingly, Europeans asked if the United States would risk a nuclear attack on its territory to defend Europe.

De Gaulle was among the doubters. He was determined to reduce U.S. control over Alliance nuclear policy by building an independent nuclear force, the *force de frappe,* a goal that he achieved in the early 1960s. The French President wanted France to act as the principal spokesman for Europe in an inner group of three with the United States and Great Britain.

The NATO nations rejected de Gaulle's 1958 bid to create a two-tiered alliance structure, insisting instead on the equality of all NATO members. In an effort to accommodate the French leader on nuclear policy, the West Germans urged the Alliance to create a multilateral nuclear force (MNF) within NATO. The United States initially hesitated to endorse the MNF because of its concern with preventing nuclear proliferation. In 1963, however, the Kennedy administration came forward with a proposal to create an MNF surface fleet equipped with Polaris missiles under NATO command. The MNF would fit into the overall U.S. nuclear defense strategy. De Gaulle rejected the plan because the United States insisted on retaining final say on the launching of these weapons. The United States quietly dropped the MNF concept in 1964. In 1966, de Gaulle took France out of the Alliance military command structure, while maintaining French participation in the political consultative mechanism. Consequently, NATO headquarters moved from Paris to Brussels, and U.S. forces withdrew from France.

FLEXIBLE RESPONSE AND DETENTE, 1966–1974

One factor in de Gaulle's decision to pull French forces out of NATO was his belief that the climate of East-West relations was improving and that the danger of war had lessened. By the mid-1960s, two separate but related processes of normalization of relations were underway between East and West. The United States and the Soviet Union were attempting to lessen tensions between themselves. At the same time, a number of Western European states, including France and the Federal Republic of Germany, were seeking new relationships with the Soviet Union and Eastern European states.

Within the context of this changing political climate, the NATO nations in December 1966 commissioned a study on the "Future Tasks of the Alliance" by a working group headed by Belgian Foreign Minister Pierre Harmel. The Allies also agreed to establish two permanent bodies for nuclear planning, the Nuclear Defense Affairs Committee, open to all members, and a smaller Nuclear Planning Group, with permanent and rotating members, to handle the details.

The Harmel Report, issued at the Ministerial Meeting of the North Atlantic Council in Brussels in December 1967, concluded that "military security and a policy of détente are not contradictory but complementary" and that NATO had an important role to play in preparing for bilateral and multilateral negotiations between Eastern and Western nations over key issues such as the future of Germany and arms control. Public perception of the Alliance would be significantly improved, the report noted, if the Allied consultative process were strengthened and if the Alliance took an active role in advancing the rapprochement between East and West by coordinating European and U.S. political approaches to the Soviet Union and Eastern Europe.

Also at Brussels, the Alliance adopted a strategy of "flexible response," endorsing a balanced range of appropriate conventional and nuclear reactions to all levels of aggression or threats of aggression. The responses were designed first to deter aggression, but failing that to maintain the security and integrity of the North Atlantic Treaty area within the concept of forward defense.

The move toward East-West accommodation met a significant setback in August 1968 when the Soviet Union invaded Czechoslovakia. The Soviet invasion gave impetus to the buildup of NATO conventional forces and strengthened support for the Alliance. A number of European countries increased their NATO contributions, while the United States cancelled planned troop reductions in Europe.

Détente was further limited by disagreement over the U.S. role in Europe as well as by Soviet support for "national liberation movements" in the underdeveloped nations. While attempting to extend its influence in the Third World, the Soviet Union insisted that détente required the exclusion of the United States from Europe and an end to defensive alliances. It called NATO a U.S.-imposed straitjacket whose continued existence precluded successful settlement of Europe's difficulties. The United States and its NATO Allies rejected this claim and insisted that any improvement in relations between East and West would have to be negotiated within the existing Alliance framework.

The Western view prevailed. During the Nixon administration (1969–1974), the West succeeded in creating arrangements that fostered both an improved climate of East-West relations and a NATO role in the process. The conclusion in September 1971 of a Quadripartite Agreement on Berlin (which had been occupied since 1945 by the United States, the United Kingdom, France, and the Soviet Union) reduced tensions between the blocs. The Western Allies extracted Soviet concessions over Berlin in exchange for an agreement to convene a Conference on

Security and Cooperation in Europe (CSCE). The caucus of NATO states has been the primary forum for coordinating Western strategy at successive CSCE meetings. NATO coordination has played an important role in defining the West's CSCE objectives.

Mutual and Balanced Force Reduction Talks (MFBR) also began as a result of a NATO initiative. These talks, intended to reduce in a stabilizing way the conventional forces of both NATO and the Warsaw Pact in Central Europe, continue to the present, but the results have not been significant. The Soviet Union has refused to address Western compromise proposals to concentrate on a limited reduction of U.S. and Soviet forces under effective verification measures.

The appropriate level of U.S. participation in NATO was debated vigorously during the Nixon administration. The Mansfield Amendment of 1971, which would have significantly cut the number of U.S. troops stationed in Germany, reflected a widely held view that Europeans must do more for their own defense and that the United States must improve its balance of payments. The Nixon administration, with the support of the foreign policy establishment, headed off a reduction of one-half of the ground troops committed to Europe. West European leaders recognized the seriousness of public sentiment in the United States, and the West German Government arranged to pay a higher share of the costs of maintaining U.S. forces on its soil.

During the mid-1970s, conflicting political and economic interests among NATO's member states created an element of tension within the Alliance. Disagreements over Middle East policy between the United States and its European partners surfaced at the time of the 1973 Arab-Israeli war and the subsequent Arab oil embargo. Tensions within the Alliance grew more acute in 1974 as a result of a major crisis on Cyprus. A coup by right-wing Greek Cypriots triggered Turkish military occupation of almost 40 percent of the island of Cyprus in July-August 1974. Greece's newly installed democratic government pulled its forces out of NATO's integrated military command structure to protest the Alliance's inability to prevent or reverse the Turkish military action. Meanwhile, the Allies welcomed the end of the dictatorship in Portugal but watched the growing radicalization of its military leadership and the increasing strength of the Portuguese Communist Party with mounting concern until democratic forces gained control of the situation in late 1975.

THE DECLINE OF DETENTE, 1975–1980

Détente became increasingly difficult to maintain after 1974. The United States and the Soviet Union clashed over the expansion of Soviet influence in Africa, and negotiations stalled on a second SALT agreement. The Soviet Union undertook a major modernization of its intermediate-range nuclear forces (INF), substantially increasing the threat to NATO by replacing older SS-4 and SS-5 missiles with the mobile, longer-range, more accurate SS-20, which were equipped with multiple independently targeted reentry vehicles (MIRV's). The concept of détente came under attack within the United States from both sides of the political spectrum.

NATO continued to carry out its basic defense functions and regained its unity through a series of political accommodations and military reforms. The Portuguese situation began to stabilize in 1976–1977. Although Greek-Turkish relations remained tense, the Greek Government recognized the value of NATO participation and rejoined the Alliance's military wing in October 1980. The Western nations also achieved greater coordination on energy policy. Newly democratic Spain joined the NATO Alliance in December 1981.

The growing Soviet military threat was a key to improved Allied cooperation. In May 1977, the NATO states agreed to increase their defense expenditures by 3 percent per annum after adjustment for inflation in order to meet the growth in Soviet military power. West Germany took the lead in calling for a NATO response to the Soviet SS-20 intermediate-range missile deployments. Discussions within the Alliance led to the adoption in December 1979 of a "two-track" approach. The Western Alliance would proceed with the installation of 572 U.S. Pershing II and ground-launched cruise intermediate-range missiles beginning in 1983, while the United States would offer to negotiate with the Soviet Union on an INF balance at the lowest possible level.

FROM A SECOND COLD WAR TO AN ERA OF INTENSIFIED DIALOG, 1980–1987

The Soviet invasion of Afghanistan in December 1979 plunged East-West relations into a period of hostility reminiscent of the early years of the cold war. The Carter administration requested a delay in Senate consideration of the June 1979 SALT II Treaty, which was already under heavy criticism. The United States imposed a grain embargo on the Soviet Union and sought to organize a Western boycott of the 1980 Moscow Olympic Games to protest the invasion.

Soviet actions continued to feed the crisis. The U.S.S.R. encouraged and supported the Polish government's imposition of martial law and its repression of popular democratic movements. It propped up a puppet government in Afghanistan and provided it with military support against a popular resistance movement. It intensified the repression of domestic human rights activists. The quick succession of three aging Soviet leaders increased the West's difficulties in dealing with the Soviet Union. The September 1, 1983, destruction of KAL 007, an unarmed civilian airliner that strayed into Soviet airspace, further impeded East-West dialog.

NATO continued to pursue its "two-track" approach on missile deployment. In 1981, the Reagan administration, in close consultation with the Allies, offered a "zero/zero" INF outcome—no Pershing II/cruise missile deployments in exchange for the dismantlement of comparable Soviet weapons systems—and in 1983, an interim INF approach to establish equal low ceilings on these weapons for the United States and the Soviet Union on a global basis. The Soviet Union rejected Western proposals and intensified its propaganda campaign, seeking to exploit a growing pacifist movement in Europe and the United States to "freeze" a status quo that established a Soviet predominance by

preventing a U.S. INF deployment. The Soviet Union broke off INF talks in the fall of 1983, as the first U.S. missiles became operational.

Upon taking office in January 1981, President Reagan began a long-term nuclear and conventional rearmament program. The administration urged the NATO Allies to take a greater share in the defense of Europe through a buildup of their conventional forces. The administration maintained that the Alliance must solidify the Western defense posture as the first step toward realistic and productive negotiations with the Soviet Union. U.S. proposals for Strategic Arms Reduction Talks (START) foresaw an overall reduction in the number of offensive nuclear weapons each side deployed, as well as a restructuring of these forces to enhance stability. The Reagan administration also sought to reduce the size of the ground forces that both sides had in Europe in the MBFR talks, and to improve European security through adopting concrete and mutually verifiable confidence-building measures. The Madrid meeting of the Conference on Security and Cooperation in Europe (1980–1983) adopted a NATO-backed proposal for the creation of a Conference on Confidence- and Security-Building Measures and Disarmament in Europe (CDE) with a mandate to formulate confidence-building measures. The CDE concluded its meeting in Stockholm in September 1986 with an agreement on a set of mutually complementary measures for monitoring significant military activities in Europe, including mandatory on-site inspection as a means of verification. The ongoing Vienna CSCE review conference is

now considering a NATO proposal to establish talks on further confidence- and security-building measures as well as negotiations on conventional stability.

NATO also sought to improve intergovernmental cooperation in other areas of deep mutual concern. A May 1981 NATO declaration deplored the recent resurgence of violent terrorist attacks, agreed on the necessity for bilateral and multilateral cooperation to prevent and combat terrorism, and expressed determination to take all necessary measures to ensure the security of diplomatic and other official personnel.

The successful conclusion of the Madrid CSCE meeting in 1983 marked the first break in the cycle of East-West confrontation that characterized the relationship since the invasion of Afghanistan. The 1984 reelection of President Reagan and the emergence of Mikhail Gorbachev as Soviet leader in the spring of 1985 provided both great powers with stable political leadership. Negotiations on INF and strategic arms reductions as well as on limitation of space systems began in Geneva in March 1985. The November 1985 Reagan–Gorbachev summit in Geneva produced an agreement to give priority to 50 percent START reductions and to an interim INF agreement. A subsequent meeting of the two leaders at Reykjavik, Iceland, in October 1986 led to wide-ranging discussion of major disarmament initiatives, but no agreement. In February 1987, General Secretary Gorbachev removed his previous requirement that U.S. concessions on the Strategic Defense Initiative precede INF progress. The June 1987 meeting of NATO Foreign Ministers at Reykjavik supported the global and effectively verifiable elimination of both long- and short-range United States and Soviet land-based INF missiles, urging the Soviet Union to drop its demand to retain a portion of its SS-20 missiles. In September, the United States and the Soviet Union announced agreement in principle to a zero level on all INF missiles.

NATO's role in an era of renewed negotiations remains central. It provides the military deterrent essential for success in negotiations. Moreover, as the process of Europe's economic and political integration continues and as Europe's role in its own defense increases, NATO serves as a unique forum in which Allied policy can be forged and differences between the American and European pillars of the Atlantic Alliance resolved. ■

Seven Myths About NATO

By Melvyn Krauss

In January of 1988, *The New York Times* carried an article entitled "Navy Secretary Suggests Forces in Europe be Cut," quoting the then Secretary James Webb. According to the article, Webb called "for a thorough review of United States commitments to foreign nations and a reexamination of the deployment of American forces around the world, especially in Europe." The Navy Secretary noted that "national resources, changes in the world economic structure, recent political changes and the improved capabilities of many of our allies dictate that we must, perhaps for the first time since the late 1940s, seriously debate the posture of U.S. military forces around the world."

Webb went on to suggest that a national debate over this issue would be in order. The United States, he argued, has commitments to sixty nations through treaties or other arrangements that require extensive military involvement. As a result, we have become "set in static defensive positions that have drained both our economic and military resources." In the Secretary's own words:

It can fairly be argued that the economic recovery of other nations has not uniformly been met with the complete resumption of their obligation to join us in protecting the way of life and the values that we share. While American allies in NATO should do more for their own defense, another element must be the responsibility of the Japanese as a friend, ally and world power, to assume a greater portion of the regional military responsibility in Asia.

Now, we must remember that Secretary Webb was speaking on his own behalf and not that of the Navy Department or the Reagan administration. But the Secretary's remarks were significant, for here was a senior military official, a highly-respected expert on defense, speaking out in favor of reassessing our strategic commitments to our allies. It is within this context that I wish to discuss some of the prevalent myths about NATO.

MYTH #1

Time and time again, one hears that NATO "has kept the peace for forty years." But this is not an argument, for correlation doesn't prove cause and effect. Simply because U.S. troops have been stationed in Western Europe for the past forty years, and there has been peace for forty years, does not mean the former has caused the latter. Many other factors have played a role. In particular, the Western Europeans have chosen a policy of appeasement when it comes to facing down their greatest enemy—the Soviet Union. They offer subsidized trade, easy credit and political support to the very nation that threatens them most.

For example, what happens when the United States attempts to contain communist aggression in Central America, the Middle East,

Melvyn Krauss is a senior fellow at the Hoover Institution on War, Revolution and Peace and a professor of economics at New York University.

Source: From *Imprimis,* Vol. 17, No. 10 (October 1988). Reprinted by permission of Hillsdale College, Hillsdale, MI.

Africa, Asia or even in Europe? Our Western European allies become alarmed at such "American imperialism." The Soviets have no need to launch a military invasion of Europe—the status quo works just fine for them. We've had peace for forty years, but it has come at a very high price. Ironically, the Soviet enemy has benefited substantially—too much in my view—from the collective security arrangements the West has devised for itself.

MYTH #2

Myth number two is that NATO ensures the U.S. of a "forward defense" in Europe against the Soviets. The reasoning goes that, in the event of a conventional Soviet attack, it is better for the U.S. to engage the enemy in Europe, not on Broadway. That is, of course, "beggar my neighbor" in the worst sense of the term. By underwriting NATO to the tune of $134 billion per year, we are, in effect, paying Western Europe to serve as a buffer and a potential battleground for the U.S. and U.S.S.R. That's what the pro-NATO crowd believes and, one must admit, there is some truth to this argument.

But most experts concede that any conventional attack launched by the Warsaw Pact nations would quickly escalate to a nuclear confrontation. This is the problem of the so-called "low nuclear threshold," acknowledged by such NATO officials as former Supreme Commander Bernard Rogers and by Senator Sam Nunn. Let's imagine a ground attack in Western Europe. Within hours or days, we would have to make the decision whether to go nuclear and launch a first strike against the Soviets (after all, no one, not even NATO's staunch-

est supporters, claim that NATO can fight a conventional war longer than a week or two with any hope of success)—or whether we would simply throw up our hands and say "Okay, Europe is yours." Where then, may I ask, is our forward defense? The truth is that there is none!

MYTH #3

We may like to think that NATO provides a *conventional deterrent* to war in Western Europe, but, like forward defense, this is another myth. We do have a system of conventional defense, but what is its deterrent value when our defense is so inadequate? The reason for this inadequacy is that while the Russians and the Americans have steadily built up their conventional armed forces in the past few decades, the Western Europeans have built up their welfare states.

After World War II, Western Europe was devastated and its people demoralized. If we hadn't stepped in to render assistance, Western Europe surely would have shared the fate of Eastern Europe and fallen within the communist orbit. Our newly developed nuclear power could extend a guarantee of safety to our allies abroad, and our greater financial resources could help the European economic recovery without shortchanging our own economic progress. NATO, in 1949, made perfect sense, because of the economic gap that existed at that time between the U.S. and Western Europe, and the nuclear gap that existed between the U.S. and the Soviet Union.

But the intention of NATO, like the Marshall Plan, was only to help Western Europeans regain their footing. Once recovered, it was

assumed that they would take primary responsibility for their own defense affairs. Dwight Eisenhower, NATO's first Supreme Commander, insisted that if U.S. troops were still in Europe ten years after its founding, "the whole enterprise will have failed." Forty years later, Eisenhower's worst fears have indeed come true. The Western Europeans are no longer poor, but they have successfully resisted building up their own military forces. "After all," the shrewd Europeans will say, "Why spend on our defense when we have the Americans to defend us? What we need to do is concentrate all our efforts upon our education, our health, our environment, our economy. . . ." Thus, liberalism alone is not responsible for the rise of the welfare state in Western Europe. Had it not been for the willingness of the U.S. to pay for the defense of those who could then plow billions of dollars into their social welfare states, liberalism would have been a vain—and unfinanced—aspiration in Western Europe.

THE INF TREATY: AN ASIDE

Unfortunately for the West, while Europe ignored its defense needs, the U.S.S.R. was busy building its conventional and nuclear forces. We are now at a crossroads when the Soviets' conventional superiority may be especially critical, because of the pending denuclearization of Europe as a consequence of the INF treaty. The function of our Pershing II missiles in Europe was not only to cancel out Soviet SS20s but to neutralize the conventional superiority that the Soviets enjoy.

Suddenly this vital strategy is supposed to be less important, we are told. According to INF proponents, including Ronald Reagan and George Shultz, who have become surprisingly unsuspicious of our enemies as of late, the Soviets are committed to withdrawing even more missiles than we are, and we are assured this is a great victory.

An example illustrates how wrong even the best of leaders can be. Suppose a very big, powerful man and a short, scrawny fellow live in the same house. In such a situation, we wouldn't find it surprising if the bigger of the two began to dominate. He might intimidate the little guy and get him to do a lot of favors for him. He wouldn't even have to ask after a while; the little guy knows the situation. The big guy says, "Gee, it's cold in here," and the other jumps up to close the window.

But one day, the little guy gets fed up. He buys a revolver, which suddenly changes the pair's whole relationship. Now the big guy closes the window himself. But what if the big guy decides to buy two guns? With the escalation of the "arms race," who dominates whom does not depend on physical strength. It depends on Who's quicker on the draw? Who's got more nerve? Who's got more firepower? And who's got more money to spend on arms?

Then along comes a do-gooder who says "Look, gentlemen, guns are dangerous. We can't have guns in the world because guns kill people. Let's disarm. Let's have peace." The little guy has only to give up one gun, but the big guy has to hand over two. If George Shultz were there to comment, he'd claim it was a great deal for the little guy, forgetting all about his initial dilemma.

The de-nuclearization of Europe, begun with the INF treaty, makes the imbalance between conventional forces a critical factor. The big guy—the Soviet Union—has only to say, "Gee, it's cold outside," and the little guy—Western Europe—will leap to do his bidding.

MYTH #4

Myth number four is that anyone who approves of withdrawing from or downscaling our commitment to NATO is isolationist. It is true, of course, that there are isolationists within this broad group, but the majority believe that reality dictates an internationalist position—namely that America cannot survive without strong allies. That is precisely why they oppose the current state of affairs. NATO has created and encouraged weak allies. When you subsidize someone, you make them dependent, and you corrupt their own sense of responsibility. Ronald Reagan should understand this better than most.

The new internationalism represented by the anti-NATO advocates is an internationalism based on a strong network of allies, not relying upon the United States as the sole policeman of the world. We are spending $134 *billion* a year on NATO. Is that creating or encouraging strong allies? Is NATO the best defense we can get for that kind of money?

MYTH #5

Leaving NATO, according to its supporters, would be deserting our friends. We ought to be loyal and stick by Western Europe. We should honor our commitments.

This is undeniably the strongest argument the pro-NATO ranks can advance. Most Americans have been brought up to revere loyalty, honor, commitment. NATO was one of the first bastions against communism, making this argument even more potent.

But to withdraw from NATO would not put an end to our commitment. Only a morally correct defense policy can help our allies—and subsidization through NATO is not the answer. Making Europeans face up to their own responsibilities, making them self-reliant and ready to defend their own nations is a better one. To argue that we would be honoring our commitment by doing any less simply is not correct.

MYTH #6

We are told by various media pundits, intellectuals and foreign policy experts that the Soviet Union wants us out of NATO. Of course, this triggers a conditioned response: We can't leave because, if we left, the Soviets would be delighted. But the Soviets have made no concerted effort to get the troops out of Europe, comparable, for example, to their effort to get the U.S. Pershing missiles out or to short-circuit the Strategic Defense Initiative. The reason is that the NATO link, by making the allies weak, has worked very much to the Soviet advantage. Adam B. Ulam of Harvard University, one of our leading Sovietologists, has written:

Although the Soviets want to encourage tensions between Western Europe and the United States, they may not want to see the United States withdraw or greatly reduce its land forces in Europe. Such a shock might make Western European leaders decide they have no choice but to unite politically. Or it might cause West Germany to reconsider its decision not to acquire nuclear weapons. Moreover, the present uneasy state of U.S.-Western European relations provides certain benefits to the U.S.S.R. America's European allies usually act as a moderating influence on Washington's anti-Soviet attitudes and initiatives.

MYTH #7

Impressive though the foregoing arguments may be, they may not add up to much in the world of domestic politics. Whether or not our troops are withdrawn from Western Europe depends on whether we can break free of one last myth: That America can afford the status quo.

Let's look at "affording" it in the literal sense. Without even taking our enormous federal deficit into account, we ought to be alarmed that we are annually spending $134 billion on NATO. That alarm should be magnified by the dramatic decline in the value of our currency. Most of our NATO troops are stationed in Germany, where in the last two years the dollar has depreciated by *fifty percent.*

Now, that has a devastating impact on the U.S. federal budget, and one part of the devastation is being visited upon our service personnel because they are being paid in dollars. Of course, they can buy some items from the PX, but what we have done to the men and women who are protecting our country and Western Europe is a disgrace.

Our soldiers in Europe are indeed hostages to prove that the

U.S. will fight to save Western Europe. The tripwire strategy goes something like this: No American president could sit idly by and watch American soldiers being killed in an attack on Western Europe. This guarantees U.S. engagement in Europe's defense. But to force our soldiers to live in jeopardy, and to be so miserly about compensating them for their service, is certainly outrageous. Is it any wonder that fewer and fewer qualified people enlist under such conditions?

Notwithstanding our soldiers' plight and the huge financial drain on our resources created by NATO, we can't afford the status quo in another sense. NATO prevents us from facing up to the very real dangers we face. We blithely sign agreements with our enemies, hoping that NATO will still protect us. Nothing could be further from the truth. ■

NATO: The Essential Treaty

By Jack Forrest

My perspective on the NATO issue springs from personal experience as well as commitment to a nearly forty-year-old alliance that has played a major role in the postwar era.

The North Atlantic Treaty Organization is not merely a piece of history; it is essential to our future and undergirds much of our national strategy. It is within this con-

text that we must consider our options. One, obviously, is to scrap the whole alliance: pack up our bags and go home. Another is to withdraw from any meaningful participation or to so scale down our financial and military contributions that other members are called upon to take over the leadership responsibility that is currently ours. The best option is to

use the debate over NATO's viability to our advantage to reform rather than repudiate NATO.

A recent incident may be illustrative of my argument in favor of the last of these three options. Two generals, one French, one American, were engaged in a recent discussion. The American was criticizing the French government for its refusal to uphold the military arm

Jack Forrest, an executive with Ford Aerospace and Communications Corporation, retired from the Army in 1983 as a lieutenant general after service stretching from the closing days of World War II.

Source: From *Imprimis,* Vol. 17, No. 10 (October 1988). Reprinted by permission of Hillsdale College, Hillsdale, MI.

of NATO. (Under de Gaulle, France had withdrawn from military membership in 1966.)

"You've made it very awkward for us to properly plan and prepare the defense of Europe," the American said.

The French general replied, "Well, we do wonder if you're going to treat us as a true ally."

"Of course, we're going to treat you as an ally!"

"That's precisely why we fear to come back [to military membership]. We remember how you treated your allies, the Nationalist Chinese, and how you treated your allies in Cuba, and how it appears you're going to treat your allies in Nicaragua and Afghanistan."

How important NATO is, is a part of a larger question: How important is America's pledge of loyalty? We have reneged on enough commitments already, usually piecemeal, in a series of gradual backward steps. If we choose to withdraw from NATO, we must be prepared to pay a heavy price in terms of our international reputation and our internal morale. It will also make it nearly impossible to attract loyal and friendly allies in the future.

A REAL THREAT

In 1947, as a cadet at West Point, I learned a great deal about the Marshall Plan. Today, people often forget what a monumental strategic achievement it was. But, then and now, it is clear that the Marshall Plan alone could not secure America's interests. It was no guarantee *against* Soviet expansionism and, furthermore, it was no guarantee *for* democracy and a free economic system. (If entrepreneurs are not safe and free to make secure investments, capitalism simply won't work.)

The Marshall Plan was never intended to be a complete strategy. Two years later, in 1949, the North Atlantic Treaty Organization was organized to stop the advance of communism in Western Europe as part of a larger containment policy. Both the Marshall Plan and NATO came at a critical time. The Germans referred to 1945 as Year Zero. Behind them lay unmitigated disaster; ahead, lay who knows what? But certainly there was hope that great things could be accomplished.

In a larger sense, 1945 was Year Zero for the world. Of the nations that dominated international relations before the war, Great Britain and the United States were in the strongest positions, along with a new force, the Soviet Union. These three nations had the power to shape the postwar world.

The United States could reward, punish or sanction actions around the planet. It chose to help establish the United Nations, which was to be an improved version of the ill-fated League of Nations. Naively, many Americans assumed that the mere establishment of the UN would guarantee peace and eliminate our national obligations. Disarmament and the withdrawal of troops began immediately. Domestic economic issues turned Americans' attention inward. When international concerns did intrude, the general feeling was that if we helped the war-devastated nations back on their feet politically and economically, everyone's troubles would be over.

This notion did not last long. We were not going to be allowed to stack our arms and return to a generally isolationist stance. We were, in fact, the major world power. Russia's brief alliance with our cause was over. Latvia, Lithuania, Estonia, Poland, Czechoslavakia, Romania, Bulgaria, Hungary, North Korea, and China either fell or came under the sway of communist domination in rapid succession in the postwar era.

The United States protested vigorously, of course. There was much talk of direct confrontations, but to no avail. Winston Churchill came to America and delivered his famous warning that an "iron curtain" was coming down all over Europe; our response was not action, but discussion and frustration.

It was true that Europe and much of Asia were in terrible shape after World War II. Some people couldn't understand why the Russians would bother to take on such liabilities, but it was apparent to our best strategists that these regions' future value was incalculable. If the Soviet Union were to capture the Western European or the Japanese industrial base, they would rival and likely outstrip the United States. Such power, wielded by a brutal totalitarian state, was a frightening prospect.

Russian ground expansion was not the only threat, however. The marriage of American nuclear weapons with German-developed missiles created an entirely new danger: nuclear destruction by international missiles. A third threat was the denial, by extortion, by force, or by economic means, of access to raw materials in the Third World and elsewhere.

NATO'S SUCCESS

NATO had a role to play in protecting against all three of these complex dangers. Yet, revisionist historians are fond of dismissing the Cold War, containment, NATO, and the whole of American military strategy as a paranoid response to an imagined monolithic communist threat. The benefit of the doubt, ironically enough, goes not to democrats but to despots. Could the revisionists be right? Imagine for a moment that NATO had not been organized in 1949. Imagine depending on the UN to keep the peace of the world, to maintain and strengthen alliances, to defend our national and international interests.

NATO has been a success not only because it has deterred war, but because it has promoted prosperity around the world. But NATO, like our entire defense strategy, has serious problems. Much of the criticism directed towards NATO is based on the fact that other member nations have not fulfilled their financial obligations. True, the United States shoulders the greatest burden, and this ought to be remedied. I do not, however, think it is cause for abandoning the alliance.

Another objection has been that NATO's ground forces are not a major deterrent in the event of war. But they have always been considered as one component in a larger plan. As such, they should not be dismissed lightly either. The Soviet Union's masterful maneuvering has pushed us just to the edge of reaction and no more in many situations. It takes small bites out of a country, landing troops and "military advisors" a few thousand at a time. It prefers to work through puppets and "indigenous" Marxist revolutionary movements and popular fronts. The United States can hardly start a nuclear war over that.

Meanwhile, Soviet conventional forces are improving all the time. Once we could boast of our superior technological advantage, but anyone who has seen a Russian tank lately knows that the technological gap has narrowed and even closed in some instances.

NATO's nuclear forces are another component of NATO's strategy, and that is why the current talk of denuclearization is so fraught with danger. Without nuclear weapons, as one keen observer has noted, war is once again thinkable. For four decades, NATO's nuclear deterrent has worked superbly. The Russians have had to resort to expending their military efforts elsewhere, and in a very limited fashion, in Asia, Central America, and Africa.

Our greatest mistake would be to assume that one alliance or one weapon or one variety of military response can secure our defense, or that by eliminating one of these, peace can be guaranteed. The very real problems that hinder us simply can't be solved by blaming NATO.

A MATTER OF TRUST

There are other false assumptions about our defense policy that must be challenged. One is that we cannot compete with a Soviet dictatorship that is free to focus its efforts and a disproportionate share of its GNP on creating an unbeatable war machine. Another is that somehow our economic superiority will win out; that if we can dominate international trade, we can bend other nations to our will.

The worst mistake of all is to assume that we Americans are too

self-absorbed, too weak, too materialistic to defend ourselves.

Some ask if it is indeed moral for the U.S. to belong to NATO. Our current political leaders certainly think so, but what about the next generation, which has grown up in a culture that stresses rapprochement with our enemies at any cost? What about the neoisolationist sentiment that has gained so much force in our political parties? Publicly, a former secretary of the navy has referred to the United States as "an island nation," suggesting that we follow 18th-century Britain's example of relying on a superfleet to defend our shores and protect our interests abroad. Our willingness to consider abandoning NATO is a sure sign that we ought to stop and consider just what kind of commitments we are ready to uphold.

True, Western Europe and the rest of our allies ought to have the courage to pull themselves together, to depend upon themselves rather than us. They ought to be able to coordinate their own defense. Certainly they have the potential to do so. But it simply won't happen. They lack the raw materials, the up-to-date industrial base, and, most of all, the necessary mutual trust. Can you imagine the French government saying, "Okay, the Germans can be in command"? Or vice versa?

Whatever quarrels various nations may have with us, however often one hears "Yankee Go Home," our allies trust the United States to a far greater degree than any other nation. Ought we betray that trust?

When everything is said and done—when the Left has expressed its genuine fear that a trigger-happy America will make Europe the first casualty in a nuclear war, and when the Right has wondered about the times we have backed away from direct confrontations with the Soviets in Eastern Europe, Afghanistan, and Central America—that trust still survives.

Unquestionably, we ought to take a good hard look at NATO; we ought to press for substantial and meaningful reforms, and not just because it makes good strategic sense. We are an ethical people with a moral vision that shapes our entire way of life, including our foreign policy and our defense. We know that peacemaking is blessed and that "if good men fail to act, evil will succeed." We have paid a great price in human lives over the years in order to live up to that demanding vision, and we must do everything in our power to make sure those lives were not lost in vain. ∎

Europessimism Takes Turn for the Worse

By Karen Elliott House

Europessimism. It's as old as the Western Alliance itself. But something very different and much more ominous is festering in European capitals today. Normally, when Europeans are fearful, they come whimpering and wheedling to Uncle Sam; this time they aren't.

Instead, the allies—especially the French and Germans—are gritting their teeth and groping among themselves for new alliances and alignments that can substitute for their traditional dependence on America. The current European mood goes beyond pessimism to something much more serious—a conclusion that survival depends less on America and more on some combination of their own political ingenuity and Soviet good will.

This conclusion comes from talks in Bonn, Paris and London with many of Europe's leading security experts and policy makers. These included, among others, the national security advisers to British Prime Minister Margaret Thatcher, West German Chancellor Helmut Kohl and French President Francois Mitterrand; former French President Valery Giscard d'Estaing; and, in Germany, Foreign Minister Hans Dietrich Genscher, Defense Minister Manfred Woerner and opposition defense spokesman Karsten Voigt.

SLIPPING AWAY FROM EUROPE

From this side of the Atlantic, the Reagan-Gorbachev treaty removing intermediate-range nuclear missiles from Europe is generally seen as just one more piece of evidence that America is pulling back. For public consumption, European officials offer a lukewarm endorsement of a treaty they already view as a fait accompli. What they say in private is very different.

The INF Treaty actually is viewed as part of Uncle Sam's long, slippery slide these past 18 months away from a traditional commitment to Europe. First came the superpower summit in Reykjavik in October 1986, when President Reagan expressed willingness to do away with all nuclear weapons, thus leaving Europe at the mercy of the Warsaw Pact's massive superiority in conventional forces. In European eyes, the Reykjavik meeting lives in infamy.

"It was Yalta II," says a French official involved in national security policy. "The two superpowers got together and in two days, without any consideration, without any consultation with us, sold out Europe again."

Since then, several other things have reinforced the fear and trembling in Europe. Following last month's Reagan-Gorbachev summit, America now actually *is* pulling its INF missiles out of Europe, not just talking about it. Then, too, the humbled economic circumstances of America and its once-dominant dollar encourage the conclusion that a U.S. troop pullout from Europe will come next. Additionally, the siren song of glasnost suggests to many Europeans, especially the Germans, that the Soviet bear isn't really all that threatening anymore. On top of all that, this month's landmark Pentagon study by such prestigious strategists as Albert Wohlstetter, Henry Kissinger and Zbigniew Brzezinski concluding that the U.S. must refocus its defense priorities away from Europe to conflicts in the

Third World is another sign to Europeans that America is abandoning them.

All this could have had positive consequences. The U.S. decision to withdraw its INF missiles and the talk of broader nuclear reductions could have led the Europeans toward a commitment to more military self-reliance. That would have made it more difficult for the U.S. to think seriously about reducing its troop presence in Europe. In turn, the sense of a firm and lasting U.S. presence could have further reinforced European efforts to do more for their own defense.

But that constructive cycle hasn't materialized. Instead, the catch phrase here these days is, "No Nukes, No Troops," meaning that America isn't about to leave its troops exposed to the Warsaw Pact's superior forces without the protection of nuclear weapons in Europe. It is an analysis that has all the earmarks of a self-fulfilling prophecy. Europeans are starting to act on the basis of what they fear will happen.

In short, they are running to each other, but heavily burdened with the suspicions and rivalries that have characterized European power politics for centuries. Without America in its traditional parental role, the Europeans are beginning to behave with all the familial intrigue of characters on "Dynasty" or "Dallas."

France and Germany are proclaiming themselves the twin pillars of a new European order. Their leaders talk of going beyond economic cooperation into an era of military integration. So far, however, only one joint brigade exists—even on paper. Indeed, the only thing the French and Germans really share is a common fear of American abandonment.

The Germans, always eager to find some way to reunite their divided nation, see glasnost as making that possibility somewhat more likely. But Germany's dream of reunification is France's nightmare. The French view a closer Franco-German alliance as a leash to restrain West Germany's pull toward the East. Paradoxically, the Germans see greater cooperation with France less as a defense shield against the Russians than as a screen behind which they can carry on flirtations with the Soviets while being protected from American protestations.

"We don't want any distrust in America that we are changing our position," says a senior West German official. "Getting rid of this distrust is essential to get room for maneuver in our relations with the East. The backing of the French socialist president makes that easier."

As the Germans maneuver behind their French shield, they expound other virtues of closer Franco-German relations. The French, they explain in loud stage whispers, are the *enfants terribles* of Europe and someone has to tame them into closer cooperation with the NATO military alliance. The problem, of course, is that the last thing the French want is to be lured into NATO.

There are other limits on France's military commitment to Germany. With the U.S.-Soviet INF agreement, France's nuclear missiles take on added significance. Despite all the talk of Franco-German cooperation, President Mitterrand has made it clear that France's strategic nuclear forces won't be used automatically to save Germany. Germany, he says, must look for protection under the American nuclear umbrella.

"Mitterrand asks America, which is far away, to do what he refuses to do for a neighbor," says a top West German official.

If Germany is concerned about French egocentrism and France is fretting over German flirtations with the Soviets, Britain is worried about even the talk of Franco-German cooperation. That's partly because closer Franco-German ties relegate Britain to a peripheral role in European affairs. But it's more because the British fear that the more Europe talks of alliances to defend itself, the more budget-conscious U.S. congressmen will be inclined to let Europe do precisely that. Once again, this could become a self-fulfilling prophecy. Indeed, Mrs. Thatcher is the only Western leader publicly calling for no more nuclear disarmament in Europe and the upgrading of the missiles that remain after the INF pullout.

Yet the Soviets seem closer than ever to their ultimate goal of denuclearizing Western Europe. Messrs. Gorbachev and Reagan are expected to meet again at midyear to conclude a treaty that would cut in half the superpower strategic nuclear arsenals. This would affect the core of those arsenals—intercontinental-range missiles targeted by the two superpowers on each other. Soviet willingness to make such deep cuts is seductive stuff to European public opinion.

At the same time, the Soviets seem virtually certain this year to offer substantial cuts in conventional weaponry. This, too, the Europeans will find beguiling.

The catch is that the Soviets want removal not just of INF missiles, but also of what soon will be the last remaining U.S. nuclear missiles in Western Europe—those, based mostly in Germany, with a range of under 500 kilometers. The official NATO strategy is to "modernize" these remaining missiles and aircraft to give them greater range and penetration capability. That would make them a more potent threat to Soviet aggression—or at least a bigger bargaining chip in conventional arms-reduction talks.

That strategy, however, already is being undercut. Key decision makers in France and Germany are deeply divided over whether to (a) modernize the short-range nuclear missiles, (b) bargain them away for cuts in Soviet conventional weapons, or (c) get rid of them as relics that have outlived their usefulness in a new age of glasnost. The Soviets, who are pressing for immediate negotiations on the short-range missiles, can afford to be magnanimous in such talks since they have roughly 1,300 such missiles, compared with the 88 Lance missiles in West Germany. "Deep cuts," the current catch phrase, would mean the effective end of all Western nuclear missiles.

NOT A CREDIBLE PROSPECT

If short-range missiles follow the INF missiles out, Europe, which is unwilling to spend more on conventional defense, would have to depend on American willingness to use its strategic nuclear forces—and risk global nuclear war—in the event of a Soviet conventional attack on Western Europe. In short, Europe would be dependent on America's willingness to sacrifice say, Boston, for Bonn. Germans never before have found that prospect credible, which is the reason the U.S put nuclear weapons in Europe in the first place.

Nonetheless, public determination remains high in West Germany to get rid of the remaining nuclear weapons, because, if used, they would land mostly on either East or West Germany. The Germans summarize their distaste for this prospect with the phrase: "The shorter the range, the deader the Germans."

If these last short-range nuclear missiles go, as seems probable, Western Europe's security will depend on one of two possibilities: the chance that the U.S would be willing to risk all-out nuclear war or the hope that the Soviets have dropped their goal of dominating Europe.

Given a choice between two such frail reeds, Western Europe, led by West Germany, is likely to grasp at the chimera of Soviet good will rather than risk relying on increasingly remote and dubious American protection. ■

The European Pillar

By William Safire

Last month, NATO held its last meeting. The Brussels session wasn't officially the final meeting —its joint communiqué was poignantly labeled "A Time for Reaffirmation"—but future confabulations cannot hide the fact that NATO is now a paper alliance.

Its raison d'être was fear of a Soviet invasion of Europe, and its essence was the guarantee that the United States would treat an attack upon Amsterdam as an attack upon Chicago. NATO's military strategy was to use conventional weapons to delay the Soviet movement

westward, then to turn to battlefield nuclear artillery and missiles, and when those defenses failed, to expect the United States to launch a nuclear attack on the Soviet Union.

None of that is present-day realthink. Despite the presence of 18,000 Soviet tanks and enough weaponry to decimate the Continent, few in Europe fear a Soviet invasion. Even fewer believe that America would launch a nuclear attack on the Soviet Union, inviting the leveling of American cities, to punish the Russians for rolling into

Europe. That realization turns our "nuclear umbrella" into a parasol.

"Today the fear of nuclear weapons is greater than the fear of the Soviets," Richard Nixon, ever the realist, told the *Washington Times* editor, Arnaud de Borchgrave, last week. "That's what made the better-Red-than-dead slogan a tempting option for some—and when you're facing death, it's probably a close call." The Russians believed Mr. Nixon was mean enough to push the button if they invaded Europe: nobody believes the next U.S. President will be that unpredictable and all know that such a policy would have no popular support.

The recent signing of the I.N.F. treaty, despite the forced smiles of European leaders, marked the military parting of the two ends of the North Atlantic alliance. A decade ago, when Mr. Brezhnev tried to dominate Europe with new midrange missiles, the Europeans and Americans countered with what turned out to be NATO's finest hour: despite the cries of our fearful freezeniks (including Jesse Jackson, who refuses to this day to admit his profound mistake), we placed an equal force of U.S. missiles in Europe to call the Soviet bluff.

Mr. Gorbachev wisely backed off, signing a treaty that removes his cities from the threat of U.S. medium-range missiles. This move toward fewer nuclear weapons brought hosannas from around the world but now reminds Europeans that the defense of Europe must be done the expensive way—raising and equipping armies by themselves.

Such military cooperation between Western European powers is called "the European pillar." The U.S. used to worry about side deals within the Atlantic alliance; now Mr. Reagan welcomes the pillar but cannot even whisper the reason: because it will be needed to prop up the region when we begin to take our 300,000 troops out.

And ready or not, the 41st President will pull them out in the 1990s. The presence of a tripwire—the potential of enough U.S. casualties to justify our triggering a nuclear strike—is no longer in the U.S. national interest. The delay that their fighting would cause would not give the world time to stop the invasion; on the contrary, the ensuing brouhaha would reassure the invaders that U.S. public opinion was against heavy nuclear response.

If so, that knocks into a cocked hat the whole notion of the use of a conventional force capable of delaying the Russians for three or four weeks. The delaying force would merely expose our strategic weakness of will (Edward Luttwak, this century's Clausewitz, is writing a book with this thesis). Only a conventional army capable of resisting and rolling back the Soviet invaders has any strategic value, and its cost is a burden Europeans are unwilling to assume.

So what should be the successor to "flexible response," which was the rhetorical but not strategic successor to "massive retaliation"? I cannot vouchsafe that to you in the remaining two paragraphs (sure I could, but do not want to louse up my visa application to the Moscow summit meeting), but its basis goes beyond dickering for an asymmetrical reduction of forces.

A superpower must act globally. Europe is one region, its component powers thinking only regionally in face of a worldwide threat. Our interest is to cooperate with the European region in resisting long-term Soviet expansion, but also to support and extend freedom in other regions like Southeast Asia, the Middle East and Central America.

For Europe, today's pillar talk is healthy if it leads to regional self-reliance; for America, worldwide action to defend freedom requires a new freedom of action. ∎

Europe Is Likely to Be New Center Stage For Confrontation Between U.S., Soviets

By Frederick Kempe

The East-West contest is moving back to Europe. Many experts believe the current Polish unrest, coinciding with economic and political problems throughout Eastern Europe, marks the beginning of a refocusing of U.S. and Soviet interests to Europe from today's distant guerrilla conflicts. Soviet retrenchment from costly foreign adventures, signaled by the planned Soviet withdrawal from Afghanistan and new flexibility on Angola, will transfer Moscow's energies to the core area of its external fears, Eastern Europe, and of its foreign ambitions, Western Europe.

Source: *The Wall Street Journal,* May 9, 1988, p. 18. Reprinted by permission.

"The U.S.-Soviet competition is shifting from the Third World to Europe," says William Griffiths, a professor at the Massachusetts Institute of Technology and a former consultant to the U.S. Embassy in Bonn. He says unrest in East Europe poses the greatest threat to Mikhail Gorbachev's attempt to open up the Soviet economy and society.

"The danger the Soviets face is how do they gain Western Europe and not lose Eastern Europe," he says. Western Europe is central to Moscow's long-term goal of eroding U.S. influence and its immediate need for financing and technology.

Sensing this shift in the East-West struggle, Rep. Lee Hamilton, the Indiana Democrat, urges a less passive allied policy that would offer carrots to East European countries to encourage closer ties with the West.

"Over the next several years, Eastern Europe will become increasingly important for American policy," he says. "Poland, the most open country in Eastern Europe, faces severe problems of economic and political stability. Hungary, Romania, Bulgaria, East Germany and Czechoslovakia will face leadership changes as well as strong pressures for political and economic change. Albania is likely to emerge from its isolation."

Dmitri Simes of the Washington-based Carnegie Endowment for International Peace believes the U.S should seize the opportunity and propose to the Soviets a joint declaration on European security under which both promise not to interfere militarily unless their allies are invaded. If Mr. Gorbachev refuses, it reveals Moscow's intention to continue preserving empire by military force. If he agrees, the U.S. will be lauded by East Europeans for the achievement. "You are showing what Gorbachev really is," says Mr. Simes.

FIRST ROUND, POLAND

As so often in the past, the first round is being played out in Poland, where security forces last week stormed a steel mill near Krakow to crush a 10-day strike that had set off a wave of labor unrest. The strikes come at a sensitive time: Washington and Moscow are preparing for the Memorial Day summit, and Mr. Gorbachev is already under fire from Communist Party conservatives for running too loose a ship.

Most dangerous to Mr. Gorbachev, the East European troubles aren't purely Polish. Demonstrations have occurred this year in East Germany, Czechoslovakia, Hungary and Romania. East European economies are stagnating, nationalist and religious feeling is growing and nonofficial organizations are proliferating.

"This is no longer a single challenge in a single country," says Sarah Terry, an expert on East Europe at Tufts University. "Gorbachev may find himself facing simultaneous challenges in several countries. The potential of unrest in Eastern Europe hangs like a sword of Damocles over Gorbachev's policies of *perestroika* [economic restructuring] at home.

All this has been helped along by Soviet agreement to start withdrawing troops from Afghanistan, which many East European dissidents read as the first sign of Soviet weakness in Moscow's efforts to spread socialism. An East European diplomat in Washington concedes the withdrawal will have "a rather provocative effect" on dissent throughout the region.

QUESTIONING SOVIET AUTHORITY

U.S. officials believe unrest in Eastern Europe is a far greater threat to Mr. Gorbachev than recent demonstrations in the Soviet republics of Armenia and Azerbaijan. Those demonstrations didn't question Soviet authority, and indeed sought Kremlin mediation.

Armenians and Azerbaijanis are among the more loyal non-Russian Soviets and haven't shown signs of wanting independence. But many East Europeans view the current period as a time to test the limits of Gorbachev's tolerance for groups that openly challenge the Communist Party's monopoly on power.

"When Gorbachev speaks of democratization, East Europeans know what it means," says Prof. Terry. "A lot of the Soviet population does not." ■

Toward Real Community?

By Frederick Painton

Nineteen ninety-two. *Quatre-vingt-douze. El horizonte 92. Zweiundneunzig.* In the languages of Western Europe, the number has become an incantation, a milestone year on the long road toward European economic union. French President François Mitterrand points to 1992 as a stern challenge that helped inspire him to announce last month that he would seek a second term of office. His main rival on the right, Premier Jacques Chirac, points to his own youth and vigor (he is 55, Mitterrand, 71) as the qualities France needs in a leader for the trials of 1992. More phlegmatically, West German Chancellor Helmut Kohl describes the year as an "extraordinary opportunity" to spur slow economic growth within the twelve-nation European Community.

In its simplest terms, 1992 is a deadline with important long-term implications, not only for Western Europe but also for the U.S., Japan and other powerful trading nations. At a 1985 summit meeting in Milan, E.C. leaders pledged to create a true single market of goods and services among their countries by the end of 1992. The original six members of the group, then known as the European Common Market, had that very goal in mind, of course, when they signed the Community's founding Treaty of Rome in 1957. But though all tariff barriers among the partners have been scaled down and the E.C. has grown larger, integration has a long way to go.

Since 1957 a web of red tape, regulation and fiscal restriction has gradually spread to protect E.C. members nearly as effectively as import duties ever did. The number of national customs officials who check intra-Community commerce at border crossings today is greater than the number of bureaucrats at E.C. headquarters in Brussels who are charged with guiding the enterprise of economic integration. Among the victims of thinly disguised protectionist curbs have been non-European firms, including U.S. companies, which have found themselves shut out of many lucrative markets. They are now feeling some hope, wisely tempered by caution, that 1992 will bring the dissolution of a thicket of strictures—and more business. Says a spokesman for Digital Equipment, based in Maynard, Mass.: "We believe that a unified market will attract capital and encourage entrepreneurial behavior. We look forward to benefiting from these commercial opportunities."

West European consumers have also been hurt by protectionism, paying higher prices than necessary for a more limited choice of products and services. In addition, with competition crimped, the technological competitiveness of E.C. members has suffered in such key sectors as computers, robotics and biotechnology. Last year the E.C. ran an estimated deficit in high-technology trade of between $10 billion and $15 billion. Explains a senior E.C. official: "It dawned on governments that they were preventing Europe from realizing its full potential."

That potential is impressive, at least on paper: a fully integrated Community would contain 323 million consumers, compared with 244 million in the U.S. and 122 million in Japan. The combined gross domestic product of E.C. countries last year was $4.2 trillion, almost equal to that of the U.S. ($4.4 trillion) and considerably more than the combined total for Japan, South Korea, Taiwan, Hong Kong and Singapore ($2.7 trillion). A recent E.C. study predicts that the creation of a truly common market would boost the Community's growth rate by 5% by the end of the 1990s and generate up to 1.8 million jobs over five years.

The promise of 1992 is already spurring a wave of mergers and takeovers in Western Europe, the start of a much needed restructuring. Italian Entrepreneur Carlo de Benedetti gave the name Europe 1992 to the company he formed with other investors for his so far unsuccessful bid for Société Générale, Belgium's huge holding company. West Germany's Axel Springer Publishing, one of the Continent's largest media conglomerates, is embroiled in what may become that country's first hostile takeover attempt. The would-be conqueror: the Kirch Group, the West German film acquisition and distribution company.

Elsewhere, the reaction to the 1992 challenge varies from anticipation to lethargy. For Italian industrial leaders, such as De Benedetti and Gianni Agnelli, chairman of Fiat, the prospect of a competi-

Source: *Time,* April 18, 1988, pp. 54–55. Reported by John Kohan/Bonn and Christopher Redman/Paris, with other bureaus.

tive free-for-all holds few concerns. "The most active part of Italian industry is well along the road to 1992," says De Benedetti. "We are held back, however, by a lack of similar progress in the state administration." Italian economists are specifically worried about handicaps in the impending competitive struggle such as a weak banking system and large government deficits.

French businessmen follow their political leaders in hailing the E.C.'s proposed reforms. According to a poll taken last year by the Employers Association, the country's most powerful business lobby, two out of three corporate leaders believe 1992 represents a great opportunity for French business. Says François Périgot, president of the group: "A united Europe is not a protected Europe but a market open to the world. I think French companies are well placed to take advantage of it." Still, French self-interest occasionally prevails. Two months ago, Finance Minister Edouard Balladur temporarily blocked a $150 million bid for *Les Echos,* France's leading financial daily, by Pearson PLC, a British conglomerate in which U.S. Media Baron Rupert Murdoch holds a minority share. Balladur's rationale: France's national interest would be compromised if non-E.C. owners had a significant stake in one of its premier newspapers, even if E.C. members held majority control.

In West Germany, where caution is frequently written in capital letters, businessmen are showing only mild interest in an expanded market. According to a poll cited by Chancellor Kohl, only 27% of West German firms are adjusting corporate planning to take account of the impending change; the fig-

ure contrasts with 87% in France. Explains a West German diplomat: "The idea of Europe seems to have diminished somewhat in Germany. Many have lost heart because things have moved so slowly."

British businessmen also appear less than excited. A study published last month by the Ernst & Whinney accounting firm found that only 38% of senior British corporate executives even knew about the proposals to knock down trade barriers by 1992. Prime Minister Margaret Thatcher's government has launched an information campaign aimed at stirring greater interest.

Spain and Portugal, E.C. members since January 1986, have their own qualms about 1992. Lisbon fears that the still insular Portuguese economy could be swallowed up by expansion-minded Spanish firms; Portugal's financial-service companies are thought to be particularly vulnerable because of their lagging technology. But unless both Spain and Portugal embrace greater competition, the longer-term danger is that they and the E.C.'s other southern members will fall further behind the more affluent northern partners.

Many U.S. businessmen take their cues about 1992 from Western Europe's mixed views. Says James Murphy, the assistant U.S. trade representative for Europe and the Mediterranean: "We are keeping a wary eye." Under Community rules for 1992, E.C.-based subsidiaries of U.S. and other foreign multinationals will qualify, in theory anyway, as European Community companies. But several U.S. firms are worried that the talk of integration is merely rhetoric to cover up discrimination that is specifically aimed at them. The ner-

vousness is well grounded, suggests Alfred Kingon, the U.S. Ambassador to the Community. Says he: "When I speak to E.C. leaders I receive reassurances that the Community will not become Fortress Europe. But when I hear talk of 'nurturing' industries, I become concerned."

Several E.C. industries are already fighting for continued protection. Some West European auto manufacturers, fearful of a Japanese onslaught after 1992, are lobbying for tighter Community-wide quotas on car imports. Last year Japan sold 1.2 million cars and trucks in E.C. countries, capturing nearly 10% of the market. E.C. auto lobbyists support an import quota of 1 million Japanese vehicles. Says Raymond Levy, chairman of France's state-owned Renault: "If we import more, we're going to have to close plants in Europe."

Other issues directly affect touchy questions of national sovereignty. Earlier this year the European Commission, the Community's executive body, caused widespread grumbling—particularly within the Thatcher government—by proposing to harmonize indirect taxes, including value-added and excise levies, among the members. For some of the partners, such a change would mean major budgetary dislocations. Beginning in 1993, according to the Community's integration plan, member governments must open public procurement contracts to bidding from firms in other E.C. countries. If they do, political leaders could be robbed of one important way to create jobs, channel funds to depressed regions and otherwise dispense patronage.

Amid the jockeying for assurances and advantages, the Community members will find it difficult to meet the 1992 deadline. By the end of last year, for example, the E.C. had adopted only 69 of the more than 160 proposals for deregulation scheduled as part of the integration process. For all that, Ambassador Kingon is cautiously optimistic. When an E.C. summit meeting in Brussels last month agreed on a series of budgetary and agricultural reform measures, Kingon conceded that the "odds now favor the E.C. making it."

The most persuasive reason behind that judgment may be that the alternative is worse. Says a top E.C. official in Brussels: "Europeans are aware of the need to play a role on the world's stage at a time when U.S. power and influence are waning." This time the battered idea of a united Europe may be recognized for what it is: of compelling supranational interest for the members of the E.C. ■

Suggested Additional Readings

Baumann, Carol Edler. *Europe in NATO* (New York: Praeger, 1988).

Buteux, Paul, *Strategy, Doctrine and the Politics of the Alliance* (Boulder, CO: Westview Press, 1983).

Calleo, David P. *Beyond American Hegemony: The Future of the Western Alliance* (New York: Basic Books, 1987).

Fedder, Edwin (ed.). *Defense Politics of the Atlantic Alliance* (New York: Praeger, 1980).

Feld, Werner. *Arms Control and the Atlantic Community* (New York: Praeger, 1987).

Golden, James Reed. *NATO Burden Sharing* (New York: Praeger, 1983).

Kleiman, Robert. *Atlantic Crises: American Diplomacy Confronts a Resurgent Europe* (New York: Norton, 1965).

Langer, Peter. *Transatlantic Discord and NATO's Crisis of Cohesion* (Washington, DC: Pergamon-Brassey, 1986).

Levine, Robert A. *NATO, the Subjective Alliance: The Debate Over the Future* (Los Angeles: RAND Corporation, 1988).

Myers, Kenneth A. *NATO: The Next Thirty Years* (Boulder, CO: Westview Press, 1980).

Palmer, John. *Europe without America? The Crisis in Atlantic Relations* (New York: Oxford University Press, 1987).

Pfaltzgraff, Robert, and Walter Hahn (eds.). *Atlantic Community in Crisis* (New York: Pergamon, 1979).

Ravenal, Earl C. *NATO: The Tides of Discontent* (Berkeley, CA: Institute of International Studies, University of California, 1985).

Stuart, Douglas T. (ed.). *Politics and Security in the Southern Region of the Atlantic Alliance* (Baltimore, MD: Johns Hopkins University Press, 1988).

Treverton, Gregory. *Making the Alliance Work: The United States and Western Europe* (Ithaca, NY: Cornell University Press, 1985).

Tucker, Robert (ed.). *The Atlantic Alliance and its Critics* (New York: Praeger, 1983).

Wiarda, Howard J. (ed.). "Southern Europe and the Mediterranean," Special Issue of the *Foreign Policy and Defense Review* Vol. 6, No. 2 (1986).

CHAPTER THREE

Asia

*
*

The Asia/Pacific area is changing so fast that it is difficult for us—as well as for U.S. policy—to keep up with it all.

Japan has emerged as an economic giant in the world, surpassing the Soviet Union and challenging United States supremacy in many economic and technological areas. It is primarily our relations with Japan that have elevated trade policy into such an important factor in U.S. foreign policy. Meanwhile, Japan has been creating its own Asian bloc of trading partners to counterbalance what it sees as large future trading blocs in North America and Western Europe. The questions are if, when, and how Japanese economic power will be transformed into political and military power as well.

U.S. relations with China—both the People's Republic of China (PRC, Communist) and the Republic of China (Taiwan)—had been good, stable, and sensible for over a decade. That is, we had come to recognize the reality of Communist control over the mainland, of Communist China's power and potential, and of its ability to preoccupy the Soviet Union—which is useful from a U.S. foreign policy point of view. At the same time, we have continued our supportive relationship with the dynamic, noncommunist Republic of China on Taiwan—although the precise relationship with the two Chinas may still be open to future negotiations. U.S. business has concluded, however, that there may be fewer incentives for investing in the People's Republic of China than had previously been thought; and the PRC's suppression of the student-led prodemocracy movement in 1989 has introduced new strains into the relationship.

In addition to Japan, the four Asian "tigers" (Republic of China, South Korea, Hong Kong, and Singapore) have been doing very well economically. In fact, they may have been responsible for convincing the Soviets that capitalism represented the future of the Third World, rather than Marxism-Leninism, and for persuading the Soviet Union not to try to expand its influence in very many new areas of the Third World. The economic performance of these Asian nations has been such as to persuade the U.S. that its priorities to these Pacific rim countries ought to be far higher than they have been historically.

The fantastic growth of these Asian nations has had a ripple effect on other countries—Malaysia, Thailand, Indonesia—which have also begun to share in the general prosperity. Other Asian countries and territories—the Philippines, Burma, Vietnam, Cambodia, Laos, as well as the islands of the South Pacific (Australia and New Zealand excepted)—have lagged behind. It is probably no accident that these are also the countries and areas that have been the most unstable and that have been—and will likely continue to be—the most contentious in international politics.

Meanwhile, the Soviet Union, with its bases at Vladivostok, the Kamchatka Peninsula, and at Vietnam's Cam Ranh Bay, has become a major Asian as well as European power. The Soviets have expanded their fleet in the Indian and Pacific oceans and gained access to new bases in the South Pacific. Whether this new and expanded Soviet military and diplomatic presence in east and southeast Asia and the South Pacific will be affected by glasnost and the presumption of a Soviet pullback from its global commitments, we will have to wait and see. Meanwhile, this area, or at least some parts of it, constitutes a potentially volatile area in future global politics.

The readings on Asia begin with an analysis prepared by the Department of State on the underlying economic and trade aspects of U.S. policy. Scholar David Lampton then assesses U.S. China policy and finds it balanced, nonpartisan, and successful. Alan Romberg of the Council on Foreign Relations next provides a careful assessment of U.S.-Japan relations. There follows a brief piece from *The New York Times* on Japan's mixed feelings about playing a stronger foreign policy role in the world. Finally, economist John Makin assesses Japan's rising economic strength and its implications for U.S. policy.

East Asia and the U.S.: An Economic Partnership

OVERVIEW

The economies of the East Asian and Pacific region[1] are important in the international trade of the United States and play a large and growing role in the world economy. During the past two to three decades, much of the region has experienced rapid economic growth, sometimes more than 10% per year, largely because most East Asian governments are committed to outward-looking and market-oriented policies. Their combined gross national product (GNP) is now about three-quarters of U.S. total output. Japan is the major economic power in the region. Other East Asian economies—such as South Korea, Taiwan, Hong Kong, and Singapore—are emulating its successful model of high rates of savings and investment, more efficient and advanced industry, high-technology exports, and increased educational and technical training. China also has been attempting to transform its economy along market lines and has experienced high rates of economic growth.

East Asian exports have penetrated almost every corner of the globe. Since 1983, U.S.-East Asian trade across the Pacific has exceeded our trade across the Atlantic. In 1987, U.S. trade with East Asia, which accounted for 35% of our global commerce, was greater than with any other region. At the same time, the U.S. trade deficit with East Asia was $107 billion, more than 60% of our worldwide trade shortfall.

East Asian economic success has been accompanied by the growth of democracy in the re-

gion. New democratic governments in the Philippines and South Korea exemplify this trend toward greater popular participation in the political process. This economic and political progress is buttressed by various bilateral military arrangements with the United States, which provide security and stability in the region.

The economic growth and political development of East Asian countries and areas will likely give the region an even greater role in world affairs in the years leading up to the 21st century. Their exports, technological advances, capital, foreign investment, and economic assistance will have an increasing impact on other regions and on international trade and finance. The United States hopes that the region will take the lead in further reducing its trade barriers, either unilaterally or in the current Uruguay Round of multilateral trade negotiations under the auspices of the General Agreement on Tariffs and Trade. A more open international trading system will enhance East Asia's future economic development and lessen the U.S. trade imbalance with the region.

The United States will continue to be the major power in the Pacific, even though the rapid growth of the East Asian economies has lessened our relative economic position. The U.S. market will probably remain the largest for East Asian exports, but it is not likely to absorb their future rapid growth to the extent that it did earlier in this decade. The United States will continue to be an important source of investment, high

technology, and manufacturing facilities for East Asia, and our service industries are poised for an expanded role in the region. Additionally, it remains an educational magnet: 39% of all foreign students in the United States are East Asians. The mutually beneficial partnership between the United States and East Asia, both multilaterally and through many personal ties and experiences, contributes to developing a stronger international economic system and the strengthening of democratic institutions among our allies and friends.

A sense of interdependence is evolving among the economies of East Asia and the Pacific. The Association of South East Asian Nations (ASEAN) has fostered cooperation among its members and dialogue with governments in the Pacific basin and with other developed countries. Community consciousness also has contributed to the formation and development of other organizations, such as the Pacific Basin Economic Council and the Pacific Economic Cooperation Conference. Future cooperation in the region could come from dialogue in some kind of new Pacific basin forum on various topics of mutual interest:

• Structural economic policies, such as privatization of public enterprises and lowering of trade barriers, that would promote further growth, efficiency, private sector initiatives, and free trade;
• Deregulation and improvement of transportation systems to facilitate the movement of goods, people, and information throughout the region;

Source: From U.S. Department of State, Bureau of Public Affairs, *East Asia and the Pacific: Regional Brief,* January 1989.

• Promotion of educational exchanges with the United States; and
• Protection of natural resources and the environment.

The United States hopes to participate with all market-oriented governments of the region in the development of this dialogue and the establishment of a mutually beneficial East Asian/Pacific agenda in the coming years.

JAPAN

Because of its strength as the second largest economy in the noncommunist world, Japan is the major economic power in East Asia. The combined GNP of the United States and Japan totals about 35% of world output. The two countries have close economic, political, cultural, and security ties. This alliance has been and will continue to be the cornerstone of U.S. policies in East Asia.

Japan's strong export performance since the 1960s has been the envy of developed and developing countries. Japan's share of world exports is now more than 10%, about twice its share of 20 years ago. U.S.-Japanese trade has grown to $116 billion in 1987, second only to U.S.-Canadian commerce. Our trade deficit with Japan, which began in 1965, has increased to almost $60 billion per year in 1986–87, although it is now coming down slowly.

The U.S. Government aims to increase U.S. exports to Japan. During the past 4 years, U.S.-Japanese trade negotiations have opened Japanese markets for U.S. exports of such items as drugs, medical equipment, semiconductors, telecommunications equipment, beef,

and citrus products. In addition, American goods have become more competitive in Japan because of the depreciation of the dollar and greater U.S. attention to the quality of our export products. Although much progress has been made, the United States continues to call upon Japan to implement further trade liberalization and to expand its domestic markets. The U.S. Government has pointed out that such measures would benefit Japan, the United States, and the international trading system.

According to U.S. data, the stock of direct investment in each other's economies grew rapidly to $43 billion by the end of 1987, almost three times more than in 1982. Japan's direct investment in the United States was nearly $31 billion at the end of 1987. There are Japanese-owned manufacturing facilities in 40 U.S. states, employing more than 100,000 Americans. Productive foreign investment can bring better jobs, more efficient operations, greater choice of quality goods at competitive prices, and the transfer of capital and technology to us. They also reflect the growing linkages between the two economies.

The United States and Japan have worked to coordinate their economic policies and exchange rates to assure stable economic growth. For example, the two countries agreed in October 1986 that Japan should cut interest rates while increasing government spending and that the United States should continue to seek reductions in its budget deficit, in order to reduce their large external imbalances. This cooperation has been bolstered by semiannual subcabinet economic meetings, numerous trade negotiations, and other official contacts between the two countries.

Japan has become a major source of economic aid, primarily to other countries in Asia. At the Toronto economic summit in June 1988, Japanese Prime Minister Noboru Takeshita outlined a new program of $50 billion in official development assistance over the next 5 years. The Government of Japan intends to increase the grant component of this assistance, require fewer conditions on its loans, and provide $1 billion in debt relief to the poorest developing countries. Japan is likely to become the world's largest aid donor in 1989. The United States welcomes this development as part of our interest in having our allies make a greater contribution to common global interests. We hope that Japan will extend a greater proportion of its expanded foreign aid program on a grant basis.

CHINA

During the past decade, the United States and the People's Republic of China (P.R.C.) have enjoyed a significant expansion in economic relations. The United States is China's third largest trading partner. In 1988, our bilateral trade exceeded $13 billion, nearly a seven-fold increase since diplomatic relations were normalized 10 years ago. In the same period, U.S. investment committed to China increased to more than $3 billion and has focused on energy exploration, electronics, textiles, food processing, hotels, and construction. This relationship has been achieved without compromising our friendship for, or cooperation with, the people of Taiwan.

China has had impressive economic growth during the last decade, averaging nearly 10% per year. Under the leadership of Chairman Deng Xiaoping, the P.R.C. has undertaken a series of far-reaching economic reforms, including decentralizing enterprise management, relaxing price controls, and encouraging trade and investment with market economies. As a result of these reforms, industrial production rose dramatically and agricultural output expanded and diversified. Recently, however, China postponed further price reforms in an effort to bring inflation under control. In 1988, the annual official inflation rate was about 20% nationwide and 25%–30% in urban areas. Despite China's opening to the West, opportunities to trade with and invest in China are restricted in many important ways by Chinese law and practice.

China continues to be strongly interested in acquiring state-of-the-art technology in order to modernize key sectors of its economy. In recent years, the United States has liberalized controls on the export of high-technology items to China. Chinese imports of computers and sophisticated electronic equipment have increased dramatically.

The United States and China have the largest bilateral science and technology cooperation program of its kind for each side, with some 400 cooperative activities under 30 bilateral agreements. For example, a December 1985 agreement provides for cooperation in the peaceful uses of nuclear energy. More than 30,000 Chinese students currently are enrolled in U.S. universities, while roughly 7,000 Americans are studying or teaching in the P.R.C.

FOUR ASIAN "TIGERS"

The newly industrialized economies of South Korea, Taiwan, Hong Kong, and Singapore are often referred to as the four Asian "tigers" or "dragons." Their success stems in large part from a commitment to private sector and/or market-oriented economic policies that have resulted in very rapid growth of industries and exports as well as the unleashing of human resources.

In recent years, the United States has played an important part in this economic development by providing a relatively open market for their products. Our trade deficits with the four tigers grew to $38 billion in 1987, accounted for primarily by deficits with Taiwan ($19.2 billion) and South Korea ($10.3 billion). As these two have become stronger economically, they have begun to lower their trade barriers and make their exchange rates more realistic, but they need to do more on both fronts to reduce their trade imbalances with the United States.

South Korea

The Republic of Korea has witnessed astounding economic changes in this decade as real GNP has doubled. In the process Korea has become America's seventh largest trading partner among individual countries. It now exports high-technology goods, such as automobiles and electronics, to the United States, Japan, and elsewhere. Soaring per capita income, declining unemployment, and reduced foreign debt have allowed Korea to move in the direction of a more liberalized economy. During the past year, South Korea has made the transition to democracy

by restoring freedom to the media and providing for full participation in elections. A multiparty political system has emerged. The United States fully supports these political developments while continuing to provide military support under a bilateral security agreement.

Taiwan

The people of Taiwan have generated enviable economic growth, averaging nearly double-digit annual rates since the 1950s. As elsewhere in East Asia, industry has expanded and produced higher value-added products. Taiwan's authorities have lowered tariffs, relaxed foreign exchange controls, strengthened the protection of intellectual property, encouraged export diversification, and appreciated the currency (40% against the U.S. dollar since 1985). Although U.S. exports to Taiwan have increased, our trade deficit with Taiwan was $19 billion in 1987. Taiwan's foreign exchange reserves at the end of 1988 were about $75 billion, exceeded only by Japan. Taiwan's political system has become more open in recent years. The United States welcomes Taiwan's economic and political modernization but has urged its leaders to lower trade barriers further and allow a more realistic exchange rate.

Hong Kong and Singapore

These two "city states" also have experienced rapid economic development; they have the highest per capita GNPs among the newly industralized economies. Lacking natural resources, the accomplishments of Hong Kong and Singapore have been largely due to strong market orientation and hard-working and disciplined labor forces. Savings and investment rates in Singapore are among the highest in the world. Hong Kong and Singapore are extremely successful examples of the virtues of export-led growth. Their economies, which have almost completely free markets and which center around very busy ports, are totally dependent on the maintenance of an open international trading system. Both Hong Kong's domestic exports and reexports from China have skyrocketed in the past 20 years.

ASEAN COUNTRIES

More than 300 million people live in the six nations that make up the Association of South East Asian Nations—the Philippines, Indonesia, Malaysia, Thailand, Singapore, and Brunei. The ASEAN countries are rich in natural resources, possess talented and hard-working populations, and to a large extent have pursued market-oriented development policies. Since 1977, these nations have averaged annual real GNP growth of more than 5%, one of the economic success stories among developing countries.

The United States has maintained cooperative economic relations with the ASEAN countries. We continue to be the largest consumer for ASEAN manufactures. U.S.-ASEAN trade, expanding rapidly, was about $28 billion in 1987, making ASEAN our seventh most important trading partner. Unfortunately, most ASEAN countries (not including Singapore and Brunei) retain relatively high tariff barriers and other nontariff constraints. U.S. direct investment in ASEAN economies totaled approximately $10 billion at the end of 1987. Many U.S. companies manufacture increasingly higher technology products and components in

ASEAN countries for reexport to the United States and other markets. The United States has engaged in regular economic dialogue with ASEAN. In addition, we are engaged in the U.S.-ASEAN initiative, a broad-gauged study of our economic relationship, including analysis of possible liberalization measures both sides can take to strengthen it.

The Philippines

After years of declining economic health, the Philippines increased its real GNP by almost 6% in 1987; even stronger growth is estimated in 1988. President Corazon Aquino's government has instituted fiscal and market-opening reforms, but more could be done to make the economy more efficient and dynamic and to encourage foreign investment. Unemployment and underemployment remain serious problems. The Philippines has a large external debt totaling approximately $30 billion. The United States has strongly supported the transition to democracy in the Philippines during the past 3 years. The U.S. Government is providing the Philippines with high levels of economic and security assistance—about $400 million during fiscal year 1988—as part of our effort to maintain mutually beneficial economic, political, and security relations. U.S. military facilities in the Philippines are very important to U.S. defense interests in the Pacific, a large part of the Philippines' and the region's defenses, and the source of substantial economic benefits—employing more than 68,000 Filipinos and injecting hundreds of millions of dollars into the local economy. The U.S. Government also has taken the lead in calling on its friends and allies to increase aid, promote in-

vestment, and open markets to Philippine exports.

Indonesia

The Indonesian economy—the largest though least developed (in terms of annual per capita income) among ASEAN members—has faced the challenge of lower and fluctuating oil prices since 1983. In order to promote growth, the Government of Indonesia has undertaken sweeping structural reforms, restrained public spending, maintained currency convertibility, encouraged foreign investment and capital market development, and instituted a series of trade, banking, and tax reforms. The United States welcomes these initiatives. Indonesia has boosted non-oil exports, which now account for more than one-half of its export earnings. External debt has risen sharply in recent years to about $45 billion at the end of 1988.

Malaysia

The Malaysian economy is moving from dependence on commodities (such as tin and rubber) to a light manufacturing base. Electronics products have become the largest export earner. Malaysia had a 1987 trade surplus of more than $5 billion. Commerce with the United States has grown rapidly. Real GNP growth was nearly 5% in 1987 and is estimated to be higher in 1988. The country's financial condition remains solid because the government has pursued responsible fiscal policies.

Thailand

Thailand had economic growth of almost 7% in 1987 and even better performance in 1988. The government has promoted export diversification and encouraged foreign investment. Foreign exchange

Economic Indicators, 1987 (U.S. $ millions, unless otherwise indicated)

	Population (millions)	GNP	Real GNP Growth (%)	GNP Per Capita (U.S.$)	Consumer Price Inflation (%)	Exports (f .o. b.)	Imports (c. i. f.)	Trade Balance	U.S. Exports	U.S. Imports	U.S. Trade Balance
ASEAN[1]	301.0	199,827	5.4	663	—	83,354	79,751	3,603	9,840	18,052	(8,212)
Australia	15.9	195,521	4.4	12,100	7.1	26,433	29,350	(2,917)	5,467	3,287	2,180
China	1,074.0	293,383	9.4	273	7.3	39,542	43,392	(3,850)	3,488	6,911	(3,423)
Hong Kong[1,2]	5.7	46,196	13.6	8,230	5.5	48,478	48,467	11	3,983	10,490	(6,507)
Indonesia[1]	170.4	65,291	3.0	383	8.0	17,600	13,100	4,500	764	3,719	(2,955)
Japan	121.1	2,384,500	4.2	19,537	0.1	229,100	149,200	79,900	28,200	88,074	(59,874)
Korea	42.1	118,300	12.6	2,830	3.0	47,282	41,021	6,261	7,665	17,991	(10,326)
Malaysia[1]	16.5	29,800	4.7	1,750	0.8	17,897	12,670	5,227	1,895	3,053	(1,158)
New Zealand[1,3]	3.3	35,200	−0.9	10,700	13.5	7,196	7,233	(37)	815	1,180	(365)
Philippines[1]	57.7	33,398	5.7	595	7.4	5,720	7,715	(1,455)	1,584	2,481	(897)
Singapore[1]	2.6	19,398	8.8	7,413	0.9	28,622	32,487	(3,865)	4,023	6,395	(2,372)
Taiwan	19.7	97,200	11.2	4,925	0.2	52,100	33,000	19,100	7,186	26,406	(19,220)
Thailand[1]	53.7	47,000	6.6	875	2.5	11,719	13,023	(1,777)	1,483	2,387	(904)
United States	243.9	4,487,700	4.0	18,400	4.4	252,866	424,082	(171,216)	-	-	-

[1]Product data are on gross domestic product (GDP), rather than gross national product (GNP).
[2]Total exports include reexports; total domestic exports were $19,700 million.
[3]GDP for fiscal year ending March 31, 1988.
Sources: U.S. Department of Commerce, U.S. Embassies, International Monetary Fund, East Asian and Pacific governments.

earnings from tourism soared in 1987 to nearly $2 billion. The United States is Thailand's largest export market. However, the Thais are very concerned about U.S. agricultural subsidies, particularly for rice, and the threat of U.S. import restrictions, especially on textiles. The main recent U.S. concern about our trade with Thailand has been lack of Thai protection of U.S. intellectual property rights, such as copyrights and patent protection of U.S. pharmaceutical products.

SOUTH PACIFIC

Australia

The main source of strength in the Australian economy is its export sector, especially agricultural products and raw materials. Exports increased by 19% in 1987. About one-

half of Australian merchandise exports go to 11 Asian nations, principally Japan. However, Australia remains an important trading partner with the United States. It is one of the few Pacific countries with which the United States has a sizeable and consistent trade surplus. The Australian Government has undertaken significant economic reforms, including a program of phased tariff reductions. It has complained about subsidized U.S. agricultural exports that restrict Australian sales. Our long and cooperative alliance relationship with Australia is based on mutual economic, political, and security interests.

New Zealand

Prime Minister David Lange's government has instituted far-reaching reforms, including decreases in protectionism, less government spending, and better

management of the public sector, in order to achieve more efficient resource allocation and to reduce inflation. As a result, real GNP was down slightly in 1987 and is estimated to decline further in 1988. New Zealand remains heavily dependent on agricultural exports. Japan, Australia, and the United States account for about one-half of New Zealand's trade. For many years the United States and New Zealand were military allies under the Australia-New Zealand-United States (ANZUS) treaty. However, in 1986, the U.S. Government suspended its security guarantees to New Zealand under the ANZUS alliance because of New Zealand's restrictive policy regarding U.S. naval ship visits. The United States hopes that the New Zealand Government will come to realize the value of restoring traditional alliance cooperation. ∎

Notes

1. Japan, China, South Korea, Taiwan, Hong Kong, Singapore, the Philippines, Indonesia, Malaysia, Thailand, Australia, and New Zealand are considered here.

China Policy: Interests and Process

By David M. Lampton

INTRODUCTION

Process and policy are inseparable, as recent events which have improbably linked the United States, Iran, Iraq, Israel, and the Nicaraguan "contras" amply demonstrate. Flawed decision-making processes produce flawed decisions, though it is untrue that good processes invariably assure favorable outcomes. Below I argue that the United States has important interests at stake in its China policy (to include Taiwan and Hong Kong), that the institutionalization of China policy in the stable bureaucracies has generally served those interests admirably in recent years, and that the task ahead is to avoid swamping these policies with domestic content as we move into the presidential sweepstakes anew and into a period of increasing congressional assertiveness during the next two years. It took the United States more than twenty years to get China policy out of the vortex of domestic political debate—the job ahead is to insulate this issue from the riptides of domestic politics, to keep it in an arena where the expediencies of the present do not continually overwhelm the needs of the future.

AMERICAN INTERESTS AND CHINA POLICY

Four sets of interests have been, and should remain, paramount considerations of United States China policy: *strategic* (and regional) power and stability interests, *economic* and trade interests, *peaceful* resolution of the Taiwan issue, and *stable transitions* to more pluralized polities throughout the region. Present U.S. policies generally promote these interests and appropriately seek to reconcile the inevitable conflicts among them and within them. The tugging and hauling among interest groups, the politicization of foreign policy in the White House, congressional pressures, and the glare of the mass media, which have made it so difficult to pursue policies of continuity and balance in U.S. policy toward other regions of the world, for the last few years at least, have not been destructive features of the policy process vis-á-vis China. The question is, how can we maintain this situation?

Looking at *strategic* and regional power interests, U.S. policies should continue to make clear to Beijing the benefits of close ties to Washington and the costs of accommodations with Moscow that would give the Kremlin more latitude in the disposition of its armed forces in ways threatening to the U.S., our allies, and friends. The limited accommodation now underway between Moscow and Beijing, thus far, has not adversely affected U.S. interests, but we should closely monitor developments. The U.S. response to this evolving Sino-Soviet relationship, thus far, has been appropriate, measured, and balanced.

With respect to relations between China and Japan, for much of American history Washington has been forced to choose between good relations with Japan *or* good relations with China—we now have the luxury of sound relations with both. This is a function of the stable relations between these two Asian nations. American policies have promoted, and should continue to promote, strong Sino-Japanese ties. This, in turn, means that there continues to be a need to place restraints on American attempts to increase Japan's military capacities in East Asia, capacities that could worry Tokyo's neighbors, including the PRC. Finally, China is seeking to improve relations with the ASEAN countries, downplaying its revolutionary objectives considerably, and building economic linkages widely in East and Southeast Asia. This, too, is consonant with American interests because regional instability creates impulses for American involvement that everyone wishes to avoid.

Turning to *economic* interests, our objectives appropriately are to foster growing American trade and economic intercourse with the People's Republic of China, Taiwan, and Hong Kong—three of the fastest growing economies in the world. Though the U.S. is properly concerned with equitable conditions for more balanced trade, we also need to remain mindful that current reform policies in both the PRC and Taiwan (not to mention the transition to 1997 in Hong Kong and developments in South

At the time this article was written, David M. Lampton was director of China Policy Studies at the American Enterprise Institute, Washington, D.C.

Source: From *World Affairs,* Vol. 149, No. 3 (Winter 1986–87), pp. 139–142.

Korea) are dependent on the maintenance of economic stability in each society. U.S. policies that would slow trade could reduce economic performance in Hong Kong, the PRC, and Taiwan. This, in turn, could affect the transitions underway in each society, transitions in which the U.S. has a very large stake. We need, therefore, to push for better market access in the PRC and Taiwan, but to do so in a way that does not run out of control by producing retaliatory measures that reduce total economic activity, degrade economic performance, and produce pressures in each society that would stall domestice reform. The administration has shown commendable restraint in its handling of the trade issue, and one can only hope that such restraint is sustainable in the upcoming session of Congress.

Obviously related to the above is the fact that an historic transition appears underway in Asia—a moderation of authoritarian forms of government and a move toward more pluralized polities. Though this trend is reversible and fragile (witness the precarious position of the Aquino government in the Philippines), movements for somewhat more pluralized polities are under way in South Korea, Taiwan, and the PRC. In each case, the American interest is to encourage adequate stability as this welcome process unfolds.

The case of Taiwan, however, reveals the fine line that must be walked. In Taiwan, a new political proto-party has recently been formed—the Democratic Progressive Party—in which its new "charter" calls for "self-determination." *If* (and this is as yet by no means certain) "self-determination" were to come to mean the independence of

Taiwan from the mainland, this probably would force Beijing to assert its claim to the island forcefully. This, in turn, would pose a grave dilemma for the United States, as we are simultaneously committed to both the peaceful resolution of the Taiwan issue and to the proposition that there is but one China. Moreover, notions of self-determination strike responsive chords among many Americans. The United States must, therefore, on the one hand, look favorably on gradual pluralization in Taiwan, while, at the same time, making it clear that we will not associate ourselves with the most destabilizing of possible outcomes of a pluralized political process. The way to accomplish this is not through media megaphones or by throwing these sensitive relationships into the Congressional arena; it is by quiet and persistent diplomacy undertaken by the Department of State with the clear backing of the White House.

THE FOREIGN POLICY PROCESS AND ITS DANGERS

The realization of American interests in China policy involves the striking of careful *balances*. The question is, what type of foreign policy process makes such balance most likely? In my view, the established bureaucracies (most particularly the Department of State in close cooperation with the National Security Council) have done an admirable job in striking these balances and institutionalizing these sorts of policies. A balanced policy would keep a careful watch on Sino-Soviet relations without becoming alarmed at every modest improvement in relations between

Moscow and Beijing. A balanced policy would encourage a modest increase in Japan's self-defense capabilities while being sensitive to the concerns of Tokyo's neighbors about a Japanese defense buildup. A balanced policy would promote American market access in the PRC, Taiwan, and elsewhere in Asia while not adopting self-defeating protectionist policies. And, balanced policies would promote the forces of political pluralization in the region while at the same time not encouraging change in its most rapid and destabilizing forms.

Nonetheless, the very nature of the American foreign policy process assures that sustaining balanced and modulated policies like those described above is most difficult. Besides the generalized media, interest group, think tank, and congressional pressures alluded to above, there are two sources of instability in American foreign policy that should be of concern to those who deal with China policy: the tendency of foreign policy issues to become shuttlecocks in the game of domestic politics (or domestic issues—like abortion—to attach themselves to foreign policy) and the possibility that policy departures will be engineered in arenas in which the restraints of expert advice and bureaucratic caution are absent.

While our current China policy would have been most difficult to realize had it not been for the radical departures conceived in the Nixon and Carter White Houses, *the policy problem now is not departures, but continuity and balance*—this is best assured through a more routinized and bureaucratized foreign policy process.

Of the above-mentioned twin dangers to balance and continuity, at the present time the principal task is to ensure that China policy not become a divisive issue in the domestic political arena. Two issues conceivably have this potential in the context of the upcoming presidential election and recent changes in Congress, particularly in the Senate: trade and the issue of "self-determination" in Taiwan.

Looking first at trade, there is every reason to expect that the protectionist impulse in Congress has been strengthened by the 1986 November election, most notably the change in Senate control. Almost certainly there will be a spate of protectionist bills winding their way through Congress. The president, with a reduced number of allies on Capitol Hill and himself weakened by a foreign policy debacle of still growing proportions, may be unable to resist this tide much longer. Of course, much undoubtedly rests on the trade deficit figures in the next couple of months. But, with the presidential aspirants in both parties already jockeying for pole positions in the primary races, trade issues could easily surge to the fore. In that event, we could expect our trade policy toward China, Taiwan, and Hong Kong (not to mention Japan and South Korea) to fall victim to the logic of domestic politics. And trade partners in Hong Kong, the PRC, and Taiwan are unlikely to remain supine as Congress works out its will on them. As the *Hong Kong Standard* noted in a 7 November, 1986 editorial entitled, "Battle Stations in Wake of U.S. Elections":

. . . Anything like the Jenkins Bill will trigger off retaliation in non-textile areas, it will then not be a matter of spreading the job-loss around, but increasing it all around and, perhaps, involving all of us in a global trade war.

One other issue is simmering below the surface, an issue that has some (though I suspect limited) potential of becoming grist for the domestic political mill—this involves Taiwan. The recently established Democratic Progressive party in Taiwan released its "charter" in early November, and the draft said, "All residents [of Taiwan] have the right to self-determination to freely decide their political status and pursue economic, social and cultural development." Though it is improbable that the populace on Taiwan would vote to declare independence (of China) even if it had the electoral opportunity, there is a significant Taiwan independence movement in the United States (primarily among former residents of Taiwan) and, of course, notions of "self-determination" have a generic appeal to most Americans. It is important that Congress and the executive branch speak with a single voice and that we adhere to our past policy of recognizing but one China, that Taiwan is a part of that entity, and that we stand for the peaceful resolution of the Taiwan issue. Tragic consequences could result were emerging forces in Taiwan to misjudge a general American predilection for self-determination with concrete support for a specific policy of independence.

SUMMARY

Unlike the foreign policy fiasco that so dominates the headlines today (a problem that has its roots in an insufficiently expert organization apparently being driven by the perceived domestic political advantage of gaining the release of U.S. hostages and the desire to continue funding the contras in the face of congressional resistance), America's China policy has been comparatively well-institutionalized and, for the most part, is balanced. The job ahead is to keep China policy out of the domestic political cauldron as much as possible and to keep it in the hands of the specialized bureaucracies that have, thus far, not done badly. Launching new policy initiatives like those of Nixon in 1971 and Carter in 1978 may require centralization in the White House, but, continuity and balance in the management of our present relationship requires institutionalization in the regularized bureaucracies.

It is well to recall that loose election talk in September 1980 by candidate Reagan took President Reagan almost two years to repair. Loose talk by a new generation of candidates, and protectionist appeals in Congress, could swamp our China policy with domestic political content. If this occurs, in the words of Destler, Gelb, and Lake, we surely will have become "Our Own Worst Enemy."[1] ∎

Notes

1. I. M. Destler, Leslie H. Gelb, and Anthony Lake, *Our Own Worst Enemy* (New York: Simon & Schuster, 1985).

U.S.-Japan Relations: A Partnership in Search of Definition

By Alan D. Romberg

INTRODUCTION

It is perhaps trite by now to suggest that U.S.-Japan relations are at once the most important partnership each nation has and more troubled than at any time in the postwar era. And one must always be cautious about sweeping generalizations and dire predictions—a decade ago experts saw "ample reason" to question the survival of the alliance, an alliance that, in fact, has grown immeasurably in the intervening years. Nonetheless, it is arguable that the current confluence of economic, political and social forces presents a greater challenge to the relationship than ever before. Without strong leadership in defining its purposes and content, the risks of derailing it are disturbingly high.

"Resolving" the trade issue would go a long way in the short term to lowering tension. But as important as that would be—and the poisoning effect of drawn-out economic tensions cannot be overemphasized—to focus solely on that dimension of bilateral ties is to miss the essence of the problems we will face in the future. Indeed one major task for both countries is to identify "the problem" accurately, including the interrelationship among economic, political and security interests and the different weights they carry in each country. Another is to devise policies and mechanisms which facilitate assumption by the Japanese of a more active role in world affairs without pushing them so far—or arousing a not so latent nationalism so much—that Japan crosses an invisible boundary into overbearing assertiveness or even into a disturbing military posture.

The style of communication and negotiation between the United States and Japan is also troubling and in need of drastic improvement, especially on economic issues. To some it is very much a game whose rules are long established and purposes well understood. But for others, especially in the political arena or the public at large, it creates negative images and lingering resentment, as well as reinforcing destructive patterns of behavior.

Putting all of this together, what, then, is "the problem" in U.S.-Japan relations? What are possible "solutions"? What are the implications of success or failure in handling these issues?[1]

ECONOMIC ISSUES

Having said that trade and economic issues are far from constituting the totality of the relationship—or the problem—they are, nonetheless, the most urgent aspect. If mishandled, they will create attitudes that will weaken the alliance, perhaps severely.

A recent *Washington Post* article[2] addressed the range of issues that have focused American attention on trade:

Growing commercial prowess and its lingering trade barriers have brought it into repeated confrontations with the United States, making bilateral relations tense.

Once joined in a relatively harmonious trading alliance these two economic powers have entered into a period of strain that is generating anger on both sides. How this difficult relationship is managed, say politicians and diplomats in both countries, will help determine the outcome of a crucial debate here between protectionists and free-traders over ... future economic policy.

The article went on to talk of how difficult it was for the U.S. to switch from patron to partner and how aggressive export drives have led to U.S. import quotas. It mentioned how hard American firms found it to penetrate the domestic computer market, and how the economy is, among non-communist countries, most closed to imports.

The most interesting fact for the purposes of this study is that "here" in the penultimate line of the above quotation was Rio de Janeiro, and the country in question was Brazil. Thus, while the magnitude of the problems with Japan may be unique, their character is not.

People not only overlook this commonality with other U.S. trading relationships, but they frequently forget that there are at least three aspects of the trade issues that are related but distinguishable both analytically and in terms of policy prescription: market access in Japan; commercial

Alan D. Romberg is the C.V. Star Fellow for Asian Studies at the Council on Foreign Relations.

Source: From *Critical Issues,* No. 1 (1988), pp. 7–31. Copyright 1988 by Council on Foreign Relations, New York.

competition in the United States and in third-country markets; and the size of the bilateral deficit. Solving one may well not solve the others.

In the dispassionate light of intellectual analysis, most people on both sides agree that to cure the U.S. global current account and trade deficits it is necessary to reduce the American budget deficit, increase savings, raise productivity and improve quality of American goods and services. And to reduce the Japanese global surplus there must be emphasis on domestic-led growth and further reduction of tariff and non-tariff barriers to imports. The adjustment of exchange rates, with the yen revaluing by over 70 percent since February 1985, has only recently begun to have some impact on U.S. trade data. (It has been reflected in Japanese data on the volume and yen value of their exports for some time.) This slowness of the turnaround has raised in the minds of many Americans a question whether further exchange rate adjustment is not required, and in the minds of many Japanese whether American goods simply aren't competitive.

Both may be right in some measure, but the tendency to justify inaction on one's own part while pressuring the other party to bear the expense of any adjustment has become all too familiar a part of the U.S.-Japan economic relationship. American negotiators tend to play up the negative economic and political consequences in the U.S. of the current problems, while downplaying the negative impact in Japan of the proposed solutions. Japanese negotiators, conversely, often belittle the intrinsic importance of the issues in dispute but

highlight the damage of proposed solutions. The Americans are scornful of political or security rationales advanced to support cautious handling of economic disputes, arguing that failure to deal straight forwardly with those disputes will inflict great long-term political damage. The Japanese acknowledge that "bashing" has led to concessions on their side (at least up till now), but potentially at great political expense in terms of changes in attitudes toward the alliance relationship, which will only be visible in later years.

Each side, of course, has a point. The Japanese share of the U.S. global trade deficit (around 1/3) has not changed appreciably in recent years. But, as a rather steady fraction of a growing deficit, the dollar value has become very large (reaching $58.6 billion in 1986). McKinsey & Company's managing director in Tokyo, Kenichii Ohmae, observes that focusing on these data misses the point. He argues that overall U.S. trade statistics have changed so dramatically primarily because American corporations have shifted their operations abroad. Thus, he says, rather than declining, American industry has increased its share of global markets in all key sectors, including manufacturing, over the past 5–10 years. And to those who argue that the unemployment effects have been severe, especially in manufacturing Ohmae responds that the trade deficit has affected less than five percent of total unemployment in the United States.

Even if one accepts Ohmae's assessment, it fails to give adequate political weight to the size of the overall deficit, to the accumulated annoyance with Japanese import restrictions and frustration over

failure to remove them through years of negotiation, and to the special concern over allegedly unfair trading practices in high technology areas, which Americans see as an arena where they are unarguably competitive. In this latter area, the issue of "national security" also arises, and Japanese efforts to secure market share is especially sensitive. This sensitivity was manifest in recent months in the unprecedented sanctions imposed by the U.S. on shipments of electronics equipment by Japanese semiconductor manufacturers, in the jawboning to death of a Fujitsu bid to buy the Fairchild company (even after arrangements had already been made to keep defense contracts in American hands), and in the outrage over a Toshiba subsidiary's diversion to the Soviet Union of COCOM-prohibited multi-axis precision milling equipment that is judged to have helped the Soviets greatly in quieting their submarines.

DEFENSE

Over the past ten years, the U.S.-Japan alliance has taken on much greater substantive significance. Albeit within the limits of the "peace constitution" (under which Japan foreswears the use of military force) and of the three nonnuclear principles (not to possess, manufacture or introduce nuclear weapons), Japan has begun to develop a credible self-defense capability that is approved by the vast majority of the Japanese people. The scrapping in 1987 of the 1976 cabinet decision to limit defense spending to no more than one percent of GNP will allow Japan to fulfill previously approved modernization plans without having to go through fiscal contortions. As one Japanese defense expert put it, Japan will no longer have to operate from a base of "shared insufficiency" but can—and must—now think in terms of what strategy should be adopted. Nonetheless, in the foreseeable future it is highly unlikely that one will see major departures. Japan will still have its hands full equipping itself to defend against any conventional Soviet attack as well as to protect sea lines of communication out to a distance of 1,000 miles south and east of Tokyo.

Joint planning, training, and information-sharing with the United States have proceeded apace, as has the growth of support provided to the 55,000 U.S. forces based in Japan. That latter support now equates to about $2 billion annually. Although much of the recent increase comes from exchange rate adjustments rather than increased Japanese budgetary outlays, from a Washington perspective, in this period of budget squeeze, one of the most important steps Tokyo took to contribute to international efforts in the Persian Gulf was to assume responsibility for new categories of labor costs at U.S. bases in Japan, and Washington is delighted that the Japanese are now seriously considering even further steps in that direction.

Defense cooperation with the United States has branched out into other areas that are symbolically important and could become substantively so. The two most prominent examples are agreement to participate in SDI research and the decision to allow transfer of indigenously developed military technology to the United States. In both cases the issues of commercial applications and of transfer to third countries are already sticky and could become more so. But, in any event, the linkage to economic relations is quite real, and with SDI so close to Ronald Reagan's heart, there is an obvious political dimension as well.

For years the two governments have worked to create a "fire break" between economic problems and other aspects of the relationship. Despite the positive mood that one supposes Japan hoped to create through participation in SDI and military technology transfer, in recent months three events threatened to leap the firebreak and create negative linkages: the Toshiba case, the Persian Gulf issue, and a Japanese decision on design of the next generation fighter aircraft (the so called FSX).

The first case has already been alluded to. From the administration's perspective, the Japanese were very slow to take the Toshiba case seriously, and even when they addressed it they were slow to come up with prescriptions for dealing effectively with any future cases. In the end, however, the measures adopted were quite comprehensive. This evidently persuaded Congress not to adopt a comprehensive five-year ban on Toshiba exports to the United States. But the Continuing Resolution adopted in late December did include a ban on Toshiba products in PXs and on Pentagon procurement from Toshiba for a year.

The Toshiba case provoked some remarkable displays of emotionalism. The television picture of Members of Congress smashing Toshiba electronic equipment on the steps of the Capitol will probably fade quickly for those few Americans who saw it. But it will doubtless stick for a very long time in the minds of the millions of Japanese for whom it was repeated over and over in all its chauvinistic zeal.

In the case of the Gulf, although the administration wanted allied support for political as much as military reasons, it was willing to act alone, if necessary, because it saw vital U.S. interests being challenged by Iran. Many in Congress, on the other hand, focused on the fact that Gulf oil was flowing primarily to Europe and Japan, and demanded that those countries share the burden. The Europeans eventually dispatched minesweepers and other escort vessels. Japan wrestled with sending either minesweepers or maritime safety patrol boats. But in the end Japan was unprepared to define self defense so broadly as to allow even the civilian agency patrol craft to go, since it was unclear how they would defend themselves if attacked. In any case, the multifaceted package adopted by Tokyo, including aid to Oman and Jordan and augmented support for the U.S. military in Japan, was welcomed by the administration, and criticism in Congress seems to have quieted down.

As to the FSX, Japan's decision to base the new fighter on the American F-16 airframe has cooled that problem. Had the Japanese decided on an all-indigenous design, a serious breach would have opened not only with the Congress but with a crucial bureaucratic ally—the Pentagon. Moreover, it would have signalled a major shift in Japanese armaments policy, since pressure would have inevitably built to export an otherwise economically unviable aircraft.

Thus all three challenges to the firebreak concept seem, in the end, to have been relatively successfully met. But they underscored the artificiality of trying to deal with an important ally in totally isolated compartments. While it is still critical not to let trade issues get out of hand, the alliance relationship and the partnership about which many of us have spoken over the years in fact comprises inseparable parts of an integrated whole. This has important implications for the policies of each and for the way in which policy is formulated.

STYLE

Before turning to issues for the future, we should pause for a moment to consider the very different political cultures and styles of operation and communication in both countries, and the impact they have on our bilateral relations. The indirect, nonconfrontational and hesitant consensus-building approach of the Japanese contrasts sharply with the frontal, blunt, action-oriented American approach, and frustrations are very easily generated.

From a U.S. perspective, looking back at the history of many disputes from automobiles, tobacco products, beef, citrus and baseball bats to semiconductors and diversion of high technology to the USSR, Japan has been slow to acknowledge problems and slow to work out solutions. And somehow the "solutions" often turn out to be too little, too late.

From a Japanese perspective, the U.S. has been too quick to turn American problems into bilateral disputes, too willing to politicize them, and too insistent on American-dictated solutions. Moreover, the U.S. has also failed to consult Japan on questions of vital importance (e.g. normalization of relations with China) and proved an unreliable supplier of crucial products (e.g. soybeans). Overlooking our equally insensitive actions elsewhere, Japanese see discrimination in this behavior when contrasted with our attitude toward other trading partners.

Japan and its defenders say that the slowness of the consensus-building process may be frustrating to Americans, but the results stick, as opposed to instances on the American side—private and governmental—when joint ventures have fallen through because not all the bureaucratic, political or financial ducks had been lined up.

The American penchant for "bashing," for strident and sometimes indiscriminate and even irrational rhetoric (including use of Pearl Harbor-type imagery), grates on Japanese sensibilities much as the layers of indirection in Japanese statements (when "I'll try my best" sometimes means "It can't be done") annoys Americans. "Bullying Americans" and "insincere Japanese" are among the unfortunate images that result. Both are costly.

A new attitude is also emerging in Japan as a younger, more assertive generation has begun to speak up—and in some cases lash out—in response to intemperate American remarks or behavior. The new nationalism has come to border on, or even cross into, arrogance. (Actually, Americans, who recognize their own penchant for self-indulgence, are not nearly as bothered by it as Chinese and other Asians, who readily connect it with rising defense expenditures, textbook revision on the war period,

and Nakasone's 1985 visit to the Yasukuni Shrine in honor of war dead—and conjure up images of the militarism of fifty years ago.)

Some Japanese have tried to channel these growing feelings in constructive directions. Nakasone, himself, called for "sound nationalism" that is compatible with internationalism. Whatever reservations one may have about the specific ways in which the former prime minister sought to implement that idea, I believe it is a valid proposition that unless Japanese have an adequate sense of identity and pride in themselves, they will not be comfortable with the larger world role that Americans and others think they must play. (On the other hand, it is possible that a Japanese role in economics and diplomacy that is sufficiently more assertive to satisfy the U.S. might only come as part of a sea change in overall attitudes, including toward military power. If so, one would have to think carefully about the wisdom of pushing Japan in that direction. Ellen L. Frost has an insightful discussion of the problem of Japanese and American self-image in her new book *For Richer, For Poorer: The New U.S.-Japan Relationship,* New York, Council on Foreign Relations, 1987.)

So long as large numbers of Japanese consider themselves either poor or, as recent polls suggest, vulnerable to becoming poor once again, they will not see themselves in the role of world leaders. At the same time, to the extent that the new arrogance is becoming stronger among those who do interact abroad, the lack of a healthy, well-established, confident self-image could become a serious problem.

It is not, in my judgment, a case of Japan having to adapt to being "#1" and the United States to being "#2," as some have suggested. Without detracting from Japanese accomplishments or minimizing American problems, I don't believe the turnaround has been, or is likely to be, that great. But *relative* power has shifted, and unless behavior patterns shift with it, faulty policies will be pursued and further strains will develop. What should those new policies and attitudes be?

ADJUSTING TO
NEW REALITIES

Both sides need to alter the style and the substance of their approach to the world and to each other. Unless Americans meaningfully address their budget deficit, savings and investment rates, productivity, basic and applied research and development, and, over the longer term, educational levels, the currently false images of the U.S. as #2 could well become justified in years ahead. The beginnings of a response to these problems, in both the public and private sector, give every indication, however, that self-interest and common sense will overcome lethargy and ideology, and that American economic—and political—health will be restored.

In Japan, the recent 6 trillion yen stimulus package was to some extent smoke and mirrors designed to ward off international pressure, especially at the mid-1987 Venice Economic Summit. But Japan's self-interest in persisting with structural adjustment toward open markets and domestic-led growth also give hope that those policies will survive. As the

Japan Economic Journal said in an editorial earlier this year: "No matter how painful this economic transformation may be, it is absolutely necessary if Japan is to help restore balance in the world economy. And this balance is absolutely essential if the Japanese economy is to continue to prosper."[3]

Which brings us back to the issue of how adjustments in domestic policy fit into adjustments in international relations. The United States cannot keep pressing Japan to assume greater international responsibility without sharing with Tokyo greater international authority, a greater say in decisions. And just as Japan is going to have to exhibit, again in the words of the *Japan Economic Journal,* "strong-willed resistance to pressures from domestic special interest groups;"[4] the U.S. is going to have to do the same. Both countries need to catch up with the reality of economic interdependence.

Japan is often accused—perhaps as much at home as abroad—of seeking to "buy" its way out of tensions rather than truly "internationalizing." Tokyo can direct resources to development assistance, refugee relief, or financial support for U.S. forces without opening domestic markets to competition from LDC (less developed country) exports, taking in large numbers of refugees, or expanding its own defense role.

Perhaps the United States and the rest of the world should be satisfied with this because the need for more resources is very great. But I am doubtful—doubtful that, over time, either the Japanese or the rest of the world will find that sufficient.

Even the boldest Japanese thinkers I have run into believe their countrymen are as much as

ten years away from the domestic consensus necessary to underpin an international leadership role, even in the economic arena. But their ideas for that future role are imaginative, indeed probably more imaginative than the reality will turn out to be. They revolve largely around knowledge- and technology-intensive endeavors, with Japan contributing importantly to international efforts to cope not only with the requirements of economic development, but with problems of the environment, health, nutrition and even the verification and monitoring of arms control agreements.[5]

If the world must wait several years for many of these ideas to flower in practice, however, it will not wait that long for Tokyo to bring its economic policies and practices into harmony with new international realities. And if the United States is not yet prepared to share substantial leadership responsibilities—and decision-making power—with Japan (the idea of a G-2 is premature for both countries and for Europe), it is at least going to have to consult much more closely and take Japan's views seriously into account.[6] And it is going to have to discipline itself to speak and act rationally and respectfully even at times of tension.

Some Japanese would perhaps see the change in their role coming more quickly. The 1987 Japanese *Diplomatic Bluebook,* the annual Foreign Ministry statement of policy and analysis of world affairs, says that "Japan is truly at a major turning point in its history." It cites the need for Tokyo to take a long-term perspective and to play "an important and responsible role as a standard-bearer sustaining the international order.[7] This rhetoric goes beyond past stress on "harmonization," but there is little indication of public support for taking initiatives. Staying the course on structural adjustment will be problematical enough.

Theoretically, national leadership could go some way toward reshaping public attitudes. And we can expect the leadership to say most of the right things in this respect. But not even his most ardent supporters argue that the present prime minister has anything like Nakasone's charisma or policy boldness, and if Nakasone had only limited success in combating the "small Japan" mentality, there is little reason to believe his successors will do better.

Still, as the *Bluebook* rhetoric suggests, some people are striving for a conceptual approach that would facilitate a transformation that would be both comfortable for Japan and accepted abroad. Their thinking goes beyond resolving trade disputes to considering how Japan can be a major player in international politics. Restrained from using military might, they have considered a kind of bridging role for Japan, especially between Asia and the West, but also in special cases elsewhere, as in the Middle East, where Japan retains reasonably good relations with both Iran and Iraq.

If Japan were to devote massive amounts of resources in the form of untied aid or investment guarantees in developing countries, this extension of the late Prime Minister Ohira's policy of "comprehensive security" might indeed have some impact. But even though the thrice redoubling of Japanese Official Development Assistance (ODA) in the past decade has brought the total to a substantial sum in absolute terms (some $3.8 billion in FY86), it still comes to less than 0.3 percent of GNP, well below the average Organization for Economic Cooperation and Development (OECD) share of GNP devoted to aid. The point is not to belittle the important contribution Japanese ODA makes, but rather that, to be perceived as a "leader" in this field, Japan would need to think in terms of something approaching an order-of-magnitude increase, an unlikely prospect to say the least.

A thoughtful Japanese observed privately that Japan lacks two necessary attributes for world leadership: military power to back up economic and diplomatic policy, and a vision with which to guide others. That individual saw no change in the offing. Others, who seem to share his analysis do not share his prognosis and worry that, to remain an economic superpower Japan inevitably will acquire military superpower status as well. Despite the limited nature of Nakasone's defense increases as part of his search for "a political role befitting [Japan's] international position,"[8] the sharp reaction by China (and others) to the scrapping of the one percent defense ceiling reflected the hypersensitivity of Japan's neighbors. Thus, Beijing, which once excoriated the U.S.-Japan alliance in extreme terms, has for some time supported it not only as a bulwark against the Soviet Union but also as a constraint on any independent Japanese military role.

In this context, one must wonder at the suggestion contained in a recent Congressional resolution that Japan spend 3 percent of GNP on defense. To what *constructive* purpose do people assume the additional $500 billion over the next ten years would be put? (One Japanese defense expert has asserted that the additional funds could finance ten aircraft carrier task forces!)

Despite these concerns, it is not clear whether Washington, Beijing and others understand—or, in any case, can deal with—the impact that economic or political relations will have on future Japanese decisions on defense policy. The issue is not the one percent ceiling, or even two percent, which some Japanese feel would fit within the constitutional parameters. The issue is Japan's orientation and its sense about its place in the world. If the Japanese feel besieged and unable to count on a relationship of trust and partnership with the United States, obviously this will have a significant impact. If Japan either feels threatened by a major Chinese military buildup, or isolated by sour relations with the PRC, this too will have an effect.

It will be critical for the U.S. to coordinate the various strands of its policy so as to avoid damaging essential aspects of the relationship through thoughtless or quasi-autonomous actions in other spheres. Moreover, the U.S. should consider the reasonableness of its positions, and whether it does not often seek far more from Japan, far faster, than America could produce if roles were reversed. To the extent that Congress can be persuaded to think along the same lines, it would be helpful, but at least the administration should get its act together.

The Japanese frequently talk about "internationalization," but a definition is elusive. As was discussed at a May 1986 Council on

Foreign Relations conference, Japan has undergone an information revolution, and baseball, blue jeans and Baskin-Robbins are all fixtures in Japanese life. But many Japanese themselves question whether there has been significant internationalization in a deeper social or attitudinal sense, whether the domestic system has the capacity to accommodate within itself alien people, systems and experiences.[9]

Some point out that Japan may not be internationalized in the sense of reducing its "obsession" with national sovereignty. They argue, however, it is being "globalized" in terms of recognizing not only that it has responsibilities to the international community but that Japan's own self-interest requires that it meet those responsibilities.

One should not quarrel with the notion that self-interest drives national policy. But the extent to which efforts to mollify the U.S. and others is a principal motivating factor in Japanese policy is disturbing. Such an attitude will lead the Japanese always to do the minimum. Experience teaches us that will often not be enough. The Japanese might do many of the "right" things, but without a concept of an affirmative role, they will continue to see themselves as put upon; others will see them as begrudging and selfish. This is a sure formula for future trouble.

LOOKING TO THE FUTURE

What is it that Japan could—or should—do with its new role in the world, should it develop one? What adjustments would the U.S. be willing to make?

On the economic side, Japan could take the lead in international efforts to maintain an open trading system by initiating policies to open its economy further and to promote investments in LDCs, including projects with a substantial element of technology transfer. Despite the domestic problems involved, it could open construction projects in Japan to foreign bids without waiting to be pressured from abroad.[10] It could actively support the Uruguay GATT Round by proposing initiatives, for example, to encourage engagement of LDCs in the process through institutional strengthening and to liberalize international trade in agriculture. Meanwhile, it could seize the opportunity presented by demographic shifts to open the economy further to agricultural imports. In sum, Japan could proceed boldly with the restructuring already begun.

Japan could encourage more consumption through a variety of monetary and fiscal policies. If it did, the Japanese people might have a greater sense of their real wealth. But foreigners, especially high-consumption Americans, should be hesitant to lecture Japanese about saving less. Not only would we be taking direct aim at a critical source of financing for our debt, but we are unprepared to take responsibility for any negative consequences. Moreover, with some two-thirds of the Japanese people worrying that they do not save enough, pressure to save less will not only fail, but it will engender further resentment.

From time to time a U.S.-Japan free trade agreement has been proposed. It is doubtful that either side is prepared for the openness that would entail. Nonetheless, it is an idea worth reviewing periodically, especially in light of accumulated experience with Israel and Canada.

The United States must make major substantive and stylistic adjustments if the bilateral relationship is to remain healthy. Every poll shows that Americans understand that our own profligacy and lack of discipline are primarily responsible for our budget and trade deficits. But some politicians seem incapable of resisting the "easy" solution, which is to blame someone else. Our largest overseas trading partner, which has a huge surplus with us and a market that is far from open, is a juicy target.

Because their prosperity—and security—still depend on sound relations with the United States, it is reasonable to assume that the Japanese will eventually bow to U.S. pressure. But the emotionalism and rhetoric of the past three years have taken a toll. It is not just that Japanese feel America's problems are mostly of America's making and that our high-pressure approach is unjustified. They are increasingly angered by the ill-mannered bashing in which some Americans have indulged.

Compounding this problem is the fact that over the years the Japanese who want to open their markets have depended on—even invited—foreign pressure as a key element in developing a domestic consensus to "do the necessary." Not long ago a Japanese official expressed extreme anger at a fellow countryman over the latter's complaint about U.S. pressure. No matter the legacy of bitter feelings on both sides and the habits of scolding that are developed; there is no other way, the official said, to open the markets.

This pattern has become dangerous. Both sides need to consider the likelihood that, as their economy goes through its structural adjustment, the Japanese may become less willing to accede to American demands. Habits developed now may incur real costs at that stage.

On the diplomatic front, exchanges across the range of issues have been quite productive. It will be helpful if Japan can be more forthcoming with initiatives, and the U.S. more willing to give Tokyo the lead. In some cases there are complicating factors, as in the Philippines, where substantial new Japanese aid and investment will be crucial, but where a high Japanese profile would be counterproductive.

Continued close contact with respect to such sensitive areas as China, the USSR, Korea and Indochina, as well as the Middle East and southern Africa, will be essential to avoid inadvertent missteps and to move ahead in parallel.

There is no reason to expect security relations to falter, though it should be amply clear that a severe problem in other areas could have a major impact. The *Diplomatic Bluebook*'s implicit linkage of Japan's self-defense efforts with U.S. deterrence of the Soviet Union is a welcome sign that the two countries continue to

share strategic perspectives, even if they have very different roles.

U.S.-Japan relations truly do contain important elements of partnership. But to nurture them will require that both sides treat the process as a dynamic one, not merely as an exercise in gardentending. And it will require greater recognition on both sides that, whatever firebreaks we may construct, it will be impossible to totally isolate different aspects of the relationship from one another. The rewards of this partnership can be great; the penalties for failure to manage it properly are almost unimaginable. ■

Notes

1. Based on a paper originally presented to a meeting of the Japanese-American Study Committee on Comprehensive Security sponsored by the Pacific Forum and the Asia Pacific Association of Japan, Honolulu, Hawaii, November 19–21, 1987.
2. *The Washington Post,* October 26, 1987, p. A-15.
3. *Japan Economic Journal,* June 20, 1987.
4. Ibid.
5. Ellen Frost addresses this subject in her book, *For Richer, For Poorer: The New U.S.-Japan Relationship,* (New York: Council on Foreign Relations, 1987). And Professor Shumpei Kumon of Tokyo University has developed this thesis extensively.
6. Cf. C. Fred Bergsten, "Economic Imbalances," *Foreign Affairs,* Volume 65, No. 4 (Spring, 1987).
7. From a provisional translation provided by the Foreign Ministry.
8. Speech at Chulalongkorn University, Bangkok, Thailand, September 26, 1987.
9. Alan D. Romberg, *The United States and Japan: Changing Societies in a Changing Relationship (A Conference Report),* (New York: Council on Foreign Relations, 1987).
10. The retaliatory Congressional ban on Japanese participation in federally funded American public works projects was a dramatic manifestation of growing frustration with Japanese foot-dragging.

Japan and the World: *Applying Assertiveness Training to a Foreign Policy*

By Susan Chira

Japan is struggling, sometimes against its own instincts, to break away from its follow-the-leader foreign policy and take more initiatives on its own.

The development comes at a time when Japan is being prodded by other nations' demands that it

contribute more to the world and propelled by an emerging new confidence born of its financial might.

In the last few months, Japanese officials have surprised foreign diplomats by a new willingness to speak out in world councils and

take steps that, while modest, would have been unthinkable only a few years ago.

Fundamentally, Japan remains a reluctant power, gingerly stepping onto the world stage, as yet unsure of its role and nervous about being in the spotlight.

VENTURES INTO NEW WATERS

But from the Persian Gulf and Afghanistan to Burma and Toronto, Japan has begun to venture into new waters. It is moving cautiously to define a role as a contributor to peacekeeping efforts and a champion of the developing nations of Asia.

What is more, these steps are coming during the administration of Prime Minister Noboru Takeshita, a man who came to office with a reputation for domestic, rather than foreign, expertise.

In recent months Japan has taken these actions, among others:

• It sent people as well as money to United Nations peacekeeping operations in Iran and Afghanistan.

• It spoke out at a gathering of Asian nations in Bangkok to define its conditions for an acceptable peace process in Cambodia.

• It offered its own plan for debtor nations at the Toronto summit meeting of industrialized democracies in June and asked its summit partners to avoid taking protectionist measures against newly industrializing countries in Asia.

It hinted to Burmese officials that it might restore foreign aid to previous levels if Burma took steps to change its troubled economy.

"I think you are beginning to see a gradual evolution—cautiously, prudently—of Japan's role in the world," said Tommy Koh, Singapore's Ambassador to the United States.

"In the past, they tended to be overshadowed by the United States or the European Community. You see them much more assertive now, much more articulate, much more willing to state their own point of view and much more self-confident."

Yet Japan continues to display a profound ambivalence about its new global status. Indeed, the whole topic of Japanese foreign policy assertiveness clearly unnerves some people at the Foreign Ministry.

One senior diplomat, asked whether Japanese resent American criticism at a time when Japan is beginning to assume more of the financial burdens the United States is increasingly reluctant to shoulder, lapsed into silence for several minutes and then asked about the weather in New York City.

Several Foreign Ministry officials, asked whether Japan was embarking on a bolder policy, agreed to speak only if their names were not used.

DOMESTIC OPPOSITION

Domestic opposition to entanglement in military conflict and the specter of foreign resentment of an assertive Japan continue to hobble Japanese foreign policy. And many of Japan's new initiatives—such as its recent pledge to double foreign aid in five years—spring as much from foreign pressure to step up its international role as from any internal call for change.

"There is a long overdue awareness and acceptance of the fact that Japan is a major power and what we do has bearing on the world at large," said Tadashi Yamamoto, head of the Japan Center for International Exchange, an influential research organization.

Japan is still trying to define what kind of foreign policy role it can play without military power and without any clear ideological mission.

"We will have to exert a certain amount of political power because it will be expected of us as a 'great' economic power," a senior Foreign Ministry official said.

"But it's a pipe dream to think we could replace the United States. We do see some changes in our relative weight in the international system. Japan's opinion is listened to more. But there are limits and we should understand them."

With a few exceptions, notably its good relations with Iran and its post-oil crisis swing toward the Arab stance in the Middle East, Japan is the economic power most supportive of American foreign policy goals. At least for now, it is likely to remain that way. And with memories still fresh of Japan's last attempt to impose its own ideology on its neighbors in World War II, Japan is wary of dictating any political system to another country.

Over all, economic imperatives continue to drive Japanese foreign policy. Its good relations with Iran and Iraq, for example, are built on the large Japanese economic stake in these countries and Japanese companies' expectations of more business if a peace treaty can be signed.

TWO DISTINCT ROLES

Yet Japanese foreign policy makers see at least two areas in which Japan can play a distinct role: as a promoter and financier of global peacekeeping efforts and as a defender and intermediary to Western powers of emerging Asian traders like South Korea, Taiwan and Singapore.

At a time when peace efforts are being made in the Persian Gulf, Afghanistan and Namibia, and when the United States is in arrears to the United Nations, Japan's contribution to peacekeeping efforts is being sought more than ever before.

Former Prime Minister Yasuhiro Nakasone first seized on the idea of Japan as a global peacemaker several years ago, arguing that Japan's close relations with Iran allowed it to play a kind of shuttle diplomacy, communicating to Iran and Iraq the other's positions in the hope of fostering dialogue.

It is only now, however, that Japan seems more willing to back up its talk with substantial aid. "At first, I think it started as window-dressing," Mr. Yamamoto said. "Yes, we were in contact with both Iran and Iraq, but what did it amount to? Now I think we're coming to put more beef in it."

Earlier this year, Japan donated $20 million to a special United Nations fund to support peacekeeping operations, earmarking $5 million for Afghanistan and $10 million for Iran and Iraq. Mr. Takeshita told the United Nations this spring that Japan's definition of peacekeeping included mediation to prevent or help resolve regional conflicts as well as donating money for refugees and reconstruction efforts.

BAN ON MILITARY ACTIVITY ABROAD

For the first time, Japan has sent people as well as money to support peace. Because Japan's Constitution forbids any foreign military involvement, Japan has refused in the past even to send civilians to peacekeeping operations for fear they might become caught up in military conflict.

This year, however, Japan sent a Foreign Ministry official to Afghanistan to help monitor the Soviet withdrawal of troops. Last week, Japan sent a Foreign Ministry official to Iran to monitor the cease-fire and a United Nations official to serve as a legal adviser to the peacekeeping forces. Japan has also pledged to send people to monitor elections in Namibia, if they take place.

Foreign Minister Sosuke Uno of Japan also impressed Asian diplomats in Bangkok in July with a commitment to send money and civilians to Cambodia if Vietnamese troops withdrew.

But Foreign Ministry officials are quick to add that Japan's lack of an offensive military force—in theory, offensive troops are banned and Japan's forces are formally considered self-defense forces—limits its clout.

"Unless you have the power to make conflicts, you do not have enough influence to resolve them," a senior Foreign Ministry official said. "We will not be able to be a driving force for political settlement. We are now trying to find out to what extent we can use our resources in a constructive way."

CHAMPION OF THE REGION

Japan is also moving to position itself as a champion of its Asian neighbors—a role it tried to enforce in World War II by military conquest.

Driven by the strong yen, Japan has begun to contribute to Asian economies as well as sell them goods. Japan is opening its own markets to their products, building factories there, and sending more foreign aid. And for many Asian

countries, Japan is serving as a model of economic development.

But recently, Japan has moved into the political arena in Asia as well, while trying to avoid touching off resentment among its neighbors.

At the request of President Roh Tae Woo of South Korea, Mr. Takeshita asked that the Toronto summit meeting include a declaration of support for the Olympic Games in Seoul. He argued at the summit talks that protectionism would cripple Asia's newly industrializing countries.

MORE MONEY FOR CHINA

Last week, he returned from his first state visit to China, where he met an old friend from a youth group exchange, Deputy Prime Minister Wu Xueqian, and announced that loans to China would double to $6 billion by 1995.

And in Burma, Japan showed the first signs that it might try to use economic aid to encourage economic and political changes.

In Bangkok, at a July gathering of Southeast Asian nations, Foreign Minister Uno broke with precedent, spelling out Japan's preference for Cambodian peace terms.

Ambassador Koh of Singapore said that other Asian nations present welcomed Mr. Uno's unusual outspokenness, and that a new generation of Asians was less afraid of Japanese influence because they feel more confident of their own strength.

ADIEU TO SHYNESS

Finally, Japan is becoming less shy about exerting its influence on the more familiar turf of economic affairs. In a dramatic break with the past Finance Minister Kiichi Miyazawa offered a new plan for debtor nations at the Toronto summit meeting, irritating the United States, which has not gotten full agreement for its own debt plan.

Japan has also been pushing to increase its contribution, and thus its growing power, in the Asian Development Bank. It is already the No. 2 power in the World Bank.

As in foreign policy, however, Japan is still not ready to lead. Shijuro Ozana, a former senior Bank of Japan official whose name was one of those mentioned as a possible Japanese candidate to head the International Monetary Fund, said that Japanese are going to lobby for such positions.

"I think we're still in the stage of hinting, not really leading or coordinating or trying to go it alone," he said. "When debate in a meeting is deadlocked, does Japan try to coordinate immediate? I doubt it. I think we still first try to become a coordinator but we are trying to take some initiatives although we are not fully prepared to do so."

U.S. Must Accept Japan's New Role in the World

By John Makin

After nearly eight weeks in Tokyo, I am convinced of one thing: The leader-follower relationship between America and Japan that has characterized the postwar period is over.

The obvious signs of transition have been noted. Emperor Hirohito's death literally marks the end of the Showa era, the name given to his reign. On everything from milk cartons to legal documents, one soon learns that this is the 63rd year of the Showa era. "63–12–5," or Dec. 5, Showa 63, translates to 12–5–88. Our taxes will be due on Japan's 1–4–15, or April 15, 1989, in the first year of the next era, name as yet unknown.

To America, far less interested in Japan than Japan is in it, the end of an era is marked only by the resignation of our much-loved ambassador of nearly 12 years, Mike Mansfield. Mr. Mansfield's successor will soon discover, provided that he or she takes the time to develop direct ties with influential

Japanese, a lot more is changing than the emperor, the calendar and the American ambassador.

Tokyo is becoming a major international financial market, shifting Asia's center of finance from Hong Kong and growing toward the size of the New York and London markets.

Meanwhile, Japanese financial markets are being deregulated at a rapid pace. The place of American and other non-Japanese financial institutions in this new, potentially profitable market is yet to be determined.

The new American ambassador had better have some friends at the Ministry of Finance and the Bank of Japan if he wants to have any idea about what is going on or play any role in representing American interests here.

Japan is becoming a producer of sophisticated military aircraft. Japanese companies, in a consortium led by Mitsubishi Heavy Industries, will design and produce

most of the FSX, Japan's jet fighter for the 1990s. American companies may serve as subcontractors for the project, but the exact terms of co-production and provisions covering technology-sharing have yet to be determined.

Japanese press reports on FSX make it clear that the Japanese view differs considerably from U.S. press reports that the United States won the primary role in FSX production. It did not, or perhaps should not have, but the new American secretary of defense and the new ambassador had better budget some time for resolution of disputes between American and Japanese companies working on FSX. Otherwise, American contractors are going to end up very unhappy.

The FSX is part of a broader class of critical issues that comes under the heading of defense burden-sharing. In his valedictory meeting with reporters, Mr. Mansfield said: "We do not want Japan to

---

John Makin is a resident scholar and director of fiscal policy studies at the American Enterprise Institute for Public Policy Research.

Source: *Washington Times,* December 20, 1988. Reprinted in *On the Issues,* 1989 #3. American Enterprise Institute, Washington, D.C.

become a regional military power. Japan's neighbors do not want it to become one. And neither does Japan."

The new ambassador will want to think long and hard about the first and last of Mr. Mansfield's assertions. How can Japan increase its ability to provide for its own defense without becoming a regional military power?

It cannot, unless it thinks it can get more defense either by paying more to the United States than it already does or, following the official line, by distributing more foreign aid. No serious defense analyst in Japan believes either of these pipe dreams.

Japan is well on its way to becoming a regional military power, if it is not already one. The talk in Tokyo is of "power-sharing" as a necessary counterpart to burden-sharing. Japan will spend more on defense to enhance its own security, as most nations do. It will do so partly because of its proximity to such dangerous and potentially unstable nations as North Korea, China and the Soviet Union, and partly because its client-defense relationship with the United States is rapidly becoming intolerable.

What nation wants to depend for its defense on another nation that views it as an economic threat?

Japan must and will move out from beneath the American wing. How America reacts to this process may become the primary focus of our foreign policy that has for too long been obsessed with managing the communist threat. For starters, we might hope that the Bush administration will spend more time and effort on Japan than it will on Nicaragua.

Paralleling the strategic issues facing America and Japan are the economic issues. Mr. Mansfield said that "in the field of security, [our] relationship couldn't be better" and "the only problem we have at the moment is rice."

Rice is a red herring. It has great symbolic importance to Japan as a national food and great symbolic importance to nations that would like to sell rice to Japan, which openly and unfairly excludes imported rice from Japanese markets. America needn't waste much time on rice, because if Japan ever allows significant rice imports, which is unlikely, low-cost Southeast Asian producers will undercut American suppliers.

Japanese investment in the United States will continue, to the mutual advantage of both countries. Although most of that money is flowing into the United States, American investment in Japan is growing and should be encouraged.

The new ambassador should aim to eliminate the many Japanese-sponsored efforts to help American exporters and financial institutions in Japan by providing sophisticated, bilingual assistance from the U.S. Embassy.

Perhaps the best advice to America's new ambassador would be to pay a visit to the Japanese Embassy in Washington and the Japanese consulates and offices of Japanese agencies in New York. Also, check around Washington to see how many key people are regularly in contact with Japanese Embassy personnel.

If it were possible for the next American ambassador to match half of the Japanese effort in the United States, we might begin to feel happier about what Mr. Mansfield correctly termed "the most important bilateral relationship in the world, bar none." ∎

Suggested Additional Readings

Charlesworth, James C. *A New American Posture Toward Asia* (Philadelphia: American Academy of Political and Social Science, 1970).

Clough, Ralph. *East Asia and U.S. Security* (Washington: Brookings Institute, 1975).

Greene, Fred. *U.S. Policy and the Security of Asia* (New York: McGraw-Hill, 1968).

Harrison, Selig. *The Widening Gulf: Asian Nationalism and American Policy* (New York: Free Press, 1978).

Hsiung, James C. (ed.). *Asia and U.S. Foreign Policy* (New York: Praeger, 1981).

Lampton, David M., and Catherine H. Keyser (eds.). *China's Global Presence* (Washington, DC: American Enterprise Institute for Public Policy Research, 1988).

Myers, Ramon H. *A U.S. Foreign Policy for Asia* (Stanford, CA: Hoover Institution, 1982).

Pye, Lucian. *Redefining American Policy in Southeast Asia* (Washington, DC: American Enterprise Institute for Public Policy Research, 1982).

Romberg, Alan D. *The United States and Japan* (New York: Council on Foreign Relations, 1987).

Simon, Sheldon W. *Asian Neutralism and U.S. Policy* (Washington, DC: American Enterprise Institute for Public Policy Research, 1975).

Wu, Yuan-li. *U.S. Policy and Strategic Positions in the Western Pacific* (New York: Crane Russak, 1975).

CHAPTER FOUR

The Middle East

✳
✳

The Middle East, along with Central Europe, is often considered one of those flashpoints where potential conflict between the superpowers could begin.

The Middle East is an extremely volatile area. Violence and conflict can explode there on very short notice—or with no notice at all. It is an area where East-West rivalries (The Soviet Union versus the United States) get entangled with North-South conflicts (wealth vs. poverty). There is also the conflict between Muslim and Jew (regarding the state of Israel); between Muslim and Christian (as in Lebanon); and among Muslims themselves, where the conflict between moderates and fundamentalists has become intense in many countries. So far, U.S. policy has been to stand against Islamic fundamentalism; it has seldom sought to understand and come to grips with this powerful movement on its own terms.

Israel is not just a Jewish state controlling some of Islam's holiest places (and is thus unacceptable to many Arabs); it is also the U.S.' only reliable ally in the area. The Palestinians, however, also claim the territory of Israel (or parts of it) as their homeland. At the same time, Israel relies heavily on Arab workers; and the demographics figures indicate that in the not very distant future Arabs will outnumber Jews within the state of Israel. Should the more numerous Arabs have equal rights with Jews in what was founded as a Jewish state? What happens to the idea of a Jewish homeland and nation if the Arabs are the majority and, as seems likely, control the major political posts?

Could a Jewish state coexist peaceably with a Palestinian state that would likely be dominated by radical elements and aligned with the Soviet Union? Where would such a state be located? Would it be carved out of Israel, out of neighboring Jordan, formed from the occupied territories (Gaza, the West Bank, the Golan Heights), or created out of some combination of these? The distances in this area are very small, however. From the Golan Heights one can see all the way across Israel to the Mediterranean; and if the eye can take in the entire width of Israel, so presumably could hostile Arab guns.

The Middle East reveals layer upon layer of complexities such as these. The conflicts are ethnic, cultural, religious, familial, tribal, and nationalistic. They are also long-term, deep-rooted, and almost impossible to resolve amicably. In addition, the Middle East sits upon the world's largest proven reserves of petroleum, essential to the economies of not only the U.S., but also Western Europe and Japan. Since our allies in these areas are even more dependent on oil imported from the Middle East than we are, their foreign policies toward that area are often different from our own, generally less supportive of Israel and somewhat closer to the Arabs.

The Middle East has no monopoly on terrorism, but its politics and international conflicts have given rise to some of the most spectacular terrorist incidents of recent years. The subject of terrorism is taken up separately later in this book, but it is important to note that terrorism also has something of a regional base in the Middle East.

Finally, there are entanglements with our domestic politics. Because of their history of persecution, and particularly the experience of the World War II holocaust, American Jews and others have a special interest in the fate of Israel as a Jewish homeland. The so-called "Israeli lobby" in the United States is much better organized and more influential than is the American Arab lobby. Perhaps in no other area does U.S. domestic politics become so entangled with international politics, adding one more layer of complexity to an already tangled situation.

A selection from the Foreign Policy Association's *Great Decisions, 1988* begins our discussion of the Middle East. There follows a careful and balanced statement on U.S. Middle East policy and the peace process by Robert Hunter, a serious scholar as well as an experienced government official. Adam Garfinkle then cuts through the cant of recent changes and rhetoric about the Middle East and provides a commentary that probes considerably deeper than the television evening news.

U.S. and the Middle East   *Dangerous Drift?*

Since World War II, U.S. policy-makers have considered the Middle East, which holds two thirds of the world's known oil reserves, to be of vital importance to American interests. A number of times in recent years the U.S. took military action to protect these interests—in Lebanon, in Libya and, in 1987, in the Persian Gulf, where the seven-year war between Iran and Iraq threatened the tankers that carry oil to Japan, Europe and the U.S.

Keeping the international sea-lanes open and keeping the oil flowing at reasonable prices are only two of a number of U.S. objectives in that strategically located region. Others include preventing the Soviet Union from extending its influence, providing support for Israel and moderate Arab governments, and promoting trade.

Until recently the Reagan Administration was preoccupied with foreign policy concerns in other parts of the world and saw little hope of progress in resolving any of the Middle East's intractable problems. Foremost among these are the Iran-Iraq war; the absence of peace between Israel and its Arab neighbors; the political future of 4.5 million Palestinians, scattered in refugee camps or living in exile; a continuing civil war in Lebanon; and recurrent acts of terrorism.

What is the current status of U.S. interests in the region? How will events now unfolding there affect them? In order to answer those questions it is necessary to trace the changes that have taken place in the Middle East over the past four decades and how different Administrations have responded.

The Region Defined

There is no standard definition of the Middle East, a term that came into widespread use during World War II. The Middle East, as used here, consists of the countries from Libya to Afghanistan, inclusive.

These lands historically comprised Arab, Persian and Turkish cultural zones. Today they are divided into 14 Arab states (containing 50% of the region's population), two Persian-dominated states (Iran and Afghanistan), plus Turkey and Israel. Egypt, Iran and Turkey are the largest countries (see chart), the United Arab Emirates in the Persian Gulf is among the world's smallest.

Despite differences in size, language and economic development important factors contribute to a sense of regional identity. The Middle East has long served as a cultural and commercial bridge between Europe and the Far East. Geographically, it is a region where aridity is widespread, agriculture is largely dependent upon irrigation and pastoral nomadism was once widely practiced.

It is the birthplace of three major religions, Judaism, Christianity and Islam. Today, Islam, practiced by over 90% of the region's people, provides a common cultural link. The Islamic system of law, or *shari'a,* is still a powerful influence, although how this law should be implemented today is hotly debated. The majority of Islam's followers, or Muslims, belong to the Sunni branch. The other major branch, the Shiite, has many adherents in Iran, Iraq and Lebanon.

Demographic Transformation

Profound changes have taken place in the Middle East over the past four decades. The most noticeable is demographic: in 1950 the population was around 87 million; today it is about 241 million. After World War II the Middle East was still largely a rural society, with only about a quarter of the people living in cities. Near-starvation, pestilence, high death rates and economic exploitation were not unusual. The average money income was only $20–$30 a year. "There is no standard of living in the European sense—mere existence is accepted as the standard," according to a 1948 survey.

Today in most countries one half to two thirds of the people live in or near cities—drawn there by the prospect of jobs. After the war, Cairo had over 2 million inhabitants, Tehran less than 1 million. Today, greater Cairo is estimated to contain some 13 million, Tehran, 7 million to 10 million.

Spread of Modernization

Modernization, which has been defined as the process by which man increasingly gains control over his environment, took centuries in the West but is being compressed into decades in the Middle East. The exploitation of the region's petroleum reserves after World War II provided the revenues that quickly propelled traditional societies into the modern world.

The process changed the social and psychological climate as well as the physical appearance of the

Source: From *Great Decisions, 1988* Foreign Policy Association, New York, 1988.

Middle East. The construction of new buildings and transportation networks altered the look of many traditional cities. Newspapers, and later radio and television, brought villagers into contact with the life of their country's capital as well as the wider world. Governments promoted the spread of secular education, which now reached many more people.

But modernization is a disruptive process that raises expectations, which, if unmet, lead to social upheaval. It placed authoritarian political systems under unprecedented strain as new governments had to establish their fitness or legitimacy to rule. In traditional Islamic society, legitimacy was bestowed by the clerical class or *ulama*. In the new states, the military who typically took control could not claim religious sanction for rule. They claimed instead to represent the will of the people and often staged elections to prove it. The leaders who guided their countries to independence often regarded religion as an impediment to modernization and promoted secular nationalism instead. People who were used to autocratic leadership began to expect more from their government and even desired a say in it.

Problems of National Integration

Many Middle Eastern countries once formed part of the Ottoman Empire. From their capital in Istanbul the Ottomans for five centuries governed much of North Africa, southeastern Europe and the Arab countries of the Fertile Crescent stretching from the Nile to the Euphrates. After World War I, European powers carved up the empire into a number of sovereign states, some of which, like Lebanon, Iraq and Jordan, had no historical basis. Consequently, many new states found it difficult to forge a sense of national identity. Middle Easterners found themselves arbitrarily joined with members of different religious, tribal, linguistic and ethnic groups. In addition, national groups such as the Palestinians and Armenians, and tribal groups, such as the Kurds and Baluchis, lived in more than one state. Some never developed an allegiance to any government.

While the forced assimilation of minorities helped create national identities, it also made people more aware of their ethnic, religious, tribal and linguistic differences, which led, decades later, to divisive tensions.

Political Evolution

The period between World Wars I and II was the high point of European influence. The British, in Egypt, Palestine, Transjordan and Iraq, and the French, in North Africa, Syria and Lebanon, exercised hegemony over much of the region. Italy dominated Libya. Of the major countries, only Persia (renamed Iran in 1935) and Turkey retained their independence.

After World War II Britain and France needed to devote their resources to rebuilding their own countries. They also faced growing Arab nationalism in their Middle Eastern colonies. Because of these factors they decided to withdraw from the region. Before doing so, they tried to shape the newly independent governments in their own image, with constitutional monarchies in British territories and parliamentary republics in French ones.

Britain granted independence to Jordan in 1946 and withdrew from Palestine in 1948. This opened the way for the formation of the state of Israel. A bitter war followed between Israel and its Arab neighbors, and some 800,000 Palestinian refugees resettled elsewhere, primarily in Jordan and southern Lebanon.

Although nominally independent, Egypt remained under British influence until 1956 and Iraq until 1958. Kuwait achieved independence in 1961 and the small states of the Persian Gulf, in 1971. France declared Syria and Lebanon independent in 1941, although French military occupation continued until 1946. Libya has been independent since 1951.

Many of the newly independent states rejected the monarchical form of government that had long prevailed. King Farouk of Egypt once quipped that there would eventually be only five kings—the kings of hearts, spades, clubs, diamonds and England. The title of the autobiography of King Hussein of Jordan, written in 1962, tells it all: *Uneasy Lies the Head*.

Since the war six monarchies have fallen—those of Egypt (1952), Iraq (1958), North Yemen (1962), Libya (1969), Afghanistan (1973) and Iran (1979). Kings continue to rule in Saudi Arabia, Jordan, and Oman. Four tiny Persian Gulf states, Bahrain, Kuwait, Qatar and the United Arab Emirates (UAE) are ruled by emirs and shaykhs. Israel and Turkey are the most democratic. The remaining countries have authoritarian secular leaders except for Iran, which is an Islamic Republic.

The Role of Outside Powers

The watershed for European imperialism in the Middle East was the Suez war of 1956. In retaliation for Egypt's nationalization of the

Suez Canal, Britain and France, along with Israel, invaded Sinai. They were forced to withdraw under strong U.S. and Soviet pressure.

The Suez war won for Egypt's president, Gamal Abdel Nasser, a reputation as a great Arab hero, and he dominated the region until his death in 1970. He promoted pan-Arabism, a movement of political unification based on common ethnic identity rather than religious or national affiliation, and vied with Syria and Iraq for leadership of the Arab world. However, pan-Arabism faltered as unification efforts by regional countries failed. (A Syrian-Egyptian union lasted from 1958 to 1961.) The Syrians resented Egyptian domination and opposed Nasser's policy of nationalizing the economy. Subsequent attempts on the part of Libya's Muammar Qaddafi to form political unions with the Sudan, Tunisia, Morocco and Egypt were all short-lived.

The Arab Predicament

The June 1967 war, which Nasser provoked by preventing shipping from reaching the Israeli port of Eilat via the Gulf of Aqaba, resulted in a stunning Israeli victory and was a political turning point for the Middle East. Israel tripled the size of its territory by taking the West Bank and East Jerusalem from Jordan; Sinai and the Gaza Strip from Egypt; and the Golan Heights from Syria.

The Arabs lost more than territory in the war: they lost self-esteem. Claims by Arab governments that they were ready to confront Israel were no longer credible. Pan-Arabism never regained the appeal it previously had and individual countries increasingly focused on their own problems and development.

The sense of frustration and despair that swept the Arab world after this war was particularly acute among the Palestinians. The Palestine Liberation Organization (PLO) had been founded by Arab leaders in 1964 to represent various Palestinian groups and press their grievances. In the early 1970s, under the leadership of a new chairman, Yasir Arafat, the PLO turned to terrorist attacks to publicize its cause. Since then, King Hussein and Arafat have competed for the allegiance of the Palestinian community.

The Oil Weapon

To regain territory lost in 1967 and to break an increasingly intolerable diplomatic stalemate, Egypt and Syria launched a surprise attack on Israel in October 1973. While Israel prevailed militarily, the Arab armies performed creditably. Arabs throughout the region gained a renewed sense of confidence and power. The prestige of president Anwar al-Sadat of Egypt soared and this enabled him to sign a peace treaty with Israel in 1979. The treaty was bitterly resented by Palestinians and opposed by most of the Arab world.

In retaliation for its resupply of arms to Israel during the 1973 war, Arab oil-producing states (but not Iran) placed a five-month embargo on oil exports to the U.S. (The Netherlands was similarly penalized for supporting Israel.) The Organization of Petroleum Exporting Countries (OPEC), which also includes non-Arab members, greatly raised oil prices. A barrel of oil, which cost Saudi Arabia pennies to produce, rose in price from $2 in 1971 to $35 by 1981.

The countries that benefited the most from the price rises were those with 80% of the reserves—Saudi Arabia, Kuwait, Iraq and Iran. They used their new revenues to hire large numbers of foreign workers and paid them well to build transportation networks, ports and manufacturing plants.

Many of these workers came from oil-poor countries such as Egypt, Turkey, the Sudan, the Yemens and Jordan, as well as the Indian subcontinent and Southeast Asia. From the early 1970s until the mid-1980s the amount of labor migration in the Arab world was unprecedented, and the expatriates' countries came to depend on their remittances. In 1986, about 3 million out of the Egyptian work force of 18 million worked abroad. The sight of people who had been poor peasants (*fellahin*) in rural Egypt returning from the Gulf laden with TVs and VCRs was not unusual.

Much of the new wealth was spent on military hardware. Between 1971 and 1980 the Middle East, with about 5% of the world's population, accounted for over half of the world's arms trade. Regional states spent $122 billion on imported arms, and the number of regular soldiers in uniform jumped from 1.3 million in 1973 to 2.1 million now.

The main beneficiaries of this militarization were Western arms companies and local middlemen. The huge expenditures led to vastly increased corruption, and complaints, such as in Iran, that revenues were being squandered on sophisticated armaments rather than, for example, agricultural development. Such complaints rose as economic conditions worsened and resources for development dried up in the 1980s.

Islamic Revival

Since about 1970 an Islamic revival has swept the region. People who felt Western concepts such as nationalism, socialism and capitalism had failed them turned to Islam as a native, authentic ideology. Islam had led them to greatness before, and they believed it could do so again. Pious Muslims criticized their rulers for conspicuous consumption and for not being religious enough. They demanded social justice, a more equitable share of the economic pie, and a voice in political decisions.

The West had previously associated Islam with a fatalistic mind-set that inhibited progress and led to economic backwardness. After religious fundamentalists had played a major role in overthrowing the shah of Iran in 1979 and a militant Islamic group had assassinated President Sadat of Egypt in 1981, Islam became associated in the Western public's mind with political militancy and violence. This was especially true of Shiite Muslims, with their historic association with martyrdom. Iran, under Ayatollah Ruhollah Khomeini, loomed as a menace to its Middle Eastern neighbors, especially those with large Shiite populations. They feared Iran would try to export its revolution.

Because there is no standard definition of Islam, and its practice varies in different countries, both governments and oppositions claim religious sanction for their programs. Political scientist James A. Bill uses the term "establishment Islam" to denote the conservative form of religion used by governments—such as Saudi Arabia, Morocco, and Pakistan—to legitimate their rule. He contrasts it with "populist Islam" or the "Islam from below" that the lower classes have invoked to challenge rulers.

While religion is an important force today throughout the Islamic world, especially in Iran, Egypt, the Sudan and Tunisia, the Iranian revolution, its most dramatic manifestation, has not been repeated in other countries. Although many Muslims are proud that Islam helped overthrow an impious autocrat, they do not want to imitate the form of religious government imposed by Ayatollah Khomeini.

Leadership Today

Since the 1970s, the Middle East has had longer-lasting and more powerful governments than was the case in the coup- ridden 1950s and 1960s. King Hussein has been in power in Jordan since 1953; Saddam Hussein has been at the top level of the Iraqi government since 1968 and president since 1979; Quaddafi has ruled Libya since 1969; Hafez al-Assad has led Syria since 1970; Ayatollah Khomeini has dominated Iran since 1979; and President Hosni Mubarak has led Egypt since 1981.

Leaders have achieved a greater degree of control partly by coercion, partly by centralizing power. Aided by better communications, larger armed forces and huge bureaucracies, they can extend their reach throughout the country.

The rulers of the oil-rich states are also able to "buy off" potential opposition groups. In Bahrain the ruler, a Sunni, goes out of his way to accommodate his Shiite minority. The Saudis subsidize the PLO so they will not cause trouble in the kingdom.

Quest for Legitimacy

Among the Arab masses today there is widespread apathy and disillusionment, according to Adeed Dawisha, professor of government at George Mason University. The old ideological goals of Arab unification, the liberation of Palestine, and the institution of Islamic government seem further away than ever. The Gulf war hangs like a shadow over the region, adding to Arab anxiety.

A major unresolved problem is the lack of stable mechanisms for orderly succession of Middle Eastern governments. Military coups have been the most frequent catalyst of governmental change (Israel is a major exception.) Lebanon, Kuwait and Egypt have experimented with limited democracy, but it has always been subject to cancellation. Governments typically rig elections to demonstrate popular support for their actions. The fact is that they distrust many of their people and rely on repressive security services to stay in power. Opposition groups must often operate underground or abroad.

Authoritarian regimes that do not have an accepted procedure for political succession or a forum for debating policy are likely to alienate their populations and engender violent opposition, according to North African specialist Lisa Anderson. Syria, Iraq and Iran are all good examples. On the other hand, regimes that tolerate some political opposition, such as Egypt and Turkey, may be able to accommodate the changes most urgently demanded by their peoples.

Oil Bust

Government spending drives the regional economies. With the decline in oil revenues due to increased worldwide production and lowered demand in the early 1980s, governments have had to trim expenditures. Saudi oil revenues for 1987 may amount to no more than $27 billion, down from $119 billion in 1981, and the Saudi economy has been in recession for several years. Saudi Arabia and Kuwait still have a "buffer" of savings accumulated during more prosperous times. (In 1985, Kuwait earned as much from its investments in the West as from its oil.) Other countries such as Bahrain, Qatar and Oman are more vulnerable. Rulers fear the upheaval that could accompany radical spending cutbacks. To help shore up their governments, Saudi Arabia has distributed largess to Syria, Jordan and Iraq. It is an open question, however, how long it can continue.

The current economic contraction may have unforeseen social consequences. Overseas workers who began returning home in 1986 face an uncertain future. Accustomed to receiving high pay, they are certain to constitute a disenchanted element in some countries, such as Egypt. In cities unemployed or underemployed workers place severe strains on social services and exacerbate housing shortages.

Foreign Relations

In the postwar period, no single outside power has dominated the Middle East, and no regional power has exercised primacy for long. The Northern Tier countries adjoining the Soviet Union—Turkey, Iran, Afghanistan and Pakistan—have always been suspicious of Soviet designs on their territory. Consequently, with the exception of Afghanistan, in the postwar period they have had close defense ties with the U.S. The Arab world to the south, in contrast, has been ambivalent about its relations with both East and West.

In the 1950s and 1960s, Egypt was the most influential Arab state. Today, the Arab world does not have a comparable "center," and it is harder for states of the region to form effective political groupings. This has been especially true since the Egypt-Israel peace treaty in 1979 split the Arab world. The Iran-Iraq war, which began in 1980, led to further divisions, with Arab states such as Syria and Libya supporting non-Arab Iran.

Although religion is a powerful force today, it can be argued that national self-interest is even stronger. The Iran-Iraq war is a good illustration. Although sometimes portrayed as a religious crusade of Sunni against Shiite, the war is regarded by most observers as a struggle between Iranian and Iraqi nationalism.

The two major foreign policy concerns of regional states are the Gulf war and the "unfinished business" of the Arab-Israeli wars. The Arab nations in the Gulf are no match for Iran or Iraq and do not want to be dominated by either. So far they have supported Iraq out of fear of the Iranian revolution spreading.

On the second issue, there is an Arab consensus that Israel should withdraw from territories it seized in 1967, and that the Palestinians should be given a homeland. Beyond these principles, few can agree on details.

Future Trends

The Middle East has undergone momentous changes over the past four decades. Some current trends listed below bear watching.

• Population pressure will be a serious problem in many countries, especially Egypt. There are not enough jobs to go around today, and this situation will likely worsen.

In Israel, the birthrate among Arabs is outstripping that of Jews. If Israel keeps the West Bank and Gaza, demographers predict that by the year 2000 Arabs will constitute almost half the population. Israelis will increasingly have to grapple with the question of whether they will live in a democratic or Jewish state.

• If there is no consensus in Israel on the future status of the West Bank, and if no Arab leader is willing to risk negotiating, a comprehensive peace settlement is not likely any time soon.

• The Persian Gulf region will continue to be of key importance for global petroleum production. By 1990, the Gulf states, including Iran and Iraq, could account for half of OPEC's output, and this could increase later in the decade. Oil-rich countries would then have a second chance for development. At the same time, due to the construction of pipelines by Iraq, Turkey, Saudi Arabia and Iran, much of this oil will be transported overland, not through the Strait of Hormuz. This should lead to lessened tension in the Gulf.

• The nuclear trends in the region are worrisome to the largely Western "nuclear club." Iran, Iraq and Libya may be seeking to develop a nuclear capability. Israel is assumed to already have nuclear bombs.

• It is possible that the wave of religiously inspired violence (though not adherence to religion) may have peaked. In Iran, a more moderate government, with clerics advising rather than running it, may eventually appear.

• The struggle over water resources may become increasingly bitter. Disagreement exists between Israel and Jordan over the waters of the Jordan River, between Israel and Lebanon over the Litani River, between Egypt and the Sudan over the Nile, between Iran and Afghanistan over the Helmand River, and among Iraq, Syria and Turkey over distribution of the waters of the Euphrates.

• Political upheaval is a certainty, due to the lack of accepted means for succession. Professor Bill believes that by the year 2000 many of the traditional political systems will have been replaced. Unless there is economic improvement for the masses in the oil-poor countries, more coups or revolutions could lie ahead.

U.S. POSTWAR POLICY

Before World War II the U.S. was little involved in the Middle East. Many Americans discovered the region for the first time during the war, when U.S. forces were stationed in Egypt and Iran. Afterward, the U.S. replaced Britain and France as the main Western influence, and American companies sought more oil concessions.

For the past four decades, U.S. administrations have subordinated Middle East policy to their overriding concern of containing Communist expansion. Presidents have typically announced "doctrines"

that aimed to discourage Soviet involvement in the region. All Administrations since the time of President Dwight D. Eisenhower have also proposed plans to resolve the Arab-Israeli dispute. In order to understand current U.S. policy toward the region and how it is formulated, it is necessary to review its evolution.

Truman (1945–53). A number of Soviet moves after the war raised U.S. apprehensions. In 1946, the Soviets demanded joint control of the strategic Turkish straits through which their ships passed from the Black Sea to the Aegean. In Iran, they delayed withdrawing their troops in 1946 and sponsored two autonomous republics, in Azerbaijan and Kurdistan. In Greece, Communist-led guerrillas had gained the upper hand in the civil war by 1947, and the Soviets requested a port on the Aegean.

In response, President Harry S. Truman proclaimed what became known as the Truman Doctrine on March 12, 1947: "I believe that it must be the policy of the U.S. to support free peoples who are resisting attempted subjugation by armed minorities or by outside pressures." Congress quickly voted $400 million in military and economic aid for Turkey and Greece. Iran, by clever negotiating and exerting pressure at the United Nations, succeeded in thwarting Soviet designs on its territory. The "policy of firm containment" that diplomat George F. Kennan proposed in July 1947 became the guiding ideology of the postwar period.

The Korean War (1950–53) revived U.S. apprehensions about Communist intentions, and the Middle East assumed a new impor-

tance as an ideological battleground. The U.S. brought Turkey and Greece into the North Atlantic Treaty Organization (NATO) in 1952, sent aid to Iran, and weighed a major aid package for Egypt.

The Truman years are also remembered for U.S. recognition of Israel in 1948. This move caused serious disagreement within the U.S. government. The State Department, which was overruled by the President, opposed recognition on the grounds that the Jewish state could not survive and that recognition would alienate Arab nations.

Eisenhower (1953–61). In the Eisenhower Administration foreign policy was largely shaped by Secretary of State John Foster Dulles. Dulles regarded most nationalist movements as Communist-inspired, and thought that neutrality between communism and the free world was immoral. His belief that Iran's charismatic prime minister, Mohammad Mossadeq, was influenced by Communists led the U.S., along with Britain, to restore Shah Mohammad Reza Pahlavi to his throne after he was briefly forced out of the country in August 1953.

Eisenhower opposed too close an identification with Israel and refused to approve military aid, arguing that this would provoke an arms race with the Arabs.

In the Arab world, the U.S. attempted to curry favor with two major rivals, Egypt and Iraq. At first it welcomed the coup in Egypt that deposed King Farouk in 1952 and brought Nasser to power. However, out of deference to the British, who were negotiating their departure from the Suez Canal Zone, and Israel, the U.S. turned down repeated Egyptian requests for military aid.

In 1955, the U.S. promoted a mutual security and economic development agreement called the Baghdad Pact, which included Iraq, Turkey, Iran and Pakistan. The U.S. supported the pact but did not formally join to avoid Egyptian criticism.

In September 1955, President Nasser made the first arms deal between an Arab country and the Soviet bloc. This was partly because of an Israeli raid on Gaza in February. In an attempt to recoup its influence, the U.S. in December promised to help Egypt build a massive dam on the Nile River at Aswan. It withdrew the offer the following July due to dismay at the Egyptian-Czech arms deal, Nasser's refusal to negotiate with Israel and congressional opposition.

Nasser's nationalization of the Suez Canal followed, along with the aborted invasion of Sinai by allies of the U.S. Two years later the Soviet Union helped build the dam. When President Richard M. Nixon visited the completed dam years later, he told Nasser, "Today I have seen America's greatest mistake."

Apprehensive about the growing Soviet presence in Egypt, the Administration in 1957 propounded the Eisenhower Doctrine, which stated that the U.S. was prepared to come to the aid of any government in the Middle East threatened by a Communist takeover. This led the U.S. to send troops to Lebanon in July 1958. In 1959, the U.S. signed bilateral defense agreements with Turkey, Iran and Pakistan, which were members of the Central Treaty Organization (CENTO), the successor to the Baghdad Pact.

The central premise of Eisenhower's foreign policy—like Truman's—was to contain communism, and for this he received broad bipartisan support. In retrospect, the Administration may have overestimated the Communist threat to the region and inadvertently given the Soviet Union a foothold. Its principal failure, however, was its lack of effective policies to deal with local nationalisms and to resolve the Arab-Israeli conflict.

Kennedy and Johnson (1961–69).

President John F. Kennedy, who pursued an active anti-Communist policy in the Third World, promoted friendship with both Israel and the Arab states. To balance the Soviet arms that Egypt and Iraq were receiving, the U.S. in June 1962 for the first time agreed to sell arms to Israel.

In Iran, the U.S. pressured the shah to introduce a program of social reforms, including land reform. This led to serious antigovernment rioting in late 1962 and June 1963, spearheaded by Ayatollah Khomeini. Khomeini was deported and resided primarily in Iraq until his triumphant return in 1979.

Lyndon B. Johnson took office in 1963 after Kennedy's assassination, and relations with Egypt sank to a new low. Following Israel's victory in the June 1967 war, the U.S. came to regard it as the guardian of American interests, a powerful ally that could be depended on to maintain regional stability. The U.S. replaced France as Israel's main source of arms and U.S. arms aid for Israel shot up from $44 million in 1963 to $995 million in 1968.

The Johnson Administration played a role in formulating UN Security Council Resolution 242, passed on November 22, 1967. The resolution called on Israel to withdraw "from territories occupied in the recent conflict" and for Arab states to allow it to "live in peace within secure and recognized boundaries." The resolution was deliberately ambiguous—it did not specify *all* territories, for example—and U.S. officials have differed among themselves and with others in their interpretation. Since 1967, however, UN Resolution 242 has served as the basis for most peace plans.

Following the war, the Soviet Union rearmed Egypt, Syria and Jordan, and regional politics became polarized between the U.S. and Israel on one side and the Soviet Union and its Arab allies on the other. U.S. ties with Iran remained close.

Nixon-Ford (1969–77).

President Nixon, chastened by the U.S. disaster in Vietnam, determined that American troops would no longer be sent to world trouble spots. Instead, under the July 1969 "Nixon Doctrine," U.S. economic and military aid would help fortify allies so they could defend themselves.

The U.S. relied on Iran and Saudi Arabia, the "twin pillars," to protect its interests in the Persian Gulf after the British withdrawal in 1971. In May 1972, Nixon, overriding the objections of the Defense Department, gave Iran carte blanche to buy virtually any weapons in the U.S. inventory, short of nuclear arms.

Secretary of State Henry A. Kissinger tried to bring the October 1973 Arab-Israeli war to an end without a clearcut winner or loser and without Soviet intervention. By so doing Israelis complained that the U.S. had robbed them of victory. In cooperation with the Soviets, the U.S. forged a cease-fire resolution at the UN on October 22, 1973.

Once a cease-fire was in effect, Kissinger worked to formulate a peace plan. His style of negotiation was to build confidence on both sides in a step-by-step process. He sought agreement on the smaller issues and set aside the big ones— such as where the final Israeli borders would be and how to resolve the question of the Palestinians. A key factor in his success was Sadat's willingness to negotiate and his acceptance of the U.S. as mediator: "The U.S. holds 99% of the cards," Sadat liked to say.

Through months of exhaustive "shuttle diplomacy" between the former combatants, Kissinger succeeded in mediating troop disengagements between Israel and Egypt in 1974 and 1975 and between Israel and Syria in 1974. But a real peace treaty had to await the next Administration.

Carter (1977–81). President Jimmy Carter made Arab-Israeli peace a top priority. In contrast to Kissinger's one-step-at-a-time approach. Carter sought a comprehensive settlement that would address all the major issues. Sadat's dramatic visit to Israel in November 1977, the first by an Arab head of state, broke an important psychological barrier and set the stage for peace.

There was little real progress, however, until Carter invited Sadat and Israeli Prime Minister Menachem Begin to a historic meeting at Camp David, Maryland, in September 1978. They signed two path-breaking agreements: one provided for Israeli withdrawal from Sinai and an Egypt-Israel peace treaty; the other was a frame-work for Palestinian autonomy in the West Bank and Gaza Strip.

President Carter traveled to the Middle East to conclude the Egypt-Israel peace treaty in March 1979. Observers credit the success of the negotiations to his personal commitment. To fulfill its part of the bargain, the U.S. began providing unprecedented levels of aid to the two countries.

In 1979–80 the Carter Administration was plagued by setbacks in what it dubbed the arc of crisis— the area extending from Egypt to Pakistan. Iran, after the overthrow of the shah in January 1979, was at the center of this arc. The following November 66 hostages were seized at the U.S. embassy in Tehran, leading to a prolonged crisis, which did not end until their release in January 1981. U.S. friends in the region accused Washington of deserting the shah and feared for their own future.

Carter had come into office with a benign impression of Soviet intentions in the Middle East. However, he changed his mind after the Soviet invasion of Afghanistan in December 1979. In January 1980 Carter warned the Soviets that "an attempt by any outside force to gain control of the Persian Gulf region will be regarded as an assault on the vital interests" of the U.S. The Carter Doctrine was accompanied by the creation of a Rapid Deployment Force, or RDF (later renamed the Central Command), which had access to facilities in Egypt, Oman, Kenya, and Somalia and was designed to intervene militarily in the Gulf region.

Reagan (1981–89). President Ronald Reagan entered office strongly committed to rebuilding America's image in the world. Al-though the U.S. had lost face in the Middle East, the Administration gave it a low priority. With peace between Israel and Egypt a reality, the Administration felt little pressure to follow up on the Camp David accords.

Secretary of State Alexander M. Haig Jr. initially sought to build a "strategic consensus" of moderate regional states against the Soviet threat. As in the 1950s, however, the states were more afraid of each other than the Soviet Union.

It was Israel's invasion of Lebanon in June 1982 that led the U.S. into a risky intervention in Lebanese politics. (The president's special Middle East envoy, Philip C. Habib, had succeeded in negotiating a cease-fire between Israel and the PLO in August 1981.) As part of a multinational peacekeeping force, U.S. troops helped evacuate PLO fighters trapped in Beirut. U.S. troops were withdrawn but were sent back following the massacre of hundreds of civilians at the Palestinian refugee camps of Sabra and Shatila.

The Reagan Plan of September 1982, the President's only diplomatic initiative on the Middle East, proposed giving Palestinians on the West Bank and Gaza self-government in association with Jordan. It also called on Israel not to build any more settlements on the West Bank. Israel and Syria rejected the plan, and Jordan did not fully go along. The plan's downfall, however, has mainly been attributed to U.S. failure to consult adequately with the concerned parties in advance.

In May 1983 Secretary of State George P. Shultz brokered an agreement providing for Israel to withdraw most of its troops from Lebanon with the exception of the border area. The plan fell apart largely due to Syrian opposition. This failure reportedly dissuaded Shultz from further ventures in Middle East diplomacy.

U.S. Marines remained in Lebanon but had no clear mission other than to bolster the government. A truck bomb, which destroyed their barracks in Beirut on October 23, 1983, killed 241 men and prompted new questions at home as to the U.S. purpose there. Although the President declared at the time that the U.S. had "vital interests in Lebanon" and that the presence of U.S. forces there was "central to our credibility," he withdrew the Marines in February 1984.

The Peace Process

Since mid-1983, the U.S. has let the countries of the region take the lead in seeking peace and has played a behind-the-scenes role in trying to facilitate negotiations. U.S. hopes have focused on getting King Hussein and "moderate" Palestinians to negotiate with Israel.

Critics have charged the Administration with a dangerous drift in its Middle East diplomacy. According to Harold Saunders, longtime Mideast expert on the National Security Council (NSC) staff and at the State Department, it is the duty of political leaders—primarily the U.S. President—to break down the barriers to peace. "Peace, like politics is never finished," he says, "it is always in the making." Carter complained in Cairo in March 1987 that President Reagan's lack of leadership has almost doomed the peace process to failure.

The Administration felt that there is little likelihood of real progress any time soon, and was therefore reluctant to undertake a major diplomatic effort in 1987. King Hussein promoted the idea of an international peace conference, including the five permanent members of the UN Security Council, Israel, Syria, and a Jordanian-Palestinian delegation. Shultz endorsed it, provided the Soviets do not play a substantive role. The Israeli leadership is seriously divided, with Foreign Minister Shimon Peres its main supporter. On a trip to the region in October 1987—his first in two and a half years—Shultz was unsuccessful in persuading Prime Minister Yitzhak Shamir to go along.

The effectiveness of the U.S. as a mediator is compromised by its anti-Arab tilt, according to Professor Michael C. Hudson of Georgetown University. The covert sale of arms to Iran is only the latest in a string of U.S. actions that many in the Arab world interpret as hostile. These include the shelling of Lebanese villages by U.S. ships in retaliation for attacks on American Marines in Beirut, presumed complicity in the Israeli attack on PLO headquarters in Tunisia, and the bombing of Libya in retaliation for a terrorist attack.

The high-level attention the U.S. government has paid to terrorist acts in the past appears to have backfired. The intense personal involvement of President Carter during the Iranian hostage crisis is widely believed to have prolonged it. More recently, the secret attempts to exchange arms for hostages failed, and the Administration asserts it has resumed its earlier policy of not negotiating with terrorists.

How great a threat is terrorism? The number of Americans involved is actually very small, with 12 killed throughout the world in 1986 compared with 38 in 1985.

Overall, the number of terrorist incidents by Middle Eastern groups fell from 74 in 1985 to 39 in 1986.

Credibility Crisis

One measure of U.S. friendship is America's willingness to sell arms. The last major U.S. sale was of five airborne warning and control system (AWACS) radar planes to Saudi Arabia in 1981. The sale was only approved after Reagan put his own prestige on the line. The Administration would like to sell arms to Saudi Arabia, Jordan, Kuwait and the UAE, but congress has opposed all but minor sales on the grounds that the arms could be used against Israel. Jordan's request to improve its Hawk missile system and Saudi Arabia's to buy additional F-15 jet fighters have been pending for years.

In September 1987, the Administration proposed a $1.4 billion sale of Maverick antitank missiles and F-15s to Saudi Arabia to strengthen its defenses against Iran and as a reward for cooperating with the U.S. mission in the Gulf. The Administration later dropped the request for missiles in hopes of obtaining Congress' approval for the F-15s.

With regard to the war between Iran and Iraq, the U.S. supports the territorial integrity and political independence of both countries. It would like to bring the war to a negotiated end in which neither side is victorious. Its publicly stated position of neutrality, however, was compromised by relevations of covert arms sales to Iran, and by a subsequent increasing tilt toward Iraq.

The Iraqi attack on the USS *Stark* on May 17, 1987, killing 37 U.S. sailors, suddenly brought the war home to Americans. The *Stark* was part of a seven-ship task force escorting U.S. registered merchant vessels through the Gulf. (Since 1984, the two belligerents had attacked some 230 ships, mainly oil tankers. Iraq was responsible for 61% of the attacks; Iran, 39%.) The "inadvertent" attack, for which Iraq promptly apologized, caught the U.S. by surprise. The U.S. had anticipated that if an attack came it would be from Iran.

Not long before the *Stark* incident the U.S. had promised Kuwait to protect half of its 22 oil tankers by "reflagging" them, or transferring them to U.S. registry. Kuwait had requested U.S. protection in November, 1986, but the request was ignored until the Soviets showed a willingness to help. Secretary of State Shultz said that U.S. escorts would defend themselves but the U.S. would not go to war with either party. The Administration's rationale for increasing its presence in the Gulf was that the U.S. had a responsibility to maintain the freedom of navigation and to keep the Strait of Hormuz open.

The intervention achieved the longtime U.S. goal of closer military cooperation with the regional countries. The U.S. has access to a naval mooring and supply facility (the term "base" is carefully avoided) in Bahrain, and an airstrip at Oman. The U.S. also assists the Saudis in operating AWACS aircraft and reportedly will receive storage facilities in Qatar. In the wake of the crisis of confidence resulting from the disclosure of its arms sales to Iran, the U.S. feels it must reassure its nervous Arab friends.

The expanded role of the U.S. military in the Gulf war zone has, however, alarmed many congress-men, who recall the disastrous stationing of Marines in Beirut. The Gulf operations, which cost $15–$20 million per month, are also a financial drain. In 1986 the U.S. got only 6% of its oil from the Gulf region; Japan got 60%, Italy 51%, France 33% and West Germany 10%. Therefore, if protection is needed, critics say, others should provide it. After initially hesitating to support the U.S., five European powers—Britain, France, Italy, Belgium and the Netherlands—agreed to send in minesweepers, and Britain put several Kuwaiti tankers under its protection.

The U.S. has looked to the UN for help in resolving the conflict. The Security Council passed a resolution in July 1987 calling for a cease-fire. The U.S. hoped to introduce a follow-up resolution aimed at Iran, which would impose an arms embargo on any party refusing to go along. It was not clear, however, if China and the Soviet Union (both of which supply Iran with arms) would agree to those stronger steps.

MAJOR ISSUES

There are some persistent long-term problems in the Middle East which all Administrations have faced. These include U.S. relations with Israel, the Palestinian problem and the Soviet role. They can only be briefly sketched here.

Israel: A 'Strategic Asset'?

One issue that has confronted every Administration is how to treat Israel. The arguments supporting favored treatment run as follows: Israel is the dominant military power in the region and consistently supports U.S. objectives, such as resisting communism and fighting terrorism. In addition to being democracies, there are strong personal links between the two countries. Because of the Holocaust, the U.S. has a moral obligation to support the Jewish state. Israel is an embattled ally that the Arab states will not let live in peace.

Those favoring a more even-handed approach argue that continued strong support for Israel is against the U.S. interest. They say that Israel's refusal to deal fairly with the Palestinians keeps the region in constant turmoil and fosters terrorism. They claim it is Israel that threatens Arab states, not the other way around. The real U.S. interest in the Middle East is in secure oil supplies, which means not offending the Arabs. Unquestioned U.S. support for Israeli policies has alienated Arab moderates and led some frustrated Arab governments to turn to the Soviets for arms.

The Palestinians

How to deal with the Palestinians, once characterized by the State Department as "the heart of the conflict," has long bedeviled U.S. diplomacy. The Camp David accords did not address the issue successfully, and this was a major reason Arab states rejected them. U.S. diplomats are handicapped, it is argued, by a prohibition against negotiating with the PLO until it recognizes UN Resolution 242 and Israel's right to exist.

A major issue is whether the Palestinians should be given a state of their own. One solution, endorsed by King Hussein and President Reagan, would be to grant the Palestinians self-government in the West Bank and Gaza in an entity confederated with Jordan. Otherwise, they will continue to live under military occupation or as exiles. Israel opposes a Palestinian state, and it is unclear whether Arab leaders, despite their rhetoric, really wish to see one.

Should the U.S. try to bring the PLO into the negotiating process, or continue to exclude it? Those in favor note that the PLO is the only Palestinian organization with the clout to make a deal with Israel. Those opposed say the U.S. should not deal with a terrorist organization whose word cannot be trusted.

The Soviet Role

The Soviet Union has good relations with Syria, Libya, South Yemen and the PLO. It has diplomatic ties with Iraq, Oman, the UAE and Kuwait, and for the first time has gained a foothold in the Gulf by agreeing to transport Kuwaiti oil. Under Mikhail S. Gorbachev, the Soviets have made new efforts to woo moderate states such as Egypt, Jordan, and Saudi Arabia, as well as Israel.

The U.S. on the other hand, has good relations with moderate Arab states that oppose communism at home; with Islamic countries that condemn the Soviet invasion of Afghanistan; and with Israel.

The Reagan Administration views the Soviets as regional troublemakers, eager to exploit tensions. An alternative view holds that the Soviets do not want instability so near their borders and do not want another Arab-Israeli war in which Arab leaders will ask them to intervene.

Some believe that cooperating with the Soviets in the Middle East would benefit the U.S., for only by working with them can the U.S. hope to achieve peace in Afghanistan and between the Arabs and Israel. The Soviet Union is the only superpower with influence in both Iran and Iraq, and says it shares the U.S. goal of reducing instability and ending the Iran-Iraq war.

The society and politics of the Middle East have changed considerably over the past four decades. As the pace of change accelerates, the region is likely to become an even greater challenge for U.S. diplomacy. Optimism that the U.S. can influence developments and impose solutions has often been belied by the limited leverage it really exercises. Yet the importance of the region to U.S. interests and its potential to disrupt international politics guarantee that it will continue to be a priority area for policymakers. ∎

Seeking Middle East Peace

by Robert E. Hunter

Until Ronald Reagan became president, there was little question that the American chief executive would become actively engaged in Arab-Israeli peacemaking. At least since the Six-Day War of 1967, U.S. interests, as well as those of allies in Western Europe and Japan, had been seen as critically engaged along the eastern rim of the Mediterranean Sea. It was a given that the United States could not—and would not—stand aloof from what had come to be known as the "peace process."

But in 1981 the new Reagan administration downgraded the importance of Arab-Israeli peacemaking. The key factor was the March 1979 peace treaty between Israel and Egypt. It had fundamentally changed U.S. geostrategic interests in the Middle East. The combined military power of the Arab states, arrayed against Israel, had proved inadequate in three wars in 1956, 1967, and 1973—and that with Egypt weighing in fully. Without Egypt, surely no Arab state could expect to prevail militarily against Israel. Thus the risk of war plummeted. So, too, did the risks of a U.S.-Soviet confrontation, such as those that arose in the three major Arab-Israeli conflicts.

At the same time, the Persian Gulf had taken on new importance. Iran was no longer a source of regional stability but was trying to export Islamic fundamentalism. Soviet troops were in Afghanistan. And Iraq had invaded Iran. Hence Arab-Israeli peacemaking no longer seemed to be a compelling first charge on time and attention

Robert E. Hunter, director of Middle East affairs at the National Security Council from 1979 to 1981, is a senior fellow in Middle Eastern studies at the Center for Strategic and International Studies.

Source: Reprinted with permission from *Foreign Policy,* No. 73 (Winter 1988–89), pp. 3–21. Copyright 1988 by the Carnegie Endowment for International Peace.

in U.S. strategy. Thus for 7 years the United States largely abdicated the peacemaking role that was almost universally expected of it.

By late 1987, however, it was clear that the strategic sums had to be redone. A qualitatively new arms race had begun in the Middle East, focusing on ballistic missiles and other weapons that threatened to outstrip the region's tolerance for avoiding war by accident or miscalculation. Iraq had used poison gas against Iran in the most massive violation of a global taboo since the end of World War I.

These developments had immediate relevance for Syria, which had completed a major rearmament program following its military disgrace in Lebanon in 1982. It had acquired not only accurate SS-21 ballistic missiles from the Soviet Union but also chemical and other warheads that raised doubts in Israel about its ability to resist preemption in the event of a crisis. The Israeli air force was being forced to move toward a hair-trigger alert status, lest the first line of Israel's national defense risked being caught on the ground.

Yet events in unexpected quarters were most important in forcing the United States to recalculate its interests and policies and in leading the Reagan administration to undertake its first sustained Arab-Israeli peace initiative, named after Secretary of State George Shultz. In November 1987 an Arab summit in Amman, Jordan, concluded that the most important threat to Arab interests came from Iran, not from the unresolved Palestinian problem. Within weeks Palestinians on the Israeli-occupied West Bank and Gaza Strip rose up, frustrated by the apparent desertion of their professed cham-

pions. Thus began the uprising known as the *intifada,* Arabic for "to shake" or "to shake off." The *intifada* is proving that Israel's security problem does not entail just successful deterrence of, and if need be defense against, enemies from without, but also a formidable challenge from within.

Another event refocusing U.S. attention on the Arab-Israeli conflict was Tehran's surprise acceptance of a cease-fire in the Iran-Iraq war, which took effect on August 20, 1988. This has raised new concerns in Israel and the West about the relative priority of Arab concerns, including those of battle-tested Iraq.

Overall, then, a key conclusion emerges: In Middle East affairs 1989 will not be like 1981 for the United States and its new president. The evolving situations there may not call for according the Arab-Israeli conflict the high-priority, high-profile peacemaking efforts of the 1970s, but neither will they permit the relative indifference of the early and mid-1980s.

THE SETTING FOR 1989

It is always risky to predict the precise circumstances of this conflict several months in advance. The uncertainty is even greater in the latter half of 1988. Most striking was the July shocker from Jordan's King Hussein in which he formally abandoned the peace process and renounced claims to the West Bank. Hussein compared his vulnerabilities with the desultory progress and faint hopes of the Shultz plan. From his perspective the picture was bleak: He was criticized by other Arabs for being too accommodating; expected by Israel to run even greater risks while

it reserved its own position; cajoled by the United States to show courage but denied U.S. weapons; resented by Palestinians on the West Bank and Gaza as an interloper; and likely to be a target for the ambitions of Syria and perhaps also Iraq following the Iran-Iraq war. For him, stepping back and confronting others with the problems of stalemate was a natural act of self-preservation.

Hussein's action foreclosed one possibility, at least for now—the so-called Jordanian option. But it did not open up an unlimited range of choices. Only a few practical scenarios for Arab-Israeli peacemaking exist, and all are well understood by the involved parties.

Historically, two broad approaches have been tried. One is called "comprehensive" in that it provides a plan for resolving all major outstanding disputes. The other is called "step-by-step" and involves progressing slowly from one issue to the next in the hope that dividing the overall conflict into its constituent parts will make each one more malleable—and success in one area can create precedents for progress in others.

To date, however, all diplomatic successes have been the result of the step-by-step approach. The comprehensive idea remains a long-standing goal for many diplomats because of the theory that if the interests of all parties are represented in negotiations, all may be prepared to entertain a successful outcome. But this approach has not proved adequate: Some parties have either refused to take part or, when they did, gained a veto on the whole. There is no reason to expect this historical record to change.

Under the step-by-step approach, several efforts to make

progress on the Middle East problem have tried to avoid dealing first with the Palestinian problem—or at least the West Bank, the territory most valued by Israelis for various reasons of security, history, and religion. In the late 1970s, serious thought was given by some leaders and officials in the United States, Egypt, and Israel to a "Gaza first" solution—either negotiating arrangements for that territory first, implementing a broader agreement there first, or even, in a formulation advocated by then Israeli Foreign Minister Moshe Dayan and others, seeing Israel pre-emptively withdrawn from Gaza.

Daunted by the West Bank's complexities, some experts have favored an attack on the Syrian-Israeli impasse. The Golan Heights represent a dispute rooted in security issues, with the political struggle essentially divorced from the conflict over territory. But this idea has come to naught, largely because of wider Syrian ambitions. The question of Jerusalem's status, a political tangle without peer, has regularly eluded resolution and is the most emotionally charged of all the Arab-Israeli issues.

The focus of diplomacy has repeatedly returned to the Palestinian problem and, more precisely, to the West Bank. This is not unnatural, given its prominence in human as well as security terms: It contains the largest number of Palestinians under occupation and is the territory most coveted. Gaza, by contrast, has been rejected by Egypt, whence it came, aspired to by Jordan only as a necessary adjunct of the West Bank, and viewed by Israel as being of secondary importance. This focus on the West Bank is likely to continue. Indeed,

in view of the political ferment of 1988, the "Palestinian problem first" tack is now inescapable.

Over the years, the practical diplomatic alternatives for the West Bank have narrowed to two, known in shorthand as "territory for peace" and "autonomy." The former has the longer pedigree. It is implicit in United Nations Security Council Resolution 242, the bedrock agreement that conditions all Arab-Israeli bargaining, although when it was negotiated in 1967 the resolution was deliberately left vague on whether Israel was to relinquish all or only part of the territories. For many years the Israeli Labor party has supported variants of the principle of territorial compromise. It was part of the abortive September 1982 Reagan plan for the Middle East, and its acceptance by all parties—in practice this means Israel, since it has the territory and since one of its governing parties, the Likud, rejects the concept of territory for peace—was made a precondition of the 1988 Shultz plan. The essence of the concept is simple, though its details are immensely complex: In exchange for a decisive and permanent change in Israel's political relations with its neighbors—under the Shultz plan, Jordan and some entity embracing the Palestinians—Israel would be expected to relinquish some unspecified portion of the occupied territories. How much, where, and with what guarantees are points that so far have not been settled.

By contrast, the concept of autonomy, like the basic step-by-step method, is a recognition of stalemate, a concession to the limited tractability of conflict. It does not rule out a compromise on territory but rather provides a means for

getting there—or to some other goal—that is more practical than immediately trying to resolve such a contentious matter. As formulated in the Camp David accords, autonomy for the West Bank and Gaza would provide an interim stage before negotiations on the final status of the territories. It is a device premised on some possibility of political change or, from a more pessimistic viewpoint, on the calculation that a decision put off by mutual agreement at least reduces the risks of war. The autonomy concept has assumed that a final settlement between Israel and the Palestinians is not now possible. Indeed, if the question "Who owns the West Bank?" were posed, each party would assert that its claim was absolute.

Under this approach, it is assumed that attitudes might change if the Israeli-Palestinian relationship were changed from the current one of occupier and occupied, especially if many of the practical functions of daily life were ceded to the Palestinians and most evidences of Israeli rule were removed. If, after a period of years, the same question were posed, a more productive answer might emerge.

The autonomy concept as embodied in the Camp David accords, however, has seemingly been discredited. As its limited promise turned to failure, it became a symbol for the Arab countries, save Egypt, of all that was wrong with the peace process, the U.S. role in it, and ideas that did not permit a full partnership for the Palestine Liberation Organization (PLO), which, by agreement reached at the 1974 Arab summit in Rabat, Morocco, is the "sole legitimate representative of the Palestinian people."

Yet this attitude should not be accepted as the last word. After all, rejecting the concept of autonomy —or more broadly, of any half-measure adopted in the hope that more can be achieved later—does nothing to create new peaceful alternatives, inspire greater political flexibility, relieve human suffering, or fulfill any party's aspirations. There are further reasons for trying to revive the autonomy concept. The Camp David accords still stand alone in that they were signed face to face by Israel and an Arab state and were not later rescinded. Unlike the armistice agreements of 1948–1949 and the disengagement agreements of the mid-1970s, the Camp David accords did not come from so-called proximity talks or shuttle diplomacy that connoted a restricted political legitimacy. That fact must not be belittled in the urge to craft something new; nor must the fact that the document binds both the Egyptian and the Israeli governments.

The staying power of rejection cannot be assumed because of the past either. For Israelis and Palestinians face a special political phenomenon. They both have been unable to take existence for granted, and therefore they have not been able to speculate about hypothetical questions. In a psychology that is not nurtured on confidence in the existence of possibilities, such questions have no meaning; they are vacuous. Thus few Israelis could have said that they would transfer the Sinai peninsula to Egypt in exchange for peace until they were confronted with that palpable choice. Today even fewer Palestinians could say that they would accept autonomy —or some other half-measure—in the absence of a demand to choose

between change and the status quo. The autonomy negotiations of 1979–1982 were cramped by so many factors, including Israel's progressive creation of West Bank settlements, that they never approached the point where a clear-cut, take-it-or-leave-it choice was offered to either party.

FAILINGS OF THE SHULTZ PLAN

It is doubtful that any peace-making diplomacy had a chance to succeed in 1988, a year marked by elections in both the United States and Israel. But in assessing its position within the region and among its allies, the United States could not fail to respond to the *intifada* and the ensuing confusion within Israel. Inaction could have further damaged America's faltering reputation for leadership in Arab-Israeli peacemaking and left the field totally open to the counsels of despair. By contrast, diplomacy, however inauspicious, could prepare the way for new governments in Washington and Jerusalem.

Yet there was more courage in launching the Shultz plan than clear sense in its crafting. Its minor failing was in setting an agenda with an elaborate set of interlocking parts that required negotiations at an unparalleled pace and against the ticking clock of the Reagan administration's final months. This was an error in a region where time, politically, is considered infinite and haste is used by others to manipulate those who advocate it. Nonetheless, a well-ordered plan could develop its own timing, extending past artificial deadlines into the next U.S. administration.

Far more serious misjudgments were two of the plan's substantive

proposals: setting acceptance of a territorial compromise as a precondition for talks rather than as a possible, even preferred, outcome, and opening the way to active Soviet participation in the process. The former had an inhibiting effect within Israel; the latter represented an unproductive concession to the Soviet Union.

Some compromise on territory is almost certainly a necessary element of a lasting peace. Yet requiring Israel to accept this outcome as a precondition for the peace process made negotiations more difficult by prejudicing domestic debate—in this case, favoring the Labor bloc under Foreign Minister Shimon Peres over the Likud leadership of Prime Minister Yitzhak Shamir. Likud argued that an issue to be negotiated was being transformed into a pre-emptive Israeli concession. Even if Israel thereby gained implicit recognition by Palestinian and Jordanian partners in negotiations, the outcome would be foreordained. It was not surprising, therefore, that this condition became more important as a factor in Israel's partisan politics than as a spur to peacemaking. It had the further liability of deepening Hussein's skepticism that Israel would formally embrace the peace process, and he had to confront the fact of stalemate. He responded accordingly in July.

The Shultz plan also accepted direct Soviet involvement in the peace process. This had happened before—at the Geneva conference in 1973 and for a few days in October 1977. But in both cases Moscow's role was soon rendered unnecessary by the diplomacy of others. By 1987, however, Soviet participation in an international conference had become a settled point as far as Jordan and the Israeli Labor party were concerned, and that became a further point of contention in Israel.

Including the Soviets rested on the theory that Hussein needed a special set of political circumstances to engage in direct negotiations with Israel. Not only did he need the PLO's blessing to include, within a Jordanian delegation, Palestinians who would not automatically be rejected by Israel because of PLO membership, but he also had to have insurance that he would not be fatally exposed to the opposition of Syria and perhaps others. The answer lay in convening an international conference, a diplomatic "umbrella," to include regional parties plus outsiders, among which would be the Soviets. Once involved, they would be expected to discipline Hussein's enemies.

Jordan's effort to gain political insurance was at odds with classic Soviet policy toward the Arab-Israeli conflict, perhaps best summarized by the slogan "No war, no peace." Under Mikhail Gorbachev, to be sure, Soviet policy toward the Arab-Israeli conflict has altered visibly. Moscow has talked about the importance of peace to its overall orientation toward the Middle East. It has engaged in elaborate diplomacy with Israel that could lead to a renewal of diplomatic relations, which Moscow severed at the time of the Six-Day War. And in 1988 the Soviet leadership publicly distanced itself from both Syria and the PLO on some Arab-Israeli issues. Some observers believed that the Soviet Union would lead these two obdurate parties to change their stance on peacemaking. By late 1988, however, that goal was still well out of reach.

Yet even those diplomats and experts who have favored a Soviet role differ on what form it should take. By one formula, the Soviets would join the United States in an opening ceremony and then withdraw permanently, leaving all practical bargaining to regional parties and the Americans. Shamir, a strong opponent of giving the Soviets a chance to isolate Israel, was prepared to give his conditional approval to this idea. A variant earned support in the Shultz plan: The U.N. secretary general would call a conference that would include the permanent Security Council members. It would "not be able to impose solutions or veto agreements reached" by subsidiary negotiations, and only parties that accepted Israel's right to exist and renounced violence and terrorism could take part. By a contrasting formula favored by Moscow and its allies, a conference would do more than simply launch subsidiary negotiations—for example, among Israelis, Palestinians, and Jordanians over the West Bank and Gaza it would retain plenary powers for review and ratification.

The distinctions were significant. The first two approaches would have given Hussein just enough of an umbrella to get him and the Palestinians talking to Israel. In the process, Israel would have gained implicit recognition from face-to-face negotiations. The other approach would have given the Soviets and their regional allies continuing veto power.

In 1988 the prevailing view behind U.S. diplomacy was that the process, once started, would concede to Israel the central point of face-to-face negotiations and would gain such momentum that the Soviet Union could not pre-

serve a blocking position. Further, once the USSR acceded to any form of negotiations involving Israel and an Arab partner, it would burn some bridges with the rejectionist Arab states even if it did not press Syria and the PLO to be more flexible. The Soviet Union would be seen to be in the peacemakers' camp.

This idea takes much on faith. Inevitably, the most tangible concessions in any negotiations about territory would have to come from Israel. But with a role to play through a conference with continuing powers, the Soviet Union could take positions strongly favoring the Arab side and attempt to isolate the United States and Israel. Depending on the issue, Washington and Jerusalem could become isolated even from America's West European allies. Because of larger issues on its global diplomatic agenda the Soviet Union might not take this approach; but the opening would be there.

THE WAY FORWARD

These flaws in the Shultz plan, which Hussein's actions underscored, ended any chance that it would succeed. The next U.S. administration will have to devise a new approach to the region. Its task will be more difficult because a major element in all previous negotiating successes is absent— the willingness of Israel and at least one Arab partner to accomplish something together. This calls for American caution but not passivity.

New administrations at their outset are often tempted to launch new diplomatic initiatives—almost acting for the sake of acting. Yet in the Arab-Israeli conflict, every word is weighed by all sides, and the U.S. role is dissected by everyone. So American ideas must be crafted and presented with great care and not be offered on a take-it-or-leave-it basis. In those negotiations that have succeeded, the United States has generally put forward ideas to help break diplomatic logjams only after being asked to do so by Israel and its Arab negotiating partner.

Nevertheless, America's influence in Arab-Israeli diplomacy must not be underestimated. Even following an administration that abstained from peacemaking for most of its existence, every party to the conflict will still look to Washington for leadership. Indeed, the very act of U.S. engagement stirs anticipation that circumstances will be transformed. Under the right conditions it can create incentives for the local parties to try something new. It is doubtful that the late Egyptian President Anwar el-Sadat would have ventured to Jerusalem if U.S. President Jimmy Carter had not been actively involved in Arab-Israeli peacemaking early in his administration. As that example illustrates, negotiations do not have to end where they seem headed at the beginning: Bargaining among the regional parties under American prodding can at times transform the political environment. And that, after all, is the message behind the idea of autonomy.

To be valued as a negotiator the next administration must begin by earning the trust of all the parties to a future settlement. This could be its most difficult task, especially in the face of the deeply held views on all sides. Trust must be earned in a way that progressively brings

parties into the process without driving out others.

Several initial steps should be adopted as general principles. These are heavily focused on U.S.-Israeli relations. But this focus is indispensable if the United States is to help create a political and psychological basis for productive negotiations. The supreme task will be to develop America's relationship with Israel without ending its ability to deal effectively with key moderate Arabs. Five steps are most important:

• The U.S. president must develop a secure political base at home. He must convince congressional leaders and major interest groups that he is embarked on a deliberate, well-considered effort to pursue a settlement. The first test, both at home and in the region, will be to make a firm commitment to Israel's security against external threats, including an attack by Syrian ballistic missiles. Critics of the American relationship with Israel fault this proposition, but it carries great weight. Not only should there be a deep-seated U.S. commitment to Israel's existence and future, but also there can be no psychological capacity in Israel to be engaged in a peace process unless this commitment is unimpeachable.

• The United States must reiterate the impossibility of an imposed peace. That does not preclude inducements to act. Rather, it means that peace must emerge from face-to-face negotiations and that it must be ratified by the involved regional parties. The political and cultural character of the conflict means that a settlement will last only if it becomes embedded in

the politics and societies of the countries taking part, as has been happening between Egypt and Israel. No armed truce supervised by outsiders can suffice.

• The United States must make clear that it will continue honoring the pledge it gave to Israel in September 1975 concerning the role of the PLO: It will "not recognize or negotiate with the Palestine Liberation Organization so long as the Palestine Liberation Organization does not recognize Israel's right to exist and does not accept Security Council Resolutions 242 and 338." For Israel to join in any viable peace process, its legitimacy must be beyond question, even if the configuration of its post-1967 borders is not.

During 1988, PLO Chairman Yasir Arafat and other PLO leaders sought to broaden their base of support internationally and to recapture and then sustain political leadership over events in the West Bank and Gaza. Thus in June, Bassam Abu Sharif, a principal adviser to Arafat, spoke of "points on which [Israelis and Palestinians] are in almost total agreement." He personally accepted a number of key principles, including lasting peace and security, nonbelligerence, direct talks between the parties, the unacceptability of an imposed peace, and—with conditions—Resolutions 242 and 338. However, this position did not gain formal PLO approval. Likewise, the PLO moved toward declaring an independent Palestinian state and creating a provisional government. In theory, this would be implicit acceptance of Israel as a separate and legitimate entity. Yet by grounding this idea in the 1947 U.N. partition plan for Palestine that provided for a truncated Israel, the PLO raised new doubts about whether it would accept Israel, even within pre-1967 borders.

Discussions among PLO leaders may yet lead to acceptance of U.S. conditions. But unless that happens, unambiguously, the United States should continue its current policy. Nor should it deal with any form of self-proclaimed Palestinian government, which would not be the product of direct negotiations between the parties and thus would not advance the peace process.

• Any U.S. diplomatic effort must begin in Israel, with the new administration reiterating political, economic, and strategic commitments and with close consultations on peace-making strategy. The latter part of this argument is often faulted as providing a veto to Israel on the course of negotiations, but that critique misses the point: Israel, which occupies the territories in dispute, inherently has a veto over any negotiating progress, as much psychologically as politically. By beginning its Middle East consultations in Jerusalem the United States will build trust that it can use to help shape Israeli policies.

• Finally, the United States must establish its credibility with moderate Arab leaders, beginning in Egypt, Jordan, and Saudi Arabia. It must show that it takes seriously the parallel Camp David pledge to the "legitimate rights of the Palestinian people and their just requirements." The first demonstration of its commitment will lie in active and continuing involvement, seeking to push forward the peace process rather than standing on the sidelines. In 1989 the United States should encourage Israel to

accept a central point: If Israel is to find a valid interlocutor able to negotiate on behalf of the Palestinians—an interlocutor it finds more attractive than the current leadership of the PLO—then West Bank leadership must have an opportunity to gain legitimacy.

For more than 20 years Israel has faced a dilemma: Should it permit indigenous leadership to emerge and risk seeing it turn toward the PLO, or should it squelch the leaders who do emerge, thus consolidating the PLO's grip on the territories and reducing even further the chances for a settlement? Through violence and intimidation the PLO has also worked against the emergence of local leadership. The *intifada* had made Israel's dilemma worse. Israel can no longer preside peacefully over the territories. It faces unpleasant choices that are compounded by Hussein's self-imposed exile from the peace process: mass expulsions of Palestinians to Jordan proper, which would trigger a major international crisis, if not a war; a continuing, festering internal conflict, which would damage Israel's image internationally and pervert its politics domestically; or some process of reconciliation with Palestinians prepared to take part.

It cannot be easy for Israel to risk allowing local leadership to rise on the West Bank. It is burdened with a choice far more intense now than at any other time since 1967. The possibility of finding an authentic and legitimate negotiating partner has appeared, but so have the risks that the PLO will still predominate and that Israel will lose control without advancing toward peace and acceptance.

That decision must rest in Jerusalem, not in Washington or elsewhere. In 1989, however, the United States should consult with Israel on this point. As a general principle it should seek an end to the expulsion of Palestinians from the West Bank; and it should urge Israel to test whether local leadership is prepared to enter into a peace process, however tentatively and indirectly at the outset, rather than simply follow obstructionist PLO elements. There may be no Palestinian response; indeed, in late 1988 it still appears most unlikely. Israel must retain the capacity to retreat, and the process must be leading clearly toward formal negotiations. These would preferably be based on the Camp David concept of "full autonomy," which provides significant incentives to the Palestinians.

It is also important to set limits on the U.S. role in peacemaking. It is incorrect to assert that the United States can achieve movement only by pressuring Israel—at the extreme, making hostage to Israeli flexibility either America's aid or its security commitment. Such an outcome could be fatal to any peace process, precisely because the U.S. commitment to Israel's survival and security must be unquestioned. That does not mean that Israel should be the sole determinant of "security." Indeed, when the U.S. commitment is clear, it can debate the means chosen and the goals sought, as happened when Israel invaded Lebanon in 1978.

The proper U.S. role should be to help create conditions for Israel and other parties that will offer choices promising better circumstances. This can entail doggedly reworking matters of substance, constantly cajoling to think afresh, probing for possibilities, and simply staying in the fray however difficult it becomes. The result could be characterized as "pressure" in the sense that taking risks that have enormous consequences is highly stressful, however desirable the goal.

Even if the United States follows this course, it is not certain that any Arab partner will come forth, nor even that Israel will coalesce around a single negotiating position or goal. Yet the United States must attempt to build confidence —in itself, in the process, and ultimately by the regional parties in one another—without which there will be no diplomatic settlement.

Following an initial review, the new president should therefore appoint a special emissary for the Arab-Israeli conflict who should, on his first trip, reassure both Israel and moderate Arab leaders and engage in cautious "fact finding." Several presidents have taken this step, with mixed results. Yet in an environment of such deep conflict, among parties so entrenched in their respective positions, the United States can be effective only if it conveys seriousness of purpose. A level of U.S. diplomatic representation appropriate for Africa or Latin America will not suffice. Further, any settlement will very likely entail continuing U.S. participation that potentially involves both money and security. That can only be pledged by the highest U.S. political authority, and the secretary of state must balance the constant demands of Arab-Israeli peacemaking with his other priorities.

Sending a special presidential envoy will raise expectations that can then be dashed, leaving hopes for diplomacy even worse off than before. Yet it is also true that the United States will be judged within the region by the new president's decision on a peacemaking role. Failed attempts could further degrade U.S. standing, but so could inaction. Moreover, dispatching an envoy cannot substitute for engaging the president personally. If a president accords a high priority to Arab-Israeli peacemaking, he must understand the demands on his own time. U.S. negotiators must be able to count on his active engagement from time to time.

THE SOVIETS: IN OR OUT?

In addition, the new president must consider the Soviet Union's role. The principal motive for involving the Soviets, to provide an umbrella for Jordan, no longer applies. Yet Moscow continues to bid for entry.

This issue is bound up with the broader state of U.S.-Soviet relations. There is now an opportunity not only to stabilize the superpowers' basic strategic relationship, but also to reduce the risk that regional conflicts will lead to confrontations that neither wants. Nevertheless, U.S.-Soviet competition for power, position, and influence has not ended. It remains difficult partly because of the new flexibility and deftness of Soviet diplomacy under Gorbachev. The United States will need to choose wisely where to engage the Soviets and where to keep its distance. In

the Middle East the superpowers have a mutual interest in preventing another Arab-Israeli conflict and in trying to constrain the arms race. But the value of involving Moscow in peacemaking is much more problematical.

Excluded, the Soviet Union could play a spoiler's role. Yet if the Soviets were faced with a U.S. diplomacy more determined than anything seen over the past 8 years, it is not clear what more they could do to block progress than is now evident in actions by their regional clients, Syria and the PLO. By contrast, seeking Moscow's participation in the peace process assumes that it would be willing to pursue Syrian and radical PLO accession to a settlement. Understandably, it has not been prepared to embrace this necessary goal so far. The rejectionist parties do not naturally take their lead from Moscow. They have looked to Moscow precisely because it has served their interests; that, not peacemaking, has been the basis of Soviet influence in the region. Thus Moscow is unlikely to adopt a peacemaking agenda compatible with that of the United States, or, if it did, to be able to deliver its client states.

Nor does the Soviet Union have much to offer either Israel or the moderate Arab states that would make it an effective peacemaking competitor with the United States —provided, of course, that the latter takes seriously its responsibilities in the region. Indeed, Hussein sought a Soviet umbrella only after the United States had removed itself from active peacemaking.

The U.S. goal should be to create conditions that make the Soviet

Union eager to take part in a peace process that promises some success, rather than courting Soviet involvement or appealing to it to join, without cost, as an equal partner. Throughout the Middle East the latter approach would be read as a major shift in the strategic and political equation. At the very least, before dealing the Soviets into the Arab-Israeli peace process the United States should test their attitudes and motives. This should include the restoration of Soviet-Israeli relations. Also important will be Soviet statements and actions that show a desire to reduce the risks of conflict, particularly in the USSR's arms supply relationship with Syria; that convey irrevocable determination to promote peace; that embrace a practical peacemaking agenda; and that demonstrate a desire to pursue influence in the Arab world on a basis other than rejectionism. So far, Moscow has resisted crossing this threshold.

Likewise, the United States should be chary of seeking joint superpower guarantees of an Arab-Israeli settlement. In Afghanistan the United States achieved legitimacy for its interests in a country bordering on both the Soviet Union and vital states of Southwest Asia. To accord a similar status to the Soviets in the Middle East could be justified only if the United States were unable to play an effective role by itself and if U.S. interests would be irremediably damaged without their assistance. That point surely has not yet been proved. Indeed, if U.S power and influence are not sufficient to provide guarantees for an Arab-Israeli settlement without Soviet involvement, then America's ability to act will be in jeopardy virtually everywhere.

These prescriptions for U.S. diplomatic action in the Middle East do not provide all the details—and deliberately so. A central ingredient of change—an Arab negotiating partner for Israel—does not now exist. Israeli politics lacks an adequate basis for peacemaking. Despite some renewed interest, Hussein remains outside the process. And there is no means apparent for confounding or converting Syria's role through any of the classic diplomatic instruments, from outright opposition to appeasement. Syria's current ambitions are not to be satisfied by virtually any peaceful outcome of the Arab-Israeli conflict. So here, too, the U.S. goal should be to advance Arab-Israeli peacemaking in a way that presents risks to Syria from abstention, not to seek—unrealistically—to gain Syria's blessing for efforts that can only cripple its pursuit of larger goals.

Some element of imprecision has virtue for another reason: The process itself can create the opportunities or prevent them from emerging. That is not a counsel of despair but a testament to the experience of earlier attempts to change the seemingly intractable.

During his first months in office the new U.S. president could face a situation characterized by one of three broad descriptions, in descending order of hopefulness and ascending order of danger:

• political changes on the ground that slowly are transforming the prospects for Israeli-Palestinian accommodation, a sort of spontaneous Camp David;

• a continuing stalemate because of political paralysis in Israel, the collapse of possibilities for an indigenous leadership in the West Bank and Gaza that is prepared to live and work with Israel, or initiatives by the PLO that reinforce its claims to Palestinian allegiance without making the commitments required for it to become a valid interlocutor for either the United States or Israel; or

• a stalemate complicated by continued violence in the occupied territories and Israeli crackdown, an intensified regional arms race, and a breakdown of chances for diplomatic change.

The new president must be prepared to respond to any of these possibilities. Unlike other periods of transition in the U.S. government, events in flux on inauguration day will be critical in determining the degree of U.S. involvement, its character, and its timing. Nevertheless, while tactics must remain flexible, the underlying principles set forth above will remain valid.

In 1989 the United States will not have the relative luxury of abstaining from Arab-Israeli peacemaking that the outgoing administration had 8 years ago. The new president's course will have a major impact on the prospects for strife or stability. In the past, sustained professional U.S. involvement has been critical to shaping the peace process. Whether that can still be true will be a key indicator, far beyond the issues in the Arab-Israeli conflict, of America's continuing ability to be an influential and respected power in the Middle East. ■

Plus Ça Change . . . in the Middle East

by Adam Garfinkle

Change in international politics is sometimes obvious, dramatic, even blunt as the collapse of the Romanian dictatorship in December 1989 attests. But in what used to be called the Levant, the relationship between the perception and reality of change is less clear. Sometimes a frenzy of activity is taken to indicate important new developments, and then nothing happens; how many times have our hearts been filled with optimism about new developments in the "peace process," only to wake up some days or weeks later scratching our heads and muttering philosophical phrases? At other times, however, important changes occur but few notice or understand them. Who knew at the time that bread riots in Cairo in January 1977 would lead Egyptian President Anwar es. Sadat to Jerusalem in November?

The Middle East has gone through many changes since the end of 1987. These months qualify as a form of accelerated experience, but the trick is to separate real changes from apparent ones. It isn't always easy.

THE INTIFADAH: TRUTH AND CONSEQUENCES

Let us start with the inception and continuation of the *intifadah,* which began in December 1987.

Basic press coverage of the uprising in the United States and in Israel focused on the details of the violence and reprisals for it.

Early analysis concentrated not surprisingly on why it began and why it did not end. A list of explanations was soon compiled, the more obvious being: a traffic accident in Gaza that most Arabs thought was no accident, followed by a blundersome Israeli approach to the funereal aftermath; and a hang glider assault by Palestinian guerrillas that left eight Israelis dead at a military camp near the Lebanese border, this following an Arab Summit in Amman that had pointedly ignored the Palestinian issue.

More obscure and less proximate causes, noticed by only a few observers outside of Israel, included: the trickled-down consequences of Israel's release in May 1985 of over a thousand convicted terrorists and criminals in exchange for three Israeli prisoners held in Lebanon; the example of civilian resistance to Israeli occupation shown the world by the Shiites of southern Lebanon; and PLO efforts to organize the youth of the refugee camps, led by Khalil al-Wazir in the 1984–86 period when its offices were allowed to function in Amman. Add to this Israel's televising of the Gaza disturbances near and far, i.e., to anyone with a television set; its premature use of jail terms and deadly force, the latter largely because of the Army's lack of training in police tactics; and it was easy to agree after the fact that a combustible critical mass had been present.

Then, in due course, the *intifadah* became a tactical problem: how to stop it without, or before, understanding it. Indeed, the discussion of tactics—or rather, the discussion of the Israeli and Palestinian discussions—dominated the U.S. press for months after the uprising showed signs of becoming protracted. Should Israel use truly massive force, as some Americans (and, though hard to prove, some Arab governments quietly) suggested, and avoid a local form of graduated response that actually gave incentive to Arab stone throwing and rioting? No, that jeopardized the "normal" behavior of the tens of thousands of Arab workers in Israel who, for all their chances to plant bombs and start fires, rarely did so. Besides, Israeli officers would probably refuse to issue such orders, and if they did, most Israeli soldiers would probably refuse to obey them.

Put all the protestors in jail? No, that only turns a fiery fourteen year-old into a revolutionary by putting him in contact with real terrorists.

Large scale deportation? Too sensitive with the American government, which vigorously condemned isolated cases of deportation for fear of the precedent it might set with so many on Israel's right-wing penumbra making noises about "transferring" the Arab population of Greater Israel.

The tactical problem was real, to be sure, but it was not the real problem. The real problem was, as

Adam Garfinkle is coordinator of the political studies program at the Foreign Policy Research Institute and a Contributing Editor to *Orbis,* the Institute's journal of world affairs.

Source: From *Jerusalem Quarterly,* No. 52 (Fall 1989).

Thomas Friedman captured it, that most Israelis and their American supporters had drifted off into an amnesic zone in which it was believed that a status quo that most everyone knew in their most private honesty to be untenable in the long run somehow became detached from real time. Time passed but the long run never arrived.

It took many long months for most Israelis—longer for some than for others—to recognize the *intifadah* for what it was: an assertion of Palestinian identity and a practical exercise in nation-building unlike anything the PLO had ever done in its entire history—and all this without firing a shot. Most important, such an exercise came about not because the occupation changed, but because the Palestinians changed.

As Ehud Ya'ari noted, the *intifadah* represents a war within a war. The outer war is the war against the Israeli occupation. The inner war, the one with the more serious long-range implications, is the war within Palestinian society that has variously displaced, intimidated, converted, silenced, or retired the old elite.[1] The generational shift in the territories has finally percolated to the level of community power and leadership, and it has caused momentous changes within Palestinian society. One of them is the rise of a political youth culture; as one Arab father put it: "It is a miserable life. I admit we are commiting suicide, but we cannot retreat. Our children want an end to the occupation and they are running the show. What are we going to tell them, we don't want independence? I would be degraded in the eyes of my children if I told them to stop."[2] That is what the *intifadah*

has really been about; it is because of a deeper sociological movement in Palestinian society twenty years in the making that the political character of the occupation changed.

The *intifadah* has also represented the power of an idea arising out of that social evolution. Before, Palestinians in effect conspired in their own subjugation. They no longer do; to use a Biblical phrase that Israelis understand well, the Palestinian "generation of the wilderness"[3] has died out, and their successors take a new view of their circumstances. The military occupation has now become normal—for a military occupation—because Palestinians are politically mobilized by an idea. And as the I.D.F. (Israeli Defense Force) has found out, an army can defeat another army, but an army, no matter how it is trained, cannot defeat an idea. This is what the Israeli high command and the Minister of Defense mean when they say, as they have ever more frequently in recent months, that there is no military solution for the *intifadah,* only a political solution.

As soon as all this began to be better understood, it produced in train a cascade of mostly erroneous conclusions in the West, the most important ones being that a fully independent Palestinian state was inevitable, and that the PLO would be the political inheritor of it. Does the *intifadah* mean that an independent Palestinian state—in fact rather than in fancy—is inevitable? No, it does not. Does it mean that the PLO's position generally is stronger? Not necessarily; it rather depends on what one thinks the PLO's "position" is.

On the other hand, the *intifadah* does mean that the Israeli occupation of the West Bank and Gaza will,

for as long as it lasts, be harder, more expensive, more violent, and more corrosive of Israeli society than it was before. This in turn means that when thoughtful Israelis complain about the absence of an "acceptable" Arab party with which to parley about Israel's eastern frontier, the meaning of "acceptable" is likely to undergo significant change in rough proportion to these increased costs.

Despite the current ascendancy of the Revisionist Likud wing within the Israeli government, this has already happened. In earlier days, Israel showed a willingness to talk with Palestinians approved by the PLO so long as they were not formally members of the PLO. These days that willingness is growing, as are the number of potential Palestinian interlocutors in this category. The number of semisurreptitious meetings between Israelis and PLO representatives have expanded exponentially. Regardless of how relations proceed between the U.S. government and the PLO, these meetings are certain to continue.

A KING'S GAMBIT

One man who understood the *intifadah* early on was the erstwhile King of Jordan—Hussein ibn Talal. The mobilization of a romanticized Palestinian vanguard was, after all, not something entirely new to him—between 1968 and September 1970 a similar phenomenon made life in the Hashemite Kingdom bitter and dangerous. As was the case nearly twenty years before, he understood this Palestinian mobilization to be dangerous, too.

Jordan is by almost all objective measures a weak state surrounded by stronger adversaries, but its pivotal position magnifies both its natural vulnerabilities and its leverage. Hussein has had ample practice over the years learning to exploit this leverage to minimize the vulnerabilities. In this regard, the main Hashemite problem, far more than Israel, has been radical Palestinian nationalism, which, from the days of the Mufti of Jerusalem half a century ago, has blocked Hashemite ambitions west of Jordan and often claimed its territory to the east. Hashemite kings have resolutely opposed an independent Palestinian state or a base for it and twice used force toward that end, once on the western side of the river in 1948 to prevent a state, once on the eastern side in the civil war of 1970–71 to prevent a base. Since then, the Hashemite monarchy has competed with the PLO for the loyalty of West Bank Palestinians in order to prevent the PLO from attaining an irredentist rump state there whose likely first victim would be not Israel but the Hashemite monarchy.

The King has worked carefully. Given the pandemonic nature of Arab nationalism and the largely Palestinian demography of Jordan, Jordan's control of Palestinian nationalism has required simultaneously accepting its legitimacy and limiting its power. For Hussein to have survived on his throne for 35 years, Jordan had to identify rhetorically with Palestinian aspirations in order to win allies among them and thus stabilize life in the Kingdom. Even while he simultaneously managed regime security and built a quiet, pragmatic relationship with Israel, the King also sought to "Jordanianize" the Palestinians, that is, to integrate them into the mainstream of Jordanian

society, giving them a stake in the prosperity and future of the country.

It is from such considerations that one can understand why the Jordanian government is a public booster of the PLO's legitimacy and why it recognized the "independent" Palestinian state. It is not because the King has affection for the PLO, but because he wants to shape its future in ways that make it less dangerous to Jordan. A genuinely moderate PLO would be an expression of Palestinian nationalism that Hussein could both live with and effectively co-opt, which is what he has been trying to do for years, and what he must do for the monarchy to survive after he is gone.

The *intidafah* has been a mixed blessing for Jordan in this regard. On the one hand, the development of an indigenous West Bank leadership has weakened PLO rejectionism and driven the PLO's basic postures in a direction that is benign for Jordan. On the other hand, the growth of the Palestinian national idea makes it harder to maintain the delicate balance of rhetoric and pragmatism within the east bank. This explains both why King Hussein did not *like* the *intifadah,* and why he acted publicly as though he did. His real attitude toward the *shebab* in the territories was probably similar to his grandfather's attitude toward the rank-and-file of the Arab revolt in 1936. As 'Abdallah put it then: "We are not concerned anymore with organized bands but with certain elements from the lower strata of the population. My opinion is that these have gone mad like a man bitten by a rabid dog. How can you negotiate intelligently with crazy people?"[4]

With Israeli television broadcasting the stone throwing and the reprisals on a daily basis, Hussein worried that the disturbances would spread to the east bank. One of the first things Jordan did after the uprising showed signs of lasting was to arrest 23 Palestinians formerly involved with splinter PLO factions;[5] the second was to ban demonstrations supportive of the *intifadah*. The guard on the refugee camps was doubled.

So much for bedrock pragmatism. Next came public relations. To reduce his exposure to the rising tide of Palestinian emotion, Hussein announced on May 8, 1988 that he would not negotiate for the PLO, essentially telling the West Bankers that if they wanted the PLO, they could have the PLO, for all the good it would do them.[6] Then, on July 28, the King ended a highly touted development plan. Three days later, Hussein declared that Jordan was not Palestine and announced a dramatic severing of administrative links to the West Bank, an area that it had ruled for 18 years before the 1967 war.

And the reaction? Some, including rather desperately the Israeli Labor party (then in the midst of an election campaign) said that Hussein's move was merely "tactical." It was designed, futilely it was thought, to prod the PLO to more moderate positions and also to chastize ungrateful West Bankers, to whom the King gave his dollars at the kissing booth without ever getting kissed. But, they insisted, the King didn't—couldn't have— meant it. Others insisted that this time the King wasn't being coy, and soon the chorus of common knowledge within the American prestige press assumed curtly that the Jordanian Option in all its forms was dead.[7]

Both reactions were marred by an inappropriate either/or approach and missed the basic point. King Hussein cannot ignore developments in Palestinian politics any more than Yasir Arafat can ignore Jordan. Hussein knows that Jordan's demography and economy tilt toward being Palestinian; Arafat knows there are more Palestinians in Jordan than anywhere else in the world. As always, what happens on one side of the river influences what happens on the other side. In this, nothing essential has changed in recent years. A total severance of Jordan's links to the West Bank was out of the question. Jordan's formal severing was accompanied by some real severing, but most basic relationships persisted or were put into escrow. A few have since been resumed. The bridges across the Jordan stayed open, trade continued under selective impediments, the banks and courts worked, and Jordan's currency, passports, and most professional licenses remained valid, albeit in adumbrated form with respect to passports, which became two-year "travel documents." Some development funds still flow. The Cairo-Amman bank branches have remained open, and a new branch started in Gaza.[8]

Besides, if the King had wanted a real "divorce" from the West Bank, he could have abrogated the 1950 "union" agreement, which is the legal basis in the Jordanian context for its claim to the West Bank, but he did not. He could have reorganized the parliament instead of delaying new elections until November 1989. He could have formally suspended West Bankers' Jordanian citizenship, but he did neither.

Still something important has changed. The "Jordanianization" of the Palestinians over the years has not been easy, but it has worked well enough. Had it not, the monarchy would probably have lost the civil war in 1970–71, when most Palestinians either supported the government or stayed neutral. But since then, a new spirit of self-assertiveness among East Bankers has arisen, partly because East Bankers are better educated, more sophisticated, and more technically competent than they have ever been; Jordan does not "need" Palestinians in the same way that it used to need them.[9] Only on account of both of these changes could Hussein have done what he did in July without shattering the country's domestic peace. This is what was new, that Hussein could shout out loud, in the midst of the *intifadah,* that "Jordan is not Palestine," that it has a separate, prior agenda of its own. And while many Palestinians on the East Bank did not like it, there is not much that they could or really wanted to do about it, especially in the face of so many East Bankers who liked it very much. Today, the King worries more about the implications of being *too* closely associated with the mayhem on the West Bank, rather than of being not closely *enough* associated. This is a real change, and in this limited sense the monarchy has separated itself from the torments of the Palestinian issue.

The enhanced internal stability of the Kingdom, though far from perfect, allowed Hussein new tactics in the old Hashemite struggle with radical Palestinian nationalism. Hussein intended by his formal severing of the West Bank from Jordan to force the PLO into a decision, into a diplomatic posture (it was hoped) that would bring it closer to Jordanian interests and allies. Jordan offered incentives: the economic lure of confederation, access to Washington, perhaps help in establishing itself in the territories. But threats were more obvious. Jordan's disengagement implied gains for the United Leadership of the Uprising, which, rhetoric aside, the PLO viewed as a competitor. Also, almost completely unnoticed in the West, Jordan's withdrawal of financial resources constituted an effort to weaken the *intifadah.*[10]

While Arafat pondered the King's move, complaining of not having been informed of it beforehand, the PLO was relentlessly attacked by Jordanian officialdom to let everyone know just who had leverage over whom. For example, Interior Minister Raja'i al-Dajani restated old propaganda positions that seemingly had been left behind in King Hussein's July 31, 1988 speech:

> *We are a natural demographic and geographic extension of the West Bank, and they are an extension of us. We are one nation and one people. We do not allow anyone to bargain over us. . . . We are one people regardless of what is said. His Majesty King Husayn stressed this and was careful to highlight it.*[11]

Next, Dajani baited Arafat, questioning his judgment by disclaiming any conflict of interest between Jordan and the PLO, but then mentioning immediately thereafter Jordan's 1972 United Kingdom plan, which, to the PLO, is shorthand for

Jordanian predations. "The PLO's problem," he said,

is that they have a complex that Jordan is competing with them. . . . Jordan is not competing with the PLO over the West Bank, and we have no designs on or interests in the West Bank. It is in our interests that the Palestinian Arab people return, and that the Palestinian land be returned to the Arab nation and Arab order. When this happens, we will congratulate you. Yasir 'Arafat had a complex that this talk was untrue and that we wanted to cheat him and go to the international conference. Is it possible that Jordan, going to the international conference with such international legitimacy, should come away empty-handed? Naturally, for us this was out of the question, and there are many clear Jordanian approaches, one of which is the United Arab Kingdom plan.[12]

Nor was Dajani finished. To express Amman's anger at the PLO's contempt for Jordan, voiced frequently from its radio station in Baghdad from the outset of the *intifadah,* he said:

When you come and boast that you will pay their salaries, you mean that you will replace Jordan, which abandoned them. I can say that this is naive talk that shows lack of knowledge of the reality of things. I say and challenge that no one in the Arab world knows this and the nature of affairs in the occupied territories as Jordan does. There have been 40 years of merger

in this homeland in this part of the Arab world. . . . O Yasir 'Arafat . . . you want to pay the salaries that we used to pay as an assistance to the employees that receive their salaries from Israel; that is, you want to share power with Israel? Helping this people is considered by the PLO as power sharing. I want to know what they will call the new reality, when Israel and the PLO pay salaries and assistance. Will they call it sharing power with Israel or assistance? Here, things will become clear, and we will see what will happen to the names and headlines that were given as part of the campaign against Jordan—power sharing, relations of annexation, relations of subordination.[13]

The Jordanian campaign worked in record time; Hussein and Arafat met in Aqaba on October 22, 1988, less than two months after Hussein's dramatic announcement. Arafat agreed to coordinate strategy with Jordan, and the King announced himself fully satisfied with the results.[14] Arafat's deputy, Khaled al-Hassan, admitted that coordination between Jordan and the PLO "was a necessity that can't be ignored,"[15] a plain admission both that the PLO could not go it alone and that needing Jordan carried a price "to be determined." Afterwards, Arafat took to speaking of raising the Palestinian *and the Jordanian* flags over a "liberated" Jerusalem, an indication that the King and Arafat were moving toward a firmer understanding.[16] Indeed, from Arafat's perspective, it may well be that the primary value of the "independent Palestinian state," then under

heated discussion within the PLO, was and remains its use as symbolic leverage in his eventual journey to Canossa, to Hussein.

Jordan has much that the PLO needs: international legitimacy, connections, a quiet relationship with Israel and a good one with the United States, infrastructure and access to the West Bank. But the one thing Jordan does not have—legitimacy on the West Bank—the PLO does. One way to perceive the Jordanian-PLO relationship is as a bartering process; each is trying to get from the other what it most needs by giving up as little as possible of what it has.

So, Jordan is not Palestine, but it is. Jordan does not compete with the PLO, but it does. Jordan leaves the West Bank to the PLO, but it does not. Even the basic question—whether Jordan will or will not negotiate over the West Bank—is not so clear. Hussein put it cleverly, and more than once: he will not negotiate over the West Bank, not unless the Palestinians ask him to do so, that is. But, all Palestinians, or just some Palestinians? If some, how many, and which ones? Hussein doesn't say—a formula that allows a reassertion of the Hashemite voice in the West Bank under any number of circumstances.

In a way, what the Jordanians did in the summer of 1988 cannot be completely undone. Some of it is irreversible—if not administratively, then psychologically. But then again, the process of Palestinian state building is to some extent irreversible, too. Whether one calls Jordanian policy tactical or not is beside the point; such a vocabulary cannot do justice to a situation in which Jordan and the PLO are essentially allied against Israeli occupation of the West Bank, but in which Israel and Jordan are essentially allied against the PLO's gaining control of it if and when Israel leaves.

What matters for now is that the King has concluded that the dangers of a titularly independent Palestinian state are less than a confederated arrangement along the lines of a "United Kingdom" plan, and that only the former is feasible nowadays anyway. This does *not* mean that the King cares any less about the Jordanian role in the West Bank. It does mean that the directness and the instruments of Jordanian influence look much different from those in the classical Jordanian Option scenario of 1968–71, or the abridged United Kingdom one of 1972–74, or the even more abridged "confederation" one of 1975–86. That, in turn, and ironically, means that any Jordanian reassumption of influence and authority will have to be coordinated that much more closely with Israel in order to make sure that any small "Filastin" does not "get out of hand."

THE PLO IN ALGIERS

Hussein put the PLO in a bind over the West Bank; he gave it responsibility without power. The Jordanian disengagement was designed in large part to drive the PLO either toward irrelevance or toward a West Bank constituency. It did the latter.

It was the King, in essence, who established the agenda of the November 1988 Algiers Palestine National Council meeting, the failure of which would have meant another intra-PLO civil war, openly in Lebanon—and perhaps elsewhere

as well, in the guise of competitive terrorism. Such a spectacle, going on simultaneously with the *intifadah,* might have sped the PLO's path to historical oblivion. Sobered by such fears, the PNC struggled to avoid self-destruction, and succeeded, barely.

Theirs was not an enviable predicament. If the PLO had "accepted" the West Bank from Jordan only to terrorize Israel more effectively, the residents of the territories would have suffered most, and the PLO would have failed. Hussein risked little because there was no chance that the PLO as constituted before Algiers could achieve even Arab support for an independent state in the West Bank, let alone achieve the state. A rejectionist approach would have reminded everyone that the only way to end the occupation was through Jordan, and the King would then have been better able to revive his role in the territories at the PLO's expense. It is certainly true, as all the pundits said, that the King is not loved in the West Bank. But in the Middle East, it is better to be needed than to be loved, just as it is better to ask forgiveness than permission.

Still, it might be thought that Hussein should have feared pushing the PLO toward the leadership of the *intifadah,* which seemed then and seems now anti-Hashemite, radical, and self-identified with the PLO. But the King has been around too long to mistake appearances for realities. The King knows that the basic interests of most West Bankers diverge from those of the PLO—that the leadership of the "uprising," though full of bravado and stirring words, necessarily has a different and inherently more conciliable

perspective than the PLO's. Excluding those in refugee camps, West Bankers *are* home and want the Israelis to *go* home. PLO cadres for the most part think of their homes as being in Israel proper; they are *not* home, want to *go* home, and want the Israelis to go back to impossible places like Poland and Tsarist Russia. Just as PLO cadres care more about Jaffa (in Israel proper) than about Nablus (in the West Bank), those from Nablus care more about Nablus than about Jaffa. And this is why, not surprisingly, the PLO has developed firmer support in the refugee camps than in the towns and villages of the West Bank, because most of the refugees, too, think of their homes as being on the green side of the green (pre-June 1967) border.

For this reason, many West Bankers are ready for a two-state solution in perpetuity. But even those who are not are more moderate tactically, because they are the ones now under occupation who would be redeemed politically sooner rather than later. That is why the West Bank leadership, old and new, tends to be more flexible than that of even PLO "moderates." That is why, specific affinities aside, Jordan expects to be able to cooperate with it.

This meant that if the PLO decided to genuinely moderate its extremism in hopes of a lasting political compromise with Israel, then it would for the first time accept the residents of the West Bank and Gaza as its core constituency instead of Palestinians who will accept nothing less than a Palestine "from the river to the sea." But if the PLO opted for political compromise and for a primary West Bank constituency, it had to find a way to assume Jordan's considerable role in the West Bank and a way to pay for it. Further, to negotiate the peace, it had to convince America and Israel that its moderation was sincere. Hussein knew that none of these things would be easy; a "new" PLO would need Jordan's moderate credentials and international connections to help it administer the West Bank, talk to Washington, approach Israel, negotiate with it, and make peace with it. And Arafat knew that Jordan's help would carry a price the PLO as an organization would not easily agree to pay.

The problem for the PLO at Algiers, therefore, was how to avoid both being squeezed by Jordan and the leadership of the *intifadah,* and at the same time avoid (another) civil war in its own midst. The danger of self-destruction was real. Some PLO members, supported by prominent Arabs in the territories, wanted the PNC to declare an independent state and a government-in-exile. But others saw such tactics as invalidating PLO claims to all of Palestine. Given these differences and dangers, the challenge was to design a set of statements that would improve its standing in the territories—this meant that the PLO had to embrace the idea of a state in the West Bank and Gaza— but without implying that the PLO was giving up the right to struggle for all of Palestine. If it failed on the second count, Fatah would risk detaching the organization from its old core constituency and ceding it to its internal opposition, led by George Habash's Popular Front for the Liberation of Palestine, and even that emanating by proxy from Syria in the form of the

National Salvation Front. But Arafat could go no further than a state; a government-in-exile, in which the Unified Leadership of the Uprising was demanding at least half the seats, might transfer too much of its authority to the *intifadah* leadership. What the Leadership might eventually do with that authority, should they get their hands on it, was something no one could know; but most of the members of the rather self-interested PLO Executive Committee, which has since taken to referring to itself and only itself informally as a government, did not want to find out.

So, the PNC declared an independent Palestinian state and avoided naming a government-in-exile. It invoked resolutions 181 from 1947 and 242 from 1967, but neither was clearly interpreted and both were encumbered by an assortment of verbal mystifications and vagueness. PNC declarations were too much for some, too little for others. After the session, various Palestinian factions and interested Arab countries sought to put their own "spin" on what had happened. Taken together, the various explications of the document to different audiences, Arab and non-Arab, added up to a series of so many impossible contradictions that an honest observer could not have been faulted for suspecting deceit.

Some Western observers interpreted the PNC declarations as proof that the PLO had finally been impelled to genuine moderation; some hoped, and others assumed, that the PLO had expressed a tacit recognition of Israel. This represented a major breakthrough toward peace, or so went one current of the common wisdom.

The majority opinion, however, was different. Talk of a breakthrough was a chimera, said U.S. Secretary of State George Shultz, *The New York Times,* and most establishment opinion. Positive movement toward peace from the Palestinian side was judged modest. The PNC was viewed as another demonstration of Palestinian political paralysis shrouded in propaganda and aimed at the United States. The balance of the evidence, it was averred, suggested that the PLO still did not want peace with Israel; rather, it wanted a piece of the territory Israel controls today in order to destroy it in the future.

The analysis behind this conclusion was impressive. The PLO's movement toward tactical flexibility was driven by its fear that the leaders of the uprising in the territories might eclipse the PLO and, in time, use their new-found power to advance a political settlement that Arafat and company cannot control. And this fear was rendered an urgent problem by King Hussein's July surprise. But greater tactical flexibility did not imply real moderation; what the PLO did was to *posture* toward moderation rather than actually take a step. It leaned, rather than moved, in an attempt to simultaneously maintain a modicum of organizational consensus and give the appearance of change far beyond what that consensus allowed.

For a quarter century, the PLO's consensus has been based on a principled denial of Israel's right to exist, and its factional differences have been only about tactics. "Rejectionists" are the romantics, rejecting the legitimacy of Israel, claiming all of Palestine, trusting military means to achieve eventual victory, and seeing diplomacy as a snare. But most so-called moderates also reject the legitimacy of Israel and claim all of Palestine. They believe, however, that a diplomacy aimed at "liberation in stages" is a more realistic path to victory. This kind of "realism" became the PLO's formal strategy in 1974—the Phased Program. As far as anyone knows, it remains PLO policy today; it is not so easy to dismiss Israeli allegations that the organization has not changed its spots. In this approach, declarations such as those from the PNC are aimed more toward the United States, Israel's support, than toward Israel itself.

PLO factional differences also explain why the PNC affirmed United Nations resolution 242 only in the context of other UN resolutions, including the one that equates Zionism with racism. Resolution 242 has always been troublesome for the PLO, but not only or mainly because it refers to Palestinians as a "refugee problem." Because it speaks only of the occupied territories, the PLO has believed that accepting it amounts to giving up the right to struggle for Israel proper. The rejectionists still resist it for this reason.

The moderates finessed the problem in Algiers; the PNC's phraseology concerning 242 avoided mentioning Israel or delimiting any borders for their state. Thus, Arafat could (and did) tell rejectionists that since Zionism is racism and Israel is therefore not a "legitimate state," it has no ultimate rights under resolution 242, in which Israel is not mentioned by name. And he could (and did) tell credulous Europeans and Ameri-

cans just the opposite. Which is true?

The State Department's view, in November 1988, was that it did not matter because the PLO's incapacity to be clear reflected its incapacity to act boldly or consistently as an organization. Thus, while professing to see some progress, it preferred to assume that the maximalist aim to "liberate" all of Palestine remained, that Algiers had aimed not at peace but at gaining international legitimacy for a Palestinian state *without* changing the "historical illegitimacy" of Israel. It was this analysis that counseled withholding any public rewards to the PLO—including a visa for Arafat to come to New York to address the United Nations. But at the same time, the U.S. government gave private indications that it had an open mind about changing its mind if Arafat changed his.

This analysis and approach remain cogent, at least up to a point. There are many Palestinians who accept Israel as a fact of life, to be lived with—like the Crusaders of centuries past—until a change in the balance of power allows "the injustice" of Israel's creation to be put right. They are willing to accept *dharurah* with Israel—a truce born of *necessity*—but not *sulh,* not peace born of true conciliation. There are few Palestinians who accept the Jewish right to self-definition as a *people,* from which flows the right to self-determination. To most Arabs— although the exceptions are growing—Jews are either members of a religion or a race. If the former, Jews have no right to a state; if the latter, then anything Jews do politically is automatically

racist and hence illegitimate. This is the difference between "accepting" Israel and accepting Zionism; the former is imaginable under certain circumstances, but the latter is not. This is a little like agreeing to accept a collect telephone call on the condition that you can change the person on the other end of the line.

Even so, Palestinian conditional acceptance of Israel is progress, and conditional acceptance today could become a deeper form of conciliation tomorrow; not for the first time would a clever hypocrisy be the advanced wave of a new truth. Until real conciliation arises, there can be no real peace —only armed truces of varying duration. But truces are better than wars.

In short, what has been happening within Palestinian nationalism of late is neither an intellectual revolution nor simple trickery. The PNC did not change the fundamental tenet of the Palestinian rejection of Israel's *right* to exist as Israel chooses to define itself (Zionist); to the contrary, its verbal gymnastics confirmed it. Nothing that Arafat has ever said can be read as voiding this deep antipathy toward the legitimacy of Israel as a Zionist state. But, clearly, there are now three PLO approaches instead of only two: rejectionism, tactical moderation, and, for the first time, real moderation. No serious observer believes that this third approach is anything but a small minority. It is the great wager of U.S. foreign policy in recent years that the lure of U.S. diplomacy can enlarge it rapidly and meaningfully.

But there was another effect of the PNC, a significant and still underappreciated one, that sets a fair wind for the eventual success of the U.S. wager. Realistically, the Algiers PNC was only a very small step toward PLO moderation, but that was not how Palestinians in the territories interpreted it. Their almost universal interpretation of the PNC was that it overturned the maximalist program of the National Covenant, which was never mentioned in Algiers, and that itself is important. Most of those in the territories favored this development; some, associated with Hamas, the Muslim Brother's fundamentalist front, and Habash's PFLP supporters, did not. Nevertheless, this perception demonstrated that there is a real constituency for moderation and suggested that if the PLO does not embrace it, an alternative leadership from the territories one day might. It meant that the residents of the territories were far more concerned about translating the *intifadah* into some form of lasting political advantage —and far more ready to be realistic about compromise—than the PLO far away in Baghdad, Tunis, or Algiers.

Arafat has been forced by the *intifadah* and by Jordanian diplomatic maneuver to make decisions he has assiduously avoided for years. King Hussein deserves much credit for whatever modicum of progress there has been in the PLO's position since December 1987. The PLO has been pressed to a decision that Jordan and the United States had been trying to extract for years. This decision led in December 1988 to the opening of a U.S.-PLO dialogue on U.S. terms.

These were positive and important changes. But it is a measure of

how intractable the conflict really is that, despite these developments, the prospects for major movement toward a settlement are still slight.

LESSONS FOR THE UNITED STATES

Looking carefully at the *intifadah,* the Jordanian approach to it, and the PLO's response to both at Algiers can teach us many things. Perhaps the most important lesson is that it was and remains wrong to see the options before Israel and the United States as either negotiating with Jordan or negotiating with the PLO. Despite their important differences, both the PLO and Jordan have to be involved in any settlement or serious movement toward it; this is fact of life embedded in geography, demography, history, and the basic interests of the parties. The important questions, again, are not either/or questions, but these: (1) where is the center of gravity in the Jordanian-PLO relationship, (2) how stable is that center, and (3) what does it imply about the limits and nature of the concessions that the Arab side might wish and might be able to make? As we enter the 1990s, the answer to the first question is this: the center of gravity in the Jordanian-PLO relationship is moving back toward Jordan, but only after having previously moved far toward the PLO. And both Arafat and Hussein are looking over their shoulders at the West Bankers, who have perhaps moved into a position to decide the matter.

The answer to the second question is: not very stable at all; and therefore the answer to the third question is hard to know.

What is not hard to know is that the Jordanian-PLO struggle is not over just because the two sides find it in their interests these days to say that it is. From the Jordanian point of view, the struggle is no more over than a tree that sheds its leaves in winter is dead. The product of this struggle is unquestionably crucial to the peace process; if Jordan or its associates or the West Bank does not prevail, more or less, within it, there isn't much hope for peace in the near term. A cursory look at current PLO and Jordanian positions reveals why.

The PLO still spends most of its energy these days struggling to keep itself together. Precisely because there is no consensus on further change, the PLO insists that it will make no more concessions to Israel or the United States: no direct negotiations outside an international conference, no stopping the uprising, no joint delegation with Jordan, no cooperation with "autonomy" schemes.[17] So until there is proof to the contrary, we must assume that the PLO as an organization is still incapable of a genuine and significant moderation.

Paralysis often fosters illusion, and it is no different here. Arafat apparently thinks—as Sadat did for a time—that if he waits long enough, the United States will deliver Israel to him on the proverbial silver platter. He has been disarmingly explicit about this. He explained in January 1989:

The issues of the Iran-Iraq war, Afghanistan, Namibia, Cyprus, Central America, and Cambodia have either been resolved or are under discussion, except for the Palestine question, which has not come under discussion yet, this because of the Israeli stand rejecting peace. This stand is the result of unlimited U.S. support, which enables Israel to reject peace.

When asked if the American attitude will change in the Bush Administration, Arafat reminded his interviewer

... of the year 1956 when Eisenhower was able to impose peace on Israel and two major countries, the UK and France, after the Suez War. We hope the new U.S. administration will do what Eisenhower did.[18]

Now consider: Jordan's interests are the opposite of the PLO's in every case. Jordan supports the concept of direct negotiations; the King knows there can be no solution without them. The King wants to stop the uprising. He wants a joint delegation if he can get one, the better to control the Palestinian factor. Interim autonomy schemes, properly conceived, are not a bad idea because Hussein knows that the implementation on the ground of any such scheme requires use of Jordan's extensive private relationship with Israel and administrative ties to West Bank institutions. And, last of all, King Hussein is not under the impression that the United States will "deliver" Israel; no longstanding ally of the United States

could imagine Washington as capable of doing any such thing.

This is why Washington's aim in the U.S.-PLO dialogue has been to entice the PLO further into the nexus of Jordanian interests that are potentially compatible with (at least some) definitions of Israeli interests. The sagacious use of the U.S.-PLO dialogue became the key to ending the *intifadah* and propelling the peace process forward.

But the *intifadah* was all the PLO really had, that and its dialogue with Washington. The United States tried to make Arafat choose between the two, the vehicle of choice being Israeli Prime Minister Yitzhak Shamir's proposal to hold elections in the occupied territories.

At the very least, Shamir's proposal allowed the United States to affirm the basic idea that efforts on the ground in the occupied territories between Palestinians and Israelis were necessary to till the soil before the seeds of international negotiations could be planted. The U.S. aim was to focus the prenegotiating action on West Bank Palestinians in order to enlarge their diplomatic profile and political mandate, urge them toward pragmatic positions, and create a magnet that would draw Arafat and the PLO along behind.

This meant, in effect, that inevitable trouble between the United States and Israel would be put in escrow for a while. It was inevitable because Prime Minister Shamir's interest in the elections approach was to cultivate an alternative to the PLO and split the Palestinians. The U.S. interest was not to cultivate

an alternative to the PLO, but to move the PLO toward a more conciliable constituency. The empowerment of West Bank Palestinians was also designed, in effect, to set the agenda of the U.S.-PLO dialogue in Tunis. By operating the dialogue this way—keeping a channel open, but using it to press the PLO toward the more conciliatory attitudes of the West Bankers—Washington maneuvered well, but it also maneuvered unavoidably right into the steel jaws of Yitzhak Shamir, for whom the PLO was a permanent anthema.

Thus, despite its having some local Palestinian support in principle, an interim truce in the *intifadah* and the holding of elections proved to be tall orders. The Arab side, locally and from the PLO, rejected the Shamir proposal, and Shamir, for his part, seemed not to be terribly upset about it as U.S. pressures convinced many of his Likud colleagues that elections were a slippery slope leading to a Palestinian state. Bush Administration spokesmen refused to take no for an answer, however, dismissing the initial Palestinian response as posturing, or mere "station identification."

Privately, the administration recognized the severity of the problem: both sides—The Israeli and the Palestinian—were internally divided to the point that concessions were extremely difficult for either to make. But having created a stake in the forward movement of the process, the Bush Administration found itself applying pressure not always where it wished, but where it could—on Israel. This including supporting quietly most Palestinian positions on the disputed modalities of elections; namely that East Jerusalemites could vote but in the West Bank, that international supervision was possible, that a withdrawal of censorship regulations might be considered, and so forth. It meant changing more overtly the rhetoric of public diplomacy, as with Secretary James Baker's stunning speech to the American-Israel Political Action Committee on May 22, 1989. It meant forcing a discussion about long term matters at the outset of the process, largely as a temptation to the Arab side that elections could lead to qualitative changes if only they would participate in them.

At the same time, the administration took care not to give the Palestinians the impression that Bush was Eisenhower and that 1989 was 1956; this explains in part the vehement opposition of the United States to the PLO's attempt to enter the World Health Organization in the spring of 1989, and its opposition later in the year to PLO and Arab attempts to raise the PLO's profile at the United Nations.

As the election plan fell on hard times and ground increasingly to a slow crawl, President Hosni Mubarak of Egypt made a dramatic effort to save the day. In September, he put forth a ten point plan designed to bridge the differences between the antagonists. The plan included all those things that the Palestinian and Israeli sides could agree upon, and left out the issues on which they did not agree. A long, complicated process then ensued within Israel and within the Palestinian camp as to how to deal

with the Egyptian proposal. Neither wished to be the first to reject the idea, but both were too internally divided to risk accepting it. Then, to save Mubarak's ten points, U.S. Secretary of State James Baker introduced five points of his own. Still the sides balked, with both Israel and the PLO, working through Egypt, seeking side agreements or interpretations to Baker's plan. The effect of this devolution from the elections proposal to Mubarak's ten points, to Baker's five, and beyond that was not to eliminate the points of disagreement, but to try to obscure them sufficiently that the process would not obviously be seen to have failed. But by the end of 1989, despite progress toward an Israeli-Egyptian-U.S. meeting in February 1990, failure was obvious, even though too many commitments to the process had been made for anyone to plainly admit as much.

. . . THE MORE THINGS REMAIN THE SAME?

So, there have been changes lately, but not the ones most prominently imagined. The *intifadah* has revealed more about changes in Palestinian political culture than about the character of Israeli politics or the occupation. Those politics are essentially democratic, and that occupation is, as it always has been, ultimately inconsistent with that democracy. The *intifadah* did not teach us this, it only reminded us.

King Hussein *was* being coy in July 1988 and at the same time very serious about adjusting Jordan's relationship in accord with the relative strengths and weaknesses of Palestinian nationalism both inside

the territories and inside the East Bank. He was being tactical in a strategic sort of way, not opting out of the picture, but instead trying to redraw it or shade it to the best of his considerable ability.

The PNC was neither the herald of genuine PLO moderation nor a premeditated propaganda exercise. Rather, it reflected real dilemmas, real differences—and a real failure to resolve them in any definitive way. Withal, the PNC's effects on Palestinians' general attitudes have been more profound than its effects on the PLO as an organization or on its formal positions. Whether these new attitudes among the people will exert real political influence, only time can tell. The *intifadah* has already made obsolete the old forms of Israeli occupation and the old forms of local West Bank politics. If it makes the old politics of the PLO obsolete, too, then it will in the end have done some good.

The U.S. government was right to open a dialogue when he met longstanding U.S. conditions for that dialogue. The essential change was in the PLO's position, not the U.S. position. What is needed now is more of the same.

Bush Administration principals arguably made fine use of the space that Middle Eastern realities gave them. But they were unable to maneuver decisively. The key test was whether the West Bankers, whose conditions for holding elections were generally milder than those favored by the PLO, could win the day or not. They could not. Even had they succeeded, whether further maneuvering would have been enough to bridge the enormous enmities between the Jewish and Arab sides, or even between

Palestinians inside and outside of the territories, would not have been assured. Still, Washington got the basic approach right for once. The failure of a successful approach only reaffirms the truth that an American effort to bring about peace in the Middle East is a necessary, but not a sufficient, condition for success. For success, the local protagonists have to help, too. ■

Notes

1. Ehud Ya'ari, "Runaway Revolution," *Atlantic Monthly,* June 1988.
2. Quoted in Youssef M. Ibrahim, "Israeli Army Pushes Town to Hatred in West Bank," *New York Times,* March 15, 1989, p. 14.
3. *Dor ha-midbar* is the transliteration from Hebrew.
4. Ladislas Farago, *Palestine on the Eve* (London: Putnam, 1936), p. 266.
5. See Ihsan A. Hijazi, "23 Palestinians Seized by Jordan; Plot to Subvert Regime is Charged," *New York Times,* January 25, 1988, p. A9; and Geraldine Brooks, "Jordan's King Deflects Unrest at Border," *Wall Street Journal,* May 10, 1988, p. 35.
6. See Alan Cowell, "Hussein Seeks to Placate Palestinians," *New York Times,* May 9, 1988, p. A3.
7. Two examples include Arthur Hertzberg, "This Time, Hussein Isn't Being Coy," *The New York Times,* August 9, 1988, p. 19; and Trudy Rubin, "Hussein's Had Enough of West Bank Mess," *The Philadelphia Inquirer,* October 11, 1988.
8. See "Cairo-Amman Bank Branches to Remain Open," *Al-Ra'y,* in FBIS-NE, August 10, 1988, p. 27; " 'Some' West Bank Projects Reportedly To Continue," Abu Dhabi, *Al-Ittihad al- Usbui'i,* in FBIS-NE, September 27, 1988, p. 25; and "Cairo-Amman Bank to Open Branch in Gaza," Dubayy, *Al- Bayan,* in FBIS-NE, September 28, 1988, p. 5.
9. Of course, the other side of this new consciousness on the east bank is that the King cannot take East Bankers' political passivity for granted, as was shown by the riots in the south of the country in April 1989.
10. For some details, see David Rosenberg, "Jordan Cuts Farm Import Quota from West Bank," *The Jerusalem Post,* January 19, 1989, p. 8. A more general source for how the intifadah funds itself may be found in an article by Avinoam bar-Yosef in *Ma'ariv,* January 13, 1989, pp. 1, 2.
11. Dajani's remarks are to be found in *Al- Ra'y,* September 10, 1988, in FBIS-NE, September 14, 1988, pp. 27–32.
12. Ibid.
13. Ibid.
14. See Alan Cowell, "Arafat Confers With Hussein on Ending Split," *New York Times,* October 23, 1988, and Alan Cowell, "Parley in Jordan Is Said to Narrow Split with P.L.O.," *New York Times,* October 24, 1988.
15. See Alan Cowell, "P.L.O. Appeals to Israelis to Vote the 'Peace Choice'," *New York Times,* October 25, 1988.
16. "Flags Hoisted; 'Arafat Speaks," Amman Television Service, January 7, 1989, in FBIS-NE, January 9, 1989, p. 42.
17. Salah Khalaf has been quite explicit on these points. See Alan Cowell, "P.L.O. Goes Back to Debating How to Create Its Exile State," *New York Times,* January 26, 1989, p. A8. Sad to say, the lack of imagination on the Israeli side may be laid to a similar cause: lack of consensus both in the government and in the society at large about what to do next.
18. " 'Text' of Arafat News Conference in Amman," FBIS-NE, January 10, 1989, p. 3. So, too, Khaled al-Hasan, Arafat's deputy, has said: "Israel is not a principal side in the conflict. ... We are aiming at the Americans more than the Israelis." Al-Hasan's remarks were printed in the Egyptian paper *Al-Musawar;* quoted in part in Meron Benvenisti, "The Morning After," *The Jerusalem Post,* March 4, 1989, p. 8.

Suggested Additional Readings

Atiyeh, George N. *Arab and American Cultures* (Washington, DC: American Enterprise Institute for Public Policy Research, 1977).

Ben- Zvi, Abraham. *The American Approach to Superpower Collaboration in the Middle East* (Boulder, CO: Westview Press, 1986).

Bookbinder, Hyman and James Abourezk. *Through Different Eyes: Two Leading Americans, a Jew and an Arab, Debate U.S. Policy in the Middle East* (Bethesda, MD: Adler and Adler, 1987).

Braun, Aurel. *The Middle East in Global Strategy* (Boulder, CO: Westview Press, 1987).

Curtiss, Richard. *A Changing Image: American Perceptions of the Arab- Israeli Dispute* (Washington, DC: American Educational Trust, 1986).

Naff, Thomas and Marvin E. Wolfgang. *Changing Patterns of Power in the Middle East* (Beverly Hills, CA: Sage, 1985).

Pipes, Daniel. *In the Path of God: Islam and Political Power* (New York: Basic Books, 1983).

Quandt, William (ed.). *The Middle East: Ten Years After Camp David* (Washington, DC: Brookings Institution, 1988).

Saunders, Harold H. *The Other Walls: The Politics of the Arab-Israeli Peace Process* (Washington, DC: American Enterprise Institute for Public Policy Research, 1985).

Sick, Gary. *All Fall Down: America's Tragic Encounter with Iran* (New York: Random House, 1985).

Spiegel, Steven et. al. (eds.). *The Soviet-American Competition in the Middle East* (Lexington, MA: Lexington Books, 1988).

Stivers, William. *America's Confrontation with Revolutionary Change in the Middle East* (London: MacMillan, 1986).

Taylor, Alan R. *The Islamic Question in Middle East Politics* (Boulder, CO: Westview Press, 1988).

CHAPTER FIVE

Latin America

*
*

Though the focus of U.S. attention on Latin America in recent years has been on the crisis in Central America—specifically, U.S. policy toward Nicaragua and El Salvador—the United States actually has broader interests in the region as a whole that may be more important than its Central American concerns.

Over the last decade Central America has been one of the most contentious issues in U.S. foreign policy. Both political parties allowed Central America to define their ideological differences over foreign policy. At the same time, and in some ways like the controversy over Middle East policy, the Central American issues have helped to mobilize thousands of domestic interest and other groups into strong participation in the political process.

The issues in Nicaragua are: the extent to which the revolution has become an entirely Marxist-Leninist one; how much pressure (if any) the U.S. should put on that regime, and what form that pressure should take; how and when to combine diplomacy with pressure; and whether our goal is to get rid of the Sandinista regime entirely or only to ensure that it does not become a base for Soviet activities.

In El Salvador (and somewhat less dramatically in Guatemala) the questions are: how extensive human right violations by the military are; how democratic the countries have become and how strongly we should support their gov-

ernments; and what to do about the guerrilla movements that have now been present in both countries for a protracted period—try to defeat them or try to bring them into the political system.

The United States has other interests in Latin America besides these trouble spots, however. Mexico may be the second most important country in the world—next to the Soviet Union—in terms of U.S. foreign policy, both because it lies on our border and is interdependent with the U.S. in many ways (drugs, tourism, immigration, pollution, water supplies, oil, natural gas, labor supplies, investment) and because any signs of instability there would send millions of Mexicans (not hundreds of thousands as currently) streaming toward the U.S. border. Brazil,—large, rich, in resources, and restless—has become a major regional power on the South American continent and is reaching for great-power status. Argentina also sees itself as a South Atlantic power and a rival to the U.S. on the continent. Chile, Colombia, Peru, and Venezuela are also important countries to U.S. foreign policy interests; and we would not like to see the smaller countries fall into the abyss of instability and financial insolvency that might serve as an invitation to Soviet adventurism.

Beyond these considerations of specific countries, there are many general issues pertaining to Latin America. These include many of the global issues treated in Part II of this book: the drug traffic, human rights, international debt, immigration, the environment, and U.S. efforts to expand democracy. Latin America seems to be something of an experimental laboratory for all the complex social and political issues that have surged to the forefront in the United States in recent years.

There is a growing consensus in American foreign policy that we need to put our relations with Latin America on the same normal, regular, mature basis that we have long had with Western Europe. This means that policy should not alternate between "benign neglect" (which often turns out not to be so benign) and occasional dramatic interventions, but instead should be routinized and made more sensible. This implies a moderate and multifaceted policy based on democracy and human rights considerations as well as on narrower security interests; foreign aid as well as private investment; and social and economic as well as military assistance. It means paying serious attention to Latin America and fashioning a multifaceted approach to the area in accordance with the complex web of interrelationships in which we are now enmeshed.

Among scholars of Latin America the fear is growing that the region could easily get left behind and become like Africa: poor, neglected, hopeless. Latin America's economies are flagging, and we have not seen the signs of growth there that are so abundant in Asia. Almost no new investment is entering the area from any source, and the capital that is there is fleeing rapidly. Moreover, Latin America is often unwilling to do much to solve its own problems, preferring to blame these on the U.S. With the Cold War seemingly winding down, however, it seems likely that the U.S. will pay even less attention to Latin America than in the past. So the future of that region looks bleak and will continue to cause innumerable problems for U.S. foreign policy.

Latin America has recently been our most contentious foreign policy area, and our readings reflect that controversy. We begin with a background statement by the author, providing a sense of the context and history of U.S.-Latin American relations. There follow statements of recommendations by the conservative Committee of Santa Fe and the liberal Inter-American Dialogue. More balanced views are found in the Kissinger Commission Report on Central America (see the list of suggested additional readings). A statement by the author concludes the chapter, outlining reasons for being pessimistic about the future of Latin America and U.S.-Latin American relations.

The United States and Latin America: Historic Continuities, New Directions

By Howard J. Wiarda

Latin America, especially Central America and the Caribbean, has recently been catapulted onto our television screens and the front pages of our newspapers—if not yet into our consciousness. A major debate has been occurring in the United States about what our policy toward Latin America should be. This debate has often been intensely partisan and ideological. It has not always been enlightening.

If one probes beneath the partisan posturing, the emotionalism of the debate, and the veil of untruths and half-truths surrounding this issue, one discovers that there are critical aspects of past and present U.S. policy toward Latin America that have not received sufficient attention. The first of these is the historic continuity of American foreign policy in Latin America, including its practice by the two most recent American administrations, those of Presidents Carter and Reagan. The second is the learning and growth process that, again, all recent American administrations have gone through with regard to Latin America policy. The third is the remarkable degree of consensus, often hidden under the avalanche of partisan differences, that exists on most aspects of U.S. Latin America policy. And the fourth is, in the wake of Irangate and a weakened presidency, how fragile and uncertain the possibilities for an enlightened U.S. policy toward Latin America still are.

THE CONTENT OF U.S.-LATIN AMERICAN RELATIONS

Let us begin by talking about the content of U.S.-Latin American relations and by stating some truths that may not leave us entirely comfortable.

1. Latin America has not historically been thought of as very important in the rank ordering of U.S. policy priorities and areas. Soviet relations, Europe and NATO, China, Japan, and the Middle East are all viewed as more important by Washington than is Latin America. Latin America's low priority is changing under the impact of the crisis in Central America and as Hispanics have become a major influence in our domestic politics. But these changes seem glacial. Latin America still has a low priority, and policy-makers do not always pay the area much sustained or serious attention.

2. The United States does not understand Latin America very well. We tend to view the region through the prism of our own preferred solutions. We do not seriously study its culture, history, politics, and sociology. Instead we think that we know best for the area, that our ways are the ways Latin America should adopt. We are certain either that Central America is "another Vietnam" or, alternatively, that we are finally overcoming our "Vietnam complexes" there. In neither case do we try to understand the Central American crisis in its own terms. As an illustration, when I worked for Dr. Henry Kissinger as Lead Consultant to the National Bipartisan Commission on Central America, I wrote a report for the commissioners suggesting that we attempt some unaccustomed deference toward the region, that we try to understand Central American institutions in their own right, that we consider allowing the Central Americans to work out their own murky solutions to their own murky problems. That suggestion received zero support from the commissioners on either side of the political aisle. The sense is very strong in this country, among both liberals and conservatives, that we know best for Central America and must impose our solutions on it.

3. Not only do we not understand Latin America very well, but we do not want to understand it. That attitude is best summed up in the oft-quoted comment of *New York Times* correspondent James Reston, who said, "The United States will do anything for Latin America except read about it." Not only do we not read about the area, but we consistently use the wrong models to try to understand and reform it. The course of U.S.-Latin American relations is a path strewn with cast-off theories that in Latin America have not worked very well or as intended: Rostow's aeronautical "stages of growth," the Alliance for Progress, the polit-

Source: Published as the Third Annual Ellsworth Lecture delivered at Johnson State University, Johnson, Vermont, April 8, 1987.

ical development ideas of the 1960s, and a host of others. None of these have worked very well because they have not been adequately adapted to Latin American realities.

These factors, based either on ignorance or on some set of academic or ideological blinders, prevent us from understanding Latin America on its own terms and in its own institutional context. When such blinders are worn by policy makers as well as academics, it is small wonder that our policies toward the region have often been misinformed and misapplied. The fact is that at the base of our policy mistakes toward Latin America is a whole range of cultural, social, and political attitudes and prejudices toward that region that are strongly rooted in myths, half-truths, and misunderstandings.

HISTORIC CONTINUITIES OF POLICY

Within this context of what may be termed traditional bias, misunderstanding, and ethocentrism, let us look at the historic bases and continuities of U.S. policy toward Latin America. The fundamentals have remained the same for a long time. They have not changed greatly since President Monroe in his famous doctrine first articulated them one hundred sixty-four years ago. A more modern and updated version, formulated a century ago when the United States emerged as a major global power, was set forth by Teddy (later President) Roosevelt and Admiral Alfred Thayer Mahan, the apostle of American seapower. The "bedrocks" of U.S. policy then and largely now included the following:

1. Keep out hostile foreign powers. In earlier eras that meant efforts directed against Spain, France, England, and Germany; more recently it has meant excluding the Soviet Union from the region as much as possible.
2. Maintain stability. Latin America has not been known for its stable politics. Indeed the very instability of the area has given foreign powers the opportunity to establish beachheads there. Hence, the United States has been very concerned in the region to secure stability. Maintaining stability means not some unalterable defense of the status quo but encompasses adjustment to and even the encouragement of change and modernization. But not change that gets out of hand or leads to revolution.
3. Maintain a string of bases, listening posts, stations, etc., throughout Central America and the arc of the Caribbean islands.
4. Maintain access to markets, raw materials, and labor supplies of the area; keep open the sea lanes; guard the Panama Canal and the routes to it; provide border protection; stand for free trade and navigation.

There are some corollaries that follow from this listing of our primary interests in Latin America. First, as a nation we have historically been far more concerned with the areas close to home, on our strategic southern flank, Central America and the Caribbean, than with South America. Second, given the nature of these bedrock interests and of U.S. indifference to Latin America generally, our policy has almost always been reactive oriented rather than anticipatory. We have tended to react to crises

after they occur—Guatemala in 1954, Cuba in 1959–61, the Dominican Republic in 1965, Chile in 1973, Central America today—rather than to develop a long-term and positive program for the region. The third corollary has to do with democracy and human rights. These aspects have generally been subordinated to the strategic fundamentals listed above; where there has been a conflict between them, strategic considerations have dominated. But at the present that is changing, and human rights are now being viewed as ways to achieve stability in Latin America, as the best barriers against communism, and as the best means to undercut the appeals of a hostile foreign power.

Over the last hundred years and more, there has been very little disagreement from administration to administration, whether Democrat or Republican, on these basic goals of American foreign policy. The strategic considerations have been remarkably consistent. The only question has been the relative emphasis to be given each of these strategic fundamentals and the most effective and appropriate means to achieve those ends.

The question relates to a familiar one in American foreign policy, the debate between "realism" and "idealism." "Realists" have generally believed that U.S. foreign policy is best served by assistance to dictators or military regimes that are visibly, publicly, and sometimes brutally anticommunist. Such dictators, it is argued, provide stability, take vigorous action against communism, and are generally amenable to U.S. interests. "Idealists" believe that U.S. interests are best served by being on the side of democracy and human rights, by abandoning the dictators and oligarchs, and by siding with Latin America's so-called new forces. The "idealists," in accord with the moralistic and "missionary" tradition that has long characterized American foreign policy, believe that it is the obligation of the United States not just to adjust to changing conditions in Latin America, but to lead and push for change—sometimes regardless of the wishes of Latin America.

American administrations—and American foreign policy—have often oscillated between these two poles. At some times we have appeared tough and hard-nosed, at others soft and idealistic. But most recent American administrations have sought to balance and reconcile these conflicting tendencies. We have sought to protect U.S. strategic interests and advance democracy and human rights at one and the same time. Moreover, in recent years we have tended to see the two not as in conflict but as complementary. Democracy, development, and human rights may be viewed as part of a single and coordinated policy aimed at securing stability and modernization and keeping out hostile foreign powers. It is the dictators and strong-arm regimes—Batista or Somoza—that have proven to be unstable: further, rather than serving as bastions of anticommunism, such regimes may provide the conditions in which communism and radicalism may flourish. That was of course the great lesson of the Cuban revolution.

Recall, however, that the goals of U.S. foreign policy have been largely set: stability, anticommunism, bases, sea lanes, no hostile foreign powers. These are givens in any administration. The main

questions in our foreign policy debate, including the present debate over Central America is the best means to achieve these goals, not the goals per se.

Therefore, there has generally been far more continuity in U.S. policy toward Latin America than has generally been thought. In fact, our policy has been remarkably continuous over the last century because the goals are given. We still disagree over the best or most efficient strategies to achieve these goals but rarely over the goals themselves. In fact, the continuities, from Eisenhower to Kennedy, from Kennedy to Johnson, from Johnson to Nixon-Ford, and from Ford to Carter have been remarkable. The faces change, there is always some nuance in each new administration, some new emphasis as we try to grapple with this part of the world that we neither admire nor pay much serious attention to. But the essentials of policy have remained quite consistent over all this time.

These notions of continuity even apply, despite the hot campaign rhetoric and the sometimes fierce contemporary debate, to the transition from Carter to Reagan— two presidents whom we often think of as polar opposites in their approach to foreign policy. Carter began his administration with a foreign policy in considerable part derived from the left wing of the Democratic party. Reagan began from a base in the right wing of the Republican party. Both of these recent presidents gravitated over time back toward the center, back toward the mainstream of American foreign policy. With particular regard to the transition from Carter to Reagan, let me now examine how that process works,

what its dynamics are, and what it means for current and future U.S. policy.

THE TRANSITION FROM CARTER TO REAGAN

In 1980–81, it appeared as though there would be a sharp break in American foreign policy. Candidate Reagan and his aides were strongly critical of the Carter approach. They faulted Carter for his "romantic" and "globalist" approach to the Third World; for emphasizing human rights at the expense of more fundamental U.S. security interests; for "losing" Grenada and Nicaragua; for alienating such key countries as Argentina, Brazil, and Chile; and for allowing the real possibility to develop of other guerrilla triumphs in El Salvador and Guatemala.

In the campaign statements of Mr. Reagan and in the transition documents prepared by his foreign policy team, it appeared as though there would now be less attention to human rights, more stress on East-West (as opposed to North-South) issues, less attention to public foreign assistance and more to private investment, greater "realism" and less "idealism" in foreign policy, more focus on the Soviet Union, strenuous efforts to roll back the guerrilla challenge in Latin America, and efforts to reach accommodations with authoritarian regimes, which could then be reformed rather than treated as enemies.

The differences in the Carter and Reagan approaches, at least as they were presented during the campaign and in position papers prepared by President-elect Reagan's foreign policy advisers, seemed clear and rather stark.

They were so stark that in 1984 the Democrats fought the 1980 election all over again, and they may well do so once more in 1988. Many politically activist Americans have also come to believe that the campaign rhetoric that prevailed in 1980 is still the basis of Reagan Administration foreign policy. But that view ignores the enormous evolution in administration policy that has occurred since 1980, the learning process that has taken place, and the domestic and bureaucratic pressures that have forced Reagan Administration policy back toward the center, toward the mainstream of American foreign policy. Precisely the same gravitation toward the middle—albeit beginning from the opposite side of the political spectrum—had occurred under President Carter. By ignoring these dynamics we not only miss a great deal in our understanding of Reagan Administration foreign policy, but we are also condemned politically to keep repeating the same mistakes that the Democratic party made in 1984.

We cannot here review all the shifts in Reagan Administration policy, but let us briefly examine the record on the major issues, both to get a sense of the shifts that have occurred within the administration and to emphasize how continuous and consistent the policy has been with the classic tradition of policy as outlined earlier. For example, in the human rights area a very strong case can be made that after a terribly shaky and sometimes unfortunate beginning, the human rights record of the Reagan Administration, in terms of actual accomplishments as distinct from rhetoric, has been at least as strong as that of the Carter Administration. In addition, the two main

positive foreign policy initiatives of the Reagan Administration, the Caribbean Basin Initiative (CBI) and the Kissinger Commission recommendations on Central America, both bear a striking resemblance to the Alliance for Progress of John F. Kennedy—particularly in the balances they strike between socioeconomic assistance and military aid, public assistance and private investment, and human rights as opposed to strategic considerations. Similarly with the democracy initiatives, a strong case can be made that the Reagan Administration has done more—or at least as much—to advance the cause of democracy in Latin America than did its predecessor. Ninety per cent of the people of Latin America, thanks in part to U.S. pressures, now live under democratic rule—the highest percentage in the history of the hemisphere.

If one turns to policy toward individual countries, the same conclusions largely apply: that there has been far more continuity than change in U.S. policy and that the policy itself has been far more pragmatic, centrist, and moderate than the ongoing political debate suggests. For example, U.S.-Cuban relations remain in a deepfreeze, but it was actually during the Carter Administration that the strong disillusionment began with the policy of gradually normalizing relations with the Cuban regime. In El Salvador both the Carter and the Reagan administrations pursued a policy designed to encourage the formation of a democratic-centrist government, to isolate and reform the far right, and to isolate and if possible defeat the guerrilla left. Policy toward Nicaragua has been the most controversial, but both the Carter and the Reagan

administrations have agreed on: (1) the growing Marxism-Leninism of the Sandinista regime; (2) its steadily closer ties with the Soviet Union; (3) the increasingly monolithic and nonpluralist nature of the regime; (4) the need to isolate the revolution and keep it from spreading; and (5) the need to put pressure on the regime (although there may still be disagreement on the precise form such pressure should take) while at the same time keeping open the possibilities for negotiation and compromise.

In all these and other cases, U.S. policy has consistently been more pragmatic, more centrist, and more middle-of-the-road than the early campaign rhetoric would have led one to believe. Indeed the parallels between the later-Carter and later-Reagan policies are striking—much to the chagrin, incidentally, of the ideological "true believers" in both the Carter and the Reagan camps. Hence we need to ask: What are the factors explaining these remarkable parallels and continuities in U.S. Latin America policy?

Answers may be provided by examining both domestic and international factors. Domestically, the press has played a major role. Concerned about its reelection possibilities, wanting a good press, and responding to the drumbeat of criticism it received on El Salvador and other issues, the Reagan Administration was no doubt sensitive to the press and modified its policies accordingly. The Congress was another factor forcing compromise by holding hearings on administration policy, requiring certification of human rights progress in difficult countries like El Salvador and Guatemala, holding up presidential appointments, and seeking to frustrate and embarrass the Republican White House as much as possible.

Such new domestic interests as the human rights lobbies and religious groups also forced a sometimes reluctant administration back toward the center. Public opinion, which favored no more "second Cubas" in the Caribbean but was reluctant to give the government the instruments to carry out that mandate (no foreign aid, no CIA covert operations, no commitment of U.S. ground forces), also played a major role.

In addition, bureaucratic factors were important. The Defense Department was reluctant to get involved in "another Vietnam" in Central America. There were changes in the Department of State, personified by the emergence and consolidation of foreign-policy decision making under George Shultz, that led toward centrism. Meanwhile, about two years into the administration (about the same time period as under Carter), the professionals and specialists within the several foreign-policy bureaucracies reconsolidated their grip on policy, slowly recapturing policy making from the more ideological appointees who had accompanied President Reagan into office. While these changes were occurring, the administration was itself going through a learning process about Central America and other key foreign policy issues.

On the international front other forces were working that similarly led to a more centrist policy. The civil war in El Salvador proved not to be subject to a simplistic East-West interpretation (Soviet machinations) but required a North-South (poverty, social conditions)

explanation as well. In addition, the administration discovered that the levers of power in El Salvador were not as easily manipulable as it had thought. Even in small countries such as this, it proved far more difficult than the administration expected to grasp these levers and effect change. The handles of Salvadoran society and politics proved to be very slippery, or they broke off in the administration's hands as it attempted to aid, assist, and rearrange them.

Finally, that amorphous factor called "world public opinion" played an important role in changing administration policies. The administration found that our friends, allies, and neutrals did not support U.S. policy in Central America. Hence, the administration began to push for democracy, human rights, and socioeconomic progress in the region as well as U.S. strategic interests, narrowly defined. Friends and allies, to say nothing of the Congress and U.S. domestic public opinion and interest groups, could be neutralized, silenced, and in some cases even brought around to supporting U.S. policy if it stood for democracy, human rights, and development and not just for its security aspects. Fairly soon this strategy had a self-fulfilling aspect: not only could domestic and international opponents of U.S. policy be neutralized, but the administration discovered that democratic and centrist regimes in Latin America were far less bellicose, far easier to get along with, and caused far fewer problems for the U.S. than authoritarian regimes of the right or Marxist-Leninist regimes of the left. Hence, the administration again shifted course in favor of a policy that supported a trend already un-

der way in Latin America, away from authoritarianism and toward democracy. For reasons of morality, politics, and *realpolitik,* the administration came to a position of strong support for democracy and democratic transitions in Latin America and launched the Democracy Project and the National Endowment for Democracy to help strengthen its policies.

THE EVOLUTION OF ADMINISTRATION POLICY

Some of the early statements of Reagan Administration officials on Latin America were strident and unfortunate. On the other hand, the Democratic opposition often responded as if these early statements were still administration policy.

Actually, there was a significant evolution from the more ideological language of the early weeks of the administration. We have not "gone to the source" (as Secretary of State Haig once suggested, with obvious reference to Cuba); we have not invaded Nicaragua; we have not sent U.S. combat forces to fight in Central America.

On the positive side, the administration achieved a major (though still uncertain) victory in El Salvador, it has a strong human rights program, and through Project Democracy and the National Endowment for Democracy it came out foursquare and strongly assisted the evolution toward democracy throughout the Hemisphere. Through the CBI and the Kissinger Commission legislative agenda, it has a balanced program of aid and investment, socioeconomic and military assistance, and moral (human rights, democracy) as well as strategic concerns.

More than that, the administration had begun to put our relations with Latin America on the same normal, healthy, mature, regular, almost "boring" basis that we have long had with Western Europe. This is not to say there are no issues of contention between the United States and the counties of Latin America; there are, and they are many. These differences will continue to exist regardless of the governments in power in Washington or in Latin America because on a variety of issues we have somewhat different interests. But such issues are now handled largely through diplomatic and normal bilateral channels rather than on the "crash" or "crisis" basis of the past. Given the past history of U.S. relations with Latin America, of crisis-response and frequent interventions, such "boring" and normal relations seem to me to represent a step in the right direction.

Even on Nicaragua—our most contentious issue—there is widespread agreement in Washington, D.C., if not yet on college campuses and among church or Hollywood groups. Almost no one disagrees anymore that Nicaragua has a Marxist-Leninist regime, that it has been aiding insurgencies elsewhere in Central America, that domestic pluralism in Nicaragua has been reduced almost to the vanishing point, and that Nicaragua has become a close ally of Cuba and the Soviet Union. The disagreement is no longer over the nature of the regime and its international alliances, but what, precisely, to do about it.

Above and beyond this immediate debate, there is also widespread agreement in Washington, D.C., that the United States can no longer ignore Latin America, that we can no longer consider it a second-rate area unworthy of serious and sustained attention. Latin America is not just important to us in a foreign policy sense but also because the area and its peoples are now intertwined with our domestic political considerations and constituencies, and because the United States and Latin America are interdependent on a host of issues (immigration, trade, investment, drugs, pollution, water resources, labor supplies, markets, etc.), which had not been the case in the past.

The problem is that all these positive steps toward putting our relations with Latin America on a more balanced, mature, and sophisticated basis may be submerged under our current political preoccupations. It is the accepted wisdom in the nation's capital that nothing much will get done in 1987 because of the Iran/Contragate issue and that little can be accomplished in 1988 because that is an election year. And of course little will be done in 1989 because it takes at least a year for a new administration to get organized.

The result is that not only are the positive accomplishments in Latin America relations of the last few years likely to be forgotten and not further implemented, but we may, in our preoccupation with domestic considerations, revert to a de facto policy of "benign neglect." That is a grave danger, because it may well be argued that it was our "benign neglect" of Latin America in the 1970s—of Nicaragua, of El Salvador, of Guatemala, and of the rest of the hemisphere —that brought on the severe crisis that we face in that region today. Had we dealt with Somoza in the early 1970s and responded strongly to the emergence of exceedingly repressive regimes in El Salvador and Guatemala around that same time—had we not been preoccupied then with Vietnam and Watergate—we would not be facing the severe problems in the Caribbean area that have since come home to haunt and divide us. Benign neglect is no longer—if it ever was—a sound basis for U.S. policy in Latin America, and it is not a policy (or the lack thereof) to which we can afford to return.

CONCLUSIONS AND IMPLICATIONS

We have seen that historically there has been a great deal of continuity in U.S. policy toward Latin America—more continuity than change, regardless of the party or president in control of the White House. American public opinion, interest groups, our system of checks and balances, and the force of international realties all tend to force American foreign policy back toward the middle, including in the administrations of our two most recent and more ideological presidencies. The basic security goals of the United States in Latin America are set; the main questions for policy have centered on the best means to achieve those goals. We should not, therefore, expect any sudden or dramatic changes of policy from any new administration in Washington, despite the campaign rhetoric to the contrary.

That commentary is not to rule out change, however. The basics of policy may be set, but in any new administration there are new faces, new emphases, new ideas, and new initiatives. These nuances, within an overall context of policy continuity, provide room to maneuver and offer openings for new tilts of direction.

Moreover, some larger "sea changes" are also occurring in our attitudes and hence our policy toward Latin America. We are, ourselves, in terms of immigration patterns and ethnic makeup, becoming something of a Caribbean nation. In some parts of the country the Hispanic vote has begun to affect our domestic and, ultimately, our international politics. We are, as a nation, more aware of and somewhat better informed about Latin America than in the past. United States policy toward Latin America has over the years, with certain notable "blips," become more sophisticated and informed. We have begun to adjust to the new realities in Latin America and in inter-American relations. There has been a "learning curve" whose general direction is upward in recent years, on the part of all recent administrations, Congress,

the media, and the general public, regarding Latin America.

We need to continue along the lines of the general trends suggested here. We need greater understanding of and greater sophistication regarding Latin America. We need a policy that is steady, positive, and long-term and not just reactive to crisis. We need a less volatile policy and one that does not elevate certain "devils" to an importance they may not deserve—be they "authoritarian governments" in one administration or "the Cubans" in another. Above all we need sustained attention to Latin America and a consistent policy, not a situation of "benign neglect" that causes problems to fester to the explosion point, followed by a new period of crisis response and finger-pointing.

We need, in short, to put our relations with Latin America on the same sophisticated, mature, normal basis that we have long maintained with Western Europe. In fact, that is and has been the general thrust of American foreign policy in recent years, despite the headlines that imply great volatility and disagreement. Such a more mature policy requires not only sustained attention to the area but, as all recent administrations have come to recognize, a balance of socioeconomic assistance and military aid, of strategic and human rights concerns, of promoting democratic development as well as U.S. security interests. Such a balanced and multifaceted policy is not only good in itself, but it also best serves the interests of both Latin America and the United States. ▪

Santa Fe II: *A Strategy for Latin America in the Nineties*

By the Committee of Santa Fe

In 1980 a group of Latin American policy experts came together in Santa Fe, New Mexico, to formulate a sensible U.S. foreign-policy strategy for Latin America in the coming decade. Members of the Santa Fe Committee, as it was later dubbed, included L. Francis Bouchey, then vice-president of the Council for Inter-American Security; Dr. Roger Fontaine, Resident Fellow at the American Enterprise Institute for Public Policy Research; David C. Jordan, then professor of Government and Foreign Affairs at the University of Virginia and a board member of

the U.S. Strategic Institute; Lt. Gen. Gordon Sumner, (Ret.), former chairman of the Inter-American Defense Board; and Lewis Tambs, then professor of History at Arizona State University. All five went on to serve the Reagan administration in Latin America.

When the Santa Fe Committee released its 1980 report on Latin America, the Republican campaign was casting about for sound and sober policy recommendations. It got them. The Reagan administration subsequently adopted some of group's key proposals, including military aid for El Salvador, the

creation of Radio Marti for Cuba and the Caribbean Basin Initiative for the entire region.

Now, on the verge of the last decade of the 20th century, Latin America has reached an important crossroads in its economic development. There are two distinct paths for the family of nations that stretch from the Rio Grande to Cape Horn as they emerge from the 1980s, a period overshadowed by the frustration of the debt crisis. Once again the Committee of Santa Fe has identified the alternatives. The first path is the movement toward more open economies,

Source: From Committee of Santa Fe, *Sante Fe II: A Strategy for Latin America in the Nineties,* Council for Inter-American Security, (Washington, D.C., 1989.)

driven by free-market strategies that will help countries grow out of the debt crisis and away from the dead hand of central planning that has crippled them. Key innovative measures of this approach include privatization of large and swollen state companies and debt-equity conversion programs. Privatization helps increase employment, production and efficiency, while debt-equity conversion aids the privatization process and attracts foreign direct investment and capital inflows. This path—which the new administration and Congress can promote and encourage—holds the promise of self-sustained growth and debt reduction.

The second path is a retreat back to the same tired straitjacket of economic nationalism. Front and center are policies that promote import substitution, trade protectionism, and antiforeign investment laws. There is no well-conceived strategy to grow out of the debt crisis and regain lost ground, but only a hazy view of a post-debt–crisis utopia achieved after confrontation with international creditors and some magical form of debt repudiation.

The stakes for Latin America are very high as it chooses which path to follow. Recovery along free-market lines is crucial, especially if the region is to emerge as a competitive, yet cooperative partner in the evolving international economic system. The first path offers the potential for more balanced and diversified economies capable of providing stable foundations for democratic government. The second leaves the door open for further political turmoil. It would be a sad commentary indeed if Latin America retreated from a widening international movement toward more open and capitalist economies that is even being embraced by the Soviet Union and Eastern Europe.

The crossroads await Latin America and the United States. We hope the second report, Santa Fe II, will serve as a light for the surest road to economic freedom and stability and secure democratic government.

THE THREAT TO THE AMERICAS

The Americas are still under attack.[1] We warned of this danger in 1980. The attack is manifested in communist subversion, terrorism and narcotics-trafficking. The struggling Latin democracies' ability to combat these attacks has been undermined by the region-wide, debt-aggravated economic stagnation. The resulting political violence and worsening poverty have produced a growing emigration crisis within and from the region. Despite the initial efforts of the Reagan administration to address these problems and their underlying causes, the situation is more, not less, severe as the U.S. embarks on the last decade of the 20th century. Much of the lack of progress can be attributed to the failure to achieve a bipartisan agreement to address the problems facing Latin America in a coherent and effective manner.[2]

Problems on the Horizon

The communist subversive and terrorist network stretches from the Chiapas in southern Mexico to Chile, making the entire Pacific coast below the Rio Grande an arena of open conflict. It is clear that communist conflict strategy for the region is to seek power, or at least involve Western security forces in protracted operations simultaneously in several countries. The magnitude of this operation has the strategic implication of reducing U.S. forward commitments on the Eurasian land mass and thereby enhancing Soviet coercive ability. This is true even if there is a reduction of Soviet strategic nuclear forces because of arms control agreements. At the same time, Soviet conflict strategy stretches U.S. capacities to cope with its global responsibilities.

This subversive-terrorist threat has grown, not diminished, in the past decade. Nicaragua and Cuba, the Soviet client states in the hemisphere, have become involved in the drug trade and have moved into cooperative and possibly dominant relationships with the drug mafias of Colombia. The vast resources narcotics-trafficking produces have augmented the capacity of the subversive threat far beyond what was initially conceivable. The possibility of having to involve American military forces to combat this menace is now publicly aired before congressional committees.

At the same time, the Latin American economies have staggered along at only marginally positive rates of growth. The United Nations Economic Commission for Latin America and the Caribbean (ECLAC), in its preliminary report for 1987, notes that in per capita terms, the aggregate GDP of the region rose by only 0.5 percent in 1987, compared with the still weak 1.4 percent increase in 1986. The report concludes that these figures signify that "the deterioration in living conditions suffered by most of the relatively poorer economies of Latin America continued in 1987." In addition there has been an acceleration in the rate of inflation. Leading the way are Nicaragua at 1,226 percent, Brazil at 338 percent, Argentina at 178 percent, and Mexico at 144 percent. What is most disturbing is the high rate of inflation among the three largest Latin nations, which also hold the highest debt. When it is recalled that the total external debt rose more than 4 percent over 1986, it seems certain that the debt-servicing problem will become more onerous in the decade ahead.

Most Americans look at the Latin emigration problem as a U.S. immigration problem. It is seen primarily as how to absorb or discourage the millions of displaced persons heading to the U.S. The initial response, and probably only the first of many, was the Simpson-Rodino law. It seeks to absorb the illegal immigrants who can prove that they started living in the U.S. prior to 1982 and to discourage further migrations by imposing fines on employers who have knowingly hired illegal immigrants since the bill was passed on November 6, 1986. However, the problem is not merely the attraction of the U.S. for voluntary immigrants, but the displacement of millions of people because of Marxist violence, poverty, government mismanagement, and the growth of general lawlessness and corruption within Latin America itself. The source of this problem lies in the pressures producing emigration.

Thus, if the trends continue, it is virtually certain we will face

- more hostile Latin American attitudes;
- more pro-Soviet states;
- more subversion;
- greater threats to the international financial system;
- more crime and subversive-driven narcotics trafficking;
- more waves of immigration; and finally
- greater likelihood of U.S. military involvement.

What we see is a continuation of the attitude of strategic indifference, which the first report of this committee warned against in 1980. Unless the United States addresses the region in a coherent, serious, and bipartisan fashion, there is no prospect of reversing these trends. The costs of addressing each one of the symptoms has already sky-rocketed, and the price the U.S. may be forced to pay will exceed anything we have yet faced in our 200-year history.

CONCLUSION

The United States and the Inter-American system are faced with tremendous problems in Latin America. The crisis in Central America remains unresolved, and turbulent currents at work in South America are being ignored to our peril. Debts, terrorism, drugs, robber states, huge population migrations, communist insurgencies and corruption are just part of the scenario. Santa Fe II is a strategy for attacking these problems and for promoting democracy, freedom, and economic opportunity throughout the region in a pro-active instead of reactive fashion.

When the Reagan administration took office, Latin America and U.S. foreign policy towards Latin America mirrored each other: both were in a shambles. Santa Fe I, which came out in 1980, was de-

signed to cope with some of the more immediate problems facing the U.S. It helped focus American perceptions on how Latin America should be viewed in a geostrategic context, warned of the looming debt crisis, encouraged the push for democracy and sparked such programs as the Caribbean Basin Initiative and Radio Marti.

But not all of the Santa Fe I proposals were adequately followed up, nor could all of the problems be solved in just eight years, which is why Santa Fe II, besides following the innovative trademark of its predecessor, is also a product of necessity. As was the case eight years ago, the Inter-American system, especially the OAS, remains underutilized, and has, in fact, witnessed a further deterioration. The authors of Santa Fe II have therefore sought to provide a regime strategy that goes beyond just setting up an electoral system and which, if pursued by the next administration, could bring stability to otherwise shaky and volatile political situations. Specifically, this will mean shoring up independent organizations within the Latin societies, educating the people, and grappling with the Marxist and other statist cultural and political forces.

The Santa Fe II document forces particular attention on the economy, arguing that democracy requires a degree of policy rationality in the economic sphere. Centrally directed socialist systems produce neither wealth nor equity. It is not enough to come up with plans for the debtor nations to pay the interest on their debts; strategies have to be devised that will allow them to break out of the debt cycle and generate real savings and growth. Statism, giant bureaucratic apparatuses and nationalization are condemned, while the formation of national capital markets, deregulation, and privatization of existing state companies are encouraged. Besides advocating the merits of private enterprise as opposed to state capitalism, the authors also propose measures ranging from the prolongation of the Caribbean Basin Initiative to the preservation of the tropical rain forests.

The problems of terrorism, insurgencies, drugs, and emigration/immigration are identified as destabilizing factors, which contribute to the volatility and lack of security of the Latin democratic regimes and to a greater or lesser extent are felt by us domestically as well. The terrorism network stretches from the Chiapas in Mexico to the southern Andes in Chile. Last year, Americans spent more money importing illegal drugs from Latin American than they did on food. These obviously are problems that won't go away. In order to begin to cope with them, U.S. policymakers have to recognize the crisis they are facing and be prepared to take extraordinary steps. Their first moves however, should be to build up the normal—and lawful—capabilities of the judicial systems that have to bear the strain.

The crises in Latin America have not been resolved; the problems have changed, but they are as bad as, or worse than, they were in 1980. We have witnessed a failure in communication and persistent confusion, and this failure has to end. U.S. policy makers owe it to the people to inform them about what is going on—decision makers need to be clear and specific about what problems the United States faces and what they intend to do about them. Santa Fe II is a guide for the path they need to take. ■

Notes

1. Committee of Santa Fe-(L. Francis Bouchey, Roger Fontaine, David Jordan, Gordon Sumner and Lewis Tambs, editor), A New Inter-American Policy for the Eighties. (Santa Fe: 1980).

2. For example, Congress failed to support or provide an alternate to the Caribbean Basin Initiative (two and one-half year delay), Radio Marti (three years), funding for El Salvador (nearly three years) and still does not at the time of writing have a bipartisan policy on Panama.

The Americas in 1989: Consensus for Action   *Executive Summary*

I. DEBT AND STAGNATION: A PROGRAM FOR RECOVERY

Latin America has been mired in depression for six years; most Latin Americans are worse off today than they were a decade ago. Having trapped millions in extreme poverty, the depression has begun to feed on itself. Continuing capital flight, low investment, rampant inflation, and declining funding for education and health are destroying the foundations of future productivity and may keep Latin American economies stagnant for years to come.

The Latin American debt crisis may soon touch off a political crisis. Economic adversity has weakened democratic governments in country after country. As governments lose credibility and authority, the appeal of extremist solutions is rising, and it becomes harder to institute the economic measures needed for recovery and growth. Latin America may be condemned to a long period of economic hardship and political turbulence, which may force civilian authorities to yield to military rule in some places.

Throughout the Hemisphere, a consensus has been gathering among debtors and creditors on what must be done to tackle the two biggest impediments to Latin America's recovery—a desperate shortage of external resources and a legacy of national economic mismanagement. Latin Americans now recognize that their economic policies must be revised to favor greater reliance on private markets and greater openness to trade and foreign investment; they also recognize that the state has played an excessive role in most of the region's economies. For their part, creditor countries and banks increasingly acknowledge that restructuring Latin America's econo-

---

Source: From *The Americas in 1989: Consensus for action,* the Aspen Institute (Queenstown, Md, 1989), pp. 83–92. Reprinted by permission of Inter-American Dialogue.

mies and priming them for growth require increased external capital; that new lending alone will never provide enough capital; and that debt reduction is essential.

Latin America must grow at least five percent annually in order to restore business confidence, improve living standards, absorb an expanding work force, and create conditions for political stability. Achieving that rate of growth will not be easy. Five priority tasks must be accomplished.

The first responsibility is that of Latin America. The countries of the region cannot recover unless they revamp their development strategies, restructure their economies, and effectively integrate them in the world economy. Debtor governments must generate and save foreign exchange by promoting exports, increasing the efficiency of domestic industry, encouraging the return of flight capital, and attracting new foreign investment. Internally, fiscal deficits must be reduced, inflation controlled, the private sector expanded and strengthened, and income and wealth more equitably distributed.

Second, the United States must address its own economic problems and join other industrial countries to reduce international financial imbalances, open world markets, and sustain world growth. The international economy must become a stimulus, not an obstacle, to Latin America's recovery.

Third, the international financial institutions—the International Monetary Fund (IMF), the World Bank, and the Inter-American Development Bank (IDB)—must sharply step up their lending to Latin America. If pushed by the industrial countries, these agencies could provide $8 to $9 billion of the $20 billion in new capital needed annually over the next several years to reverse Latin America's economic fortunes. This lending should be conditioned on debtor government's adherence to economic reform programs.

Fourth, debt reduction agreements must be negotiated between individual debtor countries and their commercial bank creditors. The smallest and weakest debtors require outright relief from much of their obligations. For Latin America's larger countries—Brazil, Mexico, Argentina, Venezuela, Chile, and Colombia—which together owe 85 percent of the regions debt, proportionally smaller reductions are required.

Fifth, the United States and other industrial countries should actively encourage commercial banks to reach debt reduction agreements with Latin American countries. Changes should be made in regulatory, accounting, and tax practices that would make debt reduction a more attractive option. The crucial inducement, however, will be protection against further losses. The industrial countries must provide some form of official guarantees on the interest or principal that remains after the debt reduction operation.

No comprehensive debt reduction scheme is likely to gain support from creditor countries or banks. But the economic status quo is intolerable. As long as the debtors' interest payments dwarf new borrowing, Latin American countries will remain stuck on a treadmill of austerity, stagnation, and rising debt. What can and should be set in motion now is a step-by-step, case-by-case approach in which each country works out specific, differentiated, and mutually-agreed debt reduction agreements with its commercial creditors. The longer such action is postponed, the greater the ultimate costs will be— for both the United States and Latin America.

II. CENTRAL AMERICA: A BLUEPRINT FOR PEACE

Central America remains at war, but broad agreement has finally emerged on what must be done to achieve a durable peace. The Esquipulas accords adopted by the five Central American presidents in Guatemala in August 1987 provide the blueprint.

Implementation of the accords has lagged. But events are heightening the appeal of their central goal: encouraging essential compromises among Central Americans. The U.S. presidential transition, major shifts in U.S.-Soviet relations, and, above all, frustration and exhaustion in Central America may finally generate the will to turn the blueprint into policy and action.

In order to rebuild Nicaragua's battered economy, the Sandinistas must reach a negotiated settlement that permits military spending cuts, stems the flow of Nicaraguans out of the country, fosters national reconciliation, and opens the way for international aid. Without U.S. military aid, in turn, the Contras' only hope for influencing the course of Nicaraguan politics lies in an agreement that enables them to challenge the Sandinista government politically.

In El Salvador, war and political violence are intensifying again, but the military stalemate may convince both sides to seek a negotiated peace. An encouraging, if limited, sign is that elements on the left and right are demonstrating a new willingness to seek power through the electoral process.

A lasting peace in Central America requires that four tightly intertwined challenges be met.

First, the nations of the region and their hemispheric neighbors must be assured that their national security is protected. Washington must move forthrightly to defend its own legitimate security interests by pressing the Soviets and Cubans to curtail their military ties with Nicaragua. Washington must also specify its terms for coexistence with Nicaragua and bilaterally negotiate mutual security arrangements. Aid to the Contras must be confined to humanitarian assistance aimed at reintegrating them into Nicaraguan life. And Managua must desist from assisting insurgencies in El Salvador and elsewhere. There can be no double standard on this essential point.

Second, Central America's armed conflicts must be transformed into peaceful competition. International pressure should be mobilized in support of Esquipulas for promoting democratic politics. Three measures would be especially helpful: creation of an independent international committee to evaluate compliance with the political provisions of Esquipulas; the tying of aid commitments to good-faith efforts by Central American governments to negotiate peace and implement their political pledges; and an international consultative group to sustain democratic change through diplomatic and aid-related incentives and sanctions.

Third, the economies of Central America must be revived. This will require major aid infusions and local economic policy reforms. Various studies by international organizations provide a consensus for action featuring emergency assistance to satisfy basic human needs; a fairer distribution of land and other resources; national policies to encourage domestic savings and exports; greater regional economic integration; a substantial measure of debt relief; and expanded access to world markets.

Fourth, Central America's two million or more refugees and displaced persons must be cared for. Substantial international assistance is needed to meet their immediate material needs, and to help in repatriation and resettlement. After arming the Contras and encouraging them to fight, the United States must take responsibility for assisting them to integrate safely and fully into Nicaraguan life. The United States, Canada, and Mexico should apply generous standards in deciding claims for temporary asylum by all Central Americans.

The Esquipulas blueprint will be useless unless the confrontation between the governments of Nicaragua and the United States can be resolved. Nicaragua must curtail its military ties with the Soviet bloc, keep from subverting its neighbors, and open up its politics. The United States must stop trying to overthrow Nicaragua's regime and, instead, focus on assuring that Nicaragua's activities do not threaten hemispheric security. U.S. leadership, within a multilateral framework, is also needed to aid Central America's reconstruction. Only in this way can a secure peace be achieved and sustained.

III. DRUGS; GETTING SERIOUS ABOUT DEMAND AND SUPPLY

The Hemisphere is losing the fight against dangerous drugs. No quick or easy solutions are currently available. But both North and South Americans are realizing that today's strategy of eradication, interdiction, and U.S. pressure on its drug-producing neighbors should be deemphasized in favor of hemispheric cooperation and a concerted attack on demand.

Most people in the United States now view narcotics as the country's single biggest problem. U.S. citizens currently spend up to $100 billion annually on illegal drugs, and a cocaine epidemic is devastating inner cities, where the drug is cheaper and more plentiful than ever. Narcotics trafficking is taking a heavy toll in Latin America as well. Drug abuse is spreading, and cocaine-related crime and violence are an open threat to governmental authority in some supplier countries. The fight against cocaine can threaten democratic governments as seriously as the the trafficking itself, by provoking drug criminals to step up violence and corruption, exposing militaries to corruption, stretching the military's responsibility and diminishing civilian authority, and occasionally driving guerrillas and traffickers to join forces.

The United States is finally shifting its attention to reducing demand, but prevention and treatment programs have been slow to take shape. There is a growing recognition that supply-side approaches like eradication and interdiction will not do much to address the U.S. cocaine problem.

As long as there is demand for illicit drugs, supplies will find their way to it. Cocaine's retail price so exceeds distribution and production costs that eradication or crop substitution programs, no matter how effective, have scarce effect on U.S. street prices. The drug business is so lucrative that traffickers can tolerate seizure of half or more of their shipments.

Heavy-handed U.S. pressure on Latin American governments and continuing public criticisms of their performances have accomplished little in the battle against drugs, while poisoning Hemispheric relations and hamstringing cooperation on other issues. Whatever the temptation to call for a "drug-free America," without specific and funded programs to curb both demand and supply, such calls should be seen for what they are—words substituting for actions.

The United States and Latin America should devise and implement a joint strategy based on a shared assessment of the Hemisphere's narcotics problems. The consensus for inter-American action starts with reducing demand in both the United States and Latin America. This will require substantially increased emphasis on education and rehabilitation, including funding to expand successful pilot programs and to test a wide range of demand reduction measures. U.S. financial and technical assistance should be made available to Latin American countries for programs to reduce drug abuse as well as for supply-containment efforts. Other useful initiatives would include intensifying police and intelligence cooperation, new laws to restrict money-laundering and control the trade in chemicals used in cocaine production, and expanded information-sharing utilizing the expertise of the United Nations' and Organization of American States drug control agencies.

Progress can be made toward curbing narcotics use and controlling drug crime. The first requirement is to stop the scapegoating that obscures a painful but unavoidable truth: the narcotics problem begins at home for all countries. Hemispheric cooperation is essential, but each nation must also concentrate on what it can do internally to confront the scourge of drugs.

IV. THE ENVIRONMENTAL CHALLENGE

Environmental degradation throughout the Hemisphere threatens the health of North and South Americans, their economic prospects, and perhaps even the future of their planet. The destruction of the Amazon's tropical forests may trigger disastrous worldwide climate changes. Air- and water-borne pollutants like acid rain are increasingly crossing national boundaries. North Americans dump their hazardous waste in Latin America and the Caribbean. Latin American countries export pesticide-laden produce to each other and to the United States and Canada. But the greatest damage is occurring inside each country: choking pollution and resource destruction are endangering millions and undermining economic and social development.

Tropical forests are under assault not only in Brazil, but also in Central America and Mexico. Forests are being ecologically devastated, and their enormous economic potential is being squandered. Soil losses threaten agricultural development throughout Latin America. The silt from degraded land clogs waterways and impedes navigation and hydroelectric generation, while denuded mountain slopes have increased flooding. In Central America and elsewhere, overkill levels of pesticide use have led to poisoning rates nearly 2,000 times higher than those in the United States.

In Latin America's cities, most sewage is not even collected, much less treated. Air pollution in all major metropolises in the region exceeds that of any U.S. city. And hazardous industrial wastes are dumped perilously close to crop lands, fishing grounds, and reservoirs.

Environmental problems are both fueling and fueled by Latin America's economic crisis. Government policies that promote environmentally damaging and economically dubious activities like cattle ranching in the Amazon waste public funds and destroy the real commercial value of the forests. Soil erosion is reducing domestic food production, while silt-filled waterways raise the cost of hydroelectricity. At the same time, poverty and landlessness are pushing ever more people into ecologically fragile areas.

With environmental dangers so numerous and financial resources so limited, the Hemisphere's governments, individually and collectively, must set careful priorities. The first task for all governments is to revise policies—taxes, subsidies, and regulations—which perversely offer economic incentives for environmentally destructive activities. In Haiti, for example, export taxes on coffee led farmers to switch to other cash crops. The results were both accelerated soil erosion and reduced export revenues.

Investments are needed in natural resource management that will bring longer-term economic payoffs from valuable forests, farmland, and waterways. International financial institutions and industrial countries can contribute not only by factoring environmental considerations into their lending decisions, but also by financing sound resource development programs and offering their expertise in ecological management and pollution control. Long-term regulatory and investment strategies are needed to replace the ad hoc, piecemeal actions that have characterized Latin America's response to environmental degradation to date.

The costs of protecting and cleaning up the environment are immense, especially for depression-wracked Latin American countries. But the costs of neglecting the problems are higher still. No country of the Hemisphere, rich or poor, can afford to postpone action to develop its resources in sound and sustainable ways.

V. DEMOCRACY AT RISK

Latin America's turn toward democracy in the 1980s has been real and significant, but it is by no means irreversible. Democratic rule today is under siege from several directions.

Democratic governments have been unable to achieve economic growth, control rampant inflation, and provide basic public services. As a result, Latin Americans have become increasingly frustrated, and the appeal of political extremists has grown stronger. The region's economic crisis and the resulting austerity measures have widened inequalities of income and wealth, thereby jeopardizing social stability. Guerrilla insurgencies are becoming stronger and more threatening in some places; in others, drug traffickers have corrupted governmental institutions and seized control of whole regions. Latin American militaries are in conflict with weak democratic governments over many issues: military autonomy, defense spending, human rights prosecutions, and the choice of antiguerrilla tactics.

Only Costa Rica, Venezuela, Jamaica, and several small countries of the Commonwealth Caribbean qualify as fully consolidated democracies. Elsewhere, democracy is still incomplete and fragile, or authoritarian regimes rule.

In Mexico, opposition groups mounted an unprecedented challenge to the Institutional Revolutionary Party in last year's elections, opening politics in that country to a new level of competition. But Mexico's continuing need for painful economic austerity could lead to a retightening of political control. Colombia's long-standing constitutional democracy is embattled; the country is torn by guerrilla movements, drug-related violence, and death squads. Democracy appears more firmly entrenched in Uruguay but tensions linger over the issue of prosecuting military officers for human rights violations during the authoritarian years.

The new democracies of Argentina, Brazil, and Ecuador are under greater stress. In Brazil, where people have been deeply disappointed by the first years of civilian rule, the military still wields a decisive influence over many political issues. In Ecuador, as well, the armed forces continue to play an active role in political affairs. Argentina's government has confronted two military uprisings in the past year.

Democracy's plight has become desperate in Peru, where the economy is in shambles and an elected civilian government seems powerless to control guerrilla terrorism and drug corruption. In Bolivia and the Dominican Republic, venerable political figures dominate, and it is unclear what will follow their departure.

In Central America, progress toward democracy is fitful at best. The elected civilian governments in El Salvador, Guatemala, and Honduras remain extremely weak—political parties are in their infancy, political competition is restricted, and the military intervenes in politics almost at will.

Six countries of the Hemisphere still suffer authoritarian regimes of different kinds. Hopes for a prompt restoration of democracy are highest in Chile, following General Augusto Pinochet's defeat in the October 1988 plebiscite. Prospects are much poorer in neighboring Paraguay, where aging General Alfredo Stroessner perpetuates his repressive rule. In Cuba, Fidel Castro militantly resists testing his mandate in a popular vote, and allows no room for political opposition. Nicaragua has an elected government and a host of active parties and interest groups, but the ruling Sandinista party limits political competition and curtails freedom of assembly and the press. In 1988, both Haiti and Panama saw incipient movement toward democracy derailed by military intervention.

Each Latin American country must ultimately achieve and protect democracy on its own; yet together the nations of the Hemisphere can do much to nurture and strengthen democracy. The fact that so many countries of the Americas are now ruled democratically provides a strong basis for more effective inter-American cooperation to fortify democracy. The opportunities for such cooperation have been enhanced by the emergence in the United States of a broad bipartisan consensus that regards human rights and democratic politics as legitimate priorities of U.S. foreign policy.

We recommend four direct measures that the democracies of the Hemisphere can undertake cooperatively in support of democratic rule: inter-American actions to promote human rights and freedom of the press; publicly accountable assistance to democratic institutions, tailored to the particular circumstances of each country; consistent and open expressions of preference for democratic governments over authoritarian regimes of either the right or left; and aid to establish democratic patterns of civil-military relations.

The most vital actions, however, will be indirect—to remove the main obstacles to democratic progress. The United States and the creditor countries of Western Europe should provide Latin America with debt relief to ease the regional economic crisis. All countries in the Hemisphere should work together to confront the drug trade and the corruption and violence it engenders; to achieve a secure peace and improve the prospects for peaceful political competition in Central America; and to develop programs which will alleviate poverty and social injustices. These actions would contribute most to building a Hemisphere where democracy can take root and flourish. ∎

The United States and Latin America—Toward the 1990s

By Howard J. Wiarda

The Latin America policy of the United States has, for the last year, been in limbo. The Administration of President Reagan had been severely damaged by Iran/Contra, the President had become a lame duck, and the steam had gone out of the Reagan revolution. No new initiatives were forthcoming; the Reagan staff spent the past year looking for more lucrative opportunities in the think tanks and private business, and a certain air of impending retirement or finality had set in at the White House.

Meanwhile, on the Democratic side, things were hardly any better. Governor Dukakis's advisers had caught Potomac Fever and could not wait to inherit those influential positions that the Reaganites had controlled for eight years. On Latin America they wanted to forgive the debt and surreptitiously pass the costs on to the American taxpayer. They apparently wished to cede responsibility for U.S. Latin American policy to such moribund international agencies as the Organization of American States. And on Central America the Democrats wished to rely on the *deus ex machina* of the Arias Plan, which passes U.S. foreign policy responsibility again on to a third party, enables the Democrats to wash their hands of Central America, blames the Republicans for scuttling the Plan, and even denies that the U.S. has any security interests at all in Central America.

It has not been a time to be wildly optimistic about U.S. Latin American policy. In political Washington, the policy process for the past year has been all but paralyzed since everyone has been waiting around for the outcome of the November elections—as if that would solve the basic problems. But of course the outcome of our elections do not much alter the fundamental dilemmas of Latin America, which are deeply entrenched and intractable, and we should not delude ourselves that either of our candidates could solve them.

Source: From Five College International Forum No. 2 (Fall, 1988).

U.S. ATTITUDES TOWARD LATIN AMERICA

U.S. policy toward Latin America has long been shaped by attitudes and prejudices that are deeply ingrained. These will not be changed quickly, easily, or maybe ever. In fact, they may be getting worse. Let us briefly review the roots of these attitudes.

First, Latin America has not—in the past and to a large extent contemporaneously—been considered important culturally or in the social sciences. Nothing of significance is ever thought to have emanated from Latin America. Hegel said Latin America had "no history"; Marx consigned Latin America to the then unflattering category of "Asiatic societies." Ever since, in both the Marxist and non-Marxist traditions, Latin America has been thought to have little to teach us, to be unworthy of serious intellectual attention and consideration.

Second, Latin America has seldom been thought to have been important geopolitically. That attitude is best captured in Henry Kissinger's quip that the axis of the world begins in Moscow, flows through Bonn, Paris, and London, proceeds to New York and Washington, and terminates in Tokyo. Not only is Latin America thus left out of this strategic calculus, but so is the entire Third World. Actually, since chairing the Presidential Commission on Central America, Mr. Kissinger has modified his views considerably.

Third, our knowledge of Latin America is appallingly limited. We do not have much understanding about the area, but we nonetheless assume that we can solve its problems. Left, Right, and Center in the U.S.-all assume they have a solution for Latin America's problems and are not usually hesitant about imposing it on the area.

Fourth, not only do we not know much about Latin America, but we are usually unwilling to invest the time to learn about it—and especially on its own terms and in its own languages. We have "instant solutions" for the area and many "instant commentators," but few of them have a solid grounding in Latin American history, politics, sociology, and economics.

Fifth, Latin America ranks low on our list of strategic priorities. It is a lower priority than Soviet relations, NATO and Europe, Japan, China, and the Middle East. That low-order priority may be changing a bit now because, through immigration as well as increased interdependence with the area, we are ourselves becoming something of a Latin American nation; and because the crisis in Central America has forced us to turn our attention to that area. But one should not hold one's breath too long waiting for Latin America to move up higher on the priority list.

Sixth and finally, U.S. policy toward Latin America is derivative. That is what Latin American ambassadors to Washington complain about the most: that U.S. policy toward their countries is merely derivative of the Cold War competition between the United States and the Soviet Union and is not based on any real interest in their countries per se.

Another personal anecdote may be in order to illustrate this point. Once after a lecture I had given in a Latin American capital, a student came up to me and said, "Oh you Americans, the only reason you're interested in Latin America is because of the Cold War." My usual polite response to such a question is to say, "Oh no, things are changing, we're really interested in you, policy will improve, etc." But this time I replied honestly, a bit to the chagrin of the student, and said, "You're absolutely right, and, furthermore, you should thank God for the Cold War because otherwise we wouldn't be interested in you at all." Fortunately or unfortunately, this brutal truth is as valid now as it was in earlier decades.

U.S. policy toward Latin America historically has thus been patronizing, condescending, superior, and ethnocentric. Even in those periods often thought of as among the better eras in U.S. Latin American relations—the Good Neighbor Policy of Franklin Roosevelt and John F. Kennedy's Alliance for Progress—it was *our* solutions that were imposed on the area and *our* prejudices and preferences, with virtually no input from the Latin Americans themselves. Such consistent we-know-best attitudes have not served us well in terms of our relations with the area. They do serve, however, as the cultural and sociological base on which our foreign policy rests, and, unfortunately, there are few signs that these basic American attitudes toward the region are changing, despite the best efforts of our Latin America experts for many years. Therefore, we should not be overly optimistic that U.S. policy will soon change very much either, regardless of the occupant of the Oval Office.

ISSUES IN U.S.-LATIN AMERICA RELATIONS

U.S. relations with Latin America are at this stage a confusing mix of good and bad. The United States is widely admired in Latin America for its wealth, power, culture (Coca Cola, blue jeans, rock music), and democracy; but it is disliked for its insensitivities, arrogance, and frequent interventions. Latin America is nationalistic and resentful of the United States at some levels, but its people at other levels like Americans and often want to be like us. U.S. relations with some countries and people are strained, but overall the U.S. has begun, by fits and starts and over the course of several recent administrations, to put its relations with most of the countries of Latin America on the same regular, normal, even "boring" basis that we have long maintained with Western Europe. By "boring" we mean that issues in bilateral relations are generally dealt with through negotiations, accommodation, discussion, and compromise rather than through confrontation, crisis, and intervention.

Since the issues and debate over Central America change virtually from day to day, let us leave that issue aside for now and concentrate on the major, long-term trends in U.S.-Latin American relations, which many scholars believe are far more important.

First, Latin America is desperately short of the capital that is needed for long-term development. Nor is there any evidence that new infusions of the investment money that Latin America desperately needs will be forthcoming soon. Capital flight has reached staggering proportions as Latin Americans themselves send their money for safe-keeping to Miami, Houston, San Diego, and Geneva. There is precious little European investment in Latin America. Japan is similarly reluctant to invest because of the corruption and inefficiencies of Latin America and because of Japanese fears that Latin America will not pay its foreign debts, including those to Japanese banks. Polls indicate that 80–85% of the American public are against all forms of foreign aid, so there will not be much help from that quarter. No grand new Alliance for Progress or Marshall Plan for Latin America will be forthcoming, either.

Fearing future instability, United States firms are now extremely reluctant to invest in Latin America, and the companies that are there are pulling their capital out as soon as possible, since they make far larger profits elsewhere and receive fewer hassles. The figures indicate that there is not a single Fortune 500 company anymore that has more than 10% of its holdings in Latin America. The days when a big United States company like United Fruit could dominate the affairs of a small country are over. There are practically no more U.S. companies of any size left in Latin America.

Latin America has long followed a policy of restricting the activities of large investors, but the practical result of that strategy now is that there are very few foreign companies remaining and almost no investment at all. Latin America has usually consoled itself by saying, "Well, if the help doesn't come from the U.S., then we will get it from Europe or the Soviet Union or maybe China." But these efforts to "diversify its dependency" have not worked either; there is precious little European or *any other* capital coming into the region. Without such investment, of course, there can be no development. So if we think Latin America is badly off now, things are almost certain to get worse in the future. Brazil, is one of the very few Latin American countries still attracting investments, and even there the new constitution and Brazil's uncertain future are raising doubts.

A second long-term problem is the bankruptcy of Latin America's earlier development models and the retardedness of economic thinking and practice. The varied developmental models of the Argentine, Brazilian, and Peruvian military regimes did not work out very well in the 1970s; the Cuban and Nicaraguan revolutions have been disasters economically; Pinochet is unacceptable politically; and Mexico's standard of living has recently dropped by 40%. This dismal summary does not even include the small countries of Central America and the Caribbean who may not be viable economically. All the "models" of the past have failed or been found wanting.

Most observers at the development agencies in Washington believe Latin America is at least fifteen years behind in its economic thinking and even farther behind in practice. With only one or two exceptions, Latin America still clings to its outmoded import-substitution strategy of the past; and its often corrupt and patronage-dominated bureaucracies and government agencies are simply not set up to achieve growth. Employment yes, but growth no. Latin America must attract investment capital, it must modernize and streamline its stifling bureaucracies and state-run companies, and it must export. But so far there are precious few signs of anything more than feeble and often reluctant moves in these directions. Brazil is, once again, the major exception.

Third, Latin America has been suffering by comparison. In the last thirty years, countries like Japan, South Korea, the Republic of China (Taiwan), Hong Kong, and Singapore have been growing at miracle rates of 8, 9, 10% (sometimes more) per year. Several of these are countries that were also poor and backward, with major social problems and at least as "dependent" on foreign capital and markets as is Latin America. Yet these Asian "tigers" have made it into the modern world while much of Latin America has not. Many people who have long been sympathetic to Latin America are beginning to ask, "Why?"

If these small Asian countries can "make it," why can't Latin America do the same? Since the Asian countries also have U.S. multinational corporations (MNCs) operating within their borders, are tied into U.S. markets, and are similarly "dependent" on the U.S., why have they been so successful and Latin America not? Given the Asian success in achieving development by using the same institutions and processes (MNCs and the U.S. markets) that Latin Americans are often inclined to blame for their failures, scholars of development are starting to ask if there is some fatal flaw (or flaws) *in Latin America* that retards development. If dependency, MNCs, and U.S. markets cannot be blamed, then wherein lies the problem? Latin America does not at all come out well in these comparisons, and its friends and allies are beginning to conclude that the problems lie chiefly *in* the region and not outside of it.

A fourth and related long-term difficulty is Latin America's increasingly bad reputation in the United States. For those of us who for many years have been battling the prejudices and biases about Latin America outlined in the first part of this article, this is a very discouraging time. The image of Latin America is getting worse. Latin America is presently viewed by the general American public as an area of drug dealers who are ruining our youth and our society, as an area of sleazy dictators (Noriega), of widespread corruption, of stupid wars (Argentina), of violence and disorder, of countries that prey upon American tourists and murder our drug enforcement officials, of backward and unsuccessful societies (the Asia comparison), and of leaders who don't much like the United States (Nicaragua) and who manage to drag us into their murky and bloody conflicts.

This image of Latin America—whatever its accuracy—is widespread in the United States, is poisoning attitudes toward Latin America, and is leading us not to want to have anything to do with the region. No aid, no investment, no nothing. Given these negative images, very little attention has been paid to Latin America's quite remarkable transitions to democracy in the last decade, to the success of a good number of its countries in moving to a stable and more advanced growth level, and to the generally good relations which most of the countries of the area have with the United States. It will likely take a very long time for Latin America's current bad reputation to be ameliorated and, meantime, Americans want as little to do with the area as possible. Such attitudes will not well serve either our purposes or Latin America's.

One further factor requires mention, and that involves the impact of the diminishing Cold War on Latin America. If the student questioner mentioned earlier is correct and the only reason the U.S. is interested in Latin America is because of the Cold War, then as the Cold War winds down and the Soviet Union turns inward and likely reduces its adventurism in such far-flung areas of the globe, it seems probable that the U.S. interests in Latin America will diminish as well. Such declining U.S. interest will not help our relations with the area but it will carry even more negatives for Latin America. For history has taught Latin America, after all, that it is terribly difficult to achieve development and change *with* the United States. But it is impossible to achieve these goals *without* the United States and, as the Cuban and Nicaraguan experiences have now made clear—regardless of how one assigns the blame—disastrous to try to do it *against* the United States.

FUTURE IMPLICATIONS

United States relations with most of Latin America are, actually, quite good. Attention in the United States in recent years has been riveted on certain key central American countries: El Salvador, Nicaragua, Guatemala. But in general our relations with the larger and, arguably, more important countries of Mexico and the nations of South America are quite decent and more or less regularized. There will continue to be differences, of course, regardless of who is in power in Washington, D.C., Brasilia, Mexico City, Caracas, Bogota, or Buenos Aires, because there are sometimes different interests and priorities between the United States and the other countries. But these differences will largely be dealt with diplomatically and through negotiations, reflecting the more normal and regularized relations we have now established with the major countries. Everyone in Washington, D.C., understands that you can't treat Brazil or Mexico as if they were "banana republics."

It may come as a surprise also to hear that many of the Latin American countries are not doing all that badly, economically. They are not developing at the miracle rates of the East Asian nations (nor does Latin America necessarily want to imitate the Asian cultural and social model), but they have pulled out of the recession of the early-to-mid-1980s.

In 1986 and 1987 seventeen of the twenty-one Latin American nations showed positive, real economic growth. Moreover most of the Latin American nations have learned to manage and cope with the debt situation in quite clever ways, so that it seems unlikely they will ever repay these onerous debts—although part of the game is never to say that publicly. The economic growth has not been dramatic, but it has occurred and some of it has even "trickled down," producing social modernization and transforming over several decades what were poor and backward nations for the most part into middle-level developing ones. Those long-term trends are likely to continue as long as the great motor force of a powerful U.S. economy continues.

Despite the polarized partisan debate and the rancorous 1988 election campaign, furthermore, there is remarkable consensus in Washington, D.C., on a sound Latin America policy. That policy involves a package of programs: human rights considerations as well as U.S. strategic concerns; about two-thirds of our foreign aid devoted to economic and social assistance and one-third in security assistance; efforts to help Latin America achieve democracy and to develop stable, viable political institutions; help with the debt in subtle ways but not at the cost of avoiding needed reforms in Latin America or of unacceptably passing the costs on to U.S. taxpayers— in short a package that includes a little bit for everyone. Such a package will not be acceptable to some purists but is probably about as good as the United States can realistically expect to do for Latin America, and it bears a striking resemblance to John F. Kennedy's Alliance for Progress and the recommendations of the Kissinger Commission.

There is even remarkable consensus, readers will be surprised to hear, about Central America, despite the debate that has raged for the last ten years and which is amplified and often polarized in the media. Virtually no one in political Washington disputes that we must, despite the frustrations of policy in that country, massively assist El Salvador along the lines described in the previous paragraph, or that we will and must continue to put pressure on the Sandinista regime. The only question is what form the pressure should take and how to combine that pressure with diplomacy. Actually, what had occurred in Washington was that the leaders of both parties had agreed to allow Central America to define the ideological differences between them because they both thought they could get political mileage out of the conflict. Republicans sought to blame Democrats for "losing" Nicaragua and perhaps other countries to Communism, while the Democrats thought they could use Central America to prove Republican ineptness and venality. Central America has been chosen by the party leaders on both sides of the aisle to define these differences because, unlike the Middle East or Soviet relations, there are few costs to a politician who says or does stupid things about that area. So Central America has become a partisan issue even though everyone inside the Washington Beltway knows these issues could be fairly easily resolved if we really wanted to. As long as it is not "our boys" who are dying, the Central America issue is likely to continue to fester as a political issue.

The Bush administration will have to wrestle with all these complex dilemmas, as well as the mist, smokescreens, and partisan posturings that shroud them. There are no easy solutions to any of these problems: far more likely is it that we will simply learn to live and cope with the more fundamental of these issues rather than resolve them. Above all, they are not amenable to simplistic solutions or the bumper sticker-level slogans that pass for a "debate" in the United States. Nor are we likely to see very many abrupt changes in a new U.S. administration, since President Bush is already aware of the issues. His advisers will quickly discover that the problems are intractable and the security and other dilemmas largely the same as those that plagued his predecessor.

The new Bush administration will undoubtedly be more pragmatic, centrist, and moderate than its predecessor—but without abandoning the more successful aspects of President Reagan's foreign policy agenda. On Latin America President Bush will emphasize democracy and human rights as well as U.S. strategic interests, give priority to socioeconomic assistance but continue some U.S. military assistance, work through normal diplomatic channels while not being averse to using the might and power of the U.S., support economic development as well as political reform, and provide some modest and partial forms of debt relief. He will combine pressure on the Sandinista regime with a genuine willingness to negotiate a solution to the crisis. In short, he will follow the multifaceted recommendations of the Kissinger Commission, which were enacted by the Congress but never completely implemented.

We have all the elements— outlined above—of a sane, sensible, long-term foreign policy for Latin America. What we need to avoid is a return to a strategy of neglect—benign or otherwise— toward the area as practiced in earlier administrations: or, as in Central America, a policy that allows "small" problems (Somoza's corruption and brutality, the repression practiced in the 1970s in Guatemala and El Salvador) to fester into larger ones that, as we have seen in the last few years, cause us endless grief. But one suspects that with Mexico fragmenting (Mexico is probably the second most important country in the world for U.S. foreign policy, behind only the Soviet Union), with the continuing crises in Central America that will not go away, and with future bilateral differences with the major South American countries, benign neglect of Latin America is no longer an option open to us. ∎

Suggested Additional Readings

Atkins, G. Pope. *Latin America in the International Political System,* 2nd ed. (Boulder, CO: Westview Press, 1989).

Committee of Santa Fe, *Santa Fe II: A Strategy for Latin America in the Nineties* (Washington, D.C.: Council for Inter-American Security, 1989).

Inter-American Dialogue. *The Americas in 1989: Consensus for Action* (Queenstown, MD: The Aspen Institute, 1989).

Kryzanek, Michael J. *U.S.-Latin American Relations* (New York: Praeger, 1985).

Lowenthal, Abraham F. *Partners in Conflict: The United States and Latin America* (Baltimore, MD: Johns Hopkins University Press, 1987).

McMichael, R. Daniel and John D. Paulus (eds.). *Western Hemisphere Stability* (Pittsburgh: World Affairs Council, 1983).

Molineau, Harold. *U.S. Policy Toward Latin America* (Boulder, CO: Westview Press, 1986).

Muñoz, Heraldo, and Joseph S. Tulchin (eds.). *Latin American Nations in World Politics* (Boulder, CO: Westview Press, 1984).

Nuccio, Richard. *What's Wrong, Who's Right in Central America: A Citizen's Guide* (Washington, D.C.: Roosevelt Center, 1986).

PACCA (Policy Alternatives for the Caribbean and Central America). *Changing Course: Blueprint for Peace in Central America and the Caribbean* (Washington, D.C.: Institute for Policy Studies, 1984).

Purcell, Susan Kaufman. *Mexico in Transition: Implications for U.S. Policy* (New York: Council on Foreign Relations, 1988).

The Report of the President's National Bipartisan Commission on Central America (New York: MacMillan, 1984).

Wiarda, Howard J. *The Democratic Revolution in Latin America: Implications for U.S. Policy.* (New York: Holmes and Meier, 1990).

————. *Finding Our Way? Toward Maturity in U.S.-Latin American Relations* (Washington, D.C.: American Enterprise Institute for Public Policy Research, 1987).

CHAPTER SIX

Southern Africa

*
*

If the future of Latin America appears discouraging, the future of Africa—particularly Africa south of the Sahara—looks bleaker still.

There was a time in the 1960s when the future of the newly independent states of Africa looked hopeful; many scholars were also attracted to the area to study these "new nations." Now, however, just about all the states of sub-Saharan Africa are mired in poverty and underdevelopment; the early democracies have given way to widespread authoritarianism; and scholars have abandoned their Africa specializations en masse. Both superpowers have apparently reached the same conclusions: that the area is hopeless, that there are few gains to be scored there, and that Africa is not worth paying much serious attention to.

The single exception is southern Africa, encompassing Angola, Mozambique, South Africa, and Namibia. Angola and Mozambique are both former Portuguese colonies that were given independence in the midst of the chaos and confusion of the Portuguese revolution of 1974–75. In both countries power was given over to Marxist-Leninist elements who have been facing strong opposition from noncommunist groups ever since. The Marxist-Leninist governments of these countries have received the backing of the Soviet Union, while the United States has sometimes supported their oppositions, especially UNITA in Angola. The issue is complicated by the presence of upwards of 50,000 Cuban troops, acting as agents of the Soviet Union in bolstering the Angolan government. Along with Vietnam and Central America, southern Africa has been the scene in recent decades of some of the globe's bloodiest fighting, involving not just local forces but the proxies of the Soviet Union and the United States as well.

Now, however, the Soviet Union, feeling the pressures of the need to reform its domestic economy as well as the debilitating effects of its long Africa venture, apparently wants "out" of southern Africa, as it has recently gotten out of Afghanistan. It has put pressure on the Cubans to reach an agreement with South Africa and Angola, with the United States serving as intermediary, to end the conflict. As part of the arrangement, Cuba is supposed to withdraw its troops from the area, South Africa is supposed to stop supplying UNITA, and Southwest Africa will receive independence as the new country of Namibia. There are many pitfalls and possibilities for violations of these treaty arrangements, but it looks as though both superpowers have an interest in greatly reducing, if not abandoning, their interests there.

The other major problem is South Africa itself. South Africa not only occupies one of the world's most vital strategic locations—on the southern tip of Africa, around which a great deal of Western Europe's and the United States' oil supplies pass—but it is also rich in vital strategic minerals. South Africa is the only predominantly Western nation in southern Africa and the only one firmly allied with the West. On the other hand, most Americans find South Africa's apartheid policies of racial segregation repugnant, and the U.S. has put pressure on South Africa in the form of economic and other sanctions to move toward a system of racial equality.

In the beginning of the debate over South Africa, the strategic and moral considerations (racial segregation) were almost evenly balanced, with the strategic ones usually receiving the greatest weight. In recent years, though, under the impact of television's coverage of the plight of South Africa's blacks as well as pressures from U.S. antiapartheid groups, the balance has tipped the other way. Now the racial situation gets all the coverage, while the strategic considerations are all but ignored. In political terms, this has often implied support for the Marxist-Leninist African National Congress.

South Africa is in a potentially very dangerous situation. On the one hand, we all want South Africa to evolve toward a system of greater racial equality. On the other hand, we need to balance that consideration with the strategic value of South Africa and the dangers of turning power over to a Marxist-Leninist group allied to the Soviet Union. Not only would that be inimical to our interests, it would also likely produce economic, political, and social retrogression in South Africa. Related as it is both to major foreign policy considerations and to strong domestic ethical and racial considerations, this is a terribly knotty issue.

This section begins with a fine statement on Africa's dilemmas by scholar John Marcum. The next two readings, by Ray Cline and by Peter Guignan and L. H. Gann, emphasize the strategic importance of South Africa and the resultant need for a go-slow approach by the United States that will not sacrifice our vital interests there. Pauline Baker of the Carnegie Endowment, however, argues, among other things, that the strategic importance of South Africa has now taken a back seat to human rights concerns. We conclude this section with a plan by the State Department for peace in southwest Africa.

AFRICA: A CONTINENT ADRIFT

John A. Marcum

For Africa, this decade has been a period of ominous economic, social and environmental decline. In 1980 depressed world commodity prices, declining agricultural production, ravaging drought and desertification, rising external debt, and both civil and interstate warfare portended continent-wide disaster. Throughout the 1980s per capita income fell from a level already the lowest in two decades. Decreasing financial reserves forced cuts in vital imports, including an eight-percent cut in 1987 alone. As the value of African exports continued to fall, from $57 billion in 1980 to $32 billion in 1986, one African statesman, the former Nigerian head of state General Olusegun Obasanjo, warned that Africa was falling into a state of "dereliction and decay."

Yet Africa remained low on the list of American foreign policy concerns. During the Reagan presidency Washington officials spoke of Africa as "a continent of great promise" with which the United States was effectively interacting on both economic and diplomatic fronts.[1] The somber reality was that human conditions in Africa were continuing to deteriorate, despite a U.N.-sponsored recovery plan (1986–1990) under which many African states were undertaking unpopular structural reforms and austerity measures.

U.N. Secretary-General Javier Pérez de Cuéllar lamented the failure of industrialized donor states to respond to African reforms with increased assistance, saying that it was leading Africa "not to recovery and development but to drift and stagnation, if not a chronic state of crisis."[2] Even in gold-rich South Africa, where the persistence of apartheid was a principal focus of the administration's Africa policy, economic conditions were worsening, exacerbated by the intensifying racial polarity.

On the other hand, Africa was approaching its fourth decade of independence with some plausible grounds for hope and avenues of opportunity. In southern Africa an agreement for the military disengagement of Cuban and South African forces from Angola and Namibia, respectively, held the possibility of converting this area of devastating conflict into an engine for development in the region. In West Africa, at an October 1988 Africa Leadership Forum convened by Nigeria's Obasanjo, he and other Africans presented tough, perceptive and prescriptive analyses aimed at deepening and expanding their commitment to disciplined recovery and development efforts.

For the first time since the rise of African nationalism after World War II, there was reason to believe that Africa's internal efforts might not be distracted by East-West confrontation. A tentative relaxation in superpower tensions, if confirmed by full military disengagement from Afghanistan and Angola, could result in a less divisive, if not more generous, international climate. African needs and issues might then at least compete for international consideration on their merits rather than on their relevance to a zero-sum cold war.

II

Despite Africa's stark socioeconomic crisis, it was instead the perceived threat of Soviet expansionism in Angola, Mozambique and Ethiopia, and domestic political pressure on the issue of apartheid in South Africa, which commanded Washington's attention. These concerns seemed to pose a more immediate challenge to American interests. From the time he assumed office in 1981, Assistant Secretary of State for African Affairs Chester A. Crocker focused his energies on two objectives: reducing Soviet/Cuban influence and cross-border conflict in southern Africa, and encouraging liberalization of the oppressive racial and political order in South Africa.

The Africa policies of the Carter Administration were dismissed as ineffectual, even though it was on Jimmy Carter's "watch" that Zimbabwe had achieved independence and South Africa had endorsed but not yet implemented a U.N. formula (Security Council Resolution 435) for Namibian independence. Assistant Secretary Crocker believed that softer language, ex-

John A. Marcum is Professor of Politics and Chair of International Programs at the University of California, Santa Cruz. He is the author of a two-volume study, *The Angolan Revolution*.

Source: From *Foreign Affairs* Vol. 68, No. 1 (Winter, 1988–89), pp. 159–170. Reprinted by permission of Foreign Affairs, Winter 1988–89. Copyright 1988 by the Council on Foreign Relations, Inc.

panded economic and cultural ties, and diplomatic suasion could nudge South Africa toward regional accommodation and internal reform. He first tested this concept of "constructive engagement" on the issue of Namibia.

In mid-1981 the United States broke ranks with other members of a Contact Group (Britain, Canada, France, West Germany) that had been seeking to persuade Pretoria to implement Resolution 435. Judging that multilateral approach to have failed, it unilaterally proposed, and South Africa readily accepted, the idea of linking the withdrawal of South African forces from Namibia to a parallel withdrawal of Cuban forces from Angola. Washington thereby dismantled collective Western diplomatic pressure on Pretoria and provided the issue of Cuban troops as a rationale for a prolonged South African military presence in Namibia.

The United States, alone among the world powers, had not recognized the MPLA (Popular Movement for the Liberation of Angola) government that emerged from a violent power struggle following the collapse of Portuguese rule in 1975. A Cuban expeditionary force and Soviet arms had played a crucial role in the victory of the Marxist MPLA over rival movements supported by the United States and South Africa. Despite initial postindependence zealotry and dogmatism, however, the MPLA government pragmatically came to terms with American and other Western oil firms exploiting the country's considerable petroleum reserves, and Cuban forces began to withdraw as early as April 1976. As this withdrawal proceeded, the Carter Administration missed an opportunity in early 1977 to accord relatively uncontroversial recognition

to the government. Soon after, the exodus of Cuban troops was ended, and reversed, because of overflights of South African aircraft and mounting antigovernment insurgency. The South African Defense Force (SADF) had helped to reorganize, train and equip remnants of the rival movement UNITA (National Union for the Total Independence of Angola), which had regrouped in Angola's southeastern savanna. Led by a formidable, longtime adversary of the MPLA, Jonas Savimbi, whose political roots were in populous and ethnically Ovimbundu central Angola, UNITA's deadly hit-and-run insurgency gradually expanded northward across the Benguela railroad corridor and throughout much of eastern and central Angola.

UNITA's anticommunist stance earned the assistance of Morocco, Saudi Arabia and other Gulf states, as well as South Africa. By mid-1986 South Africa's assistance alone reportedly totaled about $1 billion.[3] The dramatic success of UNITA's guerrilla strategy prompted Cuba and the Soviet Union to ratchet up their assistance to beleaguered Angolan government forces. This, in turn, galvanized sympathy for UNITA among conservative, anticommunist groups in the United States. UNITA became an obvious candidate for Reagan Doctrine assistance to "freedom fighters" opposing governments perceived to be Soviet-imposed. The doctrine's thesis was that relatively small amounts of aid to groups such as UNITA could, at low risk, raise the cost of and ultimately reverse Soviet expansionism of the late Brezhnev years.

As a political chameleon of passing persuasion but steady ambition, Savimbi feted foreign journalists and political leaders at his headquarters in Jamba near the Namibian border. Described by visitors as a charismatic strategist and democrat, Savimbi made a high-profile entry onto the Washington stage in early 1986. He met with President Reagan and other top executive and congressional leaders, publicized his case in a well-orchestrated media campaign and obtained a promise of substantial military help. The 1976 Clark Amendment, which banned such aid to Angolan groups, had been repealed in 1985. By mid-1986 UNITA's defenses against sophisticated Soviet weaponry were being strengthened by officially acknowledged "covert" aid, reportedly including Stinger antiaircraft and TOW antitank missiles.

This new thrust in American policy was intended to force the MPLA to negotiate a political settlement with Savimbi, thereby eliminating the excuse for Cuban troops in Angola. Most European observers feared that American intervention would have the contrary effect of closing the door to a negotiated settlement and the departure of the 35,000 Cuban troops.[4] In the event, neither the intent nor the fear would test out before the political and strategic realities of southern Africa were altered by three intervening factors: (1) the cumulative ravages and exhaustion of unwinnable war; (2) the "new thinking" that reoriented Soviet diplomacy; and (3) the overextension and retrenchment of South African military power.

III

Afflicted by over a quarter-century of anticolonial and internal conflict, Angola was facing disaster by the late 1980s. Its oil revenues (about $2 billion annually) were not enough to pay for billions of dollars' worth of Soviet military equipment, support thousands of Cuban soldiers and technicians and rebuild a ruined economy subject to continuing destruction. The statistics were grim. Since 1975 nearly half of Angola's approximately eight million people had been uprooted. Land mines created tens of thousands of amputees, and hundreds of thousands took refuge in adjoining countries. UNICEF estimated that 55,000 children under the age of five died from violence-related causes in 1986 alone.[5] Angola was being consumed by war, a war to which the United States was now contributing.

In 1985 and again in 1987 the MPLA government and its Soviet and Cuban guarantors sought a definitive military solution by means of massive, tank-led offensives designed to capture UNITA's southeastern redoubt and its "capital," Jamba. These slow, easily targeted offensives were meant to destroy UNITA's communications and supply links to Namibia/South Africa. In each case, the intervention of South African air, artillery and surrogate ground forces (the 32 Battalion—white-officered Angolan dissidents) helped UNITA blunt the attacks, but at serious human and material cost to both sides. After the second offensive the MPLA was left with a badly pummeled army and thinly stretched Cuban rearguard forces facing a seemingly endless attritional guerrilla insurgency.[6] The enormity of the human suffering and physical destruction disposed even the most war-calloused leadership within the MPLA to become more receptive to the notion of an externally brokered regional settlement.

An agreement that resulted in the withdrawal of Cuban and South African forces from Angola and Namibia would presumably deprive UNITA of its primary source of external support. The MPLA rejected as unnecessary all suggestions that it negotiate with UNITA's Jonas Savimbi, possibly overestimating the extent to which South African involvement was accountable for UNITA's success. Critics suspected that the MPLA might be a victim of its own propaganda, according to which UNITA was little more than a creature of the SADF. The Luanda government seemed unable to accept that to some extent UNITA was a political beneficiary of the MPLA's failure to reach beyond its own traditional urban and northern strongholds to less-educated, rural and religious communities, whose support was essential to national unity. MPLA leaders wanted to believe that if UNITA could be deprived of its Namibian logistical hinterland, its second-echelon leadership would become receptive to offers of individual amnesty and the movement would fade away.

Under Mikhail Gorbachev, the Soviet Union's willingness to pay the price of a protective, privileged relationship with a destitute client in faraway southwestern Africa came increasingly into question. It knew that American leadership was still smarting over what was widely, albeit simplistically, viewed as the humiliating "loss" of Angola in 1975 to Soviet domination. Angola had come to symbolize the end of détente. As Moscow's policymakers came to acknowledge the extent to which regional confrontations had poisoned U.S.-Soviet relations, they became more interested in regional disengage-

ment. Informed by the sobering experience of working with a government whose "socialist orientation" was not buttressed by the educated cadres, economic infrastructure or national cohesion necessary to realize its aims, and absorbed by the exigencies of perestroika at home, Soviet authorities became less enthusiastic about pouring additional billions of dollars of scarce resources into a distant military entanglement. Soviet Deputy Foreign Minister Anatoly L. Adamishin and Assistant Secretary Crocker became active interlocutors in the search for a way out.

The shift in South Africa's policy was equally sharp and important, though some feared ephemeral. Skeptics doubted that South Africa's shift represented more than a tactical maneuver, just as some distrusted Moscow's "new thinking." The ruling National Party in South Africa must have been uneasy that the rising, extreme right-wing Conservative Party would capitalize electorally on any moves it made to withdraw from Namibia. But there was reason to believe that the shift, however tentative and grudging, reflected new power realities in southern Africa. South Africa had extended its military projection beyond sustainable limits and was finding it prudent to step back.

Twice the United States had encouraged South Africa to overextend itself, according to official South African sources: first in 1975 when Secretary of State Henry Kissinger allegedly urged it to intervene in support of UNITA and other anti-MPLA forces, and again in the mid-1980s when Director of Central Intelligence William Casey and private conservative groups in

Washington supported its second engagement with UNITA. In both instances Cuban forces were the immediate cause of South Africa's undoing.

In its September–October 1987 intervention South Africa's formidable long-range artillery, air force and surrogate ground forces were successful in smashing the MPLA's lumbering, Soviet-designed, motorized offensive at Mavinga, north of Jamba. The South Africans pressed on to join UNITA forces in laying siege to Cuito Cuanavale, where shattered MPLA units had taken refuge. Savoring their Mavinga victory, albeit with unease over small but politically sensitive white conscript casualties, South African officials reacted with seeming scorn when Mr. Crocker announced in early 1988 that he had managed to obtain the Angolan government's formal acceptance of the principle of a total Cuban troop withdrawal, and on a speedier timetable than had previously seemed possible, in return for South African implementation of U.N. Resolution 435.

Some journalists wrote that because South Africa had altered the "military equation" in Angola, the most a Cuban withdrawal might produce would be a South African withdrawal from Angola, not Namibia.[7] President P. W. Botha publicly speculated that Cuba was contemplating the withdrawal of its forces without a Namibian settlement. Expressing doubt that Crocker had contributed to this promising situation, Botha credited South African military power, claimed that the Soviets had become "frustrated" and were "shopping" for a compromise, and declared that South Africa had no intention of leaving Angola "until

the Cubans leave."[8] In Washington, analysts at the Defense Intelligence Agency, long critical of Crocker's greater enthusiasm for negotiations than for military support for UNITA, were speculating that the imminent fall of Cuito Cuanavale might lead to the surrender of other provincial capitals and even UNITA's triumphal entry into Luanda.

As it had since the late 1970s, the South African/UNITA military success led to military escalation. Early in 1988 Cuba sent 10,000 to 15,000 new combat troops to Angola, raising its military presence to approximately 50,000. In addition to reinforcing besieged Cuito Cuanavale, the Cubans seized the initiative and did what the MPLA had long wanted them to do: they moved south toward the Namibian border. As its artillery mired down in rainy season mud outside Cuito Cuanavale, SADF suffered new white casualties and lost at least two Cheetah fighter planes—a serious loss because perhaps only 12 planes were operational and the international arms embargo dating back to 1963 made replacing aircraft difficult. Angolan MiG-23s flying from new bases at Cahama and Xangongo gained air supremacy over southwestern Angola, a dozen white South African soldiers were killed near Calueque Dam on the border, and Angolan aircraft overflew South African military facilities in Ovamboland in Namibia.

South Africa confronted the prospect of greater human and material losses if it undertook an assault on Cuito Cuanavale or attempted to press Cuban forces back from the border. SADF could no longer range freely through southern Angola to accomplish its other mission, to search and de-

stroy guerrilla units of the nationalist South West African People's Organization (SWAPO) seeking to infiltrate into and liberate Namibia. By mid-1988 South African military leaders knew that the new Cuban presence along Namibia's northern border, unless removed by negotiations, would likely translate into increased external support for SWAPO and related encounters with Angolan or Cuban forces.

Suddenly it was a Cuban-imposed "military equation" that was concentrating South African minds. If Pretoria implemented Resolution 435 it would lose the Caprivi Strip base complex that had given SADF striking power into the heart of southern Africa. It would receive an embarrassing influx of angry emigrants from among Namibia's white minority of approximately 90,000, who would attempt to stir political passions in South Africa as Algeria's *pieds noirs* had done in France in 1962. The Conservative Party was poised to exploit the occasion. On the other hand, the African National Congress (ANC) would lose its training bases in Angola, and South Africa would retain control of the vital railhead and port of Walvis Bay and thus the capacity to intervene quickly to thwart any hostile thrust from SWAPO-governed Namibian territory.

In Pretoria the influence of the military was giving way to that of the Foreign Office, as the government seemed to recognize the geopolitical limits of its power. After new rounds of U.S.-brokered diplomatic discussions, in August 1988 several thousand South African troops extricated themselves from Cuito Cuanavale and made an orderly withdrawal back across the Namibian border.

IV

Circumstances having become propitious, Chester Crocker's persistence paid off. Beginning in May with U.S.-mediated talks between South Africa, Angola and Cuba in London, and subsequent meetings in Cairo, New York, Geneva and Brazzaville, the terms of a regional settlement were systematically hammered out. They culminated in the signing of formal agreements on December 22 setting forth the steps and timetable for implementation of Resolution 435 and the departure of Cuban forces from Angola. Cuban troops are to leave over a period of 27 months, with an initial cohort of 3,000 out of 50,000 to leave by April 1, 1989. Namibia's transition to independence is to begin on that same date. A U.N. peacekeeping force of up to 9,000 soldiers, police and administrators costing up to $700 million will move into Namibia as South Africa reduces its troop strength from some 50,000 to 1,500 by July 1. Preparations will then proceed for the election of a constituent assembly based on proportional representation on November 1. Following the assembly's adoption of a constitution, Namibia is slated to gain independence.

Meanwhile, Cuban forces are scheduled to withdraw northward: to 200 miles from the Namibian border by August and then to the 13th parallel above the Benguela railroad by November. By that time, half of Cuba's 50,000 troops should have left the country. The remainder of Cuban forces will leave by stages to be completed by July 1, 1991. Critics of the agreement argue that as of April 1989 South Africa's departure from Namibia will be irreversible, whereas Cuba could halt its withdrawal at any time. Excluded from the settlement, UNITA would be left vulnerable to a Cuban-backed MPLA offensive designed to wipe it out. However, the failure of Cuba and the Soviet Union to support a 1988 dry season assault on UNITA and reports of an informal Cuban-UNITA agreement not to attack each other's forces suggest that the MPLA might not be supported in such action. Continued improvement in Soviet-American relations may depend on the laboriously negotiated regional settlement's not being wrecked on the shoals of Angola's internal conflict.

Angola's quest for peace clearly depends on reaching an internal political settlement. Once Cuban and South African forces are removed from the region, American officials reason, "pressures for political settlement between the MPLA regime of [President] José Eduardo dos Santos and Mr. Savimbi's UNITA movement will become inexorable."[9] They have also indicated that the United States will not establish diplomatic relations with the Luanda government or stop blocking its membership in the World Bank and International Monetary Fund until it has come to terms with UNITA. But the dos Santos government has continued strongly to resist having to deal with Savimbi, whom it fears politically and holds personally responsible for alleged UNITA collaboration with Portuguese military officials in the early 1970s and subsequently with the South African military beginning in 1975.

The potential for an internal settlement is complicated by continuing, congressionally supported U.S. aid to UNITA, which could also become a major stumbling block to the implementation of Cuban troop withdrawal. The U.S. aid factor has grown in importance as the UNITA insurgency has shifted northward away from its original South African umbilical cord to regions within reach of an American lifeline via Zaïre. On January 6, in advance of his inauguration, President-elect George Bush wrote Savimbi promising to continue "all appropriate and effective assistance" until realization of a negotiated "national reconciliation." In what a January 12 *Washington Post* story called Bush's "first foreign policy commitment," he pledged his support to the man UNITA radio refers to as "supreme guide, Comrade President Dr. [Savimbi]." A Bush aide described this support as meaning continued covert military help valued at about $15 million annually, which the incoming administration views as having helped bring about the accords of December 22, as well as support for African diplomatic efforts. It will not be easy for the White House or the State Department to extricate the United States from this commitment, which could perpetuate civil war unless African diplomacy prevails over MPLA and UNITA rigidities.

A powerful congressional alignment led by Senator Dennis DeConcini (D-Ariz.) threatened in October to deny $150 million in essential U.S. funding for the U.N. 435 peacekeeping function (including the monitoring of Cuban troop withdrawal over some 27 months) unless UNITA's inclusion within a settlement was assured. Combined African, Soviet and American pressure and cajoling in favor of national reconciliation of an imaginative kind is needed to overcome the Savimbi factor. Discussion has centered around such formulas as an MPLA offer of a coalition government if Savimbi would "volunteer" to step aside. Perhaps most promising are the efforts of African states to persuade the Luanda government to join in reconciliation talks with UNITA. The heads of state of Nigeria, Morocco, the Ivory Coast and Kenya, among others, have offered their good offices. But at year's end, in a move likely to reinforce MPLA reluctance to negotiate, the Frontline States collectively urged the incoming Bush Administration to discontinue U.S. support for UNITA "bandits." With the likely continuation of both U.S. aid for UNITA and (possibly reduced) Soviet support for the MPLA, however, stalemated civil war and de facto partition loom as a possible outcome.

As for Namibia, it faces an unpromising independence, reliant on mineral wealth of declining value, depleted fisheries and arid agriculture. A rudimentary, racially segregated educational system imposed by South Africa has left its population ill prepared. The country will be vulnerable to social upheaval as thousands of war-brutalized soldiers of the internal South-West Africa Territorial Force and the external SWAPO guerrilla army are demobilized. Thousands of Namibians studying in Cuba, the Soviet Union and elsewhere will also have to be integrated back into local society. A widely predicted victory for SWAPO in the November 1, 1989, elections is less likely to produce the hardline Marxist government feared by some than a fragile, inexperienced government in dire need of international assistance.

Above all, the UNITA issue dramatized how vulnerable to derailment a tortuously negotiated

agreement might be even after implementation has begun.[10] Yet, however pitted and detouring the road, a grudging, fitful regional retrenchment by an overextended South Africa appeared to be under way at year's end.

V

In another example of regional retrenchment, in mid-1988 President Botha engaged in a flurry of jet diplomacy with Mozambique, emulating John Vorster's visits to distant African capitals a decade and a half earlier. The time when Pretoria's legions could lay waste its neighbors at little short-term cost was ebbing.

Reduced to chaos by drought, administrative incapacity, political disaffection and South African-nourished rebellion, Mozambique had signed the U.S.-encouraged Nkomati agreement with South Africa in 1984 under which it expelled militants of the ANC in return for Pretoria's pledge to discontinue its destabilization policy against the hard-pressed, socialist-oriented but increasingly pragmatic government of FRELIMO, the Mozambique Liberation Front. But the Mozambique National Resistance (RENAMO) continued its scorched-earth devastation, though it became largely self-propelled. Mozambique turned to the West for help amid what seemed like expressions of embarrassed relief in Moscow, heretofore FRELIMO's principal but parsimonious benefactor. Military units from neighboring Zimbabwe, Tanzania and Malawi attempted to restore control over vital transport routes, and British trainers and Italian equipment began to help rebuild the army. The Reagan Administration dropped its earlier

hostility and in 1983–84 joined in providing modest food and technical assistance.

Despite this assistance, the Maputo government could not end the chaos. But one of the causes of its trauma, South African complicity in the RENAMO rebellion, seemed on the wane. In mid-1988 Pretoria initiated bilateral talks designed to resuscitate the largely lapsed Nkomati agreement, pledged to discontinue any residual support to RENAMO insurgents and promised technical and security assistance to permit the transmission and sale of electrical power from Mozambique's Cabora Bassa dam on the Zambezi River to South Africa. A successful meeting between Presidents Botha and Joaquim Chissano at Cabora Bassa in September appeared to undercut lingering pressure from zealous Reagan Doctrine enthusiasts in Washington to assist the "anticommunist" RENAMO. Even more important to the debate in Washington over whether to aid that group was a compelling report released by the State Department, which held RENAMO responsible for vast destruction and the deaths of some 100,000 civilians.[11] As Mozambique's plight commanded increasing international concern and Western assistance, South African policymakers had to reckon that renewed support for attritional destabilization would bring them into collision with the West.

Seeking to offset military retrenchment with diplomatic outreach, President Botha also flew to Malawi, Zaïre and the Ivory Coast in September–October 1988. While they seemed to provide South Africa with an ephemeral measure of external acceptance, his visits were not reciprocated, and the Frontline leadership of Botswana, Tanzania, Zambia and Zimbabwe did not receive him.

In Zimbabwe, one of the few countries where agricultural production has remained strong, the ruling ZANU (Zimbabwe African National Union) and the opposition ZAPU (Zimbabwe African People's Union) achieved a political reconciliation in 1988. These longtime political rivals merged, advancing Prime Minister Robert Mugabe's goal of a one-party state by 1990. The reconciliation also diminished South Africa's opportunities for political destabilization in this key Frontline State. Although South Africa used such tactics less frequently in 1988, South African soldiers raided an alleged ANC headquarters in Botswana in late March, killing four.

Regional dependence on and vulnerability to South Africa will be further decreased if Angola reaches an internal settlement and the troop withdrawal proceeds. It will open the way for reconstruction and use of the Benguela railroad, enabling Zambia and Zaïre to redirect mineral exports away from South African transport routes and ports. Also, Angola could then use its petroleum wealth to relaunch what was previously developing as a rich and diverse economy based on coffee, maize, diamonds, iron and food-processing.

VI

The second goal of "constructive engagement" was to facilitate and hasten racial and political reform within South Africa. During the early years of the Reagan Administration, P. W. Botha promulgated a series of reforms eliminating pass laws, the ban on mixed marriages and group restrictions on university admissions. As it gained momentum, the reform agenda raised expectations and catalyzed a feverish growth of black political organizations, including trade unions, student movements and community volunteer groups. But reform did not extend to such essentials of apartheid as the Group Areas Act, separate homeland citizenship and denial of the franchise to blacks at the national level. The gap between what the National Party and black political leadership considered a reasonable process, scope and pace of reform led to frustration, despair and accelerating violence. As South Africa's townships erupted, the government responded with armored troop carriers and tear gas, and millions of American television viewers found themselves caught up in South Africa's racial drama.

The Free South Africa Movement burst onto the American scene in the wake of President Reagan's reelection in 1984. Rejecting "constructive engagement" as failed appeasement, antiapartheid activists campaigned for divestment, disinvestment, consumer boycotts and, ultimately, national trade sanctions, all of which culminated in a 1986 Comprehensive Anti-Apartheid Act adopted by Congress over the president's veto. Interviews with both advocates and opponents of such measures revealed more concern for being on the "right side" of the issue than for strategic and realistic thinking about how best to facilitate fundamental reform at tolerable cost.[12]

The sanctions passed by Congress were limited and inexpensive. They banned a range of South African imports (excluding strategic minerals) and terminated landing rights for South African Airways in the United States. Most important, they marked a downturn in U.S.-South African relations, underscored by the January 1987 report of an independent, presidentially appointed advisory committee on U.S. policy toward South Africa. The report concluded that circumstances in South Africa had "moved in a direction sharply at odds with the hopes and expectations of the architects" of American policy.[13]

Bitter and defiant, the South African government severely restricted foreign news media and restored order in the townships by using the police, army and a succession of "states of emergency." The National Party government professed a continuing belief that the 5-to-1 black majority should be incorporated into economic and political structures of the country. But it was unable to persuade credible black leadership to endorse or participate in limited, unilaterally dispensed "power sharing." It persisted in efforts to crush "radical opposition" such as the pluralistic United Democratic Front and the underground, exiled ANC, which demand a universal political franchise. Its determination to crush this opposition was dramatized by a three-year treason trial of UDF and other black leaders. Four defendants were found guilty of treason; in December 1988 they were sentenced to prison, but this verdict made their crimes of antiapartheid advocacy and "hostile intent" legally punishable by hanging. If these were the consequences of mere dissent, *The New York Times* asked, "what course remains open *but* revolution?"[14] In late 1988 South Africa's best-known political prisoner, the ill and aging Nelson

Mandela, was shifted to a relatively comfortable confinement—but with little or no prospect of political freedom.

Pretoria appears locked into a policy of coerce and co-opt, hoping to gain local black support, or at least quiescence, by means of socioeconomic programs of improved housing, education and social services. The aim is to buy time to persuade appreciable numbers of blacks to accept a modified apartheid system incorporating limited local self-government in a patchwork of political entities reminiscent of the Holy Roman Empire. Leaving aside the question of whether economic well-being and political equity can be achieved in a framework of enduring separation, carrying out this policy depends on the availability of massive financial resources.

Although the South African economy is based on gold, diamonds and strategic minerals, which have been exempted from sanctions and are easily transported, it has proved vulnerable to external trade sanctions and a related loss of investor confidence. Over the past decade South Africa's population has grown at a faster rate than its economy—3.6 percent versus 1.3 percent, according to some estimates. Gross national product is currently growing at about 2.5 percent annually, well below the five percent needed to meet job demand. Unemployment within the economically active black population is already 30 to 40 percent and is expected to reach 50 to 60 percent within 15 years.

The prospects for an improving economy are not good, given the current situation: a depreciated currency, a 14-percent inflation rate, some $12 billion in external debt payments due in 1990–91 and a $5-billion net capital outflow since 1986. From the time of the Soweto uprising in 1976, South Africa has been a net exporter of capital, unable to attract new financial and technological investment crucial to growth and its co-optation strategy. Nothing short of fundamental political change is likely to alter these impediments to the economy's long-term health.

Compounding the economic difficulties is the right-wing backlash against the National Party's haphazard moves to reduce racial discrimination and introduce controlled power sharing. The Conservative Party, pledged to return to pure Verwoerdian apartheid, replaced the liberal Progressive Federal Party as the official opposition in parliament after the March 1988 elections. In municipal elections in October Conservatives won 60 percent of the seats on Transvaal city councils and promptly moved to reintroduce petty apartheid segregation in cities such as Boksburg. While the Conservative Party enjoys a heady sense of growing power, a brain drain of liberal professionals steadily carries away vital skilled manpower (half of the country's medical school graduates emigrate), and black labor and consumers try desperately to organize countervailing pressure. The Conservatives demand "self-determination" for South Africa's five million whites, which means partition of the country by whites. The more extreme, paramilitary Afrikaner Resistance Movement (AWB) with an estimated 5,000 to 9,000 members and hundreds of thousands of supporters and tacit sympathizers, is fanning a mystical, xenophobic Afrikaner nationalism.

Believed to have a strong covert following among government employees, notably the police, the AWB poses a threat of violent resistance to any reform program seen as undermining continued white domination.

As the 1980s end, South Africa confronts an inexorable logic. A coercively fragmented and stratified state of five million white citizens dominating some 28 million "others" cannot hope to achieve and sustain healthy economic development. It cannot do so even if it stops expending huge sums administering and defending Namibia (over $1 billion a year), aiding UNITA (some $250 million a year), dispatching expeditionary forces, supporting surrogate armies and mounting "preemptive strikes" against presumed ANC facilities in neighboring countries. But it is no less evident that the fundamental reform required will remain beyond reach so long as right-wing reaction paralyzes the state. A specter of near-term stalemate and long-term isolation, violence and decay haunt South Africa's future.

In late 1987 Secretary Shultz and Assistant Secretary Crocker acknowledged their "frustration" at the "grim realities" and a "debilitating pessimism" concerning prospects for the construction of a democratic South Africa. Arguing that the 1986 sanctions, which they had opposed, had served to arrest "meaningful reform" and abet a cycle of violence and counterviolence, they also acknowledged that Americans were deeply divided over how to approach a seemingly intractable tragedy. Crocker decried an "adolescent tendency" among South Africans of all persuasions "alternately to cultivate or scapegoat" foreigners and, speaking with the sobered voice of experience, mused: "we know now—more than ever—that the fate of South Africa is not in our hands."[15]

Implicitly recognizing this impasse, George Bush proposed during his presidential campaign that efforts to "compel" change in South Africa with more "unilateral" sanctions be forgone in favor of "a more effective diplomatic strategy" focused on active "multilateral" coordination with Europe and Japan. "In my administration," he averred, "the first thing I will do is meet with the heads of state of other Western countries to work out a united Western position on South Africa." Such a position would be premised on a need for "fundamental political change" and a recognition that "racial conflict in South Africa would be a catastrophe for all concerned." The style, if not the content, was in contrast with the years of apparent Reagan indifference to apartheid and multilateralism. Candidate George Bush also called for an expansion of government and private initiatives "to help black South Africans in areas such as housing, education and training."[16]

A combination of coordinated international pressure and black empowerment initiatives, if given substance and focus, might in fact improve chances for a positive outcome. If, as George Bush argues, sanctions have been counterproductive in furthering internal reform, they may have been productive in inducing more accommodating South African policies toward the region. Might concerted multilateral sanctions, chosen for their potential effectiveness rather than for domestic political gratifi-

cation, impose on South Africa a sense of realism about its internal future? Bipartisan and multilateral discussions might concentrate on the identification of a selective list of measures that could be rapidly implemented and that could have potentially sharp psychological or strategic impact. These could include an international air embargo or bans on relatively easily monitored sales of specific industrial chemicals and high-technology machinery. Any multilateral initiatives of this nature would need to be accompanied by an explicit commitment to respond promptly to a fundamental reversal of race policies in South Africa by ending sanctions and resuming fruitful economic ties.

In the absence of such substantive multilateral action, "black empowerment" initiatives risk being perceived by increasingly battered, embittered and radicalized black South Africans as manipulative palliatives. As a substitute rather than an aspect of a comprehensive multilateral policy of all South Africa's present and alternative trading partners—including Britain, Israel, Japan, South Korea, Taiwan and West Germany—such programs could become increasingly controversial.

President George Bush's electoral endorsement of "economic assistance to the member states of the Southern African Development Coordination Conference" points up another policy opportunity.[17] Increased support for transport and other SADCC development projects would strengthen the region and reorient trade (via the Beira and Benguela railroads) and communications away from dependency on South Africa. The U.S.- and Soviet-backed interna-

tional guarantees in the Angola-Namibia settlement and increased support for security forces in other Frontline States would help dissuade South Africa from returning to an aggressive regional destabilization policy.

Prospects for American policy toward South and southern Africa remain problematic. But the Bush Administration might improve them by working with a range of partners, including seasoned allies, trade competitors and traditional adversaries, to galvanize a broad international consensus behind a well-considered, patiently pursued set of strategies.

VII

The unfolding tragedy of South Africa serves to command the attention of an otherwise distracted United States to matters African. But it may also divert attention from the intimidating complex of crises besetting the continent as a whole. While policymakers concentrate on southern Africa, accelerating deforestation and desertification, spreading malnutrition and disease (including AIDS), debilitating warfare in potentially rich agricultural countries such as Angola, Ethiopia and Sudan, deteriorating terms of trade and soaring international debt are combining to make Africa a human and environmental disaster area. The crisis is so diffuse and of such magnitude that the United States and the world at large shrink from engaging it.

The cumulative destruction and exhaustion of protracted warfare is so severe that it can force protagonists to contemplate negotiated settlement. Prospects are least auspicious in Ethiopia, where the military government remains determined to crush Eritrean and Tigre nationalism despite horrendous casualities; they are better in Sudan, where some northern leaders show signs of willingness to abandon forced Islamization of the war-and-famine-decimated but resolutely rebellious south; promising in the Western Sahara, where economically motivated rapprochement between Algeria and Morocco is facilitating a political resolution to the Polisario insurgency; and consummated in Chad, where costly military defeat finally persuaded Libya's Muammar al-Qaddafi to abandon his territorial ambitions.

Presidential candidate Bush acknowledged a need for debt rescheduling and greater coordination and mobilization of Western financial assistance, but he also spoke of Africa as "a major and growing market for U.S. commodities, technology and equipment."[18] The reality is otherwise. Confronting it, General Obasanjo has observed that only Africans can "know what is really amiss" and only they "can tell it as it is" to themselves. Considering perestroika, the coming integration of Europe, and the economic and technological miracle of Japan and the NICs, Obasanjo said, and "contrasting all this with what is taking place in Africa, it is difficult to believe that we inhabit the same historical time."[19]

What is required, in the Nigerian leader's view, is an assertion of democratic values and collaboration among African states. Eschewing the notion of any quick fix, he also urges renewed efforts to persuade the international community to stabilize commodity prices, lower protectionist barriers and, in general, build "a new and fairer economic order." Above all, however, Obasanjo says Africans must rely principally on their own efforts. They must depend on their own imagination and purpose, draw upon their own human resources. Specifically, they must free themselves from continuing dependency on the "roaring industry" of up to 80,000 expatriate advisers costing over half of Africa's $7 to $8 billion in annual assistance.

In ascribing a "special responsibility" to African universities and intellectuals to devise solutions and spur action, he points to a core aspect of the African crisis in which the United States might take a lead in promoting an international response. The universities that Obasanjo sees as crucial to African efforts to reverse the continent's decline are themselves hard hit by the economic situation. The development and preservation of key African universities and research centers with adequate libraries, laboratories and trained African faculty and researchers should be an achievable goal. Bearing in mind the role that land grant colleges played in the development of the United States, an American-sponsored international effort to help African universities and intellectuals meet the challenge of this historical time would seem a logical priority.

Because the United States is preoccupied with its own debt and trade deficit, it is unlikely to expand significantly its annual $800 to $850 million in bilateral assistance to Africa (about ten percent of the total foreign aid Africa receives). But it could become a leader rather than a foot-dragger in devising more generous, coherent and practicable means of scheduling and meeting debt payments.[20] Specifically, it could encourage international financial and bilateral assistance criteria based on demonstrable productivity gains rather than ideological or strategic considerations;[21] it could respond to General Obasanjo's arguments for a "variegated" approach to development by encouraging maximum multilateral coordination, flexibility and humility before the enormity of Africa's unfolding crisis.

American policymakers will continue to concentrate diplomatic energy on the special challenges of southern Africa, but they can at the same time develop initiatives relevant to the larger African context. They can press upon the Soviet Union and others agreements to stop arms sales to such self-destructing societies as those of Ethiopia, Sudan, Sahara and Angola, and joint or parallel efforts to facilitate conflict resolution and economic reconstruction. They can build on international consensus achieved in cases such as Angola to turn energies to creative, self-sustaining uses, to rescue afflicted societies from further decline. In so doing they will contribute to the quest for concrete diplomatic and economic breakthroughs and models desperately needed by a continent in distress. ∎

Notes

1. See address by Secretary of State George P. Shultz to Organization of African Unity gathering, New York City, Oct. 4, 1988.
2. See report of the secretary-general in the mid-term review of the United Nations Programme of Action for African Economic Recovery and Development 1986–1988, A/43/150, Aug. 10, 1988, and *Los Angeles Times,* Sept. 19, 1988.
3. *Los Angeles Times,* Sept. 16, 1988.
4. For example, *L'Express* (Paris), Feb. 24, 1986.

5. See U.S. Committee on Refugees, *Uprooted Angolans: From Crisis to Catastrophe* (Washington, D.C.: August 1987), *Washington Post,* Aug. 30, 1987.

6. See John A. Marcum, "Regional Security in Southern Africa: Angola," *Survival* (London), January-February 1988.

7. Peter Younghusband in *The Washington Times,* Mar. 17, 1988.

8. Arnaud de Borchgrave interview with P. W. Botha, *The Washington Times,* Mar. 14, 1988.

9. Herman W. Nickel, U.S. ambassador to South Africa from 1982 to 1986, in *The Wall Street Journal,* Nov. 25, 1988.

10. See Gillian Gunn, "A Guide to the Intricacies of the Angola-Namibia Negotiations," *CSIS Africa Notes,* September 1988.

11. Report by Robert Gersony, "Summary of Mozambican Refugee Accounts of Principally Conflict-Related Experience in Mozambique." April 1988.

12. See results of interviewing by David Hauck and Shelley Green in Peter Berger and Bobby Godsell (ed. *A Future South Africa: Visions, Strategies and Realities* (Cape Town: Human and Rousseau, 1988) pp. 245–249.

13. *The Report of the Secretary of State's Advisory Committee on South Africa* (Washington, D.C., January 1987).

14. *The New York Times,* Nov. 26, 1988.

15. See Chester A. Crocker, "A Democratic Future: The Challenge for South Africans," CUNY Conference on South Africa in Transition, White Plains, N.Y., Oct. 1, 1987; and George Shultz, "The Deomocratic Future of South Africa," Business Council for International Understanding, New York City, Sept. 29, 1987.

16. George Bush, "The U.S. and Africa: The Republican Platform," *Africa Report,* July-August 1988, pp. 13–16.

17. Ibid., p. 16.

18. Ibid.

19. Address by General Olusegun Obasanjo at Africa Leadership Forum, Ota. Nigeria, Oct. 24, 1988.

20. See Carol Lancaster, *U.S. Aid to Sub-Saharan Africa: Challenges, Constraints, and Choices* (Washington, D.C.,: Center for Strategic and International Studies, 1988), pp. 32–33.

21. See Isebill V. Gruhn, "African Debt: Shadow Play of the 1980s," *Africa and the World,* April 1988.

Africa's Importance in Global Strategy

By Ray S. Cline

The United States is perceived by nearly all foreign powers as fuzzy or incoherent in strategic purpose and flabby in national will to pursue strategic interests abroad. It becomes clearer and clearer that American leaders have moved away from a policy of worldwide containment without evolving a coherent alternative strategy for dealing with the Soviet challenge in areas of lower-intensity conflict in the fluid international environment of the 1970s and 1980s.

The series of quasi-clandestine interventions in Africa south of the Sahara by Soviet and Cuban forces have belatedly focused the world's attention on the strategic importance of this subcontinent. At 6.6 million square miles, the central and southern Africa region is one of the eleven large geostrategic zones into which the 52 million square miles of the earth's surface is divided. It is not so large as North America or the northern Eurasian zone dominated by the Soviet Union, but four times as large as technologically rich, more densely populated Western Europe. With more than 300 million inhabitants, this zone constitutes a major population bloc— approximately at the mid-range of the other geostrategic zones in population size as well as territory.

The surge of decolonization in past decades has left central and southern Africa fragmented into forty-one political entities, some of them enjoying the classification of nation only because colonial boundaries give them an identity recognized by others as a result of the existence of lines on the colonial map. These artificial boundaries are of great importance because they provide the only viable stability in what historically is a conglomerate of hundreds of ethnic elements—tribal associations, bound together by a strong sense of cultural identity, many of them transcending the newly proclaimed national borders.

These associations proliferate untidily within and across most of the political boundaries of the

Dr. Cline is former deputy director of the CIA and a scholar at the Center for Strategic and International Studies.

Source: *From AEI Foreign Policy and Defense Review,* vol. 1, No. 1 (1979), pp. 10–13. Reprinted with permission from AEI Foreign Policy and Defense Review by Ray S. Cline, published in 1979 by the American Enterprise Institute for Public Policy Research, Washington, D.C.

forty-one states, ensuring considerable doubt as to the permanence of the present political structure and making cross-border sympathies and conflicts endemic. Because of this fragile structure of regional relationships and the recency of achievement of self-government in most cases, the mainstream of international affairs has seemed to pass by central and southern Africa until the past few years.

What has propelled the region into world consequence has been increased awareness in the industrial nations that we are entering a time of relative scarcity of economic raw materials, particularly energy sources, nonfuel minerals essential to advanced industry, and foodstuffs. The geological stabilization of the earth's crust and the slow shifting of continents over the millennia have richly endowed central and southern Africa with chrome, cobalt, manganese, vanadium, and other valuable alloys, as well as gold, platinum, and diamonds. Coal, oil, and uranium are also present in substantial quantities, and the tropical and subtropical climate ensures that production of foodstuffs is mainly a matter of technology and administrative infrastructure—badly lacking in most nations other than South Africa, where the white European managerial system in the economic structure still prevails. In short, at the end of the twentieth century, central and southern Africa is a geostrategic zone that is a rich treasure house of industrial raw materials—a prime target for the U.S.S.R. because of the area's political weakness and its crucial value as a trading partner for Western Europe, Japan, and the United States.

Under the guise of supporting Marxist-Leninist wars of national liberation, the Soviet Union and Cuba are moving massively into central and southern Africa with arms, soldiers, money, and political guidance to establish a sphere of influence of what the Chinese Communists call "socialist imperialism." The Soviet Union aims to exploit some of this wealth for its benefit and—more important strategically—prevent the exploitation of central and southern Africa by the United States and its main allies in Western Europe and northeast Asia.

American uncertainty about its global strategic purposes since the twin tragedies of defeat in Vietnam and the political crisis of the Watergate cover-up has left a power vacuum in many regions, and nowhere is this vacuum more dangerously inviting to Soviet exploitation than in sub-Saharan Africa. The U.S.S.R. has responded to the opportunity with vigor, deploying Cuban proxy armies in the first naked military interventions by Moscow's political dependencies since the North Korean attack on South Korea in 1950. The U.S.S.R. is gaining the kind of influence in Ethiopia and a few other African states that it has not succeeded in establishing so far from its own border except in the case of Cuba, now providing much of the impetus to new Soviet gains in Africa.

It is clear that central and southern Africa cannot be excluded from the American transoceanic alliance system if that system is to have global outreach and international credibility. All of the oceans of the world are one body of water, and American security and economic strength as well as self-respect require us to protect our transoceanic links to key allies in the Eurasian rimlands and outer circle regions of the globe. The sea lanes linking the all-important oil sources of the Persian-Arabian Gulf with the industries of Western Europe and North America pass along both the Indian Ocean and South Atlantic coasts of Africa and around the Cape of Good Hope.

While sub-Saharan Africa is at present only beginning to be a major factor in world developments, it is bound to assume more and more importance. The major nations among the forty-one countries composing this strategic zone account for about 7 percent of the total world power. (See my *World Power Assessment 1977*, Westview Press, for methodology.) Some of them rank reasonably high among the more powerful nations of the world and will be influential regional powers unless the whole zone disintegrates economically and politically as a result of continuing disruption along the lines foreshadowed by Soviet-Cuban moves in Angola, Zaire, and Ethiopia.

There are a disproportionate number of mini-states in Africa, but I would rank seven sub-Saharan entities among the top sixty nations of the world in terms of perceived power of all kinds—South Africa (eighteen on the world scale), Zaïre (twenty), Nigeria (twenty-three), Tanzania (thirty-nine), Zambia (forty-five), Ethiopia (fifty-two), and Guinea (sixty). Among these seven, three are roughly similar in perceived power—South Africa, Zaïre, and Nigeria. Each of these nations has about one-fifth of the total power for the whole zone. Ethiopia, on the basis of territory and population, ought to rank higher than it does, but the political ambivalence that has caused it to welcome in Soviet and Cuban forces to prop up its extremist dictatorship leaves it for the present comparatively weak in international influence. It is, of course, an international menace of the first order. South Africa, Nigeria, and Ethiopia all maintain substantial military forces, South Africa achieving a high quality and effectiveness and the other two at present achieving only a very low quality. Zimbabwean military forces are of high quality, but Zimbabwe is too small and its politics too divisive for this beleaguered nation experimenting with joint white-black government to show up even on a regional power scale. It is a target for subversion by Soviet-supported outside forces, a vulnerability rather than an element of strength. Its fate may turn out to be crucial for the future of the other nations in the region.

All of the seven most powerful countries in sub Saharan Africa derive most of their perceived strength from the extent of their territory and size of their population. Only South Africa is assessed any power weights for military (nonnuclear) strength. Four of the seven countries have critical mineral resources: Zimbabwe, chromium; South Africa, chromium and uranium; Zaïre, copper; and Zambia, copper. Nigeria has oil in abundance, and South Africa has coal in addition to its astonishing array of nonfuel minerals. Tanzania and Ethiopia are perceived as major nations only because of the size of their territory and population.

Problems as well as advantages derive from large territory; Zaïre, for example, has 910,000 square miles, making it the eleventh largest nation in the world. The vast range of the country assures the presence of many critical economic resources, but divisiveness among its 200 tribal groups and indifferent managerial skill since its independence in 1960 have made Zaïre almost a byword for instability and lack of economic progress in Africa.

Because of its severe internal political crisis and wars against the Somalis and the Eritrean secessionists, Ethiopia is now even more disordered than Zaïre. It is hard to say for the time being whether it is more disruptive and dangerous for a country to be attacked from outside by Cuban-Soviet supported armies (Zaïre) or to be supported in antiguerrilla warfare by Cuban-Soviet forces inside (Ethiopia). In any case, the Soviet strategic presence in Angola, Zambia, Mozambique, and Ethiopia, jeopardizing Zaïre and Somalia, threatens to cut this strategic zone in two along two different intersecting lines from Angola to the Horn of Africa on the Persian Arabian Gulf, and from Angola to Mozambique's Indian Ocean shores. In either case South Africa and the strategic sea lanes around the Cape of Good Hope would be isolated and could be brought under attack either by guerrilla interventions or by blockade. Hence the time of truth for southern Africa may be at hand.

Ethiopia is in many ways a testing ground for Soviet strategic ambitions in central Africa. Since there has been little resistance to Soviet maneuvers until recently, the U.S.S.R. has been able to play a very flexible game. For a time, when Soviet relations with Somalia were good enough to permit the construction and use of a naval base at Berbera, the U.S.S.R. supported both the Eritrean and the Ogaden (Somali) "liberation movements." Then Soviet forces were thrown out of Somalia, and Soviet policy reversed course and sent in massive military supplies and Cuban troops to expel the Somali rebels from the Ogaden and to try to pacify Eritrea by force. Presumably what hitherto were "liberation movements" have become potential partners in a Marxist, Soviet-oriented "Ethiopian socialist" state.

The presence of nearly 20,000 Cuban soldiers in Ethiopia and the Soviet presence in Yemen threaten to leapfrog the Red Sea and squeeze Saudi Arabia itself. Somali President Siad Barre, who has experienced the penalties of dependency on Soviet military assistance, on September 17, 1978, expressed the Arab view in saying: "The Soviets and Cubans will invade Somalia as soon as they are in a position to do so. . . . The law of the strongest applies here." The Saudis greatly fear this eventuality, and their complaints have stirred Western European nations and the United States from their lethargy and complacence, causing them to come jointly to the aid of Zaïre and denounce the Soviet-Cuban presence in Ethiopia, as well as in eight other African countries.

How all this will turn out is far from clear, but Soviet intervention and the willingness of a number of African states to "invite" the Cuban troops in to bolster their local fortunes have awakened almost everyone to the important geopolitical issues at stake in sub-Saharan Africa. In many ways the capability of the United States to cope with these tensions and to emerge with at least one or two major African nations as key allies is an early test of the viability of American leadership in a period of realistic foreign policy and transoceanic alliance building.

I do not see how this test can turn out successfully unless there

is a successful political experiment in pluralist politics and representative government in South Africa that would incorporate South Africa in the American global alliance

system. As the best organized and richest state south of the Sahara, South Africa has a grave and fateful responsibility in the framework of world power confrontations. ∎

A Case for Détente with South Africa

By Peter Duignan and L. H. Gann

How should Americans react to the South African situation? Clergymen call for sanctions. Students demand "divestment" by American business interests. Militants agitate for revolution. We ourselves see the problem in a very different fashion.

There is a form of inverted American chauvinism that interprets all the world's evils in terms of the real or supposed wrongs committed abroad by American investors and American spies. According to this interpretation, South Africa—or, for that matter, Iran, Chile, or Greece—would speedily become happy and contented democracies if only the Elders of Wall Street were to cease their plotting. This American ethnocentricity has many other forms. It assumes, for instance, that a system of franchise and of political organization that functions well in the United States would be equally successful in a multiethnic and multiracial country like South Africa.

White South Africans, however, are convinced that a "one-man, one-vote" system would imply ethnic suicide for the whites, that a powerless white minority would

be treated no better by the ruling blacks than the Indians were treated in Uganda, and that black rule would entail civil war and economic collapse. The whites may be wrong in their assumptions. But given the experiences of post-colonial Zanzibar (where the Arab minority was destroyed), or Burundi (where the Hutu were cruelly persecuted), or northern Nigeria (where the Ibo were robbed or massacred), or Algeria, Angola, or Mozambique (where most of the European population was compelled to emigrate), white fears are not unreasonable and should be treated with respect rather than with the contempt they receive from so many American academics.

In our view, American interests —political and humanitarian— would best be served by the kind of "convergence" diplomacy so many liberals advocate with regard to the Soviet Union. We should quietly press for improvements in return for economic favors. We should extend rather than diminish academic, cultural, athletic, diplomatic, and economic contacts with South Africa. We should be

conciliatory in tone and firm in intention. Quiet pressure for change, the gradual ending of apartheid, more education and job opportunities for blacks and coloureds, more self-government for urban blacks, and more democracy in the homelands: these are attainable goals. Quiet diplomacy will achieve more than will harangues in the UN. The Carter-Mondale-Young approach has hardened white resolve in South Africa, encouraged blacks to unrealistic expectations, and destroyed the middle ground of discussion and compromise.

The difficulties in applying morality to diplomacy are many. Few governments outside of Western Europe and North America are democratic. Few governments are moral or just, or rule for the benefit of their people. If you do not deal with Chile, you can hardly deal with any Communist regime. Stop talking to South Africans because of their racial policies, and you have to stop talking to half of the nations of the world who oppress their minorities, their political opposition, their religious bodies, or persons who own property.

Source: From *Business Week*, July 3, 1978; reprinted in *AEI Foreign Policy and Defense Review, Vol. 1, No. 1, 1979.*

A self-denying ordinance on moral judgments should regulate the relations between states. We should press for minor reforms in the hope that piecemeal changes will have a multiplier effect. One could argue that we should use the carrot instead of the stick—that we should try to accelerate change through increased, not lessened, foreign investment in South Africa. By pouring in vast sums of money, the economy would expand so rapidly that there would be a greater need for skilled workers than could be supplied by the white population. White trade unions would allow the blacks to enter the skilled trades, for example, if there were more jobs than the whites could handle. This has happened informally in South Africa in recent years: blacks now dominate industries that a few years ago excluded them—for example, the garment industry.

The Carter administration took a very different line because it mistook South Africa for Georgia. South Africa's problems are not those of the American black minority seeking civil rights in the 1960s. In South Africa the blacks are the majority, and many are still basically tribal people. American blacks are a fully Americanized minority, and they speak English. Blacks in South Africa are half in the tribal world and half in the modern world; they are divided into eleven major ethnic groups or nations, and English or Afrikaans is their second or third language. American policy makers are mistaken, therefore, in looking on South Africa as if it were the American South, to be restructured by a new breed of twentieth century abolitionists.

The Carter administration swung back to the policy of harassment followed during the Kennedy and Johnson era. It gave unequivocal support to majority rule of South Africa—though not to that of any other member of the Second or Third Worlds. The Transkei was refused recognition; there was a tightened arms embargo of South Africa; U.S. corporations doing business in South Africa are being pressured. Yet this policy of harassment has failed in the past. It will fail in the future, with a resultant hardening of white rule over blacks, Indians, and coloureds.

American investments in South Africa occupy too small a place—18 percent—in the nation's economy to be a major bargaining counter. South Africa today generates the bulk of its own capital and even exports it. Past restrictions on American arms sales have not only deprived the United States of a market but have forced South Africa to develop a major arms industry of its own—in cooperation with the French. An American trade embargo on South Africa is not likely to succeed. The balance of trade is in favor of the United States rather than the reverse. What America supplies, moreover, can readily be obtained from other sources, whereas the United States needs South Africa's minerals. Formal trade embargoes (violated by many African states) are no more likely to succeed than were American attempts to coerce Cuba, or than the Stalinist attempts to subjugate Yugoslavia by economic means.

George W. Ball, in *Atlantic Monthly*, put his finger on what was wrong with Carter's policy. "Diplomacy, like politics, is the art of the possible, and if we use our leverage toward an unachievable end, we will create a mess." A peaceful but imperfect solution for South Africa is preferable to trying to get a perfect solution by violent means.

Is the disruption of South Africa truly in the American interest? South Africa at present controls the Cape route, a major consideration at a time when Soviet naval power has become predominant in the western part of the Indian Ocean. South Africa, moreover, is the only African country capable during wartime of supplying its allies in the western part of the Indian Ocean with a vast industrial infrastructure—factories, supply depots, repair facilities, dry docks. It plays a major role in the global economy as the world's greatest producer of gold and as a major exporter of uranium, diamonds, chrome, manganese, and other minerals. South Africa's policy may offend the governments of countries like Guinea and Rwanda, which, between them, wield two paper votes at the UN. But the real power—as opposed to the voting power—of all African countries is small, and the Western nations cannot afford to buy their capricious favors by concessions that would further weaken the West itself.

As regards moral considerations, South Africa, for all its restrictions, is a great deal more free than Cuba or Russia, or China, not to mention a score of African countries. Consider the murderous regimes in Uganda, Ethiopia, Burundi, and Equatorial Guinea, to mention the worst ones. It is surely inconsistent to argue that while détente is a good thing to help reform the Soviets, it is a bad thing when applied to South Africa. ∎

The American Challenge in Southern Africa

By Pauline H. Baker

The Bush administration faces both formidable constraints and fresh opportunities in southern Africa, a region that ranks, along with Central America, among the most controversial foreign policy flashpoints inherited from the Reagan administration. But the contrasts between these two regions are striking. In the interregnum between the Reagan and Bush administrations, the American debate on Central America turned a corner. Military support for the contras came to an end, concerted diplomatic involvement of regional actors assumed center stage, and the Bush administration reached a compromise with Congress.

None of these factors apply to southern Africa. To the contrary, President George Bush reaffirmed his unstinting support for military aid to UNITA; the superpowers rather than regional actors are framing a diplomatic settlement that is slated to take at least until mid-1991 to complete; and a political consensus remains elusive on a range of other issues in the region, including South Africa, one of the most inflammatory foreign policy issues in the American body politic.

Ironically, these trends are continuing despite—or, rather, in large part, because of—the last-minute success of the Reagan administration in brokering a settlement on Angola and Namibia.[1] This historic peace accord was a significant breakthrough, offering the best hope yet of scaling down violence in the region and ending foreign intervention. It was also a personal triumph for former Assis-

tant Secretary of State Chester A. Crocker, whose eight years in office created a record of its own. Crocker was the longest serving assistant secretary of state in the Reagan administration, and he held the post of head of the Africa Bureau longer than any of his predecessors. Withstanding severe criticism in earlier years, including calls for his resignation because his policy of "constructive engagement" was seen as a tilt toward South Africa, Crocker exhibited extraordinary perseverance and patience that ultimately paid off.

Achieved just at the close of the Reagan years, the accord opened up a new phase of American diplomacy that the Bush administration must carry on to completion. It thus represents the beginning, not the end, of a long process of conflict resolution with much at stake. Besides transforming the strategic balance in southern Africa and bringing independence to Africa's last colony, the accord will test the endurance of superpower cooperation, since the US and the USSR are coguarantors of the agreement. Indeed, in southern Africa there was probably more active collaboration between Moscow and Washington than on any other regional conflict in which the superpowers were at odds. They therefore have a strong interest in seeing that the peace agreement stays on track.

The settlement will also test the political commitment of the signatory countries—Cuba, Angola and South Africa. Adherence to the peace process significantly alters

their political and military status. In exchange, they have the chance to usher in a new era of regional peace and economic development, after more than a decade of unrelenting war, economic deterioration and human suffering.

The peace pact also represents a challenge for the United Nations, which has scaled back the size of the Namibia operation from the original 9500 civilians and military personnel called for in UN Resolution 435 to roughly 6000. But even after this reduction, which was insisted upon by the five permanent members of the Security Council who are footing the lion's share of the bill, the project remains the most ambitious peacekeeping operation in the history of the organization. Its overall mission in support of the accord involves monitoring the cease-fire, verifying Cuban and South African troop withdrawals in Angola and Namibia, respectively and overseeing the release of political prisoners, the repeal of apartheid laws, the conduct of at least one election for a constituent assembly (and possibly another for a new government), the drafting of a constitution and the transition to independence in Nami- bia, a territory twice the size of Texas with a population of 1.5 million.

THE PEACE PACT

The regional accord signed December 22, 1988 sets forth a 27-month-long schedule for the gradual withdrawal of Cuban troops

Pauline Baker is a fellow at the Carnegie Endowment for International Peace.

Source: From *Current History,* (May, 1989).

from Angola and the implementation of the UN plan for the independence of Namibia. Requiring a series of parallel military and political steps, the complex agreement will be the central priority of the Bush administration in southern Africa, occupying much of its attention at least until July 1991, when all Cuban troops are to be out of Angola.

The terms of the agreement demand constant vigilance and careful monitoring. It calls for 3000 Cuban troops to leave Angola by April 1, 1989, a deadline that Havana announced it met months ahead of schedule as a gesture of good faith. In addition, 25,000 troops, or 50% of Cuban troop strength, are to be out of Angola by November 1989; 33,000, or 66%, out by April 1990; and all Cuban troops out by July 1991. Correspondingly, April 1, 1989 was D-Day for the start of the UN plan for Namibia, although the specifics of this side of the accord are not as precise. According to published documents, there is no fixed date for Namibia's independence. However, the schedule of events listed in State Department materials indicate that by July 1989, all South African troops should be out of Namibia except for a residual force of 1500 confined to base, and the rest are to depart by November 1989, when Namibian elections should be held.[2]

The international celebration surrounding the accord, while justified, nevertheless has obscured the underlying distrust among the signatories, who exchanged angry words at the signing ceremony in New York City and immediately began accusing each other of bad faith. Other parties that remain deeply suspicious of the accord include elements of the South African military and guerrilla forces like UNITA, the antigovernment rebel movement seemingly left out in the cold. They have the capacity to threaten successful implementation of the settlement, just as previous regional agreements that once inspired hope were suddenly torpedoed without warning.[3]

Moreover, in the rush to get the agreement signed before the end of the Reagan era, many loose ends were left unresolved. The ongoing war in Angola is the most immediate problem. While jockeying for international support by alternately proposing new initiatives and threatening new military offensives, the rival UNITA and MPLA forces seemed no closer to a settlement than they were before the accord.

The Southwest African People's Organization (SWAPO), though supportive of the pact, was not included in the deliberations. On April 1, the first day of implementation, SWAPO insurgents crossed the border from Angola to Namibia, immediately creating a crisis that put the accord in jeopardy. However, the signatories kept to the terms of the agreement. The UN, which came under attack for being unprepared, released South African security forces; they killed some 300 rebels before a ceasefire was declared, and SWAPO leaders ordered their soldiers back into Angola in accordance with the terms of the agreement.

There is considerable uncertainty about South Africa's underlying intentions in Namibia, where electoral manipulation and military subterfuge could create problems for a smooth transition.[4] Walvis Bay, Namibia's only deepwater port, remains in South Africa's hands and is sure to be raised in the future as an anomaly compromising Namibia's independence. And there has, thus far, been no clarification about the political stalemate that resulted in the Reagan administration's failure to obtain congressional appropriation of $150 million, the estimated US share of the peacekeeping costs. While the Bush administration has assured Congress that it will back UNITA, supporters of the rebel group on Capitol Hill have hinted that they might tie future funding of the Namibia operation to a resolution of the Angola civil war that ensures that UNITA has a role in the central government. Verification concerns expressed on both sides will also continue to stalk the process, as an estimated 100,000 Cuban and South African troops pull back from confrontation in an area that is roughly comparable in size to the United States east of the Mississippi. In addition, United States relations with Angola are not normalized. Administration spokesmen and congressional sources have suggested that new conditions, besides the removal of Cuban troops, could be laid down before diplomatic relations are established, including national reconciliation and an end to Soviet assistance to the Angolan government.

Beyond the agreement, the most critical issues that stir the American debate on southern Africa are covert aid to UNITA, the insurgency in Mozambique and US policy toward South Africa. Each raises questions about the appropriate role of the US in a region that traditionally lies just on the periphery of American international concerns. As the 1990s approach, however, southern Africa—while still low on the foreign policy totem pole—is gradually assuming greater salience in the hierarchy of international priorities as American involvement intensifies.

REGIONAL ISSUES

In what the *Washington Post* described as his first foreign policy commitment, President George Bush wrote a letter to UNITA leader Jonas Savimbi two weeks before his inauguration promising "all appropriate and effective assistance" in order "to provide maximum support to a process of negotiation leading to national reconciliation."[5] UNITA guerrillas are regarded by supporters of the Reagan Doctrine as "freedom fighters," and Savimbi is portrayed as a charismatic exponent of democracy and free enterprise. Nevertheless, today the guerrilla movement is poised on what may be the most delicate tightrope in its existence. While Bush's statement of support was welcome news to Savimbi, it was poor consolation for the cutoff of direct South African military and financial assistance, which was necessary to obtain the agreement on Angola and Namibia. Pretoria's agreement to end aid to UNITA was the *quid pro quo* for Angola's agreement to close down military bases of the African National Congress, South Africa's oldest liberation movement.

Deprived of South African air cover and ground support, as well as a lifeline of South African-supplied material, UNITA is more dependent than ever on the United States. Since 1986, Washington has helped Savimbi through a covert military program—reported to be at an annual level of $15 million for 1986 and 1987 and said to have

been raised to $45 million in 1988—that operates out of Zaire. There is substantial support for UNITA on Capitol Hill, including among some Democrats. But the US military program could be threatening to the Bush administration's relations with Congress if national reconciliation becomes an elusive or unsustainable goal.

Similar anti-Marxist insurgencies funded by the US in other regions are winding down just as support for UNITA appears to be increasing. In the wake of the regional agreement, administration officials are reported to be assessing the need for additional aid to offset the loss of South African assistance. Moreover, the UNITA operation seems to be shaping up more as a litmus test of conservative loyalty to the anti-Marxist strategy identified with Reagan rather than a political strategy for achieving long-term peace and stability in Angola. Critics see Savimbi not as a pro-Western freedom fighter, but as one observer put it, "a political chameleon of passing persuasion but steady ambition."[6] They argue that American military aid erodes Washington's ability to act as an honest broker, inflames rather than resolves the civil war in Angola, and undercuts American credibility and influence in Africa as a whole. South African blacks, for example, cite US aid to UNITA as evidence of their perception that the United States silently supports South Africa.

A second source of controversy is the ongoing RENAMO insurgency in Mozambique. After years of deadly warfare and economic mismanagement, this former Portuguese colony has become a de facto ward of the international community. Malawi, Tanzania and,

most of all, Zimbabwe have deployed troops in Mozambique to defend their outlets to the sea; the British supply military training to the Mozambican army; and the Western world is shoring up the economy with economic aid, including more than $450 million pledged for the rehabilitation of the Beira Corridor—the central railway, road, pipeline, port and town that serves as a vital outlet to the sea for the region as a whole.[7] Yet, for all this assistance, Mozambique continues to reel from the brutal activities of RENAMO, which consists essentially of bands of marauding guerrilla fighters originally created as a fifth column by the white minority regime in Rhodesia. Since 1980, when Zimbabwe gained its independence and South Africa took over responsibility for training and equipping the rebels, RENAMO has intensified its attacks. Several sources, including the State Department in a report issued last year, describe RENAMO as a force that regularly commits atrocities and that lacks a coherent program and clear leadership. The State Department report concluded that the right-wing rebels killed at least 100,000 Mozambicans and had turned one million others into refugees.[8]

Having had a hand in creating this undisciplined force—which, among other things, has attacked pylons from the Cahora Bassa hydroelectric project that supplies power to Pretoria—South Africa decided to distance itself from RENAMO in 1988. This was part of a wider campaign to improve its international image and mend fences with its neighbors after a decade of destabilization. Radically reversing its policy on Mozambique, Pretoria formally declared that it was no longer aiding RENAMO, though it never officially admitted to having done so as a matter of policy. Pretoria also revived the 1984 nonaggression pact with Mozambique, known as the Nkomati Accord; concluded an agreement to upgrade the Cahora Bassa hydroelectric project in Mozambique; supplied nonlethal military equipment to help defend the project's installations; and lifted restrictions on Mozambican migrant workers imposed in 1986. But there have been charges, emphatically denied by Pretoria, that the South African military is still secretly supplying RENAMO, and elements of the United States Government, including the Pentagon and extreme conservatives, remain sympathetic. In this context, Pretoria's suggestion, offered in February, that the US and the USSR broker a settlement in Mozambique similar to the one negotiated in Angola, raises puzzling questions.[9] Is there a genuine role for outside powers, or is this an attempt to entice the international community into a process that would legitimize discredited rebels who still retain ties to their benefactor?

The third and most salient point of contention concerns South Africa itself. An important threshold was crossed in relations between Pretoria and Washington when sanctions were enacted by a bipartisan vote of Congress in October 1986, over the veto of a popular conservative president. Even with that margin of consensus, built on outrage over the continuing violence and repression in South Africa, sanctions remain a matter of considerable debate.

There will be no going back on these measures unless and until there is significant progress toward granting blacks full political rights, as detailed in provisions of the Comprehensive Anti-Apartheid Act of 1986. But it is an open question whether new sanctions will be adopted and, if so, whether they will be as extensive as those proposed in the so-called Dellums Bill, a measure that requires comprehensive sanctions. It is also unclear whether, in recognition of the fixed congressional position, the administration will try to use sanctions creatively as a lever to exert influence on South Africa, along with diplomatic pressure and aid to antiapartheid groups. If so, it would stand in stark contrast to the Reagan administration, which adopted a stance of blanket opposition to economic sanctions, regardless of egregious South African behavior, a position which led to a bitter confrontation with Congress.

It is possible that the Bush administration will move further than Reagan did in seeking to harmonize American policy toward South Africa with its allies, many of which are taking advantage of American sanctions to advance their own trading relationships with Pretoria. Perhaps collaboration with the Soviet Union is also in the cards. Moscow has not only worked in tandem with Washington on the Angola/Namibia settlement, but it has revised fundamental tenets of its approach toward South Africa by downplaying revolution, pushing for a political settlement, encouraging preservation of the economy and calling for recognition of the importance of ethnicity and group rights. Moscow has also expanded ties with liberal whites, academics and journalists in South Africa and is said to be cautiously exploring the merits of improving official relations with Pretoria. South African officials have even hinted of establishing diplomatic relations with the Soviet Union.

For the United States, the search for an effective policy consistent with American values and strategic interests has put it in the curious position of both opposing and working with South Africa. An important threshold has been reached in US relations with Pretoria, however. South Africa is now viewed almost entirely as a human rights issue, with economic and strategic considerations of secondary importance. Yet there is a mutual interest in keeping the Angola/Namibia settlement on track. Washington and Pretoria are thus estranged partners, deeply divided over apartheid while linked to a regional peace process that has the potential of bringing the most far-reaching transformations in southern Africa since the collapse of Portuguese colonialism in 1975.

NEW PERSPECTIVES

Southern Africa could be a major testing ground for the Bush administration, particularly its ability to forge a bipartisan foreign policy that has congressional support. In addition to the considerations mentioned above, a domestic political agenda will also enter into play in this arena. Since the election of George Bush, Republicans have declared their intention of seeking to capture the black vote; yet Democrats, who elected a black American as national party chairman, are dedicated to holding onto their most loyal voting block. In the contest over black votes, both parties must demonstrate sensitivity to African issues, particularly South Africa. Blacks had an unprecedented impact on shaping

US policy toward South Africa during the Reagan years. Bush, who raised expectations early on by meeting with prominent black political leaders, must take into account the implications of Jesse Jackson's call for 12 percent of the American population to identify themselves as African-Americans.

The concern with bipartisanship and the quest for black support may set a new direction in U.S. policy in southern Africa. But Bush also is keen to avoid alienating the right, which has targeted the region as an area of concern and drives policy toward an opposite course. The central question for the US at this juncture, therefore, is whether a genuine political consensus can be achieved, taking these domestic and international factors into account, or whether paralysis will set in as a result of political polarization.

Public opinion will be an important factor in shaping future policy, although it has rarely been significant in the past. Active American diplomacy in southern Africa started in 1976, when former Secretary of State Henry Kissinger embarked upon last-minute shuttle diplomacy during the Ford administration to achieve a settlement of the conflicts in Rhodesia and Namibia. It continued through the Carter administration, which succeeded in forging a multilateral initiative, known as the Contact Group (consisting of the US, UK, France, West Germany and Canada), that negotiated the United Nations plan for Namibian independence that is the basis for the current accord. Public opinion did not play a strong role in either of these periods, however. Even the first term of the Reagan administration conformed to the pattern.

Crocker worked in relative obscurity, without much public scrutiny and with a virtually free hand from the administration. Not until 1984, when an uprising in South Africa propelled apartheid into the mainstream of public attention, did "constructive engagement," Reagan's southern Africa policy, come under fire.

The second term of the Reagan administration brought new perspectives to US policy in southern Africa in more ways than one. The public outcry over repression in South Africa and the failure of the United States to respond appropriately resulted in an overwhelming vote of no confidence in the administration's policy and a decisive refutation of the premises on which it was based. It took some time for this to sink in fully, and the trappings of the administration's policy remained in place. Crocker, for example, continued to oppose sanctions, stress linkage of Cuban troop withdrawal with Namibian independence, and insist that the United States would stay "engaged." Nor was there a sharp turn in its approach to South Africa, where the fundamental tenets of the policy remained largely intact.

But gradually there appeared a new flexibility in regional diplomacy. Ultimately, Crocker repudiated the tenets of his own policy, not by bowing to public opinion, which he continued to reject, but by reacting to changing regional events. Step by step, he acted in ways that overturned many of his own propositions, as geostrategic shifts, a change in the military balance of power in the region and mounting economic pressures opened up a window of opportunity.

Whereas previously Crocker had spurned multilateral diplomacy, in the last year of the Reagan administration he pursued it with a vengeance. Instead of shutting Cuba out, he came to see that it had to be brought in as an integral part of the negotiating process. Building on the improvement in East-West relations, he also enlisted Soviet support instead of portraying Moscow as a common enemy of Washington and Pretoria. The linkage formula was repackaged, so that South Africa would free Namibia before, not after, all the Cuban troops left Angola, which the United States and South Africa had insisted on for years.

Most important, Crocker distanced the United States from South Africa's strategic interests. This was in direct contradiction to his original call to identify with white fears in order to influence Pretoria. Crocker made no protest when Cuba rushed 10,000 to 15,000 fresh troops to reinforce Angolan forces threatened by a South African counteroffensive that was launched in 1987 and extended into 1988. Nor did he encourage bankers, allies or international institutions to help bail out Pretoria from the economic squeeze imposed by sanctions, debt, disinvestment and the falling price of gold. Pressed from all sides, including its own domestic situation as the death of white conscripts began to provoke protest from the white electorate, South Africa finally agreed to cut a deal.

New perspectives were also introduced during the later Reagan years with regard to the tools and tactics of American policy. Before Reagan, diplomacy and aid to the black-ruled states in the region were the primary threads of involvement. During the Reagan administration, a wider array of measures was adopted, even though they occasionally worked at cross-purposes and not all were part of official policy. Diplomacy intensified, superpower relations were brought to bear on the conflicts and economics assumed a larger role in exerting pressure. A substantial aid program to antiapartheid groups was introduced, bypassing the South African government. Congress got deeply involved, voting not only for a comprehensive new approach to South Africa that included sanctions, but for resuming military assistance to UNITA after a lapse of 9 years. Even though some of these measures, such as sanctions and disinvestment, appeared to distance the United States from the region, they were, in fact, attempts to exert more influence. Moreover, American institutions, from universities to religious groups, began searching for ways to promote development and erode apartheid, including through "black empowerment," a term that includes support for programs for black education, labor unions and community institutions. These developments could offer fresh opportunities in the future for applying pressures and incentives that had once been considered unacceptable.

REGIONAL TRENDS

Whatever the domestic and international trends, the character of American policy will be defined, to a large extent, by developments in the region, for internal events set both the limits and the opportunities for effective external influence. Three major trends in the last decade are noteworthy in planning for the future.

First, violence reached unprecedented levels in the 1980s, with massacres, cross-border attacks and insurgencies afflicting the region. The accord in southwestern Africa holds out the promise that violence will diminish as large foreign armies withdraw. But many states in the region are still affected by internal armed rebellions that are either linked to or were started by South Africa. Many of these rebellions have spilled over into neighboring countries or have economic consequences for the region as a whole. Within South Africa, violence has become endemic, with a simmering revolt that intermittently erupts into popular uprisings, regularly crushed with ever-increasing force by the government.

A second regional trend is the political escalation of local conflicts. In the 1970s, for example, a settlement in Namibia would have required only the consent of South Africa and SWAPO, the liberation movement that fought for independence. Today, the accord that promises to grant independence to Namibia depends upon the cooperation of the Angolan, Cuban, Soviet and American governments, as well as South Africa, and SWAPO was not even present at the talks. The insurgency in Mozambique has also drawn in every neighboring state, along with international economic and military assistance.

A third trend is the worsening internal crisis in South Africa. Blacks and whites are reassessing their strategies in light of the political stalemate. Antiapartheid leaders seem increasingly aware that, with the overwhelming power of the state and the removal of ANC bases from the neighboring Front-Line states, the struggle for racial equality will likely continue for some time and end, not in a violent upheaval or a revolutionary overthrow of the government, but at the negotiating table. Whites are in more disarray than they have ever been since the ruling National Party came to power in 1948, and the government is in transition. General elections in September 1989 will usher in a new generation of party leaders and possibly a new political alignment at the top. Meanwhile, larger socioeconomic forces, like urbanization and population growth, are tearing at the walls of apartheid, and international pressures on Pretoria are mounting. Without a major breakthrough, the prospect is for an accelerating spiral of economic attrition, political violence and racial conflict. On the other hand, mounting uncertainties and confusions within South Africa could offer the international community a chance to exert a margin of influence on the conflict that was not available before. ■

Notes

1. For details of the peace agreement, see U.S. Department of State, Bureau of Public Affairs, "Agreements for Peace in Southwestern Africa" (Washington, D.C.: Selected Documents No. 32, December 1988).

2. Ibid.

3. The 1984 agreements, for example, know as the Nkomati Accord (between South Africa and Mozambique) and the Lusaka Accord (between South Africa and Angola), both colapsed due to violations on the battlefield and secret supplies by Pretoria to rebel forces. In the tripartite accord on southwestern Africa, there is a mechanism for dispute resolution, known as the Joint Commission. It went into effect immediately after the agreement was

signed in December to interpret provisions of the agreement and mediate conflicts. However, no penalties are specified if the Commission determines that there have been violations. Ultimately, enforcement depends upon the parties themselves. The Joint Commission consists of the US, and USSR, Angola, Cuba, South Africa and, upon independence, the Namibian government.

4. See, for example, the paper prepared by the Lawyers' Committee for Civil Rights Under Law, entitled "Resolution 435: Treatment of Military and Police in Namibia," dated January 24, 1989. It raises questions about the reduction of UN peacekeeping forces, deployment of numerous territorial troops, reports of new irregular forces being trained in secret to disrupt elections, and other alleged abuses.

5. *The Washington Post,* January 12, 1989, p.1. The letter was dated January 6, 1989.

6. John A. Marcum, "Africa: A Continent Adrift," *Foreign Affairs,* vol. 68 (1988/89), *America and the World,* p. 162.

7. *The New York Times,* February 21, 1989, p. 4.

8. See also the research report by William Minter, "The Mozambican National Resistance (RENAMO) as Described by Ex-Participants," submitted to the Ford Foundation and the Swedish International Development Agency, Washington, D.C., March 1989.

9. See *The Washington Post,* February 11, 1989, and *The New York Times,* February 12, 1989.

Southwestern Africa: Blueprint for Peace

BACKGROUND:

On December 22, 1988, at the UN in New York, Angola, Cuba, and South Africa, with the US serving as mediator, took a major step toward peace in southwestern Africa. In separate but related actions, Angola and Cuba signed a bilateral agreement on the phased withdrawal of all Cuban troops from Angola, and Angola, Cuba, and South Africa signed a tripartite agreement that formally provided for peace in southwestern Africa. The signing of the two agreements marked the culmination of an 8-year effort, in which the US, acting as broker, sought to narrow the differences among the parties. The agreements set in motion a process that will complete the decolonization of Africa by bringing Namibia to independence, end the involvement of foreign military forces in Angola's civil war, and give Angolans an unprecedented opportunity to achieve a political settlement of their differences and an honorable peace.

ANGOLA:

Angola has been in a state of civil war since Portugal ceded independence to its former colony in 1975. The Alvor accord, which the Portuguese worked out with the three liberation movements—the Popular Movement for the Liberation of Angola (MPLA), the National Front for the Liberation of Angola (FNLA), and the National Union for the Total Independence of Angola (UNITA)—provided for a transitional government and for elections in preparation for independence in November 1975. But fighting broke out among the MPLA, FNLA, and UNITA forces, and the transitional government collapsed during the summer of 1975. The conflict became internationalized when the Cubans entered Angola in support of the MPLA, and the South Africans came to the aid of the FNLA and UNITA. In early 1976, Congress passed the Clark amendment, which prohibited all direct or indirect American military or paramilitary assistance to any group in Angola, and South Africa withdrew its forces. With Soviet aid and the support of Cuban troops, the MPLA controlled most of Angola by March 1976. The FNLA ceased to be a factor in late 1975, but over the years UNITA, under Jonas Savimbi, has steadily increased the scope of its operations and now poses a major challenge to the MPLA regime.

US POLICY IN ANGOLA:

The US believes that UNITA is a genuine nationalist movement with a legitimate claim to represent its large numbers of followers in the Angolan government. Since the repeal of the Clark amendment

Source: From U.S. Department of State, Bureau of Public Affairs, *Gist* (Feb. 1989).

in 1985, the US has provided UNITA with appropriate and effective assistance for its efforts to secure that role. The US and UNITA believe that there must be a genuine process of national reconciliation if there is to be real peace in Angola. President Bush, in one of his first foreign policy commitments, wrote to Jonas Savimbi assuring him of continued US support until national reconciliation is achieved. American diplomacy will continue to encourage African and other interested governments to provide maximum support to a negotiation process leading to peace among Angolans.

NAMIBIA:

Namibia also has been caught up in civil strife dating back to the early 1960s when nationalist guerrillas began a struggle for independence from South African rule. South Africa has administered the territory in defiance of both a 1966 UN General Assembly resolution revoking a League of Nations mandate granted to South Africa in 1920 and a 1971 International Court of Justice ruling that the South African presence in Namibia was illegal. In 1977, the then five Western members of the UN Security Council—Canada, France, the Federal Republic of Germany, the UK, and the US (known as the contact group)—launched a joint effort to bring about a peaceful, internationally acceptable transition to Namibian independence. Their efforts led to the adoption in September 1978 of UN Security Council Resolution 435, a plan for settling the Namibian problem. This plan was worked out after

lengthy consultations with South Africa, the "front-line states" (Angola, Botswana, Mozambique, Tanzania, Zambia, and—since 1980—Zimbabwe), South West Africa People's Organization (SWAPO), and the contact group. It calls for, among other things, the holding of direct elections in Namibia under UN supervision and control, the cessation of hostile acts by all parties, and restrictions on the activities of South African, Namibian, and SWAPO armed forces.

THE SETTLEMENT:

By the time the Reagan Administration took office in 1981, several political realities had emerged:

- South Africa would not accept Namibian independence without an agreement on the withdrawal of Cuban forces from Angola;
- Neither side in Angola was capable of military victory; and
- The presence of South African forces in Namibia posed a continuing threat to Angola.

The logical outline for a settlement was clear. Such an agreement would have to remove all foreign forces from the region, bring independence to Namibia, and create conditions under which Angolans could resolve their internal conflict through negotiation. It took a long and complex series of talks among the South Africans, Angolans, and Cubans, with the US acting as mediator, to work out a timetable for Cuban troop withdrawal from Angola and South African troop withdrawal from Namibia in accor-

dance with UN Security Council Resolution 435. Finally, in the Congo on December 13, 1988, the parties signed the protocol of Brazzaville establishing the basis for the New York accords of December 22 and setting up a joint commission to facilitate the resolution of any dispute regarding the tripartite agreement's interpretation or implementation.

NEXT STEPS:

At the request of Angola and Cuba, a UN team is stationed in Angola to verify the redeployment of Cuban troops to the north and their phased, total withdrawal. The UN will dispatch a Transition Assistance Group (UNTAG) to Namibia to ensure free and fair elections for a national assembly empowered to draft a constitution for an independent Namibia. The tripartite agreement provides for the following steps:

- *April 1, 1989*—Cuba cuts back its forces in Angola to no more than 47,000; UN Security Council Resolution 435 goes into effect; UNTAG begins its supervision of Namibia's transition to independence.
- *November 1, 1989*—Free and fair elections are held in Namibia for a representative assembly, which will in turn adopt a constitution within a few months. All South African troops are withdrawn from Namibia; Cuban troops in Angola reduced to 25,000, with all of them withdrawn north of the 13th parallel.
- *July 1, 1991*—Cuba completes the total withdrawal of its forces from Angola. ∎

Suggested Additional Readings

Arkhurst, Frederick S. *U.S. Policy Toward Africa* (New York: Praeger, 1975).

Bender, Gerald et al. (eds.). *African Crisis Areas and U.S. Foreign Policy* (Berkeley: University of California Press, 1985).

Bissell, Richard. *Southern Africa in the World* (Philadelphia: Foreign Policy Research Institute, 1978).

Hanks, Robert J. *Southern Africa and Western Security* (Cambridge, MA: Institute for Foreign Policy Analysis, 1983).

Jackson, Henry F. *From the Congo to Soweto: U.S. Foreign Policy toward Africa since 1960* (New York: Morrow, 1962).

_____. *Southern Africa: Regional Security Problem and Prospects* (Washington, D.C.: American Enterprise Institute for Public Policy Research, 1982).

Jaster, Robert (ed.). *Southern Africa in Conflict: Implications for U.S. Policies* (New York: St. Martin's Press, 1985).

Kitchen, Helen. "Options for U.S. Policy Toward Africa," Special Issue of the *Foreign Policy and Defense Review,* Vol. 1, No. 1 (1979).

Ogene, F. Chidozie. *Interest Groups and the Shaping of Foreign Policy: Four Case Studies of United States Africa Policy* (New York: St. Martin's Press, 1983).

Samuels, Michael. *Implications of Soviet and Cuban Activities in Africa for U.S. Policy* (Washington, D.C.: Center for Strategic and International Studies, 1979).

Zartman, I. William. *Ripe for Resolution: Conflict and Intervention in Africa* (New York: Oxford University Press, 1985).

PART TWO

Issues in Contention

❈
❈

CHAPTER SEVEN

Human Rights and Democracy

*
*

Human rights and democracy have become major concerns of U.S. foreign policy in recent years—although some would say these have always been major concerns.

The United States was founded on an ethical, moral, and religious basis that heavily emphasized human rights. We think of ourselves as a special nation, a beacon on a hill, a Zion and an example for other nations to emulate. Moreover, we believe it is our right and obligation to bring the benefits of our civilization—including democracy and human rights—to other, less blessed nations. That was undoubtedly a powerful motivation behind "manifest destiny" and America's westward expansion in the nineteenth century, behind Woodrow Wilson's effort to "make the world safe for democracy," and John F. Kennedy's Alliance for Progress. More recently, such moral foreign policy considerations undergirded Jimmy Carter's campaign for human rights and Ronald Reagan's effort to incorporate human rights in a broader campaign for democracy.

The debate over democracy and human rights in foreign policy relates to a broader issue in foreign affairs, that of idealism versus realism. "Realist" analysts, defenders of *realpolitik,* tend to believe the United States should be concerned—like most states in the world—only with a hard-headed defense of its national interests. The "idealists" argue that the United States must have moral concerns as its first priority: human rights, world starvation, the global environment. The debate between these two schools of thought has often been hot and heavy, but recently the beginning of a meeting of the minds has occurred. Even the strongest defenders of *realpolitik* are now convinced that for the United States (although not necessarily other countries) to have a successful foreign policy, it must have a strong human rights component to it. Otherwise, we appear indifferent to Soviet Jews trying to emigrate, to the fate of blacks in South Africa, to peasants and nuns who put their lives on the line in Central America, and to the fate of democracy everywhere. A consensus has emerged that human rights must be a major component in U.S. foreign policy, although it should not be the only component; other U.S. interests—political, economic, diplomatic, strategic—must also be taken into account.

The question remains, however, whether we really stand for democracy in the world or whether we simply use "democracy" as a cover for less glorious activities. Most Americans really believe our Fourth of July rhetoric that we are a democratic beacon in the world; but to others, particularly those Third World nations that have experienced United States interventions, it sometimes strains credulity to believe that the U.S. stands for democracy. Actually, the answer to the question posed above is, "both": we stand for democracy in the world, *and* we sometimes use democracy to disguise baser power-plays. But more and more, policy makers have come to see that not only are democracy and human rights good in themselves and at the base of our foundations as a nation, but they also serve our foreign policy goals, for we have learned over the years that democracies tend to be more stable, are more resistant to communism, do not support guerrilla movements in other countries, and in general cause less grief for U.S. foreign policy.

That still leaves unanswered, however, the questions of when to press for democracy and human rights, whether to use quiet diplomacy or stronger pressure, when such advocacy constitutes unwarranted interference in other nations' internal affairs, how to promote democracy effectively, and what instruments to use. These are complicated questions with which the readings that follow wrestle.

This section begins with a statement by George Lister of the State Department's human rights office on the origins of U.S. human rights policy and why we should have such a policy. Former Secretary of State Henry Kissinger is more skeptical, recognizing the importance of human rights concerns but suggesting that the U.S. must be primarily concerned with defending its national interests rather than involving itself deeply in other nations' internal affairs. The editor of this anthology follows with a statement that, while supportive of a strong human rights policy, points out the pitfalls along the trail.

Eminent American historian (and former director of the Library of Congress) Daniel Boorstin is skeptical of the possibilities for the U.S. to export its form of democracy. In contrast, Stanford political scientist Gabriel Almond favors a policy that would help the Third World both develop and democratize. The debate is an important one.

U.S. Human Rights Policy: Origins and Implementation

By George Lister

I welcome the opportunity to talk with you today, not for just the usual polite reasons of responding to an invitation but mainly because I feel the subject of our meeting, U.S. human rights policy, is very important. And certainly it is one that is close to my heart. The subject is also highly controversial and does not lend itself to easy generalizations, and since I am going to speak for only about 30 minutes, I suggest you consider these opening remarks as merely an introduction to our discussion. I anticipate that following my presentation, you will ask many questions, and I hope we can have a candid, vigorous exchange of views, which I am prepared to continue for as long as you wish.

ORIGINS OF CURRENT POLICY

First, how and when did our human rights policy begin? At the outset I should emphasize that my government does not perceive itself as the original defender of human rights. There were articulate supporters of human rights long before Columbus came to this hemisphere. And, of course, there have been many important human rights issues throughout history, e.g., slavery was a major cause of our Civil War over a century ago. So nothing that I am going to say here should be construed as implying that we have a monopoly in the defense of human rights. We do not.

However, there did come a time when human rights advocates both inside and outside our government decided that human rights should be accorded a higher priority in the conduct of our foreign policy. This movement began to take shape some years prior to the Carter Administration. A leading role in this campaign was played by several Members of Congress from both major parties, Republicans and Democrats, and particularly by Congressman Don Fraser of Minnesota, who was Chairman of the Subcommittee on International Organizations and Movements. In the latter half of 1973, and in early 1974, Fraser's subcommittee held a series of public hearings on U.S. foreign policy and human rights, with witnesses including U.S. Government officials, jurists, scholars, representatives of nongovernmental organizations, etc. These hearings were followed by a subcommittee report on the subject in March 1974, including 29 specific recommendations. The first recommendation stated that: "The Department of State should treat human rights factors as a regular part of U.S. foreign policy decision-making." The report itself began with the following sentence: "The human rights factor is not accorded the high priority it deserves in our country's foreign policy."

The Fraser subcommittee report achieved considerable impact in our government, and some of the 29 recommendations were implemented fairly soon. One of these called for the appointment of a human rights officer in each of the State Department's five geographic bureaus: for Europe, Latin America, Africa, the Near East, and East Asia. I was serving in our Latin American bureau at the time and became the first human rights officer for that area.

So the human rights cause was gaining impetus before Jimmy Carter won the 1976 elections. But, of course, soon after President Carter assumed office, human rights did begin to receive considerably more attention in the daily implementation of our foreign policy. A separate Bureau of Human Rights and Humanitarian Affairs was created with a new Assistant Secretary. I will discuss how that policy was implemented, and with what results, in a few minutes, but first let me say a few words about what happened when the Reagan Administration replaced the Carter Administration, in early 1981.

At that time I recall there were some, in and out of government, who assumed that our human rights policy was finished. This assumption prevailed both among strong advocates of human rights and those who felt human rights considerations should have no place in our foreign policy. Some even expected the human rights bureau to be abolished. But fortunately, it soon became apparent that our human rights policy had been institutionalized, that it had strong bipartisan support in Congress, that human rights legislation passed in previous years was still

---

George Lister is the Senior Policy Adviser, Bureau of Human Rights and Humanitarian Affairs.

Source: From a speech Reprinted in U.S. Department of State, Bureau of Public Affairs, *Current Policy No. 973*, pp. 1–3.

in force, that our annual human rights reports to Congress were still required by law, etc. In short, our human rights policy continued. Today our human rights bureau is alive and well, with an able and committed Assistant Secretary, Richard Schifter, who has dedicated his work in the Department to the memory of his parents, who perished in the Holocaust.

MISCONCEPTIONS

So much for the origins of our current human rights policy. Now I will discuss briefly a few of the misconceptions that have arisen regarding that policy.

First, we are not seeking to impose our moral standards on other countries. The rights we are discussing here are recognized, at least with lip service, throughout the world. Indeed, they are included in the Universal Declaration of Human Rights, which was adopted by the General Assembly of the United Nations on December 10, 1948. I am sure many of you are familiar with the declaration, but I have copies here in case you would like to take them. So, to repeat, our human rights policy is based on internationally accepted norms.

Second, our human rights policy does not—repeat, not—reflect any assumptions of U.S. moral superiority. Those of you who have been to my country know very well that we have many human rights problems at home, including, for example, race discrimination, sex discrimination, violations of minimum wage laws, etc. We have achieved much progress with some of these problems in recent years, but they still persist and are a frequent subject of criticism in

our free press. So the United States is no exception. We all have human rights problems.

Third, we are also aware that many other nations are less fortunate than the United States. Due to accidents of history, geography, climate, etc., there are countries with appalling problems of extreme poverty, illiteracy, overpopulation, terrorism, etc., which we have been favored enough by fate to escape. As a result, other peoples sometimes see us as insanely lucky. For example, having served in Poland, I know that many people there consider the United States to be uniquely fortunate. They see themselves as situated between Germany and Russia, while we are sheltered by two oceans. There is a Polish saying that "God protects little babies, drunkards, and the United States of America."

Fourth, contrary to what some people assume, we do not intend our human rights policy to be intervention. We would like to be on friendly terms with all governments, and, everything else being equal, we prefer to avoid political confrontations, strained relations, dramatic headlines reporting diplomatic crises, etc. On the other hand, of course, we do have a right to decide to which countries we will give our economic and military assistance. And when another government pursues a policy of murder and torture of its citizens, we have a right to disassociate ourselves publicly from that policy and to withhold our aid.

RESULTS

Now, what have been some of the results of our human rights policy over the past 10 years or so? Here I will attempt a very rough

and incomplete balance sheet. On the minus side there have been strains in our relations with some governments, which otherwise would have been friendly allies but which resented our criticism of their widespread human rights violations. And sometimes that resentment has been shared by important areas of public opinion in those countries. For example, I recall accompanying the then-Assistant Secretary for Inter-American Affairs, Terry Todman, on a visit to Argentina in 1977. In Buenos Aires one evening, we were invited to supper by a group of local Argentine businessmen, some of whom were extremely critical of our human rights policy as they understood it. They deeply resented the State Department's criticism of human rights violations in Argentina, and they accused us of naively underestimating the danger of a communist takeover. I felt their resentment was entirely understandable, although I did not agree with it. And that bad feeling certainly imposed a strain on our relations with Argentina. I will discuss some other costs to the United States later if you wish, but because of the shortness of time, I will pass on now to the plus side of this human rights balance sheet.

What have been some of the achievements of our human rights policy? Here I would say that, both as direct and indirect results of our efforts, there has been less torture in some countries, there have been fewer political murders, fewer "disappeareds," more names published of political prisoners being held, more prisoners actually released, states of siege lifted, censorship relaxed, more elections and more honest elections, and in

Latin America the Inter-American Human Rights Commission has been invited to more countries, etc. I feel this is an impressive record and far outweighs the minus side of the balance sheet.

I hasten to add that I am not suggesting these advances in human rights are exclusively the result of our human rights policy. The main credit for this progress belongs to the citizens of those countries in which it took place. But I do maintain that the United States has made a major contribution to the progress, and I feel we should take quiet satisfaction in our record.

From the viewpoint of U.S. foreign policy, there is another very important benefit to be included on the plus side of the balance sheet. That is that our human rights policy has been welcomed by many key sectors of foreign public opinion that, in the past, have often been hostile to U.S. policies, at least as they understood them. Such groups include, for example, some democratic political parties, some labor unions, various religious organizations, many student bodies, many intellectual circles, etc. Our human rights policy has helped greatly in improving our relations with the democratic left, including Marxists who reject Leninism.

It is noteworthy that a number of other governments have now appointed officials to monitor human rights problems. The French Government is one of these. In Moscow an "Administration of Humanitarian and Cultural Affairs" has been created in the Ministry of Foreign Affairs. However, thus far it appears the main purpose of this new office is to counter foreign criticism of Soviet human rights abuses.

To sum up, I am convinced that our human rights policy over the past 10 years has not only helped the human rights cause in many areas of the world but has also been very much in the self-interest of the United States.

DIFFICULT QUESTIONS

Having said that, I emphasize immediately that I am not suggesting for a moment that, because we accord a high priority to human rights, our entire foreign policy automatically works well. Obviously not; our human rights policy provides no easy solutions to the complex and urgent problems that confront us daily and is in no way a guarantee against mistakes in judgment, faulty implementation, misinformation, etc. Moreover, many problems and questions arise in just trying to carry out our human rights policy. I will mention only a couple of these very briefly.

First of all, just how high a priority should human rights enjoy in our foreign policy? I think it is clear that, in the final analysis, our highest priority must go to the survival of the United States as a free and independent nation in a world that is often extremely dangerous. The application of these two priorities, survival and human rights, frequently involves difficult and complicated decisions.

Another difficult question concerns economic assistance. Should the United States cancel economic aid to a country with a poor human rights record if our calculations indicate that those who will suffer most from that decision will be the poorest sectors of that society? In such instances we can sometimes receive useful insights and advice from local religious representa-

tives and those in a country who are in close touch with the needs of the local community.

CRITICISMS

Now, what about some of the many criticisms of our human rights policy? One, which I recall as fairly frequent during the early days, a dozen or so years ago, was that human rights advocates are "emotional" and that emotion has no place in serious foreign affairs. Well, I would say that emotion is fairly normal to the human race, and just about all of us become emotional for one reason or another—some of us about the stock market's Dow Jones average, for example, and others possibly about human rights. Obviously, emotion does not necessarily preclude common sense and good judgment. In any event, now that the novelty of our human rights policy has worn off, this is a criticism that is seldom heard these days.

Another criticism is that the application of our human rights policy is "inconsistent," that we do not respond consistently to human rights violations in one country and another. There might be more validity to that criticism if the protection of human rights were our only objective. But, as I mentioned earlier, human rights is only one very important consideration in our foreign policy. However, even if this were not so, even if human rights were the *only* consideration, experience indicates it would be unreasonable to expect complete consistency in the day-to-day conduct of our foreign affairs. There are over 160 countries in the world today. Our human rights policy cannot operate with computers. It is simply unrealistic to expect a large government bureaucracy to perform perfectly. Even championship football teams never play an absolutely perfect game. I would say, rather, that consistency is a goal for which we aim, and when some inconsistencies inevitably do occur, they do not invalidate the basic policy. In brief, I maintain that, while our human rights policy is far from perfect, it is both genuine and effective.

Still another criticism we hear is that we apply our human rights policy only to leftwing governments; never to rightwing dictatorships. This is a favorite theme of broadcasts from the Soviet Union and Cuba, which I read every day, and I find it highly significant that both Moscow and Havana devote much time and effort trying to prove that our human rights policy is simply capitalist propaganda, with a double standard. Obviously, the Leninists feel very threatened by our human rights efforts.

The truth is, of course, that we criticize human rights violations by both the right and the left. If you have any doubts on that score I invite you to read the latest issue of our annual human rights reports to Congress for the year 1986. I would be interested to know whether you can find any pattern of ideological discrimination in the reports on 167 countries we prepared last year.

On the same theme it is relevant to mention that we now commemorate Human Rights Day, December 10, with a ceremony in the White House, during which the President signs the Human Rights Day proclamation. Last year both President Reagan and Assistant Secretary Richard Schifter briefly reviewed the state of human rights

worldwide, and their comments referred to repression not only in the Soviet Union, Cuba, Nicaragua, and Poland but also in South Africa, Chile, Paraguay, and Iran [see Special Report No. 164—"Reviewing the U.S. Commitment to Human Rights"]. I repeat, we criticize human rights violations by both the left and the right.

There is another important criticism from the political left, and not just the Leninists, which argues that one cannot really combat human injustice without replacing capitalism with socialism, that to work against torture, political murders, etc., is all very well, but basic human rights cannot be ensured without the establishment of socialism. I disagree, and I often recall another saying I learned in Poland many years ago. It goes like this: "What is the difference between capitalism and socialism? Capitalism is the exploitation of man by man, and socialism is vice versa." There is much truth in that bitter joke, and I think it is quite obvious by now that there can be ruthless oppression and exploitation with both economic systems. Neither capitalism nor socialism, in themselves, are a guarantee of human liberty. I personally feel that if there is one human right that is a key to all the others, it would be free speech. Free speech is more revolutionary than Marxism-Leninism.

ROLE PLAYED BY NONGOVERNMENTAL ORGANIZATIONS

Now, before concluding, a few words on the very important role played by nongovernmental organizations involved with human rights work. Many of them perform

valuable services in monitoring human rights issues, protecting human rights victims, helping refugees, etc. These are badly needed activities and represent a major contribution to the human rights cause. A good number of these groups are also occasional or frequent critics of the State Department's performance, and there is certainly nothing wrong with that when the criticism is reasonably accurate.

But having acknowledged the positive role they play, and having heard and read much of their comment, I also wish to voice one measured criticism of some of these groups. A good many organizations, such as Amnesty International, are quite willing to protest human rights violations across the political spectrum, from right to left. But it is discouraging to note how many other self-described human rights activists are motivated mainly by ideological prejudice. For example, it is remarkable that some of these people accuse the State Department of favoring rightwing dictatorships over communist regimes when they themselves do precisely the opposite. It is difficult to understand, for instance, how an organization allegedly covering human rights in Latin America can be highly vocal on problems in Chile and Paraguay but steadfastly refuse to say one word on violations in Cuba and will then accuse the State Department of applying a double standard.

In this connection I will conclude by recalling a vivid personal experience several years ago in one of our embassies in a foreign capital. I was talking with a woman whose husband had "disappeared," as they say, and she herself had good reason to fear for her own safety. She was discussing her plight with me while accompanied by her son of around 10 years of age. Toward the end of our meeting, she felt she had summoned up enough courage to venture outside once again, and she stood up to say goodbye. But then panic returned, and she decided to stay for just one more cigarette. When she tried to light up, her hands were trembling so much that I finally did it for her. And her small son's eyes never left me as he desperately tried to read in my face the chances for their survival. I think the question of whether that mother and son were in danger from a rightwing or leftwing regime is totally irrelevant. ■

The Great Foreign Policy Divide

By Henry Kissinger

As controversy envelops almost every foreign policy issue, a growing nostalgia develops for the spirit of compromise and bipartisanship that marked America's entry into world affairs in the decade following the Second World War. But the nostalgia misinterprets America's current dilemma. During the period of bipartisanship, there was agreement on fundamentals; compromise adjusted differences over method. Today, conflicts are philosophical; compromises are likely to combine the disadvantages of every course of action—witness the Reagan-Wright agreement on Nicaragua. So long as that conflict persists, America will continue to wallow in self-absorption.

In designing its foreign policy, any nation must answer at least three questions: (1) What is its concept of national security? In other words, what international changes is it prepared to resist? (2) What is its national purpose? That is, what goals will it seek to achieve? (3) What resources are available for either of these ends?

The American leaders of the bipartisan post-World War II era answered these questions with great assurance. Their concept of security was formed by Hitler's aggression with organized forces attacking across recognized military frontiers and the failure of the democracies to resist at an early stage. Their political goals were legacies of the New Deal, whose dominant experience was the threat to political institutions produced by a world depression. The leaders of that period could implement these assumptions because the United States had a nuclear monopoly and for two decades afterward a vast margin of superiority enabling it to assume the role of world policeman without analyzing its long-term implications. Moreover, America could overwhelm economic problems with resources because it produced 52 percent of the world's gross national product. The immediate postwar era seemed to vindicate America's historic image of itself as chosen by destiny to spread its virtue to the rest of the world.

Two decades of domestic discord have eroded this self-assurance, and history has changed the circumstances in which it was applied. A nation that produced over half of the world's GNP represented the balance of power all by itself. But today, when the United States generates barely a fourth of the world's GNP, concern with equilibrium and with setting priorities has become as necessary as it is distasteful to the traditional American approach to international affairs.

The American domestic drama for two decades has been the inability to reconcile traditional expectations with realities. Ever since the collapse of the effort of the Nixon administration to base foreign policy on some concept of permanent national interest, the public debate has been polarized between those who seek to turn all international conflicts into a confrontation between good and evil and those who believe that America's contribution to world politics is not power but virtue. Both schools of thought are hostile to a geopolitical analysis.

East-West relations illustrate this point. They are being treated either as a morality play or as an aberration caused by temporary condi-

Henry Kissinger was a professor at Harvard and, later, a National Security Adviser and Secretary of State. He now heads a private consulting firm.

Source: From *Los Angeles Times,* November, 24, 1987. Reprinted by permission of the author and Los Angeles Times Syndication.

tions, by the defective character of Soviet leaders or by their ideologically based suspiciousness. Whatever their starting point, American presidents have, in the end, opted for the psychiatric explanation of Soviet conduct. They have sought to cultivate improved personal relations with their Soviet counterparts as a key to world peace. From Khrushchev to Gorbachev, this has focused the domestic American debate on the significance of reform in Moscow, on whether the Soviet leaders have become more enlightened rather then on Soviet international conduct.

In the entire postwar period, there has been amazingly little analysis of the content of peaceful coexistence—the avowed goal of U.S. national policy in all administrations. What exactly is it that America wants the Soviet Union to stop doing? What is the American notion of cooperative conduct? In the contemporary situation, is *glasnost* or human rights progress enough, or are other changes necessary? Can four centuries of Russian expansionism be due to personalities, or do they reflect more permanent geopolitical and strategic elements? The absence of criteria causes domestic disputes to fester. The reluctance to endow peaceful coexistence with political content produces a near obsession with arms control, which confuses symptoms with causes and threatens to open up a gap between strategy and arms-control policy in which each checkmates the other.

For two decades at least, the dilemmas of nuclear parity have been obvious. In the past, nations went to war because the consequences of defeat were worse than the consequences of conflict. But when general nuclear war guarantees tens of millions of casualties in a matter of hours, this equation is far from self-evident. Yet strategists and arms controllers pursue incompatible courses in seeking to escape the dilemma. Strategists seek to resurrect the period of atomic superiority, while the arms controllers make little provision for the possibility that, for the Soviets, arms control may not be a cooperative enterprise but a strategy to weaken the democracies that are still being considered as adversaries.

Until recently, the strategists dominated the executive branch and strove for accurate counterforce nuclear weapons, largely blocked by Congress, and for the Strategic Defense Initiative, which is at best a decade away. The arms controllers dominate congressional thinking, and too many of them resist accurate counterforce weapons, strategic defense or any other limited application of nuclear weapons; they argue that this would open the door to a nuclear war that in the end cannot be limited.

But it is not possible to make the initiation of nuclear war absurd while relying on it as the principal deterrent to Soviet preponderance in conventional forces. One or the other course must be modified. After the prospective arms-control negotiations are completed, when warheads are reduced, strategic defense is postponed for at least a decade and uncertain thereafter, how will the United States implement its declared strategy? Does anyone believe the democracies will build up their conventional forces under current conditions of fiscal stringency when the new secretary of defense is being widely praised for his willingness to reduce the defense budget? In short, strategy and arms control are on different, potentially incompatible tracks, each with its own constituency. Sooner or later, a grave price will have to be paid for the paramountcy of domestic politics over national security considerations.

A society divided over how to deal with the relatively straightforward problem of overt military aggression will necessarily have even greater difficulty with more ambiguous challenges. America no longer has a bipartisan foreign policy because either it is divided over fundamental objectives or the objectives on which there is consensus reflect no recognizable international reality. If there exists a bipartisan agreement on any subject it is on the need to promote the spread of democracy globally. But how realistic is this objective? That the United States prefers democratic regimes to repressive ones goes without saying. That America should be prepared to pay some price for its preferences is also obvious. But it is dangerous to forget that Western democracy is homegrown in only a small corner of the globe and that it took several hundred years to evolve there. It was fostered by special characteristics of Western civilization that have so far not been duplicated elsewhere.

No other civilization has developed such absolute concepts of justice and such an insistence on the limits of temporal power. No other group of societies has evolved a concept of natural and religious law defined by hierarchies not controlled by temporal authorities. No other history has witnessed such a constant struggle for freedom in ever new forms. In the West, the accumulation of excessive power at the center has been the principal concern of political theorists; in most other societies the concern has been to buttress, not to weaken or balance central authority.

But to what extent are these concepts a guide for day-to-day policy? Hardly a day passes without some congressional stricture against some foreign country or other or some administration pronouncement as to appropriate domestic conduct all over the globe. Oddly enough, as American resources are shrinking the drive toward global intervention seems to be increasing.

There are, to be sure, egregious human rights violations that must be protested and, if necessary, penalized. But can we really sustain the role as schoolmaster of domestic politics everywhere in the world? Do we really know enough to advise and sometimes press simultaneously on domestic politics from Asia to Latin America? The implication that domestic reform is America's overriding foreign policy objective has two consequences: actual negotiations with, for example, Nicaragua take on the abstract quality of a political science seminar on elusive and reversible concepts of democratization, while more tangible subjects related to national security such as Cuban and Eastern-bloc advisers and the size of Nicaragua's armed forces are neglected. In the longer term, this attitude becomes the alibi for an incipient isolationism by providing an escape into choices involving little apparent risk.

This global interventionism works best with respect to friendly regimes dependent on U.S. support and least well with hostile ones protected by the U.S. reluctance to use force. In either event, the American capacity to undermine is not matched by a capacity to construct. Revolutions are made by a coalition of resentments. But when the demolition is completed, a fierce struggle between the previous allies is nearly inevitable. Given American public and congressional attitudes toward covert action and, even more, American ignorance of the intangibles of political processes, the risk is great that America may be making the world safe not for democracy but for the most highly organized militant and ruthless groups.

America's unresolved contradictions risk opening up a huge gap between ends and means in the pursuit of incompatible objectives. This would be serious enough in a bipolar world. But Japan, Western Europe, China and possibly India all have the capacity to become major players by the end of this century. As American military and economic preeminence declines, they are less likely to listen to American preachment and apt to return to the balance-of-power policies that have shaped their history. This in turn may accelerate America's turn toward isolationism, thus undoing the creative efforts of a generation.

Three years ago, when President Reagan won an overwhelming reelection victory, I wrote that he had a unique opportunity to reconcile the American domestic debate and to take bipartisanship beyond the least common denominator. This has not happened. But the president can still leave a historic legacy by raising the debate to a conceptual level. Precisely because his is a lame-duck administration, he can afford to recall America to its vision and its duties. He has nothing to lose by raising the issue of the relationship between power and diplomacy, of the content of peace and the nature of global progress. And the presidential candidates who now claim to have "solutions" can serve their country better by participating in a national debate over philosophy and concepts rather than gimmicks. If this does not happen, America may become the scold of international politics while losing the capacity to shape events. ∎

Unresolved Issues of Human Rights

By Howard J. Wiarda

While human rights policy has come a considerable distance since the early days, numerous problems still stand in the way of a more effective policy. I indicate nine such problems, which are not mere nit-picking but which must be grappled with if we are to have a serious human rights policy.

1. *Diverse meanings of key human rights terms.* Other nations and culture areas clearly mean different things than we do by "human rights" or key human rights

Source: From Howard J. Wiarda, *The Democratic Revolution in Latin America* (New York: Holmes and Meier, A Twentieth Century Fund Book, 1990).

terms—or have different priorities. That is true not only of the so-called Peoples' Democracies but of non-Western or only partially Western (Latin America) culture areas as well. In Latin America, for instance, many of the historic organic, Rousseauean, and corporatist forms of democracy are now in the process of being gradually replaced by a Western and modern conception of democracy—competitive elections, civil liberties, pluralism, and the like. That evolution is heartening and provides room for political maneuver and progress in the human rights area; but the more traditional and historic Latin American meanings of "representation," "democracy," etc., should not be forgotten. Sensitivity, empathy, and understanding of these differences are essential. Serious scholarly research and comprehension of the diverse meanings and shadings of such terms are fundamental to an informed and effective human rights policy.

2. *Categories of human rights.* Human rights may be conveniently divided into three types: political and civil rights, social and economic rights, and basic rights affecting the human person (absence of torture, etc.). In its excess enthusiasm, the Carter Administration tried to secure gains in all three areas at once. But the fact is that there is less consensus globally on some of these rights than others, and therefore more probability for success in some areas than in others. Our experience has been that the best chances of success are in the area of rights of the human person (preventing torture, getting people out of jail, securing humane treatment for prisoners), because most of the world shares agreement on this; that there is less consensus and therefore more limited opportunities for success in the area of political and civil rights (guaranteeing freedom of the press, of assembly, of speech, etc.); and that there is very little consensus except perhaps at the rhetorical level on social and economic rights. It would be nice if all three categories could be advanced simultaneously, and we should not give up in any area; but policy makers need to know that the possibilities for success are stronger in some areas than in others.

3. *Evenhandedness.* As it has evolved, U.S. human rights policy is now more evenhanded than it was in the early years. Nevertheless, liberal administrations have tended to be more condemnatory of abuses in right-wing regimes and to pay less attention to abuses in left-wing regimes, while conservative administrations have tended to emphasize the abuses of Marxist-Leninist regimes and to have mixed feelings about criticizing (and thereby potentially destabilizing, with possibly disastrous foreign policy repercussions) right-wing ones. Even more worrisome has been the continuing attitude of some of the major human rights lobbies, which are quick to condemn abuses in Chile or El Salvador but are very quiet on abuses in Cuba or Nicaragua. They rationalize this lack of balance by saying they are only concerned with those countries where the U.S. provides assistance. But that is, of course, a terribly weak rationalization and will not do. Either one is in favor of human rights or one is not; and if one is in favor, then one must condemn human rights abuses regardless of the ideological coloring of the regime—unless, of course, the purpose of these lobbies is not human rights but some other agenda (see #9 below). In general, however (and there may be valid reasons for certain exceptions under some circumstances), we need to be evenhanded in our approach to human rights, which means concern for the human rights situation in both left-wing and right-wing regimes.

4. *Intervention vs. nonintervention.* When we pursue a strong human rights policy in another country, we need to face the fact that we are intervening in that country's internal affairs. It may be a "good" (human rights) as opposed to a "bad" (gunboat diplomacy) intervention, but it is still intervention, and we need to be aware of the sensitivities involved. It is clear, for example, that such interventions—often from the best of intentions—on the part of some Carter Administration officials were deeply resented and counterproductive. The U.S. diplomatic intervention in the Dominican Republic in 1978 (to guarantee an honest ballot count, often claimed as the most successful of the Carter efforts) reinforced that country's dependence on and subservience to the U.S., which was certainly not the intention of those involved. As an intervention in other countries' internal affairs, for however a noble cause, human rights policy requires sensitivity, knowledge, and understanding of the full implications of our action. Riding roughshod over local practices and ways of doing things, blatant interference, wholesale and indiscriminate condemnations of entire countries and institutions, arrogance, and insensitivity are likely to produce the opposite effects of those intended.

5. *What instruments?* How best and most effectively to further human rights? Do we use quiet or public diplomacy? Do sanctions work or not? The answers are complex and subject to change, and they must be redesigned for individual situations. But in general it has been found that quiet diplomacy works better than the loud kind—until a point is reached (as in the case of Pinochet's Chile) where quiet persuasion has gotten nowhere and policy makers are left with no choice but to go public. As for sanctions, the Carter Administration cut off aid to Somoza, but there was so much aid already in the pipeline that the cutoff had no real practical effect. Then the U.S. tried to "rev up" the aid to exercise influence over the direction of the Sandinista revolution, but that took added time and had no effect either. In general, it can be said that sanctions have limited effect except psychologically. Moreover, by cutting off aid to a country we lose whatever leverage we might otherwise have had.

6. *Balance with other U.S. interests.* The Carter Administration, particularly in its early years, put too great a stress on human rights concerns, sometimes at the cost of important U.S. political, diplomatic, economic, and strategic interests. The Reagan Administration made the mistake in its early months of so downplaying human rights as to give the appearance they were not important in American foreign policy considerations. Both of these approaches were too extreme. The United States needs to have a strong human rights component in its foreign policy. Indeed, I have concluded that it is impossible to have a successful U.S. foreign policy without that component. But the human rights concern cannot be permitted to submerge important strategic and other considerations. Although we will still disagree about specific cases—cases that can appropriately be decided in the political process—I think we have now achieved a fairly good balance between the strategic, the diplomatic, the economic, and the human rights aspects of our policy.

7. *How hard to push?* How much pressure do we exert on a country before we do irreparable harm to it and to us? This is a hard question, the answer to which may vary in different contexts. Do we push the white South African regime so hard that we destroy it, producing yet another shoddy Marxist-Leninist regime on the strategic tip of Africa? Does our interest in democracy and human rights in Haiti force us to occupy the country militarily as the best or only way to accomplish that goal? Do we push Saudi Arabia so hard that we eventually face a cutoff of our oil supplies (and probably produce a regime like Khoemeini's—hardly a paragon of human rights virtue)? And how far do we push the human rights issue vis-à-vis the Soviet Union, a country with a miserable human rights record but with the power to destroy us and all mankind? There are no easy answers to all these questions; they are raised here as illustrations of the complexities involved and to point up the fact that there are limits beyond which any well-meaning human rights policy probably ought not to go.

8. *The national interest.* I believe human rights ought to be a major component of U.S. foreign policy, but it must also be remembered that there will be instances, perhaps many of them, when human rights concerns will have to be subordinated to a more pressing national interest. Take El Salvador, for example. Under José Napoleón Duarte's able democratic leadership, our human rights and our strategic interests (preventing a Marxist-Leninist takeover) could go forward in tandem. But if Duarte or his successor were to be overthrown and a repressive military regime were to come to power again in that unfortunate and guerrilla-ravaged country, we might still have to come to that regime's defense, because we have an even stronger interest in preventing a communist guerrilla takeover. We could then work with that regime to improve human rights conditions, but we would also need to support such a regime. In these circumstances we would have returned to the situation in El Salvador that prevailed in the early 1980s—and with all the possibilities for a renewal of the divisive and nearly paralyzing policy debate that existed then.

9. *The politics of human rights.* Human rights are no longer just a moral and ethical interest and a matter of individual conscience in the United States. Rather, human rights are now the "stuff" of major lobbying organizations, of vast amounts of money, of armies of activists and demonstrators, and of national mobilization campaigns. Other agendas besides the human rights agenda (but disguised or hidden) are often pursued in the name of human rights. Human rights issues may be used in an attempt to undermine or destroy an American administration with which some persons may disagree. Human rights issues have proved deeply divisive between the White

House and the Congress. Human rights have been politicized, used by one party to embarrass the other, and vice versa. The human rights issue, coupled with the divisive debate over Central America, has the possibility quite literally to paralyze and immobilize the entire foreign policy-making apparatus of the United States government—as seemed to be the case in the early-to-mid-1980s. This point is made not because I believe the discussion of human rights issues can be entirely removed from the political arena—or even that that would be desirable—but to indicate that

there are frequently other agendas than the human rights agenda involved; that the issue can be extremely divisive and is used purposely by some groups for their own political purposes; and that such divisiveness can hamstring American foreign policy making. We need to be alert to these potential dangers.

Now, if all these issues can be resolved—and some, but by no means all of them, have been over the years—we can have an effective, balanced, viable human rights policy. It is a daunting task. The

history recounted here and the nine problem areas discussed show how complex, difficult, and potentially divisive the issue can be. Of course, not all of these issues need to be resolved now and for all time; they are—and appropriately so—a part of the American political process, open to further discussion and modification. But we have made impressive progress over the years, to the point where human rights are an integral part of American foreign policy making and global concern. That is, I believe, as it should be. ■

The Genius of American Politics

By Daniel J. Boorstin

The doom that awaited the Roman Empire, according to C. N. Cochrane, "was that of a civilization which failed to understand itself and was, in consequence, dominated by a haunting fear of the unknown." Much the same could be said for us. Our intellectual insecurity, our feeling of philosophical inadequacy, may be explained at least in part by our failure to understand ourselves. This failure is due in some measure to our readiness to accept the European clichés about us.

We all know that people are prone to parade their weaknesses as if they were virtues. Anyone who has recently been among Europeans can tell you that there is an

increasing tendency on the old continent to blame the United States for lacking many of the ills that have characterized European history. Our lack of poverty is called materialism, our lack of political dogma is called aimlessness and confusion. On the whole, the people, and especially the intellectuals of Europe, who are desperately on the offensive, have succeeded in convincing us—and especially our intellectuals. They have made us apologize for our wealth and welfare. You will find many well-meaning Americans abroad who think that they are defending their country when they point out that people in the United States are really a lot worse off than

Europeans think. They have made us apologize for our lack of philosophical clarity, so that we seek to concoct a political philosophy that can rival the dogmas of Europe.

It has been too long since we have stood on the special virtues of our life and our continent. Over a century has passed since Emerson declared in his "American Scholar": "Our day of dependence, our long apprenticeship to the learning of other lands, draws to a close. The millions that around us are rushing into life, cannot always be fed on the mere remains of foreign harvests." But we still see ourselves in the distorting mirror of Europe.

The image which Europe shows us is as much a defense of itself as

The author is Professor of American History at the University of Chicago and has been a visiting scholar at various universitites in Italy, France, Puerto Rico, and Japan; he later served as Director of the Library of Congress.

a caricature of us. We are too easily persuaded that the cancers of European life (and especially of European political life) are healthy growths and that we are deformed for not possessing them. The equations of poverty and idealism, of monopoly and responsibility, of aristocracy and culture, of political dogma and purposeful political institutions, are too readily accepted. It is, of course, some solace to a declining European culture—a culture dying of poverty, monopoly, aristocracy, and ideology—to think that their ills are simply the excess of their virtues. That theirs must be the virtues of all cultures. And hence that the accidents of history that may have immunized us against such vices also sterilize our culture and doom us to philistinism and vagrancy.

There is no denying that our intellectuals and, most of all, our academics, being the most cosmopolitan part of our culture, have been especially susceptible to the well-meaning advice of our sick friends in Europe. Like many sick friends, they are none too sorry to be able to tell us that we are not in the best of health.

We have, in a word, been too easily led to deny our peculiarly American virtues, in order to seem to have the peculiar European vices. Moreover, our intellectuals, who rightly consider themselves the critical organ of our community, have been much too sensitive to any charge of chauvinism. Hence they, too, have been readier to tell us what we lack than to help us discover what we have. Our historians and political scientists, while blaming themselves and one another for "irresponsibility," have failed to help us discover the peculiar virtues of our situation. They

have left the discovery and defense of those virtues to the dubious efforts of professional patriots.

Is it any wonder that the very word "patriotism" should come to be suspect among intellectuals? Is it any wonder that we suffer from cultural hypochondria?

The cure for our hypochondria is surely not chauvinism. That simply adds one real ill to the many unreal ills of which we already accuse ourselves. Waving a flag cannot cure inner uncertainty. One possibility, at least a little more fruitful, is to try to discover the peculiar virtues of our situation, the special character of our history: to try to judge ourselves by the potentialities of our own peculiar and magnificent continent. We may then discover that our virtues, like our ills, are actually peculiar to ourselves; that what seem to be inadequacies of our culture, if measured by European standards, are nothing but our differences and may even be virtues. . . .

The European concept of culture is basically aristocratic; its great successes—especially in countries like Italy and France— are in the aristocratic arts. Its literature is for the few; its newspapers are subsidized by political parties; its books, when successful, have a circulation a fifth of that in America, even in proportion to the population. European culture, most of it at least, is the heritage of a pre-liberal past. For all their magnificence, the monuments of that past are products of a culture with which we, fortunately, are in no position to compete. It is surely no accident that we have accomplished relatively little in the arts of painting, sculpture, palace and church architecture, chamber music, and chamber poetry. It is

equally no accident that we have contributed so little in political philosophy.

Some Americans, however— and they are probably increasing in number—make un-American demands for a philosophy of democracy. They believe that this philosophy will be a weapon against Russia and a prop for our own institutions. They are afraid that, without some such salable commodity, they may not be able to compete with Russia in the world market.

These people are puzzled that we should have come as far as we have without knowing the philosophy that lies beneath our institutions. They are even frightened at what they might find—or fail to find—when they open the *sanctum sanctorum* of national belief. It is these who are among our most dangerous friends; for, even if they should find the Holy of Holies empty, they would refuse to admit it. Instead of trying to discover the reasons why we have managed to be free of idolatry, they will make their own graven image, their own ass's head, and say that is what belonged in the temple all the time. These people are dangerous because they would misrepresent us abroad and corrupt us at home.

If we have no exportable political theory, then can we export our political institutions? Should we try to induce the Italian or the German people to become democratic in the American image? If the thesis of this book is correct, the answer here too is, of course, No. The answer is No, not merely because the attempt to distill our philosophy or to transplant our institutions is apt to fail. It is No, because the principles on which we approach politics and have succeeded in building our own institutions, deny such a possibility.

If we have learned anything from our history, it is the wisdom of allowing institutions to develop according to the needs of each particular environment; and the value of both environmentalism and traditionalism as principles of political life, as ways of saving ourselves from the imbecilities, the vagaries, and the cosmic enthusiasms of individual men. This is our idea of constitutional federalism, without which our great union would have been impossible.

If what has held us together as a nation has been no explicit political theory held in common but rather a fact of life (what Whitman properly called "adhesiveness"), how can we expect to bind other nations by theories? We have felt both "individualism which isolates" and, as he says, "adhesiveness or love, that fuses, ties, and aggregates."

We have traditionally held out to the world, not our doctrine, but our example. The idea of America as the last best hope of mankind has not been the idea that America would outdo other ages and places with its philosophy. It was life, and not thought, which would excel here. This has perhaps taken some of the sting of arrogance out of our consciousness of destiny. For men are in the habit of claiming more personal credit for the quality of their thought than for the quality of their institutions. Even to the most obtuse, institutions seem the product of many forces. In the past we have wanted to be judged not by what we could tell the world but by what we could show the world. Moreover, we have considered ourselves not a factory of institutions but a laboratory, an experiment. By showing what man might

do under our new circumstances, we might give men everywhere new hope for improving their lot after their own fashion.

No one has stated the case better than did John C. Calhoun, speaking at the time of the Mexican War, about a century ago:

It has been lately urged in a very respectable quarter, that it is the mission of this country to spread civil and religious liberty over all the globe, and especially over this continent— even by force, if necessary. It is a sad delusion. . . . It is a remarkable fact in the political history of man, that there is scarcely an instance of a free constitutional government, which has been the work exclusively of foresight and wisdom. They have all been the result of a fortunate combination of circumstances (Works, IV, 416).

It is our experience, not our dogma or our power, that may be the encouragement and the hope of the world. We can, Calhoun concluded, "do more to extend liberty by our example over the country and the world generally, than would be done by a thousand victories."

To tell people what institutions they must have, whether we tell them with the Voice of America or with the Money of America, is the thorough denial of our American heritage. It would be an attempt "to meet the monolithic East by attempting to set up a monolithic West." As Stephen Spender has observed, "When the Communists today congratulate themselves on being 'monolithic,' they are congratulating themselves in being dead: and it is for us to see that they do not turn the whole world into their cemetery." An imposed democracy ex-

presses a corroding cynicism. And democratic institutions, however much they may rest on pessimism, must be the opposite of cynical. Tyrannies—fascism, naziism, communism—can impose themselves on others with no hypocrisy, for they rest unashamedly on force. But if we were to become cynical in order to make Europe seem to stand for something better than it might on its own, we would risk losing everything, even if we should win.

Is it not even possible that the people of Europe will be more willing to defend themselves if it is their own institutions they are defending? If they are unwilling to defend their own, they surely will not want to defend ours.

We have, of course, our modern abolitionists, those who believe that the abolition of slavery in Russia is the sole issue in the world. They surely need no philosophy. The clarity and righteousness of their objective is enough. Soviet communism provides them the sense of "giveness," of obviousness in their objective. For them, Communists embody the spirit of Satan as vividly as the American Indians did for the first Puritans, or as the southern slaveowners did for fire-eaters like Phillips and Garrison. Some of them would seem almost as willing as Garrison to burn the Constitution in order to attain their admirable objective.

There are others who take a more practical Lincolnian view. Like Lincoln, these people hate slavery anywhere, but they doubt their capacity to make a perfect world. Their main concern is to preserve and improve free institutions where they now exist.

If the Lincolnian view involves us in the seeming contradiction of defending our institutions without insisting on propagating them, this is nothing but the contradiction within the idea of freedom itself, which affirms a value but asserts it only to allow a competition among values.

We must refuse to become crusaders for liberalism, in order to remain liberals. We must refuse to try to export our commodity. We must

refuse to become crusaders for democracy, in order to conserve the institutions and the genius which have made America great. ■

Making New Nations Democratic

By Gabriel A. Almond

MUST IT BE ALL OR NOTHING?

There has been no end of debate in recent years on the question of political modernization and democratization in the new and modernizing nations of Asia, Africa and Latin America. One of the schools of thought goes like this. The very idea of democracy in these nations was a naive one. How can we take a delicate mechanism and subtle culture like democracy, which took centuries of groping and trial and error to develop in the West, and transplant it into societies with radically different political cultures, social structures and political traditions? What we have to settle for in the so-called developing and uncommitted world, goes this line of reasoning, are political stability and the military-strategic interests of the United States.

There have been two approaches in our appraisals of the prospects of these new and modernizing nations, a "tough" one and a "tender" one; and these have been the points of view expressed in our political debate about foreign aid and America's role in the

developing and transitional world. The "tender" approach grows out of the liberal enlightenment tradition in America, the faith in man's inclination to freedom and justice, a belief in education and educability, a belief in the democratic consequences of economic progress. This school of thought imputed to the democratic constitutions that were established in Asia and Africa after World War II a reality which they could not have possessed. And as Korea, Vietnam, Burma, Indonesia, Pakistan, Egypt, Ghana, Cuba and Brazil—I won't attempt to name them all—have turned to authoritarian and even Communist regimes—this school of thought has become demoralized. It had no prepared ground to fall back on, and, as a consequence, has tended to play into the hands of the "tough" school of thought, tended to lend credibility to [the] point of view of simply holding the line. . . .

Two distortions of reality underlie the "tender" approach. The first is the failure to perceive accurately and without illusion the human and social material of the new nations, and the complexity of the institutions we were expecting

them to operate. I shall return to this problem at a later point. The second is our failure to appreciate how recent and how partial is our own attainment of democracy in the West. Not much more than a century ago England, the mother of parliaments, looked very much like one of our non-Western nations. It had a serious problem of illiteracy, or of low literacy, a working class living in rude poverty, a small aristocratic elite based substantially on landed property monopolizing political power. In contemporary England the old society is only slowly giving way to pressures for equalizing opportunity, and there is a good long way to go. In our own United States the denial of equal opportunities on grounds of race is still a popular policy among some Southern whites and a minority of Northern whites. Two of the great European powers, Italy and Germany, not long ago explicitly rejected democratic processes, and Germany left memories of destructiveness and barbarism that all human history will be unable to wipe out. France, of the glorious revolutionary tradition, for a time lived in a state of suspended democracy by popular

Gabriel A. Almond is Professor of Political Science at Stanford University.

Source: From *Stanford Today,* Series 1, No. 10 (Autumn, 1964), with the permission of the publishers, Stanford University. Copyright 1964 by the Board of Trustees of the Leland Stanford Junior University.

request, so to speak, because of the long and humiliating failures of her republican regimes.

I stress these points only to remind ourselves that we are not comparing an exotic, backward, chaotic and authoritarian world with a modern democratic one, but rather for both the old and the new nations we are dealing with an unfulfilled process of enlightenment and democratization. This should reduce our impatience and panic at the excesses and instabilities of the new nations. . . .

What I have called the "tough" approach is also based on a number of myths and false expectations. One of these is that stable, military and conservative regimes are really stable. We need only recall the events of recent years and months in South Korea, in Vietnam, pre-Castro Cuba, or Brazil. The forces which are alive in the world today are too powerful to be contained for long. What looks like stability and viability today may end in an Iraqian blood bath tomorrow. Surely we may have to support such regimes, but we cannot rest our policy of support on the theory that their stability is more than superficial. In addition there is a tendency for extremism to breed extremism, repression, repression. It may very well be that these repressive regimes are the ones most susceptible to Communist penetration like the Cuba of Batista, that the illusion of security and stability in these areas may really be doubly illusory, so to speak.

A second myth that underlies the approach which would put our bets—and primarily military bets—on military and authoritarian regimes is what I call the dom-

inoes theory of international politics. This theory is a very simple one. For example, it was argued when China fell to the Communists in 1949 that it would simply be a matter of time—and not much time at that—before Korea, Indo-China, Thailand, and the rest of Southeast Asia and then India would fall to the Communists. The same argument has been advanced in relation to Laos and Vietnam, and it has been said that unless the Castro regime is overturned, the rest of Latin America cannot be held.

The Chinese collapse was an immensely costly one in a strategic and political sense. A collapse of the present situation in Laos should be prevented if possible; we cannot withdraw from our present situation in Central America without serious risks and costs; and Cuba is a threat of major proportions. But the trouble with the dominoes theory is that it is a tense and rigid—a crisis-oriented—policy. It tends to move us from crisis to crisis, tempts us to commit our reserves prematurely. It is a panicky, defensive posture. In the long pull of foreign policy we have to be prepared to lose a position here and there, and gain some as well. We need to be deployed in depth, and husband our reserves.

We have long since passed beyond the clarities and simplicities of the cold war era and the containment policy. The Communist camp is no longer a camp, an orbit, or a bloc. It is a complex system in which the increasingly sharp struggle between Russia and China has granted a larger and larger autonomy to the smaller Communist powers and Communist parties. . . . On the Western side, the old conditions which produced NATO and

the Marshall Plan have long since disappeared. Europe is economically vigorous and increasingly independent. In other words, the old unities and simplicities of the cold war are no longer with us. The structure has become loose, less predictable.

We have to revise our conceptions and strategies regarding the political prospects of the new nations in accordance with these fundamental changes in the international political system. In our relations with these nations in Asia, Africa and Latin America we are encountering the conflicting diplomacies not only of the French, the British, the Portuguese, but also the conflicting diplomacies of Russia and China. And it may very well be that the competition between Russia and China in the new nations is as hostile and antagonistic as is the Russian antagonism toward us. In this more loosely structured international political system with more competitors and a lower level of competitive intensity, we need another way of thinking about the developing nations.

CAN IT HAPPEN ALL AT ONCE?

We need an orderly and realistic way of fostering the process of modernization and democratization—to develop more effective policies not only for ourselves, but also for the leaders and statesmen of the new nations. Most of these men—these U Nus, Nyereres, Bandas, Mboyas, Nkrumahs, Sukarnos —have been strongly influenced by democratic ideology. The democratic political theory of the West—unlike Marxist theory—did not provide them with a theory of political growth that might help them develop sound strategies of how to move from traditional and authoritarian social and political structures toward the orderly freedoms and restraints of the democratic polity. What we need, in other words, is a good theory of *democratization*, rather than an ideological theory of democracy. The collapse of the formal democracies of Asia, Africa and Latin America might have been avoided in some cases, or at least their demoralizing consequences mitigated, had they begun with this kind of developmental conception of democratization.

What would this theory of democratization look like? In the first place it would be a theory of social change in which economic, social, psychological and political factors would have to be considered in their interrelations. It would avoid the assumptions made by economists that industrialization in and of itself brings about the development of democratic institutions. It would avoid the assumptions of lawyers and public administrators, who tend to overlook the human and social material that they sought to contain in the constitutional and administrative "bottles" of the West.

It would have to start from the vantage point of the leaderships of the new nations themselves—recognizing the resources available to them and the varieties and intensities of the pressures to which they are exposed. The statesmen of the Anglo-American West as they developed the institutions of law and popular control in the last few hundred years had a luxury of time. First, they had luxury of time to form nations out of smaller units, and patriots out of tribesmen and villagers. Second,

they had a luxury of time to create governmental authority and habits of obedience to law among their populations. Third, they had a luxury of time to turn subjects into citizens as the culture and infrastructure of democracy emerged; as the suffrage expanded, the political parties, interest groups and mass media developed. And fourth, they had time to meet the demands for popular welfare that became pressing in the course of the nineteenth and twentieth centuries. The statesmen of the new and modernizing nations are hit by all of these problems at once. They confront *simultaneous* and *cumulative* revolutions. They have to make choices which Western statesmen were never called on to make.

I don't wish to give the impression that all the modernizing nations of Asia, Africa and Latin America confront these same problems in the same way and extent. But let me put it in its extreme version, taking perhaps as our model the problem which confronts Julius Nyerere of what was Tanganyika yesterday [and is Tanzania today]. He is confronted with what we may call the four problems of democratic nation-building. In the first place he has the job of creating Tanganyikans out of members of more than a hundred different tribal stocks; without this he has no nation. He has to create a framework of bureaucratic authority, dealing with a population that in its overwhelming majority consists of simple and illiterate tribesmen and villagers. He has to create citizen-participants out of this same human material, give them the right to vote before they can read, before they properly know what government is. And as he strives to

raise the level of literacy and exposes his people to the amenities and physical good of modern civilization, he has somehow to respond to the growing demands for physical goods and welfare.

He confronts, in other words, a *national* revolution, an *authority* revolution, a *participation* revolution and a *welfare* revolution all at one time. It goes without saying that he cannot give in all four directions at once. Furthermore, it should also be unambiguously clear that he is not even free to choose the particular mix of revolutions or the order that he prefers. Whether he likes it or not he must give a higher priority to the creation of a nation and of effective government authority before he gives way fully to demands for participation and welfare. Indeed we may say that he must first create a nation and effective governmental authority if he is ever going to be able to respond to demands for political participation and welfare.

What this means is that whatever names we may give to them, or whatever their constitutional or legal form may be, the political systems of the new and modernizing nations will have to have strong centralizing and authoritarian tendencies. But this is not the same thing as saying we must give up the prospect of democracy in the new nations. What can be done is to build into these centralizing and authoritarian systems a democratizing strategy and pattern of investment.[1]

A WHIG APPROACH TO DEMOCRATIZATION

We might call this approach to the problem of democratization the Whig approach, because it represents an effort to apply to the political development of the new nations the lessons of Western experience. As the British monarchy moved toward centralization in the fifteenth-to-seventeenth centuries, the so-called Age of Absolutism, British centralization stopped short of destroying its local autonomies—the local powers of the aristocracy and the country gentry, the self-governing rights of cities, merchant guilds and the like. A vigorous tradition of autonomy remained, fought the centralizing crown to a standstill, and preserved a traditional pluralism until a modern one was ready to combine with it in the nineteenth and twentieth centuries. It was the chaffering and bargaining of spokesmen of the crown with Whig aristocrats and middle-class merchants in Parliament that created the culture of the parliamentary bargaining and discussion, which enabled Britain to pass through the later crises of industrialization with a minimum of violence and discontinuity, relying on electoral and parliamentary processes. On the other hand you will recall from political history that the destruction of local and pluralistic tendencies in France and the extreme centralization that took place in that country are often used as an explanation of the instability of republican and democratic processes in France.

But is the Whig theory applicable in the new nations? Does it apply in India, Burma, Indonesia, Nigeria, Kenya and Uganda, Tanzania and the like? The answer must be, it applies in some areas more than in others. It depends in part on the vigor of local and parochial institutions, the tribal structure and the religious composition. And it

also depends on what happened in the colonial period or in the earlier history of these nations. It has a more obvious relevance to India with its strong local cultural traditions, Nigeria with its strong and well-balanced tribal structure, perhaps in Kenya and Uganda and other countries with similar structures. But even in those nations without vigorous local structures and traditions—the Whig theory has some important lessons for us. It suggests a moderate form of authoritarianism, a kind of tutelary authoritarianism (such as that of Nyerere . . . , or the pattern of the Mexican revolution), a moderate pattern of penetration and centralization in which resisting groups are not destroyed, but bargained with, and occasionally conceded to, even at some cost in efficiency.

If the centralizing tendencies in these first two phases of political development—the creation of national identity and effective government—stop short of destroying local initiative, but assimilate them into a bargaining process, then the democratizing processes of education and mass communication, industrialization, urbanization and the emancipation of women can build on this pluralism and something like a viable democratic process may in time emerge. At least some of the new nations may be able to move continuously and incrementally into modernization and democratization, preserving and assimilating the pluralisms of the traditional society until the pluralism of the industrial society can emerge.

There will be many failures. We cannot properly sit in judgment of those leaders who, confronted with this cumulative revolutionary

process, decide to concentrate their resources on economic development, who suppress disruptive movements, or fail to cultivate democratic tendencies. Western statesmen have never been called upon to cope with such a range of issues and choices all at once. Our own foreign policy and foreign aid programs can make a significant contribution in this modernizing and democratizing process by increasing the scale of resources available to the leaders of these nations, and by making knowledge, insight, and technical knowhow into the modernizing process available. But we have to be prepared to accept failures, and waste. The world around us will not collapse into Communism like a row of dominoes, nor will it transform itself in a brief few years into a community of democratic and peaceful nations.

A while back we often heard the boast from Moscow, "We will bury you," and from our side some of us would reply, "No, we will bury you." If I am not mistaken, we don't hear this particular boast from Moscow these days, particularly since the Cuban missiles crisis. I don't think either side is going to bury the other in an ideological sense. There are loosening and pluralistic tendencies at work in the Soviet Union and in other Communist nations. These are the consequence of the unremitting pressures of an increasingly educated, technically skilled and economically well-off population— pressures for privacy, pressures for dignity, pressures for professional, artistic and intellectual integrity, and for participation in decisions affecting their lives. These pressures will not bring about a free society with a multi-party system—

but surely it will be a great deal looser than it is today.

Among the Western nations there is good reason for encouragement. The processes of democratization are slowly but surely at work. The status system of England is being eroded away through the spread of educational opportunity. The racial-caste system of America is under very sharp attack. It will give way slowly; there will be setbacks; but change is irresistibly on the move here. And in the new and modernizing nations of Asia, Africa and Latin America the processes of enlightenment and democratization will have their inevitable way.

The rude shocks of two world wars and the political horrors of the interwar period shook the enlightenment faith of many of us. I must confess that I am not a political relativist any more, though I flirted with this point of view . . . in the dark periods of the last decades. Who would want to deny that man is engaged in a long-run effort at attaining control over nature and of himself, and that liberty and responsibility are at the very center of his search, and this despite the distortions and caricatures that we often produce? The early enlightenment fathers were somewhat naive and impatient. It will be a longer and costlier struggle than they anticipated, and the problems are a good deal less tractable than they supposed. But the vision was sound, and the confidence well-founded. ■

Notes

1. See Myron Weiner, "Political Modernization and Evolutionary Theory," in Herbert R. Barringer, George Blanksten, and Raymond Mack, (eds.), *Social Change in Developing Areas* (Cambridge, MA: Schenkman, 1965).

Suggested Additional Readings

Binnendijk, Hans (ed.). *Authoritarian Regimes in Transition* (Washington, D.C.: Department of State, Foreign Service Institute, 1987).

Forsythe, David P. *Human Rights and U.S. Foreign Policy* (Gainesville: University of Florida Press, 1988).

Garfinkle, Adam, and Daniel Pipes (eds.). *Friendly Tyrants: An American Foreign Policy Conundrum,* 3 vols. (Philadelphia: Foreign Policy Research Institute, forthcoming).

Goldman, Ralph M., and William A. Douglas. *Promoting Democracy: Opportunities and Issues* (New York: Praeger, 1988).

Hoffmann, Stanley. *Duties Beyond Borders: On the Limits and Possibilities of an Ethical International Politics* (Syracuse, NY: Syracuse University Press, 1981).

Macfarlane, L. J. *The Theory and Practice of Human Rights* (New York: St. Martin's Press, 1985).

McGrath, Edward G. (ed.). *Is American Democracy Exportable?* (Beverly Hills, CA: Glencoe Press, 1968).

Mower, A. Glenn. *Human Rights and American Foreign Policy* (New York: Greenwood Press, 1987).

Muravchik, Joshua. *The Uncertain Crusade: Jimmy Carter and the Dilemmas of Human Rights Policy* (Lanham, MD: Hamilton Press, 1986).

Newsom, David D. *The Diplomacy of Human Rights* (Lanham, MD: University Press of America, 1986).

Schultz, Lars. *Human Rights and United States Policy toward Latin America* (Princeton, NJ: Princeton University Press, 1981).

Wiarda, Howard J. *The Democratic Revolution in Latin America: Implications for U.S. Policy* (New York: Holmes and Meier, A Twentieth Century Fund Book, 1990).

_____ (ed.). *Human Rights and U.S. Human Rights Policy* (Washington, D.C.: American Enterprise Institute for Public Policy Research, 1982).

CHAPTER EIGHT

Third World Debt

*
*

The Third World—especially the Latin American part of it—has been accumulating a staggering international debt in the last decade and a half: $450 billion by last count, with $45 billion in new debt being accumulated every year. Figures like these boggle the mind—until we realize that the huge size of the debt is enough to break the Latin American governments, the private commercial banks who hold the debt, the international financial system, and even the U.S. Treasury!

The debt is so large that it cannot ever be paid back. It is unpaid and, worse, unpayable. We know that, the banks know that, the debtors know that, and the U.S. government knows that. But the fact cannot be admitted for fear the whole house of cards that is the world financial structure may come crashing down. Actually, our ability to absorb the shock of the unpaid debt and still keep the world afloat financially is considerably better now than it was in the early 1980s.

If the Third World debt is so large that it cannot be paid back, then it becomes no longer an economic issue but a political issue with enormous international implications. Once we are agreed that the debt cannot and will not be paid back, the only question is, how will this debt be managed? That, of course, is a matter for politicians, not financiers.

"Managing" the debt means different things to the different parties. To the private commercial banks it means keeping the loans on the books and not admitting they are uncollectible (the banks' stock would plummet if they admitted that), gradually reducing their exposure to these ruinous loans, rolling up profits in other areas to offset the losses on the Third World loans, and looking for ways to get the U.S. Treasury and the taxpayer to help bail them out. To the Latin American governments it means absorbing some painful austerity programs while also promising to pay the loans back—and meanwhile not doing much to implement either policy. To the U.S. government it means trying to make all the parties maintain the fiction that the debts will be paid back, trying to make new loans available, postponing the day of reckoning, and disguising from American taxpayers the fact that they will ultimately pick up a large share of the tab.

The strategy is to play for time, hope for the best, and try to keep the cauldron from boiling over. The hope is that if the economic recovery of the West continues, Latin America as well as the banks may be able to grow out of the crisis. No amount of U.S. foreign aid would ever be sufficient to make up this huge debt. However, if the U.S. and the world economy were to decline into a recession, then all bets would be off, and the collapse of the banks, the Latin American debtors, and the international financial system might still occur.

To ward off these disastrous possibilities the U.S. has been pressuring the banks to make new loans available to help the debtors pay at least part of the interest on their old loans, pressuring the Latin American countries to reform their economic houses, urging the World Bank and other international lenders to make generous new loans available, and stepping in during genuine emergencies on an ad hoc and case-by-case basis to replenish the impoverished debtors. This strategy was known as the "Baker Plan," named for former U.S. Treasury Secretary James Baker.

The whole arrangement is precarious, based on some large assumptions (continued global economic expansion), and hangs by very slender threads. Austerity has caused considerable suffering among the poor in Latin America, for example, and cannot be continued indefinitely. So while the Baker Plan was useful in the short run, experts on the issue concluded that something more would probably have to be done to solve the problem in the long run. The fact is that most Latin American governments are all but bankrupt. If their economies go down the drain, so probably will their currently democratic political systems, an eventuality that would be disastrous for U.S. foreign policy.

The problem is that doing "more" about Third World debt—which essentially means forgiving the debt—will inevitably mean higher taxes for most Americans. Congress doesn't have enough funds to finance needed U.S. domestic programs; it is therefore inconceivable that Congress will happily vote for a plan that will be presented as bailing out "corrupt and ineffi-cient" bankers and Latin American governments. Various forms of "debt relief" are being presented—such as the establishment of an international agency that would absorb many of these debts—that would disguise from the taxpayers that they will ultimately shoulder the burden.

More recently the U.S. has moved to try to get the banks to forgive some of the outstanding loans ("debt relief"), to offer lower interest rates to the Third World countries in return for U.S. guarantees on new loans, and to get the international lending agencies (such as the World Bank) to shoulder a greater share of the debt burden. In this way U.S. taxpayers are indirectly helping to bail out the Third World debtors, but without being fully informed that they are doing so.

This is one of the thorniest issues in U.S. foreign policy. Typical of the new agenda of issues, it has both major financial and foreign policy implications. It is also an issue that cuts across both foreign and domestic policy. No quick or final resolution of this issue yet seems in sight.

Our readings begin with a brief statement on debt and growth in Latin America by the Department of State. Next comes a balanced assessment of the Third World debt problem by the Foreign Policy Association. Robert Wesson of the Hoover Institution shows why the debt is as much a political as an economic crisis. The general editor of this book takes off from that point, showing the political dimensions of the crisis and also the political obstacles that stand in the way of resolving it.

Debt and Growth in Latin America and the Caribbean

BACKGROUND

Latin America has suffered from a profound recession in the 1980s. After vigorous expansion in the 1970s, when annual per capita growth rates averaged 3.6%, gross domestic product (GDP) on a per capita basis fell 7.6% between 1981 and 1986 (all figures are preliminary). These statistics, compiled by the UN Economic Commission for Latin America and the Caribbean, disguise wide variations from country to country. Oil-exporting countries have undergone a decline of more than 13% in per capita GDP during the period. In the case of Venezuela, the decline was even more (22%). Oil-importing countries did slightly better with a cumulative fall of 4.6% in per capita GDP. Some, however, experienced positive growth, such as Brazil with a 4% increase.

DEBT-RELATED PROBLEMS

Revitalization of growth in Latin America is complicated by severe, debt-related problems. By 1986, Latin America's external debt totaled $382 billion, more than half of the total indebtedness of all developing countries. Interest payments alone absorbed some 35% of export earnings.

While debt is a serious problem and debt service a heavy burden to the Latin American developing countries, other factors, principally inappropriate domestic economic policies, have imposed serious constraints on economic growth and development. Lack of confidence resulting from these policies dried up domestic savings and investment and led to huge capital flight in many countries. Total capital flight for Latin America since 1979 is estimated conservatively to have exceeded $100 billion. Adverse external economic developments aggravated the resulting deficits in the borrowing countries' balance of payments.

ECONOMIC STABILIZATION

Most countries in the region have now undertaken adjustment efforts with the support of the international financial institutions and creditor countries, including the US. Considerable progress has been made toward economic stabilization and renewed growth. As economic adjustment has proceeded, it has been accompanied by growing recognition in Latin America that private initiative and private savings and investment must be stimulated if there is to be hope for sustained growth. In the last 3 years, many Latin American governments have taken preliminary steps away from the excessive statism, market intervention, and import substitution strategies they have relied upon for decades.

Debt problems have forced governments to the realization that it is impossible to sustain double-digit fiscal deficits through excessive borrowing or monetary expansion. Most countries have moved to adopt more realistic exchange rates, expand exports, and cut inflation. Inflation for the region has come down from its peak of 275% in 1985 to 69% in 1986. Reforms, particularly in Argentina, Bolivia, and Brazil, have cut inflation rates enormously.

STRUCTURAL ADJUSTMENT

Of even greater importance for the longer term, several governments have begun to reduce entrenched structural barriers to growth. Specifically, they have taken steps to reduce price controls and subsidies; to liberalize trade; to attack over-regulation and excessive bureaucratic controls; and to improve the investment climate, including reducing restrictions on foreign private investment.

Several countries have recognized the heavy burden of inefficient and highly subsidized public enterprises that siphon off domestic savings and often increase external indebtedness. They have moved to transfer government-owned industries to private ownership and management. Mexico, for example, has made an important beginning in this area. In addition, Argentina, Chile, and Uruguay are seeking to turn more state enterprises over to the private sector.

Other countries have realized that external commerce is better regulated not by governments but by market mechanisms, and they have liberalized trade regimes. Haiti has converted import quotas to tariffs, the Dominican Republic has eliminated many import surcharges, and Ecuador has sharply reduced duties on a wide variety of manufactured imports. Mexico's recent steps to liberalize trade, which received both International Monetary Fund (IMF) and World Bank support, provided a sound basis for its accession to the General Agreement on Tariffs and Trade.

Source: From U.S. Department of State, Bureau of Public Affairs, *Gist,* February, 1987, pp. 1–2.

INTERNATIONAL EFFORTS TO ENCOURAGE GROWTH

International financial institutions and the US Government, particularly through its Program for Sustained Growth, have encouraged reforms. The IMF and World Bank are cooperating in assisting debtors to formulate growth-oriented adjustment programs within a consistent framework. The IMF has negotiated new standby programs or enhanced surveillance arrangements with 15 countries in Latin America since the advent of severe debt-related problems in mid-1982. The World Bank has assumed an increasingly important role in the stimulation of sustainable economic growth in the debtor countries through emphasis on policy-based, fast-disbursing, structural adjustment loans and sectoral loans. Since 1980, the World Bank has committed $2.7 billion in policy-based loans to Latin American and Caribbean countries.

The steps being taken in Latin America toward greater reliance on market forces are most encouraging and have begun to take effect. Growth fell precipitously in 1982 and 1983 when many countries experienced debt-servicing difficulties. Since 1984 however, the region has experienced modest growth. In 1986, growth reached an estimated 3.4%, which, on per capita basis, represents an increase of 1.2%. The US will continue to devote considerable attention to international debt problems and to support policies aimed at the realization of sustained growth and improved living standards for the people of Latin America and the Caribbean. ■

Latin American Debt   *Living on Borrowed Time?*

As the Latin American debt crisis approaches its seventh year, many commercial bankers and policymakers in the U.S. believe the worst is over. Since August 1982, when the crisis first erupted, the banks have steadily improved their position by restricting new lending to the region, setting aside a greater portion of their assets against the possibility that the loans will never be repaid and exchanging a part of the debt for investments in some countries. These actions by the commercial banks have generally had the backing of the U.S. government.

Increasingly though, analysts both in the U.S. and in Latin America speak of the 1980s as a "lost decade" for the region, which extends from Mexico to the southern tip of Chile. Over the past seven years, economic development there, with few exceptions, has come to a standstill. Social indicators—those statistics measuring trends in such areas as education, employment, health, housing, and nutrition—have fallen to alarmingly low levels.

In many countries, frustration over economic hardships is the primary threat to political stability. In Mexico's July 1988 presidential elections the long-ruling Institutional Revolutionary party (PRI) faced its biggest challenge in over 50 years, when voters turned out in record numbers in support of an opposition candidate who favored cancelling payments on all foreign debts. In the region's fledgling democracies, such as Brazil, Argentina and Peru, governments unable to solve the chronic financial crisis have increasingly come under attack by both left- and right-wing parties.

Some economic analysts fear that the struggle to meet international debt obligations is exhausting the region's human resources, and that not only a decade but an entire generation may be lost to the crisis. Dr. G. A. Cornia, a senior planning officer for the United Nations Children's Fund (UNICEF), points out that, "when children don't get enough to eat, it affects their concentration, their ability to learn. When they are sick most of the time, they don't go to school, and in many cases the schools simply aren't there to go to anymore." As a result, says Dr. Cornia, "The quality of labor in Latin America could suffer for decades to come."

Inefficiency and Growth

Just how much of Latin America's current economic crisis has been caused by the region's debt problems? Latin America has long suffered from weak political leadership and ill-conceived economic policies. State control of key industries, such as energy, mining, transportation and banking, has led to high levels of bureaucratic red tape, inefficiency, corruption and

Source: From *Great Decisions 1989,* Foreign Policy Association, New York, 1989.

price distortions, while political considerations have created unfair tax policies, overprotection for domestic industry and costly consumer subsidies.

Still, between 1950 and 1982, the region experienced phenomenal economic growth rates. According to Abraham F. Lowenthal, cochairman of the Inter-American Dialogue, from 1960 to 1980 Latin America's economic growth rate was nearly twice that of the U.S. The region's output of electric energy, metal, machinery and automobiles increased tenfold during those years. This rapid rate of industrialization was comparable with that experienced by the U.S. during its most intensive period of industrial transformation, from 1890 to 1914.

Today, Latin America's debt to the industrialized countries is a staggering $410 billion (the combined Third World debt is over $1.2 trillion). Interest payments alone cost the region between $25 billion and $30 billion a year. To save revenue and earn the U.S. dollars necessary to make these payments, the Latin Americans have had to cut drastically government support of development and social welfare programs, reduce nonessential imports and increase exports.

Merrill Collett, a U.S. journalist who covers South America from Venezuela and has written for *Newsweek* magazine, says wryly, "Wherever I go these days, things seem dirtier, dustier, and more destitute. The problem can be described in one little four-letter word, *debt!*"

Two Groups of Debtors

Third World debtors can be divided into two groups: the poorest nations, such as the sub-Saharan

African countries, and the so-called middle-income group, which includes most of Latin America and Asia. The poorest nations are characterized by extremely low rates of economic output per person, or per capita gross domestic product (GDP). For example, in the sub-Saharan region per capita GDP averages $220 (as compared with $10,000 to $20,000 a year for the world's seven leading economic powers). For the poorest nations such basic necessities as food and shelter remain major concerns.

By contrast, the middle-income group is seen as having great economic development potential. Argentina, Brazil and Mexico, for example, with average per capita GDPs of around $2,000, are wealthy in comparison with the sub-Saharan African states. On the whole, Latin America boasts an abundance of natural resources, including large reserves of oil, minerals, forests and agricultural lands. Also, the region's population of 400 million is relatively small, about half that of India but spread over a much greater area, causing less demand on the available resources. (Brazil alone is two and a half times the size of India but with only one sixth the population.)

Impact on the U.S.

For the U.S., the Latin American debt crisis has been costly. Exports of U.S. products to the region have dropped by nearly 30%, from a high of $42 billion in 1981 to around $30 billion today. By 1984, sales of steel and motor vehicles to Latin America had dropped by 50%, construction equipment by 80%, and farm machinery by 86%. U.S. farmers were particularly hard hit.

According to Richard E. Feinberg of the Overseas Development

Council (ODC), a Washington think tank, this drop in trade has cost the U.S. nearly 1 million jobs. Says Feinberg, "Every dollar shipped to money-center banks [by the Latin Americans] is one dollar less to spend on wheat grown in Iowa or trucks made in Michigan."

FROM PROSPERITY TO AUSTERITY

Between the mid-1940s and the early 1960s, very little money was lent by commercial banks to Latin America. Most of the funding for development came from the World Bank and the International Monetary Fund (IMF), and from the U.S. as foreign aid or as direct foreign investment. Between 1946 and 1955, international corporations doubled their investments in the region to over $6 billion.

By the 1960s, the major Latin American countries were showing impressive rates of economic growth. In 1963, Mexico issued its first overseas bond in 50 years. After that, commercial bank lending to Mexico picked up at the rate of about $1 billion a year. By the late 1960s, Brazil, Argentina and Peru had also become important borrowers.

Two major events in the early 1970s completely changed the nature of international finance, setting the stage for the crisis of the 1980s. First came the removal of the international gold-exchange standard. In 1944, to promote stability in the international monetary system, the price of gold was fixed at $35 per ounce, and all other countries set the value of their currencies in terms of the dollar. Because so many dollars were being put into circulation, the actual value of the dollar declined during the 1950s and 1960s, but the price of gold stayed the same. Foreign governments, anticipating a steep devaluation of the dollar, were putting pressure on the U.S. to exchange the dollars they were holding for gold. Since the U.S. did not have enough gold to back up the number of dollars in circulation, it was feared that a run on gold would break the dollar and wreck the international monetary system. In response to the growing financial crisis, President Richard M. Nixon voided the gold-exchange standard in 1971. Notes John H. Makin in *The Global Debt Crisis:* "The 1971 collapse of the [international monetary] system was precipitated by a U.S. President who had to untie the dollar from gold in order to print the IOUs needed to pay for Vietnam and the Great Society."

Once the gold-exchange standard had been removed, there was nothing to prevent the U.S. Treasury from pumping dollars into the global economy. As a result, the U.S. economy boomed in 1972 and 1973, growing at a rate of nearly 6% each year. But inflation was also booming; in 1973 it reached 8.8%, more than double that of the previous year; in 1974, it hit 12%. The high inflation rates drove up the price paid for Latin American exports, providing the region with more dollars and thus improving its creditworthiness. High inflation also made borrowing dollars attractive, since real interest rates, the interest charged by banks for their loans minus the inflation rate, fell to negative levels as inflation increased. (For example, if inflation was running at 10% and interest rates were only 9%, the *real* interest rate would be a negative 1%.)

Petrodollars

The second major event was the oil price shock of 1973–74. During that period the Organization of Petroleum Exporting Countries (OPEC), spurred by the high inflation rates and the price hikes for other commodities, suddenly quadrupled the price of its oil. This led to a giant increase in OPEC's trade surplus, which for 1974 alone was an incredible $68 billion.

The OPEC countries quickly deposited their new wealth in U.S. and European banks, which, finding themselves awash in "petrodollars," began recycling them in the form of loans to the Third World. Many Latin American finance ministers, rather than adjust to the higher oil prices by reducing economic growth in their countries, preferred to borrow. They suddenly enjoyed enormous popularity, as bankers literally stood in line to offer them new and bigger loans. By 1980, the region's three largest debtors, Argentina, Brazil and Mexico, had accumulated a combined debt of nearly $150 billion.

Mexico's Crash

Mexico was the first country to buckle under Latin America's burgeoning debt. In August 1982, during what is known in financial circles as "the Mexican weekend," Mexico notified the U.S. Treasury that it could no longer meet payments on its external loans. Falling prices for Mexican oil and rising interest rates had left the country

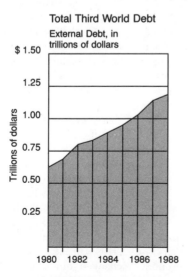

Total Third World Debt

External Debt, in trillions of dollars

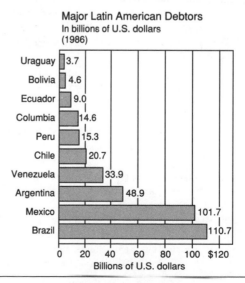

Major Latin American Debtors

In billions of U.S. dollars (1986)

Uraguay	3.7
Bolivia	4.6
Ecuador	9.0
Columbia	14.6
Peru	15.3
Chile	20.7
Venezuela	33.9
Argentina	48.9
Mexico	101.7
Brazil	110.7

Billions of U.S. dollars

with a severe shortage of foreign exchange.

Mexico's announcement shocked the world financial community. Failure to collect interest payments would have forced the country's 1,400 creditor banks to declare much of its $80 billion debt in default. Such a default would have cost the six largest banks in the U.S. $12 billion. Loans by Citicorp, Mexico's largest creditor, represented two thirds of the bank's net corporate assets ($3.3 billion).

The banks soon realized that Mexico's problem was not an isolated case. Within 16 months, 45 developing countries were experiencing debt-servicing difficulties. In Latin America, Brazil, Argentina and Venezuela soon followed Mexico's example by announcing their inability to meet their financial obligations.

Where Did All the Money Go?

During the 1960s and to a much greater extent in the 1970s, the Latin Americans borrowed heavily to finance ambitious development projects, rejuvenate aging and defunct industrial plants and create new businesses geared for the export market. Funds were channeled into major industries, such as steel, cement, mining and shipbuilding. Roads and hydroelectric dams were built, airports suddenly dotted the landscape, and agricultural production was greatly expanded.

Thanks largely to the surge in investments from abroad, the region's combined GDP tripled between 1960 and 1980, according to the Inter-American Development Bank. Nontraditional exports, such as automobiles, shoes, textiles and clothing, shot from less than $1 billion in 1965 to more than $15 billion in 1980. By 1982, Brazil

ranked 12th on the global economic scale and Mexico (this country's third most important trading partner), 14th.

Not all of the new funds were invested in Latin America's development. Bankers, businessmen, even government officials transferred assets into newly borrowed dollars so that they could send them back to the U.S. in the form of investments and savings. Such investments in the U.S. were considered more profitable than investing at home, chiefly because of the high inflation rates that have long troubled the region's unstable local economies. This "capital flight" ate up billions of dollars in foreign exchange. According to World Bank estimates, between 1976 and 1984, $54 billion (57% of its total external debt at the time) left Mexico in the form of capital flight, $28 billion (60% of its total debt) left Argentina, and $35 billion (more than its total debt) left Venezuela.

In recent years, close to 100% of all new lending has been used exclusively to service outstanding debts. What's more, interest payments have taken a huge portion of the region's total export earnings. In 1970, according to the World Bank, the debt-service ratio—the amount of export earnings required to meet interest and principal payments on foreign debts—was approximately 19% for the region as a whole. By 1986, the debt-service ratio had reached 30%, though for certain countries it was actually much higher. In 1986, Argentina had a debt-service ratio of 64%, Mexico of 51.5% and Brazil of 42%.

Austerity

In order to service international loans, debtor nations must boost their foreign exchange revenues.

This requires four basic steps: first, they must increase exports more rapidly than imports; second, they must decrease expenses by cutting government spending; third, they must protect their currencies by keeping inflation low; and finally, they must adopt policies to promote economic growth and attract capital and investments.

Since 1982, the IMF has played a pivotal role in helping banks and debtor countries reschedule loan payments and negotiate emergency lending packages. To qualify for new loans, debtor nations have had to submit to rigorous IMF austerity programs. These programs are designed to help debtors meet the conditions necessary to increase their revenues.

The IMF was created in 1944 at Bretton Woods, N.H., to promote balanced growth in world trade by bringing stability to the foreign exchange system. Today, it functions like an international credit union. Each of its 146 member countries is assigned a "quota" payment based on economic size and participation in world trade. The quota shares determine the number of votes a country has in the IMF (the U.S. as the largest contributor has the most votes). Members in financial trouble can borrow up to 125% of their quota contributions annually. To qualify for a loan in excess of its quota share, a country must agree to accept the IMF's austerity measures.

During the 1960s and 1970s, the IMF was largely inactive in the developing world. Commercial banks were willing to provide loans, and Third World leaders saw little reason to submit to the IMF's tough conditions. Once the debt crisis broke, however, things changed dramatically. It was the

IMF (which committed $1.3 billion of its own funds) that convinced the commercial banks to put up an additional $5 billion in "involuntary" loans for Mexico's first rescue package. By 1983, the IMF had conditional lending programs in place in 47 countries.

Bitter Medicine

Austerity is a hard pill to swallow. Though terms vary from country to country, the typical austerity program includes deep cuts in government spending, privatization and other measures.

Proponents of the IMF's programs claim that austerity measures are necessary for sustained economic growth in Latin America. They point out that during the recession of 1981–82, the debtor countries failed to adjust their economic policies fast enough to keep up with the changing international environment.

Hans H. Angermueller, vice-chairman of Citicorp, has noted that countries such as Mexico and Brazil created their own economic troubles by subsidizing inefficient industries, allowing inflation to get out of hand and valuing their currencies too high against the dollar. Says Angermueller, ". . . if [austerity programs] are consistently followed over time, such steps will bring countries back to the global capital market and put them back on the path to long-term, sustainable growth."

Critics of the IMF's programs charge that the burden of such measures—no matter how sound they are—falls disproportionately on the poor. In Mexico, for example, the first structural adjustment program brought a 40% hike in the price of corn tortillas and a 100% increase in the price of bread. Meanwhile, though inflation was raging at nearly 90%, wages were allowed to rise by only 25%, causing a sharp reduction in workers' real purchasing power.

Standard Components of an IMF Austerity Program

1. Abolition or liberalization of foreign exchange and import controls.
2. Domestic anti-inflationary programs, including:

• control of bank credit; higher interest rates and perhaps tighter reserve requirements;
• reduction of the government deficit: curbs on spending; increases in taxes and in prices charged by public enterprises; abolition of consumer subsidies.
• control of wage rises, so far as within the government's power;
• dismantling of price controls.

3. Greater hospitality to foreign investment.
4. Reduction of arrears on foreign debt.

To save revenue, Latin American governments have made deep cuts in domestic spending. Particularly hard hit have been health, education and food subsidy programs, such as food stamps and price controls. According to a UNICEF study, expenditures on health fell in 14 Latin American countries between 1980 and 1984, while during that same period, expenditures on education were cut in 10 countries. Argentina, for example, cut health spending by 14% and education by nearly 10%, and Bolivia cut health by 77% and education by 14%.

Because subsidized food prices do not provide incentives to farmers and add to budget deficits, the IMF has insisted they be cut in one third of the austerity programs it has imposed. Brazil, which has eliminated wheat subsidies and reduced rural credit, now spends 50% less on food programs than it did in 1980.

New Currencies

High inflation has been a stumbling block in all of the IMF's Latin American adjustment programs. Latin American finance ministers have traditionally balanced their budgets by simply printing more money. This tendency, coupled with currency devaluations and rising prices for food and basic services, has led to periods of hyperinflation in recent years. In response, governments have employed a range of anti-inflation devices, the most radical of which were the Austral Plan in Argentina and the Cruzado Plan in Brazil.

In June 1985, Argentina's president Raúl Alfonsín announced a plan designed to halt the country's nearly 2,000% a year runaway inflation. The plan centered on replacing the old currency, the peso, with a new currency, the austral (valued at 1,000 old pesos) and on strict wage and price controls. Though not ordered by the IMF, the Austral Plan was initially met with enthusiasm by the Argentines and by members of the world banking community. Barber Conable, president of the World Bank, called it an "excellent program." By the end of the year, inflation had dropped to 82%.

In 1986, with inflation approaching 500%, Brazil announced a plan similar to Argentina's and replaced its old currency, the cruzeiro, with the cruzado. Though both plans were initially successful in reducing inflation and bringing the economy under control, neither was sustained long enough to produce lasting effects. Political pressures soon induced the governments of Argentina and Brazil to lift their wage and price controls. By mid-1988, the inflation rate for both countries had shot back up to around 600% (Brazil's was expected to top 900% by the end of the year).

The IMF's high visibility makes it an easy target for resentment in Latin America. Though it cannot be held responsible for the poor policies and economic circumstances that brought the debtors to its doorstep, for many in the region the IMF has become a bogeyman and austerity, a dirty word. Just mention of an IMF accord can spark violent protests. In the Dominican Republic, for example, the so-called IMF riots of 1984 over increases in the price of basic necessities led to the deaths of nearly 200 people.

Who's to Blame?

Assessing blame for the debt crisis is not easy. In just four years, from 1978 to 1982, the total dollar amount of U.S. bank loans to the Third World grew from $110 billion to $450 billion. Looking back, it seems inconceivable that bankers and Third World policymakers allowed the debt situation to get out of hand in such a short period of time. In a 1985 article for the North American Council on Latin America's *Report on the Americas,* economist Cheryl Payer quotes the often heard explanation that "stupid bankers made stupid loans to stupid countries."

Critics have accused the bankers of participating in what economists call a Ponzi scheme, named

after an early twentieth-century entrepreneur. Charles Ponzi used new deposits to pay dividends to earlier investors. As long as the system expanded, it worked; but as soon as he ran out of new investors, the scheme fell apart.

According to Payer, lending to Latin America operated in much the same way. Bankers, anxious to avoid writing off bad loans, continued to lend long after it was prudent to do so. For their part, the Latin Americans found it more attractive to go on borrowing against the hope of future stability than to make hard economic choices in the present. Here again, as long as the banks were willing to lend, the system worked; but, when lending suddenly stopped in 1982, the system collapsed.

Debtor nations and bankers tend to blame outside forces for much of the crisis. Between mid-1979 and the end of 1980, OPEC nearly doubled the price of oil, sending the world economy into its deepest recession since the years immediately following World War II. Consequently, demand for manufactured products and commodities from Latin America was sharply reduced, and the region's much needed export earnings began to dry up.

Meanwhile, to curb the high inflation, the U.S. Federal Reserve restricted the flow of dollars in the late 1970s by charging higher interest on its loans to banks. As demand for their exports dropped, interest rates soared, putting the Latin Americans into the awkward position of having to pay more for their loans while earning less foreign exchange. Every 1% increase in U.S. rates, for example, added nearly $1 billion to the annual interest payments of Brazil and

Mexico, the region's major debtors. The dramatic increase in lending between 1979 and the end of 1981 kept the system intact. By 1982, it became apparent that the higher levels of lending were unsustainable.

DEBT FATIGUE

Since 1982, commercial bankers have been reluctant to extend credit to Latin America. New lending has mainly been tied to debt rescheduling, with a large portion of the funds coming from the IMF, the World Bank or other international institutions. As one Latin American business manager said in September 1982, "Six months ago there were so many bankers in here you couldn't walk across the room. Now they don't even answer my telephone calls."

Since very little new money is going into Latin America and quite a bit is going out in the form of debt-service payments, there has been a negative transfer of funds from the region since 1982. Between 1982 and 1988, net outflows totaled a whopping $150 billion, according to the United Nations Economic Commission for Latin America and the Caribbean. Many analysts believe that the high rate of capital outflow will continue through the 1990s, absorbing nearly one third of all export earnings. Notes the Debt Crisis Network, a citizens' coalition formed to address the international debt crisis, debt has become "a vacuum cleaner, siphoning resources out of the Third World."

While the debt continues to grow and standards of living to fall, a sense of fatigue and disillusionment has spread throughout Latin America. Dry statistics on balance of payments and social indicators do not express the pain felt by many in the region today. Said one Brazilian mayor, "When I visit the people in the shantytowns, they talk to me about the children who have died of dysentery for lack of clean water. All I can say is, 'Don't lose hope.' I don't have a solution."

So far, of all Latin America's leaders, General Augusto Pinochet of Chile has best managed to sustain the strict economic reforms necessary to assure meaningful economic recovery. Pinochet, who seized power in 1972, has followed a policy of privatizing state-owned industries, encouraging capitalism and promoting trade through lower tariffs and taxes. As a result, Chile has been able to service its more than $21 billion in foreign debts more or less on schedule.

For Latin America's other leaders, coping with the debt has been a fine balancing act between satisfying foreign creditors and maintaining political stability at home. Some leaders have independently taken drastic steps. In his inaugural address, Peru's President Alan García announced that Peru would hold debt-service payments to just 10% of export earnings, and that the IMF would no longer be allowed to interfere in domestic policies. The move met with great popular support, but produced no economic benefits. Disastrous government policies and growing political discontent have since discredited García's stance at home and abroad.

So far, Brazil's president José Sarney has taken the most dramatic step. In February 1987, he declared a moratorium on the interest payments on the country's foreign debts. Again, though the move met with popular approval, the costs in

terms of lost investments, credit flows and confidence within the business community were too high for Sarney to sustain. By February 1988, a new finance minister had been appointed—Brazil's fourth in three years—and the moratorium was called off.

Though they have met several times to discuss the debt, Latin American leaders have been unable to develop a unified strategy to deal with the crisis. After a 1984 meeting in Ecuador, leaders from the major debtor nations issued the Quito Declaration, a call to "harmonize the requirements of debt servicing with the development needs of each country." At a later meeting in Cartagena, Colombia, a group of 11 debtor nations issued statements calling for a reduction of interest rates, resumption of credit flows and greater market opportunities for their export goods. At subsequent meetings, these points have been reiterated time and again. The major debtors, however, continue to pursue bilateral arrangements with their creditor banks, making a joint effort by the Latin Americans unlikely.

The primary question concerning the debt situation now, as one prominent analyst points out, is not whether the Latin Americans are willing to pay, but where the money to pay will come from. Faced with growing discontent, governments are reordering their priorities to meet domestic needs. Even in Mexico, which has long been considered the region's model debtor because of its willingness to adhere closely to IMF measures, officials complain that the social, political and economic costs of debt servicing are insupportable. As Foreign Minister Ber-

nardo Sepúlveda Amor told *The New York Times* last August, "[Our] first priority is the development of the economy and the welfare of Mexican society." Adds Mexico's new president, Carlos Salinas de Gortari, "If we don't grow because of the weight of the debt, we don't pay."

What Has the U.S. Done?

U.S. policy on Latin American debt has mainly been directed by the Treasury Department. When the crisis broke in 1982, Treasury officials, working closely with the IMF, moved to head off what was perceived as a major if temporary threat to the international economic order. Because of the large sums of money involved, it was feared that if one of the big debtor nations, such as Mexico or Brazil, defaulted on its loans the banking system worldwide would suffer.

To ward off disaster a series of "bridge" loans were hastily put together as each country's interest payments came due. These loans were meant to ease tensions by bridging over what was then expected to be a temporary crisis period. This set the stage for the case-by-case approach to debt negotiations and restructuring that continues to dominate official U.S. policy. Proponents of this approach believe that it allows the debtor countries and their creditor banks to tailor debt-relief strategies to fit a variety of circumstances.

Though the Treasury Department was applauded for moving quickly in 1982 to prevent a major economic disaster, it has since been criticized for mistaking the crisis for a short-term liquidity problem—with Mexico temporarily out of cash—and for following what is generally characterized as a day-by-day "muddling through" approach to managing the debt situation. According to the ODC's Feinberg, the Administration failed to grasp the severity of the crisis, especially from Latin America's perspective.

In 1985, Treasury Secretary James A. Baker 3d unveiled his "Program for Sustained Growth" at the annual IMF/World Bank meeting in Seoul, South Korea. The Baker Plan, as the initiative came to be known, called on debtor countries to adopt domestic economic reforms. As an incentive he proposed $29 billion in new loans from commercial banks and international lending institutions.

The unveiling of the Baker Plan marked a change in emphasis in official U.S. policy, away from just strict austerity and toward a program of renewed economic growth in the Third World. The plan has never been fully implemented. With a few exceptions, the debtor countries have not been willing to make the economic reforms necessary to encourage bankers to participate with new loans.

In 1987, the Baker Plan was expanded to encompass a "menu of options," designed to allow commercial banks to deal with their Third World loans in unconventional ways. These options include a number of financial techniques that allow banks to convert loans to debtor nations into investments in goods, real estate, industry or longterm bonds guaranteed by the U.S. Treasury. One bank, for example, swapped $20 million of debt for part ownership in two hotel companies in Mexico. Other banks have exchanged debts for investments in fishing fleets and fruit farms. So far, participation in these options by banks and debtor nations has not been as great as was hoped for.

Alternative Plans

A number of other debt-relief plans have been suggested over the years. Since 1984, the Latin Americans have favored one containing three basic elements: first, outright forgiveness of a portion of their debt; second, rescheduling of the remaining debt at longer payback periods, with interest rates pegged to each country's economic performance; and, finally, the separation of old debt from new loans, with an increase in lending for development. The Latin Americans claim they cannot continue to remit 5% of their combined GDP in the form of debt-service payments. They point out that in relative terms, this is twice the level of German reparations payments after World War I.

In 1986, Senator Bill Bradley (D-N.J.) proposed a debt-relief plan that incorporates some of the original Baker Plan and most of what the Latin Americans want. Under the Bradley Plan, the debtor nations would receive a cut of 3% on interest rates on all outstanding debts for 3 years; banks would be required to write off 3% of all loan principals for 3 years; and $9 billion in new loans would be made available from multinational institutions. In return for these concessions, the Latin Americans would have to agree to pursue economic policies that promote growth and free trade, reduce capital flight and work to eliminate government corruption.

Altogether, Bradley's proposal would provide $57 billion in debt relief, nearly twice as much as the expanded Baker Plan, without involving new loans from commercial banks. Bradley, who has long expressed concern over the economic and political stability of Latin America, believes that any debt-relief plan "must be big enough to be seen by Latin America as a cure, not simply a Band-Aid."

Other debt-relief proposals have been introduced by Congressmen John LaFalce (D-N.Y.) and Don J. Pease (D-Ohio) and by James D. Robinson 3d, chairman of American Express Company. Those three plans call for the creation of an international agency under the auspices of the World Bank to coordinate debt-relief efforts worldwide. The agency would purchase debt from creditor banks at a discount (from 40% to 45% of the actual value) and pass the savings on to the debtor countries as a partial debt forgiveness. The remainder of the debt would be repaid to the agency at market interest rates over an extended period. Again, like the Baker Plan, all three plans would require debtor nations to undertake policies that would promote economic growth through free-market principles.

Lost Confidence

Critics of these plans claim they would do more harm than good by forcing the banks to take huge losses and thus damaging the debtor nations credit ratings even further. They point out that after the massive defaults of the 1930s, it took nearly three decades for commercial banks to regain confidence in Latin America. What is more, all of these plans, critics say, would cost the U.S. taxpayer money. The Robinson Plan, which former Treasury Secretary Baker dismissed as a "bank bailout," would require $12.5 billion in initial capital, $2.5 billion of which would come from the U.S. Though the LaFalce and Pease plans wouldn't require any direct funding from the U.S., and Treasury would lose tax revenues due to bank write-offs.

Supporters of the plans claim that since the commercial banks have virtually stopped lending to Latin America, creditworthiness is a moot point. Also, they argue, debt relief would pay for itself by enhancing trade possibilities and thus creating jobs in the U.S. Instead of making massive interest payments, the Latin Americans could stimulate local economies by investing at home.

Under the Reagan Administration, the U.S. opposed any form of nonvoluntary comprehensive debt relief. At the summit meeting in Toronto in June 1988 of the world's seven leading economic powers, the U.S. rejected a French proposal to forgive a part of the debts of the poorest African nations. Instead, the U.S. called for some reduction in interest rates and longer payback periods on the debts of these countries. Last October, in keeping with the case-by-case approach, the U.S. initiated another multibillion-dollar rescue package for Mexico, which included a $3.5 billion bridge loan that Washington made available to the Mexican government.

Having weathered the debt situation for almost seven years without a major financial disaster, many in the banking community believe that the crisis is now behind them. The Latin Americans, on the other hand, claim that without comprehensive debt relief, future economic growth and development in the region will be impossible.

The Reagan Administration largely supported the bankers' view, pressing for economic reforms within the debtor nations and pursuing a case-by-case strategy toward debt management. Should the U.S. continue to do so? Is the Baker Plan approach with its emphasis on encouraging economic growth through a system of incentives adequate to deal with the social and political tensions spreading throughout Latin America because of the debt? Or is it time to develop a new strategy? ∎

The Latin American Debt as a Political Problem

By Robert Wesson

If lenders and borrowers had been guided solely by economic calculations, even if their projections were erroneous, the problem would have never acquired anything like its present magnitude and ways out would seem fairly clear. But actions have been politically distorted on both sides. On one hand, lending has been misshaped by the perceived political interests of the American government; on the other, leaders of borrowing nations have been influenced by factors different from the long-term welfare of their nations. It is typical that corruption, or near-corruption, is a major reality in the whole affair, although seldom mentioned in economic analyses.

The relevant fact is that lending by private institutions to sovereign nations is a dubious proposition at best. It is an invitation to loss so far as governments are inefficient and less than totally honest. Banks would not loan large sums to corporations with a record of mismanagement and losses, without being able to control the application of the money or seize collateral in case of failure to pay. It is ironic that they have so happily done so in the case of entities called nations. It is somewhat more understandable that the political authority should welcome the openhandedness of financial institutions for its own short-term benefit.

SEVERITY OF PROBLEM

The severity of the problem is not adequately perceived because it is undramatic. It has crept up and has been little publicized except as affecting U.S. financial institutions. When millions starve in Africa, the world sits up in shock. But not much notice is taken if the standard of living of scores of millions in Latin America is less dramatically affected. Unemployment, inflation, and decline of real incomes are the rule in a large majority of

Robert Wesson is a Fellow at the Hoover Institution on War, Revolution, and Peace at Stanford University. This paper was part of a larger project on the debt.

Latin American countries. Domestic investment has been slashed, and foreign investment in many countries has virtually disappeared. The poor have suffered more than the rich, and many more children are undernourished and subject to disease and mortality. Health services suffer, and education deteriorates. The region has been set back in its development by 10–20 years, with no improvement in sight. The overwhelming cause of this calamity has been the tremendous foreign borrowing, the ostensible purpose of which was to bring tremendous economic development.

The problem is not only Latin American, of course, although about half the Third World debt, now reported to be well over $1 trillion, pertains to that region. African countries owe only about a third as much as Latin America, but Africa is so much poorer that, relatively speaking, the problem is about equally bad. A number of Asian countries, including Thailand, Malaysia, the Philippines, and Indonesia, have fallen into the same trap, with debt loads around half of their GNP. Several East European countries, especially Poland and Yugoslavia, are also heavily burdened.

Not only is the situation a human tragedy of enormous proportions; it is strongly negative for the selfish interests of the United States. It is one of the major causes of the stagnation of world trade and the difficulty of increasing American exports. It represents a grave setback for all efforts to promote the economic development of the countries commonly called "developing," which have seen rates of growth, generally good in the 1960s and 1970s, sharply re-

duced or turned negative. It threatens the worst difficulties the world financial system has seen since the depression of the 1930s. It also impedes the broad trend toward democratic institutions and may come to destabilize democracy in various countries that have emerged from authoritarian government, such as Brazil. The tragic gap between the advanced and the less developed world has widened. Many countries, great and small, that were full of hope a few years ago, are full of gloom.

THE DEBT TRAP

Many causes have been cited to explain why the Third World has incurred a debt far larger, in proportion to its economic product, than ever before. Most important was the surplus of petrodollars in the mid-1970s, with low, sometimes negative real interest rates that encouraged overlending or overborrowing. Bankers had forgotten the defaults of the 1930s, when all Latin American countries except Argentina failed to meet their commitments; and they assumed that in the brave new postwar world nothing such could happen again. They consequently went around practically begging politicians to accept hundred of millions of dollars in return for a few signatures. This massive transfer of "resources" to countries in need of capital was viewed as inherently good, and the banks were praised for their diligence and skill in arranging it—they had the satisfaction of being virtuous while engaging in very good business. In 1982 about half the profits of the biggest banks were from foreign operations.

But after 1979, real interest rates rose sharply with the decline of inflation, and commodity prices fell. Typically, a country would run large trade and fiscal deficits, borrow enthusiastically to meet them, permit private capital outflow, and keep exchange rates overvalued—sometimes ridiculously so—for reasons from elite profit to subsidizing imports of necessities. As the generally short-term loans began coming due, countries met difficulties in servicing them; but banks kept on lending without much concern, until the crunch marked by the Mexican debt crisis of August 1982.

Since then, voluntary lending has come to a halt (except for ordinary commercial financing), but banks have been driven to putting together new loan packages to stave off default and keep interest payments coming. International agencies, chiefly the IMF and the World Bank, have contributed to the extent of their ability. The lenders have done their best to maintain that there is really nothing abnormal, that the loans represent real value, and that with good management and favorable conditions all will be taken care of. It has been a great success, however, to have prevented thus far a collapse.

The difficulty of dealing with the problem is compounded by the fact that indebtedness is addictive, a sort of trap into which countries slide blissfully but out of which it is very difficult to climb. Lenders, government, international institutions, and borrowers all look to immediate benefits or solutions for the immediate and pressing problems. There is little concern about adding to outstanding principal of the debt, as long as it is possible to meet the exigencies of the day, to show a profit on the lenders' books, and to increase disposable funds in the hands of the debtors. If the debt is obviously unpayable, what does it matter if it is doubled?

Economic effects of the debt make more borrowing necessary. The indebted country usually suffers not only inflation but also capital flight (because of lack of confidence in the national currency), shortage of needed imports (because of pressure to conserve foreign exchange), bureaucratic controls (to manage foreign exchange), and lack of capital and high interest rates (as capital is drained out by both capital flight and debt service). All these decrease ability to make payments and cause further loss of confidence. This may induce political instability, or fears of it, further exacerbating the situation. Foreign investment, of course, shies away.

After the 1974 oil price shock, countries were relieved from having to make appropriate adjustments because of the ease of borrowing. Needs decreased in subsequent years of relative stability of oil prices, but the countries kept on borrowing in what had become a habit. Indebted countries always seem prepared to get deeper into debt, and the urge grows so far as conditions deteriorate. The borrowers are not nations but politicians, and it is always more agreeable to borrow than to tax—they may well be unable to tax effectively, but they can hope to borrow. Not only do the persons negotiating the loan receive immediate benefits; they probably transfer the troubles to others who will be in office when the loans come due.

The people receiving loans are always advantaged thereby. They reap a political gain, buying a little freedom to spend for popular purposes. There may be more concrete benefits, such as desirable commissions and administrative charges to be taken from the loan amounts. The political leadership can probably deal more freely with loan funds, not strictly tied by the lenders, than they can with monies more painfully squeezed out of national taxpayers. Money loaned to government departments or enterprises, which the central authorities probably encourage to seek foreign financing, may augment benefits for administrators. There are contracts for influential persons. Foreign exchange can be made available at rates much better than the street or black market rates, amounting to an indirect gift. And there is an unspecifiable and usually unpublicized amount of plain corruption, slicing off more or less of amounts loaned—perhaps a substantial percentage, as has become known in connection with loans to Mexico and the Philippines. The leadership does not bargain strictly for the interests of the nation, because they are not responsible owners but temporary custodians.

Distortions also appear on the side of the lenders. In the past, bank officers were rewarded for placing loans, with little consideration of soundness. A new foreign loan on the books, with upfront fees and prospects of higher interest than obtainable at home, looked good. The bank officers, like the borrowing politicians, may not be in charge when the loans become troubled. And when the loans become problematic, it is most urgent to keep the books looking good by maintaining the face value of the paper and pleasing stockholders, who are to be persuaded so far as possible that all is well. Lenders, like the borrowers, want to keep the system functioning and money flowing, even at a cost of increasing the outstanding amounts. They have also been encouraged to keep on lending, first by a conviction that in the crunch the government would have to come to their rescue, if only to save the financial system from disaster; and second, by direct pressures from the authorities.

The United States shows something of the same preference for a quick fix in its inability to balance the federal budget. Incidentally, this nation also in effect borrows heavily by running a big deficit in trade with an overvalued currency. This has helped very much to keep inflation down, while the corresponding influx of foreign capital has helped to finance the fiscal deficit without monetizing the debt. This is very agreeable, and it would or will be painful for this country, like Latin American countries, to see the flow halted or reversed. Yet it must be halted if the United States is to begin paying what is by far the world's largest negative balance, even if it is not strictly a debt in the manner of the obligations of Mexico, Brazil, and so forth.

Lending to the Third World has contributed to the flow of funds to the United States, as loans have come back in large measure in the form of capital flight. But as soon as repayment of the loans became the question of the day and debtors were under pressure to cut down imports, U.S. trade suffered severely; this, together with the failure of normal growth, is a large component of the U.S. trade deficit. It cannot be held coincidental that the change of status of the United States from a creditor to a debtor nation has coincided with the debt problem coming to the fore in 1982. Incidentally, the negative balance of the United States would be far greater if outstanding loans were valued realistically. It is the good fortune of the United States, however, that foreign capital has not been borrowed by the government but has been applied as productively as the owners could arrange.

POLITICAL LENDING

The crucial factor in the generation of the debt crisis was the new willingness of the banks in the 1970s to undertake lending on a large scale to Third World governments. Overflowing with petrodollars, the banks undertook, after 1974, what had not been customary in international finance: large-scale lending to governments for general purposes. Many countries, finding their finances in disarray, were happy to borrow to get over problems, especially deficits on the commercial balance. On the other hand, some countries (including Mexico, Venezuela, Ecuador, Nigeria, and Indonesia) borrowed because they had abundant funds. Seeing them as very creditworthy and blessed with everrising oil incomes, the banks were eager to lend to them. They could always use more money.

After 1980, adverse economic developments undid the rosy prospects, as interest rates rose, and so forth; but trouble was inevitable sooner or later, because unproductive loans are, broadly speaking, not repayable; and untied loans to Third World governments

are seldom productive. It is ordinarily taken for granted that transfer of capital to needy "developing" countries means economic development. In fact, the transfer of several hundred billion dollars between 1974 and 1981 contributed to the rather rapid growth of that period. But an unearned influx of money is not usually productive of much sound economic progress, as demonstrated by the OPEC countries that suddenly found themselves rich. The transfer of capital is only momentarily useful unless it is put to good use. There was no reason to expect that it would be, and very little attention was given to how it was used. And the end of the bonanza and the outflow of comparable amounts have led to the general depression and massive setback of the following years.

Lending is of different kinds. Strictly commercial trade financing is short-term and self-liquidating, and it generally goes on normally even when governments renege on their longterm obligations. Lending for projects, if well planned, should also be self-liquidating in a medium or longer term; and it has not usually caused major problems. The bulk of the lending, however, has been to governments and state enterprises to cover general needs, often simply to make up budget deficits. It is clear that the first type is necessary and ordinarily productive; the second is more subject to abuse but probably positive; the third is negative.

It is difficult to argue that lending to governments of the needy countries is the best way to apply scarce capital. Recipient governments of the Third World are almost always subject to some degree of corruption. At best, their priorities are bound to be more

political than economic, and they are likely to invest in white elephant projects. Their administrative competence and discipline are not high—if they were, the country would probably rapidly rise from the poverty level.

It is very difficult for the lenders to make sure that the funds supplied to a government are well applied,—if they try to do so. The only seriously indebted Third World country that has really made good use of its borrowings is South Korea, which has been better able than any other to meet its obligations (although even South Korean would have trouble if it were not for two large influx of funds from the U.S. military presence). A government is obviously much less likely to use funds productively than private enterprises, and the lenders are much better able to make sure that private borrowers apply the money productively. Borrowing rather encourages the postponement of needed measures of adjustment. Freeflowing money coming from abroad without strict accounting promotes careless attitudes and increases corruption.

Sovereign lending is also probably contrary to the long-term political interests of the United States. It seems to be a fine lubricant while money is going out, but it is an irritant when it comes time to sacrifice to make payments. Even though U.S. interests may hold only a minor fraction of the loans, this country is the largest and most visible target; and the saying that "Loan oft loses both itself and friend" holds on the international as well as the personal scene.

Moreover, providing large sums to the state inevitably strengthens its economic role, contrary to policies of fostering private or market economies. Political lending does nothing to build a strong world market economy. On the contrary, it is strongly in the interests of the United States that capital flows should be to the private sector.

THE GOVERNMENT'S RESPONSIBILITY

The political leadership has perceived a large interest in loans being made for several reasons. Countries are enabled to buy American goods. There is a diplomatic advantage, as countries are happy with their role in the world economy and in relation to the international financial community centered on the United States, to a lesser extent on its allies. Much of the money loaned out flows back as capital flight, helping to keep interest rates down and to finance the federal deficit. It is like a gigantic foreign aid program that does not need legislative approval and does not burden the American taxpayer, only adds to the assets on the books of the banking community—if these are doubtful, this is a matter for the future.

As a result of such considerations, when the banks were wishing to slow their lending as the problem began looking serious, various agencies of the government, Federal Reserve, Treasury, and State Department, urged and armtwisted them to keep on lending. Since the rescue of Mexico in 1982, the government has pressed "involuntary lending," partly coercing by use of regulatory powers—forcing banks, contrary to normal banking ethics, to

make loans they know are unsound. This means that lenders take new paper at 100% of face value when the valuation in the secondary market is much less—in the faint hope that by putting more out they may improve the chances of ultimately getting more back.

At the same time, the government has been very indulgent in classifying loans. Only those of the most hopeless cases (Bolivia, Liberia, Nicaragua, Peru, Poland, Sudan, and Zaire) have been declared "value impaired"; none has been declared in default. The general position of the administration, at least until late 1985, was that there was no real problem, that the country-by-country approach was working, and that the debtors could manage if they really wanted to. Even the allegedly revolutionary "Baker Plan" of October 1985 sought little concrete except the increase of lending. The recent suspension of payments by Brazil was received with a smile.

Having no authority to guarantee loans, the government has insisted that it has made no commitment. It has long been assumed, however, that the government could not allow the principal banks to become bankrupt (as they would if most Third World loans were held worthless) but would exert pressure on debtors, assist through international agencies, or otherwise come to their rescue. In any event, banks, having loaned freely with government encouragement or against their will because of government insistence, clearly have a reasonable expectation that they will in one way or another be protected when or if loans go sour.

THE IMF

The International Monetary Fund has also played a large political role, helping to postpone troubles while making them potentially worse.

The IMF was established in the aftermath of WWII for rather clear purposes of keeping better order in exchange rates, smoothing violent fluctuations and helping over critical situations. It tended to become a broader lending institution in the 1960s, but there was no intention that the IMF should be a continuing crutch for hard-pressed governments or act as guarantor of international loans. It is questionable whether the world's statemen would have created an international agency to help countries suffering general financial problems —for which, economic assistance might or might not be in order. In devoting its resources to postponing debt problems, the IMF has largely neglected what it was intended to dedicate itself to, the management of exchange rates. It has had no part in the excessive rise of the dollar up to February 1985 or its steep fall thereafter.

Since the beginning of the 1980s, however, the IMF has made possible the "packages" put together for the benefit of many countries, because new loans by the IMF made it possible for the banks in many cases to come out ahead by putting up money to pay themselves interest. Only this made the $12 billion dollar Mexican deal of August 1986 halfway palatable. Reliance on the assistance of the IMF has, of course, contributed to the carelessness of lenders.

The IMF has also played a part in justifying new lending by laying down conditions for loans, the fulfillment of which might, it was hoped, improve the ability of the debtor nation to pay. On this basis of prospective improved creditworthiness, the banks felt encouraged to extend new credit, or at least had an excuse to do so.

But the IMF conditions may have done more harm than good. Out of a hundred or so efforts, it would be hard to point to a single case in which they have come near fulfilling their purpose of so improving the economy of the debtor as to make loans payable as written. IMF programs do not open markets, improve export prices, or reduce corruption. Necessitous governments will agree, so far as national pride admits, to the imposed conditions (of reducing subsidies, reducing deficits and inflation, freeing interest rates, loosening or eliminating exchange controls, and so forth), and they may make gestures toward compliance. But they are not likely to change seriously the management of their economies to satisfy the representative of international financial interests, and when loans have been spent unproductively it is hard to imagine the new policies that are going to make them repayable. At best, good results of belt-tightening programs are likely to be years off, by which time the IMF conditions will have been forgotten.

Important economic reform can hardly be imposed by the kind of pressure the IMF can exert; to the contrary, salutary measures are discredited by being associated with the greedy lenders. Real change must come by change of habits and values of the people concerned. By insistence on austerity programs with a negative impact—perhaps a strong one—

on the standard of living of the masses, with less negative effects on the better-off, the IMF discredits the free market philosophy and strengthens leftist politics. It is sometimes claimed that the IMF does a service by permitting governments to lay the blame on it for needed unpleasant measures; but this is a shortsighted view. For the debtor country, to refuse IMF intervention is proof of manhood.

In part the inefficacy of the IMF is due to its being a one-sided agency. If it is to take a hand in the debt problem, it properly should be an intermediary, promoting the interests of the debtors with the creditors as well as vice versa, looking for equitable and practical solutions, not simply seeking to protect the interests of lenders. This partiality has injected bitterness into the whole affair, giving it more sharply the character of rich versus poor and complicating politics.

DEALING WITH THE CRISIS

Latin America remarkably paid out net some $30 billion yearly between 1982 and 1986, while the outstanding debt not only was not reduced but increased by over $100 billion dollars. But this is not sustainable. The vision of the so-called developing nations transferring large amounts year by year, up to half their export receipts, without cutting down their outstanding obligations, is not realistic. It seems unavoidable that they will increasingly insist on new money as the price for paying any large amount on old debts. Least of all can a genuinely democratic government propose to send to foreign financiers large resources needed by native children.

Thus far, the banks have defended their interests ably and

have kept up profits and dividends, thanks in part to the contributions of international agencies. Even restructuring has been turned to advantage, with hefty fees. Doubtless chiefly for this reason, there is great reluctance to change the *modus operandi*. However, it is becoming increasingly difficult to manage the situation. Repeated restructurings are called for, because almost nothing has been paid on principal by any country for many years, but they become tedious. Each postponement of debt makes necessary more postponements, and banks would like to reduce exposure. Debtors are docile as long as more money is forthcoming, but willingness to pay decreases as prospects for new loans weaken. The long inability of the banks to finalize the Mexican package of August 1986 is indicative of growing divergence between lenders and borrowers. The precipitous fall of Brazil from shining star to black hole is striking; and if Brazil can gain by halting payments, other countries can do the same.

Hopes that circumstances will come to the rescue, through a dramatic recovery of commodity prices, a great increase of developed country exports, or a sharp fall of interest rates, have worn thin. In the early 1980s, the general talk was that the debt problem would be solved by growth. The economies of the First World would expand rapidly and absorb more of the products of the Third World debtors, the expanding economies of which would grow out of the debt. This was the sense of the Baker Plan of October 1985: growth, promoted by new lending and "structural reforms" would solve the problem. This was a very faint hope, however. The industrial economies cannot expect to grow, on average, more than perhaps 3% yearly, and they seem more inclined to protectionism than to welcoming a flood of Third World imports. In order to reduce the load, the debtors had to grow more rapidly than the interest rate. This has not been attainable.

Up to late 1986, Brazil was cited as proof that it was possible to combine heavy net payments with good expansion; but after the collapse of the Cruzado Plan the opposite lesson could be drawn, that a large outflow is fatal for healthy growth. It is obviously time to give thought to seeking a settlement to salvage as much as possible. There can be no easy remedy, but some sensible steps could easily be taken to reduce the crisis and dangers.

The U.S. government, having contributed to the problem, might take steps toward solving it. Good sense dictates facilitating the exports of debtor countries. When countries push exports to earn dollars, it has the results of both depressing prices and evoking antidumping measures. Brazilians cannot be impressed with the rationality of the American government if it erects barriers to their shoes, alcohol, or steel while they are expected to pay about a billion dollars of interest monthly, much of it to U.S. entities. Costa Ricans, with a debt larger than the GNP, who were supposedly to benefit from the CBI (Caribbean Basin Initiative), must wonder that the United States imposes a high tariff on their cutflowers as soon as they succeed in doing what the United States preaches.

Thought should also be given to turning the very substantial part of the debt owed to the U.S. government—partly for military sales—into foreign aid. The United States could accept payment in national currency for many purposes useful for the country concerned, from endowment of education, social and economic infrastructure, and study in the United States to assisting the privatization of state enterprises. To subsidize the shrinkage of the public sector would greatly help to invigorate the ailing economies, restore confidence, and improve the political outlook.

The government could also by regulatory changes encourage the banks to chip away the debt through the secondary market for debt obligations. Debt is sold at discounted prices, mostly for redemption in national currency, probably for investment in the country under conditions agreed between the national authorities and the holder of the debt paper. This is a means, in effect, of sharing the loss: the bank accepts less than full value, the country pays something. This has the added advantage of putting capital to work usefully; one can be fairly sure that those who invest in this form will do their best to make sure that it is soundly applied.

The borrowing country may also simply buy its own debt at a discount. This practice is distasteful to the banks in principle, but it is probably salutary. It at least reduces the amount outstanding (except so far as interest keeps increasing it). If Peru has available $150 million, it could use this to reduce by a small fraction its arrears of interest, or it could (paying $.15 on the dollar) retire $1 billion of its debt. So far as the country goes into the market for its debt, it sustains the value at a more or less realistic level.

Any such measures are palliatives, however, and substantial losses—which have to borne primarily by the lenders—are unavoidable. Happily, banks' reserves and capital have been built up in the past five years, so writeoffs of a considerable part of the debt, although very painful, would not be so catastrophic. Spread over a number of years, they might even be reasonably bearable. It would probably be better to begin recognizing losses instead of trying, at considerable cost of new loans, to maintain the fiction of full value.

The creditors are naturally reluctant to make concessions on the grounds that whatever is given to one debtor probably has to be extended to others. But this is not a realistic argument, because the reasons for making concessions probably apply widely; the debtors are in more or less the same situation. It may be necessary to choose between making concessions or facing unilateral actions, and it would be better to yield something before bargaining power is reduced by inability to counter debtors' initiatives.

There are many specific ways, of course, in which the weight of the debt might be lessened. It would seem necessary to make concessions on interest rates. Uncollectable interest might be capitalized, if banks cannot bring themselves to acknowledge that it should be written off. More or less of interest might be accepted in national currency, to be invested in the debtor country. On the other hand, if countries make a serious effort to pay interest, it might be in order to credit them with some reduction of principal.

More broadly, it might be recognized that countries cannot be expected to pay over an extended time more than (say) 20% of export receipts, which was considered the limit of sound borrowing in the old days. Indeed, it is burdensome for a developing country to pay out anything like 10% of export receipts over an extended time. It would also be sensible, if the idea of improvement of ability to pay by structural reform is taken seriously, to offer concessions on the debt (instead of new loans) as incentives for reform.

Consideration should also be given to tieing loans or interest rates to terms of trade. Countries complain with justice that they are expected to pay back under less favorable commercial conditions than when they borrowed (although the opposite can also occur, it does not seem to be noticed).

The common argument against making any concessions is that it would inhibit banks making voluntary loans in the future. But this would generally be beneficial except for a few who stand to profit. It is ridiculous to argue opposite propositions: that sovereign lending is essential for the development of the Third World and that debtor countries can pay out large amounts without ruining their economies.

The aim must be not merely to handle the debt but to get rid of it. It may be advantageous to lending institutions to have countries permanently indebted, but it is as disadvantageous for countries as it is for individuals to carry a permanent load of debt. Only when they are unburdened can the Third World resume economic development. The end of sovereign lending should be negotiated in ways not hindering but preferably assisting sounder types of financing, foreign investment, commercial support, or project loans with built-in means of repayment. Debtor countries generally strongly desire to stay on the right side and in the good graces of international finance, and they will make sacrifices to do so.

But resistance to sacrifice of immediate interests is very strong, and the acceptable approaches can help only marginally. The secondary market can assist, especially in enabling regional banks to unload; but it is impossible to apply within the debtor countries any large fraction of the debt. For one thing, they lack the financial resources to furnish appropriate amounts of their own currency without excessively contributing to inflation. For another, the amounts are too great. Typically, the foreign debt is ten times as much as the total amount of foreign investment accumulated over the years.

The whole debt problem may, however, be reduced in quite unplanned ways. Just as the appreciation of the dollar worsened the situation, the decline in its value in terms of other major currencies since early 1985 correspondingly helps. Although most debtor nations tie their currency more or less to the prevalent international medium, the dollar, if they get more dollars for the marks or yen or other currency they earn by selling to Germany or Japan or elsewhere, the weight of the debt becomes proportionally less.

It also seems probable that inflation will come to the rescue. The floating interest rates of the bulk of the debt prevent the debtors from getting full benefit of inflationary conditions, but any substantial inflation, raising commodity prices, will lighten the burden. If there is really high inflation in the United States, the whole question could be largely set aside.

It is, in any case, imperative that international finance be normalized by somehow helping the less developed countries to get out from under their present load of debt. Initiative for this can come only from the United States, which has the strongest interest, both economic and political. Until economic normalcy can be restored, U.S. exports suffer where this country should have a marked natural advantage, and it is difficult for investment to prosper. On the other hand, if the debt problem can be set aside, one could expect a surge of growth in the presently afflicted countries to compensate for the many lost years.

There is also a strong political interest. If the depression continues, extremism is sure to grow; and the United States, as the conspicuous target, gets more than its share of the blame. Democratic institutions are strained, and they are likely to become increasingly shaky. Conservative and moderate elements generally favor honoring the debt and cooperating with the world financial community; and there has thus far been much less anticapitalist outcry than might be expected. But the private sector in many countries has been decimated. If a nation feels deeply frustrated, and paying seems to be a losing game, leftist forces will be energized, and the United States could face instabilities much more menacing than problems of Central America.

RESHAPING THE SYSTEM

One would suppose that, the great spree of sovereign lending having turned out so badly, there would be a great cry to change the system; but there is silence on the subject. Possibly the experience of recent years will suffice to discourage banks from getting into the trap. They are not easily discouraged, however. In the summer of 1986, when Brazil gave superficial appearances of having overcome inflation, banks were talking of prospects of resuming lending on a commercial basis, as though the Brazilian debt of $108 billion were not enough. One may assume that they would have done so if the situation had improved, and that the Brazilians would have accepted more loans. At the same time, undeterred by sad prospects in Latin America and Africa, the banks have seemed resolved to get Asian countries—previously less deeply indebted—into the same condition. It seems that the bankers still have visions of a return to the idyllic times of the 1970s, when freehanded lending and grand (paper) profits were the order of the day.

Difficulties having come from political loans, the obvious remedy is to restrict private financial institutions lending to foreign governments. It may be advisable to place prior limits on the amount of lending to any given borrower. Or if banks are to be free to lend to governments, despite the likelihood of abuses, such loans could be placed on a sounder basis by

being "securitized" and subjected to market controls from the outset. The market would give early warning of troubles with loans and impose rationality. This would be a return to earlier practices, when banks floated bond issues and investors took their chances, weighing risks against returns. A reason for banks to prefer holding loans has been the feeling that there was more or less government guarantee behind them.

It is questionable, however, whether banks should lend to governments at all. Prior to 1974, bankers rightly doubted that they had any business making unsecured loans to governments, and experience with them since then has obviously been disastrous. It seems certain that more or less political distortion will result from channelling funds through official channels, quite aside from the abuses that have been frequent. It is not clear when, if ever, it is really desirable for private institutions to make general loans to governments. If emergency help is needed, the IMF could provide this at much less cost than it currently bears in trying to sustain private lending.

In a few cases, as that of South Korea, the capital transfer has worked out well and has contrib-

uted to sound development. But even in such a case it is not clear that it might not have been preferable to loan to Korean enterprises directly instead of through the state.

If the U.S. government wishes for some reason to promote sovereign lending, it must be assumed that the operation is politically directed. The administration then should explicitly license the transaction, more or less like sales of armaments. The government would assume a degree of responsibility, presumably guaranteeing the loan.

Without any prohibition, the government could fairly well end sovereign lending simply by expressing disapproval, treating sovereign loans as doubtful for regulatory purposes, and making it quite clear that there would be no official support if they became troubled. The more forthright and safer approach, however, would be simply to prohibit banks from lending to foreign governments.

One very simple thing is needed: to remove the politics from both sides of international lending. This cannot easily be done. But it is essential, and if it can be achieved, lending guided by economic considerations should be healthy and productive for both lenders and borrowers. ∎

The United States, Latin America, and the International Debt: Toward a Resolution?

By Howard J. Wiarda

Latin America has been going through its worst economic depression since the 1930s. Now compounded by the international debt situation, the economic downturn

the region has experienced since the early 1980s has major implications for the U.S. and for U.S. foreign policy. It has not only resulted in a plummeting of GNP in many

countries and a lowered standard of living for many persons, but it also threatens to reverse the trend toward moderate, stable, democratic government that has been so

Source: From James Finn (ed.) *Private Virtue and Public Policy in Catholic Social Teaching,* Transaction Press, New Brunswick, NJ., 1989.

heartening in Latin America in the past several years. These issues of economics, politics, and their international and domestic interrelations are fraught with major consequences for Latin America, for the U.S., and for international financial and political affairs.

The international debt has become a very "hot" issue, and many groups are rushing pell-mell to offer advice and solutions. Such counsel is of course part of the democratic process of give-and-take, and to the extent that it is positive and constructive it is to be welcomed. The danger at present, however, is that such advice, by its selectivity and one-sidedness, may exacerbate the crisis rather than help the several parties involved arrive at a resolution.

The fact is that currently Latin America, the commercial banks, and the U.S. government are on a course that, albeit strewn with boulders and often proceeding by fits and starts, offers promise of resolving the debt crisis or at least reducing it to manageable proportions. That is a major step forward. Yet by their sometimes biased or politically motivated interventions in this very sensitive and controversial issue, such bodies as the U.S. Congress, which has also entered the fray and is casting about for an overall general solution, may in fact make matters worse just when the debt crisis shows promise of being resolved or at least becoming less dangerous.

THE DEBT ISSUE: BACKGROUND AND CAUSES

The debt that Latin America owes to foreign creditors has the potential to be disastrous for everyone: for the banks that hold the debt: for the Latin American governments that must repay it: for the international financial system, which is threatened with collapse if the debt is not paid: and for the U.S. government, which may have to face the possibility of bailing out all the other actors.

The sheer size of the debt is staggering: about $450 billion, with another $45 billion more per year being added in new interest. Brazil owes $120 billion, Mexico $100 billion, Argentina $60 billion, and Venezuela $40 billion. On a per capita basis, Costa Rica's debt burden is the region's heaviest.

The causes of the debt are various, and there is plenty of responsibility to go around. The private commercial banks in the 1970s were flush with petrodollars, eager to lend, and not too particular about the credit-worthiness of their customers. The Latin American governments were similarly eager to borrow, for military hardware, advanced social programs, war (the Argentine case), costly consumer goods, subsidies, and bloated bureaucracies—and even to feed outright corruption. The U.S. government encouraged these transactions as a way of substituting for public foreign assistance, then being diminished, and as a means of serving the foreign policy goals of stability and economic development in Latin America.

The global depression that began in 1979–80 and deepened in the following years was the precipitating factor that turned the debt "situation" into a debt "crisis." The bottom fell out of the demand for Latin America's products, production dried up, and interest rates on new loans to pay off the earlier debts soared.

Before proceeding further, it is necessary to clear up a number of myths about the debt. The first is that the debt will ever be paid back in full. It is so large that it is inconceivable that Latin America could ever pay it back. In this sense the major agenda item in the so-called North-South dialogue—the massive transfer of resources from North to South—has to a large extent already occurred.

Second, even though everyone knows the debt cannot be paid back, Latin America cannot be permitted to default. That would stigmatize the region as "uncivilized," make it ineligible for new loans, result in the seizure of many of Latin America's assets, and subject the area to a broad range of penalties. The costs of default to Latin America would be severe.

Third, even though the banks know these loans are uncollectible, they cannot write them off as such. If they did, not only would the management of the banks come under severe criticism from their stockholders, but those banks with an especially high Latin American debt exposure might have to fold.

Fourth, the U.S. government must help maintain the mythology that the debts are payable. The reason is that the alternatives are unthinkable, for the U.S. would then have to bail out the banks, the Latin American governments, and the international financial system. The U.S. taxpayer would undoubtedly have to shoulder the burden of such bail-outs, a particularly unhappy project in this era of economic belt-tightening at home and when many of our own social assistance programs are thought to be underfunded. That is not a series of prospects that politicians or policy makers in the U.S. wish to face. Hence the need, in dealing with the debt, for charades, smoke-screens, fig leaves, and dissembling.

"MANAGING" THE CRISIS

If the debt cannot be paid and default cannot be admitted, then the only possible solution is to "manage" the crisis. The question then becomes what "managing the crisis" means.

To the banks, "managing" the debt means keeping the Latin American loans on the books as potentially collectible even though only a trickle of interest may be coming in, and no principal at all. It means continuously rolling over the debt, foregoing fees, lowering interest rates, and making new loans available—anything but admitting that the loans are no good.

To the Latin American governments, "managing" the debt means some limited belt tightening, some compliance with International Monetary Fund-imposed austerity, and constant renegotiations over "repayment." In this way Latin America remains "credit-worthy" but without ever paying more than a small amount of interest and never any principal.

For the U.S., "managing" the debt means that no one has to face the unpalatable task of dealing with the issue squarely or bailing out either banks or Latin American governments with taxpayers' money. Moreover, in that way the U.S. can continue to maintain the further fiction that the debt is a purely financial matter between debtors and creditors, and not a "political" issue. If the U.S. were to admit that the debt is a political problem, then it would also have to admit that the debt is negotiable and essentially uncollectible, thus letting completely off the hook some Latin American regimes that are badly in need of structural reforms to encourage greater probity and efficiency.

Hence all the parties to the debt crisis have a strong interest in maintaining the idea that it is "manageable." To do otherwise would be to admit the debt is unpayable, that the loans cannot be collected, that the banks and Latin American governments are unsound and unstable, and that the international financial system is insecure. Since none of these things can be admitted, the formula of "managing" the debt must be kept alive.

The strategy on the part of all the participants in the debt crisis is to play for time, keep postponing the day of reckoning, and hope for the best. That is not a "great and glorious" solution to the debt crisis, but it may not be an inappropriate one, and it is probably better than most others that have been proposed.

The hope is that the world economic recovery that began in the U.S. in 1983 and that has by now spread to many regions of Latin America will enable these countries to *grow* out of the crisis. Since aid and assistance are always meager, economic growth is the only long-term solution. Meanwhile, Latin America under the impact of the crisis has begun to expand and diversify its exports, make some structural changes, and reform its finances and bureaucracy—all necessary changes on which all observers can agree.

At the same time, the private banks are rapidly converting their outstanding Latin American debt holdings to paper, selling them off at discount rates, and thus getting out from under the heavy burden of vast, uncollectible loans—while at the same time rolling up immense profits in other areas to make up for the losses they will one day have to absorb on their uncollectible Latin American loans. Many bankers say (though not some of the big New York banks whose loan exposure in Latin America is dangerously large) that if they are given five years, they will be out from under their Latin American loan burden. In short, the strategy is to wait the crisis out, meanwhile doing a series of small things that will attenuate the crisis and make it all but disappear.

If this is the strategy, how then is the debt actually *managed?* The key components have by now become familiar. They include ignoring the de facto defaults of such comparatively small debtors as Bolivia, Ecuador, and Peru; postponing the due dates of payments; and renegotiating constantly over new "packages" of loan assistance and their repayment schedules. At the same time, austerity has to be carried out by the debtor nations. Meanwhile, the U.S. government puts pressure on the private banks and the international lending agencies such as the World Bank to make more loans available, and on the Latin American governments to carry out more reforms.

One should not underestimate the impact that austerity has had, especially on the poor, in such countries as Brazil or the Dominican Republic. There have been food riots, protests, and violent demonstrations. On the other hand, the effects have not been so bad as are sometimes portrayed, and a number of the Latin American governments have become quite adept at managing austerity just as they have managed the debt itself.

The IMF, for example, has not been as draconian in the implementation of its austerity measures as its popular image would lead one to believe. It has learned how far it can go and when to back off lest the government that it is pressuring actually fall. The governments of Brazil and Mexico, for example, have been clever in imposing initial austerity, then relaxing the rules when protests mounted or an election was forthcoming, and reimposing austerity once the electoral returns were in. Under the gun of an IMF mission, Mexico fired 50,000 public employees but then rehired 30,000 of them the next week—and by the end of the year had found ways to put the rest, and new persons besides, back on the public payroll.

A similar process may be observed with regard to the issue of privatization. Some state-owned firms that form part of the bloated public sector in Latin America have actually been sold back into private hands. In most cases, however, "privatization" has meant the "sale" of a state-owned enterprise from one public-sector corporation to another, or its consolidation into a larger state-owned company, or its "sale" to a labor or business group that is itself part of the state system.

In Argentina, not only did President Raul Alfonsin manage these conflicting pressures very cleverly, but he has also discovered that austerity can even be popular with voters, who are looking for greater honesty and efficiency from the government.

The result of these measures is that not a single Latin America government has taken the advice of Fidel Castro to repudiate its debts. Not even Cuba has done so, nor has a single Latin American government yet fallen as a result of IMF-imposed austerity. Austerity's bark has so far been worse than its bite.

Furthermore, the Latin American countries have been able to manipulate the debt crisis for their own purposes. Brazilians like to say, only partially in jest, that while a little debt is a bad thing, a big debt is good. Brazil's debt is so large that it holds virtually make-or-break power over the major U.S. banks and over the international financial system. Mexico has as its ace-in-the-hole a 2,000-mile border with the U.S. and the knowledge that it is the last country in the world the U.S. would want to see destabilized. Most of the other Latin American countries also know that in the last analysis the U.S. would not allow them to "go down the tubes," that our own security interests would require us to step in with a rescue package before we would allow Latin America to become unstable and thus susceptible to upheaval from which only the Soviet Union would benefit.

Seen in these lights, the debt crisis is not at all the one-way affair that it is often pictured. Latin America is clearly not without finely honed skills and considerable bargaining power in dealing with the issue. Nor is this simply a case of the "Colossus of the North" and its banks keeping Latin America "in chains" for their own private or strategic purposes. Though there are of course elements of dependency, asymmetry, and injustice involved in this issue, explanations

that flow from such perspectives are by themselves surely too simple and one-sided. They do not at all take account of the nuance, cynicism, sophistication, and capacity for maneuver that *all* parties to the issue have demonstrated.

TOWARD RESOLUTION?

Though not without its cynical as well as comic-opera aspects, the debt crisis is a very serious issue. It is being played out at several different levels, however, only a few of which have to do with the "great issues" of moral injustice, North-South imbalances, and ideological purity. Rather, the issue is pre-eminently a political issue, to be worked out by political means—all the while not admitting, at least from the U.S. viewpoint, that it is a political issue at all.

To begin with, one must distinguish between the near- and longer-term aspects of the debt crisis. In the near term, the Latin American governments and the U.S. have managed not altogether badly. Default and/or bankruptcy have been avoided, no governments have toppled, and the crisis has not produced total collapse. At the same time, the banks, the U.S. government, and the Latin American governments have all learned some lessons, the debt has been "managed," and even austerity has proven survivable.

All the steps that have been taken, though—while useful in the short run—probably cannot be sustained over the longer term. For example, it is estimated that it will take Mexico at least until the year 2000 to recover from its present economic troubles. It is inconceivable that Mexico, or any other country in the region, can maintain austerity—even on the on-again, off-again basis here described—for that long a period without something fundamental giving way. Waiting in the wings in all these major countries are a whole new crop of demagogic politicians who are likely to be far more radical on the debt issue than the incumbents have been.

Nor can the facades and smokescreens be kept in place forever. Eventually someone will surely say, "But the emperor has no clothes on," and all the myths about the debt issue will be exploded. The issue is politically volatile as well as economically precarious, and it hangs by slender threads. If the world economic recovery proves short-lived, if the banks' stockholders demand an honest accounting, if the American taxpayer senses that he or she will be left holding the bag, if several Latin American governments simultaneously refuse to pay, if these or any number of other possibilities should come to pass, then the entire edifice of "managing" the debt in the manner used so far could come tumbling down.

That is why many experts agree that while the strategy employed for dealing with the debt crisis has been more or less successful to this point, a more general or comprehensive solution will have to be found for the longer term. No one knows what the precise formula will be, but of the need for some new and innovative strategies all parties are agreed.

There are three ways to meet the debt crisis: (1) Treat it purely as a private matter, between creditors and debtors, and follow an essentially hands-off or *laissez faire* policy. (2) Deal with it on an ad hoc basis, responding to crises as they arise. (3) Adopt a general or comprehensive approach. This last solution has been advocated most often by persons who also believe in central planning, a managed economy, and the capacity of experts and technocrats to solve such problems as the debt crisis once and for all.

The administration of President Reagan was accused of following a *laissez faire* approach toward the Latin American debt, but that is surely too simple a reading. The Administration, for understandable political and economic reasons, much preferred to have this matter remain in the hands of the private banks and the Latin American governments, rather than get involved itself. It did not hesitate, however, to step in with a major U.S.–government-assisted relief package for Mexico in 1982 and 1987, when the *laissez faire* approach proved inadequate and the threat of disaster loomed.

In this way the Administration combined elements of solutions (1) and (2); that is, hands-off but with strong involvement in times of genuine emergency. Moreover, it had very good reasons for not opting for a comprehensive solution, fearing that the issues are so complex and the debtor country problems so infinitely varied that a general plan could well make things worse rather than better. In addition, such a "total" or overarching solution would immediately absolve the Latin American governments from ever having to make any structural reforms at all. It would also probably leave the banks—and ultimately the U.S. government and its taxpayers—holding the bag. In the meantime, the debt crisis is on its way to being resolved: economic growth in Latin America in 1986 was quite good for all except four of the countries, structural reform is going forward, and the banks have begun to get out from under the crisis.

The Reagan Administration also respected the majesty of facts, however, and began to inch forward toward a more comprehensive solution. That is what the so-called Baker plan was all about. Without ever saying that he was advancing a general formula, without admitting he was moving ever so slowly toward a political solution, and still proceeding in a piecemeal fashion, former Treasury Secretary James Baker nevertheless *did* take a series of political steps to resolve the issue. In his pressure on the commercial banks, the World Bank, and the IMF to make additional funding available—as well as in his assurances of official U.S. concern—he did move toward a more general solution. The Brady Plan announced in 1989 augments the Baker Plan by moving toward a policy of partial debt forgiveness.

CONCLUSION

There is in short a great deal to be said for continuing with the present policy. That policy may be interpreted as combining elements (1) and (2) above with just a hint of element (3). The strategy is based on patience and prudence. It recognizes that the only solution in the long run is for Latin America to *grow* out of its economic doldrums. It shows restraint about urging more comprehensive steps that may not work and in avoiding outright capitulation. It requires that all parties to the dispute be prepared over the long run to absorb some losses. The banks will have to absorb loss either by selling off their Latin American debt holdings at discount prices or, eventually, by writing off some Latin American loans altogether. The Latin American governments will have to absorb some pain, through austerity and the need for reform. And it is likely the U.S. will similarly absorb some of the agony of the Latin American debt, either through inflation or by increased taxes. None of this will come without controversy and acrimony from all the parties.

It is very likely that this is how the debt crisis will finally be "solved." The U.S. will generally maintain a hands-off attitude at the level of public discourse, while showing a willingness to step into genuine emergency situations and at the same time nudging all the parties toward a longer-term and more general solution. Most of the banks will reduce their Latin American debt exposure over time to the point where it no longer threatens their existences. And Latin America will continue to change, to modernize, and to grow, even if this occurs on a stop-and-go basis and through a variety of crazy-quilt solutions. The debt crisis will not disappear through these means but, rather like the guerrilla threat in El Salvador, it may atrophy, become less severe, and go into what economist Albert Hischman, in another context, has called a "quasi-vanishing act."

If these scenarios prove essentially correct, Latin America will not only move slowly toward a resolution of its debt crisis but the cause of Latin American democracy will be strengthened as well. Historically, when the Latin American economies have gone under, their political systems have usually been swamped as well. But the present economic trends in the area, toward recovery and renewed growth, offer hope that Latin America's new and struggling democracies may be able to survive as well.

The area will still face immense economic problems that are a function of its underdevelopment. There is evidence, however, that gradually, incrementally, and by fits and starts, Latin America is moving toward both accelerated economic growth and a genuinely civic and democratic political culture. Moreover, a very powerful argument can be made that it is precisely such ad-hocism, gradualism, and incrementalism that are at the heart of the democratic process. Certainly, such a careful strategy, which proceeds slowly to "feel its way," is to be preferred to some more total and comprehensive package that produces in Latin America either disaster and chaos on the one hand or a full-fledged command economy à la Cuba or Nicaragua on the other.

It is always a delicate balancing act in Latin America between change, collapse, and survival. In the long run as well as in the shorter term, however, by following the prudent, moderate, and pragmatic course here described, Latin America might just make it, both economically and politically. ■

Suggested Additional Readings

Cline, William R. *International Debt* (Cambridge, MA: MIT Press, 1984).

Feinberg, Richard E., and Ricardo French Davis. *Development and External Debt in Latin America* (Notre Dame, IN: University of Notre Dame Press, 1988).

Holley, H. A. *Developing Country Debt: The Role of the Commercial Banks* (London: Routledge and Kegan Paul, 1987).

Kuczynski, Pedro-Pablo. *Latin American Debt* (Baltimore, MD: Johns Hopkins University Press, 1988).

Makin, John H. *The Global Debt Crisis* (New York: Basic Books, 1984).

Stallings, Barbara, and Robert Kaufman (eds.). *Debt and Democracy in Latin America* (Boulder, CO: Westview Press, 1989).

Watkins, Alfred J. *Till Debt Do Us Part* (Lanham, MD: University Press of America, 1986).

Wesson, Robert (ed.). *Coping with the Latin American Debt* (New York: Praeger, 1988).

Wiarda, Howard J. *Latin America at the Crossroads: Debt, Development and the Future* (Boulder, CO: Westview Press, 1987).

CHAPTER NINE

Disarmament

*
*

The disarmament debate has waxed in intensity in the United States and elsewhere, but often it has shed more heat than light on the subject.

The debate has been so emotional because we all recognize that nuclear weapons have the capacity to kill us all and to wreak irrevocable and fatal damage on the earth. On the other hand, the chances of that happening are actually quite small. No one has exploded a nuclear device in anger since 1945; and many scholars are convinced that the nuclear era really ended—in terms of the actual use of these weapons—in the year that they were first used.

We must begin with the realistic assumption that we will never rid the world entirely either of weapons or of nuclear devices. The nuclear genie is out of the bottle, and it cannot be put back in. In addition, too many interests and countries have enough stake in nuclear weapons for those weapons to be eliminated entirely. The question, realistically, is not the total elimination of armaments or nuclear weapons (which is impossible to achieve) but rather whether they can be reduced somewhat, managed effectively, and kept under quite stringent controls. Since nuclear and other weapons of mass destruction (including biological and chemical agents) cannot be entirely eliminated, we will simply have to learn to live with some of our fears and anxieties about them, neither allowing such fears to paralyze us and force us to take refuge in some isolated mountains, *nor* reducing our efforts to shrink the stocks of such weapons and bring them under effective control.

The debate was especially intense in the 1980s. In part, this was due to frightening movies about the issue, in part to dramatizations of such unlikely catastrophes as a "nuclear winter," and in part to simple alarm on the part of many intellectual leaders that Ronald Reagan's finger was on the nuclear trigger. Many in the journalistic, religious, and academic communities simply did not trust Reagan with such heavy responsibilities and therefore, with the campaign for nuclear disarmament or a "freeze," sought to remove his hand from the cocked nuclear gun. In the end, however, Reagan proved to be as responsible about nuclear weapons as had previous American presidents.

Western Europe, the other area most strongly impacted by the nuclear weapons debate, saw the issue in quite different terms than did the U.S. Under one strategic scenario, any conflict between the U.S. and the U.S.S.R.—including one employing strategic or limited nuclear weapons—would probably be fought out on the plains of Central Europe, not a prospect to Europe's liking, since it would be the main battleground as well as main victim of such an exchange. Under another scenario—much more to Europe's liking—the U.S. and the

U.S.S.R. would send missiles at each other, flying over Europe in both directions but, in a kind of umbrella effect, not actually raining down there. Because it is so close to the Soviet Union and is the setting for the most likely kind of nuclear exchange (one that is limited, but that could well escalate), Europe feels more strongly about the issue than does the United States. In Europe, whole political parties and mass movements have been organized around the nuclear issue. These movements will continue to be influential, but they will probably decline in strength now that it is no longer Ronald Reagan whose finger can decide their fate.

The issue is not whether to have nuclear weapons, but whether they can be kept under control and how best to do so. One group suggests that nuclear weapons are so frightful that we must move quickly to abolish them, even going so far as to disarm unilaterally—that is, without any mutual and verifiable movement toward disarmament on the part of the Soviet Union. This argument suggests that the Soviet people are just like the American people in their desire for peace, that people-to-people diplomacy and exchanges can lead to greater understanding and trust of each other, that we must exercise moral leadership in beginning the disarmament process, and that world public opinion will oblige the Soviets to follow.

Others argue, however, that the threat of the use of nuclear weapons is not so imminent; that while the Soviet people may want peace, their government is not a democracy; that what the people want may have nothing to do with the decisions of the communist leadership; that people-to-people exchanges are nice but have little effect on Soviet policy; that unilateral disarmament would leave us dangerously vulnera-

ble; and that world public opinion has not historically affected and cannot now be counted on to affect Soviet behavior. Thus, this group argues that the U.S. must remain strong and vigilant and maintain its military (including nuclear) preparedness. At the same time, the U.S. must be prepared to negotiate the reduction of nuclear and other weapons—but from a position of strength, not weakness, and with appropriate guarantees and systems of inspection. This stance and the military buildup that accompanied it during the 1980s were denigrated by the nuclear freeze advocates as "war mongering", but when Reagan and Chairman Gorbachev signed the nuclear reduction agreement of 1988—the most far-reaching in history—the peace-through-strength argument seemed to be vindicated. That same conclusion was reflected in the outcome of the 1988 presidential election won by George Bush.

It is likely that we will have to reconcile ourselves to the fact that we cannot and will not have perfect peace. On the other hand, there is a great deal that a prudent and more limited disarmament agenda can accomplish.

Arms control is a controversial subject. We begin with a balanced statement by the Foreign Policy Association. Then Robert Bowie, scholar and statesman, provides the historical background on nuclear strategy and arms control and analyze the dimensions of the problem. Kenneth Adelman, who served as President Reagan's director of the Arms Control and Disarmament Agency, argues that agreements on arms control with the Soviet Union must be linked to human rights progress there. Finally, former Secretary of State George Shultz offers a balanced, careful view of this difficult issue.

Arms Agreements   *Too Little Too Late, or Too Much Too Soon?*

In May 1988, President Ronald Reagan paid his first visit to Moscow for his fourth meeting with Soviet General Secretary Mikhail Gorbachev. There the two leaders exchanged ratifications of the treaty on intermediate-range nuclear forces (INF), which had been approved by the U.S. Senate just in time for the summit. The agreement is the first ever to eliminate a whole category of nuclear missiles, and it contains unprecedented provisions for on-site inspections by both sides.

During Reagan's last year in office, the superpowers also made progress toward slashing their strategic, or long-range, forces, the backbone of their nuclear arsenals. There were also some promising developments in the long-stalemated East-West talks on conventional, or nonnuclear, force reductions in Europe.

Five years earlier, such developments had seemed out of the question. Reagan spent most of his first term denouncing the Soviet Union, the "evil empire," while allocating an unprecedented amount to build up U.S. military strength in peacetime. "Arms control" was at best a propaganda exercise, with both sides publicly advancing proposals that the other then promptly rejected. In November 1983, the U.S., at the request of the North Atlantic Treaty Organization (NATO), began installing INF in Western Europe to counter those on the Soviet side. (The members of NATO, which was founded in 1949, are Belgium, Britain, Canada, Denmark, the Federal Republic of Germany, France, Greece, Iceland, Italy, Luxembourg, the Netherlands, Norway, Portugal, Spain, Turkey and the U.S.) In response, the Soviets walked out of the INF negotiations and the strategic arms reduction talks, or START. For the next few years, the stalemate led even some traditional arms control supporters to question the value of the process itself.

The tide turned at the Reagan-Gorbachev summit in Reykjavik, Iceland, in October 1986. There the two leaders, to the alarm of a number of Reagan's advisers and European allies, departed from their prepared agenda and discussed the possibility of eliminating nuclear weapons—or at least ballistic (rocket-propelled) missiles—altogether.

Reaction to the flurry of arms control activity since Reykjavik has been decidedly mixed. Public opinion has been overwhelmingly favorable, according to an opinion survey called "Americans Talk Security," although Americans are also generally wary of rushing into a bad deal with the Soviets. Experts, on the other hand, are divided. Some see the INF treaty as a significant contribution to U.S. security because it eliminates the threat to Western Europe from Soviet medium-range missiles and has contributed to a lessening of U.S.-Soviet tensions. Others view it as a minor first step, important as a precedent but affecting only 5% of the world's nuclear weapons—and only those of the superpowers, not the British, French or Chinese arsenals. Some critics, like former Secretary of State Henry A. Kissinger, fear that removing U.S. nuclear weapons from Western Europe will weaken the Atlantic alliance. He finds this especially worrisome when there is little chance that the U.S. will strengthen its conventional forces, which are far more expensive to maintain than nuclear weapons. Still others, including a number of former Reagan Administration officials, have denounced Reagan's abandonment of his earlier—and in their view, healthy—skepticism of the Soviet Union and the wisdom of dealing with Moscow.

What should we expect from arms control? Is it a promising avenue for reducing the dangers posed by nuclear weapons? Should the Bush Administration move quickly to build on the progress made to date or should it stand back and review its priorities?

Current U.S. and Soviet Strategic Nuclear Forces

	Strategic Nuclear Delivery Vehicles	Weapons (Warheads)
U.S.		
Ballistic missiles		
ICBMs	1,000	2,334
SLBMs	640	5,632
Bombers	353	4,808
Total	**1,993**	**12,774**
U.S.SR.		
Ballistic missiles		
ICBMs	1,418	6,440
SLBMs	932	3,492
Bombers	165	960
Total	**2,515**	**10,892**

Sources: Congressional Research Senate and American Association for the Advancement of Science

Source: From *Great Decisions, 1989,* Foreign Policy Association, New York, 1989.

Promise and Pitfalls

Ever since the U.S. dropped nuclear bombs on Hiroshima and Nagasaki, Japan, in 1945 in order to hasten the end of World War II, people have been searching for ways to limit if not eliminate the dangers posed by these weapons. Arms control, which seeks to reduce the risk of nuclear war and to regulate levels of weapons through negotiated agreements between the superpowers, is only one of those ways, and not everyone agrees that it is the best one.

Conservatives, who do not trust the Soviets to live up to their end of any arms control bargain, place their faith in a strong U.S. military posture as the best guarantee of U.S. security. They believe the U.S.S.R.'s motives are fundamentally hostile and that it has a considerable advantage over the U.S. and its allies in conventional forces. In the words of the U.S. Ambassador to Turkey Robert Strausz-Hupé, "The West cannot gamble its security on a disarmament agreement until it faces across the conference table men who represent an open political system, are responsive to the popular will, and have forsworn aggression."

President Reagan's Strategic Defense Initiative (SDI) represents another approach to limiting the nuclear danger: building defensive weapons to shoot down offensive ballistic missiles. The U.S. began to build an antiballistic missile, or ABM, system once before, but negotiated ABM limits with Moscow as part of the 1972 SALT I (first strategic arms limitation talks) agreements and abandoned its system shortly after that.

Arms control advocates tend to be skeptical that either outgunning the Soviets or building defenses against their missiles holds any real prospect of eliminating the danger of nuclear war. Arms control rests on the assumption that war is less likely to occur if there is balance and stability in the kinds and numbers of forces that two opponents maintain. Arms control's primary goal, therefore, is to *manage* rather than eliminate, the arms race in a way that minimizes these instabilities. As McGeorge Bundy, national security adviser in the Kennedy and Johnson Administrations (1961–69) has written, "The purpose of arms control agreements is to strengthen stability, not to get rid of the weapons. We don't know how to get rid of the weapons." Arms control has also been touted over the years as a way to save money and to advance cooperation and communication between the superpowers.

Arms control has come under fire from the left as well as the right. In contrast to some conservatives who see the Soviet Union as the primary threat to U.S. security, some liberals see nuclear weapons themselves as the chief danger. General and complete disarmament is the ultimate expression of the view that if all nuclear weapons were eliminated, the danger of war would also disappear. But many who do not see disarmament as the solution nevertheless believe that arms control has ligitimized both sides' buildup rather than constrained it and has not done enough to encourage the adoption of less-threatening and less-destabilizing military postures.

The ABCs of Nukespeak

To limit the threat it faces from the Soviet nuclear arsenal, the U.S. has depended on a combination of arms control and unilateral decisions about what kinds of weapons to build and where to put them. The key concept has always been to make sure these weapons never have to be used by *deterring* the Soviet Union from aggression.

Military deterrence is the process of convincing a potential aggressor, by the threat of retaliation, not to attack. In the nuclear age, deterrence depends on the capacity to strike back after a nuclear attack (or **first strike**). Retaliation must be both certain and potentially so devastating that an enemy considering aggression knows that more will be lost by attacking than could possibly be gained. He must, therefore, be convinced of your retaliatory (**second strike**) capability and your will to use it. Nuclear deterrence, in other words, depends on both military capabilities and *credibility*—the other side has to believe that you can and will inflict unacceptable damage on him if provoked—whether with nuclear or conventional weapons.

In order to make sure that not all of its weapons will be destroyed in the event of a Soviet first strike, the U.S. has relied since the 1960s on a mix of weapons known as the **strategic triad**: land-based, sea-based and aircraft-based intercontinental-range (or strategic) nuclear weapons, with a range of 3,400 miles or more. Each leg of the triad has its own strengths and weaknesses for retaliation. Land-based intercontinental ballistic missiles (ICBMs) are highly accurate. However, if they are located in stationary "silos," they are easy to find and therefore not very *survivable*. If they are equipped with multiple independently targetable reentry vehicles, or warheads (known as MIRVs), they are also very threatening and therefore likely to be early targets of attack in the event of war. This is why many arms control experts believe MIRVed ICBMs are so destabilizing.

Submarine-launched ballistic missiles (SLBMs) are hardest to find and destroy but have until very recently been far less accurate than ICBMs. Like ICBMs, SLBMs can be equipped with multiple warheads. Submarines can also carry cruise missiles. (Slower moving than ballistic missiles, cruise missiles fly much like a pilotless airplane. They are nearly invisible to radar, in part because they fly so low.) Bombers, which can also carry cruise missiles, present targeting problems for an opponent because they can leave their bases upon warning of an attack. (Unlike a missile, a bomber can be called back in case of a false alarm.) But the Soviet Union's extensive air defenses make it difficult for bombers to reach their targets, which is why the U.S. is developing "stealth" technology to make aircraft less visible to enemy radar.

U.S. strategy today provides for a choice of targets, some of which are located near or within Soviet cities and industrial sites ("countervalue" targets) and some of which are Soviet military installations ("counterforce" targets). The idea is that a threat to use nuclear weapons is more credible if the President has a wide range of options in responding to any provocation.

Not everyone agrees that these options help make the U.S. secure. Liberal critics charge that with an arsenal that can already wipe out life as we know it many times over ("overkill"), the U.S. *reduces* its security by choosing strategies that must make the Soviet Union think the U.S. is actually planning to use them.

Today, the overall sizes of the superpowers' strategic nuclear arsenals are roughly comparable, although the structures of the two forces are different. The Soviets' strength is in their land-based ICBM force, dominated by large (or "heavy"), powerful and accurate multiwarhead missiles. The U.S. is stronger in submarines and bombers (see chart). By what process has the U.S. chosen the weapons that make up its arsenal? What role has arms control played in limiting the nuclear threat?

ARMS CONTROL: THEORY AND PRACTICE

The U.S. and Soviet Union traded disarmament proposals after World War II until the cold war intervened. The U.S., which had rapidly demobilized after the war, depended on its monopoly of nuclear weapons to deter a Soviet conventional attack on American allies in Western Europe and otherwise to "contain" the expansion of Soviet power. Although the Soviets tested their first atomic weapon in 1949, the U.S. remained well ahead in the arms race for another two decades.

Much of arms control theory was formulated during the 1950s and 1960s. It was incorporated into U.S. defense policy by Robert S. McNamara, secretary of defense during the Kennedy and Johnson Administrations. McNamara reasoned that since the Soviet Union was well on its way to catching up with the U.S., it no longer made sense to try to maintain U.S. nuclear superiority; in fact, it was dangerous to do so. He believed that deterrence would be stable so long as each side maintained an "assured destruction" capability,

that is, "a clear and unmistakable ability to inflict an unacceptable degree of damage upon any aggressor ... even after absorbing a first strike." In addition, each side should be certain that the other was not planning a first strike, so that neither would ever have an incentive to preempt such an attack, even at the height of a political crisis. McNamara estimated that the U.S. needed no more than 1,000 ICBMs to accomplish this, and the U.S. stopped adding to its arsenal of Minuteman missiles when it reached this number in 1967. His hope was that by ending its buildup, the U.S. could demonstrate its benign intentions to the Soviet Union. If that didn't work, he hoped he could convince Moscow in arms negotiations to design its forces according to the same logic. McNamara therefore saw arms control as a way of assuring that both sides would adjust their forces so that they clearly served deterrent purposes only.

Practice: The ABM Debate

The concepts McNamara relied on have dominated U.S. arms control policy for 20 years. But practice has not always been consistent with theory. The present U.S. and Soviet arsenals are the product not so much of careful planning but of complex dynamics between the superpowers and among institutions with competing interests within each country.

McNamara's ideas ran into trouble because the pace and scale of the Soviet buildup during the 1960s triggered alarm in the U.S. After withdrawing their missiles from Cuba in the 1962 crisis, the Soviets increased their defense spending by 3%–4% a year. They kept building after they reached

U.S. levels, and by the end of the decade had more ICBMs than the U.S. They also built up their arsenal of SLBMs, improved their air defenses, expanded civil defense measures, and began building an ABM system around Moscow. The Soviets also began deploying heavy land-based ICBMs that could destroy U.S. land-based missiles, even those housed in hardened (heavily protected) silos.

As a result, the Johnson Administration (1963–69) came under heavy pressure from the Joint Chiefs of Staff (JCS) and Congress to build new offensive weapons and a U.S. ABM system. Although it did not build additional missile launchers, the U.S. began developing MIRVs in 1965 since at the time they appeared to be the cheapest and least destabilizing way of countering Moscow's buildup.

Primarily in the hope of avoiding an ABM race, which he thought would be destabilizing, McNamara tried to get arms negotiations started with Moscow. He reasoned that if one side was invulnerable to the other's missiles, it could strike first without the fear of retaliation that was crucial to deterrence. Moreover, the cheapest way for the other side to counter an ABM defense system would be to add enough offensive weapons to overwhelm it, thereby triggering another round of the arms race. McNamara was unsuccessful in persuading the Soviets of his logic during the June 1967 Glassboro, N.J., summit meeting between President Lyndon B. Johnson and Soviet leader Alexei N. Kosygin. However, once the U.S. started building its own ABM system, the Soviets agreed to talks to limit both ABM systems and strategic arms.

Nixon, Kissinger and Détente

The first SALT talks did not begin during the Johnson Administration because the Soviet Union invaded Czechoslovakia the day before they were to be announced. By the time Richard M. Nixon entered the White House in 1969, Soviet nuclear parity with the U.S. was nearly a reality. The image of the U.S. abroad had been weakened by the long war in Vietnam, whose unpopularity had also created deep divisions in this country and built pressure to cut defense spending. The new President and his national security adviser (later secretary of state) Kissinger therefore had a different arms control agenda from that of their predecessors. *Détente,* or a lessening of tensions, with the Soviet Union would be their primary foreign policy instrument, and arms control would be its most visible symbol. The idea was to use the common U.S. and Soviet interest in avoiding nuclear war as "a springboard for building a network of mutually advantageous relationships." Détente was to work primarily through "linkage": offering the Soviets agreements in areas of special concern to them, such as trade, to discourage them from stirring up trouble in the Third World that might require U.S. involvement. The Administration saw a SALT agreement more as a symbol of a new "era of negotiation" than as a way of addressing strategic problems. In the Nixon-Kissinger view, significant advances in arms control would have to wait for an overall improvement in superpower relations.

For the U.S.S.R., the talks offered acknowledgment from the U.S. and the rest of the world that the Soviet Union had become a superpower, on an equal footing with the U.S. Faced with recurring unrest in Eastern Europe and a deepening rift with its former ally, the People's Republic of China, as well as with a need to raise living standards at home, Moscow was also anxious to reduce tensions with the U.S.

SALT I: Successes and Failures

Agreement on the ABM treaty by the superpowers indicated that they both implicitly, at least, accepted the concept that building defenses would undermine the stability of deterrence by removing the certainty of mutual assured destruction. The interim agreement on offensive arms set a cap on the number of launchers, but it did not prevent major qualitative improvements: the MIRVing of launchers and dramatic increases in missile accuracy. MIRVs were left out of the agreement partly at the insistence of the JCS, who made their support for the treaty contingent on continuation of the U.S. MIRV program along with funding for what were to become the B-1 bomber, the Trident submarine and the Abrams tank. It was an omission many in the U.S. came to regret. By the late 1970s, it became widely apparent that the Soviet MIRV program, combined with a new generation of Soviet missiles then under development (notably the huge SS-18), posed a threat to the U.S. force of land-based missiles. The U.S. began to consider building a more powerful MIRVed ICBM, which would be mobile and therefore more survivable (the future missile experimental, or MX).

The major consequence of SALT I was political rather than military: "the process was the product," in the words of one observer. Made possible by a warming in the superpower relationship, the talks became the centerpiece of U.S.-Soviet relations. SALT I, however, was not, as advertised by Nixon and Kissinger, the first step "in a [détente] process leading to greater stability." Indeed, many observers believe the kind of rhetoric used to sell SALT and détente to the U.S. public inflated expectations and helped create a backlash as relations between the superpowers soured in subsequent years.

The Numbers Game

Part of the backlash was due to the U.S. agreement to freeze missile levels. This gave the Soviet Union a larger number to offset what Moscow claimed were U.S. technological and geographical advantages (some more-advanced weapons and the fact that the U.S. has no nuclear-armed adversaries on or near its borders, as does the U.S.S.R. in Western Europe and China). This provision made many in the U.S. angry, and Congress, shortly after ratifying SALT I, passed the Jackson Amendment. The amendment, authored by the late Senator Henry M. Jackson (D-Wash.), required the President to "seek a future treaty that . . . would not limit the U.S. to levels of intercontinental strategic forces inferior [in number] to the limits provided for the Soviet Union."

What this meant for future negotiations was a preoccupation with numbers at the expense of other considerations, such as the greatly improved missile accuracies that were undermining the stability of the strategic balance. It also made negotiating any agreement more difficult, since a treaty that was to be politically acceptable in the U.S. would require greater reductions by the Soviets.

President Gerald R. Ford and Soviet General Secretary Leonid I. Brezhnev agreed at Vladivostok, U.S.S.R., in 1974 on a framework that would govern the negotiations on SALT II. The Vladivostok accord set equal launcher limits and began to deal with some of the stability issues. Construction of new stationary land-based ICBM launchers would be banned, thereby encouraging both sides to add missiles in more-survivable categories like SLBMs. Ceilings on MIRVed missiles were also agreed on. But the large numbers in the agreement led Jackson to attack it for putting a cap on a mountain top, despite the fact that it had achieved the equal ceilings he had insisted on earlier.

Carter and SALT II

In his 1977 inaugural address, President Jimmy Carter expressed the hope of eliminating "all nuclear weapons from this earth." He believed that the nearly completed agreement left by the Ford Administration was too limited, and, although it took two more years, he succeeded in working out a more comprehensive SALT II treaty, which he and Brezhnev signed in 1979. Building on the Vladivostok accord, the treaty set additional limits on the number and types of Soviet ICBMs and placed further restrictions on MIRVing. It permitted each side to build only one new type of ICBM, which left the U.S. free to proceed with the MX.

Ratification of SALT II became a casualty of deteriorating U.S.-Soviet relations. Even before the end of the Ford Administration, it was increasingly obvious that Washington and Moscow understood détente to mean different things. Moscow did not gain the "mutually advantageous" trade it sought, mainly because of legislation that made U.S. trading privileges contingent on an improvement in Soviet human rights policy. Washington did not win an end to the involvement of the U.S.S.R. and its Cuban proxies in the Third World.

In the meantime, Soviet arms developments were creating alarm in the West. The Soviet Union had begun in 1977 to deploy a new and versatile generation of intermediate-range nuclear forces, with ranges of 300–3,400 miles, ideal for hitting the countries of Western Europe from Warsaw Pact territory. (The members of the Warsaw Pact, which was founded in 1955, are Bulgaria, Czechoslovakia, East Germany, Hungary, Poland, Romania and the Soviet Union.) West European concern over the impact of these weapons on NATO's deterrent strategy led to a 1979 decision to station U.S. INF in Western Europe starting in 1983 unless a prior arms agreement removed the Soviet INF threat.

The Carter Administration gave the green light to development of the 10-warhead MX once it had worked out a survivable, mobile basing mode. The MX was to be fast, accurate and powerful enough to destroy SS-18s and other missiles in their hardened silos. But political squabbling over an appropriate basing mode continues and has held up deployment of half the planned MX force.

The fall of U.S. ally Mohammad Reza Shah Pahlavi of Iran in January 1979, followed in November by the taking of 66 American hostages by Iranian radicals and in December by the Soviet invasion of Afghanistan, attracted growing public attention to what appeared to be a serious weakening of American power relative to that of the Soviet Union. The prolonged debate over SALT II, which presidential candidate Ronald Reagan pronounced "fatally flawed," focused this debate still further and contributed to Reagan's landslide victory over Carter in 1980.

Reagan and Arms Control

Reagan viewed U.S. policy toward the Soviet Union during the 1970s as misguided. Many of his political advisers were charter members of the Committee on the Present Danger, where they had been sounding the alarm about the rapidly expanding Soviet military power since 1976. The committee cited heavy military expenditures, military writings and force structure as evidence that the Soviets were seeking strategic superiority that would enable them not only to "fight and win" a nuclear war but to extend the political and military influence of the U.S.S.R. throughout the world. In the face of this sustained buildup, for the U.S. to have decreased its own defense spending and placed its faith in arms control was sheer folly and placed the U.S. in a grave situation, according to the committee.

Reagan made strengthening the U.S. military a precondition of negotiations. Although the modernization of all three legs of the strategic triad had begun under Ford, Reagan raised spending on

strategic forces by almost 50% between 1981 and 1987. He also bolstered U.S. conventional forces and proceeded with plans to station INF in Europe.

To deal with the impasse over the MX and how to base it, Reagan appointed a study commission chaired by former national security adviser Brent Scowcroft. The commission recommended, among other things, deploying the MX in existing fixed silos as soon as possible and beginning development of a new, small, mobile ICBM, with only one warhead. Mobility would make Midgetman more survivable, and its single warhead would make it look less threatening to the Soviet Union and therefore a less tempting target, both qualities that would contribute to a more stable strategic environment.

Reagan also revived the concept of missile defenses, abandoned after the 1972 ABM treaty. In announcing SDI in March 1983, he expressed the hope that building a defense against nuclear weapons would free the U.S. from the need to rely on deterrence by mutual assured destruction. Over $16 billion was appropriated for the program before Reagan left office.

Because of the general perception in this country that U.S. military strength had declined while the Soviet Union's had grown, Reagan's defense buildup (totaling over $1 trillion during his first five years in office) initially commanded widespread popular and congressional support. But the pace of the buildup, the stridency of the Administration's anti-Soviet rhetoric, the broad coverage in the press of former Secretary of Defense Caspar W. Weinberger's view that the U.S. should develop nuclear capabilities that would en-

able it to "prevail" in a nuclear war, combined with the Administration's neglect of arms control during its first 10 months in office, raised fears in the U.S. and in Western Europe. The result was a season of massive antinuclear demonstrations in Western Europe and the U.S. during 1981 and 1982, and the growth of public and congressional sentiment in the U.S. favoring a freeze on all further testing and deployment of nuclear weapons.

'Alliance Management'

In late 1981, several weeks after some 250,000 West Germans turned out in Bonn to protest the planned installation of U.S. INF in West Germany, the U.S. offered to cancel the deployment if the Soviet Union would eliminate all of its INF (the "zero option"). Because the U.S. missiles were not scheduled to be installed for another two years, the proposal asked the Soviets to trade something for nothing. Neither the U.S. nor West European governments expected Moscow to accept the proposal, but the move did put the ball back in the Soviet court. "The purpose of this whole exercise," as a U.S. State Department official put it, "is maximum political advantage. It's not arms control we're engaged in, it's alliance management." The Soviet Union did not accept the offer, and the first U.S. INF were installed in West Germany and Britain in November 1983.

Earlier that year, Reagan had called for new talks on strategic weapons. Criticizing the "pseudo arms control" of previous Administrations that had merely set limits to the growth of nuclear arsenals rather than lowering them. Reagan announced that in new START negotiations the U.S. would seek to cut strategic arsenals by 50%. The Administration also began releasing yearly reports on Soviet compliance with previous arms treaties that pointed to numerous violations. It insisted that it would not sign further agreements without rigorous verification procedures, including on-site inspections, which the Soviets had always refused.

Critics, among them a number of former arms control officials, charged that Administration arms proposals were so one-sided as to be nonnegotiable and accused Reagan of deliberately trying to sabotage all chances for arms control. Many, including some prominent scientists, were also alarmed by SDI, or "Star Wars." They pronounced it unattainable, ruinously expensive and potentially destabilizing. They objected that the plan would violate the ABM treaty, sound the death knell for arms control and touch off a new round of the arms race. The Soviet Union walked out of both the START and INF negotiations when the first U.S. INF were deployed.

REYKJAVIK AND BEYOND

Talks did not begin again in Geneva until March 1985. Reagan and Gorbachev met at Reykjavik in 1986 to ratify the progress made during the preceding year, but instead the discussions branched out in unanticipated directions. Gorbachev raised the possibility of a nuclear-free world by the year 2000, and Reagan proposed in turn that both sides eliminate all ballistic missiles within 10 years. The talks collapsed over disagreement on SDI, which the U.S.S.R. maintained would violate the ABM treaty if de-

ployed and which it insisted be included in any talks on offensive weapons. The U.S. took the position that SDI was nonnegotiable.

At Reykjavik, however, the groundwork was laid for the INF treaty that was eventually signed in December 1987 and for the START talks that are still going on. In both cases, the Soviets have said yes to much of the substance of the Reagan proposals they had previously rejected.

Explanations for the dramatic turnaround vary. The Reagan Administration claimed the Soviets' return to the negotiating table vindicated its military programs and its insistence on real arms reductions rather than SALT-type caps on further growth.

Other explanations focus on the disastrous state of the Soviet economy and the accession of a dynamic new leader in the Kremlin who is addressing Soviet problems in innovative ways. Gorbachev has talked about the need for a "breathing space" that would give his reforms time to get off the ground, and most analysts—although they disagree on his long-term motives—agree that reaching arms accords with the U.S. could permit him to spend more money on "butter" instead of "guns" for a time.

Some believe the shift on arms control reflects fundamental changes in Soviet foreign policy and military strategy. Gorbachev often refers to "new political thinking," emphasizing the limitations on the use of military power in today's interdependent world. "Less security for the U.S. compared to the Soviet Union would not be in our interest since it could lead to mistrust and produce instability." Gorbachev has also denied that the Soviet Union is seeking

superiority, asserting that Moscow's goal is strategic "sufficiency."

More conservative voices suggest that while Gorbachev may be adopting surprising new tactics, his foreign policy goals are familiar: the elimination of U.S. nuclear weapons from Western Europe and the sowing of discord between the U.S. and its NATO allies by casting doubt on the reliability of the American nuclear guarantee. Dimitri K. Simes of the Carnegie Endowment for International Peace warns that Gorbachev seeks a breathing space now to ensure Soviet military superiority later. Conservatives also claim that Gorbachev can afford to reduce nuclear weapons because the Soviet Union and its allies still maintain overwhelming conventional superiority in Europe.

Too Much Too Soon?

The INF treaty was ratified by the Senate, but not everyone greeted it with enthusiasm. Scowcroft, whom Reagan had earlier appointed to chair his commission on strategic forces, has charged the Reagan Administration with not acknowledging "the interrelationship between the various elements of U.S. strategic policy." The "decision [to pull INF out of Europe] implies that we are increasing our reliance on something else. U.S. strategic forces, conventional forces, or conventional arms control will have to compensate for the imbalance that still exists between NATO and Warsaw Pact conventional forces." Instead, the Reagan Administration rushed into START negotiations—which would reduce strategic weapons—and did so at a time of budget cutbacks at the Pentagon that make conventional increases unlikely.

Other supporters of arms control, while applauding the treaty as a positive first step, pointed out that it affects only a small percentage of the superpowers' huge arsenals. McGeorge Bundy has written that the "agreement is highly important in . . . terms of what it suggests about the possible future of arms control—and not really important at all . . . in terms of the weapons balance between NATO and the Warsaw Pact."

Current Negotiations

START. The formula worked out at the 1986 Reykjavik summit would theoretically reduce numbers of strategic weapons on both sides by roughly 50%, leaving each with 6,000 warheads on a maximum of 1,600 strategic nuclear delivery vehicles (land- or submarine-based launchers, bombers, etc.). Because of complex counting rules, however, actual reductions under a START agreement could come closer to 30%, leaving both sides with between 8,000 and 9,000 weapons. Cuts would be deepest for the most destabilizing weapons, however: the sides have agreed on a maximum of 4,900 warheads on ballistic missiles and, of these, only 1,540 on heavy land-based ICBMs. The counting rules should encourage both sides to restructure their forces by shifting emphasis toward more-survivable, slower-moving weapons such as those launched from bombers.

Before such a treaty can be signed, a number of issues need to be resolved. One concerns SDI and its relationship to the 1972 ABM treaty. The Reagan Administration adopted a "broad" interpretation of the treaty that would give it the right to develop and test in space new SDI technology. Administration critics and Moscow claim development is prohibited by the treaty under its "narrow" interpretation, an interpretation that has been accepted by prior Administrations. The treaty permits either side to withdraw from it on one year's notice. Moscow wants the U.S. to agree to adhere to the treaty, narrowly interpreted, for 10 years; the Reagan Administration would only agree to a 7-year commitment, and then only to the broad interpretation. How much of a stumbling block SDI will continue to be to agreement will depend on the new Administration's policy on early space testing and deployment. In approving the INF treaty, the Senate adopted a provision prohibiting the President from reinterpreting treaties without the advice and consent of the Senate.

Moscow and Washington also disagree on whether sea-launched cruise missiles should be included in an agreement and on how to count air-launched cruise missiles. Within the overall warhead limits, they also disagree on what categories of weapons should be additionally limited: the U.S. wants further limits on land-based ICBMs, which it considers the Soviet's greatest strength and the greatest threat to stability; the Soviet Union wants additional limits on SLBMs, in which the U.S. is stronger. The question of whether or not to permit mobile missiles has also not been resolved, and the superpowers continue to disagree on numerous verification details.

Conventional Stability Talks (CST). The agreement to eliminate INF from Western Europe and the prospect of deep cuts in strategic arsenals have focused renewed attention on the state of the conventional military balance in Europe. NATO's position is that the Warsaw Pact military alliance holds a considerable advantage in conventional troops and weapons in Europe (although there are many Western analysts who question how serious the imbalance is). Since 1973 NATO and the Warsaw Pact have participated in the inconclusive Mutual and Balanced Force Reductions (MBFR) talks on reducing the size of their conventional forces in Central Europe (see map).

In June 1986, the Soviet Union proposed new negotiations on force reductions over a much wider area, "from the Atlantic to the Urals." These have become known as the CST. Gorbachev called for immediate cuts by both sides of 100,000 to 150,000 troops, and gradual reductions to 500,000 per side by the early 1990s. But Gorbachev has also acknowledged that there is a "certain asymmetry, both in forces and armaments," in Central Europe, and hinted that the Warsaw Pact might be prepared to make some one-sided reductions, as long as NATO would do the same in categories where it holds the edge. Gorbachev and other Soviet officials have also urged that both alliances adopt a "nonoffensive defense."

NATO has been cautious in its response, believing that unless the Warsaw Pact makes very disproportionate cuts in troop strength and offensive weapons like tanks and artillery, Western defenses will be worse off than if there were no agreement. In a March 1988 declaration, NATO foreign ministers presented their conventional arms control goals: the "establishment of a secure and stable balance of conventional forces at lower levels; the elimination of disparities prejudicial to stability and security; and, as a matter of high priority, the elimination of the capability for launching surprise attack and for initiating large-scale offensive action."

The CST negotiations will involve all seven Warsaw Pact members and all 16 members of NATO. Negotiating cuts in the larger zone holds both promise and pitfalls. NATO and Warsaw Pact forces are more evenly balanced in the new zone than in the MBFR area; on the other hand, getting such a large number of Western countries—not all of whose troops are integrated into the NATO military command structure—to agree on all issues has already proved difficult. A CST agreement would force Soviet troops to withdraw much further than the several hundred miles required under the old formula. On the other hand, U.S. troops would have to be pulled back across the Atlantic.

Many remain skeptical that Moscow will actually make the cuts it is talking about. Some think Soviet proposals are primarily for propaganda value, part of its traditional strategy of trying to drive a wedge between the U.S. and its NATO allies. Others think the Soviet offer may be genuine. Conventional forces are far more expensive than nuclear arsenals to maintain, and saving money in this area could make Gorbachev's task of restructuring the Soviet economy easier, or permit him to redirect some military resources into developing the technology he will need for the next generation of conventional weapons. Some observers note that pressures on the U.S. defense budget would also make a conventional arms deal a good one for the U.S.

U.S. Policy Options

The conclusion of the INF treaty and the prospect of a START agreement have prompted a lively debate over what U.S. arms control goals should be in the coming years. Some options under discussion follow.

On strategic weapons, the U.S. should:

1. **Proceed cautiously before agreeing to a START treaty.** The START cuts outlined by the Reagan Administration, Scowcroft and others argue, would decrease stability, leaving remaining U.S. forces more vulnerable by lowering the number of targets Moscow would have to hit in a first strike. Scowcroft believes it would be dangerous to reverse the practice of erring on the side of possibly too much nuclear strength in order to test how far the U.S. can cut back without damaging deterrence. Arbitrarily picking a smaller number of weapons is the wrong approach; it is the quality, not the quantity, of forces that matters to stability. In this regard, the Reagan Administration's proposed ban on mobile missiles is a mistake, it is argued, as is the abandonment of the single-warhead Midgetman in the fiscal year 1989 defense budget.

Moreover, the U.S. does not currently have the ability to monitor Soviet compliance with a START agreement, according to a February 1988 Senate Intelligence Committee report. If cheating could not be detected, the U.S. could find itself in an extremely dangerous "breakout" situation, where the U.S.S.R. could quickly deploy hidden weapons, putting the U.S. at a severe disadvantage.

2. **Work toward concluding a START agreement.** With 50% cuts, the U.S. should still be able to threaten enough Soviet targets after a first strike to maintain deterrence, according to a study done by The Brookings Institution expert John D. Steinbruner with Michael M. May and George F. Bing of the Lawrence Livermore National Laboratory. This would be true particularly if the U.S. continues to modernize its strategic forces to make them more survivable, which the treaty will not prevent in any meaningful way. (Although the issue of mobile missiles has not been decided, many believe the Soviets will not agree to a treaty requiring them to give up their already-deployed mobile ICBMs.) These changes would tend to lower both sides' first-strike capabilities, adding to stability.

On verification, Michael Krepon of the Carnegie Endowment for International Peace believes that rules can be worked out which will prevent most cheating by making it extremely costly. The variety of required intrusive, onsite measures would also provide the U.S. with greater knowledge about the workings of the Soviet national security and military establishment, in the view of Arms Control Association deputy director Jack Mendelsohn. Over the long run, careful restructuring of forces at reduced levels should also save money.

3. **Work toward deeper cuts.** ". . . Nuclear weapons serve no military purpose whatsoever . . . except only to deter one's opponent from using them," in McNamara's words, and a far lower number of nuclear weapons would suffice to

ensure deterrence. The U.S. should also adopt a policy of "no-first-use" of nuclear weapons either in anticipation of a nuclear strike or in response to a nonnuclear attack. Such a policy would leave no doubt that the U.S. nuclear arsenal is for deterrence only. The Brookings-Livermore study suggested that deterrence could be maintained with cuts down to 3,000 warheads apiece, provided the U.S. continues to modernize its remaining forces to make them more survivable.

Cuts could go still lower in the future, to 1,000 weapons apiece or even to zero, says Union of Concerned Scientists' Richard Garwin, if all nuclear powers agree to reduce their arsenals and to stop modernizing and testing nuclear weapons (a nuclear freeze) and if steps are taken to ensure that nonnuclear nations do not develop their own nuclear weapons. Randall Forsberg, who founded the nuclear freeze movement in the early 1980s, believes nuclear disarmament is possible "if it is designed to take place over a period of decades . . . if it is international, not unilateral, and if it eliminates the more aggressive and escalatory uses of armed forces first, leaving the more defensive elements for later stages. . . ."

Conventional Forces

A decision to move toward lower levels of nuclear weapons, most agree, must be synchronized with a policy on conventional forces. Here, the U.S. should:

1. **Seek deep cuts in Soviet forces for modest cuts in NATO forces.** This would be a reasonably low-risk test of Soviet intentions; modest NATO cuts could be reversed should the need suddenly arise, whereas deep cuts would be politically and logistically difficult to undo. Cuts should focus on the most clearly offensive ground troops and weapons (like tanks and artillery), which should be pulled back from Central Europe to ease tensions there.

2. **Seek deeper cuts in Soviet forces for deep cuts in NATO forces.** The current high levels of troops and armaments in Central Europe capable of offensive action are a holdover from the earlier cold-war climate when armed conflict seemed a real possibility. Deep cuts on both sides, sparing weapons and troop structures best suited for defense, would do much to promote stability. Such reductions would also save the West millions of dollars. ∎

Arms Control and United States Foreign Policy

By Robert R. Bowie

INTRODUCTION

The interest in arms control is not hard to understand. More "total" wars and more lethal weapons have enhanced tremendously the attraction of peace. In the search for a peaceful world, men's minds have naturally turned to measures to control or eliminate armaments. The memory of World War I placed this topic high on the agenda of the League of Nations. In the aftermath of World War II, the U.N. Charter, like the League Covenant, identified arms control as a major goal. Since then, nuclear weapons, missiles, and intercontinental ballistic missiles have aggravated the fear of war and intensified the pressures for arms control.

The proposals have been many—from "open skies" to "total disarmament." But none has yet produced complete agreement. Inevitably, the lack of progress raises questions whether arms can be controlled under modern conditions, and if so, how. What will determine the feasibility and viability of an arms control system? Often this question is treated merely as a technical matter. Certainly the complexity of modern weapons thrusts the technical problems more into the foreground. Characteristics of weapons, effectiveness of particular safeguards, techniques for inspection, methods of possible evasion —all involve complicated issues of science and technology requiring study and analysis. They may well impose limits on what can be done.

But the most crucial questions are political. How does arms control fit into the foreign policies of the key powers? Control implies some form of cooperation among them regarding military forces, fa-

---

Robert Bowie was director of the Center for International Affairs at Harvard University and deputy director of the CIA.

Source: From Louis Henkin (ed.), *Arms Control,* Prentice-Hall, Englewood Cliffs, NJ, 1961.

cilities or policy. How will the prospects of such cooperation be affected by hostility or distrust? In seeking an answer, one confronts the basic issue: what is the relation between arms control and the structure of international politics? Many would pose the question thus: can military forces be regulated or reduced by agreed measures before removing the political sources of friction and tension?

For two groups—holding opposite views—the answer is clear. Those on one side see clashing national purposes as the root causes of conflict, and military force as merely their reflection. As an instrument of policy the function of military force may be defensive, to protect the nation or its allies; or it may be designed to conquer territory, or dominate other states by force, or to coerce them to the purposes of the stronger power. Or force may be used in more subtle ways to influence the outside world. In any case, they conclude, armed force is not the origin of hostility but merely its consequence; and armaments cannot be controlled while political conflicts remain.

The opposite view sees in armaments themselves a major cause of tension and conflict, producing "arms races" that ultimately lead to war. Exponents of this view often conclude that far-reaching or total disarmament would eliminate major sources of conflict; in any event, that disarmament can be achieved without resolving basic political conflicts.

Any appraisal of the validity of these opposing views is handicapped by the limited experience with arms control. Moreover, in both its politics and its armaments, our era differs profoundly from the past. Even so, before examining the

problem in its modern guise, it may be fruitful to review briefly two earlier instances of arms limitation to which the United States was a party. They may at least indicate whether the dichotomy has been posed too sharply or too simply.

Two Early Instances of Arms Limitation

The first instance was the Rush-Bagot exchange of notes in 1817 which limited the British and United States naval forces on the Great Lakes to a total of four armed revenue cutters for each nation. The time was one of tension and trouble caused by a whole series of problems along the Canadian border and coast, including—the most dangerous one—the confrontation of battle fleets on the Great Lakes. The War of 1812 had proved that, for the time being at least, war could not resolve these issues, and the peace treaty at Ghent did not resolve them either. But the arms race was expensive and disruptive of the commerce that both sides wished to promote. It was also dangerous.

The agreement served the interests of both sides. It was part of a wider political settlement and accommodation. But it did not eliminate all Anglo-United States conflict. Indeed, dispute on the border and other issues continued for more than fifty years. Yet the arms limitation survived these conflicts.

The second instance is more recent and more melancholy—the naval and four-power treaties that came out of the Washington Conference in 1922. In this case military and political arrangements were freely interspersed, and stands were taken or concessions made in one sphere in order to influence the agreements in the

other. The United States agreed to freeze the military *status quo* in those areas of the Pacific (e.g., the Philippines and Guam) that would be essential to any future movements against Japan. The United States and Great Britain undertook, *de facto,* not to combine and threaten the home islands of Japan. In return, Japan agreed to withdraw from Shantung and accepted a 5–5–3 ratio in capital ship tonnage.

Here the parties accepted the necessity for political measures to go hand in hand with the naval limitations, but they failed to work out viable solutions.[1] The agreement, while particularly benefiting Japan, had some political advantages for Great Britain and the United States, and relieved them also from a burdensome race in shipbuilding. But the arrangement was completely ineffective to handle Japanese expansion ten years later. Its solutions did not survive the basic clash of interests, when Japan decided to utilize force to advance its expansion.

What light do these two instances, with their differing results, shed on the links between arms control and the broader purposes of the parties? This experience raises doubts about both the views stated earlier: that arms control is entirely separable from political conflict or is wholly dependent on its removal. It suggests that the relation of the two, while intimate, is more complex than either view asserts. Measures to control military force certainly could not be divorced from the political context in which they were to operate. The fact of political conflicts alone, however, did not necessarily exclude common interests in some cooperation in the military field.

But such cooperation will be limited and shaped by the political context, and may or may not survive strains arising from it. Arms control in turn may alter the wider context—for better or worse—in ways difficult to predict.

These historic instances tell us very little about the feasibility or basis of cooperation between the Soviet Bloc and the United States and its allies. Obviously, both political and military conditions today are different from those of the earlier periods. Yet this experience does indicate certain relevant lines of inquiry in finding what arms control might be feasible and viable in the political environment of our age. Among them are: (a) How far do major purposes of the key powers coincide or conflict, and what is the character of the conflict? (b) What is the potential role of force in the pursuit of their interests and purposes? (c) How does hostility affect the extent and basis of any cooperation for arms control? (d) What is the possible interaction of arms control with other goals of foreign policy for both sides? In this chapter these and relative questions are examined from the aspect of the interests of the United States.

THE BASIC CONFLICT OF PURPOSES

If serious analysis of the prospects for arms control should begin with the political context, its central feature is the deep-seated hostility between the Communist bloc, headed by the Soviet Union, and the non-Communist world, especially the Western nations. In appraising its bearing on arms control, it is necessary to consider (1) the wider setting of the conflict, (2) the Sino-Soviet purposes and strategy, and (3) the purposes and policies of the United States and its allies.

A World in Transition

The pervasive struggle between the Sino-Soviet bloc and the West is part of the radical reshaping of the international order occurring in our century. Since World War I, forces unleashed by industrialism, nationalism and communism have overturned the world order inherited from the 19th century, without producing any stable new order to take its place. Recent decades have speeded up the dismantling and made manifest the contending forces. Ultimately, if mankind avoids suicide, some more stable order may emerge. Its creation and structure will be the work of the coming decades. Meanwhile its contours are, to say the least, shrouded in haze. Many of the crucial elements now stand as questions that only time and events can answer.

At this stage, the nations involved can be viewed in three categories: the Communist bloc; the developed Western states; and the less developed areas of Asia, Africa and Latin America. Within each grouping, and between groupings, conditions and relations are in evolution.

Since 1945, the Communist bloc has expanded to embrace one-third of the world's people, and grown steadily in economic and military power. Rapid Soviet progress has greatly enhanced its confidence and capacity for external influence. The Eastern European satellites are still under Communist control. Despite doctrinal quarrels, the U.S.S.R. and China are still allied by strong ties of interest.

Yet the bloc is less monolithic than formerly, and not immune to change. Will rivalry for leadership strain the Sino-Soviet relationship in the coming years? Will Soviet economic growth and social progress gradually erode the fervor for Communist expansion? Will the reluctant satellites remain subdued indefinitely?

In the developed West, the situation is far from static. In the postwar period, the Atlantic nations forged major new links in NATO and companion economic agencies. The European nations, despite the war and loss of colonies, enjoy unprecedented prosperity. Europe now seeks increased influence and participation in international affairs. The Common Market is drawing together into a tighter grouping for economic progress and common action. The pressures for change within and among the Atlantic nations show no signs of abating. What will be their outcome? Will European integration go forward to closer political unity? How will a united Europe conceive its role in the world and its relations with the United States?

The less-developed nations, with forty per cent of the world's people, are a long way from stability. The older states of Latin America and the newer ones of Asia and Africa are in the throes of social, political and economic upheavals. In their search for national cohesion, effective government, modernized societies and economic growth, they will have to develop new social, political and economic structures under severe handicaps. Their conditions militate against the easy importation of patterns established elsewhere. The institutions of the West evolved slowly; self-government did not spring full-blown into existence. The Western nations had a long period for developing the political and economic foundations, for training technical and managerial talent, for fostering requisite loyalties and attitudes—before they had to cope with expanding populations, rapid technological change and urgent pressures for better living standards. In the less-developed nations, the drive for rapid advance under forced draft could readily collapse into frustration and despair. There are explosive forces in vast pools of unskilled, uprooted urban laborers; in landless rural workers; and in an intelligentsia lacking outlets for their abilities and acutely aware of the disparities between rich nations and poor.

These problems and dangers limit the options open to the less-developed countries and make far more likely some sort of rigid state control. Can these conditions, in the long run, be exploited by the Soviet Union? Or will the emergent states be stubbornly independent and intensely nationalistic? How much can the developed nations of the West help them in their tasks?

Enough has been said to make the point: ours is an era of transition to some new order. Many forces are at work to unsettle existing patterns and break familiar molds. Beneath the divisive tendencies are others pulling societies closer together. Strands of economics, politics, and communications make each one increasingly more dependent on others for its well-being and security. Even without the East-West struggle, these dynamic forces would make it impossible to preserve the *status quo* and difficult to maintain stability.

Communist Purposes and Strategy

The Sino-Soviet leaders have long assessed existing and emerging conditions as highly favorable for Communist expansion. At various times the Communist parties have joined in manifestos diagnosing the situation and prescribing the proper measures for Communist advances. Speeches by the Soviet and Chinese leaders have elaborated and interpreted these extensive documents and their programs.

Confidence in the ultimate Communist victory has long been a fundamental tenet of the Party, based on Marxist reading of history. Successes in past decades have fortified belief in this dogma. Khrushchev's boasts that our grandchildren would live under communism merely dramatize many familiar manifestos:

Whatever efforts imperialism makes, it cannot stop the advance of history. A reliable basis has been provided for the further decisive victories for socialism. The complete triumph of socialism is inevitable.

The Communists may believe that history is working for them and that they cannot fail to triumph, but they believe as firmly in the efficacy of their own efforts to assist that process. The Communist policy for this epoch is "peaceful coexistence." Many in the West and in the newer nations interpret this as a policy of "live and let live." Nothing could be further from the official Communist meaning. Coexistence is the strategy for carrying on the struggle under existing conditions. As stated in a December 1960 Manifesto:

Peaceful coexistence of states does not mean renunciation of the class struggle, as the revisionists claim. The coexistence of states with different social systems is a form of class struggle between socialism and capitalism. In the conditions of peaceful coexistence favorable possibilities are created for developing the class struggle in the capitalist countries and the national-liberation movement of the peoples of the colonial and dependent countries. The successes of the revolutionary class and national-liberation struggle, in turn, help to strengthen peaceful coexistence. . . . Peaceful coexistence of states with different social systems does not mean reconciliation of socialist and bourgeois ideologies. On the contrary, it assumes intensification of the struggle of the working class and of all the Communist Parties for the triumph of socialist ideas. But ideological and political disputes among states must not be resolved by war.

In his report on the 1960 Conference of Communist Parties Khrushchev was equally explicit on this point:

Thus, the policy of peaceful coexistence, as regards its social content, is a form of intense economic, political, and ideological struggle of the proletariat against the aggressive forces of imperialism in the international arena.

The Communist confidence in their eventual triumph is reflected also in an interesting theory of the *status quo*. It is dynamic rather than static. Averell Harriman described the concept after his interview with Mr. Khrushchev:

While he insisted that the Soviet Union only wanted to preserve the status quo, he made it very clear that his idea of the status quo was not the preservation of existing boundaries and balances. An essential element of the world's status today, as Khrushchev sees it, is the Communist march toward world domination. Anything that opposes Communism on the march he considers is altering the status quo and is therefore an act of aggression.[2]

For achieving its goals, Communist strategy has historically had several major elements:

1. Given time, the Soviets are confident that the U.S.S.R. will become the first industrial power in the world.

2. The struggle must be conducted so as to minimize the risks of all-out war. The Bloc is strong enough to deter such war by the West. At the same time, by agitation among all classes, the Communists hope to weaken the cohesion of the Western allies, force the removal of military bases and create dissension and friction.

3. The primary arena for the struggle at this stage has been shifted to the less developed areas. The Communists hope to exploit the instability and pressures in these areas. In the present phase, the main emphasis is on alienating these countries from the West. For this the Communists can take advantage of anti-colonial sentiments. The West, and especially the United States, is depicted as seeking to reimpose shackles on their newly won freedom, while the Communists pose as a bulwark against this danger. Also potent is the appeal of "socialism"

and the Soviet model as the best means for rapid growth. The wide range of discontented groups, from rural farmers and workers to urban labor and the educated elites, offers ready targets for propaganda. Technicians and advisers, economic assistance, student and other exchanges, official visits—all complement this effort. For people who start with an anti-Western bias, and who attribute their backward condition to their earlier colonial status or to Western imperialist or commercial exploitation, this Communist program often has great impact and effect.

Ultimately, as the Communist statements assert, the only acceptable solution to the problems of these countries is communism. And the only route to communism is the dictatorship of the Party. The Party may—in some cases—come to power by peaceful or even parliamentary methods, but once in power it will transform the existing institutions into the instruments of one-party rule.

4. Eventually the United States and other Western nations will be isolated and "encircled," thereby fostering their capitalist decline.

Basic Western Policies

Since World War II, the United States and its allies have gradually developed policies for a changing world and for meeting the Soviet challenge.

They have a general image of the world they desire. In essence, the goal is a peaceful world community which would enable nations of diverse cultures, social structures, and ideals to flourish and progress. Such a community must create and develop institutions and arrangements reflecting the actual interdependence of its

members under modern conditions. It should have a place for regional arrangements to enable more intimate common action.

This vision emerged from the war and inspired the United Nations Charter. But the initial plans for achieving this kind of world were based on ill-founded hopes for Soviet cooperation and undue reliance on the new international agencies for maintaining peace and moving toward the desired order. Nor did those plans take the full measure of the pace of change—economic, political and military—in the postwar period.

Events undermined these premises. Then began the hard process of comprehending new realities (themselves rapidly changing) and devising other policies to cope with them.

These policies have developed and evolved gradually, as the United States and its Western allies grasped the true nature of the world situation only by stages. For some time the Soviet challenge, and especially its military aspect, preempted their attention and effort. And for most of the postwar period, their policies and actions tended to be defensive reactions to Communist threats and initiatives. More recently, there has been growing awareness that the West must reassert and pursue its affirmative purposes, and devote more of its efforts to building its kind of world order—based on peace with diversity, and mutual assistance.

Thus the Western task is now seen to have two components: *the positive,* to develop an acceptable international order; and *the defensive,* to counter and defeat Communist efforts to impose their own pattern on the world.

This process has produced a framework of concepts and policies which largely influence Western actions and relations.

1. Postwar experience with the Soviet Union, especially in Germany and Eastern Europe, has created profound distrust of its expansionist purposes and methods. Soviet domination of the satellites, especially the brutal suppression of Hungary in 1956, serves as a perpetual *caveat* regarding Soviet objectives, as do their actions in the Congo and Laos, and their behavior in the United Nations. Soviet policy since the death of Stalin has been designed in part to erode this distrust.

2. The idea of collective defense has become deeply imbedded in the policy of the United States and its allies. It is generally accepted that no nation, including the United States, can provide for its security alone or be indifferent to aggression against others. Since present Soviet attitudes toward war are credited to deterrence resting partly on joint defense, especially through NATO, continued cooperation for defense is looked on as essential to perpetuate the stand-off.

3. A related purpose of United States policy since the war has been a strong Europe, within a broader Atlantic framework. The lesson of two world wars has been well learned. Hence the consistent support for the European Community as an essential contribution to reconciling France and Germany and uniting the European nations for constructive common purposes. Creation of OECD (Organization for European Cooperation and Development), as a successor to OEEC (Organization for European Economic Cooperation), with the United States as a full member,

will mark a further recognition of the intimate mutual dependence of the Atlantic nations.

4. Concern for the new nations of Asia and Africa and for Latin America has gradually but steadily developed and has been clarified by public reports and debates. Our interest is now seen mainly in terms of the independence and stability of these less-developed countries. Where such nations desired to join the United States for collective defense, the United States has often agreed to do so, and has provided military assistance for local forces in many countries. The issue of ally or neutral, however, has been downgraded. Attention is now focused more on helping these nations achieve political and economic progress.

5. The role and potentialities of international agencies has come to be better understood. While not a substitute for national policies and effort, they have an essential role in identifying common purposes and providing instruments for cooperation in pursuing them. The United Nations and its specialized and associated agencies perform vital functions in helping to contain or moderate conflict (as in the Middle East and the Congo); to assist in development (through the International Bank for Reconstruction and Development, UN Special Fund, and UN technical assistance); and to provide a forum for negotiation and discussion in the Security Council and the General Assembly. Regional institutions also have an important part in gradually fostering and expressing a growing sense of community and forging bonds of common purpose and action.

In general, the Atlantic nations have achieved a remarkable de-

gree of consensus on goals and policies. In doing so they have transcended serious obstacles to agreement and cooperation inherent in their differing historic positions and outlook and special national interests. The Soviets, by threats and bluster, by "coexistence" and "reducing tensions," have sought to erode their cohesion and sow discord. Soviet policy has played upon the persistent hope of Western people for genuine peace, and their tendency to attribute to the Communist leaders their own aspirations. From time to time differences have occurred among the allies regarding negotiation with the Soviet Union, at Summit or lower levels, and on particular issues such as Berlin, German unity, arms control. But such disputes have not been allowed to disrupt the coalition. Indeed, the practice of concerting effort has been steadily expanding into wider fields.

If the above analysis of the environment and purposes of the Soviet Bloc, and of the United States and its allies, is valid, it clarifies the nature of "coexistence" and of East-West relations. Guided by its present concepts, the Soviet Bloc will exploit and manipulate the forces of change to expand Communist control, even if it forgoes large-scale violence. The West will resist and seek to promote the world it envisages. This struggle will go on so long as the Soviet Union is unwilling to accept a world of diversity where each nation is free to develop and maintain the institutions and social structure it finds most suitable and congenial.

What does this conclusion imply regarding negotiations and agreements on outstanding conflicts? In general, neither side will agree to solutions that it believes will improve the relative strength of the other or its prospects of success. The Soviets will generally not assist in prolonging the survival of the "outmoded capitalist" system, and the United States will reject agreements enhancing Soviet capacity for hostile action.

This appraisal does not mean that no agreement is possible. It does define the perspective and the criteria that will be applied by each side in deciding whether or not to agree. The results will depend on the specific issue under discussion. In the case of arms control, it will depend especially on the role of force under modern conditions, and on whether the two sides share any common interests in this regard despite their basic hostility.

THE ROLE OF FORCE IN FOREIGN POLICY

The evolution of military technology has brought about a radical change in the nature of force and its relation to the purposes of foreign policy. In a sense, the evolving weapons systems have taken on a life of their own. Arms and the arms race have in themselves become a source of danger and tensions.

The salient facts about the new weapons are well-known. With nuclear fission and fusion, the power to destroy has been multiplied a million times, compared to TNT. A single hydrogen weapon can release several times the destructive force of all high explosives ever used in the entire history of mankind. The combined nuclear stockpiles of the United States and the U.S.S.R. are said to equal some

sixty billion tons of TNT—or twenty tons for every inhabitant of the globe. And the capacity to deliver this lethal power against targets has developed *pari passu*— first by long-range jets and now by missiles to any spot in the world.

Here our aim is to clarify the effects of this new reality on the role of force in foreign affairs and on the interests of the key powers, especially the United States and Soviet Union. Specifically, how far do the existing and emerging military conditions create possible parallel or common interests in the control of armaments and of their use, despite basic hostility of purpose? For the sake of brevity, the key points can be summarized under a few propositions.

All-Out Nuclear War— A Common Disaster

The evolving military technology has made every nation more vulnerable than ever before. Effective defense in a traditional sense—the ability to keep an enemy from approaching or penetrating or inflicting harm—does not exist. The prospects for achieving it are not necessarily encouraging. A nation having the requisite weapons and delivery means can do enormous damage to any adversary despite his best efforts at defense. By surprise, an attacker today might seriously curtail the striking force of his victim, but he could hardly count on avoiding costly retaliation by the remaining forces. And as retaliatory forces become more secure, the mutual damage will be more equalized. Increasingly, both defender and attacker would suffer unprecedented destruction from all-out nuclear war. Experts may dispute whether the society could survive

the resulting devastation. Certainly the social order would not be recognizable.

One consequence has been to shift primary emphasis to deterrence. When defense is so limited, the best hope is to inhibit attack by enhancing the fear of its costs. This has been the basis of the United States strategy for many years. And the Soviets have explicitly made it theirs, as their nuclear capability has grown. Various Party statements constantly stress the nuclear danger:

Monstrous means of mass annihilation and destruction have been developed which, if used in a new war, can cause unheard-of destruction to entire countries and reduce key centers of world industry and culture to ruins. Such a war would bring death and suffering to hundreds of millions of people, among them people in countries not involved in it. Imperialism spells grave danger to the whole of mankind.

The last sentence harks back to the Marxist doctrine that the "imperialist powers" will be forced to all-out war by the contradictions of capitalism.

Since their Twentieth Party Congress, however, the Soviets have modified this dogma that wars are inevitable while capitalism exists, on the ground that the Communist states are now strong enough to deter "imperialist" wars. While the Chinese seem to have doubts on this point, the Party statement of 1960 embodied the Soviet view. It asserts that the prevention of global nuclear war, which is the "most burning and vital problem for mankind," can be achieved if the Communists remain strong enough to deter the "imperialist" states from initiating it.

The time is near when each side will have great and relatively secure nuclear striking forces and little capacity to defend its cities or territory. Under these conditions the striking force has little value for either side except to offset or cancel that of the other. Neither can afford to use it or seriously to threaten its use except in defense of the most vital interests. That does not mean that it serves to safeguard only the territory of the possessor. Other areas (like Europe in the case of the United States) are so vital that the nuclear umbrella could protect against their conquest. But the all-out strategic force loses much or all of its value as an instrument of policy for wider purposes. Consequently, both sides could have a common interest in trying to keep the burden of such forces to a minimum, and to reduce the risks inherent in the existence of these forces.

Mutual Deterrence— Serious Risks of Instability

The deterrent system has its own special risks. Airplanes on bases and "soft," fixed missiles are both vulnerable to surprise attack. This has two consequences tending to undermine stability. A potential aggressor might be tempted to try to knock out the retaliatory means of his victim in the hope of keeping the damage to himself within bearable limits. For the same reason a potential victim must always be prepared to act very quickly when faced with an apparent threat of attack. And if a country thinks that it is about to be attacked, the vulnerability of its own forces might lead it to attempt a pre-emptive strike in order to disarm the suspected aggressor. Inherently such a system entails grave risks of accident, miscalculation or misjudgment, which could lead to war, desired by neither side.

This situation has led to major efforts to develop less vulnerable systems of delivery. With airplanes, the stress was on developing warning and air defense. In the missile era, the same approach to defense might be supported by an anti-missile missile, if it should prove feasible. Meanwhile, the main emphasis has shifted to the "hardening," concealing, or making more mobile the missiles themselves. A "hardened" missile requires more attacking missiles of a given accuracy to be sure of destroying it. Mobility or concealment makes it difficult, even impossible, to find the target. In either case an attacker would have little chance of knocking out all or most of the defender's weapons and would therefore run serious risks of retaliatory damage from those remaining. Moreover, with his missiles less vulnerable the defender would not have to react so fast. He would have more time to appraise the situation to make sure that he was in fact under attack. Mobile and scattered missiles on both sides may affect stability in two ways: being less vulnerable, they will tend to make the deterrent more stable; but added problems of command and control may make it harder to keep a central hand on their possible use or misuse.

Even if the stand-off became stable, neither side can assume that it will remain stable. The United States and the Soviet Union are now engaged in a frantic effort to improve weapons and to develop new ones. The arms race is in large part a research race. Each will almost surely continue to try to invent other weapons to give it an advantage, even if it has no aggressive intent. It must do so lest a breakthrough by its opponent destroy the balance and tempt it to try to use its advantage for blackmail or attack. Consequently, even if stability were achieved, research can well undermine it.

There is another potential source of instability. In time, it must be expected, the number of nuclear powers will increase. Britain, France, China and a half dozen others have nuclear weapons. In the absence of restraints, other nations seem likely to follow. There are some differences as to the effects of such an increase. Much turns on the powers involved. But in general it seems likely that the increase will cause more instability.

Limited Force— Clouded by Uncertainty

The effects of nuclear balance on more limited use of force are harder to analyze. Some argue that a stand-off on all-out war may open the way for Communist aggression at lower levels. Others conclude that the risks of local war mushrooming into larger conflicts will dampen this tendency. The situation of the two sides is not exactly parallel, and even the Soviets and Chinese appear to differ. In his report on the Moscow Conference (January 1961), Khrushchev dealt at length with this issue. It is necessary, he said, to distinguish between "world wars, local wars, liberation wars, and popular uprisings . . . to work out the correct tactics" regarding them.

After discussing the need to prevent all-out war, he turned to local war:

A word or two about local wars. A lot is being said nowadays in the imperialist camp about local wars, and they are even making small-caliber atomic weapons for use in such wars; a special theory of local wars has been concocted. Is this fortuitous? Of course not. Certain imperialist circles, fearing that world war might end in the complete collapse of capitalism, are putting their money on unleashing local wars.

There have been local wars and they may occur again in the future, but opportunities for imperialists to unleash these wars too are becoming fewer and fewer. A small imperialist war, regardless of which imperialist begins it, may grow into a world thermonuclear rocket war; we must therefore combat both world wars and local wars.

While the "stark warning" to Britain and France had stopped the Suez local war, he continued, such wars may not be excluded in the future and can be averted only if all peoples, Communists and others, unite to prevent such "aggressive wars."

National liberation wars—such as those in Vietnam, Algeria, and Cuba—are entirely different. These are uprisings against colonial or imperialist oppressors.

Can such wars flare up in the future? They can. Can there be such uprisings? There can. But these are wars which are national uprisings. In other words, can conditions be created where a people will lose their patience and rise in arms? They can. What is the attitude of the Marxists toward such uprisings? A most positive

one. These uprisings must not be identified with wars among states, with local wars, since in these uprisings the people are fighting for implementation of their right for self-determination, for independent social and national development. These are uprisings against rotten reactionary regimes, against the colonizers. The Communists fully support such just wars, and march in the front rank with the peoples waging liberation struggles.

Soviet actions in Laos and in the Congo in the 1960s carried out this policy of fostering Communist takeover by material and other support for local Party cadres.

The Soviet challenge may take other forms, as in West Berlin, where, Khrushchev said, the positions of the three Western powers "have turned out to be particularly vulnerable. There, it is essential to continue, step by step . . . to compel them to take the actual position into account. If they are stubborn, we will adopt decisive measures." By concluding a peace treaty with the GDR, we will "do away with the occupational regime in West Berlin, and, thus, eradicate this splinter from the heart of Europe."

In regard to limited force, the United States and its allies face some difficult problems. Even if the Soviets may have concluded that direct limited aggression entails undue risks of mushrooming, it is by no means clear that the Chinese share this view. In the Taiwan Straits or Southeast Asia, they may at some point threaten or undertake aggressive local action. Moreover, Soviet actions in some vulnerable situations, like Berlin, may pose the necessity of Western resort to limited force to protect

vital interests. And so-called popular uprisings against non-Communist independent governments can well be forms of indirect Communist aggression, which might require intervention to prevent minority take-over.

The political context will severely circumscribe the use of force in the future. It is likely to be feasible, whatever the justification, only if it is applied quickly, neatly and decisively. Any protraction of conflict produces disaffection at home and intense pressures from other countries. In effect, the world now places a premium on the *fait accompli*. If a takeover can be carried out before others can act, it is not very likely to be undone: to undo it would entail intervention, and endanger peace while the whole world watched. These restraints operate far more effectively on the democratic nations than on the Sino-Soviet bloc, where actions can be quicker and are less affected by outside or domestic opinion.

Extent of Common Interests

As the foregoing discussion indicates, there are potential areas of common or parallel interests in the military field between the United States and the Soviet Union.

1. Those interests are most apparent in regard to the most extreme forms of military force. Both sides might readily recognize a mutuality of interest in measures which reduced the danger of war by accident or miscalculation, or the extent of damage if such war occurred.

2. How far they could go in finding common ground regarding the control of the less extreme

kinds of force is much harder to appraise, given the persistent and pervasive conflict in basic purposes. They appear at least to have a common interest in not having local war mushroom into all-out conflict, and possibly in reducing the burden of "limited" forces.

3. Joint measures to control the arms race itself would require both sides to conclude that all-out force cannot be developed into a profitable political instrument. Conceivably, either side might hope to achieve a technical breakthrough that would destroy the "stalemate," and might prefer to follow that route so that force or threats could be used as an instrument for coercion or blackmail. That course, however, entails the risks and the costs of an unrestricted arms race. Given its dangers, both sides might conclude that they would be better off by seeking to stabilize the deterrent system and to reduce its burdens.

In assessing their interests in arms control, both sides must weigh costs and benefits in political as well as military terms. In particular, the Soviets would have to conclude that the existing and emerging situation entails risks that materially outweigh the benefits which accrue from its unrestricted exploitation. And those advantages are not insubstantial. Khrushchev was able to frighten exposed allies of the United States and hesitant neutrals by the ancient device of sword rattling, in the form of missiles. These benefits, as well as others within the bloc, accrue to the Soviets by the very existence of these weapons, not from their use. Whether they will be prepared to pay for arms control the price of forgoing these advantages as well as accepting the burdens involved in arms control is far from clear.

The West, having no aggressive designs, needs weapons only for defensive purposes. Its arms, in large part, are a necessary response to those of the Communists. In general, the West should be able to agree to any arms controls that do not weaken its capacity to defend itself and the non-Communist world. If the Communists should ever be prepared to give up the arms that threaten force, the West, for its part, could afford to do likewise; legitimate regimes endangered by Communist-managed subversion could require support but only by limited or special forms of force. For the continuing struggle with communism by political and economic means, major arms have little relevance.

ARMS CONTROL BETWEEN HOSTILE NATIONS

The existence of common interests in arms control does not assure that the United States and Soviet Union will be able to cooperate in pursuing them. Practical ways for working together will not be easy to devise. Any system of arms control for the foreseeable future will have to operate within the general framework of their antagonism in basic purposes. Their political hostility, while not excluding common interests, does seriously restrict the kinds of measures on which the two sides can agree to cooperate.

The reasons are not far to seek. Neither side will be willing to rely on the good faith of the other. Hard experience has taught the West that the Communists consider any means justified in the pursuit of their goals. Treaties will not bind them unless their interests so dictate. Hence the non-Communist states will not depend on promises alone. The Communists also distrust the non-Communist world, and assert that "the imperialists" would destroy them, if they were able. Mutual distrust is the concomitant of deep-seated antagonism.

This condition imposes severe limits on what measures can be undertaken and how they can be applied. To be adopted, and to remain effective, an arms control system will have to satisfy each party at each stage that, on balance, compliance with its provisions serves its interests better than evasion or disruption of the system. More specifically, each must conclude: (1) that its security and other interests will be advanced if all carry out the measures as planned; (2) that the risks and costs of violations outweigh their potential advantages; and (3) that possible violations by others will not unduly jeopardize its security.

Limits on Enforcement

Hostility and distrust create roadblocks to schemes for total disarmament. A disarmed world, governed by law, would require some international agency with authority to settle disputes, to enforce compliance with its decrees and to ensure against the use of force to violate them. To be effective this agency would have to be stronger than any of the nation-states within the system, or any likely combination of them. Only in this way could it protect the states that had disarmed from violations by others. Its power would have to be great enough to coerce any violator disregarding its obligations or seeking to impose its own will on other states.

Obviously no such institution now exists. Nor could it be created under existing political conditions. Neither the Soviet Union nor the United States would be prepared to confer on such an agency power to coerce them to conform to its decrees. Each of them would naturally fear that the other might dominate the enforcing agency and use it for its own purposes. Such an institution would be feasible only in a world inhabited by states essentially satisfied with the existing order. Even then they would have to be convinced that the international agency would confine itself to carrying out the common purposes and would not be utilized to modify the international order in ways that they would find unacceptable or threatening. There seems little prospect of achieving this basic condition within the foreseeable future. Even if Soviet fervor should decline in the coming years, that does not seem likely in the case of China. Moreover, the many new states show no signs of accepting that kind of stability. Doubtless a world of turmoil and danger is most in need of some method of maintaining law and order. But such a world is least well suited, or least able, to create effective institutions for its maintenance. Whatever its merits for the long run, this is not a feasible solution for our present or emerging predicament.

Dependence on Self-Help

If that is true, then the parties to any arms control will have to depend ultimately on self-help—on their own strength and that of their allies—to protect themselves against any potential violator.

Complying parties could well muster sanctions adequate to deter potential violators, or to induce compliance. Initially they might impose pressures by suspending their own observance of restrictions roughly equivalent to the provisions violated. The threat of ultimate breakdown of the agreement would face the violator with a difficult choice. Moreover, an attempted evasion could have the effect of creating a stronger coalition against the violator than existed beforehand. It could provoke crash programs for rearming, such as were prompted by Korea. The conviction that the violator planned large-scale aggression against them might lead other parties to take preventive action. All of these risks would presumably operate to restrain a violator from major evasions unless he expected to gain overwhelming superiority that could be utilized for some political advantage.

The two sides would not, however, be entirely on a par regarding sanctions. Democratic governments might face special problems in taking effective action, particularly where evidence of a violation was complex, ambiguous or based on clandestine sources. In such a case, the democracies might find it hard to dramatize the violation to public opinion so as to get adequate support for proper counter-measures. Governments that had achieved narrow electoral victories or had defended the arms control agreement as safe and workable might be unwilling to undertake this task.[3]

Balanced Impact

Given hostility and dependence on self-help, no state will accept or carry out any measures for arms control that it believes will materially affect its relative ability to protect itself. Any reductions or restrictions will have to be so phased as not to impair the ability of each party to protect its interests by self-help should an evasion occur at any stage. In short, an arms control system must be designed not to upset the strategic balance between the parties while it is being put into effect or when it becomes fully effective.

This necessity for balance imposes serious obstacles in negotiating any arms control measures. It is not easy at best to appraise how specific restrictions or other changes will affect the absolute and relative capability of the various participants. The military forces of any nation combine weapons and forces in various ways to produce a total capability. Consequently, any partial restraint on some type of weapon or force is likely to have a different impact on one nation than on another. The equating of this impact is not the same as equating numbers of weapons. Absence of experience with new weapons has greatly enhanced the difficulty and complexity of making such judgments. The effect of nuclear weapons, missiles, and other new weapons on capabilities for defense and offense is at best uncertain. In addition, weapons technology is changing so fast that the impact of future developments is even harder to assess.

The elements of uncertainty and of rapid change make it much harder to equate the various types of weapons or to judge how any specific limitation would affect the several sides. Military experts on opposing sides tend always to be cautious. They are likely to overestimate how much any proposed limitation will injure the capability of their state; they are likely to appraise its effect on the potential enemy in much lower terms.

If agreement is reached, the progress of technology may change the actual impact of the arrangement from what was anticipated and alter the costs and gains to each side. Restraints imposed in one field or on one type of weapon will probably induce the various parties to focus research on fields not so restricted and to develop weapons and strategies that take the greatest advantage of the new conditions. Even if the political leaders are really committed to stabilizing the military balance, their military experts are virtually compelled to seek ways of upsetting it. They must assume that the research staffs of other parties will be engaged in similar efforts. To maintain the balance they must keep pace with the improvements or innovations that may be discovered and applied by other participants. This factor introduces a built-in element of instability or disruption into the system. Certainly one aim of any arms control measures should be to try to mitigate this "race."

Role of Inspection

The fact of hostility, then, creates the necessity for balance in arms control and enhances the difficulty in attaining it. Likewise, this distrust produces both the need for inspection and obstacles to its operation.

The essential function of inspection is to reinforce the self-interest of the parties in the continued operation of the arms control system. It does this in two ways. On the one hand, it aims to make evasion unattractive by confronting the potential violator with risks of detection and the dangers of counter-measures and other sanctions that will outweigh the value of a violation for him. Conversely, inspection can enhance the confidence of each complying member in the arms control system so as to make him desire not to jeopardize its continuance. Thus the inspection system can make it more attractive to the parties in terms of their own self-interests to maintain the system and its safeguards rather than break it up by resorting to evasion or violence.

The inspection system cannot, however, guarantee against evasion. It will never be foolproof. No system could be devised that would create absolute certainty that every violation or evasion could be detected at once. Indeed any attempt at that level of certainty would almost surely require a degree of inspection that would be wholly unacceptable to either the Soviet Union or the United States.

But the proper test of an inspection system is not absolute certainty of detection. The potential evader will appraise how much he will gain from his violation against the risks and costs of being caught. He will hardly assume those risks merely for the pleasure of violating the agreement. To be deterred, he need not think he is certain to be caught. It is enough if he is convinced that the dangers of discovery are too high to make the effort at evasion worthwhile.

In his appraisal of a possible violation, one crucial question is whether it would offer him a real superiority if he succeeds. What are the risks of being detected before his violation would be significant in changing the strategic balance? The chances of his being caught would be substantially greater, for example, if evasion must take place over a long period or on a very wide scale before it will materially improve his relative position. Naturally that will turn partly on how far the other members have reduced their capability: if reductions have been carried very far, then even moderate evasions will have much more value for the violator.

The hostility and distrust that make inspection essential also make it more difficult to develop and apply. The costs and value of inspection differ for the two sides. The open society of the United States offers the Soviet Union a vast amount of data on the military programs of the United States through overt means. United States press reports, hearings of Congress, and other published material make the Soviet Union much less dependent on inspection. Furthermore our kind of government would find it far harder, if not impossible, to undertake secret evasions even if it wished to do so. On the other hand, the United States lacks similar information regarding the Soviet military programs and capability, and would have to rely more on inspection—which in the U.S.S.R. would be difficult.

For similar reasons the Soviets are likely to feel that the burden of inspection bears unfairly on them. They consider their military secrecy an important asset, and will view its loss as a major sacrifice. In their evaluation, inspection of United States capability is not likely to seem an equal sacrifice on our part. Thus in appraising the value and the costs of an inspection system, the criteria of the United States and the U.S.S.R. are likely to diverge substantially. In Soviet eyes reciprocity will favor us. They are likely to feel that the United States should give up some further military advantage in return for ending their military secrecy through inspection.

Violations and Sanctions

Any effort to cooperate on arms control within a context of hostility also poses certain special problems that are difficult to handle by explicit terms in formal agreements. For example:

1. *Procedure for Establishing Violations*—A tribunal to decide on violations may be desirable, but may not be an adequate solution. The evidence may not establish the evasion, but still leave other parties uneasy, especially where distrust is so profound.

2. *Sanctions for Violation*—To prescribe the sanctions for possible violations is not feasible. Since the purpose would be to redress any resulting imbalance and to coerce compliance, effective remedies will depend on the circumstances of the violator and of the complying parties. Moreover, since self-help will be the principal sanction, the attitude of the parties themselves will be crucial. In theory, a tribunal could be given discretion to fix appropriate sanctions, but the parties will hardly agree to this in practice where their security may be at stake.

3. *Adjustment to Change*—As has been said, changing technology or other factors may skew the impact of the controls from what was foreseen. Some means for adjusting the terms to fit the new conditions is essential to keep the system viable. Again, it is hard to envisage any formal procedure for

this purpose that would be workable.

These and similar factors suggest that an open-ended scheme may be the most practical approach. The right to withdraw without cause, perhaps after a modest notice, would offer one means for coping with many of these complex issues. Such an approach would avoid a hopeless effort to predict conditions and relations that cannot be anticipated. It would stress the basic facts that the viability of any system rests on its constant appeal to the self-interest of the parties, and its sanctions on their capacity for self-help. The threat to withdraw could be used as an effective lever to require revision of the control terms to adapt to new conditions.

The early stages of arms control seem likely to impose the greatest strains on the system. Suspicion among the parties will be high. The inspectorate, newly organized, will need time to learn its tasks and to gain experience as well as the confidence of the parties. The novelty of inspection will create frictions; uncertainty as to its reliability will create doubts. Moreover, when the limitations are modest, inspection is likely to seem to interfere unduly in the life and affairs of the members. The hope would be that the desire of the parties to make the agreement work will help it survive.

ARMS CONTROL AND OTHER UNITED STATES OBJECTIVES

The pursuit of arms control, and its operation if attained, would clearly affect the conduct of other aspects of United States foreign

policy in various ways—some negative, some positive. Arms control would not, of course, impinge on all aspects of policy to the same degree. Inevitably its impact would be greatest on policies that concern directly the contest with the Sino-Soviet bloc. This defensive task, while crucial, is only half the job of the United States and its allies. Their affirmative role in constructing and molding an emerging order is as important. Arms control may well have important consequences for that affirmative role as well. But those consequences are indirect and difficult to trace with confidence. Hence, what follows is not a balanced treatment of the impact of arms control on the full spectrum of United States purposes, but only its more important interactions with the East-West conflict.

Relaxing of Effort

An arms control agreement under current conditions would be negotiated and carried out within the context of continuing conflict and struggle. The cold war would likely continue by all means except the use of major war—political, economic, psychological and ideological. Even if arms control served to reinforce the restraint on war, the United States and its allies would still face the urgent necessity of carrying on the struggle against Communist encroachment by all other means.

Indeed, the reliability of any arms control system itself would depend on maintaining the deterrent within the limits of the agreement. Thus it will require continuing cooperation of allies for their military security and defense. The arms control agreement will not be a substitute for adequate military forces. It will depend on the maintenance of a proper balance of military capability on both sides. Collective defense would still be required in order to maintain the deterrent against violation of the agreement, and against the use of force, even if the arms control system made this defense feasible at lower levels.

For democratic societies this situation would pose serious dilemmas. Many people would be inclined to hail the arms control agreement as a sign that the cold war had ended and that "live and let live" had become the policy of the Soviet bloc. This attitude, if it became widespread, could lead to reducing the effort by the Western countries in various parts of the world. It could create pressures to reduce military spending below the restraints imposed by the agreement.

The fact that arms control entails cooperation with the potential enemy could create obstacles to the continued vitality of the alliances. It could easily mislead public opinion in the democracies into thinking that alliances were no longer required or that military efforts could be relaxed. If this did occur, it might breed difficulties and frictions and impair or undermine the alliances.

If, by the pressures resulting from arms control, the United States or its allies should be led to reduce their military effort unduly, the result could be catastrophic. The imbalance could produce a situation that might tempt the Soviets again to resort to the use of force and to threats to coerce their opponents or to divide them by friction and doubts.

Moreover, the conduct of the struggle by nonmilitary means will continue to demand very substantial resources. If the making of an arms control agreement should be interpreted by public opinion as justifying relaxation, then the United States and its allies would be unable to carry on the types of economic and political policy necessary to combat the expansionism of the Sino-Soviet bloc.

It would, of course, be the responsibility of Western leaders to clarify the real nature of the situation and its implications. And no doubt it could be done. But it would be unwise not to recognize the danger and the necessity to combat it courageously in the face of charges (at home and abroad) of "reviving" the cold war.

Allied Differences About Specific Controls

Some types of arms control might create frictions within the Western alliances or impair their political or moral basis.

For example, measures for preventing the spread of nuclear weapons or the capacity to produce them could be viewed by allies as cooperation between the Soviet Union and the United States to restrain *their* freedom of action.

Again, some forms of disengagement or plans for disarmed zones imply a willingness to put certain members of the alliance (e.g., Germany) into a special category. Even entertaining such proposals can have serious divisive effects on the alliance even though no agreement occurs or is even thought possible.

Similar problems will arise regarding China. Hardly any arms control system could long endure if China were not covered both by the restrictions and inspection. Otherwise the field for secret eva-

sions would be wide open. Yet inclusion of China will inevitably require revision in current policies of the United States and of certain of its allies. There is no need here to elaborate on the difficulties involved or their possible repercussions.

Faced with these or other arms control measures, some allies are likely to feel that the United States had disregarded their interests or ceased to be fully dependable. Such attitudes would foster concern lest the Soviet Union and the United States might at some stage reach agreements which sacrificed wider interests of our allies. If these views spread, they might encourage some governments to pursue a more independent course or even to seek directly to reach accommodation with the Soviet Union.

It must be assumed that the Soviet Union and Communist China would exploit these various possibilities for tension and division to the fullest extent. It must be stressed again that the existence of an agreement would *not* mean the end of efforts to expand the area of Communist control or to divide and weaken their opponents.

Political Interest in Arms Control

On the other hand, failure to pursue arms control and to make serious efforts to achieve it could have damaging effects, especially in relations with allies and with the less-developed countries. In allied countries, and in the United States as well, people are deeply concerned about the dangers of nuclear war. The governments in these countries must convince their citizens that they are doing everything feasible to avoid unnecessary risks of annihilation. If they fail, they are not likely to marshal support for other essential measures, including military forces. The neutrals, who are relatively weak, back strenuous efforts to bring about reductions in military strength and especially to bring nuclear weapons under control. They are bound to continue to feel exposed and endangered by the possibility of rash action by the powers that have such weapons.

Hence, aside from its direct interest in arms control, the United States must convince both allies and neutrals of the seriousness of that interest and of its pursuit of feasible measures for achieving it. Otherwise it will impair its influence and capability for many other kinds of action and cooperation essential to its foreign policy.

"Opening Up" the Communist Bloc

One of the hopes of Western policy has been that the passage of time would "mellow" the Soviet rulers and weaken their ideological fervor for expanding Communist control. Doubtless many have been unduly optimistic about how rapidly this evolution would take place, and too ready to find signs of its occurrence. Social change and education may well work their way in the longer run. But the reforms since the death of Stalin have, generally, strengthened the position of the Party within the Soviet Union. Their internal success has provided them with far greater resources and influence for external activities. And so far nothing has dimmed their interest in Communist expansion. Indeed recent years have often seen a marked increase in the scope, intensity and variety of Soviet efforts

to shape the outside world. In the meantime, China has begun to play a much greater role in this sphere, and its leaders display even more doctrinaire commitments to the spread of communism.

Erosion of that fervor must remain an ultimate aim or aspiration of Western policy. But how to pursue it? All the measures intended to frustrate expansion may contribute indirectly to that objective. Yet the West can do relatively little to advance it more directly.

Among the feasible actions are those designed to expose Soviet society, its leaders, and intellectuals, to the outside world—to open up the Soviet Union. The expectation is that such exposure may show the unreality or invalidity of some of the premises of expansionism and weaken its hold. Arms control may contribute modestly to this endeavor. Its adoption would undermine to some degree the picture of the "imperialists" eager to wage aggressive war, which is a constant theme of Soviet propaganda. Moreover, the inspection system could expand slightly the regular contacts of Russians with outsiders and penetrate somewhat the curtain of secrecy. How much impact it would have, and how rapidly is extremely difficult to foresee, especially if the Soviet rulers undertake to minimize it.

Building for International Order

The creation of a viable international order will require stronger and more effective instruments for common action. The new birth of nationalism may obscure the growing interdependence but cannot affect its reality.

One aim of United States and Western policy must be to foster

the development of and strengthen suitable agencies to respond to this need. Under "cold war" conditions, steps within the non-Communist world promise to be most fruitful. Arms control, however, is one area where joint action with the Communists may be feasible on the basis of mutual interests even while the underlying hostility persists. Such limited measures could at least lay a foundation for more extensive cooperation if and when that hostility should moderate. Even modest initial agencies could provide valuable experience with problems and techniques of international regulation, which might have more general use should the political climate change radically. In addition, the operation of agencies for international cooperation, if successful, might in the long run contribute to altering the political climate. This would not require the ending of conflicts of interest or disputes. It would mean rather that all states were prepared to accept the general structure of world order and to settle disputes and conflicts within that framework.

CONCLUSION

This article has explored the relation between political tension and hostility and cooperation for arms control under current conditions. Its conclusion is that the underlying hostility does not exclude measures for arms control that would reflect existing mutual interests in avoiding unintended war or futile arms burdens or dangerous arms competition. Yet any such measures will have to be designed for adoption and operation within a framework of continuing struggle and conflict among the participants.

If the analysis is valid, what then are the prospects for arms control? Certainly they fall short of early total or general disarmament. To achieve that would require international enforcement by an agency with adequate authority to coerce and constrain any potential violator. The political context now and in prospect does not appear to offer any realistic basis for the creation of such an institution. It could be established only within a new context, involving basic changes in world politics.

Within these limits, however, there appears room for substantial arms control if the parties wish to pursue it. Certainly significant steps could be taken to stabilize the deterrent and even to make modest initial reductions in nuclear-missile capabilities. As the inspectorate gained experience and earned the confidence of the participants, there should be opportunities for further measures. If an arms control system were operating with effective inspection, it might be possible to reduce conventional forces and to cut defense expenditures.

These measures would not mean that force had been banished. It could mean that the risk of all-out war had been materially reduced and that even large-scale conventional war was much less likely. Such crises or uses of force as did occur might have much better prospect of being kept within bounds. These conditions, while short of an assured peaceful world, are certainly goals well worth striving for. They would be worthwhile in themselves, and would provide a foundation for further progress, if and when the political environment became more propitious. ■

Notes

1. H. G. Wells, who was an observer at the conference, remarked at the time: "At any rate I do not see how the disarmament proposals of Mr. Secretary Hughes can possibly be accepted without a Pacific settlement, nor how that settlement can be sustained except by some sort of alliance, meeting periodically in conference to apply or adapt the settlement to such particular issues as may arise. If America is not prepared to go as far as that, then I do not understand the enthusiasm of America for the Washington conference. I do not understand the mentality that can contemplate world disarmament without at least that much provision for the prevention of future conflict." H. G. Wells, *Washington and the Riddle of Peace,* New York, Macmillan, 1922, p. 193.

2. Averell Harriman, *Peace with Russia?,* New York, Simon & Schuster, 1959, p. 167.

3. For discussion, see Fred C. Iklé, "After Detection—What?" *Foreign Affairs,* Vol. 39, (January, 1961), pp. 208–20.

Arms Control and Human Rights

By Kenneth L. Adelman

It's great to be back in my home town and to have this opportunity to address the Chicago Bar Association. One thing I learned growing up in this city is that it is a wonderful town for jokes. It's a big melting pot of a city with a great sense of humor. So I thought I'd start out with a little story that some of you may not have heard, since this one actually comes from the Soviet Union. It is a joke that was told a few years ago by one of the Soviet negotiators by the name of Yuli Kvitsinsky to our negotiators in Geneva.

The story goes this way: A man visits the city of Leningrad and goes to the zoo, where he sees a marvelous sight. There in the lion's cage is the lion sitting side by side with a lamb. Well, this fellow is just astonished, and he hurries on his way, feeling happy and uplifted.

The next day he sees the same thing, so he decides to ask the zookeeper, "You know, that display in the lion's cage is the most marvelous thing I have ever seen. How do you ever train the lion to do it?"

The zookeeper answers, "We don't train him—we just give him a different lamb every day."

Kenneth L. Adelman was director of the U.S. Arms Control and Disarmament Agency.

Source: From an address before the Chicago Bar Association in Chicago, Illinois, on January 22, 1987. Reprinted in *World Affairs,* Vol. 149, No. 3 (Winter 1986–87), pp. 157–162.

Now that's a peculiar story, but it's not a bad way of approaching the serious subject that I'm here to talk with you about today—arms control and human freedom. The moral of this story is clear: when it comes to assessing what is really going on in the Soviet system, things are not often exactly what they seem.

In the past few months we have seen an extraordinary effort on the part of the Soviet Union to persuade people in the West that its human rights situation is changing. A few weeks ago, Andrei Sakharov, the Nobel prize Soviet physicist, was allowed to return to Moscow after being forced to remain in internal exile for seven years in the closed city of Gorky, as the price for speaking his conscience. Sakharov was even permitted to engage in a number of interviews with Western newspapers and Western television. A tiny number of other dissidents have been released. Yuri Orlov and Natan (Anatoly) Shcharansky—both long-time victims of the regime—are now in the West as a result of exchanges. There are a handful of others, Jews or dissidents, less well known, who have been allowed to leave.

In addition, there has been great fanfare about a new *glasnost,* or openness, talked about both in Gorbachev's speeches and in the Soviet press—which is to say in the totally government controlled and censored propaganda publications that pass for "newspapers" and "magazines" in the Soviet Union. When riots occurred recently in the city of Alma Ata in Kazakhstan, the fact was actually noted in these state-owned publications. Normally, of course, we would not hear about such an event from

official Soviet sources, just as the Soviets refused to say anything about their disaster at Chernobyl until it was known in the West. Soviet commentators were quick to point out, especially in Soviet publications meant for Western consumption, that this unusual magnanimity on the part of the Soviet government in revealing the fact of the Alma Ata riots was also a sign of the new "openness."

Today I want to pose three questions. First, is there real change in the Soviet Union—or is it all smoke and mirrors? Second, why should we make such a fuss over human rights in the Soviet Union? And, finally, what is the connection between human rights and arms control?

First, the question of whether what we see in the Soviet Union is genuine change. There is a real eagerness among Americans to believe that the Soviet Union is changing or on the verge of a great change. This eagerness is nothing new; it has been part of the American outlook for many years. Recently, Charles Burton Marshall, a former policy adviser to Dean Acheson who was in the State Department back in Harry Truman's time, came up with an interesting figure. He noted that U.S. officials or commentators had predicted a turning point for the better in U.S.-Soviet relations on fifty-two separate occasions since 1933. That is really an astonishing number—nearly one turning point a year. Needless to say, if only a tiny fraction of those supposed turning points had been authentic or enduring, we'd be in very different circumstances from those we are in today. There is a lot of wishful thinking in the United States about possible change in the Soviet

Union, maybe because we are such a hopeful people.

Of course, when it comes to human rights, we sincerely hope that conditions in the Soviet Union will improve. Obviously we rejoice when anyone unjustly imprisoned or exiled—like Dr. Sakharov or Yuri Orlov or Anatoly Shcharansky —is released. Any time human suffering is ended, it is good. But we have to be very careful, in the Soviet context, when we think we see lions lying down beside lambs.

Let's look at the real situation there. What we have seen thus far is the release of a few of the most famous dissidents—individuals who have been the subject of intense publicity in the West and continual Western pressure on the Soviet regime. For releasing these few conspicuous individuals, the Soviet regime has received a lot of good publicity. However, this is hardly the tip of the iceberg. Literally thousands of such prisoners remain. Right now, according to our best estimates, there are between 4,000 and 10,000 prisoners of conscience—in simple words, political prisoners—in the Soviet Union. The names of only about 900 of these are known in the West. The rest suffer in anonymity, their plight hidden from world opinion. Forgotten people in the cold.

About one-third of the 4,000 to 10,000 prisoners are being persecuted for their religious practices or convictions. A number of these have been confined to psychiatric hospitals, where they are subject to torture by the administration of painful drugs. For the nameless thousands in the forced labor camps and the prisons, beatings, inadequate food, clothing, and shelter, heavy manual labor, unsatisfactory medical care, isolation, extended interrogation, and threats against their families are part and parcel of their existence.

We must be clear about what is at stake here: in the Soviet Union, you don't even have the option of leaving. The Soviet Union is a country in which even application for permission to emigrate is likely to bring the full weight of the state security apparatus down upon you and your family. People cannot vote with their feet there, and just leave. Repression is a sad fact of life in the twentieth century, as it has been in past centuries. But no secret police in the world can compete in power, ruthlessness, and thoroughness with the Soviet KGB. Little wonder that Anatoly Shcharansky calls the Soviet regime, "the most ruthless and despotic in the world today."

For the mass of these Soviet victims of repression, conditions have not been improving. According to Shcharansky, about *half* of the Jews imprisoned either for practicing their religion or stating their desire to emigrate to Israel were imprisoned in the year since Gorbachev came to office. There are now some 400,000 Jews who are being denied the right to emigrate. Yuri Orlov, a member of the Moscow Helsinki Watch group, was released from prison to the West; but Shcharansky reminds us that more than forty other members of the now-disbanded Helsinki Watch group remain in prison. Moreover, as Shcharansky writes, "Under the 'enlightened' and 'progressive' leadership of Mikhail Gorbachev, some of them got new, additional sentences and conditions for the others have become much worse."

So the question arises: why the few releases? There may be a number of reasons, but clearly one reason is that the Soviets increasingly understand that improving their image on human rights may be necessary to gain concessions from the West in arms control. Improving their image, that is—not the underlying reality. As Shcharansky wrote recently in *The Wall Street Journal*:

The Soviet leadership is far from oblivious to the need for creating an atmosphere of good will as a condition for progress toward disarmament. These efforts to manufacture favorable public opinion in the West are based on public-relations gimmickry designed to mask the disregard for human rights that festers on the "human face" of the Gorbachev dictatorship.

The intent of the regime is to suggest that it somehow shares Western values—that this ruthless and atavistic dictatorship is actually sophisticated, Western in its orientation, "progressive," and so forth.

This propaganda effort has been underway for a long time. You may remember the brief reign of Yuri Andropov as General Secretary of the USSR. Before Andropov rose to the top position in the Communist party, he was head of the KGB. It was under Andropov that the KGB began to use confinement to psychiatric hospitals as a method of torturing dissidents. That was Yuri Andropov's contribution to the advancement of enlightenment, progress, and human rights. Yet when Yuri Andropov came to power, there were stories in American newspapers suggesting that Andropov was a closet Westerner, who loved scotch and

jazz, read Jacqueline Suzanne novels, and—if you can believe this—had private conversations with Soviet dissidents in his flat at night. If Western reporters were prepared to write such things about Andropov—the head of the KGB—you can imagine what else Soviet propaganda experts might expect Westerners to swallow.

So for a while now, we have seen a new Soviet propaganda drive on the question of human rights.

The Soviets were also forced to respond in recent years to President Reagan's approach to negotiations. One key element of President Reagan's approach was to keep human rights front and center. President Reagan insisted, rightly, that negotiations between the United States and the Soviet Union could not be confined to arms control, that arms control could not be considered in isolation. At the end of the Geneva summit November, 1987, with Gorbachev present, President Reagan raised four questions by which he said the United States would measure progress in its relations with the Soviet Union. President Reagan asked the Soviet leadership:

Will we join together in sharply reducing offensive nuclear arms and moving to non-nuclear defensive strengths for systems to make this a safer world? Will we join together to help bring about a peaceful resolution of conflicts in Asia, Africa, and Central America so that the peoples there can freely determine their own destiny without outside interference? Will the cause of liberty be advanced, and will the treaties and agreements signed—past and future—be fulfilled?

Progress in peaceful resolution of regional conflicts, the advancement of liberty, and full Soviet compliance with existing international agreements—and not just in arms control—is essential if relations with the Soviet government are genuinely to improve.

But—and here is my second big question today—why should we be concerned about the human rights situation in the Soviet Union? Is this simply a humanitarian concern of ours? Some people in the West seem to believe that human rights is a side issue, and that arms control is the only real question of importance.

The truth is quite different. As President Reagan said at the United Nations General Assembly not too long ago, "nations do not mistrust each other because they are armed; they are armed because they mistrust each other." Why do we mistrust the Soviets? Not simply because they have nuclear weapons. Other nations have nuclear weapons—the French, the British. We do not fear them. We mistrust the Soviet leadership precisely because of their attitude toward human decency and human rights. Weapons are the symptom rather than the source of our problems with the Soviets. And if we are ever going to solve the problem of the arms race, we are eventually going to get at the source of the problem.

That source is the *kind* of government that rules the Soviet Union—a coercive dictatorship, which, since it came to power by force in 1917, has consistently used force both against its own people and, where possible, against other nations, to get its way. It is a regime that has always thrown up a smokescreen of propaganda, that has never hesitated to lie to the world

and that has hidden the truth from its own population. It is because this dictatorship has been so willing to use force, because it shows scant interest in keeping its word when breaking it is convenient, that we have to be on guard and extremely careful that our own defenses never weaken.

We have no quarrel with the Soviet people. On the contrary, we sympathize with them. The Soviet people and the American people have much in common and share a common complaint. That complaint is the nature and conduct of the Soviet government—which in fact threatens the Soviet people even more menacingly than it threatens us.

When we speak of the Soviet Union, we must distinguish sharply between the people and the regime. The regime, those in power, constitutes a small minority—perhaps a hundred thousand or so, called the *nomenklatura*. The names of these people are on special lists. They live on a totally different level from the ordinary Soviet citizen. They have access to special shops where there are no lines and where high quality Western goods are available. They drive nice cars. Some of them have villas, or *dachas,* in the country. The Soviet Union is run by and for this tiny privileged minority, not for the Soviet people as a whole. It is this minority, this tiny clique, whose ambitions for power and whose fear of their own people threaten world stability and fuel the nuclear arms competition.

All exchanges with the outside world—all contact—are controlled by this tiny elite via the KGB and the military. To this day, vast tracts of the Soviet Union remain entirely out of bounds to us.

The point is that the human rights problem of the Soviet Union is directly connected to arms control. As President Kennedy once said, "a nation that is afraid to let its people judge the truth and falsehood in an open market is a nation that is afraid of its people." And as President Reagan said more recently, "a government that breaks faith with its own people cannot be trusted to keep faith with foreign powers."

Why do you suppose we have a problem with Soviet noncompliance with arms control agreements? Can we be surprised when a nation that spends billions each year on a propaganda apparatus that systematically lies to its own people fails to comply fully with an arms control agreement it signs with us? Can we be surprised when a nation that subscribes publicly to an international human rights agreement—as the Soviet did by signing the Helsinki Accords of 1975—and then makes no effort to abide by it—can we be surprised when such a nation violates its arms control commitments? Can we be surprised at misbehavior from a nation that drops mines disguised as toys on the Afghan countryside—as the Soviets have done—in order to maim children and drain popular support away from the resistance? That is almost unbelievable—disguising mines as toys to maim children and wear down the guerrilla resistance—but it is documented fact, and you can find it in the State Department's *Country Reports on Human Rights Practices for 1985*. Can we be surprised that such a nation failed to respond to our various gestures of goodwill in the 1970s and to follow our lead in slowing down the pace of the arms competition? Can we be surprised when such a government seeks to acquire new nuclear weapons at an astonishing pace—as the Soviets are now doing, and have been doing for the past quarter century?

Nuclear weapons in and of themselves have never been our problem. Nobody in this country loses any sleep about the British and French nuclear arsenals. Why? Not just because these two countries are our friends, but because of the kind of governments that rule them—governments that respect basic human rights, that do not seek to expand their territory, that respect the rights of their people. Let me tell you: if the world were comprised entirely of governments like the United States, Britain, and France, arms control would not be such a problem. I am quite confident that in such a world, a world composed entirely of democracies, the nuclear danger would quickly be gotten under firm control, and the arms race put to rest.

Openness and arms control go together. When you're dealing with open societies ruled by democratic governments, you don't have to worry about "national technical means" of verification. In open societies like our own, relevant information on our defense programs is readily available. I have often said that the Soviet Union could verify U.S. compliance with arms agreements simply by subscribing to half a dozen publications—*The New York Times, The Washington Post, Aviation Week,* and a handful of others. In open societies like our own, ruled by law, compliance with international agreements is something you can't take for granted. That is one reason why since 1982 we have pushed for a resolution on disarmament and openness in the

United Nations General Assembly. In 1982, our resolution on disarmament and openness actually was adopted by the General Assembly. It explicitly stated the connection between advancing disarmament and advancing openness and free discussion and free dissemination of information in all nations. It encouraged all nations to advance the cause of openness as a way of advancing the cause of disarmament and arms control.

So—my third question—what is the connection between human rights and arms control? It is this: until the basic attitude of the Soviet regime toward human rights, coercion, and the use of force changes, arms control is going to be very, very difficult, and we are going to have to exercise extreme caution. The attitude of the Soviet regime toward human rights, coercion, and the use of force is one reason why arms control achievements have been so limited thus far. Until the Soviets start respecting the U.N. Charter, the Helsinki Accords, and existing arms control agreements, their compliance with new agreements will be suspect.

Few people, I think, are aware of how difficult it has been to get the Soviet government to accept an arms control agreement that actually reduces offensive nuclear weapons. Neither SALT I nor SALT II achieved actual reductions in weapons. This is a fact. Since signing SALT I in 1972, the Soviet inventory of strategic ballistic missile warheads has increased four-fold. Four-fold. That is what we were calling "arms control" throughout the 1970s—agreements that permitted Soviet ballistic missile warheads to quadruple. Much of this Soviet increase was taking place in the late 1970s, when our military

spending and spending for strategic weapons were actually *declining* in real terms. When our spending dropped, it made no difference to Soviet behavior: Soviet spending continued to go up and up. As Harold Brown, President Carter's Secretary of Defense, noted in testimony before Congress in 1979, "When we build, they build; when we stop building, they nevertheless continue to build. . . ."

At Reykjavik, President Reagan finally got the Soviets involved in serious negotiations on deep reductions in nuclear weapons. These were really the first such negotiations in history. When President Carter proposed deep reductions to the Soviets in March 1977, the Soviets wouldn't even discuss the possibility. But much remains up in the air. Whether the Soviets will sign on the dotted line of a truly equitable and effectively verifiable arms reduction agreement —and whether they will comply with it fully—remains to be seen.

But there is something to remember. Shcharansky puts it this way, quoting a former prisonmate in the Soviet Union: "even if disarmament reduced the arsenals of both superpowers to the point where both sides would be armed only with Stone Age weapons, the danger to Western democracy from an aggressive, militaristic, and numerically superior adversary would force the West to utilize its technical superiority to rearm." In other words, even if the Soviets sign on the dotted line, our problems are by no means over. We still have to contend with the ambitions of the Soviet regime.

That is one reason why it makes sense to pursue the Strategic Defense Initative. Strategic defenses can offer us a new kind of insurance. And insurance is something we can always use. Given the nature of the Soviet government, we need all the insurance we can get against Soviet aggression. And we could certainly also use insurance against Soviet cheating on arms control agreements. Effective defenses could supply both. Deployment of strategic defenses could complicate many times the calculations of Soviet planners contemplating an attack. It could make aggression and preemption extremely difficult, and in this way help prevent war. Defenses could also give us a cushion, a margin of safety, in a world in which offensive weapons had been deeply reduced, and in this way provide an aid to arms control. With defenses in place, there would be less incentive to cheat, since increases in offensive weapons would be partially countered by existing defenses.

I do not accept for one minute the idea that such defenses would stand in the way of achieving arms reductions or stand in the way of sound arms control. That's what people said in the early 1970s. In the early 1970s, people said the only way you're going to get arms reductions from the Soviet Union is to ban or limit defenses. So in 1972 we signed the ABM Treaty and agreed to limit defenses. Did we get reductions? Not at all. Fifteen years later we are confronting a Soviet arsenal of strategic ballistic missile warheads four times as large and many times more accurate than in 1970, and our land based missiles are now vulnerable to preemptive nuclear attack. If the Soviets are ready for real arms control—if they are ready to genuinely reduce their threat to us in exchange for our reducing the threat to them—then this can be best achieved by ar-

rangements that include *both* deep reductions *and* defensive deployments on *both* sides. A defense oriented world, properly approached, would be safer for us both. And don't think that the Soviets aren't committed to defenses. Over the last ten years they've spent $150 billion on strategic defenses—fifteen times more than we have. They believe in the promise of defenses—for them. They would love to kill our SDI and then move forward with their own SDI, which predated ours. What we're talking about instead is the promise of defenses for both nations.

As we negotiate with the Soviets, it is critical that we never lose sight of this vital truth: global stability depends on the strength of the Western democracies to deter totalitarian aggression. This will remain true with or without new arms agreements. We're the only ones that are in a position to insure our own safety whether by deterrence through offense or ultimately through defense.

But I am confident of our future. In the last six years we have seen a reversal of the troubling trends of the late 1970s when U.S. confidence was weakening and nation after nation fell to Soviet and Soviet-sponsored aggression—South Vietnam, Angola, Ethiopia, Cambodia, and finally Afghanistan. Our military strength is being restored. New democracies are burgeoning around the globe. New insurgent movements have risen up to oppose Marxist-Leninist tyranny. The free nations are confident, and the free economies continue to grow. Everywhere I sense a faith, for all the imperfections and failings, in the basic decency and power of the democratic form of government.

Olga Medvedkov put it well. Olga Medvedkov arrived last year in the West with her husband after having struggled bravely against the Soviet authorities as a member of the Soviet Union's one independent peace group, the Group to Establish Trust between the USSR and the USA. Members of this tiny group—the only group in the Soviet Union that has campaigned for peace in defiance of the authorities—have been harassed and arrested, confined to psychiatric hospitals, their brief demonstrations broken up by police.

Mrs. Medvedkov put it well. "Peace," she said, "cannot be in labor camps."

True and lasting peace will come on the day when groups like Mrs. Medvedkov's "Trust Group" can demonstrate freely in the streets of Moscow as its counterparts do in the streets of Washington, London, Paris, or Bonn. True and lasting peace will come on the day when, like the defense budget of the United States, the military budget of the Soviet Union is subject to the judgment of a free electorate. True and lasting peace will come on the day when Soviet citizens are free to emigrate and travel as they wish. True and lasting peace will come, in short, on the day when the same openness that governs the affairs of true democracies around the world pervades the Soviet Union. Then the lion will truly lie down beside the lamb. Under these circumstances, arms control will no longer be a matter of international agreements; it will be the spontaneous expression of the will of free peoples. It will be the natural extension of democratic freedom and the democratic faith. ■

Arms Control: Progress and Global Challenges

By George Shultz

In late May, 1988, in Moscow, President Reagan and General Secretary Gorbachev exchanged the instruments of ratification for the first treaty in history to reduce nuclear weapons. That treaty is a message of hope for the future.

One day earlier, the President had set forth his vision of the future, in a speech to the students at Moscow State University. He saw a world where the wonders of technology, especially the technology of information, would combine with the plain practical benefits of political and economic freedom, to bring increased peace and prosperity for all.

The work of this special session is concentrating on the weapons of war, as well it should. But we must never forget a point the President made to the students of Moscow—a point he has repeatedly made around the world: "Nations do not distrust each other because they are armed; they are armed because they distrust each other."

To succeed in our endeavor, we must pursue our visions with realism. There is no room for wishful thinking—especially thinking that technology and politics stand still. They do not.

Advanced weapons technology is spreading throughout the globe. It has been used in conflicts that are underway even as I speak to you. Terrorists are making use of advanced explosives and missiles. The diffusion of nuclear and chemical weapons capabilities, of ballis-

tic missile technology, even of biotechnology, is a global problem. These are not simply East-West issues: they concern every state here represented. And we must all recognize that if we are not part of the solution, we are part of the problem.

The spread of these technologies coincides with the resurgence of age-old ethnic, religious, and communal conflicts. These conflicts are tragedies in themselves; the misuse of new technologies of destruction only adds to the suffering and to the risk that these conflicts will expand, further threatening the peace.

So the changes we see present us with both problems and opportunities. But whatever else changes, some basic facts do not. We are all in this together. We have a common interest in international stability and security. That common interest is as compelling now as it was over 40 years ago, when the United States and others joined together to form this great body, in the aftermath of the most devastating war the world has ever known. Turning that common interest into practical reality is always the real challenge. Sweeping statements of principle have their place, but noble words can never substitute for concrete deeds.

Six years ago, President Reagan brought to the second special session the profound wish for peace of the American people. He also described his concrete agenda for progress.

As we review those 6 years, I think we have made remarkable progress—more than many expected. But much remains to be done. There is work aplenty for all of us.

Let me briefly review the progress of the past 6 years—first, what we have achieved bilaterally with the Soviet Union; next, what we have done together with our NATO allies to strengthen stability in Europe; and then our efforts to deal with disarmament challenges on a global scale.

PROGRESS SINCE 1982

U.S.-Soviet Arms Control

Progress in U.S.-Soviet arms control has been substantial. I have already mentioned the INF [Intermediate-Range Nuclear Forces] Treaty. Over the next 3 years, the United States and the Soviet Union will eliminate, forever and on a global basis, all their intermediate- and shorter range nuclear missiles. For the next 13 years, we and the Soviets will verify this disarmament by means of the most extensive onsite inspection regime ever. It may be that future historians will come to judge this treaty's breakthroughs in verification and openness to have been almost as important as the nuclear reductions themselves.

When President Reagan spoke to the second special session, negotiations on strategic weapons

---

George Shultz is an economist and a former Secretary of State.

Source: From an address before the third UN General Assembly Special Session on Disarmament, New York City, on June 13, 1988. Reprinted in U. S. Department of State, Bureau of Public Affairs, *Current Policy No. 1080,* 1988.

had just begun. As with his "zero option" for INF, he had proposed dramatic reductions, which many thought were out of the question. Six years later, we have made major progress toward a treaty to cut U.S. and Soviet strategic nuclear arsenals by 50%. I do not know whether we will be able to conclude such a treaty this year, but we will make our best effort. It is the United States' top arms control priority.

We and the Soviet Union have agreed to pursue stage-by-stage negotiations on nuclear testing. The first step is to agree on effective verification, to make it possible to ratify the Threshold Test Ban Treaty of 1974 and the Peaceful Nuclear Explosions Treaty of 1976. At the Moscow summit, we agreed on the detailed procedures necessary to design and conduct a joint verification experiment at each other's test sites. And we have made progress on a new protocol to the Peaceful Nuclear Explosions Treaty.

Earlier this year, we opened the nuclear risk reduction centers in Moscow and Washington. They will further decrease the chance of war through accident or miscalculation, and will play a direct role in implementing the INF Treaty. At the Moscow summit, we also agreed to provide 24 hours advance notice of strategic ballistic missile launches.

These achievements are tangible testimony to the success of the policy that President Reagan has steadily pursued to build a better relationship with the Soviet Union. It is a policy that covers a broad agenda—human rights, regional conflicts, and bilateral issues, as well as arms control. It is a policy built to last, and it has stood the

test of time. It is a policy that we have pursued with the full support of our NATO allies. Without the full and active support of our allies, the INF Treaty in particular could never have been achieved.

Multilateral East-West Negotiations

Together with our allies, we have taken important steps in multilateral negotiations as well.

The Stockholm Conference on Confidence- and Security-Building Measures and Disarmament in Europe concluded successfully in September 1986. This was a major breakthrough for onsite inspection of military forces and activities. The 35 participating states agreed to specific measures to reduce the risk of war as a result of misunderstanding, miscalculation, or surprise attack.

These measures have real military meaning. They require advance notice of military activities above a certain level of troops or tanks, observation of military activities above a specific level of troops, and annual forecasts of certain military activities. They also give the right to request onsite inspections to verify compliance. To date, 5 of the participating states have conducted a total of 10 inspections. The successful implementation of the Stockholm accord has increased confidence and given all concerned a better understanding of military activities by other states.

We and our NATO allies have pressed for progress in conventional arms control in Europe. This is part and parcel of a balanced overall approach. Three days ago, my NATO colleagues and I agreed on the need for a substantial and balanced outcome of the CSCE

[Conference on Security and Cooperation in Europe] followup meeting in Vienna, at an early date, including significant progress on human rights and human contacts, and on mandates for negotiations on conventional stability and security-building measures.

In conventional arms control, the leaders of the alliance stated our aim clearly at the March NATO summit: "to establish a situation in Europe in which force postures as well as the numbers and deployments of weapon systems no longer make surprise attack and large-scale offensive action a feasible option." Our leaders at the NATO summit were very specific about what steps must be taken:

• Enhance stability in the whole of Europe, from the Atlantic to the Urals, in a way which safeguards the security of all but takes into account the particular problems facing each region;
• Focus on the key weapon systems in seeking to eliminate the ability to conduct large-scale offensive actions;
• Deal with stationed forces, including forward-deployed Soviet units, while taking into consideration reinforcement capabilities;
• Concentrate on results that will eliminate the disparities that threaten stability, not on schemes for "equal reductions" that would have no such effect;
• Redress the conventional imbalance, which can be achieved through a set of measures including reductions, limitations, and redeployments, as well as the establishment of equal ceilings;
• Require highly asymmetrical reductions by the East, entailing, for example, the elimination from Europe of tens of thousands of

Warsaw Pact weapons that could be used in a surprise attack, including tanks and artillery pieces;

• Propose, as a concurrent element, measures to produce greater openness of military activities, and to support a rigorous monitoring and verification regime; and

• Include in this regime the exchange of detailed data about forces and deployments, and the right to sufficient onsite inspections to be confident of compliance.

We are under no illusion that we have set ourselves an easy objective. But we have identified what we need to achieve in order to make a real contribution to a lasting peace. And we have done so in the explicit recognition, as our leaders put it, that "the military confrontation in Europe is the result, not the cause, of the painful division which burdens that continent."

Global Disarmament

All these achievements are important, and they have received their due share of attention. But that must not be allowed to obscure the fact that building a safer world is not a U.S.-Soviet problem alone or even an East-West problem. It is every nation's responsibility.

• Since June 1982, 21 additional states have joined the most important multilateral disarmament agreement so far achieved—the Nuclear Non-Proliferation Treaty (NPT). The 1985 NPT Review Conference unanimously concluded that the treaty is essential to international peace and security.

• In April 1984, at the Geneva Conference on Disarmament (CD),

Vice President Bush tabled a draft treaty to ban chemical weapons. In doing so, he noted that if ever in the history of mankind there was something on which people from every single country could agree—not just government officials but families in Vladivostok and Leningrad, Peoria and Paris, London, Caracas, and Belgrade—it is on the need to ban chemical weapons.

Since then, negotiations at the CD toward a comprehensive, verifiable, and truly global ban have increasingly centered on the real issues. These include the need for concrete solutions to the problems of ensuring effective verification and undiminished security. For the treaty to have real meaning, all chemical-weapons-capable states must be part of it. Formidable obstacles remain. It serves no good purpose to minimize them. But the United States is fully committed to pressing ahead.

• In 1986, the second review conference of the Biological and Toxin Weapons Convention was held. It acknowledged concerns about past Soviet noncompliance, stressed the need for all states to deal seriously with compliance issues, and emphasized that failure to strengthen compliance measures undermined the convention and the arms control process in general.

• In 1987, the United States and six other industrialized democracies formed a missile technology control regime to limit the proliferation of missiles capable of delivering nuclear weapons. I might add that at the Moscow summit, we and the Soviet Union agreed to hold exploratory talks to exchange ideas and information about how to cope with this growing problem.

• The United Nations has contributed welcome support to some essential principles of arms control. For 2 years in a row, the General Assembly has adopted, by consensus, resolutions calling for compliance with existing treaties and resolutions underlining the importance of verification of arms control agreements.

• I have described how the INF Treaty and the CSCE process have brought greater openness to military matters. The United Nations is also playing a role. Last year the General Assembly adopted a resolution calling for "furthering openness and transparency" on military matters, including objective information on military capabilities. The United States warmly welcomed this resolution and calls on all member states to heed it. Every country can help build the confidence on which true peace depends, by publishing honest figures about defense expenditures, for all the world to see. We welcome the Soviet commitment to make such figures public. We think now is the time to do so.

So, as I review the past 6 years, I see a lot of forward movement. But even as we celebrate our progress, a somber fact overshadows this special session. Proliferation is winning the race against disarmament in the technologies of destruction I described at the outset. We must all face up to this threat and act to counter it.

CHALLENGES OF PROLIFERATION

Chemical Weapons

This threat is not an abstract one. During the same 6 years that we have made the progress I have outlined, bloody conflicts have been fought throughout the world. In some, chemical weapons have been employed. This is a direct and flagrant violation of the 1925 Geneva Protocol, which bans the use of chemical weapons. But only a binding international convention banning the weapons themselves can ensure that they are never used again.

All nations have a responsibility to combat the proliferation of these terrible weapons. The General Assembly has voted to strengthen the Secretary General's investigations of suspected use of chemical weapons. This is a limited but positive step. Whenever evidence emerges that chemical weapons are being used, all nations must step up to their responsibilities, by bringing political pressure and moral suasion to bear on offending states. States with chemical manufacturing capabilities have a special responsibility to work against proliferation. Stringent export controls for the chemicals needed to make these weapons are a good place to start.

I have described how, at the Conference on Disarmament, the difficult outstanding issues of a chemical weapons ban have been identified. All 40 participating nations must apply themselves to resolving them. In doing so, they are blazing a path which must be followed by all members of the international community.

Ballistic Missiles

Ballistic missile proliferation is a new and urgent challenge. It is a worldwide threat. In some cases, it involves missiles of the same sort that the INF Treaty is forever eliminating from U.S. and Soviet arsenals.

The United States is especially concerned about the introduction of advanced missiles into the Persian Gulf war. This has lead directly to the indiscriminate slaughter of civilians, making it even more difficult to bring that tragic conflict to an end. We are already seeing signs of a dangerous new arms race which will put at risk countries far removed from the gulf region itself.

Surely, mutual restraint is a better way for the nations of that troubled area to see to their security. The United States is prepared to do its part, both to curb ballistic missile proliferation, and to help bring about peaceful resolutions of the conflicts in the gulf and nearby regions.

Nuclear Weapons

Bad as the proliferation of chemical weapons and ballistic missiles is, nuclear proliferation poses an even graver threat to international stability. The United States considers nuclear proliferation the most important item on this special session's agenda.

Does anyone doubt that the spread of nuclear weapons threatens regional and global security? What state believes that, if it now acquired nuclear weapons, its rivals would not seek to do the same?

The vast majority of the countries here represented have undertaken a solemn commitment to stop the spread of nuclear weapons. One hundred and thirty-six nations have freely chosen to adhere to the Non-Proliferation Treaty, which celebrates its 20th anniversary this month. There is no good reason why every nation should not make such a commitment. It is a contribution each and

every state can make to a safer world.

The Treaty of Tlatelolco also remains a key part of the nonproliferation regime. The United States believes all eligible states should fully adhere to it. By opening their nuclear activities to inspection by the International Atomic Energy Agency, the parties to both treaties provide verifiable assurances that these activities are for peaceful purposes only.

Each state that has not yet made a binding commitment to nuclear nonproliferation must explain why for itself. But one pretext for not doing so is gone. The image of an endless nuclear buildup by the United States and the Soviet Union looks very false in the light of the INF Treaty.

At the very moment when the United States and U.S.S.R. have agreed to reduce their nuclear arsenals, it would be tragic for other countries to pursue the capability to cross the nuclear threshold. Nuclear proliferation is one of the most direct and serious threats to regional and global stability. It is a challenge which no nation has the right to ignore.

We must be most concerned about areas where regional tensions are high, and where countries that see each other as potential rivals have not made a binding commitment to nonproliferation or opened all their nuclear activities to international inspection. Today it is in South Asia that the danger is most acute. We encourage the states of South Asia to take concrete steps to meet this urgent challenge. The United States is prepared to work with countries inside and outside the region to find a lasting solution to the danger of proliferation that satisfies all parties.

THE PATH TO PEACE

Building a constructive relationship with one's neighbors and other potential adversaries should be an element of every national security policy.

Each individual country must decide the proper balance between investing in plowshares and investing in swords. In making such decisions, it is essential to have a clear idea of the threat. That is one good reason for openness about military budgets—and about nuclear programs. It is also why states should talk to each other about their political differences, in order to reduce regional tensions and thus reduce the perceived need to maintain large military forces. Let me cite a few figures without drawing any conclusions.

In the 5 years from 1977 to 1981, some $128 billion worth of arms were delivered to developing countries. In the following 5 years, ending in 1986, this figure rose to $180 billion—an increase of some 40%.

The Soviet Union was by far the most significant source of arms deliveries throughout that decade. In the first 5 years, Warsaw Pact countries accounted for 51% of the weapons shipments, while NATO countries were responsible for 41%. In the second 5 years, these figures declined somewhat, to 50% for the Warsaw Pact and 37% for NATO.

During this same period, the developing countries themselves showed a dramatic growth as the sources of their own weapons. In percentage terms, their share almost doubled from the first period to the second, rising from 6% to 11%. In absolute terms, the figure went up some two and a half times. This is development of a sort, but it is hardly disarmament.

I said at the outset that the United States recognizes the need for realism. The UN Charter specifically recognizes the right of self-defense, as well as the right to form regional collective security arrangements. History has not been kind to states that neglected their fundamental security responsibilities. The United States does not believe in peace through weakness, and does not recommend it to anyone else.

So it is necessary to be strong. But it is not sufficient. As the leaders of the NATO alliance put it, at their March summit:

Security in Europe involves not just military, but also political, economic, and, above all, humanitarian factors. We look forward to a Europe undivided, in which people of all states can freely receive ideas and information, enjoy their fundamental human rights, and determine their own future. . . . A just and lasting peaceful order in Europe requires that all states enjoy relations of confidence with their own citizens, trust them to make political or economic choices of their own, and allow them to receive information from and exchange ideas with citizens of other states.

Allied leaders went on to say that military forces should only exist to prevent war and to ensure self-defense, not for purposes of aggression or for political or military intimidation.

I think there is much in this vision that applies beyond the North Atlantic area. It suggests a way for nations to build their security on a solid foundation. The best basis on which to build a durable peace, wherever there are areas of potential or actual conflict, is a broad one. Trying to limit dialogue to a narrow agenda—whether on security measures or something else—not only misses important opportunities, it allows the whole relationship to be poisoned if things go wrong.

Within the broad approach I have outlined, confidence-building measures, or arms control and disarmament, should be considered on their own merits, as one way to enhance security. Doing them for any other reason can only lead to trouble.

THE ROAD AHEAD

There are challenges enough for all of us. Some tasks, such as work to reduce nuclear arsenals, must be strictly bilateral, in negotiation, verification, and implementation. But others—above all, the negotiations to ban chemical weapons and the need to control nuclear proliferation—are global problems.

As we continue these discussions, even as we exchange frank or candid opinions, let us recall the purpose of this great organization, as set forth in the UN Charter:

To save succeeding generations from the scourge of war . . . to reaffirm faith in fundamental human rights . . . to establish conditions under which justice and respect for the obligations arising from treaties and other sources of international law can be maintained, and to promote social progress and better standards of life in larger freedom.

In that spirit, let us get on with the job. ■

Suggested Additional Readings

Allison, Graham *et al. Hawks, Doves and Owls: An Agenda for Avoiding Nuclear War* (New York: Norton, 1985).

"Arms, Defense Policy, and Arms Control," Special Issue of *Daedalus* (Summer, 1975).

Clemens, Walter C. *The Superpowers and Arms Control* (Lexington, MA: Lexington Books, 1973).

Garfinkle, Adam M. *The Politics of the Nuclear Freeze* (Philadelphia: Foreign Policy Research Institute, 1984).

Gasteyger, Curt Walter. *Searching for World Security* (New York: St. Martin's Press, 1985).

Jones, Rodney W., and Steven A. Hildreth. *Modern Weapons and Third World Powers* (Boulder, CO: Westview Press, 1984).

Keliher, John G. *The Negotiations on Mutual and Balanced Force Reductions* (New York: Pergamon Press, 1980).

Lefever, Ernest W. *Nuclear Arms in the Third World: U.S. Policy Dilemma* (Washington, DC: Brookings Institution, 1979).

Nye, Joseph S. *Nuclear Ethics* (New York: Free Press, 1986).

Sloan, Stanley R., and Robert C. Gray. *Nuclear Strategy and Arms Control* (New York: Foreign Policy Association, 1982).

Talbott, Strobe. *Deadly Gambits* (New York: Knopf, 1984).

Williamson, David, *Realistic Arms Control Today* (Washington, DC: Center for Strategic and International Studies, 1982).

CHAPTER TEN

Drugs

*
*

The international drug trade is a relatively new and very complicated issue in U.S. foreign policy. It is complicated for several reasons: like so many of the new issues, it involves both domestic and foreign policy considerations; we are inexperienced in dealing with this kind of issue; and no matter what we do, we do not seem fundamentally able to solve the problem.

Drugs are both big business and a big problem. The money to be made in the drug trade is huge. At the same time, the drug traffic is closely associated with violence, spreading crime, and high-level corruption. It is ruining some of our youth and poisoning our society.

At first, the strategy for dealing with the drug issue was to focus on the domestic or consumption side. This involved disrupting supplies and networks, arresting users as well as sellers, and instituting a program of widespread drug testing. But these strategies quickly ran afoul of civil liberties groups and lobbies who argued that indiscriminate testing violated the civil liberties of those tested. Attacking the drug issue on the domestic front thus seemed to be stymied.

The next step was to try to stop drugs internationally, on the production side. But that step was taken ill-advisedly and without adequate preparation. For one thing, farmers abroad could earn ten or twenty times as much growing the plants from which drugs are produced as from more traditional crops. Drug sales also bolstered the generally poor economies of producing countries. They added to the tax base of these countries, which made their governments happy, and added to their ability to pay their large foreign debts, which made bankers happy. Moreover, since many government and military officials in the producing countries were in on the "take" from drug sales, clamping down meant putting cabinet members, high-ranking officers, and maybe even the president or prime minister himself in jail—obviously a sensitive issue. This brought the State Department, which wants to have good relations with these countries, into conflict with the Drug Enforcement Agency, whose agents want to put everyone responsible in jail. In addition, the technology of the "drug factories" is so elementary that they can be moved quickly in the jungle, making it impossible to eliminate them physically. Moreover, the sprays used to kill the plants are also known to cause cancer in humans, which no government could sanction. The problems of resolving the drug issue at the source or production point thus proved to be at least as complicated as resolving it on the consumption side.

The result has been bitter disappointment and disillusionment in policy-making circles. It seems that nothing we do can solve the drug problem. In the meantime, however, a number of changes are taking place. Drugs are no longer spreading among the general population but are increasingly confined to certain groups, mainly those who are poor, disadvantaged, and who have little hope or prospects in their lives. We have also become more aware of the impact of drugs: they are no longer seen simply as "lifestyle choices," but rather as the cause of long-term and permanent damage to our brains and organs. The educational campaign on television and elsewhere directed against drug use has become far more effective. The appointment of a "drug czar" should help resolve bureaucratic conflicts between the State and Justice departments noted above, but the fact that the czar lacks cabinet status gives him less clout.

At present, therefore, the strategy is a comprehensive one: to attack the drug problem where possible on the consumption side, attack it where possible on the production end, and at the same time continue the educational campaign. Those efforts will not make the problem disappear, but they may at least begin to reduce its proportions.

This section's readings commence with a statement on narcotics in Latin America by the Department of State. Rensselaer Lee then focuses on the reasons why it is so difficult for the U.S. to carry out an effective policy to limit the flow of drugs coming into the United States. Douglas Payne takes the analysis a step further by showing the power of the drug lords within their own countries and their capacity to intimidate governments or even assume sovereignty for themselves. Finally, David McClintick offers some practical suggestions for solving this out-of-control problem.

Narcotics in Latin America

BACKGROUND

Latin America and the Caribbean area are the source of all the cocaine, four-fifths of the marijuana, and one-third of the heroin consumed in the US. Democratic governments in the region are being threatened by illicit drug operations and, in some countries such as Colombia, by narcoterrorism. Latin America and Caribbean states, conscious of this threat and concerned about the growing domestic consumption of drugs, have demonstrated a new commitment to counter the narcotics problem. Intensified efforts in cooperation with the US, including major interdiction and in-country eradication programs, are under way to disrupt production and trafficking and decrease the international flow of drugs.

ECONOMIC AND POLITICAL IMPACT

The immense wealth of drug traffickers enables them to corrupt civil and police officials and pay others to assassinate those who cannot be bought. Corruption and violence weaken governments by undermining their legitimacy and intimidating them. Money from drug trafficking can exacerbate economic problems by contributing to inflation and destabilizing the money supply and local exchange markets. Most drug profits are spent on nonproductive activities such as real estate speculation and imported luxury goods or on expanding the illegal drug business; most drug money, however,

does not come back to the country of origin. In areas where exchange transactions are rigidly controlled, clandestine narcodollar movements finance a large underground economy outside of government authority. Laundering of the proceeds from drug trafficking is a problem in Panama and the Bahamas and could spread to other countries in Latin America.

REGIONAL COOPERATION

In April 1986 in Rio de Janeiro, the Organization of American States (OAS) adopted a comprehensive action program to increase regional narcotics control cooperation. In November the OAS General Assembly approved the creation of an Inter-American Drug Abuse Control Commission. A Caribbean Regional Conference on Drug Abuse was held in March 1987 in Belize. Regional enforcement cooperation against drug trafficking includes: multiagency, multinational Caribbean interdiction operations; a regional communications network connecting narcotics enforcement agencies in Andean countries; and US-funded antiterrorist training in Latin America to help countries improve security, share information, and combat narcoterrorism. There are coordinated border operations to interdict traffickers involving Colombia, Peru, and Ecuador. In October 1986 ministers of justice and attorneys general from 13 Latin American countries and the US met in Mexico to discuss mutual narcotics and enforcement problems.

ANDEAN COUNTRIES

The world supply of cocaine is processed from coca grown primarily in Peru, Bolivia, Colombia, Ecuador, and Brazil. Each country has pledged to control narcotics and has established eradication and enforcement programs that the US is supporting. Colombia has been particularly effective in controlling marijuana and coca production and in cooperating with other Andean countries. Nevertheless, the cocaine supply is growing at an estimated 10% yearly, and traffickers are looking for new markets to absorb this increasing supply. The US has assisted all the Andean countries in training and tactical intelligence and provided equipment to improve their ability to confront trafficking organizations. During 1986, at the Bolivian Government's request, the US provided US Army helicopters to airlift Bolivian National Police on a series of raids (Operation Blast Furnace) that seriously disrupted trafficking in northeastern Bolivia.

CARIBBEAN COUNTRIES

Jamaica and Belize are important marijuana producers that have taken positive steps to eradicate illicit crops. Jamaica and the Bahamas are major transshipment points for cocaine entering the US. Both countries have begun aggressive campaigns against drug traffickers. Reports indicate that the Eastern Caribbean, Belize, Dominican Republic, Guyana, and Suriname are becoming alternate trafficking routes for drugs formerly sent more directly from South

Source: From U.S. Department of State, Bureau of Public Affairs, *Gist,* May, 1987.

America. An example of a successful interdiction operation conducted through the cooperation of the US and foreign governments is the one in the Bahamas and Turks and Caicos.

MEXICO

Mexico is a primary marijuana producer, as well as a major source of heroin and a transshipment point for cocaine. In cooperation with the US, Mexico is improving the effectiveness of eradication and enforcement measures and is working to overcome problems of corruption that have impeded past efforts.

PANAMA

Panama is a transit point for cocaine and a major center for money laundering, but a series of eradication campaigns have kept Panama from becoming a significant marijuana exporter and have kept marijuana production under control.

NEW TRAFFICKING ACTIVITY

Pressure from increased enforcement efforts in major trafficking countries has pushed trafficking activities into Argentina, Brazil, Ecuador, Paraguay, and Venezuela.

US POLICY

The inter-American region is an important arena for the application of the US Government's strong antinarcotics policy aimed at drug demand reduction, eradication, and disruption of trafficking. The Anti-Drug Abuse Act of 1986 strengthened US antinarcotics efforts at home and abroad. The annual International Narcotics Control Strategy Report assesses the situation in the major drug producing and trafficking nations around the world, 19 of them in Latin America and the Caribbean. This report was prepared in response to a congressional mandate under which, for the first time, the President is required to certify whether certain major drug producing, trafficking, and money laundering countries have cooperated fully with the US on narcotics control. The legislation links this cooperation to the receipt of US assistance. ∎

Why the U.S. Cannot Stop South American Cocaine

by Rensselaer W. Lee III

The control of narcotics, once an issue far outside the diplomatic mainstream, has become a vital component of U.S. relations with Latin America. Indeed, eradicating drug production and export is officially the highest U.S. diplomatic priority in Colombia and one of the top priorities in Bolivia and Peru. U.S. economic aid is allocated accordingly: narcotics-related assistance rose from 30 percent of total aid to Colombia in fiscal year 1984 to over 90 percent in FY 1988. Moreover, Congress now ties foreign aid to recipient countries' drug-control efforts. Thus, in the last two years, the United States has withheld $17.4 million in aid from Bolivia, primarily because coca crop eradication targets were not met.

It is noteworthy that Washington does not practice drug diplomacy worldwide but restricts it largely to Latin America and the Caribbean. There is no serious threat to cut off economic and military aid to Pakistan (the world's largest heroin producer) or to stop supplying Stinger missiles to the *mujahidin* of Afghanistan (who cultivate opium). In these places, obviously, there are higher priorities than narcotics control.

Within Latin America too, there are priorities. Although Latin America supplies most of the marijuana, about 40 percent of the heroin, and all of the cocaine entering U.S. markets, cocaine is easily the biggest concern at the moment. The fight against America's cocaine epidemic —an estimated six million people regularly use this highly addictive drug— consumes the bulk of the federal government's drug-fighting resources. But the cocaine industry is a powerful antagonist. Having cultivated extensive ties with the economic and political power structures of the Andean countries, it poses a difficult challenge to U.S. policy.

Dr. Rensselaer Lee is President of Global Advisory Services, Inc., and an Associate Scholar of the Foreign Policy Research Institute.

Source: From *Orbis,*, Vol. 32, No. 4 (Fall 1988).

WHO PRODUCES COCAINE?

The business of cocaine differs from one country to the next. In Colombia, five major trafficking syndicates headquartered in the cities of Medellín and Cali control—directly or through affiliate organizations—an estimated 70 to 80 percent of that country's cocaine exports. Bolivia's cocaine trade is dominated by some twelve to twenty-five families, most of whom also run cattle ranches or commercial farms in the Beni, Cochabamba, and Santa Cruz regions. In Peru, on the other hand, the industry is highly fragmented and, to a large extent, dominated by Colombian traffickers.

Colombia is clearly the linchpin of the South American cocaine industry. The Medellín-Cali syndicates, which control up to 60 percent of the world's cocaine, procure raw materials in Peru and Bolivia, manufacture refined cocaine in Colombia, ship it in large loads of 300 kilos or more to the United States, and market the cocaine wholesale within the United States. They may also be expanding into the even more profitable phases of distribution, where a kilo of cocaine is subdivided into small lots, adulterated with an inert substance, and sold in small packages for about double the wholesale price.

The big Colombian syndicates do not constitute a cartel in the sense of being able to maintain prices. Cocaine wholesale prices in the United States dropped from $55,000 per kilo in 1980 to $15,000 in mid-1988. Also, there is bad blood between the Medellín and Cali groups, stemming from Medellín's attempts to encroach on Cali's sales territory in New York City. Yet there is considerable business collaboration within each group—traffickers collaborate on insuring cocaine shipments, engage in joint ventures, exchange loads, and jointly plan assassinations. Moreover, cocaine barons share a common agenda that includes blocking the extradition of drug traffickers and immobilizing the criminal justice system.

The top tier of the Colombian cocaine elite comprises approximately one hundred people, many of them on the U.S. government's list of "extraditables." Seven men stand at the apex of the trafficking pyramid. Five are based in Medellín: Jorge Ochoa Vázquez and his brothers Fabio and Juan David; Pablo Escobar Gaviria; and José Gonzalo Rodríguez Gacha from the town of Pacho in Cundinamarca. Two are in Cali: Gilberto Rodríguez Orejuela and José Santa Cruz Londoño. Pablo Escobar, Jorge Ochoa, and Gonzalo Rodríguez Gacha are reputedly three of the world's richest men: they made *Forbe's* 1988 list of 125 non-U.S. billionaires.[1] By the end of the mid-1980s, the Medellín and Cali organizations together grossed about $2-$3 billion annually from international cocaine sales, primarily to the U.S. market. Two-thirds or more of that amount was profit.[2]

The 20–30 percent of Colombia's cocaine industry not under the syndicate is shared by scattered small processors and refiners, some of whom have links to guerrillas of the Revolutionary Armed Forces of Colombia (FARC). FARC may also have its own cocaine-processing capabilities in some regions. The small producers do not have access to the cocaine elite's distribution capabilities; they rely heavily on mules (hired-couriers) to smuggle cocaine into the United States.

THE BENEFITS OF COCAINE

All together, South American drug traffickers earn an estimated $3–$5 billion each year.[3] Some $2–$3 billion remains abroad, stashed in offshore tax havens such as Panama and the Cayman Islands, or invested in U.S. real estate, securities, and business. In 1983, Colombian drug traffickers reportedly held $12 billion worth of assets in the United States.[4]

Between $1 billion and $2 billion annually may return to the principal cocaine-producing countries—Colombia ($200-$600 million), Bolivia ($250-$450 million), and Peru ($600-$700 million). In terms of these repatriated dollars, cocaine exports equal an estimated 4 to 12 percent of Colombia's 1987 legal exports, 23 to 27 percent of Peru's, and 53 to 95 percent of Bolivia's. Bolivian drug traffickers reputedly control two-thirds of the country's foreign exchange.[5] The economic impact of these funds is not clear, however, for the relationship between the drug industry and prosperity is far from direct.[6] When spending their repatriated dollars, traffickers tend to short-change core economic activities. As *The Economist* recently noted, "the economic impact of $1 billion spent bribing politicians and buying status symbols will usually be less than that of $1 billion spent building roads and electricity generators."[7]

And much is spent on bribes. Because cocaine is a criminal industry, the producers spend 10 to 20 percent of all operating expenses to create a secure climate for business operations. The money goes for weapons and private security forces, information networks, bribes to law enforcement officials, contributions to political campaigns, and "war taxes" paid to guerrilla groups.

Conspicuous consumption is another hallmark of the cocaine industry, giving rise to absurdly unbalanced development in the remote South American jungle regions that cultivate coca. The town of Tocache in Peru's Upper Huallaga Valley has six banks, six Telex machines, several stereo dealerships, a discotheque, and one of the largest Nissan outlets in Peru. Tocache also has no paved streets, no drinking water, and no sewage system.[8] In Medellín and Santa Cruz, cocaine capos flaunt ostentatious lifestyles—buying luxury high-rise apartment buildings, Mercedes-Benzes and BMWs, helicopters, and antiques. Last January, after a bomb exploded in front of Monaco, one of Pablo Escobar's Medellín houses, police reportedly discovered in the wreckage a veritable fortune in Ming dynasty vases, Greek sculptures, paintings (including works by Botero, Morales, and Obregón), and a collection of thirty antique cars.[9]

In the attempt to buy status, drug traffickers in South America, Jamaica, and Honduras also devote funds to social welfare programs, earning the traffickers a significant popular following. Pablo Escobar, for example, built 450–500 two-bedroom cement-block houses in a Medellín slum that has now been renamed the "Barrio Pablo Escobar." Reportedly he has built more public housing in Medellín than the government. Escobar also financed many other Medellín projects—sewer repair, educa-

tional facilities, clinics, and sports plazas. Carlos Lehder organized and funded a major earthquake relief effort in the city of Popayan and also built a housing project for the poor in his native Armenia, the capital of Quindío department. Gonzalo Rodríguez Gacha donated an outdoor basketball court to his native town of Pacho, Cundinamarca, and repaired the facade of Pacho's town hall. Roberto Suarez, the "king of cocaine" in Bolivia, paves streets, restores churches, and donates sewing machines to poor women in his Beni home town of Santa Ana de Yacuma. Suarez reportedly provides college scholarships for needy students in the Beni region.[10]

The cocaine industry also generates genuine economic activity. It directly employs up to a million people in the Andean region. About 500,000–600,000 farmers (mostly in Peru and Bolivia) cultivate and harvest coca leaves. Several hundred thousand are engaged in downstream functions: macerating coca leaves, building maceration pits, buying and selling leaves or paste, refining and smuggling cocaine, building clandestine airstrips, and smuggling percusor chemicals (used to convert coca into cocaine). An estimated 350,000–400,000 Bolivians (5–6 percent of that country's population) work directly in one phase or another of the trafficking cycle.[11] For many, however, these activities do not provide full-time work; in Bolivia, some farmers cultivate coca in the Chapare during the summer months and farm their traditional crops in the Upper Cochabamba Valley during the winter. Coca cultivation often makes the difference between subsistence and a decent standard of living.

Thus, drug-related business serves as an important economic safety valve, especially in Peru and Bolivia, providing income, jobs, and foreign exchange when the formal economy falters. According to a Bolivian government document, "Triennial Program of the Battle Against Drug Trafficking," while Bolivia's gross national product declined 2.3 percent per year from 1980 to 1986, production of coca grew an estimated 35 percent per year over the same period. The official unemployment rate more than tripled from 1980 to 1986 (from 5.7 percent to 20 percent), but so did the number of families reportedly growing coca.[12] During 1986, over 20,000 Bolivian miners lost their jobs; as many as 5,000 may have sought work in the coca fields. From 1984 to 1986, when world prices for oil, tin, and natural gas declined, Bolivia's exports shrank by 25 percent and Peru's by 20 percent; cocaine exports compensated for the loss.[13]

Cocaine production has an economic ripple effect. A proportion of drug traffickers' earnings goes for the purchase of the means of production (farm equipment, chemicals, and other tools of the trade) and export (clandestine airstrips, transportation, etc.). Local industrialists create new manufacturing capacity to provide goods, while new services (banks, law firms, and accounting firms) spring up to cater to the cocaine syndicates. Even the expenditures on conspicuous consumption have an effect. The demand for luxury housing has been a boon for building contractors and for producers of such construction materials as cement, bricks, and glass.

Some drug money is invested in quite ordinary economic outlets. though these tend to be in agriculture and services rather than in the more traditional areas, such as extraction, manufacturing industries, and infrastructure projects. The Rodríguez Orejuela family put together an extensive business empire in Cali, which at one time included banks, construction companies, pharmaceutical companies, sports clubs, private security companies, automobile dealerships, twenty-eight radio stations, and two higher educational institutions, the Fundación Educativa de Estudios Superiores and the Faculdad de Formación de Empresarios. Several of the Medellín-based traffickers (José Gonzalo Rodríguez Gacha, Pablo Escobar, and the Ochoa clan) own dairy farms, cattle ranches, and horse ranches. In Bolivia, where the cocaine dealers are largely coterminous with the rural elite, traffickers invest drug profits into expanding herds, cross-breeding cattle, or improving cotton and sugar cane yields. Characteristically, the major drug lords also invest in executive air-transport services (which may be used for drug trafficking), restaurants, and resort hotels (especially on Colombia's Caribbean coast and on San Andrés Island).[14] Even while they remain theoretically dedicated to combatting drug traffic, Andean governments encourage the inflow of narcotics profits. As a Colombian banking official remarked in a 1986 interview, "Why should we drive all this money into the black market and into foreign banks?"[15] Toward this end, tax amnesties were declared in Colombia at the beginning of the last four presidential administrations. In Peru and Bolivia, traffickers who repatriate hard currency are protected by government decree from

tax penalties and to some extent from criminal investigation. Such money now replaces the international loans that are no longer forthcoming from commercial bankers. Peru's nationalistic economic policies exclude it from receiving loans from any international sources, and Peruvian banking officials make no secret of their view that cocaine dollars partially substitute for foreign investment and bank loans.[16] In an apparent effort to draw in more cocaine dollars and to keep them in Peru, the government has overvalued the local currency (the INTI) and provided high INTI interest rates for depositors. In sum, drug dollars create pockets of prosperity, stimulate certain industries, stabilize the currency, and help finance exports. Were the industry suddenly shut down, economic chaos would reign in Bolivia and Peru, and possibly in Colombia too.

THE DRUG PRODUCERS' CLOUT

The cocaine industry's enormous wealth, its large popular base upstream, and its formidable organization downstream combine to give it great political influence in the Andean countries. It has two especially powerful constituencies: the farmers who defend their right to cultivate coca, and cocaine dealers who exert a range of influences over the criminal justice system and the state generally.

Coca Farmers

Farmers who cultivate illicit coca make up the most visible cocaine constituency, for they are highly organized and sometimes well armed. They can exert tremendous pressure on governments.

In Peru's Upper Huallaga Valley, where more than 90 percent of farm income derives from coca cultivation, coca farmers are represented by provincial and district self-defense fronts (FEDIPs). FEDIPs are heavily influenced by the parties of the United Left (Izquierda Unida), and may also have been infiltrated by the Sendero Luminoso and Tupac Amaru guerrilla movements.[17] FEDIPs lobby for the legalization of coca cultivation and challenge government eradication teams with sit-ins, demonstrations, roadblocks, and other mass mobilization tactics. The coca growers' opposition had much to do with the virtual halt of a U.S.-Peruvian eradication project in the Valley in 1987, when only 355 hectares were destroyed, compared to 2,575 in 1986 and 4,830 in 1985.[18] Unless Peru can move ahead with an aerial-spraying program, control of coca in the Upper Huallaga is largely a lost cause; unfortunately, to date there is no demonstrably safe and effective herbicide against coca. In Bolivia, the political dynamics are even worse, for 70,000 coca-growing families are organized into eight regional federations comprising several hundred syndicates. These receive direct political support from national mass membership organizations, including the 1.3-million-member Bolivian Workers Congress and its main affiliate, the Confederation of Bolivian Peasant Workers.[19] In a country of only 6.4 million people, such support significantly deters narcotics control programs. U.S.-Bolivian efforts to pressure coca farmers by destroying crops or regulating the sale of coca leaves trigger organized resistance on a national scale. The Bolivian coca lobby has the power to shut down parts of Bolivia's fragile transportation system. For example, coca farmers and their worker-peasant allies have sealed off Cochabamba, Bolivia's third largest city, four times since 1983 to protest various anti-coca policies of the Bolivian government. The Bolivian authorities did eradicate 1,000 hectares of coca last year, but only by undertaking a complex process of bargaining with federation and individual syndicates and by paying peasants $2,000 for each hectare eradicated.[20] Involuntary eradication on any significant scale is probably politically impossible in Bolivia.

Traffickers

U.S. officials sometimes characterize the narcotics industries as a direct threat to democracy in the Western hemisphere and as a danger to U.S. security interests in the region.[21] Such characterizations are not entirely accurate. To be sure, traffickers do not hesitate to use violence against government officials and public figures to promote their political objectives, such as deactivating the U.S.-Colombian extradition treaty. But unlike leftist guerrillas, whose objective is to seize power, traffickers are not ideologically committed to destroying the political system in which they survive.

Nevertheless, when an industry as large as the cocaine one searches for protection, it spawns corruption on a massive scale. Cocaine traffickers can manipulate the key institutions of public life, including the political parties, the press, the police, the military, and the judiciary. Traffickers exercise enormous influence in such major cities as Medellín and Cali; they

even dominate entire regions, including parts of Caqueta, Meta, and Guaviare in Colombia and much of the Beni region in Bolivia.

The strategy of self-protection operates on seven different levels. First, drug lords make large outlays for weapons and guard forces to protect laboratories, clandestine airfields, drug shipments, and key personnel. Traffickers are in general better armed than national police forces, use better communications equipment, and deploy faster aircraft.

Second, traffickers attempt to neutralize the effectiveness of law-enforcement institutions by paying police or military officers to overlook cocaine refineries or drug-smuggling operations. Chapare traffickers in Bolivia pay police $20,000–$25,000 for a seventy-two-hour window of impunity for loading major shipments by air, land, or river.[22]

Third, the drug lords maintain elaborate networks of informants that provide advance information of the exact plans for raids or checkpoints, thus enabling the traffickers to escape police dragnets and to live fairly comfortably in such major cities as Medellín and Cali. The Ochoa family of Colombia reportedly has informants in the Ministry of Justice and the Ministry of Foreign Affairs.[23] A few U.S. narcotics specialists in Bogota believe that the Medellín syndicates have infiltrated the U.S. Embassy, and that traffickers' informants read some of the Embassy's cable traffic.[24] The cocaine chiefs could conceivably be privy to secret U.S.-Colombian deliberations on drugs and plans for major anti-drug initiatives. No wonder that a Colombian opinion survey taken in March 1987 reports that nearly half

the population believes drug traffickers are too powerful to combat.[25]

Fourth, traffickers undermine the judicial system. When caught in the net, they pay the police to release them. Pablo Escobar, Colombia's biggest cocaine dealer, was arrested by accident in November 1986 at a police checkpoint in Southern Antioquia; he was quickly released after paying a bribe of some $250,000–$375,000.[26]

If traffickers cannot escape the police, judges presiding over drug trafficking cases in Colombia are offered the choice of *plomo o plata* (lead or silver)—death if they convict, a bribe if they set aside the charges. Not surprisingly, few judges opt to convict. In the past two years, criminal court judges either released from jail or dropped the charges against four major cocaine dealers: Gilbert Rodríguez Orejuela, José Santa Cruz Londoño, Evaristo Porras (a midlevel capo from the city of Leticia), and Jorge Luis Ochoa. In fact, Ochoa was released twice within sixteen months, and corrupt judges appear to have played a role on both occasions. Recently in Medellín, police arrested a middle-ranking trafficking chief implicated in the murder of Guillermo Cano (the editor of the Bogota daily *El Espectador*).After several days in jail, he was released because no judge in Medellín was willing to try the case.[27]

If traffickers do end up in jail, they usually can bribe their way out. The second time Jorge Ochoa escaped, according to a Western diplomatic source, his clan paid $3 million to get him out of jail and an additional $20 million to arrange every step of his escape route so that he would not be murdered or recaptured. At the moment of writing, no major traffickers are in jail anywhere in Colombia.

With respect to drug-trafficking cases, then, the Colombian criminal justice system has almost ceased to function.

The fifth level of self-protection exercised by the drug lords in Colombia includes influencing public opinion and the political process. Publications such as Carlos Lehder's *Quindío Libre* and the Escobar family's *Medellín Cívico* carry out an unremitting campaign against the U.S.-Colombian extradition treaty, portraying it as "a monstrous legal absurdity" and "the ultimate surrender of sovereignty."[28] These publications depict drug dealers as progressive and public-spirited citizens. *Medellín Cívico* praises Escobar's "great human and social sensitivity" and his dedication to "redeeming the forgotten people of Antioquia."[29] Mafia-controlled columnists in more respectable publications convey the same message. In addition, as noted above, sponsoring public works and social services in communities that governments have failed to reach wins good will for the drug lords. Although the cost of such projects represents a tiny fraction of overall cocaine resources, the political impact is incalculable.

Sixth, cocaine traffickers become power brokers. In Colombia, where political campaigns are not funded from the state treasury, drug money is an important underpinning for the entire democratic process. Traffickers contribute indiscriminately to campaigns—often through front organizations—to hedge their bets. Pablo Escobar is affiliated with the Liberal party, but he gave money to both candidates in the 1982 Colombian presidential campaign.[30] Sometimes traffickers prepare their own slate of candidates for local political office, as does the "political group" of Evaristo Porras in Colombia's Amazonas Department.[31]

Seventh, and finally, the cocaine mafia protects itself by using violence to shape the laws governing narcotics control. In Colombia, its number-one political objective is to persuade the government to adopt a policy of not extraditing drug traffickers to the United States. Consequently, in the past year-and-a-half, henchmen have murdered prominent Colombian supporters of extradition: the editor of *El Espectador,* a Colombian Supreme Court justice, the former head of Colombia's anti-narcotics police (who was preparing a "black book" on the mafia's criminal activities), and most recently a Colombian attorney general. Violence and threats have paralyzed the Colombian criminal justice system and effectively blocked extraditions.

RELATIONS WITH GUERRILLAS

Perhaps because of the cocaine industry's multi-front attack on the government's control, Washington expressed concern about a connection between the cocaine industry and Marxist guerrilla groups. Indeed, in its early days, the Reagan administration analyzed the drug problem within the framework of the East-West conflict. Administration officials spoke publicly and privately about a "deadly connection" and an "unholy alliance" between cocaine kings and guerrillas.[32] A U.S. government report in 1985 on Soviet influence in Latin America warned of an "alliance between drug smugglers and arms dealers in support of terrorists and guerrillas."[33] This report, however, may have exaggerated the depth of the narco-guerrilla connection.

To be sure, drug dealers, especially the larger operators, do share some of the guerrillas' anti-establishment views: for example, they are both strongly anti-American. In Colombia, major guerrilla groups and cocaine syndicates oppose as "Yankee imperialism" the extradition treaty that allows traffickers to be tried in the United States under American judges and U.S. law. In both Colombia and Peru, therefore, guerrilla organizations have cultivated ties with coca growers.

In addition, the drug lords generally advocate a more egalitarian social structure. Pablo Escobar, for example, espouses the cause of slum dwellers and of "marginal people" in general. The Escobar family newspaper, *Medellín Cívico,* professes strong support for the Liberal party but has a decidedly populist orientation. Recent articles in the newspaper, though not praising the cocaine traffic as such, have criticized "the fabulous profits" of industrialists, claimed that "we are good friends of the working class," and advocated "employment for all, education for all, health for all, and bread for all."[34]

The nationalist-populist fervor of Colombian narcotics traffickers reached its most extreme form in the bizarre political philosophy of Carlos Lehder, who founded a political movement in his native department of Quindio—the Movimiento Latino Nacional (MLN). The MLN's *raison d'être* was campaigning against the extradition treaty, but the party also had a full-blown international political program that included the struggle against "communism, imperialism, neocolonialism, and Zionism" and favored the replacement of Colombia's traditional political parties with mass popular organizations. In the 1986 presidential elections, his party supported the extreme leftist UP candidate, while Lehder himself maintained ties with several Colombian revolutionary organizations, including the Quintin Lamé and the April 19th Movement (M-19). He may even have helped to finance the M-19's raid on Colombia's Palace of Justice in November 1985—a raid culminating in a holocaust in which twelve Supreme Court justices and scores of other people were killed.

Lehder's extreme radicalism, however, was not shared by his colleagues, who generally prefer to work within the system. Many Colombian observers believe that the Medellín syndicates viewed Lehder as an embarrassment, were eager to cultivate a pro-establishment image, and consequently betrayed the trafficker to authorities.[35] Lehder now is in jail in the United States, probably permanently.

At any rate, whatever ideology the drug lords may espouse, on the level of "turf," clashes with guerrilla groups have been common. Guerrillas increase the cocaine industry's overhead costs—traffickers must either pay protection money (war taxes) to guerrillas or make large outlays to guard their drug shipments, laboratories, supply routes, clandestine airfields, and exports. The Colombian cocaine leadership—which invests much of its new-found wealth in farms, ranches, and landed estates in Colombia's relatively unprotected hinterland—is vulnerable to extortion by FARC guerrillas.

Because their interests in these legitimate properties are similar to the interests of Colombia's traditional elite, drug traffickers have spearheaded efforts to organize ranchers and farmers to resist attacks by local guerrilla forces. When the FARC attempted to extort money from Rodríguez Gacha at his newly acquired ranch near Acacias in the Colombian Llanos, Rodríguez organized other landowners in the area into a self-defense league. A Medellín businessman who owns a farm near the Gulf of Uraba in Antioquia admitted in an interview that he and other landowners paid dues to the local chapter of Muerte a Los Secuestradores (Death to Kidnappers), a trafficker-backed vigilante organization. The FARC subsequently gathered strength in the area, and the MAS group collapsed: now the businessman pays off the FARC.

More generally, the Colombian traffickers cooperate with businessmen, landowners, and right-wing elements of the military to wage a systematic extermination campaign against visible members of the extreme left: labor organizers, civil rights workers, intellectuals, and politicians. About one-third of the Union Patriotica (UP) mayoralty candidates (the UP is an umbrella organization for Colombia's Marxist groups) were massacred, many by drug traffickers in the six months preceding the March 1988 elections. According to Colombia's justice minister, Rodríguez Gacha paid 30 million pesos (about $120,000) to one of his henchmen to arrange the October 11 assassination of Colombia's foremost leftist leader, Jamie Pardo Leal, the head of the UP.[36]

In Peru, the Upper Huallaga Valley hosts many bloody confrontations between cocaine-trafficking gangs and Sendero Luminoso guerrillas. In mid- and late 1987, clashes were recorded in or near the Valley towns of Sion, Uchiza, and Paraíso. According to an article in Bogota's *El Tiempo,* Colombian crime syndicates recently dispatched 300 heavily armed traffickers to the Upper Huallaga Valley to help Peruvian traffickers protect cocaine shipments and supply routes against Sendero Luminoso attacks.[37] The efforts by "Machis," one of the Valley's leading cocaine dealers, to organize residents of the Uchiza district against the guerrillas led to an ambush against him at Paraíso by Sendero Luminoso on October 10, 1987. Machis got the worst of it, and was encircled by the guerrillas. At this point, he let himself be rescued from certain death by the Peruvian anti-narcotics police flying in U.S.-piloted helicopters; he is now in a Peruvian jail.[38] Such evidence of narco-guerrilla hostility is no doubt viewed with some relief by the Peruvian authorities. A real alliance between the two groups would create an almost unmanageable political threat in the Upper Huallaga region.

Clashes with guerrillas have even led drug dealers to "develop certain forms of cooperation and tacit alliance with the state."[39] Thus, during a 1984-85 state of emergency in the Upper Huallaga Valley, Peruvian military commanders relied heavily on local cocaine dealers for information on the whereabouts, strengths, and weaponry of Sendero Luminoso forces.

Conversely, Colombian military units occasionally protect cocaine laboratories against FARC extortion attempts; in a November 1983 incident, a Colombian Special Forces team from Villavicencio helped a cocaine trafficker move an entire laboratory complex from an area controlled by the First FARC Front to a safer location near the Brazilian border. The operation, which involved five officers and forty-three NCOs, required twenty-six days.[40] From the state's perspective, guerrillas present a larger threat, or at least a more obvious threat.

Narcos allied with guerrillas appear more dangerous than plain narcos, but the cocaine industry is essentially a para-establishment political force. Episodic and opportunistic links to Marxist guerrilla organizations are far less important than penetrations of legitimate economic and political institutions. The cocaine traffickers' vast financial resources, military and logistical capabilities, and power to corrupt represent a challenge to government authority—but not an ideological challenge to democracy. In the end, the narco-guerrilla theory advanced by Reagan administration officials such as former ambassador to Colombia Lewis Tambs and Assistant Secretary of State for Inter-American Affairs Elliott Abrams was designed primarily to get the attention of Latin American governments.

WHY THE SUPPLY CANNOT BE STOPPED

U.S. and Latin American efforts to curb the supply of cocaine have failed abjectly. Some 200–300 tons of cocaine may flow into U.S. markets yearly; as University of Michigan researcher Lloyd Johnston notes, "the supply of cocaine has never been greater in the streets, the price has never been lower, and [the] drug has never been purer."[41] The U.S. government supports a number of programs meant to reduce supply in the Andean countries, but these programs amount to perhaps $40–$50 million a year, a pittance when compared to the South American cocaine industry's earnings of $3–$5 billion a year. Yet more resources may not be the answer. Structural barriers block effective drug enforcement in poor countries, and such barriers could well be insurmountable.

First, Andean governments worry about the impact of successful drug-control programs. The consequences would be exacerbated rural poverty and new legions of the unemployed, both of which would strengthen antidemocratic or communist movements. Imagine 200,000 coca-growing peasants marching on Bolivia's capital, La Paz. In Peru and Colombia, the war against drugs have proved difficult to reconcile with the struggle against communist insurgency. The threat of eradication alienates coca growers from the government and enhances the appeal of insurgent groups. In the Upper Huallaga Valley, for example, the U.S.-backed eradication effort has doubtless driven many peasants into the ranks of Sendero Luminoso.

Second, many Latin Americans see the economic benefits of drug trafficking. Colombia's controller general, Rodolfo Gonzales, has publicly hailed the contribution of drug dollars to national economic growth. Leading bankers in Peru talk about the importance of cocaine earnings in stabilizing the country's currency. Bolivia's president Victor Paz Estenssoro remarked in 1986 that "cocaine has gained in importance in our economy in direct response to the shrinking of the formal economy."[42]

Third, Latin Americans tend to see U.S.-imposed drug enforcement measures as infringements on their national sovereignty. According to a recent poll, two-thirds of Colombians oppose the extradition of drug traffickers to the United States.[43] This feeling may be heightened because some of the leading candidates for extradition, such as Colombia's Pablo Escobar and Bolivia's Roberto Suárez, provide support for charitable activities and so are popular in their countries. Arresting and extraditing such traffickers would be difficult politically. Officials undoubtedly recall the violent anti-American outbursts in Honduras following the April 1988 extradition of Juan Matta Ballestreros, a narco-philanthropist who cultivated a Robin Hood image.

Fourth, governments often exercise little or no control over territories where drug production flourishes, for these are remote from metropolitan centers, relatively inaccessible mountainous or jungle terrains that are patrolled by guerrillas or other hostile groups. In this way, drug traffic encourages territorial disintegration. The Peruvian government, for example, is losing control over the Upper Huallaga Valley, the region that ships its most important export, coca paste, to Colombia and in return receives money, weapons, and some economic leadership. Colombian aircraft maintain this connection by flying in and out of Peruvian airspace with virtual impunity. Colombian middlemen increasingly buy paste directly from peasants in the Valley rather than through Peruvian dealers. The Upper Huallaga is becoming less a part of Peru and more a part of Colombia.

Finally, corruption severely undermines criminal justice systems in cocaine-producing countries. Law enforcement in Latin American countries often represents simply a way to share in the proceeds of the drug trade: the police take bribes not to make arrests and seizures. When the police do make successful busts, the drugs are often resold on the illicit market.

These barriers mean that antidrug activities in Latin American countries are largely cosmetic. Governments draw up elaborate plans to eradicate coca—the police make a few highly publicized arrests and cocaine seizures, fly around the countryside in helicopters, terrorize villages, and knock out an occasional cocaine laboratory—but with little effect. The core structure of the cocaine industry remains, and the industry's agricultural base continues to expand. Farmers in the Upper Huallaga Valley plant four or five acres for every hectare of coca eradicated, according to a professor at the Agrarian University of Tingo María, the capital of an important cocaine-growing province in the Valley.[44]

At the same time, governments resist the only effective method for controlling coca cultivation, herbicide. Herbicides toxic enough to kill the hardy cocaine bush may also be dangerous to agricultural crops, wildlife, fish, and even humans. The herbicide tebuthiuron ("Spike"), manufactured by Eli Lilly, is " one of a class of toxins that has caused liver damage and

testicle tumors in rats." Lilly has refused to sell the herbicide to the State Department, apparently fearing a rash of liability lawsuits stemming from improper use.[45]

As a result, Bolivia has ruled out chemical eradication entirely. In Colombia, an experimental spraying program has been halted because the government is reportedly afraid of "criticism by environmentalists, the political opposition and peasants involved in drug cultivation." In Peru test spraying has been underway since October 1987; however, the Peruvian government's willingness to move toward full-scale chemical eradication seems contingent on assurances "that the herbicide is not harmful to other plants, animals and human beings." Given the recent publicity surrounding "Spike" and other toxic chemicals, the Peruvian government may opt to remain at the testing stage indefinitely.[46]

THE U.S. POLICY DILEMMA

A 1988 Department of State report noted that Latin American governments do not yet recognize that coca growing and cocaine trafficking "pose serious threats to their own survival."[47] Be that as it may, many Andean leaders are concerned that the suggested cures would be worse than the disease.

To a degree, that concern must also be the concern of Washington, which wants to encourage stable, economically viable governments in the region; to promote democracy; and to suppress leftist insurgent movements. America's war against its drug addiction is not necessarily compatible with these other priorities, at least in the short run. In fact, the argument can be

made that the United States and its Latin American allies have a common interest in minimizing the intensity of the drug war. Yet this may be hard for Washington to do—particularly in an election year.

The Reagan administration is being pilloried by its opponents for not making drug control a top foreign-policy priority. Legislators and local officials demand reprisals against governments that tolerate the narcotics industry; U.S. Senator John Kerry (Democrat of Massachusetts) and New York City Mayor Edward Koch want to send troops to Colombia to root out the Medellín cartel.

These critics are responding to real public pressures. A *New York Times*/CBS News poll shows that Americans perceive drug trafficking as a more important international problem than arms control, terrorism, Palestinian unrest in Israel, or the situation in Central America. Another poll reports that Americans perceive stopping the drug dealings of anti-communist leaders in Central America as more important (by a vote of three to one) than fighting communism in the region. A third poll notes a public preference for U.S. government policies that reduce the supply of illicit drugs entering the United States over policies that focus on persuading Americans to stop using drugs.[48]

Nevertheless, the State Department report is certainly correct if it means that the status quo is not in the long-term interests of the Latin American countries. At issue is not so much democracy as the deterioration and de-modernization of political and economic institutions. As U.S. Ambassador to Colombia Charles Gillespie recently remarked, "The traffickers have already penetrated the fabric of Colombian life . . . [T]his penetration will lead not to the downfall of Colombia and its institutions but rather to a serious and lasting corruption."[49] Other political problems include the governments' weakening hold on their territories, their deteriorating reputation, and discrimination against their citizens and products.

Unfortunately, there may be no useful way to upgrade the war against cocaine that is not counterproductive. Virtually every prescription under discussion carries major disadvantages.

Enhancement of Drug-Fighting Capabilities in Producer Countries

Under this proposal, Andean governments would be provided with firepower, transport, communications, and intelligence support to establish their authority in drug-trafficking zones and destroy the cocaine industry's infrastructure. But the prevailing pattern of corruption in Andean countries makes many U.S. observers skeptical of the utility of such buildups. RAND economist Peter Reuter has suggested that better-equipped governments might mean no more than greater payoffs from the drug traffickers.[50]

"Americanization" of the War on Drugs

In this approach, the U.S. receives permission to take over drug enforcement that producer countries cannot perform. Examples to date include Operation Blast Furnace, the U.S. Army-supported operation against cocaine laboratories in Bolivia in the summer of 1986, and the trial of Colombian drug traffickers in U.S. courts. Americanization works to a point—Blast Furnace virtually shut down Bolivia's cocaine industry for three months—but such operations carry extreme political risks for host governments. All segments of Bolivia's political establishment condemned the operation, and no leader with less stature than Victor Paz Estenssoro could have survived the political fallout. (The Colombian and Peruvian governments have declined U.S. offers of military assistance.) Extradition is widely unpopular in Colombia and anathema in most of Latin America. Last June the Colombian Supreme Court struck down legislation enabling the government to implement the extradition treaty with the U.S.

Income Replacement

"If we are to make a difference in cocaine control," declares a Department of State report, "a massive infusion of economic assistance will be required."[51] Such assistance compensates countries for the economic and social costs of shutting down cocaine production. Possible measures include hard currency loans to compensate for the reduced flow of dollars and lowering import barriers for legitimate products, such as textiles and sugar.

But what about the hundreds of thousands of small farmers who cultivate coca? A coca farmer in the Bolivian Chapare can net up to $2,600 per hectare per year, over four times what he can earn from cultivating oranges and avocados, the next most profitable traditional crops.[52] Thus crop substitution offers few attractions. The U.S. government is now indirectly paying $2,000 for each hectare of coca eradicated in Bolivia, but the Bolivian government estimates that the social costs of eradication—the cost of redirecting farmers into the licit agricultural economy—would be at least $7,000 per hectare.[53] For Bolivia, where coca grows on 50,000–70,000 hectares, the cost of total eradication would be a mind-boggling $350–$490 million. Even if the money were available, it might be misspent; there are persistent rumors that some coca farmers in the Upper Huallaga Valley and the Chapare have used the cash payments for eradication to underwrite the costs of planting new coca fields in other locations.[54]

Sanctions

Perennially popular with Congress, this course of action includes withholding aid, prohibiting trade, cutting off international lending, and restricting the flow of travelers. Yet the record shows few cases where sanctions have achieved the desired objective. To cut off aid to the Andean countries would probably provoke intense anti-Yankee feeling, poison the diplomatic atmosphere, and reduce the resources available for anti-drug campaigns.

In addition, sanctions are a blunt instrument for specific problems. Thus, when Jorge Ochoa was released from a Colombian jail on December 30, 1987 (the second such release in sixteen months), the U.S. government singled out Colombian passengers and products for special customs checks at U.S. ports of entry. Yet the Colombian government had no jurisdiction over the criminal court judge who ordered Ochoa's release, and it had taken extraordinary measures to ensure that Ochoa could not escape from jail. Hence, the U.S. sanctions were misplaced—they will not bring Ochoa back to jail, nor will they make Colombia's criminal justice system less porous. Worse, they doubtless added to the unpopularity of the war against drugs. As Carlos Mauro Hoyas, Colombia's recently murdered attorney general, remarked, "Reprisals against innocent tourists create anger and resentment as well as a sort of solidarity with the drug bosses, not as traffickers but as fellow Colombians."[55]

Negotiating Cutbacks in Drug Production

This approach requires a dialogue with the Escobars, the Ochoas, the Rodríguez Gachas, and the other chief executives of the cocaine industry. The idea of a dialogue has enormous public support in Colombia. Supporters include a number of distinguished figures: a former head of Colombia's State Council (the country's top administrative court), a former acting attorney general, two Catholic bishops (of Popayan and Pereira), and several congressmen and academics.[56] The traffickers themselves made a formal offer to the government in 1984—to withdraw from the cocaine industry, dismantle their laboratories and airstrips, and repatriate their capital. In return, they wanted guarantees against extradition, which would have amounted to a safe haven in Colombia. The Colombian government has said officially that it will not negotiate with traffickers.

Certainly, selective amnesty arrangements for criminals can and have been tried as tools of law enforcement. (The United States has its own witness protection program, for example.) Cocaine chiefs

could reveal much about the structure and operations of the international cocaine industry—its supply channels, distribution networks, personnel policies, financing, and the names of corrupt U.S. officials who abet the trade. They could also provide information about guerrilla operations, for the two often use the same territory, the same clandestine methods, the same smuggling channels, even the same overseas banks.

Yet it is hard to see how the proposal would work in practice. One problem is timing: when the traffickers made their original offer to the government, they were under great pressure. Colombia had a functioning extradition treaty with the United States, and traffickers were being tried in military courts, which have a higher conviction rate than civilian courts. Thanks to Colombian Supreme Court decisions, neither of these conditions is operative today, and the Barco government does not have a great deal of bargaining leverage vis-à-vis the country's cocaine syndicates.

Further, monitoring an amnesty arrangement—the repatriation of capital and the shutting down of a multi-billion-dollar industry—would present fundamental problems. How many Colombian and American law enforcement officials would it take to oversee such a program, and who would monitor the monitors? Too, the traffickers might be unable to deliver on their promises. Is the cocaine industry so tightly structured that a few kingpins can command a larger number of lieutenants to order an even larger number of subordinates to stop producing a product that earns so much? Possibly, but an amnesty might constitute little more than a retirement program for the chief

executives of the cocaine industry. They would have to make a practical demonstration of their market power—say, by shutting down 80 percent of Colombian cocaine production for a six-month period. Amnesty is at best a futuristic option—the idea has some theoretical merit, but it would be extremely difficult to implement.

These difficulties suggest that curbing the supply of cocaine from producer countries may not be effective, no matter how much money the United States government devotes to overseas programs.

Are there better ways to spend the U.S. drug-enforcement dollar? The options seem to be increased interdiction, stepped-up enforcement against drug dealers and pushers, and such demand-reduction steps as stiffer penalties for users, "Just Say No" programs, and drug testing. Many U.S. experts expect these measures also may not work very well.[57] Moreover, as the national controversy over drug testing indicates, there are political and legal limits to controlling drug consumption, just as there are limits to controlling production in the Andean countries. Short of legalizing cocaine use (which carries the danger of stimulating even more addiction) or changing the habits and preferences of U.S. consumers, there seems to be no way out of the cocaine morass.

The solution, if there is one, lies not in the Andean jungles but in the United States. The six million people who now consume cocaine must be persuaded to change their habits and preferences. Perhaps they will grow tired of cocaine and switch to designer drugs; or perhaps they will find more productive and healthy forms of recreation. ■

Notes

1 Harold Seneker, "The World's Billionaires," *Forbes,* July 25, 1988, p.88.

2 David Henry, "Pablo Escobar Gavíria" and "Ochoa Brothers," in "How to Make $7 Billion in 7 Years," *Forbes,* October 5, 1987, p.154.

3. Author's estimate, reflecting assumptions about export volume, direction of international sales (United States vs. Europe), percentage of cocaine sold in Latin America, and U.S. wholesale and distribution prices.

4. *El Tiempo,* February 17, 1986.

5. Interview with Jorge Alderete, Ministry of Interior, La Paz, October 6, 1987; interview with Alexander Watson, U.S. ambassador to Peru, Lima, October 15, 1987; interviews with U.S. narcotics experts in Bogota, October 21, 1987; State Department, *International Narcotics Control Strategy Reports* (Washington, D.C.: Bureau of International Narcotics Matters, March 1, 1988) hereafter INCSR; and R. W. Lee, "The Drug Trade and Developing Countries," *Policy Focus* (Overseas Development Council), June 1987, p. 10.

6. Kevin Healy, "The Boom within the Crisis: Some Recent Effects of Foreign Cocaine Markets on Bolivian Rural Society and Economy," in *Coca and Cocaine* ed. Deborah Pacini and Christine Franquemont (Peterborough, NH: Transcript Printing, 1986), pp. 101–143.

7. Colombia: The Drug Economy," *The Economist,* April 2, 1988, p. 63.

8. Scott L. Malcomson, "Cocaine Republic," *The Village Voice,* August 26, 1986, p. 18; "Tocache: Some Things Go Better With . . .,"*The Andean Report,* December 1985, pp. 242–43.

9. Quién Fué?" *Semana,* January 25, 1988, p. 24.

10. Author's March 1988 trip to the Barrio Pablo Escobar and to Pacho. Hernán Gavíria Berrio, "Letter to Fabio Castillo," *Medellín Cívico,* April 1987, p. 13; "Civismo En Marcha," *Medellín Cívico,* March 1984, p. 2; Jorge Eliecer Orozco, *Lehder: El Hombre* (Bogota: Plaza y Janes, 1987), pp. 60, 120; "A Self-Styled Robin Hood," *Time,* February 25, 1985, p. 33; *The New York Times,* August 15, 1982.

11. Rensselaer Lee, "Drugs," in *The U.S. Economy and Developing Countries: Campaign 88 Briefing Papers for Candidates,* ed. Richard Feinberg and Gregg Goldstein (Washington, D.C.: Overseas Development Council, 1988), p. 2. See also Congressional Research Service, *Combatting International Drug Cartels: Issues for U.S. Policy* (Washington, D.C.: Government Printing Office, 1987), p. 32; and Institutio Nacional de Planificación, "Plan Nacional de Eliminación del Narcotrafico," (Lima, 1984), p. 4.

12. Government of Bolivia, *Triennial Program of the Battle Against Drug Trafficking,* November 1986, pp. 5–6.

13. *Latin American Regional Reports: Andean Group,* March 3, 1988, p. 8. Export data from author's conversations with U.S. Treasury officials, March, 1988.

14. Fabio Castillo, *Los Jinetes de la Cocaina* (Bogota: Editorial Documentos Periodistos, 1987), pp. 124–148.

15. Interview with the author, April 1986.

16. "Governments' Sweetheart Deals and Subsidies Attempt to Stop Widening the Gaps in the Financial Circuit," *The Andean Report,* October 1986, pp. 141–42.

17. Raúl Gonzáles, "Coca and Subversion in the Huallaga," *Quehacer* (Lima), September-October 1987, pp. 55–72.

18. *INCSR,* 1988, p. 109.

19. Healy, p. 136; and Lee, "The Drug Trade and Developing Countries," p. 7.

20. *INCSR,* 1988, p. 73.

21. *The Washington Post,* February 24, 1988; "Aboga Abrams por Más Ayuda a Gestiones de América Latina Contra Narcóticos," USIS news release in Spanish, Bogota, February 1986, p. 4.

22. *INCSR,* 1987, p. 70.

23. *El Tiempo,* January 10, 1988.

24. Author's interviews with U.S. narcotics experts in Bogota, March-April, 1986.

25. Author's interview with the staff of Invamer, a Colombian polling organization, Medellín, March 9, 1988.

26. "El Dossier de Medellín," *Semana,* January 27, 1987, p. 25.

27. *El Tiempo,* February 9, 1988.

28. See, for example, "La Patria Acorralada," *Quindío Libre,* October 1, 1983; "No a la Extradición," *Medellín Cívico,* March 1984, p. 7; and Gilberto Zapata, "El Triunfo Es de Colombia," *Medellín Cívico, July 1987, p. 3.*

29. Berrio, "Letter to Fabio Castillo."

30. "El Dinero Caliente Pretende Entrar en Política," *Guión,* July 15–21, 1983, p. 21; and Jorge Child and Mario Arango, *Los Condenados de la Coca* (Medellín: Editorial J. M. Arango, 1985), p. 107.

31. *Jinetes,* p. 105.

32. USIS, "Aboga Abrams," p. 4; *The Washington Post,* November 14, 1987.

33. Ibid.

34. "Los Barrios Pobres y la Eradicación de la Pobreza," *Medellín Cívico,* October 1986, p. 3; "La Paz Es la Justicia Social," *Medellín Cívico,* November 1986, p. 3; "Mientras el Pueblo Padece Hambre, Varias Industrias Se Enriquecen," *Medellín Cívico,* April 1987, p. 4; Berrio, "Letter to Fabio Castillo"; and "Existen Mas de Dos Milliones de Desempleados," *Medellín Cívico,* May 1987, p. 6.

35. Orozco, *Lehder: El Hombre,* p. 235.

36. *El Tiempo,* November 13. 1987. Se also: *The Washington Post,* November 14, 1987, and Ayatollah, *El Tiempo,* November 15, 1987.

37. *El Tiempo,* February 22, 1988.

38. Interview with staff of CORAH (Coca Reduction in the Alto Huallaga), Tingo María, October 12, 1987; interviews with U.S. pilots, Upper Huallaga Valley, October 13, 1987; interview with U.S. narcotics official, Lima, October 15–16, 1987; interview with General Juan Zarate of Peru's narcotics police, Lima, October 16, 1987; and *The Miami Herald,* October 14, 1987.

39. Alfredo Molano, *Selva Adentro* (Bogota: El Ancora, 1987), p. 134.
40. For accounts of this operation, see *Jinetes,* p. 235; and Fabio Castillo, "Operación Encubierta para Proteger Laboratorio de Coca," *El Espectador,* August 1, 1985.
41. Quoted in *The New York Times,* April 12, 1988.
42. "Reactivación Econaómica por Dinero Caliente," *El Espectador,* October 3, 1987; "Directive del BCR del Peru Habla Sobre Narcodolares," *El Comercio,* October 8, 1987; *The Washington Post,* July 17, 1986.
43. *The Washington Post,* February 2, 1988.
44. *The Washington Post,* April 16, 1987.
45. *The Washington Times,* June 8, 1988.
46. *INCSR,* 1988, pp. 8, 75, 91; and *The New York Times,* June 28, 1988.
47. *INCSR,* 1988, p. 8.
48. *The New York Times,* April 10, 1988.
49. Quoted in *The Los Angeles Times,* February 21, 1988.
50. Congressional Research Service, *Combatting International Drug Cartels: Issues for U.S. Policy,* Report for the Caucus on International Narcotics Control, U.S. Senate (Washington, D.C.: Government Printing Office, 1987), p. 13.
51. *INCSR,* 1988, p. 8.
52. Gerald Owens, "Costs of Production: Coca," Unsolicited report to AID, December 31, 1986, p. 6.
53. Peter McFadden, "New Eradication Program Winning Over Coca Farmers," Associated Press, December 31, 1987.
54. Interviews with Peruvian officials, Upper Huallaga Valley, October 10–14, 1987. (In Peru, farmers get up to $300 for each hectare of cocaine destroyed.) Also, telephone interview with a U.S. expert on Bolivian rural development, June 26, 1988.
55. *The New York Times,* January 13, 1988.
56. See, for example, "Hay que Hablar con los Narcos Dicen 2 Obispos," *El Tiempo,* February 13, 1988; "Lo nico que Hacemos Es el Oso," (an interview with Alfredo Gutiérrez Márquez, then acting attorney general) *El Tiempo,* February 22, 1988; Richard Craig, "Illicit Drug Traffic: Implications for South American Source Countries," *Journal of Interamerican Studies and World Affairs,* Summer 1987, p. 4; M. Arango and J. Child, *Narcotrafico Imperio de las Cocaina* (Medellín: Editorial Percepción, 1984), pp. 13–14.
57. *The New York Times,* April 12, 1988.

The Drug "Super State" in Latin America

By Douglas W. Payne

The hemispheric narcotics trade has spawned a borderless drug state whose political power now threatens the sovereignty of the Latin American nations in which it operates. William Bennett, Washington's first "drug czar," should know about the drug state: that's what he's fighting on the so-called supply side of the issue. President Bush, having singled out drug abuse as a national "scourge" in his Inaugural Address, should be aware too; the drug state is a major national security threat. The way to start is by listening to Latin American leaders who confront directly what has become a menace of geopolitical magnitude.

Upon completing his term in 1987, Colombian president Belisario Betancur said the drug dealers had become "stronger than the state." A few weeks before he was murdered in January 1988, Colombian Attorney General Carlos Mauro Hoyos declared, "We are confronting a superstate."

After the murder of Hoyos, Vladimir Gessen, head of the subcommittee on drug-trafficking in the Congress of neighboring Venezuela, referred to the regionwide narcotics operation as the "Republic of Drugs." Juan Manuel Santos, a senior executive of *El Tiempo,* Colombia's largest newspaper, stated at the end of 1988, "These people are more powerful than the state."

Latin Americans are not talking about a "cartel." The word, in fact, is used much less in Latin America than in the U.S. For in reality, there is no cartel, not in the sense of an organization that seeks to control the price of a commodity. What Latin Americans are speaking of is a political force, fueled by drug money, that has become a major contender for political power in the hemisphere.

The "super-state," centered in Colombia, radiates throughout Latin America and the Caribbean. Its foreign policy instruments, like those of any other state, include

Douglas W. Payne is Freedom House director of hemispheric studies.

Source: Reprinted from *Freedom at Issue,* March-April 1989, pp. 7–10, with permission of Freedom House, New York.

force, economic leverage and, most recently, propaganda and diplomacy. The goal of its foreign policy is to achieve legitimacy among the sovereign states of the hemisphere. States that grant legitimacy to the drug state, de facto or otherwise, necessarily forfeit their own. Law enforcement would become irrelevant; there wouldn't be any Latin American drug laws left to enforce.

The process is underway. Two years ago, the Colombian Supreme Court, having succumbed to threats, bribes and a trafficker-sponsored political campaign, threw out the U.S.-Colombia extradition treaty. U.S. officials in Colombia are now conceding that the war on drugs is not going to be won on the enforcement battlefield. Yet officials in Washington seem unaware of what that concession means.

THE MEDELLÍN ORGANIZATION

Diego Córdoba is a 32-year-old Colombian lawyer. He is employed by the drug-trafficking organization based in Medellín, Colombia. He earns twenty to thirty times the salary of the average Colombian lawyer. He is one of more than a hundred lawyers that the Medellín organization employs, many recruited directly out of law school. But Córdoba has become more than a lawyer. He is one of the new breed of diplomatic spokesmen utilized by the Medellín organization in its foreign policy pursuits.

In June 1988, Córdoba gave a lengthy interview to O Globo, a major Brazilian daily newspaper. He said there were actually more than fifty drug-trafficking "cartels" in the region, but that they were all connected into "something greater" based in Medellín. He said he was a representative of that entity. He said that within three years Brazil would replace Colombia as the largest exporter of drugs. He stated there was no imaginable U.S. policy that could destroy or even curtail the organization he represents.

Córdoba suggested that the Brazilians be pragmatic. Drug-trafficking, he said, was doing more to alleviate poverty and hunger in the region than any Latin American government. Accepting the inevitable therefore made good sense. After all, his organization was already well established, had its own international banking system, and its own agricultural monopolies. And although he didn't mention it at the time, his organization has offered to pay the entire external debt of Colombia in exchange for immunity and legitimacy. He also didn't mention his organization's military capability, its state-of-the-art weaponry and communications systems. Latin Americans already know about these things.

The message of the Medellín organization to the governments of the region is that mutual recognition is in your interest as well as ours: Our commodity is now the largest foreign exchange earner in the Andean region, and it also has the best growth potential. (The Economist has noted that the cocaine boom is probably a big reason why Colombia has been able to avoid rescheduling its foreign debt.) Think if we were to cooperate. We have only begun to exploit the European market. That's where Brazil comes in: Atlantic access. Brazil is the giant of the region, of course, but it is a stricken giant, strapped with debt, wracked by poverty. Let us cooperate in solving these problems. Isn't

mutually beneficial, peaceful coexistence preferable to violent confrontation?

This is an organization with the combined economic, political and military powers of a state that is now acting like a state and asking to be treated like a state. Will Diego Córdoba someday be addressing the United Nations, offering proposals for cooperation in alleviating the social and economic problems of Latin America? Will he present the first drug-based developmental model? If so, his speechwriter could be Mario Arango.

Arango is a Medellín writer and lawyer who serves as legal counsel to the top leadership of the Medellín organization. He is also a member of the Medellín City Council. After Bogotá, Medellín is the second largest city in Colombia. It is located in the northern province of Antioquia. Arango's book, *Impacto del Narcotráfico en Antioquia*, is the first attempt to make a serious intellectual case for the narcotics trade. Published in September 1988, it became an immediate bestseller in Colombia.

According to Arango, the drug business has ushered in an egalitarian "social revolution," opening up new opportunities for minorities and the lower class. In recent interviews he has stated, "I consider the drug trade to be the support for a country in crisis. . . .It is possible to state, without risk of error, that the money from the drug traffic has acted as a brake on the social and political deterioration of the country." Arango, whose home is decorated with an embroidered portrait of Joseph Stalin, does not allude to murder, corruption, the collapse of the judicial system, and the rampant addiction of Colombia's youth.

Arango's analysis has been respectfully received at the highest levels of the Colombian establishment. The message resonates among editors, columnists, political figures and university intellectuals. Concern about extradition and eradication is being replaced by a mood that is somewhere between acceptance and resignation. Prominent politicians and at least two Roman Catholic bishops have called for opening a dialogue with the Medellín organization. Juan Gabriel Tokatlian, director of the Center for International Studies at the University of the Andes, has stated, "My perception is we're moving toward detente." This is the language of state-to-state relations. There are other Colombians, however, who accuse Arango of being a "propagandist" for the Medellín organization. Arango dismisses the charges as "narco-McCarthyism."

THE NEW
POLITICAL STRATEGY

The drug state's recent quest for legitimacy is in sharp contrast to its former confrontational approach. In 1985, the Medellín overlords ordered the murder of a popular Colombian justice minister, resulting in a nationwide crackdown. The crackdown had teeth because the extradition treaty was still in place. To avoid the dragnet, the top Medellín figures found safe haven in nations where they had already established relations; most of them went to General Noriega's Panama.

Carlos Lehder stayed behind, surfacing at a jungle press conference. Wearing a black tee-shirt with automatic weapons slung from his shoulders, Lehder declared war on governments, particularly Colombia's. He stated that in cooperation with the (Cuban-backed) M-19 guerrilla organization and "nationalist sectors" of the Colombian military, he would run the Colombian government out of Bogotá, as well as anybody else connected with "U.S. imperialism." As for the U.S., its appetite for cocaine would eventually destroy it, he was seeing to that.

Lehder is in jail now, extradited, tried and convicted in Florida. His vitriol has been replaced by the new Medellín diplomacy. In fact, it is commonly believed in Colombia that the organization decided Lehder's reckless performance was a liability and that Pablo Escobar, Gonzalo Rodriguez Gacha and the Ochoa family set Lehder up for the fall in order to implement the new *political* strategy that is blossoming now.

While exhibiting the combined economic, political and military characteristics of a state, the drug state is nonetheless a floating state. As a Colombian Cabinet minister remarked in 1988, "The advantage for narco-traffickers is that they don't recognize national sovereignties or frontiers as we governments must. They have moved with expediency in Latin America and the Caribbean. They have cash, guns, planes and boats. Just purchasing arms, for instance, takes the Colombia government two years, while traffickers buy what they want in hours. Our own foreign policy has really been no match for theirs."

THE DRUG STATE
CONSTELLATION

How can the expanding drug state be conceptualized? Television and newspapers rely on the image of tentacles, or arrows marking distribution routes. A more accurate image would be that of a sprawling, fluctuating constellation, with Medellín as the central star. The Medellín organization accounts for roughly 80 percent of the cocaine sold in the U.S. Another bright but lesser star is the Cali organization based in Colombia's third largest city to the south. The barons of Cali and Medellín spent 1988 fighting a bloody war for sole possession of New York City distribution rights. Arango says not to worry: all great revolutions are born of violence.

Other stars in the constellation include the organizations in Peru and Bolivia that cultivate the bulk of the world's coca leaf and turn it into paste for refining in Colombia. Then there are the myriad members of the distribution network that operate in nearly every country of the hemisphere and in Europe. In turn, radiating out from this basic configuration are an entire host of elements that are drawn into or spawned by the operation and become part of the constellation. These include left-wing guerrilla organizations, right-wing death squads, political parties from left to right, agricultural and professional organizations, government figures and institutions, all either drawn by the lure of wealth, swayed by intimidation, or simply absorbed.

This is the empire overseen from Medellín. Inevitably, any public or private organization with a political or economic agenda in Latin America must either do business with the drug state or seek to destroy it; it is too powerful to ignore or avoid any longer. Trying to destroy it is dangerous business; accommodation is rapidly becoming the option of choice.

Within the constellation, alliances of convenience are formed, broken and formed again in different configurations depending on whose interest converge or diverge at any given time. Differences in political ideology exist but are shelved during tactical alliances. The mindset that unites all the players in the drug state is antagonism for the U.S. In the drug state, right-wing nationalism converges neatly with left-wing anti-imperialism when the common enemy is the U.S.

One example of the temporary, tactical alliances that shift within the constellation: The Revolutionary Armed Forces of Colombia, known by the Spanish acronym FARC, is the guerrilla organization of the Moscow-line Colombian Communist Party. It has operated for decades in the vast Colombian hinterlands. In the first half of the 1980s the FARC entered into a tactical alliance with the Medellín organization. Obvious political differences were set aside as the FARC agreed to provide protection for drug laboratories in the jungle in exchange for money and arms. It is worth noting that the cocaine boom has been concurrent with an almost complete halt to kidnappings for money by left-wing revolutionary groups in South America.

However, the alliance between the FARC and the Medellín organization broke down as Colombian politics evolved into a new stage in mid-decade with a truce between the FARC, other left-wing guerrilla groups and the government. In order to take advantage of the new political space, the FARC formed a political front organization that actively sought the support of the peasant constituency. This meant pressing for land reform and union rights, and therefore came into direct conflict with large landowners and ranchers, many of whom are major figures in the drug state.

In fact, as part of their effort to gain respectability, Colombia's drug barons have invested as much as $5 billion in an estimated 2.5 million acres of fertile land in Colombia alone. The result has been that in recent years, the FARC has clashed with the Medellín organization. With the truce between left-wing guerrilla groups and the government breaking down in 1988, however, another shift in the alliance structure appeared to be taking place. In early 1989, the Colombian media reported that an arms shipment seized in Jamaica and valued at $8 million was financed by the Medellín organization on behalf of the FARC.

There are nearly a dozen left-wing guerrilla organizations operating in the Andean countries, the largest in Colombia and Peru. Relationships between them and the drug state are variable and unstable. Interests converge and diverge. The Maoist *Sendero Luminoso* (Shining Path), for example, currently rules over its own mini-state in the coca-rich Upper Huallaga valley of Peru. The Colombian overlords are not pleased with the terms recently dictated by *Sendero* from their mountain enclave but are wary of taking on the most virulent guerrilla organization in the hemisphere. *Sendero*, meanwhile, easily funds its all-out assault on the Peruvian government.

Another form of alliance configuration was evident in the 1980 "cocaine coup" in Bolivia. Right-wing military officers seized control of the government with the backing of the major coca leaf growers, a group of former Nazis led by Kalus Barbie and, according to reports in *Le Monde* and *Der Stern,* agents of the Latin American arm of the Reverend Sun Myung Moon's Unification church. In the democratic Bolivia of 1989, as in all other Andean nations, a major issue in national elections is campaign funding by drug money.

The Bolivian "cocaine coup," however, was a provincial blip compared with the geopolitical reach of today's Medellín-based drug state. Since 1985, already existing relations with the narco-military government of Panama have been strengthened. Relations were established with both the Sandinistas and at least one faction of the contras in Nicaragua. Contacts were made in Honduras that facilitated the explosive growth of cocaine shipments through Mexico. The drug state now controls the Mexican "trampoline" into the U.S. In the Caribbean, relations have been strengthened with the Bahamas and Jamaica, and ties developed in Cuba, Haiti, Belize, Suriname and several smaller island countries. And with the opening of the European market, relations are being coordinated in Brazil and Paraguay and established in Uruguay and Argentina.

CUBA'S ROLE

The most significant case may be Cuba. There is abundant evidence of Cuba's involvement in the drug trade, most recently in the hundreds of hours of testimony given during the Lehder trial and prior to the Noriega indictments in Florida federal courts. The evidence reveals that in exchange for providing safe haven and logistical assistance, Fidel Castro earns needed hard currency, some of which goes to aiding Latin American guerrilla organizations.

More importantly, Cuba is apparently the first nation to give de facto recognition to the drug state. Jose Blandon is a former chief of Panamanian political intelligence and close Noriega advisor. After breaking with Noriega in early 1988, he testified before the Senate Foreign Relations Subcommittee on Terrorism, Narcotics and International Affairs. According to Blandon, Castro has maintained relations with the Medellín organization throughout the decade. The level of the relationship can be understood best, Blandon says, if one considers that it was

Castro's personal mediation that resolved a 1984 dispute between Noriega and the Medellín organization. That means mutual recognition all the way around, state-to-state relations.

The relationship is logical. Castro's overriding motive force is antagonism toward the U.S. One of his major objectives remains the projection of Cuban influence and power in Latin America at the expense of the U.S. The drug state's chief nemesis is also the U.S. The only thing the Medellín overlords have ever feared is extradition to the U.S. They want to diminish U.S. political and economic influence in Latin America too.

Beyond the convergence of interest, there is basic *realpolitik*. According to Blandon, Castro understands that in order to have influence in Colombia, one must have influence with the Medellín organization. As the drug state expands, that will become true in other countries as well; in many it already has. Even if Castro were to lessen his relationship with the drug trade—to keep from undermining his current diplomatic offensive, for example—he has nonetheless recognized that there is a powerful new contender in hemispheric geopolitics. It merits high attention in Washington ∎

The Drug War—Losing While Winning

By David McClintick

When John C. Lawn, the head of the Drug Enforcement Administration, wants to get a sure laugh inside his agency, he says, "We've turned the corner."

"What can I tell you, we've turned the corner," Lawn quips, as an aide recites record-setting arrest statistics at a recent meeting in Washington of the two dozen top officials of the DEA. They all laugh.

"We've turned the corner again," he says in Ft. Lauderdale in remarks to 58 supervisory agents from the DEA's huge Miami division. They all laugh. He says it at a conference in Toronto of the special-agents-in-charge of the 20 DEA field offices in the United States and Canada, and again in Vienna at a gathering of senior

DEA agents from Europe and the Middle East. More laughter.

The "corner" in the drug war hasn't been turned, of course, and claims to the contrary have been a quiet gallows joke in federal law-enforcement circles since at least 1973 when President Nixon, in all seriousness, proclaimed publicly, "We have turned the corner on drug addiction in America," a statement that proved to be incorrect in the extreme. "We've turned the corner" remains the DEA's internal laugh line today because it expresses— in a stab of bitter, dark humor— the frustration the DEA feels as the lead law-enforcement agency in America's frustrating war on illegal narcotics.

Measured by the usual standards of law-enforcement effectiveness —arrests and convictions of significant criminals—the DEA is a phenomenal success. But when judged by the more fundamental question of whether the nation is winning the war on drugs, the agency must be rated a failure. The failure is so pervasive and urgent, in fact, that the DEA is launching a new, alternative strategy—a dangerous, highly classified, when-all-else-fails effort to stop drugs overseas, at the source.

In a dichotomy perhaps unprecedented in the annals of American law enforcement, most current statistics of both success *and* failure in the drug war are records. Nearly two decades into America's

David McClintick, the author of "Indecent Exposure: A True Story of Hollywood and Wall Street," is writing a book about federal law enforcement to be published by William Morrow and Co.

Source: From *The Washington Post*, "Outlook," pp. B1, B4.

second and worst narcotics epidemic (the first lasted roughly from 1885 to 1920), drugs have spawned perhaps the most virulent crime wave in U.S. history. Some 12,395 people arrested by the DEA were convicted of drug crimes in the fiscal year ended last Sept. 30, up from 5,580 in 1981. Drug criminals comprise more than a third of the federal prison population, a growing percentage and by far the largest single category (robbery, at 15 percent, is second). Drugs are behind a recent murder wave in Washington and spawn robberies and killings in cities across the country.

The harder the DEA pushes, the more drugs seem to enter the United States. Last year, DEA agents seized nearly 40 tons of illegally imported cocaine in the United States, up from two tons in 1981. They also seized 682 illicit drug-processing laboratories, almost four times the number of labs seized six years earlier. They confiscated just over $500 million in cash and other assets belonging to drug traffickers, more than the DEA's entire budget for 1987, as well as 4,964 firearms, including 249 automatic weapons. On their face, these statistics reflect an exceptional achievement—a deft melding of new laws, bigger budgets and the skill of thousands of people. Yet they are a profile of defeat.

Despite one of the largest mobilizations of law-enforcement power in history, America's drug problem is worse than ever in many respects, and worse overall than in any other nation in the industrialized world.

One in six working Americans uses drugs regularly, and the problem is even more acute among the unemployed, the poor and the young, especially school dropouts.

More drug-addicted babies are being born than ever before. Cocaine is more readily available in the United States, and at a lower cost, than in several years. The 40 tons that the DEA seized last year are believed to represent only a small portion of the total smuggled into the nation. Meanwhile, the narcotics mafia of Colombia, the source of most cocaine, continues to function freely and appears to be stepping up a campaign of terror against Colombian government officials who try to combat it. On Jan. 25 the drug mafia kidnaped and assassinated Colombia's attorney general, the latest in a series of extraordinarily brazen acts of violence.

The DEA's efforts to combat the drug epidemic have been hampered by two factors that make the battle singularly difficult:

• Drugs aren't simply a crime problem, like bank robbery or income-tax evasion. Drugs also are a public health and medical problem, and, in a larger sense, a social dilemma that seems to invite a variety of possible approaches such as education and therapy having little to do with law enforcement. Until the demand for illegal drugs eases, the DEA's efforts to reduce the supply may be doomed to failure.

• The drug war has also been a bureaucratic turf war. Partly because of the lack of consensus on how best to attack the drug problem, the government bureaucracies responsible for fighting drugs haven't received the kind of stable political support the FBI and IRS get in waging their more conventional and less controversial wars.

Federal narcotics agents in the United States have carried a total of 30 different badges in the nearly three-quarters of a century since the federal government outlawed drugs in 1914. After decades of intermittent scandal, malfeasance and mismanagement, the DEA emerged in 1973 when the Nixon administration, responding to a narcotics epidemic already well underway, created a new "superagency" from several contending agencies. The result was paralysis at the top of the narcotics bureaucracy. Internecine warfare raged. The new agency had three heads in its first three years. It took most of a decade, and the new, younger blood that came with attrition, to begin to heal the old animosities and allow the DEA to function with any degree of institutional stability and effectiveness. In 1981, the FBI, which had shunned drug responsibilities under J. Edgar Hoover for fear that they would corrupt the bureau, agreed to accept "concurrent" jurisdiction over drug enforcement.

During the Reagan years, the drug bureaucracies at large have continued to expand. In addition to the DEA and FBI, 11 Cabinet departments and about three dozen agencies currently are involved in the drug war at the federal level—the State and Defense departments, the CIA, the National Security Agency, the Department of Health and Human Services, the Department of Agriculture, the Customs Service, the Immigration and Naturalization Service, the Coast Guard and many others. And, of course, state and local governments and a myriad of private groups are in the fight as well.

The DEA, as the primary agency for both investigations and intelligence and a leader in drug education, is at the center of the fight, and its recent growth has been explosive. From 1979 through 1987, the DEA's budget rose an average of 32 percent annually to about half a billion dollars, the only major agency outside the Defense Department to get such increases, as Congress and the White House strove to meet the drug epidemic. But since the dramatic increases in arrests, convictions and confiscations of drugs, money and property in this country have failed to reduce drug abuse—and since severe prison-overcrowding poses the distinct possibility that there will be no place to put newly convicted drug offenders—the DEA is beginning some new efforts to stop drugs at their overseas origins.

In concert with the State Department and other agencies, the DEA is launching a major and highly sensitive initiative in South and Central America to try to disrupt the manufacture, processing and shipment of cocaine before it leaves the so-called "source countries" such as Colombia, Bolivia and Peru.

The DEA is in the early stages of training between 150 and 200 of its own special agents for duty with antinarcotics teams assembled from the police and armed forces of about a dozen Latin nations. In Bolivia and Peru, the first wave of DEA agents is already participating with the teams in raiding clandestine jungle cocaine laboratories, disrupting shipments to and from the labs by air, river and other means, and collecting and coordinating intelligence on the cocaine traffic in the region.

In recent months, U.S. sources say, the joint teams (and in some cases all-Latin teams acting partly on DEA intelligence, have seized several tons of fully processed cocaine and destroyed labs, processing facilities, chemicals and ingredients capable of producing

considerably more cocaine than was seized in the United States during all of last year. The authorities believe that the techniques being employed in the operation hold the possibility of reducing more effectively the amounts of cocaine reaching the United States than other methods have.

The new venture, which is scheduled to last indefinitely, builds on the DEA's experience with a number of previous operations, that were somewhat similar but much smaller, including one in Bolivia in 1986 that was terminated after four months.

U.S. agents so far have suffered no casualties in the current effort, though there have been some close calls. Just last week, three DEA agents and a Bolivian police unit that was in the midst of arresting a drug pilot and seizing his wares were attacked by a large mob of angry, rock-throwing coca farmers. A few shots were fired but the joint team was rescued by helicopter and an armed Bolivian military convoy before anyone was seriously injured.

In foreign enterprises, such as the new Latin initiative, the DEA is making greater use of its little known but potent network of foreign agents, intelligence analysts and informants—and its 93-plane air wing. Apart from the new contingent in Latin America, the DEA currently deploys 211 special agents in 65 foreign cities, more than twice as may agents as all other civilian U.S. law-enforcement agencies combined station abroad. For example, there are 18 DEA agents in Bogota, 10 in Mexico City, 18 in Bangkok, four in Paris, three in Istanbul.

"As an intelligence network on international drug trafficking, the DEA (is) unparalleled," writes Ethan A. Nadelmann, an assistant professor at Princeton University's

Woodrow Wilson School of Public and International Affairs, in a soon-to-be-published book on international law enforcement. "In a few countries, most notably in Latin America but also in those countries where governments are not on good terms with the United States, the DEA agent's access may exceed that of both the (U.S.) ambassador and the CIA."

Panama has tarred unjustifiably the DEA's generally good record abroad. When Gen. Manuel Antonio Noriega, the Panamanian dictator, was indicted by federal grand juries in Florida on drug charges, he defended himself in part by displaying letters from DEA chief Lawn and other U.S. officials commending his supposed antidrug efforts.

The Noriega affair illustrates the seamy world in which the DEA must operate—and critics' naivete about the murky, constantly shifting reality of the international drug war. The DEA finds it necessary to deal routinely and often with many unsavory characters in its worldwide effort to inhibit narcotics traffic. Noriega turned out to be one of those characters, and the DEA long has been aware of his likely involvement in illegal activities. As Noriega was helpful in particular DEA operations, which he demonstrably was on occasion, the agency thanked him—in letters known within the DEA as "attaboys" that essentially were formalities. But when hard evidence of his criminality—usable in U.S. courts—mounted relatively recently, it was the DEA's own lengthy investigation that underlay a large part of his indictment.

The DEA also has aggressively investigated official misconduct in Mexico, where, as in Panama, the United States has a sensitive, multifaceted relationship comprising far more than narcotics policy. Even more than Panama, Mexico has allowed itself to become a major source and conduit of illegal narcotics and associated violence that has demanded urgent U.S. attention.

The 1985 torture-murder of Enrique Camarena Salazar, a U.S. drug agent stationed in Guadalajara, has obsessed the DEA, which has conducted an intensive investigation of the killing and related events. A federal grand jury in Los Angeles early last month indicted nine people, including two reputed Mexican drug lords and three Mexican police officials, for complicity in the murder. The DEA's investigation, made despite inaction, obstruction and outright corruption in Mexico, provided the evidence to support the Los Angeles indictments.

In Panama, Mexico and elsewhere, the DEA's choice—which must be exercised daily and pragmatically in hundreds of ambiguous, difficult situations—is a choice between working in, around and through an environment of pervasive corruption to accomplish something positive, or withdrawing and accomplishing nothing. The DEA has consistently chosen the former course.

The agency's reputation spans ideological boundaries. Although they once portrayed narcotics as a symptom of capitalist decadence,

the governments of the Soviet Union, the Peoples Republic of China and other communist nations over the past year or two have quietly asked the DEA's help in combatting their own drug traffickers and in training officers of their governments in drug enforcement skills. Some training already has been completed, and the Soviets, Chinese and several Warsaw Pact governments have begun to share intelligence with the United States and other western nations that has resulted in the seizure of legal drugs and the arrest of traffickers.

For years the DEA has tried to hold down a somewhat reckless "cowboy" reputation, stemming from the early 1970s when federal drug agents perhaps were best known for their occasional "knockless searches" of what turned out to be the wrong residences. They're not cowboys, but fictional portrayals of their work usually understate just how difficult it is. DEA agents work undercover most of the time, making many arrests during the commission of the crime. As a result, drug lawenforcement is considerably more dangerous than most other types, and DEA agents are much more likely to experience a violent episode than are officers of any other federal law enforcement agency. Two DEA agents were killed in a gun battle with alleged heroin

dealers in Los Angeles on Feb. 5. Two agents died in the line of duty in 1987 and a number of other have been wounded or injured while making arrests or seizing booby-trapped drug labs.

As the drug war on U.S. streets and in South American jungles grows more violent and preoccupying, we risk losing sight of the DEA's less-visible but equally urgent mission—education, which most experts consider an essential long-term key to reducing drug abuse. The DEA's Sports Drug Awareness Program provides guidance and training in drug education to the nation's 48,000 school athletic coaches, who in turn are in direct touch with over five million youths, many of them role models in their schools. This and similar federal programs, though vastly underfunded by the Reagan administration, may be contributing to the possible recent decline in cocaine use among high school seniors.

Although Americans broke a devastating drug habit in the 1920s, it's more difficult this time. The drugs are more numerous and varied, the criminals far better organized and financed. Only with the strongest commitment to curbing both supply and demand— through dogged, discriminating worldwide law enforcement and pungent, well-focused drug education—do we stand a chance of turning the corner. ∎

Suggested Additional Readings

Henan, Anthony. *Big Deal: The Politics of the Illicit Drugs Business* (Toronto: Pluto, 1985).

McDonald, Scott B. *Dancing on a Volcano: The Latin American Drug Trade* (New York: Praeger, 1987).

Mills, James. *The Underground Empire: Where Crime and Governments Embrace* (New York: Dell, 1986).

President's Commission on Organized Crime. *America's Habit: Drug Abuse, Drug Trafficking, and Organized Crime* (Washington, DC: Government Printing Office, 1986).

"The Traffic in Drugs: America's Global War," three-part series, *The New York Times* (April 10–12, 1988).

CHAPTER ELEVEN

Trade and Economic Interdependence

＊
＊

Trade and trade policy have become in recent years among the most important issues with which the United States must grapple—some would say *the* most important issues.

The United States no longer has a self-sufficient economy. We are interdependent with the rest of the world in many complex ways. Nor will it do anymore for us simply to throw up protectionist barriers, keep out foreign products, and try to go it alone in the world—the isolationist urge. The fact is that we need Middle Eastern, Mexican, and Venezuelan oil; we need Japanese cars and technology; we require European capital and investment; and we cannot get along without Latin American workers, raw materials, and now increasingly manufactured goods as well. To a degree never the case before, the United States is part of an interdependent world economy in which we must produce and compete or else fade away economically. And if our economy falters, then our political system, foreign policy, and position and stature in the world are certain to suffer as well.

The problems are numerous. Over the years our overwhelmingly dominant economic position in the world has slipped considerably—at least relative to other nations. That is, while our standard of living is still the highest in the world, other nations have crept closer and closer to our level, both in terms of living standards and productivity. At the same time, the United States

has become the world's largest debtor, a fact that is not so disastrous as some alarmists point out but that is worrisome nonetheless. Some of our industries are no longer competitive in world markets, and the quality of American goods in some sectors has gone down. Year by year the American leadership role—economically and, by extension, politically—seems more threatened.

The questions we must raise are numerous. Can we regain our position of world economic preeminence? Can we improve productivity and quality? (Quite a bit, actually, in some industries but probably not very much in others.) Can we reverse our trade deficits? Not without changing our life styles considerably and being willing to produce more, sacrifice more, and consume less. The fact is that for many years now the United States has been living on borrowed time and borrowed money—borrowed both from abroad and from future generations.

Trade issues are complex, among the most complex that we must deal with, because like drugs they involve both political *and* economic issues and because we cannot hope to control the other sovereign nations involved. The United States, for example, even under the weight of powerful domestic political forces that wish to impose protectionist barriers, has largely kept its markets open to the importation of foreign goods, but we then expect our goods to enter other nations' markets freely as well. When other countries use high tariffs to keep out our products, we may be justified in retaliating against their products or in imposing trade penalties. Another problem arises when foreign countries subsidize the products of their industries while our government does not, thus putting U.S. industries at an unfair disadvantage in global market competition. The U.S. has thus come to stand for "free trade," but we insist that it must also be "fair trade." If it is not fair, then we have processes—very elaborate, time consuming, and reluctantly employed—by which we try to impose penalties on foreign producers.

Much is happening in the trade area of which we need to keep abreast. Western Europe in 1992 will become a free trade zone with the developed world's largest market. Will the U.S. be shut out of or included in that market? Similarly, in Asia—partly to offset the European bloc—Japan is forming its own bloc of trading partners. Meanwhile, the U.S. has signed a trade pact with Canada and is moving toward a general North American accord involving Mexico as well. There are new negotiations concerning the General Agreement on Trade and Tariffs (GATT). At the domestic level the U.S. is also trying to cope with this increasingly interdependent world economy by expanding the international divisions of the Commerce and Treasury departments and giving new responsibilities to the Office of the United States Trade Representative.

Economics, international trade, international finance, and political economy are plainly the subjects to study for this future world, as the older, strictly political and diplomatic issues seem to be becoming less important by comparison.

We begin this group of readings with a statement from the Foreign Policy Association that surveys the major issues. Next comes a statement on U.S. trade policy by John Whitehead of the Department of State. The following two essays represent serious but divergent points of view by Washington policy makers: Robert Hormats, former assistant secretary of state for economic affairs, on international economic challenges; and Herbert Stein, former chair of the Council of Economic Advisers, on U.S. foreign economic policy. In the final selection political scientists Robert Pranger and Roger Labrie make the connection between the position of the U.S. in international trade and strategic security.

U.S. Trade and Global Markets   *Risks and Opportunities*

Wednesday morning, October 14, 1987, the U.S. Department of Commerce released trade figures for the month of August. The numbers were disappointing, and stockholders, already jittery over the ramifications of the trade and Federal budget deficits on the economy, began selling off their stock. The Dow Jones industrial average dropped 95 points that day, a record one-day fall.

Worse followed. On Monday, October 19, the Dow went into a free fall, finally coming to rest 508 points lower than it had been when the day started. The news from New York set in motion a worldwide market collapse: stocks plunged on exchanges from London to Tokyo to Johannesburg. The Hong Kong exchange suspended trading for the remainder of the week.

Acknowledging that the frenzy that drove down the Dow was at least partially motivated by concern over America's record $145 billion trade deficit, members of the Reagan Administration and Congress pledged to move more quickly to find grounds for agreement on trade legislation then in a Senate-House conference committee. Whatever form the final bill takes, it is almost certain to modify America's long-standing policy of free trade.

A Record Imbalance

In 1986, Americans exported $224 billion worth of goods—everything from corn to semiconductors. They imported goods worth $369 billion, primarily consumer products and petroleum, leaving a trade deficit of $145 bil-

lion. This *merchandise trade balance* is the difference between the goods that Americans buy from abroad and the goods that they sell. When services such as banking and insurance are added into that equation, the deficit contracts somewhat to $144 billion. This more inclusive equation is known as the *balance on current account*. The *balance of payments* records all of a country's economic transactions, including foreign aid and other capital movements. Since that too is negative, by an estimated $200 billion, the U.S. is a debtor nation, with more money flowing out than coming in.

Complicated definitions should not obscure the fact that the trade gap is essentially a reflection of the purchasing decisions of individual Americans—in this case a reflection of their preference for goods manufactured abroad, whether because they are cheaper, better made or not available at home. It also is a reflection of the inability of American companies to sell their products to foreign markets, whether because of price, quality or unfair restrictions on trade. Why does a trade deficit matter?

• It costs jobs. By one calculation, each $1 billion of lost trade equals 25,000 jobs. (This is offset, somewhat, by the jobs created to handle the sales of imports.)
• It threatens Americans' standard of living. A country with a trade deficit is a country that is spending more than it is earning. The U.S. is able to do so by attracting money from foreigners in the form of investments in the stock

market or Treasury bills. But the dividends and interest on these investments runs to billions of dollars. And since it must send this money abroad, the U.S. has less to spend at home—on public works, education, and research.
• It causes political fallout, damaging alliances and undermining America's global leadership. This is already evident in the strained relations with Japan. Asks C. Fred Bergsten, director of the Institute for International Economics, "Can the U.S. continue to lead its alliance systems as it goes increasingly into debt to the countries that are supposed to be its followers?"

Global Marketplace

Ironically, it is America's very success as a trader that is the source of today's trade deficit. In the postwar years, the U.S. has been transformed from a nation largely independent of trade for its well-being to one of the world's leading exporters. That transformation fueled a tremendous surge of economic growth and was the foundation for America's global economic leadership, particularly from 1945 to 1960.

The great expansion in U.S. trade has bridged the oceans that once separated the U.S. from other cultures—and competition. The U.S. has grown simultaneously more dependent on trade and less able to export. In 1950, 6.3% of the goods made in the U.S. were exported, and 5.6% of the goods bought by Americans were imports. By 1980, 19.7% of U.S.-made goods were exported, 21.9% of

Source: From *Great Decisions 1988,* Foreign Policy Association, New York, 1988.

goods bought in the U.S. were imports. What steps should the U.S. take to become more competitive in the global marketplace?

Unfair Trading Practices

Although the U.S. had a trade deficit with almost every country with which it traded in 1986, one third of the total was with only one country, Japan. Many believe this is because Japan and other competitors trade unfairly. They share President Ronald Reagan's assessment: "... if the U.S. can trade with other nations on a level playing field, we can... out-compete ... anybody, anywhere in the world." This view of the U.S. as international victim overlooks the fact that the U.S. itself puts restrictions on more than 18% of its imports. Nevertheless, America's traditional support of free trade has been undermined by the belief that others play by different rules. Can free trade be made fairer?

Concerns over competitiveness and fairness have led to a third area of debate: Should free trade remain the goal of U.S. trade policy? The Administration has answered yes. Its policy on competitiveness and trade was summed up facetiously, but not inaccurately, by one of the members of Reagan's commission on competitiveness as follows: "... the Administration believes: (a) there is no problem; and (b) if there is a problem, it's essentially a short-term problem; and (3) even if there is a problem, there is no important role for government in solving it."

Opponents of free trade tend to favor a more managed approach. They say that as America becomes increasingly dependent on the workings of a world economic system over which it has little control, it is all the more important for the U.S. to assert at home what control it can— whether by placing quotas on certain imports, or by restricting the surplus any one country can run with it. Both sides are profoundly influenced by their interpretation of free trade.

Free Trade in America

Like generals, who are said always to be fighting the last war, economists tend always to be preventing the last depression. For the past half century, the Great Depression of 1929–34 has dominated economic thought. Trade policy today is designed in part to avoid the devastating effects of that era's mistakes.

The great crash of 1929 worsened a bad economic downturn. But many economists believe that it was the passage of the Smoot-Hawley Tariff Act of 1930 that turned an economic downturn into an economic disaster. That trade act, passed by Congress and signed by President Herbert Hoover, raised tariffs on imports up to 60%. America's trading partners retaliated by putting their own tariffs into effect, and by 1933 world trade had contracted by almost two thirds.

President Franklin D. Roosevelt's secretary of state, Cordell Hull, argued that not only did tariffs hurt economic growth, they also led to war. He reasoned that countries in economic disarray were more likely to have totalitarian leaders, who were in turn more likely to cause wars. As a consequence, Hull became a passionate advocate of a free trading system in which goods would move from country to country without restriction.

Bretton Woods

The first of the major conferences on a new international order was held in Bretton Woods, New Hampshire, only three weeks after D-Day, June 6, 1944. (This somewhat out of the way place was chosen in part because John Maynard Keynes, one of the key figures in the conference, considered it an "unfriendly act" in the age before air-conditioning to be invited to a summer meeting in Washington, D.C.)

The Bretton Woods conference established the rules by which the exchange rates between currencies would be determined. Money and trade are indivisible issues. Ever since countries gave up bartering for goods, money has been the payment with which one country buys another's exports. But the value of a country's currency can be manipulated to some extent by the home government to give its exports an advantage. (In particular, by devaluing its currency—that is, lowering its value in relation to other currencies—a country can slash the price of its exports.) Such competitive devaluations were common during the years of the Great Depression. The Bretton Woods system put an end to the practice by establishing a system of fixed exchange rates.

The price of gold was fixed at $35 an ounce, and all other countries set the value of their currency in terms of the dollar. A currency's value depended on its country's economic growth, inflation and interest rates. The system allowed other countries to alter their exchange rates in exceptional cases, but the U.S. was required to maintain the dollar's value. Since most industrial countries used the U.S. dollar as a major component of their financial reserves, a drop in its value would reduce the worth of such reserves, causing panic.

One key aspect of the system was the convertibility of dollars into gold. Any country that preferred to hold gold instead of dollars could redeem the dollars at the rate of $35 for one ounce of gold. This was believed to be a way of encouraging discipline, since the U.S. would be loath to do anything that would prompt a run on its gold. At the time of the conference, the U.S. held 70% of the world's mined gold.

The Rules of Trade

The General Agreement on Tariffs and Trade (GATT), established some three years after the Bretton Woods conference, was the second pillar of the postwar economy. Its objective was the reduction of tariffs. The movement toward lowering tariffs had begun in the 1930s as the U.S. negotiated bilateral treaties with its trading partners. But GATT was a more comprehensive approach.

The concept underpinning GATT is *"most-favored-nation"*

treatment: if a country gives a trade advantage to one country, it should give the same advantage to every other country. In this way, all countries trade on an equal footing with a given country.

For 25 years, GATT succeeded far beyond the expectation of its founders. Although the ideal of free trade was never realized (restrictions on agriculture and other sectors remained in place), trade was much freer and the growth of the world's economies appeared to justify the faith of its advocates. For West Germany and Japan in particular, exports were the source of miraculous economic growth. By 1958 six European countries were strong enough to create the Common Market, which fostered intra-European trade by abolishing tariffs within the Community while establishing a common tariff toward other countries.

As world trade expanded, so did GATT. Once considered a "rich man's club," since most of its original 23 members were major industrial powers, GATT now num-

bers 96 members. Although invited, the Soviet Union originally chose not to take part in GATT or Bretton Woods, preferring to establish its own economic bloc with the Eastern European satellites. Czechoslovakia, Hungary, Poland and Romania did later join GATT, but East-West trade remains a small percentage of international trade. (The Soviet Union has since expressed interest in joining.)

Troubles Begin

The U.S. was the major beneficiary of the expansion of world trade in GATT's first quarter century. The U.S. was easily able to sell its goods abroad, at first because it was the one industrial economy not damaged by the war, later because of its technological innovations. Exports soared, new jobs were created, and the economy grew. Thanks to the Marshall Plan, which poured more than $13 billion into Europe, the Europeans had the money to buy American products—making trade possible. But as Professor Howard Wachtel of American University points out, this system "... depended on American products being so superior in price and quality that the dollars exported abroad returned as purchases of U.S. products." If this did not happen, unspent dollars would pile up abroad. This is what happened in the late 1950s when dollars flowing out in the form of loans, grants, military expenses and private investment exceeded foreign demand for American goods.

By 1958, U.S. dollars abroad exceeded the value of America's gold reserves. This meant that if they so desired, foreigners could empty Fort Knox. Countries began to cash in their dollars for gold. In

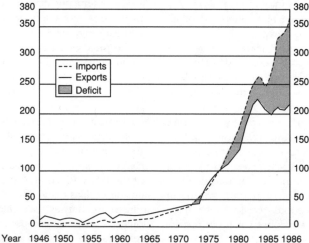

Trends in U.S. Trade
Billions of $U.S.

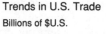

- - - Imports
— Exports
■ Deficit

Year 1946 1950 1955 1960 1965 1970 1975 1980 1985 1986

1959 the U.S. paid out 10% of the gold in Fort Knox to foreigners.

Newly elected President John F. Kennedy, who had made the gold crisis an election issue, was able to restore the U.S. allies' confidence in the dollar and slowed the run on Fort Knox. (Kennedy was reported to have said that the two things which scared him most were nuclear war and the payments deficit.) But the Vietnam War and the social welfare programs promoting a Great Society were the Bretton Woods system's death knell. Unwilling to raise taxes enough to pay for the high levels of spending, the U.S. government instead took the inflationary step of printing more dollars, many of which were cashed in by foreign governments for gold. By 1969, half the U.S. gold reserves were gone.

Finally, in 1971, President Richard M. Nixon took the dramatic step of ending the convertibility of dollars into gold. Nixon had not intended to end the system of fixed exchange rates or to devalue the dollar, but rather to force other countries to raise the value of their currencies and promote changes in the system. However, the effect of his action was to cause a devaluation of the dollar, which was formalized in the Smithsonian agreement of 1971. It was not possible to salvage Bretton Woods. By 1973, the prices of most currencies were floating like other commodities—sugar, pork bellies, coffee—with their value going up or down depending on supply and demand.

The effects on U.S. trade were beneficial initially. The dollar's depreciation made U.S. goods cheaper and more competitive. The trade balance improved. But the new global marketplace is much less stable and orderly than its predecessor, and the U.S. role less clearly defined. Can the U.S. be the leader of the global economy? Should it be satisfied with being first among equals? Or is it in danger of forfeiting its economic leadership? The answer, many believe, rests on whether the U.S. can be competitive in the global marketplace.

A RELUCTANT TRADER

No nation was ever ruined by trade.

—*Benjamin Franklin*

Franklin could afford to be sanguine. In his day, America's "adventurous spirit," along with its bountiful resources, attractive manufactured goods and competitive merchant fleet, "excited uneasy sensations in ... Europe," according to Alexander Hamilton. This confident approach has been shaken in the 1980s by questions about America's competitiveness.

At its most basic level, competitiveness means that the U.S. must be able to manufacture goods and sell services at prices cheap enough to make them attractive worldwide, yet high enough to ensure companies a profit and workers a fair wage. The stakes are high: today some 70% of U.S. manufactured products must compete with a foreign product, as compared with 25% in 1960.

It is too soon to count the U.S. out as a global competitor, but its standing has been severely eroded. Among the causes are the quality of U.S. goods, the volatility of the dollar and the decline of markets for U.S. goods.

Finding a Niche

One theory as to the origins of the trade deficit might be described as a national version of jet lag—neither government, workers, nor management have yet adjusted to the reality of the global marketplace. In this view, the trade deficit is a result of fundamental problems in important sectors of the U.S. economy, whether it be the poor quality of some U.S. goods, management's inability to design effective export strategies, or the workers' lack of commitment to trading that their East Asian competitors have. When South Korean strikers returned to work in August 1987, for example, many agreed to put in 65-hour weeks until their companies' lost export earnings were regained.

Should Americans be expected to work like this as well? If not, should Americans be willing to accept a lower standard of living? Or should the government be doing more? Should it target certain industries for aid?

According to the theory of free trade, the U.S. should export those products in which it has a comparative advantage. First articulated by early 19th-century Scottish economist David Ricardo, stockbroker and self-made millionaire, the theory of comparative advantage explains that it pays for a nation to specialize.

Ricardo argued that a country should concentrate on those products it could produce relatively more cheaply than other countries. With its well-educated work force and advanced technology, the U.S. might conclude that its comparative advantage lies in manufacturing computers, aircraft and optical equipment rather than in labor-intensive industries such as textiles or steel.

The actions of American multi-national corporations (MNCs) would seem to reflect that. These companies, such as General Motors, Coca-Cola and IBM, are headquartered in one country but have subsidiaries in several. Such companies, which include most of America's largest, manufacture their products where they believe it is most efficient.

Increasingly, many MNCs have been moving their factories abroad, to Mexico, Hong Kong and other countries where labor is less expensive. Even Zenith, the last American manufacturer of TV sets, relies on its Mexican plants for some of its parts. Said chairman Jerry K. Pearlman, "It's a global business. . . . Everybody has got a foreign chassis in their sets." Such decisions exacerbate the trade deficit, however, since a product made abroad by an MNC and sold in the U.S. is considered an import.

This also raises troubling questions. The implication is that American workers should earn less (Zenith has used the threat of moving more production to Mexico in order to win contract concessions from union workers) or that the U.S. should turn away from all labor-intensive industries. The result of the latter would be the loss of thousands of jobs and of industries important to national defense, such as steel. The fact that the Japanese have invested in such industries in the U.S.–automobiles, steel—and that the products they make in the U.S. are sold abroad suggests that with proper management, despite high salaries, U.S. industries can compete.

Even if the U.S. concentrated on those areas where it appears to have comparative advantage, would that solve its trade imbalance? The semi-conductor industry, for example, was until recently a profitable export business. But it foundered under the bombardment of Japanese exports.

For those who see the U.S. trade deficit as a reflection of a fundamental problem in its economy, the solutions are several. They include spending more money on research and development, improving education and worker training, enhancing the quality of American goods, expanding U.S. managers' knowledge of foreign production techniques and targeting aid to affected industries. Others think the trade deficit has nothing to do with comparative advantage; they blame it on the dollar.

The Dollar's Impact

In every year from 1894 to 1971, the U.S. had a trade surplus. The sharp deterioration in the balance of trade since then, notably since 1981, has been attributed by analysts such as former presidential economic adviser Martin Feldstein to the 70% rise in the value of the dollar vis-à-vis other major currencies (the Japanese yen, British pound, French franc, etc.) that took place between 1980 and 1985. Feldstein argues, ". . . the cause of the trade deficit lies not in the character of the American work force or of American management . . . .Such fundamental aspects of a nation's industry cannot change in as short a time as five years."

The sharp rise in the value of the dollar added the equivalent of a 70% sales tax to all goods sold abroad. As a result, U.S. goods have been expensive overseas, while foreign imports have been cheap in the U.S. The overpriced dollar acted like a subsidy to foreigners trying to sell in the U.S. Even its drop in value through the fall of 1987 left the dollar higher than many believed it should be.

Most economists credit the rise in the dollar's value to the Federal budget deficit. The growth of the deficit (from $74 billion in 1981 to $237 billion in 1986) pushed up the price of money—its interest rate —and therefore pushed up the value of the dollar. (High interest rates lead to a high dollar because they make investing in the U.S. attractive. To invest, foreign countries must first convert their currency into dollars, which has the effect of increasing demand on the dollar and pushing up its value in comparison with other major currencies.)

On September 22, 1985, at the Plaza Hotel in New York, U.S. Treasury Secretary James A. Baker III and Federal Reserve Chairman Paul Volcker met with the finance ministers from Britain, France, Japan and West Germany (known as the Group of 5). Recognizing that the dollar's extra strength was distorting trade and inflaming protectionist sentiments, this group agreed that "further orderly appreciation of the main nondollar currencies against the dollar is desirable."

The Group of 5 announcement gave momentum to a drop in the dollar that had begun some months before. From 1985 to 1987, the dollar dropped in value by 30% against other major currencies. The group then called a second meeting in 1987 in which they agreed to "cooperate to foster stability," in this case to slow the rapid drop in the dollar.

Has the dollar's drop in value helped the U.S. balance of trade, as had been expected? Yes, but not as much as had been hoped. U.S. demand for foreign products remains strong, and foreign companies have been willing to cut their profits on their exports to America to maintain their market share. In August 1987 the merchandise trade balance dropped to $15.7 billion from the July record of $16.5 billion. Such a small contraction after such a large drop in the dollar caused fears among investors, who were concerned that a further drop in the dollar's value might lead to inflation or higher interest rates. This was one of the causes of the 1987 stock market crash.

Closed Markets

The stagnation of America's major markets has hindered U.S. exports. Latin America, in particular, has been deep in debt for the last few years and forced to cut back its imports while pushing exports.

In its heydey in the 1970s, when foreign banks were recycling petrodollars in the form of large loans to Latin America, that region absorbed some 40% of U.S. exports. But the 1979 oil price hike, high interest rates and the world recession in the early 1980s, combined with a wasteful use of the foreign loans, led to a debt squeeze. In 1982 Mexico announced it could not pay the interest on its loans, and other major borrowers soon followed suit.

The International Monetary Fund (IMF), a multilateral agency created by the Bretton Woods agreements, became the pivotal agency involved in aiding the debtor countries. In most cases, to earn IMF assistance, Latin American countries had to implement economic austerity programs.

Countries had to reduce imports sharply and to increase exports as much as possible in order to earn the money they needed to pay back the banks. As a result, purchases from the U.S. dropped by $14 billion in two years.

In a 1987 special report on trade, the editors of *Business Week* recommended that the U.S. and other industrial nations finance a new assistance program, along the lines of the Marshall Plan, to aid developing countries. Massive infusions of aid are needed before the Latin Americans will have enough money to get their economies back in shape and resume their purchases of imports, which will help the U.S. The editors caution: "The U.S., Japan and the other main players are writing off markets of more than a billion people who simply can't afford their goods."

Two other major markets, West Germany and Japan, also went on a stringent diet in the early 1980s, though in their case it was self-imposed. The leaders of West Germany and Japan do not believe that fiscal deficits produce sustainable growth. Instead of encouraging consumer purchases the way the U.S. has (by, for example, cutting taxes), they have followed the opposite approach and have increased taxes and encouraged saving. The U.S. has urged its allies to prod their consumers to spend more, thus, it is hoped, providing a larger market for U.S. goods. Japanese Prime Minister Yasuhiro Nakasone said in April 1987 that Japan would spend $23 billion to encourage domestic consumption.

America's trade balance is also affected by the way other countries trade. Of particular concern are those actions considered unfair.

How can the U.S. make the rules fairer?

KEEPING THE BICYCLE MOVING

On September 15, 1986, trade ministers met in Punta del Este, Uruguay, to ready the agenda for the eighth round of GATT negotiations. This round promises to be far more difficult than its predecessors, yet many believe that the fate of free trade hinges on its results.

GATT talks are the forum in which the rules of free trade are discussed and hammered out. In its early days, the negotiations focused on tariffs. As a result of the seven earlier rounds, particularly the Kennedy Round (1936–67) and the Tokyo Round (1973–79), tariffs have been lowered from an average of 40% to 5%.

Trade analysts C. Michael Aho and Jonathan David Aronson have suggested that the U.S. initiated the Uruguay round of negotiations, not in the hope of a great breakthrough, but to prevent a breakdown of the multilateral trading system. They have called this "the bicycle theory of negotiations"—"unless forward momentum is maintained, the trading system, like the bicyclist will tumble over."

For free traders, the greatest benefit of these talks would be to shore up their constituencies in the U.S. Domestic support for free trade has always been lukewarm. In a 1953 survey, at a point when the U.S. was clearly the dominant economic power and easily able to export, more people favored increasing the restrictions on imports than increasing their volume. A survey in 1986 by the Chicago

Council on Foreign Relations found that 78% of the public surveyed believed protecting jobs should be America's foremost foreign policy concern for that year.

That free trade, paradoxically, has remained a goal of America's policy can be traced to several causes. Up until 1987, when it was displaced by West Germany, the U.S. was the world's major exporter. Free trade policy was ardently supported by those sectors that were then most competitive in world markets—automobiles, agriculture and manufacturers of heavy equipment—while it was ardently opposed by few, since it made up too small a part of the gross national product to hurt many. Also, in the wake of the depression, it was seen as unstatesmanlike to be labeled a protectionist. Said Chrysler chairman Lee A. Iacocca, "a member of Congress would rather be called a pervert than a protectionist."

The traditional coalition of supporters has broken down today, as many of the most pro-free trade industries are losing to international competition. In an effort to recapture support for its policy, the Reagan Administration tried to fashion a new free trade coalition. It included representatives from the high-technology industries, services (telecommunications and banking), and MNCs. Reagan's agenda for the GATT talks reflected this new coalition's interests: fair trade, standardization of services, reform of agricultural trade, more open investment practices for MNCs, and improved protection of patents and copyrights. (This last has long been of concern to companies whose patented inventions have been copied and sold by Asian countries.) By contrast, tariffs will play a small role in these negotiations.

Fair Trade

GATT does not offer clear-cut definitions of many unfair trade practices or a well-defined way of disposing of them. For example, neither of the following practices has been penalized by GATT:

- In South Korea, construction firms are subsidized by the government when they bid on foreign projects.
- In Western Europe, airline reservation systems do not list the flights of American carriers.

The result, claims U.S. Special Trade Representative Clayton K. Yeutter, is that "as currently constituted, GATT does not address many of the realities of modern trade."

In the absence of agreed-upon definitions, countries tend to define for themselves those practices they consider unfair. For example, legislation considered by Congress in 1987 designates as an unfair trade practice the denial by other countries of workers' rights, such as the right to form unions. But an offending country might respond that it is the U.S. legislation that is unfair in that it attempts to impose on others an alien value system or raise other countries' costs so that they are not competitive.

Aho and Aronson make this case for better-defined rules: "If they were up to date and widely accepted, GATT rules and procedures would allow government leaders to do what they know is in the national interest even in the face of pressure to help narrower, special interests." The difficulty in negotiations will be to come to some consensus about definitions.

Services

Trade in services now makes up 32% of global trade, and it is a growing sector. The U.S. is a leader in this field, which includes consulting, banking, insurance, telecommunications and transportation.

Up until 1981, America's service earnings were sufficiently great that they could offset its deficits in merchandise trade. Even last year, services rang up some 6.9 billion in profits for the U.S. But America's ability to increase its trade in services is hampered by the restrictive nature of this field. For example, in many countries, areas such as banking or telecommunications are tightly regulated and often government owned. This makes foreign participation difficult.

The Reagan Administration, which had made the establishment of rules to govern trade in services one of its first priorities, signed a trade pact with Canada in October 1987 that the U.S. hoped will be a model for GATT. Under the terms of the accord both countries agreed to undertake to eliminate discrimination in financial services and to establish a binding dispute settlement mechanism for services.

Agriculture

U.S. agricultural trade has been exempt from most GATT regulations since 1955, when the U.S. asked for and received a waiver. Today, many members of GATT subsidize their agriculture—either by supporting prices or supplementing farmers' income. This distorts trade: it causes overproduction, which then leads to export subsidies or restrictions on imports.

The Reagan Administration had proposed a phaseout of all price and export subsidies for agriculture. The Administration hoped that this controversial proposal, as unpopular with domestic farmers as foreign ones, will be approved. The benefits to the U.S. would be great. In 1986, agricultural subsidies equaled 12% of the budget deficit. (Income supports are not part of this proposal.)

So far this proposal has not proved popular with most other GATT negotiators. But analysts hope that at a minimum it may be possible to negotiate some sort of standardization of subsidies. For example, countries could agree to support agricultural commodities through direct income assistance to farmers rather than by keeping crop prices high.

MNCs

The increased importance of multinational corporations in international trade presents a unique set of problems. The interests of MNCs do not necessarily coincide with the interest of their home country. For example, the U.S. wishes to increase its automobile exports and might prefer for General Motors to do all its auto manufacturing in Detroit. General Motors, however, concerned with maximizing its profits, might decide to move some of its manufacturing to Mexico and export those parts back to the U.S.

One part of the Administration's platform that probably is appealing to MNCs is its effort to reduce trade-distorting investment practices. This would include negotiating an end to rules that require companies to keep a certain percentage of their profits in a given country; that set the number of residents who must be in management positions; and that regulate the percentage of a company that can be owned by foreigners.

Other National Agendas

Of the developed countries, Japan will probably be most supportive of the U.S. desire for clearly established definitions of fair trade. Japan can best hope to head off protectionist legislation against its exports by showing that it does trade fairly. This would be more easily done with a clear definition of the rules. One sign of Japanese interest was that former Prime Minister Nakasone was the first head of state to support the U.S. call for a new GATT round. Canada also is likely to be supportive since, as the major trading partner of the U.S., it also fears a rash of protectionism.

The European Community's agenda, which includes the protection of jobs in its agricultural sector, is likely to put it on a course diametrically opposite that of the other industrial countries. The Community is not expected to welcome further trade liberalization.

The major unknown is the developing countries. This is the first set of GATT talks in which they will play an active role. If they agree to open their protected markets, they could give as large a boost to world trade as it received in the 1940s from Bretton Woods and GATT. (Already some 40% of U.S. exports go to the Third World.) But the developing countries are unlikely to make such a concession unless they can increase their exports of labor-intensive goods, such as textiles and footwear, to the U.S. These exports would hurt the very industries that have already been damaged by Third World competition. The developing countries will also be unable to afford increased imports without some resolution of their debt crises.

The Last Hurdle: Congress

Once the Uruguay Round is over, and that could take several years, the President will face the most severe hurdle, getting the agreement through Congress.

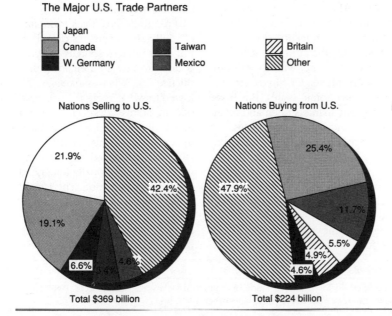

The Major U.S. Trade Partners

- Japan
- Canada
- W. Germany
- Taiwan
- Mexico
- Britain
- Other

Nations Selling to U.S.

21.9%
19.1%
6.6%
4.6%
42.4%

Total $369 billion

Nations Buying from U.S.

25.4%
47.9%
11.7%
5.5%
4.9%
4.6%

Total $224 billion

The Constitution gives the Congress the authority "to lay and collect ... duties" and to "regulate commerce with foreign nations." In practice, however, most trade legislation since the 1930s has been initiated by the President.

With trade increasingly an important domestic—and election—issue, Congress may be less eager to approve the results of the Uruguay Round than it has earlier rounds. Congress did not approve the delegation to the President of authority to negotiate at the GATT talks until the fall of 1907, one year after the agenda for the Uruguay Round had been set, and then attached it to an omnibus trade bill that the President is unlikely to approve. The bill, now in conference, includes measures that limit presidential discretion, require the President to take steps to open foreign markets and retaliate against identified unfair trading practices. ∎

U.S. Trade Policy at the Crossroads

By John C. Whitehead

Following the devastation of the Great Depression and World War II, the United States took the lead in establishing an international economic system based squarely on the principle that freer trade benefits all countries. The system we established has spurred a remarkable period of economic growth and innovation, not just for us but also for other nations prepared to seize the opportunity. Nonetheless, a debate is raging—in the halls of Congress and in the farms and factories of America—as to whether free trade is still a relevant guiding principle in today's world.

Free trade is not a spent force. The national debate over trade, and other economic policy, has intensified over the last 2 weeks in the wake of the turmoil in the stock market.

The stock market developments vividly demonstrated the interdependence of the major industrial economies and the importance of sound and coherent economic policies. In his recent press conference, President Reagan reaffirmed our intention to work closely with our allies to coordinate policies and ensure stable growth. We all recognize our responsibility to follow sound policies that will inspire public confidence.

In particular, it is necessary that we avoid protectionist policies that would damage the prospects for economic growth and global prosperity. The world community and financial markets would see an outburst of protectionism here as a sign that the United States no longer has the will to exercise responsible leadership on international economic issues. But if we keep our markets open and maintain sound economic policies, the underlying strength of our economy will carry us through.

Against this backdrop of the national debate on trade policy and the recent financial market developments, Americans should recall some basic lessons about trade.

ECONOMIC AND POLITICAL BENEFITS OF FREE TRADE

Free trade enriches our lives. Through free trade we obtain the widest possible range of goods at the lowest possible prices. Free trade raises the standard of living in all countries. Ultimately, it is the consumer who benefits from free trade—and who pays when countries depart from it.

Free trade promotes economic efficiency. It encourages capital, labor, and other resources in every country to flow to their most productive use. When markets are allowed to work freely, the principle of comparative advantage assures a global division of labor that maximizes output. Today this division of labor has produced an extraordinarily efficient, globally integrated pattern of production. The United States cannot have a comparative advantage in all products, but through free trade, we can specialize in what we do best and avail

John C. Whitehead was Deputy Secretary of State.

Source: From an address before the Conference on International Trade, Wilmington, Delaware, November 2, 1987. Reprinted in United States Department of State, *Current Policy No. 1022,* November 1987, pp. 1–3.

ourselves of the best products available anywhere.

By fostering efficient patterns of consumption and production, free trade maximizes income and spurs economic growth. International competition prods producers in every country to innovate. Free trade is the springboard for new products and processes that make our lives healthier, fuller, and more comfortable. For example, the development of fiber optics will dramatically enhance global communications networks. Recent discoveries in superconductors pave the way for new and improved products in such areas as computers, electricity transmission, medical equipment, and fusion reactors.

While the international marketplace is incredibly competitive, free trade is not a contest in which the success of one country is a defeat for others. We share in the prosperity of others, because rising incomes abroad provide enhanced markets for us. Europe and Japan obviously have become tougher economic competitors, but their economic advances also have been indispensable to our own growth.

The benefits of free trade are not just theoretical. The experience of the last 40 years bears out their practical significance. Those countries that have embraced open markets have prospered, while those that have followed inward-looking economic policies have stagnated. This lesson applies to developed and developing countries alike. For example, due in large part to the market-oriented, outward-looking economic policies, the rate of growth in Asian countries such as Korea and Singapore has far outpaced

the economic growth in developing countries with statist policies.

The strong economy we now enjoy would be impossible without free trade. We are in our 59th month of economic growth, making the current recovery the longest peacetime recovery in U.S. history. Since the start of this expansion, roughly 240,000 jobs a month have been created for American workers. A higher percentage of Americans are working now than ever before. Our unemployment rate is 5.8%, the lowest level in 8 years. Inflation last year dipped to the low level of 2%. Economic growth this year has proceeded at a healthy 3.5% rate. It is important to remember that, despite the recent volatility in the stock market, the U.S. economy is fundamentally sound and strong.

Our open market approach is not the only cause of our prosperity. A sound monetary policy, vigilant efforts to restrain growth in government spending, and deregulatory policies to spark competition and innovation also have been essential. But it is equally true that prosperity could not have been achieved in a world saddled with trade restrictions.

Despite this prosperity, concerns often are raised about the competitive position of the U.S. economy and about our persistent deficit with the rest of the world. As recently as 1981, we ran a surplus on our current account, the broadest measure of our overall trade in goods and services. In 1986, our current account deficit reached $141 billion, and it is likely to reach a similar level this year.

Ironically, perhaps, our external deficit is, in large part, a result

of the strength of the U.S. economy relative to the economies of our major partners. Economic growth in Europe, Japan, and many major developing countries has been sluggish during the past 6 years. Our economy has performed much better. As a consequence, investors have sought to put their capital in the United States; at the same time, our growth in demand has provided a ready market for the products of our trading partners. The trade deficit tells us nothing about the overall competitive position of the U.S. economy.

We should clearly understand that our deficit was not caused by unfair trade practices abroad. As objectionable as such practices are, they have not increased so dramatically during the last 6 years that they can explain the shift from a small surplus to a large deficit.

We also need to recognize that the benefits of free trade do not cease when we run a trade deficit. Trade restrictions would deprive us of the benefits of trade but would not reduce the deficit unless they were so draconian as to devastate the economy.

The United States has a choice to make. We can continue to embrace and strengthen the free trade system—a system that produces enormous benefits for our economy. Or we can retreat from the world economy and construct barriers to foreign trade an investment—an isolationist approach that damages both our national and the global prosperity.

These alternatives are posed starkly in two important issues currently before Congress: the free trade agreement with Canada and the omnibus trade bill.

U.S.-CANADA FREE TRADE AGREEMENT

The United States and Canada recently concluded an agreement establishing a bilateral free trade area. This historic agreement creates the world's largest free trade area. It will strengthen the economies of both Canada and the United States and, over time, create thousands of jobs in both countries. Some economists estimate that the agreement eventually will raise the level of economic well-being by as much as 5% in Canada and by a smaller, but still very significant, percentage in the United States.

The centerpiece achievement of the free trade area is the total elimination within 10 years of all tariffs on bilateral trade between the United States and Canada, currently in excess of $120 billion. Since Canadian tariffs currently average 10% (as opposed to 4% in the United States) and sales to Canada account for one-fourth of our total exports, the elimination of tariffs will create significant new opportunities for U.S. businesses. Canada, for its part, gains duty-free access to the largest national economy in the world.

Another landmark achievement is in the services area. The free trade agreement between Canada and the United States is the first international understanding to establish binding rules for all new measures affecting a comprehensive set of service sectors. Henceforth, neither country will discriminate against service providers from the other in some 150 service sectors. This element of the agreement, covering a large portion of our $11-billion bilateral trade in services, will provide secure market access in important service sectors, such as the rapidly growing area of enhanced telecommunications and computer services.

In another important economic area, investment, Canada has agreed to limit its practice of screening, and possibly blocking, new U.S. investments in Canada. Under the agreement, Canada will make permanent its recent policy of not screening most new investments and will reduce significantly the screening of direct acquisitions.

The free trade agreement liberalizes rules in many other areas, including agriculture, automotive trade, energy, government procurement, standards, and trade law remedies.

The free trade agreement between Canada and the United States is innovative, far-reaching, and courageous. It is based squarely on the precepts of free trade. As it tears down barriers to trade, investment, and other economic activity, the agreement will raise the standard of living and promote growth in both countries. The agreement will make both the United States and Canada more prosperous.

Furthermore, the success of this bilateral market-opening initiative will lend momentum to multilateral market-opening negotiations. We believe that in many areas the free trade agreement between Canada and the United States can serve as a model for the multilateral Uruguay Trade Round.

THE TRADE BILL

In contrast to the Canada free trade agreement, the omnibus trade bills pending before Congress would, if enacted, severely damage the U.S. and global economies. The bills represent a retreat from the postwar free trade system that we built and under which we have prospered. Perhaps more important, they represent a retreat from U.S. leadership.

Both the House and Senate trade bills are comprehensive, all-encompassing measures that affect trade, investment, finance, and foreign policy. While the provisions are detailed and complex, there is a common—and very disturbing—thread throughout each bill. Directly or indirectly, these bills seek to replace consideration of the national interest with the dictates of special interests.

In the trade area, the bills contain a myriad of "technical" changes in our trade law. All of the changes head in one direction: toward increased barriers to trade and greater limitations on the President's trade policy authority.

The cumulative effect of the proposed changes is "procedural protectionism." The provisions take our current trade statutes and twist them in a way that would make import restrictions a surer bet for industries seeking protection. In many cases, the proposed provisions explicitly prohibit the President or the Cabinet from considering the national interest when deliberating whether to take a trade action to aid a specific industry. The cost to consumers, job losses to other U.S. industries, the risk of retaliation, foreign policy considerations—none of these factors would be given full weight in the trade policy decisionmaking process.

"Quick trigger" protectionist measures would inflict economic damage both directly and indirectly. In and of themselves, trade restrictions hurt unprotected sectors of our economy. Restrictions would divert resources to protected sectors of the economy and away from dynamic sectors left unprotected. As a result, the standard of living for the country as a whole would drop.

Furthermore, new import restrictions here would incite a dangerously escalating spiral of retaliation that easily could lead to a trade war. U.S. exporters would lose overseas markets as our trading partners erect their own barriers.

The House and Senate omnibus trade bills represent an effort to subvert international trade rules and replace them with our own. If others followed such an approach, we would be the first to protest.

OUTCOME BEING WATCHED CLOSELY

The debate over the course of U.S. trade policy is being watched closely in financial markets and in foreign capitals. Our decisions will have serious consequences— ones that may be felt more quickly that many realize and in realms beyond the economic. The recent events in the stock market have demonstrated vividly the interdependence of the major industrial economies and how closely economic developments in one country are watched by other countries.

Foreign investment flows have been attracted to the United States by the prosperity of our economy, and they have contributed significantly to that prosperity. Foreign investors, however, are not interested in keeping their money in a country about to enmesh itself in protectionist trade restrictions. Furthermore, they fear, with good reason, that controls on capital movement would soon follow imposition of major restrictions on trade. Indeed, the pending omnibus trade bills already contain provisions—in the form of screening and registration requirements —for controlling capital inflows. If investors were to lose confidence in U.S. economic policy, there could be a rapid flight of capital, leading, in turn, to turmoil in foreign exchange markets. This would rekindle inflationary pressures in the U.S. economy, drive up interest rates, and put the economy in a tailspin.

Foreign governments look to the United States for economic, political, and strategic leadership. If Congress passes legislation to implement the free trade legislation, the world community will perceive that the United States continues to have the commitment and courage to uphold our international responsibilities.

On the other hand, if we enact an omnibus trade bill in its current form, foreign governments will conclude that we have surrendered international economic leadership. The will assume that we no longer have the will to compete or to lead in the search for responsible solutions to global economic problems. Given the recent turmoil in the financial markets, it is particularly dangerous, at this point in time, for the United States to even consider adopting irresponsible, protectionist economic policies.

CONCLUSION

In conclusion, the United States is at a crossroads. Before us are two paths for conducting trade relations. The first path is based on recognition of the benefits of global competition and a willingness to confront its challenges. If we continue along this path, we uphold and strengthen the postwar free trade system that has already produced two generations of unprecedented prosperity for us and others. We also remain true to a free trade tradition supported by every American President since Franklin Roosevelt. A premier example of this strong, forward-looking policy is the agreement establishing a free trade area with Canada.

The second path entails a withdrawal from global competition and a retreat from global responsibilities. Barriers to trade and other economic interactions are constructed. This path leads to economic stagnation here and abroad and more fractious political relations. A prime example of this weak, defensive approach is the omnibus trade bills before Congress.

The rest of the world is watching our deliberations in these two areas. The stakes are high. I am confident that once the American people understand clearly the nature of the choices before them, they and their elected representatives will choose the path that will foster U.S. international leadership and global prosperity. ∎

The International Economic Challenge

By Robert D. Hormats

Prophets of America's decline and advocates of defensive economic policies are out in force this year. Nonetheless, the next president will have the opportunity to disprove the former and to obviate the need for the latter. But to do so, he will have to take the initiative to strengthen America's productive base and assert vigorous leadership in the global economy.

The U.S. economy is extraordinarily resilient. It has repeatedly demonstrated an ability to adapt to change, to create new jobs, and to support innovative entrepreneurs. But the country now faces formidable competitive challenges from abroad, is burdened by massive domestic and foreign debt, depends heavily on inflows of foreign capital, and finds attainment of important domestic and national security objectives threatened by unprecedented financial constraints. Commitments at home and abroad exceed available resources, and difficult choices on budget and policy priorities have been postponed.

When resources were in relatively greater abundance, Washington committed itself to assist, subsidize, and provide preferential tax treatment to numerous social groups and economic sectors. Overseas, the United States assumed significant security obligations. Now, despite large budget deficits, powerful domestic constituencies resist cuts in their favored programs, whether or not they can

pass tests of cost or effectiveness. At the same time, practices that took root in an environment of fewer resource constraints and less global competition now impair the country's response to new circumstances. And America's ability to reorder its foreign commitments is limited by the persistence of dangerous international situations and by difficulties in transferring responsibilities to allies.

In a democracy, where, absent a broadly perceived sense of urgency, power centers can block significant change, overcoming policy and attitudinal inertia is typically difficult. In *Why England Slept* (1940), John Kennedy described this "false feeling of security, which was contagious and spread through all groups. The result was that people felt sacrifices were not necessary. . . . [T]he achievement of that singleness of purpose, which is so difficult to acquire in a democracy until moments of great danger, was postponed."

Achieving a national singleness of purpose on the need to strengthen greatly America's global competitiveness, to make difficult choices among competing resource priorities, and in doing so, to reduce internal and foreign imbalances in a manner that promotes stable growth will test the new president's leadership abilities. It will require from him an active, hands-on role in formulating, articulating, and executing domestic and international economic policy.

His most difficult challenge will be to reduce America's trade and budget deficits without causing a recession or inflation and without gutting programs vital to American security, needy groups in this society, or its economic base. But he must go well beyond this—to forge a coherent strategy to redress the underlying deficiencies in domestic saving, productivity, investment, and education, as well as the weaknesses of a world economy on which America's prosperity increasingly depends.

These issues will have profound political and security implications. A strong foreign policy and military cannot be sustained without matching economic strength. Whether America can protect its security interests around the world, continues to be a constructive leader of the Western alliance, and remains a great power will depend in large measure on whether it can maintain prosperity at home and resolve pivotal global economic problems, such as currency instability, trade deficits, and Third World debt.

A president who does not address these problems effectively is unlikely to be able to conduct a successful foreign policy. He will not have sufficient resources for defense and foreign aid. He will be pressed by public frustration with trade barriers and inadequate burden sharing to escalate economic demands on allies and to pull back from international responsibilities, aggravating frictions that could

ROBERT D. HORMATS is vice chairman of Goldman, Sachs International Corporation. He was assistant secretary of state for economic and business affairs from 1981 to 1982.

Source: From *Foreign Policy,* No. 71 (Summer, 1988) pp. 99–116. Copyright 1988 by the *Carnegie Endowment for International Peace.*

shake the very foundations of Western security arrangements. He will preside over an economy suffering from a decline in living standards relative to other countries and from growing debt—raising doubts about the U.S. ability to retain its preeminent global influence. Latin American economic problems could lead to upheavals in the Western Hemisphere, and prolonged economic disputes with major allies could weaken ties on which American security depends. The greatest threat to U.S. security over the next few years may well come not from Moscow but from a confluence of economic difficulties that jeopardizes international political stability, disrupts U.S. alliances, and undermines the capacity of the United States to pursue its global interests.

When President Ronald Reagan assumed office, his primary economic tasks were domestic—to reduce inflation and to pull the country out of recession. The next president will face international economic challenges at least as formidable as those on the domestic front, and the interaction between the two will be extremely complex.

The incoming president will inherit management of an economy that has achieved a dramatic lowering of inflation and unemployment, more than 6 years of economic growth, the benefits of deregulation in key sectors, and renewed confidence in free-market forces. But he will also inherit an economy burdened by massive internal and foreign debt—the latter amounting at his inauguration to more than $500 billion, and climbing.

These debts will weigh heavily on the next administration. Virtually every debate on fiscal policy, every major action of the Federal Reserve Board, and every private-sector financial decision will be influenced by America's dependence on foreign capital and the attendant risk of volatility in currency and financial markets. The twin deficits will limit severely both the policy tools that can be employed to sustain growth in the United States and the resources to achieve foreign-policy objectives.

This legacy will cause the president to take office on a note of pessimism. The risk is high that the large trade and budget imbalances will catch up with the United States during the next 4 years and bring to a close the longest postwar span of economic growth. The president will also face political pressures to retaliate against unfair commercial practices abroad, to resist foreign purchases of large American companies, and to insist that allies contribute more to Western security. An assertive Congress, believing that previous presidents did not firmly defend American trade interests, will push the next president to do more.

In response the new president might feel compelled to offer quick fixes. Instead, he will need to recognize that America's economic problems cannot be resolved overnight. It took years to build up the large fiscal and trade deficits and it will take years to reduce them. Ill-conceived efforts to cut these deficits could leave a legacy of recession, high inflation, protectionism, and fractured alliances.

MEETING THE GLOBAL CHALLENGE

Early in his administration the president should forge a political consensus on America's approach to the world economy. Lacking a consensus, the United States will be vulnerable to sharp shifts in policy. Individual decisions, as is often the case, will reflect short-term pressures with little consideration for their impact on American competitiveness and other longer-term goals.

For much of their history Americans have concentrated on the imperatives of building a nation. Wave after wave of immigrants joined with those already in America to build the most powerful economy in history. That permitted dramatic gains in most citizens' living standards and underpinned victory in two world wars. In the 1960s Washington felt it could redress the plight of social groups that did not enjoy the surge in prosperity and still afford a large military effort in the Vietnam War.

Abroad, Americans after World War II understood their interest in protecting friendly countries against the Soviet Union and in helping to reconstruct their economies to avert agitation for radical social and economic change. The United States made a broad range of foreign aid, military-base, and security commitments; opened its markets more rapidly than others; and for a time tolerated practices overseas that disadvantaged American exports.

But the traumas of Vietnam and the Iran hostage episode, enormous trade and budget deficits, and public sentiment that the country is paying too much to protect its competitors have combined to generate pressures for the United States to play a narrower and less costly world role. America's sense of global commitment and purpose has become clouded. Whether the United States now has the resources, or the will, to continue to play a leadership role of the size and scope of earlier years is now hotly debated.

While postwar America focused on security goals, much of the rest of the world focused on economics. Japan enjoyed a national consensus on the need to rebuild its economy with an export orientation. That has enabled successive governments to pursue policies promoting high savings, investment, and quality education while working with labor and management to support research, development, and productivity improvements.

West Germany enjoys a consensus, galvanized by memories of hyperinflation in the 1920s, that is predicated on a commitment by the government and the Bundesbank to hold down inflation. The confidence of savers and investors is thereby fostered. Management-union relations have emphasized quality and competitiveness.

In West Germany, Japan, and the newly industrializing countries of East Asia, where competitiveness is a preoccupation born of the view that international stature, security, and economic strength are intertwined, a consensus on economic policy has permitted business to compete with confidence and government backing. But exporting was not a major goal for most U.S. companies in the early postwar period because they enjoyed such a vast domestic market. Those who saw opportunities overseas frequently invested there to avoid import barriers. Taking U.S. economic strength for granted, Americans have neither defined their global role in economic terms nor emphasized international competitiveness.

In contrast to other world leaders, U.S. presidents have rarely asserted America's economic interests on the world stage. That neglect has convinced much of the world, and many Americans, that international economic issues are low presidential priorities. And domestic economic policy has lurched sharply from one administration to the next with little weight given to its impact on U.S. international economic interests.

Reagan has restored Americans' confidence in their country's global political and security stature; the new president must do the same on the international economic front. He cannot accomplish this merely with confident or patriotic rhetoric. Rather, he must convey a clear sense of national economic purpose, a coherent domestic and global economic strategy, and a willingness himself to implement that strategy vigorously.

Ultimately, the key to America's economic success lies on its shop floors and farms and in its laboratories, classrooms, and board rooms. The new president must underscore the need to meet foreign competition by strengthening the country's industrial and technological base and demonstrating to business, agriculture, and labor that his policies will support their competitive efforts. Over time this course will enable the United States to reduce its trade deficit through increases in capacity and productivity that raise wealth, job quality, and exports—rather than relying on slow growth or an ever lower dollar, which render the country poorer.

The president must first place America's international economic problems—and the notion of

decline—in perspective. Certainly the United States has legitimate grievances against foreign trade impediments and must push for their removal. But the lion's share of U.S. economic problems are homemade. Placing the blame on others diverts attention from putting America's house in order. If the United States does not narrow its gap between saving and investment, which leads to borrowing, along with a related gap between consumption and production, and if it fails to redress underlying weaknesses in productivity, education, and investment, no action by any group of countries will help it much.

The phoenix-like recovery of Western Europe and Japan over the last 40 years and the dramatic economic growth in parts of the Third World have reduced America's share of world gross product. But that proportion was bound to shrink as the rest of the world progressed. Had others not prospered, America's share of global production would have been larger, but the absolute level would have been lower.

Prosperity across the Western world represents an important success for American policy, which sought to create strong allies after World War II and avoid a domino effect in East Asia. If the U.S. defense budget is deemed large now, consider how much larger it would be were those areas today suffering from economic weakness and social upheaval.

Still, Americans should be concerned that the distribution of global wealth has not been translated into a similar apportionment of global responsibility and that the allies have been slow to lower trade barriers, assume a greater security role, and dramatically increase foreign aid. U.S. allies have come to believe that their economic strength affords them greater independence in decision making and that U.S. policy prescriptions do not necessarily serve their interests. Genuine differences persist over what constitutes appropriate domestic economic policy, how to define fair or unfair trade, how to share responsibility for Western security, and whether NATO cooperation should extend beyond the North Atlantic area. With economic power increasingly diffused, compliance with American wishes cannot be assumed or demanded. It must result from skillful negotiations that foster shared leadership of the world economy and increased allied support for Western defense.

Early in 1989 the president will be presented with the bipartisan National Economic Commission's report on ways to cut the budget deficit. This report, along with the Gramm-Rudman-Hollings budget legislation, will help create the political support for unpopular actions. But the president will still have to carry the case to the public.

The budget debate of recent years has been confusing. Despite his calls for a balanced-budget amendment, Reagan lost credibility on the issue because of the budgets he submitted to Congress. For its part Congress has found it difficult to cut favored programs in the magnitude necessary to make large budget reductions. And because economists' predictions of dire consequences of large deficits have failed to materialize, some politicians have become convinced that tough budget choices can be avoided.

A severe weakening of the U.S. economy because of continued large budget deficits cannot be ruled out. But even if that fear is not shared, the case for action is compelling. Large deficits today impose heavy burdens on the next generation and draw from the private sector large sums that could be used more productively. America's consumption and borrowing in the 1980s will be paid for by its citizens in the 1990s. The rising cost of servicing the federal debt—now about $150 billion per year, or nearly 14 percent of the budget—will limit the government's activities in important areas.

Government expenditures on entitlement programs and the military have risen dramatically. Improvements in public education, training, and economic infrastructure—crucial to American productivity and technological breakthroughs and to meeting the challenge of foreign competitors—have received less attention. Consequently, the next generation will inherit weak school systems, poorly maintained roads and bridges, and bleak inner-city housing. Paul Copperman, an expert cited by the 1983 National Commission on Excellence in Education, put it bluntly: "For the first time in the history of our country, the educational skills of one generation will not surpass, will not equal, will not even approach, those of its parents."

With such a backlog of unmet needs, the drive to cut the deficit should not be indiscriminate. It should steer clear of cuts in those areas that will strengthen productivity, such as education, research, and development. The next president should initiate a zero-based budgeting exercise, analyzing each

program on its merits to assess the savings and consequences of specific cuts. He must differentiate between programs needed to achieve important national priorities and those that cannot pass tests of need or efficiency.

The new president should aim to lower the structural deficit by $30 billion per year (unless, of course, an economic downturn makes such a course inadvisable), targeting spending cuts in such areas as entitlements for upper-income groups and redundant weapons systems. At the same time, he must keep the door open to tax increases, perhaps on final sales, as a last resort to meet the target. Beyond some point Americans should fear a weakening of defense, of the educational system, and of the ability to care for the destitute more than they fear a tax increase. The new president should emphasize that this is not simply an exercise in sharing pain but a prerequisite for a brighter economic future.

The U.S. trade balance as measured in volume terms has improved substantially. In 1987 exports grew by approximately 17 per cent and imports by only 8 per cent. The factors behind the trade gains included the considerable efforts by many American manufacturers to boost productivity, the sharply lower dollar, and the growth in foreign demand. But the U.S. trade deficit is likely to stay above $100 billion for the next few years. Coupled with interest payments on existing external debt, big trade imbalances will lead to significant current account deficits, necessitating further large-scale borrowing from foreign sources. The president must expect that for much of his term spending by households and government will have to grow more slowly in the United States than in its trading partners. Only in this manner can the U.S. trade deficit be reduced enough to cover the rising interest payments on its foreign debt. Otherwise the current account deficits will grow and the buildup of dollars in foreign hands will accelerate. Then sustained downward pressure on the dollar and upward pressure on interest rates will plague the administration.

A dramatic reversal of progress in cutting the trade deficit, or a rise in inflation, would pose even more serious risks if it caused the dollar to fall abruptly. The Federal Reserve Bank would be confronted with the choice of either tightening interest rates to stop the descent, thereby risking a severe economic slowdown and defaults by heavily leveraged American and Third World debtors, or allowing the currency to drop much further, risking higher inflation and a further slip in U.S. purchasing power.

But trade improvements that depend on slow growth or a lower dollar weaken American living standards. Over the medium term, only by raising the volume, value, and quality of American production can the United States boost exports substantially without a major decline in domestic demand or severe strains on the economy. This will require new investment in plant, equipment, and training. Maintaining an environment of stable growth, low inflation, and low interest rates is the most effective way for the president to foster this investment. He must also resist any tax law changes that create disincentives to investment. More ambitiously, he might seek to restore the investment tax credit or the

accelerated cost recovery on domestic investment; these will be more viable politically if coupled with a less liberal deductibility of interest on certain consumer borrowing and a rise in the minimum income tax.

Technological advances in microelectronics, such as robotics, computer-assisted design and manufacturing, and industrial processing systems, can produce breakthroughs in quality and productivity while trimming consumption of imported energy and raw materials. But new technologies and jobs call for a high level of skill and knowledge. In the late 20th century, knowledge is the primary determinant of comparative advantage. An unprecedented effort, therefore, is required to compensate for America's previously careless attitude toward education, particularly in technology and science. In 1957 the Soviet launch of the world's first artificial satellite prompted President Dwight Eisenhower to initiate an intensive education program; today's imported cars and videocassette recorders should have the same impact. Schools need money and teachers need better financial rewards as an incentive to build up their proficiency. Family and community attitudes toward educational quality must change. All elements of society need to play a part, with industry becoming involved in establishing curricula and training students on the job, high schools and colleges striving to upgrade worker and management skills throughout their careers, and the president himself demonstrating a personal commitment to educational excellence.

Job quality and productivity can be improved by greater use of the

bonus system, an approach the president might consider endorsing. Practiced in a few American business sectors, particularly in service industries, and widely in Japan, this arrangement bases a portion of employee pay on overall company performance, enabling workers to benefit from high profits in the good years. Moreover, labor might overcome its skepticism if given a greater role in workplace policy, opportunities for increased employee stock ownership, and more job training.

Rapid competitive shifts in the global economy will continue to threaten U.S. industries as new plants are built abroad, new technologies mastered, and production shifted to lower-wage and lower-valued-currency areas. The United States can cope by maintaining a fertile domestic setting for investment and by providing incentives for retraining and upgrading technological skills. For example, domestic trade laws designed to dampen import surges should tie such relief to industry efforts to step up investment, increase training, and contain costs.

The United States should not fall back on the notion that it is the inevitable victim of global competitive shifts. The lower dollar and productivity improvements already have increased the competitiveness of a number of American industries. Opportunities exist to recapture world market shares, and many companies are taking advantage of them. Washington will need to guard against the erection of new trade barriers by other governments under pressure from domestic industries that fear the loss of markets to the United States owing to the dollar's decline. Also, the United States should not accept the notion that its own private sector is unable to draw on government research to commercialize technical breakthroughs as fruitfully as others do. The Defense Department, the Department of Energy National Laboratories, and the National Aeronautics and Space Administration provide formidable support for new technologies; but commercial spinoffs, though celebrated, have been relatively modest. The president might establish a committee of scientists, engineers, and business leaders to identify ways to spur public-private collaborative efforts in research, development, and product commercialization.

INTERNATIONAL POLICY COORDINATION

For several years the Reagan administration worked on the belief that its trading partners' cooperation was not required to restore or maintain U.S. prosperity. The feeling that the United States could operate autonomously was shared by most postwar presidents, and for a time they were right. The United States was able to run balance-of-payments deficits larger than those of any other country, which French President Charles de Gaulle called an exhorbitant privilege. But this privilege could not last indefinitely. Foreign investors have grown reluctant to finance enormous American trade deficits. Their reduced purchases of U.S. securities have forced central banks to defend the dollar. And Americans themselves have come to resent the unemployment that accompanies large trade deficits.

The administration shifted in 1985 from "benign neglect" of the superstrong dollar to active international policy coordination. Treasury Secretary James Baker skillfully used the Group of Five, a body of finance ministers of five leading industrial countries, and the Group of Seven, composed of a slightly broader group of Western finance ministers, to steer down the dollar—although the primary impetus came from the market—and to induce higher internal growth abroad. He will bequeath to his successor a framework to manage currency movements and to encourage policy compatibility. The West's annual economic summits will offer the new president a platform to address these issues as well.

The United States cannot turn back the clock to a time when it enjoyed independence of economic action and the ability virtually to force its will on other countries. Successive American presidents, who have felt that the U.S. military protectorate entitles it to compliance from allies on major economic issues, have been frustrated by the allies' growing desire for freedom of action. But although other countries have grown stronger economically relative to the United States, they, too, remain vulnerable to disruptive external events, such as oil shocks, currency crises, and market crashes.

Interdependence has lessened the capacity for unilateral action of all countries. But political structures around the world are still rooted in the centuries-old concept of the nation-state. The verdict is still out on whether these political structures can adjust to economic interdependence: Arguments are now advanced that policy coordination has fallen well short of its intended goals. However, for the world to turn its back on that process, leaving governments to chart independent policies, raises the probability of international economic friction and instability. Common approaches thus are required to manage an open international economy; and the United States, as still the most powerful player in this process, has an essential role.

The president should clarify who within the executive branch speaks for him on trade and other international economic issues to reduce private-sector confusion in America and abroad and to achieve a central point for consultation with Congress, which plays a critical role in these issues. President Richard Nixon recognized the need for a central point in the White House. Appointing a senior-level assistant for international economic policy—similar in status to the national security adviser—not only could fulfill this function but also would greatly enhance the president's own ability to keep up with the multitude of international economic issues. This appointee could coordinate most effectively if he or she were a member of the National Security Council and the cabinet-level Economic Policy Council.

The president should be a forceful player in moving the current Uruguay Round of the General Agreement on Tariffs and Trade (GATT) negotiations to a successful conclusion. Presidents John Kennedy, Lyndon Johnson, and Jimmy Carter played limited roles in securing U.S. goals in past rounds. Then, however, American influence was greater. Now the circumstances have changed dramatically: Trade is far more important to the United States, domestic constituencies are more likely to demand unilateral action, and other countries are less willing to support U.S. trade positions—lower barriers on services and agriculture and stricter intellectual property rules.

It will be especially important for the United States and other industrialized countries to find common ground with developing countries such as Brazil, Singapore, and South Korea. The latter are now major players in the system and must be given a greater role in decisions that affect their future. Without their having a stake in implementing such decisions trade friction could become endemic. Negotiations also can help ensure that the European Community lowers external barriers as it pursues its 1992 goal of eliminating impediments to internal commerce.

Within a few months of taking office the president should convene a summit of leaders of the major industrialized and developing trading countries, as well as the head of GATT, to give impetus to American initiatives. In short, trade will need to be raised to the level of "high" foreign policy to obtain constructive results.

The next administration additionally will face growing concerns that American companies can be purchased at bargain-basement prices because of the lower dollar. Its response will have long-term implications. The United States objected to the restrictive policies of Canada's now defunct Foreign Investment Review Agency and has frequently complained about investment impediments in other countries. Hence there would be more than a little irony if America emulated these practices. Moreover, stringent U.S. limits on foreign acquisitions could be a pretext for other countries to stiffen

their investment barriers. The matter is of considerable importance to U.S. service companies because their exports often depend on their ability to invest overseas. An assessment by the new administration of other countries' investment practices, an analysis of the actual and potential magnitude of the threat to U.S. security interests from large takeovers, and consultations with the American business community should allow the administration to develop a responsible approach. The goal should be to avoid deterring acquisitions that do not threaten fundamental security or economic interests and that enable the United States to retain its credibility in resisting restrictive conditions abroad.

Currency distortions also have been a source of concern to Americans and their trading partners. The current system of managing floating rates—in which finance ministers periodically agree on a "holding zone," a temporarily agreed upon set of exchange rates—has produced mixed results, prompting demands for bolder reform. But improved cooperation will not come easily. Frequently the United States has assumed that it knows better than its trading partners how they should run their economies; and they have made similar assumptions about America's economy. A better understanding of how each major economy responds to different domestic policy measures is needed, therefore, before the next plateau of promoting policy compatibility can be reached. That understanding cannot be achieved by mechanistic or automatic formulations, although

some institutional improvements could help, such as improving further on the system of economic performance "indicators" already developed by the Group of Seven as a means of fostering further currency stability.

The new president will have a significant interest in securing currency stability, which would reassure potential investors in new plant and equipment that their investments will not turn unprofitable from a sharply higher dollar, as happened in the early 1980s. But he also will want to avoid the trap of prematurely attempting to stabilize the dollar—an effort that in early 1987 merely exacerbated market uncertainty and forced up U.S. interest rates. Large trade imbalances and currency stability are incompatible, so cutting the U.S. budget and trade deficits is a prerequisite to more stable rates. To foster a smooth reduction in the U.S. trade deficit and to maintain a smooth inflow of capital, the United States will need to conduct a special dialogue (including a regular set of cabinet and congressional sessions) with Japan, now the world's chief financial power and America's leading creditor.

With a large budget deficit the United States faces serious resource constraints on its ability to assist countries suffering from economic instability. It faces similar limits on its defense expenditures and its capacity to serve as protector of the free world. But some allies tend to shy away from providing substantial new financing to the Third World. And because of budgetary limitations, lack of political support, and the absence of a perceived threat, most are reluctant to increase significantly their contribution to Western defense.

Many of America's friends expect it to sustain indefinitely its substantial international responsibilities. But most underestimate the potential for domestic pressure on Washington to pull back from these commitments. Without a broader sharing of Western security costs, the next president will struggle to manage domestic political and budgetary pressures. The logical complement to a future U.S. deficit-reduction package—which inevitably will involve some curbs on military spending—is West European acceptance of a greater share of American defense and basing costs. This would avoid weakening NATO and would enable the United States to channel more resources to defend Western interests outside Europe. Washington, in turn, would have to accept Western Europe's desire for a greater voice in NATO decisions.

The next administration should begin early to develop a strategy for increasing West European defense contributions to NATO, and a similar exercise should be conducted at home to determine where basing and defense commitments could be reasonably pared down. As the United States comes to terms with its economic limits, so must Atlanticism come to terms with its economic success.

The next president will also recognize the high risk that within the next few years one or more heavily indebted Third World countries, particularly in Latin America, will experience economic turmoil accompanied by social and political unrest. Mexico could present an especially troublesome problem if high unemployment leads to social instability; the next president's single biggest foreign-policy problem would then be Mexico.

Economic growth in Latin America, the largest Third World market for the United States, would increase significantly U.S. imports. It would also support democracies in an area vital to American and Western security interests. Consequently, the United States must reinforce its commitment to aid effective bilateral programs and multilateral development institutions and encourage Japan, West Germany, and other industrialized economies to increase assistance substantially to the Third World. Oil-revenue surpluses went largely to governments of the Organization of Petroleum Exporting Countries (OPEC) in the 1970s. Today's trade surpluses have accrued largely to the private sectors of Western allies, while their governments run budget deficits. But these governments can offer guarantees for private-sector loans to high-debt countries. These might prove most effective if extended in conjunction with loans made by the World Bank, other multilateral development institutions, and the U.S. Export-Import Bank.

Japan has a unique ability to help. Constitutional restraints prevent that country from assuming a significantly larger military role. Besides, many Japanese, as well as their friends in the Pacific, feel uncomfortable with the prospect. But by recycling a large part of its surpluses, Japan could do more to shore up Third World economies and thus contribute to Western security. Tokyo already has made a constructive commitment to indebted countries, but as a percentage of gross national product its foreign economic aid is still low.

The next president should initiate a study at his first economic summit of ways to reduce the net outflow of funds from indebted countries. A central element should be the establishment of targets, under the aegis of the International Monetary Fund (IMF) and the World Bank, to reduce that outflow on a case-by-case basis for countries pursuing sound domestic policies. World Bank credit enhancement, new guarantees from official government agencies, and techniques similar to the December 1987 Morgan Guaranty plan for selling Mexican debt at a market-related discount all should play a role.

Less imminent, but no less troubling, is the potential threat from the creeping increase in Western dependence on imported oil. America and its allies have filled large strategic reserves for emergencies. But growing dependence on Middle East oil could allow OPEC once again to raise prices and exert political pressure on the West. Thus the new president will need a forward-looking energy strategy. He should give renewed support to the International Energy Agency, the focus of Western cooperation during last decade's oil crises, and establish a group of experts at home to report on steps necessary to reverse America's vulnerability to imported fuel. These steps should include securing Japanese investment in large U.S. energy projects in return for a share of the output that could prove vital to Japan in an emergency.

Finally, the West needs a strategy to dampen tensions over East-West economic relations. Some of the alliance's most contentious issues over the last 20 years have involved trade with the East bloc. The frequency of export control differences suggests a need for the next president to try to hammer out a consensus on economic relations with the USSR. For example, how should the West respond to Moscow's interest in attaining observer status in GATT or the IMF? Does this present an opportunity to bring the Soviets into the framework of global trade, investment, and financial rules? Should the West take the initiative by outlining the political, human rights, and economic measures it wants Moscow to adopt before becoming a member? The next president will very likely want to suggest criteria for evaluating political and economic changes in the Soviet Union, for testing Soviet reforms and intentions, and for responding to Soviet economic initiatives.

In the final analysis, the new president will not have the option of resting on the status quo. He cannot allow policy drift or inertia. His must be an administration of active economic leadership. His challenge will be nothing less than restoring America's confidence in its ability to guide its economic destiny by confronting head-on the need to raise American productivity and competitiveness and to lead the effort to strengthen the world economy.

The next president will take the United States close to the eve of the 21st century. His leadership at home and abroad will be crucial to whether America gets there as a prosperous world leader or as a country in slow decline economically and in retreat as a great power. ■

Reflections on Foreign Economic Policy

By Herbert Stein

The term *foreign economic policy* is a figure of speech, and a misleading one at that, and so are the other common terms in this field, like *international trade* and *international finance*. People are likely to get the impression that international trade is the trade between one country or nation and another and that international finance consists of financial transactions between nations. We have the impression of Uncle Sam buying all these automobiles from the Mikado, or whoever represents Japan in our minds, and we are disturbed. We think it is the proper function of the government, as the representative of the nation, to do something about it.

But that is not what is really going on at all. International trade is not trade between the United States and Japan. It is me buying a video-cassette recorder from a Japanese company. It is not trade between nations; it is trade between individuals and companies, some of which are in different countries. Similarly, international finance consists of transactions between private parties located in different countries. And foreign economic policy is basically not the policy of one country toward other countries but the policy of the government of one country toward its own citizens in their transactions with citizens of other countries.

THE BASIC QUESTION

The basic question of foreign economic policy is whether the government should have a different policy toward the transactions of its own citizens with citizens of other countries than it has toward the transactions of its own citizens with each other. If there should be a different policy, for what purposes and in what ways should it differ?

The general lesson of economics is that the policy should be the same and that the same policy should be a policy of noninterference. The argument is simple. If two citizens of country A voluntarily enter into a transaction with each other, the presumption must be that each expects to benefit from the transaction and each is the best judge of whether he will benefit. There is no reason for the government to interfere. If a citizen of country A voluntarily enters into a transaction with a citizen of another country, the citizen of country A presumably will benefit, and the government has no reason to interfere.

Herbert Stein, author of *Presidential Economics: The Making of Economic Policy from Roosevelt to Reagan and Beyond,* is a senior fellow at the American Enterprise Institute.

Source: From *The AEI Economist,* May 1984, pp. 1–8. Reprinted with permission from The AEI Economist by Herbert Stein, published in 1984 by the American Enterprise Institute for Public Policy Research, Washington, D.C.

It may seem that there is a basic difference in the two cases. In one case two citizens of country A are involved, and each presumably benefits. In the other case there is only one citizen of country A, and, even if one presumes that he benefits, the result is half as good for country A. According to some ways of looking at this transaction, the net benefit to citizens of country A may be zero or worse. If I buy a Honda, there may be a gain for me but a loss for the workers and investors at Chrysler, whose car I did not buy. And the government might decide that Chrysler's loss is more important, because Chrysler's loss is one of production and employment.

But this way of looking at the transaction is exceedingly limited. If I buy a Honda, someone in Japan acquires some dollars. These dollars may be used, directly or indirectly, to buy a product of the United States—say oranges. In that case the transaction does involve two U.S. citizens—the purchaser of the Honda and the seller of oranges, both of whom presumably benefit. The Japanese recipient of the dollars may decide to invest them in some U.S. assets. Perhaps he buys U.S. Treasury bills. That purchase helps to hold down U.S. interest rates and permits a home builder in, say, Topeka, Kansas, to sell a house. Again, there are two U.S. parties to the transaction, the buyer of the Honda and the seller of the house, both of whom presumably benefit. The Japanese may decide to hold dollars—meaning deposits in a U.S. bank—which enables the Federal Reserve to permit an expansion of total U.S. bank deposits. This transaction, another form of lending by the Japanese to the U.S. credit market, also holds

interest rates lower and so permits the sale of the house in Topeka. The indirection in these cases does not change the essential nature of the relation.

So I return to the two general propositions that the government should treat transactions of U.S. citizens with foreigners the same as it treats transactions among U.S. citizens and that the government should leave all of these transactions alone. But there are exceptions to both of these propositions, and the discussion of foreign economic policy is a discussion of the exceptions.

EXCEPTIONS TO INTERNATIONAL LAISSEZ FAIRE

We all recognize exceptions to the proposition that the government should leave the economic transactions of its citizens alone. The government has responsibilities to protect the national security and to provide a general climate of economic stability. It also has a responsibility to implement the community's concern for the well-being of its most disadvantaged members. These responsibilities may require the government to interfere with the economic activities of private citizens.

There are also reasons why a government may properly distinguish between private transactions involving only its own citizens and private transactions involving citizens of other countries as well. When we engage in foreign transactions we are not dealing with an enormous impersonal slot machine into which we put dollars in exchange for automobiles or put wheat in exchange for dollars. The other parties in our foreign ex-

changes are real people, residents of real countries and citizens of real governments. As a nation we have interests in the consequences of our economic transactions for these people, countries, and governments; and there may be cases in which these interests are not well served by a policy of noninterference.

These interests in foreign policy are dominated, in my opinion, by national security considerations. Although the nature of our national security relations and therefore of our economic interest differs from country to country, it seems to me useful to classify countries into three categories:

1. The enemy—countries or blocs considered to be hostile and strong, where we have to consider how the transactions of our citizens with them will affect either their hostility or their strength. This consideration is one that we cannot expect our citizens to take into account and which calls for intervention by our government.

2. Nonaligned, less-developed countries (LDCs)— countries that are economically poor and politically potentially unstable. As members of a relatively affluent society we have a humanitarian concern with extremes of poverty in other countries. We also have a concern that their poverty may lead to political instability that would be dangerous for us, given the present division of the world. These concerns justify action by our government to promote economic advancement in those countries by means other than unrestricted private transactions—if we know how to do that.

3. Equal partners—non-Communist industrial countries that are allied with us politically and mili-

tarily. The economic advancement of these countries is in our interest, but not in a degree that requires aid from us or discrimination in their favor. Mainly what we want from them is open economic access so that our citizens will have the opportunity to gain from transactions with their citizens. We also want the cooperation of their governments in economic policies toward the first and second groups of countries for our common security interests. And we want to prevent economic relations from becoming serious irritants to our important political relations.

Thus there can be reasons for exceptions to the general principle that the government should not discriminate between domestic and foreign transactions and should not interfere in either. But the important point is that the general principles are very strong and that exceptional circumstances must be present to justify departures from these principles. Certainly our experience shows that exceptions are claimed much more frequently than they are justified. With that background we can look at the present state of economic transactions between U.S. and foreign parties.

PRESENT STATE OF ECONOMIC TRANSACTIONS

Troubled Waters?

I will first describe this state of affairs in the common, and largely erroneous, way that makes our foreign economic transactions look like one sea of troubles calling for most drastic action. I will then present what I regard as a more balanced and realistic view of the situation.

Although the story is one seamless web, we may start with the fact that in 1983 Americans bought more merchandise from abroad— about $60 billion more—than they sold abroad. It is expected that the excess of imports will be about $100 billion in 1984. One conclusion sometimes drawn from these figures is that since this deficit in 1984 would be almost 3 percent of the GNP expected for the year, the deficit would make GNP about 3 percent lower than it would otherwise be and would cost the country about 3 million jobs. In fact, the situation could be worse than that because the deficit in trade could have a multiplier effect and depress the economy by more than its own amount.

The deterioration in our export-import position has been especially severe in a few industries called "basic," of which steel and automobiles are the leading examples. Even after recovery by more than 40 percent in 1983, production of primary metals in the United States was almost 30 percent less than it had been ten years earlier. This loss of position due to foreign competition has concentrated misery in some areas of the country. Moreover, it has given us an "unbalanced" recovery that may end prematurely because it is unbalanced. Also, the loss threatens the industrial base needed for national security.

At the same time that our old basic industries are stagnating, we are falling behind in the race for development of the new high-tech industries. This is evidenced in daily life in that a large fraction of America's color television sets and almost all, if not all, of our videocassette recorders come from Japan. Less evident to the casual ob-

server, the Japanese are ahead in robotics and are challenging us in various aspects of the semiconductor industry.

Thus we are unable to meet the competition in either the old basic industries or the new high-tech industries. Some people see us becoming a service economy, which they think of as intolerable for a world political leader. Some look at the international economic competition in an even more political and psychological way. They point out that, in the past twenty years total and per capita output has grown less in the United States than it has grown in Japan, France, Germany, and Italy. They consider our lagging in this race a blow not only to our political leadership but also to our national self-esteem.

A key reason for the U.S. excess of imports, most would agree, is the high value of the dollar, which makes exports from the United States expensive and imports to the United States inexpensive. This, in turn, is a consequence of high U.S. interest rates, usually attributed to our budget deficits. The high interest rates attract capital from the rest of the world, and the inflow of capital constitutes a demand for dollars that keeps their price high. Also the troubles of many LDCs have made them unattractive for foreign capital and have contributed to the flow of capital to the United States.

The high value of the dollar arising from capital inflow is considered by many to be a problem aside from its negative effect on the export balance. Some people consider it simply improper that the dollar exchange rate should be determined by capital flows rather than only by trade flows. Others think it anomalous and wrong that the richest country in the world should be an importer rather than an exporter of capital. The high value of the dollar is also seen as a potential threat to the U.S. recovery. It is pointed out that the dollar is high because foreigners are adding large amounts of dollars to their portfolios of assets. At some stage they may find that the increase in their holdings of dollars has gone far enough from the standpoint of prudent diversification. Then the inflow will slow down, the dollar will plummet, and U.S. interest rates and prices will rise sharply. This could be a severe shock to the U.S. economy.

The combination of high U.S. interest rates and high dollar and capital flows to the United States is the cause of much complaint in Europe. There this combination is thought to interfere with the recovery of the European economy and especially with the growth of productive investment in Europe. These complaints irritate our relations with allies.

Beyond this, there is complaint, also mainly coming from Europe, about the international monetary system in which exchange rates are free to fluctuate as much as they do, especially in response to capital movements. Such freedom is said to make exchange rates unstable and so to interfere with trade. Moreover, by relieving governments of the need to maintain convertibility of their currencies into other currencies at a fixed rate, the present system permits inflationary policy everywhere.

Although the high value of the dollar is generally considered to be the main cause of our excess of imports over exports—and an improper cause, at that—other explanations are also given. These con-

sist mainly of charges of unfair treatment by other governments that subsidize their own industries and discriminate against ours. The general backwardness that some see in the U.S. economy is attributed to the superior industrial policies of other governments, notably Japan, that have known how to identify and develop the growth industries of the future.

Another chapter in this catalogue of what is wrong with our foreign economic condition and policies refers to our relations with the less-developed countries. Many of these countries—the most important being Argentina, Brazil, and Mexico—have not been able to service the large debts they accumulated in the late 1970s. Their difficulty in servicing these debts has been increased by the slowdown of growth and inflation in the industrial countries, which has tended to reduce the export earnings of the LDCs. The difficulty has also been increased by the rise of world interest rates, which has raised the interest burden on the LDC debt.

In an effort to increase exports and reduce imports, thus earning foreign exchange to pay their debts, these countries have embraced policies of austerity. This means basically cutting down consumption and entails a contraction of total output and employment. As a result there is continuous open or latent political disaffection in these countries. But these efforts at austerity have not been sufficient to attract new voluntary private lenders, so that the existing creditors, including many U.S. banks, with the assistance of governmental institutions, have had to continue lending in order to avoid an overt default. This situation is risky because the

facts may become unconcealable, some creditors may dash to get their money out, and the fall in the value of the debts may be obvious. The capital of many U.S. banks will evaporate, bank lending in the United States will dry up, and the U.S. economy will go through a contraction, possibly severe.

Finally, our economic relations with the Soviet bloc nations are a source of dissatisfaction to everyone. The U.S. government has limited U.S. exports to the Soviet bloc to impede the Soviet military buildup and to exert more general pressure. U.S. exporters have complained about loss of markets. European allies have complained about the attempts of the U.S. government to control exports of their resident companies. Despite these efforts, the Soviets have obtained a great deal of assistance from trade with the West, and the only political consequence has been to convince the Soviets of America's hostility while alienating our allies.

This dismal diagnosis of our foreign economic relations leads to a set of prescriptions as follows, not all of which, of course, are recommended by any one doctor:

• The usual prescription, and one that is being followed to a considerable extent, is protection against imports, which these days takes the form more often of quotas than of tariffs. This is justified as necessary to save particular industries, considered for one reason or another to be deserving, as well as to correct America's balance of trade deficit. These protectionist proposals are sometimes explained as consistent with a free-trade philosophy on the ground that other countries employ unfair and discriminating measures.

• The spread of national protectionism gives rise to proposals, mainly from Europe, for coordination of trade policies, which is a way of achieving international protectionism. That is, there would be international agreements on the amount of steel or whatnot to be exported by each country. This prescription is considered to rationalize and harmonize the present struggles that cause international discord.

• There are suggestions that the United States should intervene in foreign exchange markets to depress the dollar and so increase our exports and reduce our imports.

• There are suggestions that the United States should impose controls on capital inflows to try to get the exchange value of the dollar down closer to the level appropriate for the balance of merchandise trade.

• Pursuing the exchange rate problem further, some would like to reestablish a system of more-or-less fixed rates on the order of the system that existed before 1971.

• More generally addressed to the claim of relative backwardness of the U.S. economy are suggestions that the United States should have an industrial policy to promote high-tech industries in which productivity is expected to grow rapidly.

• Probably the most common suggestion for economic relations with the Soviet bloc is that the United States should adopt the European attitude, which is to limit restraints on trade to items of the most obvious military importance, leaving all other kinds of transactions free. In fact, the standard pattern of thinking about U.S. foreign trade today seems to come down to protectionism for our friends and free trade for our enemies.

• There are two kinds of policies proposed for the problem of the LDC debts. One is to keep lending the LDCs money to pay the interest on their debts—thus increasing the amount of the debts—in the hope that something will come along to enable the debtors to meet their payments. The other is for national and international governmental institutions to stay out of the picture, forcing the private creditors to recognize the reality of the debtor's inability to pay.

• There is, of course, one measure on which almost everyone agrees as the solution to almost all problems, namely to reduce the U.S. budget deficit.

A Different Diagnosis

In my opinion, both the common diagnosis of our situation and the prescriptions derived from that are wrong. To start, I do not regard the excess of imports over exports, the high value of the dollar, the high interest rates, and the inflow of capital as problems. We are a country with a low propensity to save. We have decided to run a large budget deficit, which means that the federal government will be absorbing more of our private savings than it used to absorb. We have also decided to reduce the taxes on the return to investment, increasing the demand for saving to finance additional investment. For these reasons interest rates are high here, which attracts funds from abroad that help to finance our deficit and productive investment. The inflow of capital from abroad is encouraged because we have political stability here and a relatively good prospect of keeping inflation down.

The inflow of capital from abroad has as its necessary counterpart an excess of U.S. imports over exports. The only way foreigners can earn dollars to invest here is by selling us more goods and services than they buy from us. This combination of an inflow of capital and a net inflow of goods and services is not depressing the American economy or increasing unemployment here. The inflow of capital supports some industries, like investment and housing, while it depresses some other industries producing tradable goods.

There is nothing unbalanced about this pattern of output. It is a perfectly balanced adaptation to our savings, deficits, and other conditions. The dollar exchange rate which brings about this adaptation—this excess of goods imports balancing the excess of capital exports—is the proper exchange rate. There is nothing particularly vulnerable or unstable about this situation.

The severe difficulties of certain industries—steel being the most prominent example—are partly due to the shift in our net international position. But they are only in part due to that. The concentration of the problem in certain industries reflects in large part special characteristics of those industries, such as their relatively high wages and sluggish management.

Nothing in this situation calls for protectionism. In general, protectionism will not change the balance of trade while the factors causing capital inflow remain strong. Protectionism will only shift the trade deficit from some industries to others. Its net effect will be to protect inefficient and backward industries while making life difficult for more efficient industries. It will reduce the pressure on the less efficient to adapt. In that way it will do more harm than good.

That some imports are subsidized by foreign governments is not a reason for excluding them. The subsidization is probably uneconomic for the country that does it, but it would surely be uneconomic for the United States to reject cheap products because some other country was subsidizing them.

The whole notion of fairness in foreign trade has been distorted. What fairness used to mean was the opportunity for our citizens to sell abroad what they can sell most cheaply. What it now seems to mean is depriving our citizens of the opportunity to buy what they can buy most cheaply from abroad.

I have already suggested that the exchange rate which brings about a net inflow of goods equal to the net capital inflow is the proper exchange rate. But in any case there is little reason to believe that the real exchange rate can be altered by the method often recommended, the purchase of foreign currencies by the Federal Reserve to raise the prices of those currencies. This action will either raise prices in the United States, so that our competitiveness will not improve even though the exchange rate falls, or raise interest rates in the United States, which will keep the exchange rate from falling. The idea of attempting to reestablish a more-or-less fixed exchange rate is basically irrelevant to our present situation except as a means of pegging the dollar at a level that the market will not support. We have seen in the past how the attempt to peg exchange rates led governments into interferences with trade and capital movements.

In general, the rest of the world is not being hurt by the combination of high interest rates, a strong dollar, excess of imports of goods, and excess of imports of capital. We are a country that has a high demand for capital in relation to our supply of it, which makes capital higher priced than it otherwise would be. That situation is good for all the people who supply capital—the savers of the world—and bad for all the people who borrow. We import goods and capital. That is beneficial for all the people and countries that sell us goods and supply us capital and bad for all the people and countries that compete with us for the goods and capital. The situation is analogous to our position in the world coffee market. We consume much coffee and produce none, so that we import a great deal of it. That is good for all the people and countries that produce coffee and bad for all the people in the rest of the world that consume it. No one has suggested that we have an obligation to consume less coffee for the sake of the world's coffee drinkers. So we have no obligation to consume less capital for the sake of the world's capital users.

It is true that the governments of many of our allies complain about our economic policies, and that is a problem because we do not want them to be unhappy with us. But their complaints should not make us change important aspects of our policy that are not actually injuring them. We should try to explain our policies, and that is one of the things that summit meetings are for. We should be prepared to be more cooperative than we have been in avoiding protectionism that does hurt them as well as us. But we should not enter into arrangements for "coordination" of policy that imply, as they generally do, departures from our basic principles and objectives.

We should not be alarmed about the prospect—which is still quite uncertain—that per capita incomes will rise faster in other countries than in the United States and will surpass those in the United States. On the whole it is better to live in a world where other countries are rich than in a world where other countries are poor—unless the other countries are our enemies, and our enemies are not gaining on us. Envy is a natural emotion, but I believe that most of us do not have strong feelings of envy about national income statistics but reserve that emotion for visible individuals closer to home. As individuals we should be concerned about using our own resources as effectively as possible, which does not necessarily mean becoming richer as fast as possible. As citizens we should want our government to assist us in using our resources wisely, within the context of the kind of society we prefer. In the conduct of our private affairs and in the conduct of our public affairs we should be open to learn from others, including foreigners; but we should be careful that what we are learning is a valid lesson and not just a passing fad. Today's fad, presumably learned from observation of other countries, especially Japan, is called industrial policy. Although this idea comes in various forms, its distinctive meaning is a comprehensive government program to direct the pattern of industrial development by use of subsidies, credit, protectionism, and controls. There is, in fact, much doubt about whether such a policy has on balance made a constructive contribution to economic development anywhere. This subject is well discussed in the 1984 Annual Report of the Council of Economic Advisers. I have no doubt that as practiced in the United States it would be overwhelmingly a program for preserving backward and declining industries, simply because those industries would have the political power and the motivation to use the system for their purposes.

TRADING WITH THE ENEMY

What I have said to this point is mainly an expression of my belief that in economic relations with the countries that I call equals the basic principle of nondiscrimination should dominate. The situation is somewhat different when we consider the other classes of countries. Our relations with our enemies are dominated by our desire to make them less hostile, less aggressive, and less powerful. The main instrument we have for influencing them is our own military power, including the threat to use it and the offer to limit it in exchange for concessions from the enemy. But this is an exceedingly costly and potentially risky instrument. We should seek to use whatever other instruments we have, including the economic instrument. The Soviet bloc obviously gains from its trade with the industrial democracies. We should try to use our ability to deny this trade or to engage in it as a means of influencing their abilities and intentions.

We do this to some extent, of course, by seeking to ban sales of materials of high military signifi-

cance. We have made sporadic attempts to use more general limitations on trade to affect Soviet behavior, as in the case of the U.S. grain embargo after the invasion of Afghanistan. But these efforts have been quite limited. There is a substantial disagreement about whether control of trade can influence Soviet behavior. I believe that the Soviets are rational people and respond to penalties and rewards, but how much they respond I do not pretend to know. But I believe that our limited use of the economic instrument results very much from exaggerated opinions of the cost to us of doing so and from the inability to manage an acceptable sharing of the cost.

I am not arguing for denying trade to the Soviet bloc, in whole or in part or in exchange for any specific condition. But I do believe that we must put ourselves in a position to do so if that course seems useful. The first step is to recognize how trivial would be the *overall* costs to the United States or to its allies of giving up the trade. In 1982 U.S. exports to the bloc were one tenth of one percent of GNP. Germany had the largest ratio of bloc exports to GNP—a little under one percent. It must be remembered that the loss from giving up the trade is only a small fraction of the amount of the trade, because if labor and capital are not employed to produce exports for the bloc they can be employed to produce other things.

We get an exaggerated opinion of the costs of withholding our trade from the Soviet bloc because we hear about these costs mainly from the directly affected parties—the would-be exporting firms. The cost to them may be serious, and they are naturally vocal and politi-

cally active about it. The problem is that, although the cost to the United States of not exporting pipe-laying tractors to the Soviet Union would be negligible, the cost to Caterpillar Tractor would be severe. We will not gain freedom to control exports to the Soviet bloc when it is in the national interest to do so unless we are able to distribute the costs of such a policy to the nation as a whole.

Similarly, we have a burden-sharing problem in relation to the other industrial democracies. In general, control of exports to the Soviet bloc will not be effective unless the other industrial countries participate along with us. But for each of the others—Germany, France, Japan, the United Kingdom, and Italy—trade with the Soviet bloc is more important economically than it is for us. Therefore those governments believe that a U.S.-initiated policy of export controls will put unfair burdens on them. I do not believe that we will be able to carry on a concerted policy unless we find a way to share burdens among countries as well as within them.

I think it would be a good idea to establish an international fund to which the industrial democracies would contribute in an equitable way—perhaps in proportion to their GNPs—out of which an international board would pay compensation to firms and countries that are injured by export limitations imposed for national political reasons. The size of this fund would not have to be enormous. Total exports of the big six countries to the Soviet bloc in 1982 were about $20 billion. The loss from giving up all of these exports—which is the loss involved in transferring resources to other uses—would probably not be more than $3 billion. And I do not suggest that all of this trade would be banned. What is involved is not economic warfare or the elimination of trade but putting the industrial democracies in a position to use their economic assets positively or negatively, as carrot or stick, to advance their national security interests.

THE POOR ARE OUR PROBLEM

The most difficult and probably the most important question is what our economic relations should be toward the third part of the world, the poor, unaligned countries that are potentially unstable politically. We once had a standard notion about these countries: With our economic aid, technical assistance, and advice we were going to make them richer, more stable, and friendlier. Experience led to the conclusion that this notion was unrealistic. We were disappointed in our efforts to produce either growth or friendship. Then we were diverted from the question of public policy in this area by the belief that the inflow of private capital was solving the economic problem of the less-developed world and that this process was superior in many ways to government aid. But this inflow of foreign private capital was predicated on the assumptions that an inflationary boom would continue in the industrial countries and that real interest rates would continue to be very low or negative. When these assumptions proved to be incorrect, the voluntary private flow stopped and servicing of the debts already incurred by the poor countries became very difficult or

even impossible without an unreasonable degree of austerity.

In the past two years or so the economic problem of the less-developed countries has become identified with the problem of their outstanding debts. Such identification is unfortunate because a resolution of the debt problem would return these countries at best to the condition of underdevelopment from which they were suffering before the big and unsustainable capital inflow began. Dealing with the current debt problem is a necessary first step, but it is not the positive policy we need.

The present policy consists of stretching out the existing debt, which increases the amount of the debt because of the interest accruals, the provision of short-term financial assistance by the International Monetary Fund and other government agencies in the developed world, and measures within the debtor countries to reduce imports and promote exports. This policy is appropriate if, within a period of time for which the existing emergency financing can be counted upon, adjustments within the debtor countries will make the existing debts good. Such an outcome is extremely doubtful. Thus the policy leaves both creditors and debtors in a state of extreme uncertainty. The debtors particularly have no way of knowing what financial resources they can count on and what painful adjustments they will have to make. This solution is not satisfactory; but neither is the alternative sometimes proposed, in which the governmental finance from the developed world is halted and the debtor countries are left to make the best deals they can with their creditors, which would presumably involve some

scaling down of the debts. That course of action would leave many of the LDCs in a worse situation than they were in ten years ago, because they would still have larger debts and less prospect of either private or public capital inflow. The United States and other industrial democracies have too big an interest in the future of these countries to be satisfied with this outcome.

In my opinion we are going to need debt settlement arrangements worked out with the debtors, the private creditors, and the industrial democracies, probably represented by the international agencies. These arrangements should involve scaling down the existing debts by the private creditors, adopting long-run adjustment and development programs by the debtors, and providing a flow of capital from the developed countries in some combination of grants and loans. The arrangements would have to be worked out firmly to make sure that the provision of funds did not serve to relieve the private creditors of the losses they have deservedly incurred or relieve the debtors of the requirement for feasible adjustment. This is only one of many aspects of public policy in which it is impossible to escape the need for good judgment by someone.

The settlement of the existing debts should be regarded as a step toward reviving the efforts of the United States and of other industrial countries to speed up the economic development of the poor countries. That we have been disappointed in much of our previous effort does not permit us to abandon the effort. It calls upon us to devote more resources, mental and financial, to it.

I am afraid that statement will sound soft-headed to many of my friends. I will only reply by quoting some recent words of Richard Nixon, not usually regarded as an overly sentimental witness:

Two billion people living in poor countries in Africa, Asia, and Latin America have an average per capita income of less than $500.

The people in these countries have enormous problems. The communists at least talk about the problems. We too often just talk about the communists.

This is not worthy of America. America is a great country. We did not become great by simply being against what was wrong. We became great by being for what was right.

America and the West must make clear what our true aspirations are for people living in this part of the world. We are not for the status quo where millions are mired down in poverty, misery and injustice. We are not just against the communist way, which would make things worse.

We are for a better way, in which all people can hope to share in the progress we are making toward a better life for our own people. Their lot is not our fault. It is our responsibility. This is the supreme challenge which confronts America and other advanced nations for the balance of this century.[1] ∎

Notes:
1. Richard M. Nixon, Speech to Economics Club of New York, March 13, 1984.

The Political and Security Framework for International Trade in the Decade Ahead

By Robert J. Pranger and Roger P. Labrie

Discussions of international trade issues, whether they be non-tariff barriers, trade in services, or currency exchange fluctuations, usually presume the absence of violence and other forms of hostility among trading partners. Wars, declared or otherwise, incidents of terrorism, and acute international political crises inevitably disrupt the flow of goods and services between nations. A stable political and security environment for international trade is usually taken for granted.

The historical record of the past four decades amply demonstrates, however, that political crises and armed conflict in the international arena can have a far-reaching and negative effect on trade. Moreover, because nations have become increasingly interdependent in terms of their economic welfare, trade sanctions have become a prominent weapon for dealing with political and military adversaries. The Arab oil embargo of the 1970s and restrictions on U.S. grain sales to the Soviet Union after the invasion of Afghanistan are recent examples.

Philip Habib, former undersecretary of state and now a senior fellow at the American Enterprise Institute, has identified four central areas of concern for U.S. foreign policy in the decade ahead: (1) managing Soviet-American relations; (2) preserving and strengthening key alliances as well as bilateral security arrangements; (3) dealing with the "geopolitical equation" in major regional disputes; and (4) confronting a "grab bag" of functional issues such as ideological divisions, terrorism, and North-South economic differences. The political and security framework for international trade will be determined in large measure by how the United States addresses each of these issues.

THE MANAGEMENT OF SOVIET-AMERICAN RELATIONS

A key element of any assessment of the political and security framework for international trade

Robert J. Pranger was director of International Programs at AEI and coeditor of the AEI Foreign Policy and Defense Review. Roger P. Labrie was a research associate in foreign and defense policy at AEI and acting managing editor of the AEI Foreign Policy and Defense Review.

Source: From *Foreign Policy and Defense Review,* Vol. 5, N. 4 (1985), pp. 3–10. Reprinted with permission from AEI Foreign Policy and Defense Review by Robert J. Pranger and Roger P. Labrie, published in 1985 by the American Enterprise Institute for Public Policy Research, Washington, D.C.

in the decade ahead is the problem of managing U.S.-Soviet relations. Politically and militarily the United States and the Soviet Union are still the only superpowers on the world stage. Each has the means to project its military forces into virtually every region of the globe and to destroy the other (and many other nations, as well) with nuclear weapons. Each is the leader of rival ideological blocs whose political, economic, and security interests extend to such potentially volatile regions as the Middle East, Central America, South Asia, Southern Africa, the Persian Gulf, and the Far East. In addition, trade relations between the United States and the Soviet Union in agricultural commodities and high technology can have important consequences for the economies of many other nations.

As world events since World War II attest, the superpowers have been, and are likely to remain in the foreseeable future, direct and indirect participants in the affairs of every region of the world. Each seeks to protect its economic and security interests and to project its political influence around the globe, often at the expense of the other. In such circumstances the potential for armed conflict is ever present, whether between the superpowers themselves or between their proxies and allies. An escalation of this global rivalry to armed conflict would adversely affect the climate for trade in the decade ahead.

The Nixon administration's détente policies in the 1970s sought to manage U.S.-Soviet rivalry and minimize its impact on global stability. Those policies attempted to place the political, military, and economic relations between the superpowers on a more stable footing by emphasizing perceived common

interests in these areas. Although superpower competition persisted, détente was seen as a framework for regulating and restraining that competition. Given the incentives for cooperation provided by the specter of nuclear war, America's withdrawal from Vietnam and the domestic political upheavals caused by the war, the Soviet economy's need for modern Western technology, and the Sino-Soviet rivalry, it was hoped that Moscow would acquire a vested interest in maintaining and expanding the web of cooperative relationships offered by the West and would restrain its policy of fomenting instability in the third world.

In his testimony before the Senate Foreign Relations Committee on September 19, 1974, former Secretary of State Henry Kissinger explained U.S. détente policy this way:

[Détente] proceeds from the conviction that, in moving forward across a wide spectrum of negotiations, progress in one area adds momentum to progress in other areas. . . . We have looked for progress in a series of agreements settling specific political issues, and we have sought to relate these to a new standard of international conduct appropriate to the dangers of the nuclear age. By acquiring a stake in this network of relationships with the West, the Soviet Union may become more conscious of what it would lose by a return to confrontation. Indeed, it is our hope that it will develop a self-interest in fostering the entire process of relaxation of tensions.[1]

Détente's promise of a more stable international order proved to be elusive. In the agreement on

"Basic Principles of Relations," signed by Nixon and Brezhnev in May 1972, both countries pledged to "do their utmost to avoid military confrontations" and "exercise restraint in their mutual relations." They also agreed to eschew "efforts to obtain unilateral advantage at the expense of the other, directly or indirectly."[2] Yet Soviet military spending and weapons production continued to increase during the 1970s. Moscow threatened direct military intervention against Israel during the 1973 Middle East war. Soviet and Cuban involvement in Africa, first in Angola in 1975 and later in the war between Ethiopia and Somalia, signaled that Moscow would continue to exploit opportunities to expand its influence in the third world at the expense of the West.

Meanwhile, the economic incentives for Soviet restraint failed to materialize. In 1975 Moscow repudiated the 1972 U.S.-Soviet trade agreement after Congress tied the granting of most-favored-nation status to the Soviet Union to an easing of emigration policy and restricted Export-Import Bank credits for Soviet purchases from the United States. The promise of significant restraints on the strategic arms competition also went largely unfulfilled. The Soviet military intervention in Afghanistan and the failure of the Senate to approve the SALT II Treaty in 1979 signaled the end of détente.[3]

The Reagan administration entered office in January 1981 on the heels of significant events in Afghanistan and Iran that catalyzed the popular disillusionment that had been growing for some time in America about the conduct of U.S.-Soviet relations. The Soviet invasion of Afghanistan confirmed for many

Americans the failure of U.S. détente policies in the 1970s to restrain Soviet ambitions. Soviet troops entered Afghanistan while the SALT II Treaty was still before the Senate for approval, apparently demonstrating that Moscow's desire for arms control agreements was subordinate to its hegemonic ambitions.

The Iranian hostage crisis, which began in November 1979 and ended with the release of American diplomats after Reagan's inauguration, also had implications for U.S.-Soviet relations. The seizure of the hostages and the seeming impotence of the United States to free them confirmed in the minds of many Americans the charges made by Reagan in his 1980 election campaign that the United States was suffering a loss of respect in the world owing to its defeat in Vietnam and a "decade of neglect" of American military power. This decade of neglect, coinciding with the period of détente, was portrayed as a consequence of unrealistic U.S. policies toward the Soviet Union.

The Reagan administration vowed to rectify these perceived deficiencies of policy toward the Soviet Union. It sought to place that policy on a more realistic and stable footing by building up U.S. defense capabilities across the board, adopting a more assertive approach to the Soviet Union and its proxies, and seeking sharp reductions in the levels of Soviet nuclear weapons through arms control negotiations.[4]

Several events in recent years demonstrate how international trade can be adversely affected by U.S.-Soviet relations. An embargo on additional U.S. grain sales and tighter controls on the transfer of high technology to the Soviet

Union were among the Carter administration's responses to the Soviet invasion of Afghanistan. In response to the December 1981 imposition of martial law in Poland to crush Solidarity and a rising tide of Polish nationalism, the Reagan administration announced a package of sanctions. These included the suspension of government-sponsored shipments of agricultural and dairy products, a halt to the planned renewal of Export-Import Bank credit insurance, suspension of landing privileges for Poland's national airline, and withdrawal of Poland's fishing rights in U.S. waters. Washington also refused to discuss rescheduling Poland's $12 billion debt to Western governments and its application for membership in the International Monetary Fund. In October 1982 the United States withdrew Poland's most-favored-nation trading status.[5] The deteriorating climate in U.S.-Soviet relations caused by events in Poland and by Soviet and Cuban support for the Marxist regime in Nicaragua also contributed to the Reagan administration's attempt in 1982 to impose restrictions on the transfer of Western technology for the Soviet natural gas pipeline. Additional economic sanctions were imposed on the Soviet Union by Western governments after its destruction of an unarmed commercial airliner (Korean Air Lines flight 007) on September 1, 1983. On May 1, 1985, trade sanctions were imposed by the United States against Nicaragua.

The challenges to successful management of U.S.-Soviet relations in the decade ahead will be many. Continued regional conflict in Central America, Southern Africa, and Asia will pose risks of

greater superpower involvement. Many experts believe that a crisis in the Middle East and the Persian Gulf regions could be the most likely catalyst for U.S.-Soviet confrontation. Both superpowers have close allies in this area and have been competing for influence there for decades; in addition, Japan and the countries of Western Europe depend heavily on Middle East oil. The restraint shown by the United States and the Soviet Union during the current war between Iran and Iraq is encouraging but may not be a precedent in a future conflict between close allies of the superpowers. Trade between the Soviet Union and the West will also prove troublesome, not only for U.S.-Soviet relations but also for relations among the industrial democracies as they try to coordinate their policies on technology transfers and dependence on energy supplies from the Soviet Union. In addition, failure to negotiate real reductions in the strategic and theater nuclear arsenals of the superpowers could heighten political tensions and make resolution of other East-West issues more difficult. In addition, continued harsh domestic controls and restrictive emigration policies by the Soviet Union will further complicate the political relations between Washington and Moscow.

President Reagan entered his second term in 1985 with brightened prospects for improvement in U.S.-Soviet relations. New arms control negotiations got under way in Geneva, and high-level officials of both countries resumed talks on expanding nonstrategic trade and economic cooperation that were suspended after the Soviet invasion of Afghanistan. The NATO allies have held fast to their commitment to deploy American intermediate-range missiles in Europe. A new, more youthful and vigorous Soviet leader has ascended to power in Moscow and has already made impressive gains in consolidating his authority over the Politburo and other policy-making bodies. With détente's decline, however, no new organizing principles for managing Soviet-American relations have been devised.

What might such principles entail? The most pressing concerns for both Moscow and Washington are the nuclear arms competition and the potential for armed conflict between the superpowers or their proxies growing out of regional conflict. Both concerns need to be addressed simultaneously. The American people and the citizens of the other Western democracies demand of their elected officials nothing less than a sincere and sustained effort to reduce the levels of nuclear weapons that each superpower possesses in abundance and to remedy the most serious threats posed to stable deterrence by existing and new types of weapons. The experience of the 1970s demonstrates, however, that arms control negotiations by themselves are inadequate for managing the U.S.-Soviet rivalry. Understandings must be reached on the legitimate interests of each superpower in various regions of the world and on the need for restraint by both parties in matters of vital interest to the other. Penalties for violating these understandings must be made clear beforehand and carried out if violations occur. A political consensus among Americans on this policy will need to be forged and sustained if it is to have any chance of succeeding. Only by addressing the political competition between Washington and Moscow can a climate be created for meaningful arms control. Moreover, arms control agreements that equitably address the concerns of each country can contribute to a further easing of East-West tensions, provided those agreements are honored.

Although an easing of Soviet-American rivalry may prove possible, competition between the two countries will persist. The United States will continue to face the challenges of preserving and strengthening its existing alliances and bilateral security arrangements and contributing to the peaceful settlement of regional conflicts that pose the greatest dangers to peace.

PRESERVING AND STRENGTHENING KEY ALLIANCES

The principle of collective security has been fundamental to American postwar foreign policy, a security defined in broad political and economic dimensions as well as in military terms. The expression "free world" has often been used to describe this network of alliance and bilateral arrangements, and, although the expression has a certain rhetorical significance independent of empirical references, it also connotes a commitment on the part of our major alliance partners to certain principles of governance and economics as well as to a common defense. Indeed, the idea of a common defense has usually meant something broader than purely military issues, although these are central: U.S. policy has generally regarded its collective security arrangements as economically and ideologically important, and so have America's allies. Hence, in the key alliances of the United States—with Western Europe and Japan and in the third world—economic, military, and political factors are inextricably combined. In given circumstances we may debate just how vital these connections are to U.S. interests, but we are always conscious that they exist.

Destabilization in one of these dimensions may lead to greater insecurity in the others. Trade frictions with major allies, for example, can have repercussions on military security if these frictions are allowed to reach the threshold of economic warfare. There are at least two problems—one internal and another external—for preserving and strengthening key alliances when they are formed in three dimensional rather than in one-dimensional terms.

One danger in developing multidimensional alliances among democratic nations is obvious: the domestic political dynamics of any partner can become so fluid that its economic and ideological policies might weaken the military alliance. Sharp shifts in political philosophy from one ruling party to another or sudden changes in regime can bring instability to alliances composed of democracies. Perhaps as important as dramatic change are longer-term trends in public opinion and political affiliation as one generation of leaders gives way to another. Unilateral foreign policy is difficult enough to manage during sea changes in democracy, but the kind of multilateral policies necessary to sustain complex alliances such as NATO, or even the kind of sensitive bilateral understanding required to maintain the

U.S.-Japanese mutual security arrangement, constantly taxes the abilities of the leaders of these countries. It is testimony to the quality of both free alliances and their leaders that, so far, the domestic politics of Western Europe, Japan, and the United States have not subverted the collective security relations among these countries despite some rather dramatic changes since 1945. Nonetheless, domestic politics in democracies is not an automatic process that naturally produces sophisticated alliance statesmanship: pygmies can as easily build on the shoulders of giants as other giants can, and every democracy furnishes both.

A second threat to multidimensional alliances comes from the external environment: an adversary can seek to take advantage of weakness in one dimension and possibly weaken the overall structure of such alliances. Soviet policy toward NATO under Gorbachev will probably continue to perfect a rather sophisticated strategy of concentrating on domestic economic and political divisions (or "contradictions") in Western Europe that tend to separate Europeans from Americans, as in the areas of strategic trade and ideological debate. Such a policy is really directed at the assumptions of NATO that a large military buildup is necessary not only because of Soviet military power but as an expression of ideological solidarity in the West. Under these circumstances the United States must pay great attention, for example, to the "German question"—reunification of the two Germanys—because the Soviets hold a very high card in the game of German interest, on the left as well as the right, in uniting East and West Germany.

It is increasingly recognized by all Western alliance partners that the tasks of preserving and strengthening collective security are political and economic as well as military. Disruption in one of these interdependent areas can negatively affect the others. Because this instability may be driven by both domestic and foreign factors at the same time, affecting different dimensions of an alliance simultaneously, the demands placed on alliance managers are great today and may be impossible tomorrow. Whatever the future of key Western-oriented alliances may be, the emerging and increasingly multidimensional nature of collective security must be appreciated.

In this complicated, three-dimensional alliance network each partner finds that its allies, with few exceptions, are also its foremost trading partners. Although it may be possible to isolate economic and military factors provisionally, the very fact that close ideological and military allies may also be important trading partners tends to create both solidarity and potential division. To a certain extent one may assume that military relations between the United States and Western Europe are managed in NATO while economic relations find other venues, but it is never clear in the domestic politics of any given country that such careful distinctions are made or, if made today, will continue tomorrow. If America's key alliances are with democratic nations that tend to exaggerate the importance of economic issues in their domestic politics, the politics of defense will never be very far from basic national controversies and decisions in the realm of political economy.

Trade frictions, always closely tied to the foundations of national economy, are both directly and indirectly related to national security policy.

Collective security has been deemed an essential principle of international order by the United States and its key alliance partners; yet the management of such a security system is becoming increasingly complicated as the three dimensions of politics, economics, and military affairs interact with one another and obscure conventional dividing lines between the so-called high politics of national security and the low politics of complex interdependence. The blurring of disciplinary as well as policy boundaries does not mean that international security alliances are not still strong agencies for national defense, but it does suggest that alliance management will need to pay greater attention to interdisciplinary strategies if the aim is to preserve and strengthen collective security.

MAJOR REGIONAL DISPUTES

If the guiding principle of world order in major Western alliances is collective security, then in the dynamic and sometimes turbulent third world certain Western interests in orderliness also exist, principles such as peaceful resolution of disputes, unimpeded access to resources and markets, freedom from discrimination on grounds of religion or ethnic background, self-determination of peoples, and the inadmissibility of taking territory by force. Yet the history of the third world since the end of World War II has been, to put it mildly, a challenge to these principles.

In the major third world regions—Africa, Asia and the Pacific, the Middle East, and Central and South America—the future for international order, at least as defined by Western interests, seems ambiguous. The link between trade and security for Western nations and Japan in the third world will paradoxically hinge on furthering the principles of world order and, at the same time, amending them because of their ethnocentricity. On one side the West and Japan are confronted with the need to protect their own interests in the third world, but on the other these interests exist in a realm of interdependence where the interests of third world actors, some of whom have rejected or reinterpreted Western views of international norms, have independent and even paramount power.

Western principles of international behavior by no means exhaust the list of values that some countries, such as the United States, would like to make more operative in the third world: especially in the area of human rights, a good deal of debate has taken place in the United States. To what extent are American domestic political standards wisely urged on others? Can we find in non-Western cultures human rights standards as exacting as our own, if not more so? In opting for a more aggressive approach to human rights in the third world, are we simply entering the long debate in American history between "conservative realists" and "liberal idealists"—supposedly the argument between the Nixon/Ford-/Kissinger approach and that of Carter/Vance (according to Vance) —or are we trying to find a formula that might combine strategic necessities with justice along the lines, say, of the Reagan policy of "constructive engagement" in South Africa? Are efforts to blend realism and idealism a bit like trying to square the circle, or is there hope, at some distant future point, that there will be consensus in American foreign policy on issues of human rights?

When applied to specific conflicts in the third world, some of them of great danger to world peace, do any Western principles of international orderliness make much sense? Some have pointed to the danger that in the wake of Vietnam the United States would not only leave its world policeman's role but retire from the realm of international law entirely, either to a position of complete lack of interest in the outcomes of these conflicts or to a policy of unilateral armed intervention without any long-term objectives as far as the international order is concerned. It could be argued, for instance, that an Iran that rejects all Western concepts of international law and order must be confronted by outside powers with the consequences of its own behavior: Hobbes's state of nature, a condition of permanent warfare by various means from terror to full-scale war. Some hold a similar view of Soviet behavior in the third world, where Moscow's policies appear both highly legalistic and anarchistic.

In the jumble of third world conflicts—part local, part regional, part superpower rivalry—the relations between trade and security are self-evident, whether it is access to oil in the Persian Gulf or precious minerals in South Africa or simply unimpeded transit through strategic waterways worldwide. Part of the problem is one of trying, by dint of Western influence, to make this jumble more intelligible and predictable and even normative. But such security will probably not have the same principles of collective security based on the integrated economic, political, and military destinies one finds in the major Western alliances, and one should be careful not to envisage such solidarity between Western nations and third world nations as necessarily desirable or feasible. Surely the nations of the third world are searching for their own principles of international order, but the West will inevitably recognize these principles as somewhat at variance with its own. Hence the role of national power, including military power, will continue to be important in trying to establish a security framework for trade in the future.

FUNCTIONAL ISSUES AND WORLD TRADE

In the political and security framework for international trade in the decade ahead, three functional issues in world politics pose challenges to the unimpeded flow of goods and ideas: (1) ideological divisions; (2) terrorism; and (3) North-South economic differences. All three easily find a congenial home in third world politics, but there is also what might be called feedback into the politics of the West. For example, in NATO countries ideological division, terrorism, and North-South economic differences are increasingly important issues in domestic politics.

Ideological divisions include the enduring and protean East-West conflict led by Washington and Moscow, but such divisions will also involve conflicts of ideas that are either peripheral to, or completely separate from, the seemingly endless struggle between capitalism and communism. In the adversarial relationship between East and West, it is important to recognize both its endurance and its tendency to develop various permutations over time. The most sophisticated thinking in Moscow understands the necessity of adaptation and even reform as essential to the problematic nature of any major revolutionary movement. To the extent that the Soviet Union still lays claim to the founder's role in Socialist revolution, as it has in every party program including those in the détente period, it also acknowledges the importance of thwarting capitalism's power (which is also constantly changing its forms) by readjusted programs and methods. In this sense communism will continue to be a moving target over the next decade, thereby creating for the major democratic capitalist powers new and ingenious threats to their development and expansion. Although the most important area for East-West maneuvering in this game of ideological strategy will be the third world, this game knows no real boundaries.

Within the third world itself ideological divisions will continue along lines divergent from the East-West conflict as well as related to it. In all major regions of the third world, distinctions between types of ideological struggle—those relevant to the Moscow-Washington axis and those relevant to some other dimension of conflict—become confusing. What is apparent, however, is that the political context of future world trade will be fecund with ideological divisions that could hamper

the maintenance and expansion of this trade. In revolutions as disparate as those in Iran and Nicaragua, a range of ideological viewpoints works against American economic relations with third world countries. Such revolutionary movements have expansionist aims as well, engendering conflict with neighboring countries, as in the Iran-Iraq war or the insurgency in El Salvador, with potentially serious consequences for Western interests.

The forecast of troubles for international trade from terrorism, which is in part related to the problems of ideological division, is also potentially grave. Aside from sporadic terrorist acts in major industrialized countries as well as in the third world, acts often connected with global networks bent on countering what is thought to be Western imperialism, there is already one country, Lebanon, where productive economic relations with Europe, Japan, and the United States have been almost totally eliminated by a decade-long civil struggle dominated by abundant terrorism in all shades of the ideological rainbow. Indeed, terrorism in Lebanon has reached such a disconcerting state of development that certain acts have no rationale whatsoever save retaliation or pure randomness. With its steady diet of outside intervention as well as internal disruption, Lebanon constitutes a pathological case study in how terrorism against Western powers can create a political system totally antithetical to future trade. It is the dream of leaders such as Khomeini and Qaddafi, both heavily involved in Lebanese affairs, that Lebanon should become an example of what will happen to Western interests on a much grander scale.

Connected again with ideological divisions and, to some extent, with terrorism as well are major North-South economic differences with the major industrialized countries that are capable of creating a political and security environment hostile to the expansion of trade. There are, of course, the well-known splits between North and South evident in the United Nations and other international organizations on issues ranging from debt burden to the very philosophy of development itself. To the extent that such conflicts threaten economic or even military warfare with the United States and its major allies, they become security problems with significance for the future of international trade. For example, although the Arab oil embargo and price shocks of 1973–1974 were negotiable under the aegis of recycled petrodollars—thereby bringing the trauma of economic interdependence into some kind of equilibrium, where both sides gained something and lost something in their long-term political and security interests—a future oil cutoff for political reasons may not have such a mutually beneficial outcome. It was also the case in 1973–1974 that neither of the Persian Gulf giants, Saudi Arabia and Iran, experienced a revolutionary shift of regime during this crisis: had the Iranian involvement in the early oil price shock episodes been accompanied by the appearance of Khomeini as a national leader hostile to the United States, the mood in Washington toward this episode might have been considerably less benign.

In conclusion, the functional issues of ideological division, terrorism, and North-South economic differences could threaten Western views of an international order based on free commerce in goods and ideas in ways that leave no opening for peaceful negotiation of these conflicts. The result could be economic and even military warfare that would gravely affect international trade. It is likely that the official American mood on these three issues will continue to harden no matter which party is in power. It is also the case that the United States and its major allies have increasingly turned to security planning for meeting possibly adverse contingencies in these three functional areas.

To the extent that a stable international order, governed by certain widely accepted norms of behavior, is important for the development and expansion of trade, the next decade will demand the greatest of diplomatic and military skills if such an order is to be maintained. The tasks involved in this stabilization will be those of sheer maintenance of interests as well as the expansion of them. The first-priority business in both diplomacy and defense will include an urgent prevention of further deterioration. In all four areas of Ambassador Habib's foreign policy framework—management of Soviet-American relations, preserving and strengthening key alliances, major regional disputes, and functional issues—principles of orderliness are under challenge. The political and security framework for international trade in the decade ahead will depend as much on those who can maintain an equilibrium of competing interests as on those who propose grander designs. ∎

Notes

1. "Detente with the Soviet Union: The Reality of Competition and the Imperative of Cooperation," Statement of Secretary of State Henry Kissinger before the Senate Committee on Foreign Relations, *Department of State Bulletin,* October 14, 1974, p. 508. Full text reprinted in Robert J. Pranger, ed., *Détente and Defense: A Reader* (Washington, D.C.: American Enterprise Institute, 1976), pp. 153–78.

2. "Basic Principles of Relations," in Roger P. Labrie (ed.), *SALT Handbook: Key Documents and Issues, 1972–1979* (Washington, D.C.: American Enterprise Institute, 1979), p. 50.

3. For a detailed analysis of Soviet détente policy in the 1970s, see Harry Gelman, *The Brezhnev Politburo and the Decline of Detente* (Ithaca, NY: Cornell University Press, 1984), pp. 105–73.

4. Analyses of the Reagan administration's policies toward the Soviet Union during its first term can be found in the articles by Dan Caldwell, Michael R. Gordon, and Angela E. Stent in "Dealing with the Soviet Union," *AEI Foreign Policy and Defense Review,* vol. 5, no. 2 (1985).

5. See Sarah Meiklejohn Terry, "The Soviet Union and Eastern Europe: Implications for U.S. Policy," in Dan Caldwell (ed.), *Soviet International Behavior and U.S. Policy Options* (Lexington, MA: Lexington Books, 1985), pp. 40–41.

Suggested Additional Readings

Aho, C. Michael, and Marc Levinson. *After Reagan: Confronting the Changed World Economy* (New York: Council of Foreign Relations, 1988).

Bergsten, C. Fred. *America in the World Economy* (Washington, DC: Institute for International Economics, 1988).

———, and William R. Cline. *Trade Policy in the 1980s* (Washington, DC: Institute for International Economics, 1982).

Cohen, Stephen D. *The Making of United States Economic Policy* (New York: Praeger, 1988).

Cooper, Richard. *Economic Policy in an Interdependent World* (Cambridge, MA: MIT Press, 1986).

Dell, Edmund. *The Politics of Economic Interdependence* (New York: St. Martin's Press, 1987).

Greenaway, David (ed.). *Economic Development and International Trade* (New York: St. Martin's Press, 1988).

Spero, Joan Edelman. *The Politics of International Economic Relations* (New York: St. Martin's Press, 1977).

Yochelson, John. *Keeping Pace: U.S. Policies and Global Economic Change* (Cambridge, MA: Ballinger, 1988).

CHAPTER TWELVE

Population and Immigration

*
*

The issues of population and immigration are closely intertwined but also separate in various ways, and both of them have become very controversial.

While population growth in the United States, Western Europe, and some East Asian countries has largely leveled off in recent decades, the population in the Third World has continued to grow. Some changes have occurred that have begun to slow the birth rate in the Third World also, but even with these changes the overall population has continued to increase. In Latin America the population is doubling every thirty years; in Africa the rates of growth are even higher. In those countries immediately south of the U.S., Mexico and Central America, the population will increase by 70% in the next twenty years.

These continuing high population growth-rates are putting enormous pressures on the countries of the Third World. Their economies cannot find jobs for all the new people, social services are lagging, schools are inadequate, and hence unemployment and illiteracy are increasing. At the same time, urbanization is accelerating, the cities are swelling beyond their capacity to absorb all the new people, and the urban areas are becoming unliveable. These pressures have led in numerous countries to food riots, mass protest movements, increasing conflict, and even civil and international war (in the case

of the 1969 conflict between El Salvador and Honduras) essentially over population issues. The pressures of unchecked population increase are devastating the economies of many Third World countries, and they threaten to undermine their political systems as well. The potential for such mass violence, destabilization, and renewed opportunities for Marxist-Leninist guerrilla movements carries immense implications for U.S. foreign policy.

For roughly twenty-five years the United States has been encouraging family planning programs in these countries. These programs have had some success in reducing the population growth rate in quite a number of countries from over 3% to less than 2.5%, but even at that lower rate of growth the population keeps doubling. Moreover, even with the birthrate slowing down gradually, today's and the next generation's population problems are already with us. It is important to consider that unchecked population growth is not only a domestic social, economic, and political problem for the countries affected, but that it also has the potential to become a major international and foreign policy problem.

That gets us to the subject of immigration. The population and immigration issues are obviously closely linked. Population pressures, in the absence of jobs and future prospects, lead people to emigrate, to leave their native countries and look for greener pastures. The greenest pastures are almost universally considered to be the United States. Frequently, the migration of peasants to their capital cities is only the first step in the process; the next step is to get to the United States. With our 2000-mile border with Mexico, and with aliens also coming in through Canada or from the Caribbean, the United States has begun to lose control of its own borders.

The issue is complicated. We want as a nation to remain open to new immigrants, but not in ways that get completely out of hand. Some groups (grower interests, for example) favor increased immigration, since they need inexpensive labor to work in the fields. Labor groups, on the other hand, fear that immigrants will take jobs from unionized Americans. At the same time, the Hispanic arrivals are putting enormous pressures on the schools, social services, and justice systems of the "gateway" states (Florida, Texas, California, and others). Hispanics will soon pass blacks as the largest minority in this country; the question is also beginning to loom large in some areas as to whether we are a predominantly European and English-speaking country or a bicultural and bilingual one.

The United States needs to regain control of its own borders. At the same time, given the swelling populations of our Third World neighbors, we need to recognize that if we completely seal off the borders, we remove the safety valve for their excess population and thus add to the potential for revolutionary explosions south of the border, which is not in our interests either. These conflicts require a delicate juggling act whose management will strain both our domestic and our international politics, and which represents a severe, long-term challenge to us.

Our readings in this section begin with a survey of global population trends by demographer Paul Demeny. Then, political scientists Iêda Siqueira Wiarda and the present author show the relationships between population increases and social and political breakdowns, revolution, and war—how population policy is related to U.S. foreign policy.

Foundation official Michael Teitelbaum, focusing on the immigration issue, shows the interconnections between immigration, refugees, and foreign policy. Georges Fauriol, a think tank scholar in Washington, shows how immigration to the U.S. has recently gotten out of hand and that the U.S. needs to regain control of its own borders. Finally, James N. Purcell, Jr., of the State Department, shows us what that department is doing in the realm of refugee assistance.

World Population Trends

By Paul Demeny

Human populations, like all living species, are endowed with a reproductive potential that, if unchecked, would allow them to replenish the earth in a quite literal sense within a few dozen generations. Save for exceptional and short periods, nature and (for humans especially) social organization control that potential.

For human populations, the industrial revolution heralded the arrival of such exceptional times. The growth spurt it generated in human numbers came to its climax in the third quarter of the twentieth century. It is now abating, but population growth has a powerful built-in momentum that virtually assures major increases in population size in many countries—countries that contain the large majority of the world's people. The pattern and the modes through which population growth in these countries will be brought back to the historically dominant, (and in the long run ecologically mandatory) near-stationary levels remain uncertain. The speed at which countries converge toward and eventually attain zero population growth will have a powerful impact on human prospects in the next century.

In 1988, the world's population is estimated at 5.1 billion, slightly more than twice its 1950 size, 2.5 billion. On the global level, doubling in such a short period of time was a unique event in human history: such an explosive population increase has not happened before and will not happen again.

The spectacular and necessarily temporary acceleration of the rate of population growth that caused the increase began shortly after the close of World War II. In retrospect, the course of the population growth curve can be accurately traced. Its all-time high—at the annual rate of 2.1 percent—occurred in the late 1960s; growth rates have continued on a slowly decreasing path ever since.[1] The global rate of increase in the late 1980s is estimated at 1.7 percent. Measured in terms of absolute numbers, however, growth is still accelerating. The peak growth rate between 1965 and 1970 generated annual additions to the world's population of 72 million. In the late 1980s, the estimated global population increase amounts to 88 million each year.

Demographers failed to anticipate this extraordinary post-1950 demographic growth spurt, nor were they quick to perceive its onset. To be sure, they knew that by historical standards global population growth was already rapid before mid-century.[2] The average annual growth rate in the nineteenth century was slightly above one-half of one percent: it brought the world's population from an estimated 950 million in 1800 to somewhat above 1.6 billion in 1900. The average growth rate in the first half of the present century was still higher: only slightly below nine-tenths of one percent. But, from that already rapid tempo of increase, the jump to a 2 percent or higher rate of annual growth was nearly discontinuous and caught all experts unprepared.

Thus, in 1945, Frank Notestein, then the most eminent figure among American demographers, foresaw a year 2000 population of some 3 billion.[3] In retrospect we know that that figure was surpassed as early as 1960. In 1954, at the Rome World Population Conference, the first major international scientific meeting in demography in the post-World War II period, E. F. Schumacher (later the author of *Small is Beautiful*) posited a 1980 global population of 3 billion.[4] The projection ventured only a quarter century forward, yet it turned out to be in error by an amount roughly equivalent to the total world population at the beginning of the twentieth century. Some 10 years later, in 1965, at the next World Population Conference, held in Belgrade, the prominent Soviet demographer, A. Y. Boyarsky, was more cautious. He offered his year 2000 forecast defined by a range: somewhere between 4.2 billion and 5 billion.[5] But this generous spread failed to guard against error. The actual size of the world's population surpassed the lower-end figure by 1977; the upper-end estimate was surpassed just 10 years later.

Such failures of global foresight (of which many more could be cited) reflect the accumulation of errors, pointing in the same direction, in estimating country population trends. Global (and regional)

Paul Demeny, an economist and demographer, is Distinguished Scholar at the Population Council, New York. He is editor of the quarterly journal *Population and Development Review.*

Source: From *Current History,* Vol. 8, No. 534 (January 1989), pp 17–19, 58–59, 64–65.

population estimates are obtained simply by adding up country level estimates. At least until the late 1950s, demographers' assessments of population growth prospects displayed a consistently conservative bias, particularly with regard to the so-called developing countries.

Mid-century estimates made for the world's two demographic giants, India and China, illustrate this tendency. For example, in his encyclopedic and authoritative study of the Indian subcontinent, Kingsley Davis fitted a "logistic" curve to adjusted census data for India's prepartition territory up to 1941.[6] The logistic curve is a felicitous characterization of the long-run growth experience of biological aggregates that encounter increasing resistance from the environment as their size increases. An initial phase of expansion during which growth accelerates is followed by a decelerating growth phase and eventual stabilization as the aggregate reaches an upper limit reflecting ultimate environmental constraints. Applying this construct to India, Davis found it satisfactory to posit 700 million as the upper asymptote to the logistic curve. In fact, by 1988 the population of the Indian subcontinent exceeded this limit by some 350 million.

In similar fashion, around 1950, demographers professed to perceive a huge potential for demographic growth in China. But the quantitative estimate of that potential reflected a deep pessimism concerning the severity of the environmental constraints thought to limit China's population growth. Specific estimates of demographic growth projected to be experienced in that country between 1950 and 1980 ranged from 65 million to 140 million. The actual increase was about 440 million.

On their face, these examples of past demographic prognostication do not bode well for success in discerning future population trends. Indeed, it has been persuasively argued that population forecasts beyond some 20 years into the future rapidly lose reliability.[7] But, in fact, as the 1950s unfolded, the excessive conservatism that characterized demographic forecasts became gradually apparent to demographers, and the accuracy of the projected population figures increased markedly.

Part of the credit for the improved grasp of the shape of future population trends was due to notable, if still far from satisfactory, progress in gathering empirical data on demographic phenomena during the last few decades. Analytical tools have also sharpened.

THE DEMOGRAPHIC TRANSITION

The central paradigm devised by demographers for understanding the unprecedented growth of populations in the twentieth century, and indeed throughout the modern era, is that of the demographic transition: a more or less protracted historical process during which a population moves from an initial premodern stage characterized by high mortality and matching high fertility to an ultimate equilibrium of fertility and mortality at a low level.

When mortality is high—or, what amounts to the same thing, when expectation of life at birth is low—sustaining a population even at near-zero growth requires customs and institutions that maintain fertility at a high level. The very success in that endeavor suggests that the supporting institutions tend to be well-entrenched and resistant to change. This is not so with respect to mortality. Unlike low fertility—that is to say, a smaller family size—survival and a healthier life are universal desiderata. If technological and medical advances permit reduction of the death rate, the opportunity to take advantage of such advances will be eagerly sought.

As the complex of changes that are loosely described as "modernization" gathers force, this lack of symmetry between the behavioral underpinnings of mortality and fertility becomes a powerful generator of demographic growth. Under the impact of modernization, death rates tend to fall first, to be followed later by a decline in birthrates. Thus, with the onset of the demographic transition a gap opens up between birthrates and death rates, resulting in what demographers call "natural" increase. (The increase is called "natural" in order to distinguish it from increase *tout court,* which, in a population open to in- or out-migration, is also affected by the net migratory balance. Historically, migration as a source of growth has often been important. But in most contemporary populations, especially those of large countries, its impact on population growth tends to be relatively minor. In the global population, the net migratory balance is always zero.)

As long as people remain mortal, however, death rates cannot fall forever: they must eventually level off. When fading birthrates catch up with the already low death rates, population growth once again halts: the demographic transition is completed.

This stylized picture of the transition is, of course, consistent with a great variety of patterns of demographic change experienced by individual countries. The secular decline of mortality started early and proceeded at a steady and slow pace among those in the vanguard of industrialization. When fertility decline ensued, its tempo was typically more brisk. The pioneer countries also had pretransition social systems that, by limiting marriage, kept fertility and the level of mortality relatively low. (Indeed, these demographic characteristics reflect, and partly explain, the factors that set the pioneer countries on the road to the industrial revolution.) Thus the potential for growth in early demographic transitions was relatively limited: in nineteenth century Europe the gap between birthrates and death rates rarely generated a growth rate appreciably above one percent.

This historical record colored demographers' views on the effects of the demographic transitions that gathered momentum in the early post-World War II period in Asia, Latin America and Africa. In fact, the actual patterns of transition experienced by these countries differed in crucial respects from those traced by the demographic pioneers.

First, the initial levels of both mortality and fertility rates turned out to be appreciably higher than were the corresponding rates in the "pioneer" countries. The growth potential that declining mortality could trigger was, accordingly, more powerful than was the case in earlier demographic transitions.

Second, the driving force of the demographic transition, mortality decline, turned out to be more precipitous than would have been expected from earlier transition experience. The application of advances in the medical technology developed in the industrialized countries played a crucial role in making such rapid declines in mortality possible. Medical technology did not render the level of development irrelevant as a determinant of mortality, but it shifted the relationship between development and mortality: in the less developed world, in the second half of this century, given levels of income are associated with much lower levels of mortality than were observed in early transitions.

Third, in countries of Asia and Latin America where fertility did begin to decline, the tempo of that decline has generally been appreciably faster than was the case in earlier experience. A speeding up of fertility transitions had already been observed in the first half of the twentieth century; it was reasonable to expect that fertility declines in the late-comer countries would occur at an increasingly rapid pace. Deliberate policies that many developing countries adopted beginning in the 1960s—policies aimed at triggering and facilitating fertility declines—appear to have played an important part in fostering the spread of birth control, hence speeding the transition toward lower fertility.

Finally, in many instances, the high rates of population growth generated by the demographic transition in its middle phase affected countries that had already attained a very large size—like China, India and Indonesia. Accordingly, measured in terms of absolute increases, the impact of the transition process was very se-vere, often without historical precedent.

As a result, the demographic makeup of the world underwent a dramatic change during the course of one-third of a century. A concise quantitative picture of the massive demographic shifts that occurred between 1950 and 1985 is presented in the first two columns of Table 1, and in the columns that indicate the growth rates and population increases during that period.

The regional units shown in Table 1 are divided into two broad groups, labeled "North" and "South." For all practical purposes, this classification is the same as the familiar if plainly tenuous division of the world into "developed" and "developing" nations. However, "North" and "South" are also less than fully accurate labels.

The striking demographic contrast between these two broad regions is highlighted by the difference in growth rates: between 1950 and 1985, the poor "South" grew more than twice as fast as the rich "North." This gap is especially remarkable in view of the fact that the period also witnessed a strong resurgence of demographic growth in the "North," caused by the unexpected baby boom of the 1950s and 1960s. But the major demographic event of those decades was not rising fertility but the precipitous fall of mortality in virtually all countries of Asia, Latin America and Africa. Falling death rates combined with still high birthrates produced the extraordinary expansion of the population of these continents. Between 1950 and 1985, the net addition to human numbers in the "South" was some 2 billion, equivalent to the total world population around

Table 1 Estimates and Projections of the Population Size, Average Annual Growth Rate, and Absolute Population Increase by Regions, 1950–2020.

Region	Total population (millions)			Growth rate (percent)		Absolute Increase (millions)	
	1950	1985	2020	1950–1985	1985–2020	1950–1985	1985–2020
North America	166.1	264.8	327.2	1.33	0.60	98.7	62.4
Europe	392.5	492.2	513.8	0.65	0.12	99.7	21.6
USSR	180.1	276.9	343.2	1.23	0.61	96.8	66.3
Japan	83.6	120.8	129.9	1.05	0.21	37.2	9.1
Oceania	12.6	24.6	37.3	1.91	1.19	12.0	12.7
"NORTH"	834.9	1179.3	1351.4	.99	.39	344.4	172.1
China	554.8	1059.5	1459.8	1.85	0.92	504.7	400.3
Southeast Asia	215.0	469.8	839.4	2.23	1.66	254.8	369.6
South Asia	521.1	1184.2	2317.9	2.35	1.92	663.1	1133.7
Africa	224.1	557.4	1441.3	2.60	2.71	333.3	883.9
Latin America	165.4	403.6	719.0	2.55	1.65	238.2	315.4
"SOUTH"	1680.4	3674.5	6777.4	2.24	1.75	1994.1	3102.9
WORLD TOTAL	2515.3	4853.8	8128.8	1.88	1.47	2338.5	3275.0

1930, and nearly 2.5 times as large as the total population of the "North" at mid-century.

These unequal patterns of demographic growth induced marked shifts in the regional composition of the world's population. Table 2 presents summary information on these shifts. The share of the "South" within the global population increased from two-thirds in 1950 to three-fourths in 1985. The share of the combined population of Europe and the Soviet Union dropped from 22.8 percent to 15.8 percent. In 1950, the size of the population of North America (that is to say, the combined populations of the United States and Canada) was virtually the same as that of Latin America (including the Caribbean). By 1985, the size of Latin America's population exceeded the population of North America by 140 million.

PROJECTED TRENDS

Demographers looking into the future around 1950 were not notably successful in discerning its shape. Do they have reason to be more confident in the late 1980s? Are the improvements in forecasting, noted above, likely to stand the test of time? A sign of seemingly supreme confidence that these questions can be answered affirmatively is the existence of a flourishing minor industry preparing long-range demographic projections. The World Bank, for example, annually makes detailed population projections up to the year 2150 for nearly 200 countries and territories.[8] But these calculations, issued in periodic hefty volumes, do not really intend to imply that we can predict with some de-

Table 2 Percentage Distribution of the World's Population by Regions; Estimates and Projections 1950–2020.

Region	1950	1985	2020
North America	6.6	5.5	4.0
Europe	15.6	10.1	6.3
USSR	7.2	5.7	4.2
Japan	3.3	2.5	1.6
Oceania	0.5	0.5	0.5
"NORTH"	33.2	24.3	16.6
China	22.0	21.8	18.0
Southeast Asia	8.6	9.7	10.3
South Asia	20.7	24.4	28.5
Africa	8.9	11.5	17.7
Latin America	6.6	8.3	8.9
"SOUTH"	66.8	75.7	83.4
WORLD TOTAL	100.0	100.0	100.0

Sources, Tables 1 and 2: *World Population Prospects: 1988* (New York: United Nations, 1988).

gree of assurance that indeed there will be 43,000 females between the ages of 20 and 24 in the Solomon Islands in the year 2125, or even that Nigeria's population in fact will be stabilized at 529 million— more than five times its present size—by the middle of the twenty-first century. Such calculations are merely hypothetical.

But for a more near-term future, say, for the 35-year period from 1985 to 2020, demographic projections can now be made with a somewhat greater assurance of success than was the case in 1950. This is because fertility and mortality changes during the last few decades greatly reduced the plausible range within which the future evolution of these variables will be constrained. The most important development in this regard was the major improvement in mortality conditions experienced in every major region, and especially in the South, during the first three decades of the twentieth century. The best single measure of that improvement is the expectation of life at birth. From the early 1950s to the early 1980s, the expectation of life at birth increased by more than 16 years in the "South:" from 41 years to nearly 58 years. The magnitude of this achievement cannot be overemphasized.

From the point of view of predicting the demographic future, these developments have a special significance. While further significant progress in reducing mortality is still possible and, indeed, is likely, much of the type of mortality change that can have a major effect on population growth through improvement of child survival (as distinct from increasing the proportion of persons surviving to old age) has already oc-

curred. For example, in China and in Latin America, life expectancy at birth in the early 1980s was as high as life expectancy in Japan or in Europe in the early 1950s. An important exception is Africa. There, too, life expectancy has increased —from 38 years in the early 1950s to 50 years three decades later— but the scope for future improvement is still great enough to exert a major impact on population growth.

Recent fertility trends also narrowed the range of uncertainty concerning developments in the next few decades. Many formerly high fertility countries experienced major reductions in birthrates; these countries contain the majority of the population of the "South." The most spectacular change took place in China, where by the early 1980s fertility was more than 60 percent below its level of the early 1950s. But the corresponding declines were also important—exceeding 30 percent —in Latin America and Southeast Asia. Outside China, fertility in most less developed countries is still a long way from replacement level—from families having two children on the average—but a good deal of the distance in that direction has already been traveled. The major exceptions are the countries of South Asia and West Asia (where the overall decline was a modest 16 percent) and especially the countries of Africa (where the average level of fertility remains largely unchanged). In the "North," the post-World War II upsurge of fertility proved temporary. Between the early 1950s and the early 1980s, fertility in North America declined by almost 50 percent, and the corresponding declines exceeded 30 percent in Europe, Japan and Oceania. In the North as

a whole, fertility has now fallen below the level that, in the long run, would maintain the population at its present size. Growth is still continuing at a modest rate.

The developments just outlined make the task of demographic forecasting considerably easier than was the case around 1950. Both demographic history and population theory suggest the likelihood that once premodern patterns of fertility behavior are broken, the main tendency is toward increasing limitation of births, with reversals that are only temporary, if they occur at all. There is, perhaps, a lower limit to fertility decline: societies, unless they are resigned to disappearing from the human family, will manage to keep fertility at replacement level. As to mortality, the conventional wisdom holds that over time longevity has nowhere to go but up, with a likely upper limit of the expectation of life in the neighborhood of 80 years, and with the laggard countries catching up, more or less speedily, with those in the vanguard of progress.

It is, of course, possible to counter such assumptions with a good dose of skepticism. Significant mortality reversals did occur in many countries in the past, although for a persuasive example of a calamity that actually reduced global population one has to go back to the fourteenth century. A virus, nastier than the one that caused the influenza pandemic after World War I, may ambush mankind. In the past, war has been an ineffective regulator of total population size; in a future war, waged with nuclear or bacteriological and chemical weapons, this need not be so.

In formerly high fertility countries, like China, where fertility decline is induced by deliberate policy, a relaxation of social controls may cause fertility to rise again. Finally, and most important, it is not clear that countries where fertility is still high will naturally embark on a course of fertility decline that replicates earlier transition experiences, or that such countries have the capacity to induce fertility decline if and when a slowing down of rapid population growth is recognized in the collective interest.

Still, the character of the most plausible surprise-free demographic scenario for the near-term future is fairly well agreed on. Its central, if unabashedly optimistic assumption, is an orderly and fairly rapid convergence, in all countries, of low fertility and mortality levels: levels just sufficient to maintain population size in a stationary state. Table 1 summarizes the results of one set of such projections—those of the United Nations "medium" series—for the year 2020, and indicates the growth rate and the absolute increases in population size that they imply for the 35-year period from 1985 to 2020.[9] Table 2 indicates the further shifts in the regional composition of the world's population that the projected changes in population size will generate by 2020.

The calculations incorporated into Table 1 and Table 2 posit steady and fairly rapid further improvements of mortality in all countries. By 2020, expectation of life at birth is assumed to be 70 years or longer in all regions except Africa, where it will fall short of that figure only by about 6 years. In short, the projections assume that for all practical purposes the mortality transition will be completed by the early twenty-first century.

For fertility, the projections assume that China will succeed in keeping its fertility appreciably below replacement level throughout the 35-year period and that the regions of the North will stabilize their fertility at about present levels. In the rest of the world, the projections assume that all regions, with the exception of Africa, will experience continued rapid declines in fertility and will reach replacement or near-replacement levels by 2020. As for Africa, a major—44 percent—drop in fertility is assumed, which, by 2020, would bring African fertility to a level equal to United States fertility in the early 1950s.

Clearly, these are highly optimistic assumptions. Successful realization of both the fertility and mortality scenarios envisaged in the projections would require a felicitous combination of enlightened public policies and a good measure of luck. Yet the figures of Tables 1 and 2 suggest that population growth will remain a major challenge to successful development in the decades to come and a factor that will exert an increasingly important influence on international relations. Between 1985 and 2020, the net addition to the world population will be 3.2 billion, making the global population exceed 8 billion. Thus, in the brief period of 35 years, the net addition to population will be twice the size of the global population in 1900. The countries of the South, mostly still poor, will have to absorb some 95 percent of this increase, more than 3 billion. Africa alone will increase its population by nearly 900 million, a number equivalent to the combined current populations of Europe, North America and Japan. The share of the population of the now advanced industrial countries in the world's total will diminish at an accelerating pace. By 2020, the two current superpowers will represent a bare 8 percent of the world's population, and Europe's share will be less than half of what it was in 1950.

On the other hand, while the global population will probably still be growing around 2020, and continued demographic expansion will most likely bring the global population beyond the 10-billion mark before the end of the twenty-first century, realization of the fertility and mortality trends envisaged in the projections would mean that the historic world demographic transition had been essentially completed. Humankind could begin single-mindedly to concentrate on making life better, rather than devoting much of its energy to the task of accommodating greater numbers. ∎

Notes:

1. Unless otherwise noted, population figures cited in this discussion draw on the latest estimates and projections prepared by the United Nations. See Population Division, Department of International and Social Affairs of the United Nations, *World Population Prospects: 1988* (New York: United Nations, 1988).

2. For historical estimates of population change see Colin McEvedy and Richard Jones, *Atlas of World Population History* (New York: Viking Penguin, 1978). For a brief review of growth in the modern period, see Paul Demeny, "The World Demographic Situation," in Jane Menken (ed.), *World Population and U.S. Policy* (New York: Norton, 1986).

3. Frank W. Notestein, "Population—The Long View," in Theodore W. Schultz (ed.), *Food for the World* (Chicago: University of Chicago Press, 1959).

4. E. F. Schumacher, "Population in Relation to the Development of Energy from Coal," in *Proceedings of the World Population Conference, 1954,* vol. 5 (New York: United Nations, 1955).

5. A. Y. Boyarsky, "A Contribution to the Problem of the World Population in the Year 2000," in *World Population Conference, 1965,* vol. 2 (New York: United Nations, 1967).

6. Kingsley Davis, *The Population of India and Pakistan* (Princeton: Princeton University Press, 1951).

7. See especially Nathan Keyfitz, "The Limits of Population Forecasting," *Population and Development Review,* vol. 7, no. 4 (1981).

8. For the latest set of these projections see K. C. Zachariah and My T. Vu, *World Population Projections, 1987–88 Edition: Short- and Long-Term Estimates* (Baltimore: The Johns Hopkins University Press, published for the World Bank, 1988), or the more accessible summary in Appendix Table 27 of *World Development Report 1988* (New York: Oxford University Press, 1988).

9. See *World Population Prospects,* op. cit.

Latin America: Population and Internal Unrest

By Howard J. Wiarda and Iêda Siqueira Wiarda

At current growth rates, the population of Latin America is projected to increase between 1981 and 2001 by 225 million people. Brazil will grow to almost 200 million people, Mexico to 113 million (half the current U.S. population on one fifth the territory) and Central America's population will be similarly burgeoning. This staggering population growth is likely to have serious political, economic, social, strategic, and other implications.

The strong opposition to family planning which came principally from nationalists, the military, the church, the Right, and the Left during the 1960s has changed to general support for voluntary family planning programs in much of Latin America. Too rapid population growth is now widely viewed as aggravating the problems of development and putting severe strains on services and facilities. Surveys show a growing preference among the public for smaller families, especially in cities. The

wish to limit family size is particularly strong among women. Both civilian and military elites in Latin America now believe unchecked population growth—and hence an uneducated, alienated, unemployed "mass" of people in the capital cities—spells long-term disaster for society and the nation and, likely, short-term chaos in the form of food riots, mass protests, and general discontent that may destabilize governments.

PRESSURES ON LAND AND AGRICULTURE

Although the person-to-land ratio is lower in Latin America than in India, China or Western Europe, most of Latin America's untapped land is unusable, either so steeply mountainous, densely tropical or barren of topsoil (as in the Amazon Basin) that it cannot support life at even the most meager level of subsistence. The frontiers that did exist (western Brazil, the Colom-

bian and Venezuelan *llanos*) have been settled in the last thirty years.

Latin American landholding has long been characterized by the problems of *latifundia* (large, often unproductive estates) and *minifundia* (holdings that are too small to be economically viable). Food production in most of Latin America has not kept up with population growth. And since most new agricultural production is oriented toward exports rather than home consumption, conditions for most rural populations are worsening.

While subsistence agriculture was never very profitable, it at least enabled many to survive. Today, peasants are forced by large families and competing interests onto less fertile hillsides, often crossing the thin but deadly barrier between subsistence and starvation. In the face of these hardships, there has been widespread abandonment of the land as rural people flock to the cities in search of

Professor of Political Science, University of Massachusetts; Luso-Brazilian Culture Specialist, Library of Congress.

Source: From *Draper Fund Report,* No. 14 (September, 1985), pp. 20–24. Reprinted by permission of the Population Crisis Committee.

opportunity. Agricultural countries that were once self-sufficient are now forced to import basic food-stuffs at relatively high prices.

Even in key food producers like Brazil, some people are literally starving to death. Governments pay little attention to "poor people's food" because only export products will help them cope with their international debts. Incomes are so low and unevenly distributed that many *campesinos* cannot afford the food they need and may be experiencing worsening health, as demonstrated by rising infant mortality throughout the region.

ECONOMIC FRUSTRATIONS

The economic dilemmas facing Latin America include widespread poverty, the world's highest *per capita* debt, unemployment and underemployment that may reach between 40 and 50 percent of the workforce, negative economic growth rates over the past five years, immense income inequalities, declining terms of trade, extensive capital flight, little new investment or foreign assistance, increased protectionism on the part of those countries with whom Latin America must trade, rising prices for the goods Latin America must import, and (in some countries) devastation of the economic infrastructure by guerrilla forces.

Governments are caught in a "population-treadmill effect." High fertility countries that face a doubling or tripling of the school-age population by the end of the century will require major increases in spending for education, even if the objective is simply to maintain current, already low enrollment levels. The same population-treadmill effect applies to electric power,

transportation, jobs, housing, health care and other basic services. Given present and projected population growth, Latin American economies must move ahead at accelerated rates just to stay even. Nowhere, under present economic projections, is that likely to happen.

In this period of economic contraction, tough decisions must be made about how to spend scarce resources. Today's deprivation will have important effects later on. Insufficient spending on education, for example, will mean a less skilled labor force in years to come when Latin America will increasingly need a better trained population to achieve economic diversification. Additionally, there is mounting evidence that infant malnutrition stunts brainpower. Unchecked population growth means that the severe income inequalities will worsen, as will poverty, unemployment, bitterness and frustration.

URBANIZATION AND MIGRATION

The unprecedented flow from the countryside has made Latin America the Third World's most highly urbanized region with over 65 percent of its population residing in cities, particularly capital cities. Metropolises like São Paulo and Mexico City have grown to 16 or 17 million. Lima, Bogotá and capital cities in the smaller countries have also seen their populations double in the last two or three decades. The same is true of Santo Domingo, totalling 300,000 in 1950, now with over a million people, some of the worst slums in Latin America and virtually unmanageable problems.

Social services are breaking down in all Latin American capitals to the extent that over half the inhabitants lack water or sewage facilities. We sometimes read of "ungovernability" in the advanced industrial nations, but that is nothing compared to the increasing ungovernability of most Latin American capital cities. The relation between size, crowding and internal tension is complex. Crowding may not be a direct cause of violence, but it does provide a set of conditions in which tension, violence, and various forms of aberrant behavior are more likely to occur.

Mexico City adds at least 350,000 migrants from rural areas and small towns each year—in addition to its net annual increase by births of 2.5 percent, another 425,000 people. Projections place Mexico City's population at 26 million by the year 2000. But the city already lacks the governmental infrastructure, economic strength and social services to handle its current population. It has some of the world's worst pollution, its traffic problems are legendary, and it is literally sinking several inches a year as groundwater is progressively drawn from its swampy base. Conservative estimates put infant deaths at 30,000 a year from the effects of inadequate sewage facilities and air pollution alone.

Mexico City is not unique in Latin America. Urban life requires a large and complex set of services—water, sewerage and electricity to say nothing of schools and housing—that cannot be easily or quickly scaled up as population growth and migration accelerate. Latin American cities are proverbially short of money. Local governments have little or no taxing power and in most cases also lack the administrative and technical capacity to cope with the doubling of population size, which may now occur in a single decade.

There are, of course, benefits to urbanization. These include economies of scale, differentiated labor markets, and concentration of suppliers and consumers. However awful the conditions in city slums, the opportunities there are greater than in the countryside. Three out of four migrants make economic gains in the city and have better access to the limited services provided by the government. Women can also more easily find employment as factory workers, maids or vendors. The sheer size and uncontrolled nature of Latin America's cityward migration, however, threaten to produce such paralysis and chaos as to cancel the gains.

YOUTH AND RADICALISM

Because of high birthrates and public health improvements, half the population in virtually all Latin American countries is under eighteen years of age; in some, half is under fifteen. The implications for politics and public policy are immense. The dependency ratio, which compares the economically inactive, or dependent, population to the economically active and productive population, has undergone a dramatic increase. This rising dependency ratio has increased internal tensions, as a smaller pool of productive persons is being called upon to support more dependents and an ever larger requirement is placed on governments to carry the burden of the vast youth population.

There is mixed evidence on the relationship between youth and radicalism but it is certain that in Latin America most of the present generation of university-trained young people are Marxists. As many as 45 percent of college-aged people are activists. The implications of this disaffected group coming to power are enormous, particularly since the generation currently under fifteen is likely to be even more embittered and radical.

In our preoccupation with the political and ideological aspects of the Nicaraguan Revolution, we tend to forget that it also marked a sharp generational change. Both the Somoza regime and its more moderate opponents represented one generation; the Sandinistas represent a whole new age group coming to power. In 1979 most of the *comandantes* were in their late 20s or early 30s; the Revolution's strongest supporters are also at the younger end of the age spectrum. In fact, the Sandinistas lowered the voting age for the 1984 election from eighteen to sixteen in order to increase their margin of victory.

It is not likely that there will soon be a wave of "Nicaraguas" sweeping over Latin America—although in quite a few countries radical change led by the new generation can be expected. More likely is that demagogic politicians and political movements will seize upon the aggravations, pent-up frustrations, and radicalism of youth for their own purposes. The spectacle of high school or university students and unemployed graduates leading protest marches of recent migrants or urging peasants to take agrarian reform into their own hands is now common in Latin America. These are indirect effects of spiraling population growth. Those in power confronting such "direct action" do not

necessarily see the culprit as population growth *per se,* but rather as a malevolent opposition using "marginals" (the urban and rural unemployed) as shock troops. The predictable outcome is usually government overreaction, repression and the reassertion of authoritarian controls.

RISING SOCIAL TENSIONS

Tension, frustration and violence in society are likely to have a political impact. Unemployment in most Latin American countries may now reach 20 to 25 percent. Underemployment, often referred to as "invisible unemployment," may add another 20 to 25 percent, including "penny capitalists" who sell a few cigarettes a day, or shine shoes for a few customers. This "lumpen proletariat," the residents of urban slums surrounding all Latin American capital cities, is a powder keg waiting to explode. Few if any social or city services reach their neighborhoods. Living conditions are wretched; the slums are filthy, unhealthful and increasingly crime-ridden. The incidence of abandoned children (10 million in Brazil alone) has reached epidemic proportions. These are no longer isolated, diffused, "sleepy" peasants, fatalistically resigned to their present circumstances, but people with ambition and expectations who have been uprooted and among whom revolutionary and demagogic appeals are likely to find receptivity.

POLITICAL INSTABILITY

It takes relatively little—a change in bus fares, an increased tax on gasoline, rising prices for basic foodstuffs—to set off lawless protests in the cities' teeming slums. Protests and food riots have recently occurred in Brazil, Colombia, Peru, Nicaragua, Mexico and the Dominican Republic. They are generally unorganized, what social scientists call "anomic movements," without leadership or clear political goals. But these protests can be captured by organized political movements with the potential to undermine governments. Such movements, if they occur when other circumstances are propitious (for example, when the middle class is also feeling austerity's bite, the armed forces are divided, and the government is weak and/or illegitimate), can produce revolutionary consequences.

The prime recruiting grounds for such destabilizing movements are capital city slums, where the legions of unemployed and underemployed are concentrated, where the surplus population gathers with nothing to do, and where abandoned street children are looking for adventure and diversion. It can be a short march from there to the national palace. Movements arising from social tensions derive from unchecked population growth, and we are likely to see more and more of them in the future.

Latin American political systems have depended on an ever-expanding economic pie to continue functioning in an efficient, democratic context. As long as there were more pieces of the pie to hand out, the standard of living for most groups could be expected to increase. With the negative economic growth rates of the past several years, however, competition has intensified for the fewer available "pieces." Violence and full-scale revolutionary challenges have increased and existing political systems have begun to unravel—in El Salvador, Nicaragua, Bolivia, Peru and elsewhere.

There is no doubt that mass discontent and challenges to established ways and institutions have been fueled by the population and urban explosions. Although the relationship is indirect, it is no less important. The youthfulness of Latin American populations, the absence of jobs and opportunities, the growing impatience, the economic downturn, and rising social tensions have all combined to make traditional accommodative politics in Latin America difficult at best and well-nigh impossible in certain countries.

In summary, there is a close but indirect relationship between unchecked population growth, spiraling socioeconomic problems and the potential for political breakdown, destabilization and internal unrest in Latin America. It is not necessary to overstate the case or paint it in "crisis" terms in order to recognize the severity of the problem. Population growth rates in Latin America have begun to decline in recent years. Moreover, the problems of the area are not due to population growth alone; economic underdevelopment, social tensions and the weakness of political institutions are also prime causes. Nevertheless, uncontrolled population growth is an important factor adding to the possibility of increased tension, fragmentation and destabilization. As such, it is not only harmful to Latin America but also carries major implications for international political alignments and involvement in the region by the major powers. Hence sound and politically viable policy responses are required. ■

Immigration, Refugees, and Foreign Policy

By Michael S. Teitelbaum

The mass movement of people across international boundaries, whether voluntary or forced, is appearing with increasing frequency on the agendas of international affairs.[1] The sweep of the issues involved is breathtaking. They range from matters of war and peace, through the complexities of international economics and finance, right across the divisive fissures of "North-South" and race/ ethnicity, and as far as competing philosophies on the rights of the individual against those of the state.

Michael S. Teitelbaum is a population analyst and foundation official.

Source: From *International Organization* 38, 3, Summer 1984 0020-8183/84/030429-21 © 1984 by the Massachusetts Institute of Technology and the World Peace Foundation.

There is certainly nothing new about the phenomenon of human migration, which has characterized the species for millennia. But international migration on a large scale required two developments of relatively recent origin: the worldwide establishment of the nation-state system and the growth of human population to very high levels. Aristide Zolberg describes "deliberate action" in regulating immigration as fundamental to the nation-state system: "It has been universally acknowledged ever since the state system arose in its modern form that, under the law of nations, the right to regulate entry is a fundamental concomitant of sovereignty."[2] Other analysts see large-scale international migrations as beyond the control of nation-states, perceiving them either as inevitable consequences of immutable historical trends in the world system or as the results of overwhelming economic forces not susceptible to state regulation.

In this regard, one simple empirical fact is worth noting: the mass of the world's population does *not* move across borders. In only a few settings does outmigration involve as much as 10 percent of the population, and in only a few small countries of destination do international migrants comprise large fractions of the populace. The exceptions occur in cases in which receiving societies do not regulate entry (e.g., Puerto Rican migration to the mainland United States) or regulate it poorly (e.g., Mexican migration to the United States, Bangladeshi migration to the Indian state of Assam), or when violent convulsions drive large masses from their homelands (e.g., recent Afghanistani migrations to Pakistan and Iran). Nevertheless,

even a small percentage of a large population represents many millions of people. While the image of footloose masses roaming uncontrollably across borders tends to understate the considerable degree of state regulation in effect, the absolute numbers involved in international migration are now very large and growing apace.

The linkages of such movements to foreign policy, in both its ideological and pragmatic aspects, are also hardly new. One clear example of the ideological component appeared in the very definition of a refugee that prevailed in American law from 1952 to 1980. A refugee was defined as a person fleeing "from a Communist-dominated country or area, or from any country within the general area of the Middle East."[3] During this important period, refugee issues in the United States obviously were perceived, in substantial part, through the foreign-policy lenses of the Cold War.

U.S. law was changed in 1980 to conform to the less ideological definitions of international law. It now defines a refugee as:

> *any person who is outside any country of such person's nationality . . . and who is unable or unwilling to return to, and is unable or unwilling to avail himself or herself of the protection of, that country because of persecution or a well-founded fear of persecution on account of race, religion, nationality, membership in a particular social group, or political opinion. . . .*[4]

In practical terms, notwithstanding this change in ideological tone, most of the persons admitted as "refugees" or granted similar sta-

tus since 1980 have come from Communist countries such as Cuba and Vietnam.

Foreign-policy criteria have also guided the refugee policies of many other countries: for example, the openness of Sweden and several other countries to political refugees from post-Allende Chile, and the centrality of East European refugees to the Östpolitik of the Federal Republic of Germany. The large-scale temporary worker policies with which North American and Western European countries have experimented also involved bilateral treaties and other instruments of international relations.

But if the connections between foreign policies and immigration and refugee policies are not new, they have surely taken a quantum leap in importance for Western diplomacy in recent years, for at least two reasons. The first is the gradual—but by now dramatic—transformation in the size and nature of such international movements. The second is a series of international events over the past five years, often termed "crises," that have served to bring these transformed patterns into clearer focus.

The fundamental transformation has been in the size and direction of international migration flows over the past ten to fifteen years. From the 1920s to the 1960s (excluding the World War II period), most such movements were of modest size, were regulated by the laws of the receiving countries, and were principally from Europe to the New World or to European colonial outposts.

Since the 1960s, the pattern has been overwhelmingly one of large-scale movement, often in violation of the laws of the receiving countries, and typically from developing countries to the West. The movements of immigrants and refugees between Third World countries and of temporary workers to oil-exporting states have also increased dramatically.

The numbers involved in recent migrations have been so large, and so frequently destabilizing, that they have perforce seized the attention of high-level policy makers. Examples include:

• the long-festering problems of the Middle East, with 1.9 million persons now officially designated as Palestinian refugees by the United Nations Relief and Works Administration, the migration of 750,000 Jews from predominantly Arab countries to Israel, and the departure of several hundred thousand Lebanese to the Gulf States, Europe, and North America;

• the 300,000–500,000 Polish nationals who are residing outside Poland and unwilling to return, with larger flows widely predicted;[5]

• the one to two million refugees produced by the Ethiopian civil war and the Ethiopia-Somalia conflict over the Ogaden;

• the increasing flows of migrants from troubled nations of Central America such as El Salvador and Guatemala, many of whom simply migrate illegally and never seek or obtain refugee status;

• and the longstanding and predominantly illegal migrations of several million Colombians to Venezuela and the United States. Many other examples are discussed in greater detail below.

The reasons for this rapid growth of international movement from developing countries seem fairly clear: political instabilities, erratic and unequal economic growth, and rapid demographic increase in much of the Third World since 1945, coupled with growing differentials in earnings and employment prospects between developing and industrialized countries. In addition, industrialized countries have actively recruited "temporary" labor during several economic boom periods, and international transportation and communication have seen widespread improvements.

These basic trends have been highlighted by a series of important international "crises" over the past five years in settings as different as Asia, the Caribbean, Africa, Europe, and the Middle East. In Asia, the past few years have seen the Indochinese "boat people" crisis, highlighted by the internationally televised spectacle in 1978–79 of Malaysian officials pushing unstable boats full of people back out into the South China Sea. The Soviet intervention in Afghanistan in 1980 led to the flight of 2.5 to 4 million people (nearly 20 percent of the country's population) to Pakistan and Iran. And the decade-long and mostly illegal migration of several million Bangladeshis to the northeast Indian state of Assam led to serious internal instability and sectarian strife, including gory massacres in 1983.

In the Caribbean, the mass migration and "pushout" of some 130,000 Cubans to the United States occurred within a few months in 1980, following the siege of the Peruvian Embassy in Havana by 10,000 Cubans. Among them were a minority with serious psychiatric, health, and criminal problems that made them legally inadmissible to the United States; but the Cuban government refused to allow their return to Cuba. Much of this, too, was broadcast by satellite around the world. The same general period saw a rapid acceleration of migration by poor Haitians to South Florida, much of it by small fishing boats that made clandestine landings on beaches, with some resulting in tragic mass drownings.

In Western Europe, raucous political ferment has recently arisen from the realization that "temporary" worker programs have produced a permanent (and, if anything, growing) foreign resident population of over 13 million persons, many from developing countries such as Turkey and Yugoslavia. Over the same period, the huge growth in claims for political asylum in West Germany became a heated political issue, and the dramatic political and economic crises of Poland raised the prospect of many more such claims.

In Africa, literally millions of refugees have been generated by internal and international strife, and 1983 saw the abrupt and destabilizing mass expulsion by Nigeria of one to two million illegal aliens attracted by Nigeria's oil-fired economic boom. Meanwhile, in the Middle East, the traumas of civil war and invasions in Lebanon have generated large numbers of new migrants and have underlined the dangers posed to internal and international stability when refugee problems are allowed to fester over several decades.

All of these recent experiences, widely perceived as crises, have focused unprecedented domestic and international attention upon immigration and refugee issues, and in some important cases upon their foreign-policy dimensions.

A BROADER RANGE OF CONNECTIONS

Some of the most recent episodes of mass international migrations have been extraordinarily dramatic. However, the interconnections between foreign policies and immigration policies are no longer merely episodic dramas; instead, they have become continuous and multidirectional in form. Three main types are worthy of consideration.

1. Foreign Policy as It Affects International Migration

Foreign policies have frequently served (often unintentionally) to *stimulate* international migrations. In particular, foreign military or political interventions, or internal or external responses to intervention, often result in mass migrations. Foreign-policy makers rarely evaluate such effects seriously when considering intervention. Instead, they perceive the possible refugee consequences (if they consider them at all) more as a problem for "others," if the flow is to other countries, or alternatively as an obligation that the intervenor owes to local collaborators, if the intervention proves unsuccessful. Importantly, the intervening power does not necessarily see even the possible future need to admit such dependent populations as refugees as a serious cost of policy failure. Refugees, once admitted, are usually regarded as responsibilities of domestic organs of government, often at local rather than national levels. The balancing of foreign and domestic goals usually takes place at higher levels of government and, frequently, after the fact.

Hence the possibility of future refugee flows need not loom large in the calculus of foreign policy.

Of course, not only such active foreign-policy interventions produce immigrants and refugees. The absence of such policies may also do so when foreign intervention (direct or indirect) might serve to *restrain* mass outmigration. Such conditions may arise when domestic economic or political conditions deteriorate into economic desperation, large-scale internal repression, or the rise of totalitarian governments. The most obvious cases are provided by Europe before World War II and Uganda upon the rise of Idi Amin. In both cases, self-destructive internal processes, which prevailed in the absence of external intervention or pressure, generated large numbers of refugees.

Poland, Central America, and Afghanistan have recently exhibited the attributes of both external intervention and internal deterioration. The general pattern is one of internally generated economic or political instability, or both, followed by externally induced pressures or intervention intended either to exploit or to reverse that growing instability. Together, these internal and external factors stimulate large-scale outmigration.

Foreign policy may also be directly employed to *facilitate or to restrain* existing refugee outflows. Diplomatic pressures, economic sanctions, and direct military intervention have all been employed to such ends, which four examples illustrate. The first is the decisive military intervention by India in the Pakistani Civil War of 1971. Nearly 10 million refugees flooded into India from East Bengal, and when diplomatic efforts failed, the

government of India "considered the threat to her economy and general stability posed by the humanitarian flood from Pakistan to be a *casus belli*" (although it is likely that other strategic concerns related to Pakistan were more important).[6] The second example is American trade pressures on the USSR, such as the Jackson-Vanik Amendment, to facilitate the exit of Soviet Jews and other dissidents.[7] The third is the multilateral pressures exerted on Vietnam to restrain the outflow of "boat people"—pressures that took their most visible form in the 1979 Geneva Conference on Indochinese Refugees. A fourth example is provided by the bilateral negotiations between the United Kingdom and the People's Republic of China concerning the future of the British Crown Colony of Hong Kong. Among many British goals in these negotiations is the prevention of changes that might stimulate outmigration by millions of Hong Kong residents holding British passports. (Such concerns also contributed to recent controversial changes in British citizenship law.)

It is interesting to note that former U.S. Secretary of State Alexander Haig sought to justify U.S. foreign-policy interventions in Central America and the Reagan administration's Caribbean Basin Initiative by reference to their argued effects in preventing population outflows to the United States. In a 22 February 1982 speech to the National Governors Association that gained the lead headline in *The New York Times* ("Haig Fears Exiles from Latin Areas May Flood the U.S."), Haig asked his audience to "Just think what the level [of undocumented immigration] might be if the radicalization of this hemisphere continues, with the only alternative a totalitarian model in one state after another. . . . Why it would make the Cuban influx look like child's play." He added that to keep the flow down, "the Americans have an important responsibility to deal with the social, economic and humanitarian aspects of the crisis as well as the security aspects."[8]

More recently, Haig's successor, Secretary George Schultz, gave a similar rationale for the Caribbean Basin Initiative. Indeed, of the four examples he presented to demonstrate the closeness of U.S.-Caribbean linkages, two related to immigration (the other two concerned the security of the sea lanes and the $7 billion market for U.S. exports in the Caribbean):

> *Second,* many of our people have roots in the area. One out of five people alive today who were born in Barbados live in the United States; the same is true for one out of six Jamaicans, and one out of ten Salvadorans.
>
> *Third,* given proximity and existing ties, the United States is a natural safehaven for those fleeing social and economic pressures in the basin. These pressures create illegal immigration, itself a great problem for us. The basin area is now the second largest place of origin of illegal immigration.[9]

In June 1983, President Ronald Reagan stated that if the United States were to acquiesce in the establishment of a "string of anti-American Marxist dictatorships" in Central America, "the result could be a tidal wave of refugees—and this time they'll be feet people, not boat people—swarming into our country seeking a safe haven from Communist repression to our south."[10]

The movement of temporary migrants (legal or illegal) may also be stimulated, restrained, or regulated through the instruments of foreign policy. Such measures have been employed by most of the industrialized countries that at one time or another have decided to seek temporary labor from labor-surplus countries. West Germany and other European countries, for example, negotiated treaties with source countries for the admission of "guest workers" during the 1960s and early 1970s. The earlier bilateral treaties between the United States and Mexico provided temporary Mexican labor during World War I and World War II, with the latter case later expanded by bilateral agreement into a large-scale *bracero* program that continued until 1964.

It is now generally accepted that the *bracero* program was important in stimulating the large-scale illegal immigration from Mexico that accompanied it and that has continued since its termination in 1964.[11] Thus, the foreign-policy/migration connections came full circle. American foreign policy (i.e., World War II) led to domestic pressures from employers seeking Mexican labor; these pressures were resolved in foreign-policy initiatives that sought the best terms for the provision of temporary labor; and they in turn stimulated what has become one of the most sensitive foreign-policy issues between the United States and Mexico.

Foreign-policy instruments have also been employed to *facilitate* existing streams of permanent migration (both legal and illegal), though often less explicitly than in the case of temporary migration. A prominent recent example is provided by the diplomatic initiatives undertaken by several Commonwealth states after Britain began to restrict Commonwealth immigration in the 1960s. Such concerns were most obvious among island nations in the Caribbean that had learned to depend upon outmigration as a "safety valve" for unemployment and poverty. (These changes in British law led to a redirection of British Caribbean migration toward the United States and Canada, though it is doubtful whether the British, American, or Canadian governments anticipated such effects.)

The United States has felt similar diplomatic pressures from sending countries to facilitate outmigration, often from the foreign ministries of the same Caribbean nations, as well as from Mexico, the Philippines, and elsewhere. These pressures usually oppose American proposals to restrain illegal immigration, such as more stringent controls on the issuance of frequently violated visitors' visas to nationals of the Philippines or the Dominican Republic, or measures to limit illegal entry across the U.S.-Mexico border. Such diplomatic pressures typically place American ambassadors in an awkward relationship to their host countries. One frequent outcome is ambassadorial pressure upon the embassy's consular officers to relax their scrutiny of visa applications, in the interest of maintaining cordial diplomatic relations and encouraging tourism. Hence the predictable pressures of day-to-day ambassadorial life often lead to actions that run counter to official policies with regard to regulating illegal immigration.

ASEAN nations exercised a more open form of diplomatic pressure during the Vietnamese "boat people" crisis. Diplomats from Malaysia, Thailand, and other countries made it abundantly clear that their willingness to provide first asylum depended entirely upon firm commitments by the United States and other countries to resettle Vietnamese boat people outside the region. The heavily publicized actions by Malaysia in refusing to allow 2,500 Vietnamese to disembark from a chartered freighter served to underscore the seriousness of this demand and resulted within two weeks in a doubling of U.S. resettlement commitments by President Carter.[12]

Guest-worker source countries such as Turkey have also exerted diplomatic pressures on West Germany, especially when the German government decided to terminate recruitment in the early 1970s. Germany largely ignored these pressures at the time, but more serious international ramifications cannot now be dismissed so easily. They involve the tentative agreement for Turkish entry to the European Economic Community in 1986. While the free movement of labor within the Community has long been a principal provision of the Rome Treaty, West Germany has made it clear that it cannot agree to Turkish entry if the Turks insist on this right. This issue, presently under active diplomatic negotiation, may lead either to an important roadblock to Turkish integration with Europe or to a compromise deferring the free movement of labor into the next century.

Finally, international migrations have been *regulated* by several highly codified foreign-policy in-struments (including formal treaties, understandings, conventions, protocols, and other international agreements). Such instruments are especially prominent in regulating the treatment of refugees. The most recent and comprehensive is the 1951 United Nations Convention Relating to the Status of Refugees and its 1967 Protocol, to which more than ninety nations have now formally subscribed. These international agreements seek to establish the criteria by which claims to refugee status should be decided and the obligations of nation-states in the treatment of refugees.

Perhaps the most fundamental obligation is that of *non-refoulement*—the provision that persons shall not be returned to their homelands unwillingly if they have a "well-founded fear of persecution." This provision clearly restricts the otherwise well-recognized right of a sovereign state to exclude or deport noncitizens it does not wish to admit. *Non-refoulement* provides the principal protection for bona fide refugees fleeing persecution—but also the main incentive for ineligible immigrants to claim refugee status, in order to halt exclusion or deportation actions.

Multilateral agreements have also regulated temporary worker migrations. They include the ILO Convention Concerning Migration for Employment, the European Convention for the Protection of Human Rights and Fundamental Freedoms, and a series of accords and treaties between France and fifteen francophone African countries. These agreements usually concern criteria for recruitment; protection for the employment, social, and family rights of the tem-porary workers; economic agreements between the sending and receiving countries regarding remittances sent home and other flows from receiving countries; conditions for renewal of work permits; and other related legal guarantees.[13] Currently, a group of labor-exporting and Scandinavian countries is sponsoring an initiative in the UN General Assembly to elaborate a new "International Convention on the Protection of the Rights of All Migrant Workers and Their Families."

2. International Migrations as Tools of Foreign Policy

Both sending and receiving countries have employed mass migration movements as tools of their foreign policies. There is, first, what might be termed "mass migration for unarmed conquest or assertion of sovereignty." Generally stated, this policy involves governmental encouragement of civilian rather than military movement into claimed territories for the purposes of establishing effective control or sovereignty.

In 1975, for example, King Hassan II of Morocco organized and led the "Marche Verte" or "peaceful 'march of conquest'" by 350,000 unarmed Moroccan civilians into the disputed territories of the Spanish Sahara.[14] Earlier examples of such actions included the movement of U.S. nationals into the Mexican territory now comprising Texas; Britain's efforts to populate its colonies in North America and Australia through forced migration of convicts; Israel's settlement policy in the West Bank; and several such mass movements throughout Russian history. As recently as 1982, the government of Argentina was insisting upon the right of free immigration of Argentine nationals to the thinly populated Falkland/Malvinas Islands as a condition of removing occupying Argentinian troops. Indeed, this demand is rumored to have been one of the main stumbling blocks in the failed negotiations that preceded the undeclared war over the Falklands.[15]

More subtle are the uses made of migrant groups for foreign-policy purposes. On the sending side, there is reason to believe that mass expulsions have been employed as tools to destabilize or embarrass foreign-policy adversaries. High officials of Malaysia, Thailand, and Singapore have made claims of such foreign-policy intent regarding the apparent expulsion of hundreds of thousands of Vietnamese nationals of Chinese origin by the Democratic Republic of Vietnam.[16] In addition, the same mass outmigration has sparked fears of directly subversive intent and claims that "among the refugees are a heavy sprinkling of communist spies and deep-cover penetration agents."[17] The official newspaper of the Chinese Communist party, the *People's Daily,* said that Vietnam is exporting refugees for three reasons: to extort money from them, to create social and economic problems in Southeast Asia, and to infiltrate agents into ASEAN nations.[18]

Similarly, it seems quite likely that the Cuban government's actions in expelling criminals, psychotics, and seriously ill people during the 1980 Mariel "boatlift" to South Florida were guided in part by a desire to discomfit the United States. There have recently been claims that the East German government has been facilitating the illegal entry of Turks, Pakistanis,

and others into West Berlin, in the full knowledge that they intend to claim asylum in West Germany and that the West German political and judicial systems are ill-prepared to deal with such mass asylum claims.[19]

Outmigration may also be encouraged for foreign-policy goals of a more positive character. In the Middle East, the governments of Pakistan and India may see the large-scale movement of temporary workers to the oil-rich Gulf states not only as a temporary expedient to reduce unemployment and generate foreign exchange but also as a means of solidifying and deepening their diplomatic and economic relations with these oil-rich states.[20]

From the perspective of receiving countries, refugee admission policies have been guided in many important cases by the belief that refugee outflows serve to embarrass and discredit adversary nations. Such a belief has surely been central to U.S. policies toward migrants from Cuba, Vietnam, and the Soviet Union. In his acceptance speech at the July 1980 Republican National Convention, presidential candidate Reagan expressed this perspective in evocative religious images:

Can we doubt that only a Divine Providence placed this land, this island of freedom, here as a refuge for all those people in the world who yearn to breathe freely; Jews and Christians enduring persecution beyond the Iron Curtain, the boat people of Southeast Asia, of Cuba and of Haiti, the victims of drought and famine in Africa, the Freedom Fighters of Afghanistan, and our own countrymen held in savage captivity.[21]

Strangely enough, some critics of U.S. refugee and foreign policies use the same form of argument. For example, opponents of current U.S. policies toward Haitians and Salvadorans claiming asylum argue that the U.S. government's unwillingness to recognize the validity of such claims is based on foreign-policy considerations, in that such recognition would serve to embarrass governments with which the United States has close political ties and would also encourage domestic opposition to these ties. A typical example of this argument appears in a 1982 memo from the Central American Refugee Center in Washington, sponsored primarily by Salvadoran exiles resident in the United States.

The United States is the only nation in the world which does not recognize Salvadorans as legal refugees and thus will not grant them political asylum [sic]. There are two major reasons for this. One is that granting political asylum to Salvadorans communicates worldwide that the government of El Salvador violates the human rights of its citizens. Since the U.S. aids and supports the government of El Salvador, it does not want to communicate this message. Also, granting asylum to the estimated 500,000 undocumented Salvadorans in this country would open up a large sector of voiced opposition to U.S. policy maneuvers in El Salvador. This group of dissent can be kept silent through forcing them to live underground in fear of deportation to the threat of persecution and death in their own country.[22]

Whatever the validity of such assertions, the important point for our purposes is that both proponents and opponents of U.S. foreign policy see refugee or asylum admissions as important tools.

Foreign-policy interests have also motivated responses to refugee influxes across the borders of Pakistan, India, Somalia, Thailand, Angola, and many other nations. The typical pattern is one in which refuge is willingly provided to persons fleeing an adversarial neighboring regime, in part as a means of maintaining a reservoir of opposition that often expresses itself in the form of cross-border guerilla activities. These incursions, in turn, frequently lead to actual or threatened cross-border military attacks against refugee camps by the other country. Sometimes, as in the case of Thailand, the refugees are seen as providing a buffer against hostile incursions from neighboring powers. In African settings, in particular, the refugee populations frequently are ethnically similar to those in the receiving areas and may be caught up in long-term territorial disputes concerning colonial boundaries that arbitrarily divided tribal or ethnic populations.

Refugees have also been used as tools of what might be termed "private foreign policies." Such use arises when nongovernmental groups opposed to particular foreign regimes see mass exodus from those countries as a weapon to dramatize the reasons for their opposition. Some of the most active advocates of Haitian migrants to the United States (especially those who are themselves Haitian exiles) appear primarily concerned with the discrediting and ultimate overthrow of the Duvalier regime rather than with the plight of the migrants themselves. To this end, they seek to

maximize the attention of the American media on Haitian migrants, by advising them to claim to be fleeing direct persecution when this may not be the case (it seems to be for some, but not for many others), by organizing hunger strikes and letterwriting campaigns in detention camps, and by frustrating efforts to disperse the Haitian "entrant" population outside South Florida even when formal offers of sponsorship and employment exist.[23]

There are, of course, many other reasons for concern about Haitian migrants, including general humanitarian concern, ethnic solidarity, and perceptions of government abuse of civil liberties. Such matters are central to the interests of many of the religious groups involved in the debate, but some advocates, particularly expatriate Haitians, are quite explicit about the foreign-policy dimension to their concern. Indeed, the policies of the Duvalier regime figured centrally in a federal court battle over which Judge James L. King of the Southern District of Florida presided. After acknowledging that migration from Haiti is substantially economic in origin, King found that the poverty of Haiti "is a function of the political system" and that therefore the Haitian migrants' "economic situation is a political condition," which in his view qualified them as "refugees" under the definition of the Refugee Act of 1980.[24] Judge King's findings directly contradicted those of the State Department and thereby raised the issue of intervention by the federal judiciary in foreign policy (conventionally one of the major areas of executive primacy in the American political system).

3. Foreign-Policy Impacts of Past Migrations

The formulation of foreign policy is also affected by the presence of substantial numbers of refugees and immigrants. Not only do they naturally affect the receiving country's policies toward the sending country, but often the sending country seeks to mobilize its expatriate population in support of its own positions in dealings with the receiving country.

Domestic ethnic pressures on foreign-policy formulation loom large in the United States, affecting foreign policies toward settings as diverse as Northern Ireland, the Turkish-Greek conflict, the Middle East, Cuba, Mexico, Haiti, and Poland, to name only a few of the obvious cases. In a recent article in *Foreign Affairs,* Senator Charles Mathias (R-Md.) described as "plausible" the argument that immigration was the "single most important determinant of American foreign policy."[25] Similar pressures are also apparent, if to a lesser degree, in other countries that have experienced large-scale immigration in the past, among them Argentina, Canada, Australia, and Israel.[26]

Such domestic political effects of international migration represent expressions of the political views of migrants in conventional political forms. But more unorthodox and potentially violent examples should also be noted. There is widespread concern in the oil-rich Gulf states, for example, concerning the destabilizing political activities of temporary workers from elsewhere in the Middle East, especially Iranians and Palestinians. In Kuwait, for instance, concern about the political militancy of Palestinian guest workers (who comprise as much as 20% of the population of Kuwait) and their Kuwaiti supporters led Amir Sabah in 1976 to suspend the constitution and prorogue the assembly.[27]

As a result of such concerns, it appears, the Gulf states have decided both to restrict the growth of foreign worker populations and to give preference to those from the non-Arab states of South Asia and even East Asia. These latter groups are considered lesser threats in that they generally cannot establish connections with the indigenous population, due to language barriers, and are easily recognizable and deportable. Moreover, deportations of Indian and Korean workers have fewer foreign-policy repercussions than do deportations of fellow Arabs. As a result of such considerations, Kuwait, Saudi Arabia, and other Gulf states now have large and growing Indian, Pakistani, Filipino, and Korean populations.[28]

A second example is provided by the large gastarbeiter populations in West Germany, especially those from Yugoslavia and Turkey. The recent past has seen violent conflicts between Croatian nationalists and supporters of the Yugoslavian government, and now there is considerable evidence of active political organization within Germany on the part of both right-wing and left-wing Turkish groups opposed to the present Turkish government. After the imposition of military rule in Turkey, Germany may have become one of the most important locales for the organization of violent Turkish political action. The government of Turkey had already lodged formal protests regarding the German refusal of extradition requests for persons wanted as terrorists in Turkey. (The existence of the death penalty in Turkey prevents such extradition under German law.)

The revolutionary activities of Iranian exiles granted refuge in France provide a further example. The Ayatolla Khomeini directed the Islamic Revolution in substantial measure from his suburban Paris villa—perhaps the first mass revolution directed over international telephone circuits and by means of tape cassettes. The French government now provides refuge for Khomeini opponents, such as former Prime Ministers Bahktiari and Bani Sadr, though their political activities are far more severely constrained than were those of Khomeini and his associates.

Finally, U.S.-Cuba relations have generated and have in turn been profoundly complicated by the movement to the United States of over a million implacable opponents of Fidel Castro since 1959. For reasons described earlier, the U.S. government has long welcomed Cuban migration as demonstrating the unattractiveness of Castro's Cuba. For whatever reason, so substantial was this flow that by 1980 nearly 10 percent of those born in Cuba were resident in the United States. Yet the presence in the United States of organized and vocal anti-Castro movements surely complicates any efforts by U.S. foreign-policy makers to normalize relations with Cuba.

Moreover, the 1980 boatlift experience, itself facilitated by the actions of such Cuban-American groups, has raised further barriers to a relaxation of tensions. The expulsion of thousands of criminals and mental patients during the boatlift was particularly damaging, even though they constituted only a small fraction of the total flow of about 130,000 persons. From the Cuban perspective, these social undesirables (termed escoria or "scum" by Premier Castro) left Cuba without exit visas and were transported to Florida by Americans, and hence are not Cuba's responsibility. From the American perspective, they are clearly Cuban nationals who are excludable under American law, and hence Cuba under international law must accept them back. It is highly doubtful whether any significant improvement in bilateral relations between Cuba and the United States can occur until these profoundly different perspectives are somehow reconciled.

U.S. FOREIGN POLICY CHOICES AND CONFLICTS

The United States now faces foreign-policy choices about immigration and refugees that are complex, emotional, and deeply intertwined with domestic concerns. The complexity and emotion arise in part from conflicts among the several U.S. national interests that are at stake.

The strategic and security interests of the United States relate principally to the effects of mass migrations on the stability of both sending and receiving countries. There is no doubt that the influx of hundreds of thousands (or even millions) of desperate people into politically or economically fragile developing countries can pose severe threats to stability. This is especially true in regions that are already densely populated (i.e., in Asia more than in Africa), and particularly when the receiving and migrating populations have a long history of ethnic tensions.

Such were the security concerns of nearly every ASEAN nation about the flow of hundreds of thousands of Vietnamese to their shores. Although there is reasonably clear evidence, by the standards of such things, that the outflow of boat people was encouraged and even organized by the Vietnamese government, the United States and its allies had little leverage on that long-time adversary. The foreign-policy choices facing the United States therefore resolved to essentially three options. The first was to allow the boat people to be pushed back out to sea as a deterrent to future flows, thereby violating U.S. humanitarian concerns and the American sense of national obligation to the sequelae of the Vietnam war. The second was to employ intense diplomatic and economic pressure on friendly ASEAN nations to persuade them to allow entry by Vietnamese boat people against their best judgment, thereby accepting the strategic risk of the political instability predicted by these countries if they agreed. The third was to provide firm assurances to ASEAN allies that all Vietnamese migrants would be resettled permanently in third countries, by seeking to internationalize resettlement in the first instance and by promising U.S. resettlement as a "last resort" if alternatives could not be found. Obviously, the United States chose and acted upon the last of these options, in part for strategic reasons and in part out of humanitarian concern.

Similar strategic reasoning has long affected U.S. policy toward illegal immigration from Mexico and other Caribbean countries. The security concern, stated simply, is that restraint on such illegal movements would remove the "safety valve" of large-scale outmigration that is important for the stability of the fragile economies and political systems of these strategically important nations. Such concerns, combined with the economic interests of employers of such migrants, have until recently sufficed to thwart efforts at policy reform or even serious enforcement of existing law.

This point brings us to the *national economic interests* of the United States, especially with regard to illegal immigrants. Illegal foreign workers constitute only a small minority of the U.S. labor force (perhaps 5% at most). But two decades of ready access to such compliant labor has generated numerous employers and subsectors in certain industries in a few regions (e.g., fruit and vegetable producers in the Southwest) that are heavily dependent upon the effective subsidy that such labor provides. It is no surprise that, like all subsidized sectors, these employers feel that their vital economic interests would be threatened if the United States were to enforce its immigration laws. Consequently, they have organized vigorously to block such measures, claiming that they would not be in the economic interests of the United States.

The vital economic interests of a regional subsector should not, of course, be confused with the vital interests of the nation as a whole. It is particularly difficult to find convincing national-interest arguments for large-scale labor importation during a decade of high national unemployment (over 8% at this writing) and low economic growth. Like the European guest-worker policies, most of which started in the late 1950s and terminated about fifteen years later, such a policy may provide short-term subsidies to certain sectors at the expense of others, only to retard the gradual, long-term adjustment of a mixed economy toward higher labor productivity.[29] Indeed, Philip Martin has recently argued that the continued importation of cheap labor "spells disaster in the long run" even for its advocates among fruit and vegetable growers, since such dependence would retard mechanization needed to compete internationally:

Without mechanization the U.S. must both accept an isolated, alien-dominated labor force for seasonal handwork and erect trade barriers to keep out produce grown abroad at even lower wages. If farmers successfully oppose the immigration reforms that could begin to alter this picture, they may win the short-run battle over labor but will lose the long-run war for survival in the increasingly competitive international fruit and vegetable economy.[30]

The *ideological interests* of the United States also motivate various perspectives on immigration and refugee policies. In their crudest form, these interests underlie the long conventional but now waning political view that outmigration from Communist countries demonstrates the bankruptcy of the Communist system. As discussed earlier, the ideological (if antagonistic) twin to this perspective sees U.S. refusal to admit refugees and asylum-seekers from Haiti and El Salvador as based upon ideological support for the anti-Communist governments of those countries.

The final set of U.S. national interests is in part related to ideological issues—that of U.S. *humanitarian concerns.* The power that such concerns exert on U.S. public and political opinion should not be underestimated. President Carter's human rights policy, however poorly implemented it may have been in the eyes of its critics, surely struck a responsive chord in the general public and in the Congress. The notion that the United States should offer succor to the persecuted and the oppressed goes back to the founding of the Republic. Supportive images (and sometimes myths) remain powerful, from the high school civics text to the Statue of Liberty. The coming of age of satellite television has globalized this concern, to the point that film clips of overloaded boats being pushed out into the South China Sea may have caused more concern in the United States than in Malaysia.

Having said this, it does not follow that the sole test of such humanitarian concern is the willingness of the United States to continue to admit very large numbers of desperate people for permanent resettlement. It may indeed be true that the nation is suffering from what Senator Alan K. Simpson (R-Wyo.) has termed "compassion fatigue." But Simpson does not claim that such fatigue extends to the provision of emergency relief *in situ* to refugees in countries of first asylum or to generous assistance over the long term, as in the case of Palestinian or Somali refugees. Moreover, the "quantity" of humanitarian assistance that the United States can offer may in practical terms be maximized by such direct assistance, since it is far less expensive in economic terms to provide the means of subsistence to a rural refugee in a rural area of a neighboring country than to the same person in an urban American environment.[31] With limited resources, it makes good humanitarian sense to consider how available funds can best be stretched to assist the maximum possible numbers of refugees.

Such an approach may well conflict with those focused on strategic or security interests, or those that still see international migration in ideological terms. But such conflicts are characteristic of the subject matter and illustrate well why concerted and coherent policy is difficult to fashion.

More difficult still are the conflicts that arise between the various threads of foreign policy and those of domestic policy and politics. Here the pressures of diverse ethnic groups and economic interests coalesce into political support for one or another migrant group—Haitians, Mexicans, Soviet Jews, Ethiopians, Italians, Poles, illegal alien workers from various countries, temporary workers, Basque sheepherders, Québecois timbermen, and so on. In the tapestry of American domestic politics, each interest group presses for admission of its preferred category, and the absence of any overall numerical limit allows the formation of alliances and coalitions without requiring difficult tradeoffs.

Meanwhile, the prospects of U.S. international assistance and trade policy being directed toward the long-term economic development of major source countries are subject to substantial control by the economic and regional interests (both business and labor) that would be most directly affected. This proposition includes not only direct tariff and similar barriers but also nontariff barriers such as "orderly marketing arrangements," import quotas, price supports for certain commodities, and similar instruments of the U.S. government's economic apparatus. Of course, it is hardly reasonable to expect a U.S. industry to embrace low-wage countries' imports that would make it uncompetitive, even if the encouragement of such labor-intensive industries might be in the best interests of both the developing countries concerned and of the United States in the longer term.

To summarize briefly, decisions about immigration and refugee policies raise quite fundamental and divisive conflicts among important national interests. No objective calculus exists to tell us which option should be selected from those available. As in many other issues of national and international importance, where one stands often depends upon where one sits.

LESSONS FROM RECENT EXPERIENCE

Conventional American foreign-policy perspectives on migration now present growing foreign-policy risks. In the past decade, mass outmigrations such as those from Vietnam, Cuba, and Mexico well have illustrated those risks. Several lessons should have been learned from those experiences.

The first lesson is the need to revise two now outdated but widely held views: that admission of large numbers of refugees from Communist countries is a useful tool of American foreign policy, and that temporary migration can be started and stopped as desired, like the importation of any other factor of production.

The use of refugee admissions as a tool of foreign policy is an increasingly dangerous game. It can backfire badly, in both domestic and foreign-policy terms, if the sending country's leadership is sufficiently cynical to exploit the situation to rid itself of "undesirables" (as in the 1980 Cuban boatlift). Moreover, foreign-policy considerations that lead to differential treatment for similar migrants from different countries (as in U.S. treatment of Haitian and Cuban migrants in 1980) can stimulate divisive political protest.

Real peril also results from allowing a temporary migration stream to become established, unless a large and long-term influx is welcome. Mexican commentators are quick to point out, quite correctly, that the illegal migration streams now of such great concern in the United States were initiated by such American policies as the *bracero* program of 1942–1964. This experience, coupled with that of European guest-worker policies, offers strong evidence that migration flows are harder to stop than they are to start. Even if notionally temporary, such movements establish deep migration "pathways" based on social and family networks. They also foster a dependency on continuing inflows among the principal employers of immigrant workers, who have in effect become beneficiaries of a "labor subsidy" of substantial proportions. Like any subsidized group, such employers have powerful economic interests in the continuation of the subsidy and can be expected to lobby fiercely to this end.

The second lesson is that American measures to restrain illegal immigration can be expected to incur some foreign-policy costs in the short term. International migration has traditionally been visualized as under the control (in both legal and practical terms) of the receiving country, with the role of the sending country a passive one. It now appears, however, that sending countries may have more control over outmigration than was previously thought and indeed may visualize it as a kind of "national resource," to be managed like any other.[32]

Outmigration may be encouraged to improve or stabilize domestic economic or political conditions, thereby providing what is known as the "safety valve" of emigration. Meanwhile, remittances sent home by those working abroad may comprise an important component of total foreign currency inflows and may thereby facilitate expansionary economic policies at home.[33] Emigration may also be encouraged to remove political dissidents (as in Cuba, Vietnam, Haiti, East Germany until 1961, and possibly Poland), or as a means of capturing the assets of the departing migrants (as in Vietnam, Haiti, Uganda, and possibly Cuba).[34] Finally, and most malevolently, governments may coerce the departure of a despised ethnic or religious minority, or of a "politically undesirable" social group or class (as in Uganda, Vietnam, and Cuba).

Countries favoring outmigration, for whatever reasons, can be expected to oppose efforts by the countries of destination to regulate the entry of their nationals. Such opposition may be expressed through diplomatic channels, through criticism in the domestic or international media, through retaliatory measures, or even through support for certain political groups in the receiving country.

Any government must, of course, be circumspect in asserting that its nationals have a right to migrate to another sovereign state, for to do so openly would be to deny its own sovereign right to control entry across its own borders. Hence, such assertions may be couched obliquely in terms of "historical patterns," colonial vestiges, or an argued universal right to seek employment. But however such governments characterize their views, they resolve to assessments that their national interests are best served by the emigration of their citizens.

Real foreign-policy costs therefore attend the reform of receiving countries' immigration laws to regulate undocumented immigration. However, these costs are likely to be short-lived, and in the longer term such reforms might actually serve to deepen and improve international relations. Once sending countries realize that continuation of the status quo is not sustainable, they will have strong incentives to focus on economic development policies aimed at the rapid creation of jobs, policies that are far more appropriate to their needs in the long term. Meanwhile, such reforms may eliminate one of the most corrosive issues between certain sending countries and the United States—the exploitation and abuse experienced by undocumented migrants whom the law does not protect.

For the United States, the most obvious case is that of undocumented Mexican migration, which accounts for perhaps half of all illegal immigration. For the reasons indicated above, the government of Mexico has traditionally been reluctant to state a public preference for the status quo, while Mexican political commentators of all political persuasions have made a major theme of the abuse and exploitation experienced by undocumented Mexicans residing in the "Colossus of the North." A fairly standard Mexican response to American enquiries has been that of course immigration policies are the prerogatives of a sovereign state, but it would be hoped that the human rights of Mexican migrants and the views of a friendly neighbor would be taken into account.

Given this history, a recent resolution of the Mexican Senate is of particular interest. It arose in the final stages of consideration in the U.S. Congress of the Immigration Control and Reform Act of 1982 (also known as the Simpson-Mazzoli Bill). Most Mexican observers had believed that the bill had no chance of passage; they expected it to be blocked by an unlikely coalition of employers of undocumented aliens, Chicano activist groups, and civil libertarians. But when the bill passed the U.S. Senate by an overwhelming 80–19 margin and then was brought to the House floor in the 1982 lame-duck session, the Mexican Senate quickly adopted a strongly worded resolution on "this grave matter that negatively affects our good neighbor relations," which expressed its "alarm and concern for the repercussions which will impact both countries if the Simpson-Mazzoli legislation is passed." The Senate resolution described undocumented Mexican migration as a "transcendent matter [that] should not be considered from a unilateral perspective, but rather should be treated from a bilateral and even multilateral perspective."[35] To this end, it referred the matter to the Foreign Relations Committee of the Mexican Senate, to the next meeting of the Mexico-U.S. interparliamentary conference, and to three multilateral institutions.

This Mexican Senate resolution is to date the most forthright formal assertion by a competent governmental organ that the regulation of migration should no longer be considered a matter for unilateral action. Similar arguments by sending countries can be expected to proliferate in the coming years at various international forums, and they will require careful scrutiny and balanced response by American foreign-policy makers.

A third lesson should be learned from the coerced emigration seen most recently in Vietnam and Cuba: that American foreign policy would be well served by the preparation of contingency plans aimed at deterring such actions. As demonstrated by the 1980 Cuban boatlift, a lack of forward planning can be highly damaging in terms of both domestic and foreign policy. Such contingency planning should be wide-ranging, involving elements of both humanitarian concern and *realpolitik*. The principal goal should be to deter or reverse any policy of expulsion adopted by any government, of the right or of the left. To this end, quiet preparations should be made for prompt employment of the full array of diplomatic instruments, such as bilateral pressures, initiatives through third countries, and mobilization of the organs of the United Nations, including the Security Council. At the same time, the United States should be prepared to provide emergency humanitarian assistance to the victims of such expulsions, while standing ready if necessary to employ appropriate police measures to interdict subsequent expulsions.

The fourth and most general lesson is that new realities now demand that American foreign-policy makers factor into their calculations the possibility of mass international migrations. In the short term, proposed military or political interventions must be considered in the light of their potential to stimulate or restrain such movements toward the United States or its allies. In the longer term, the importance of labor-intensive economic development in the developing countries takes on new significance for American foreign policy once it is recognized that nationals of such countries are increasingly able to migrate internationally.

In the future, responsible foreign-policy professionals will have to focus more seriously upon immigration and refugee issues than they did in the past, much as in the 1970s they found new realities pushing energy and international economics higher on the foreign-policy agenda. Meanwhile, those concerned about immigration and refugee policies must consider foreign policy as central to their concerns. The recent changes in the scale, character, and even the "uses" of international migration have transformed these issues—probably irreversibly—into matters of the highest domestic and foreign concern. ∎

Notes:

1. The multiplicity of forms characterizing international migration makes it appropriate to keep in mind four categories of such movement throughout this article: legal permanent immigration; legal temporary migration; illegal or undocumented immigration; and refugee flows (including asylum).

2. Aristide R. Zolberg, "Dilemmas at the Gate: The Politics of Immigration in Advanced Industrial Societies" (Paper presented at the annual meeting of the American Political Science Association, Denver, CO, September 2, 1982), pp. 2–3.

3. Immigration and Nationality Act, Section 203(a)(7) (repealed).

4. Immigration and Nationality Act, Section 201(42).

5. U.S. Committee for Refugees, *Flight to Uncertainty: Poles outside Poland* (New York, 1982).

6. United Nations, Commission on Human Rights, "Question of the Violation of Human Rights and Fundamental Freedoms in Any Part of the World, with Particular Reference to Colonial and Other Dependent Countries and Territories," E/CN.4/1503, December 31, 1981, Annex 1, p. 3, para. 9.

7. The Jackson-Vanik Amendment to the Trade Act of 1974 requires that most-favored-nation treatment may not be granted to a "nonmarket economy country" that limits the rights of its nationals to emigrate. This provision, intended to facilitate Jewish emigration from the USSR, has unintentionally served to complicate relations with other nations of great U.S. foreign-policy interest, such as the People's Republic of China and Romania.

8. *New York Times,* February 23, 1982, p. A1.

9. Statement by the Secretary of State before the Senate Committee on Finance, August 2, 1982, Department of State, *Current Policy 412,* p. 1.

10. Speech before a Republican Fundraising Dinner, Jackson, Mississippi, June 20, 1983.

11. Senate, Committee on the Judiciary, *Temporary Worker Programs: Backgrounds and Issues,* 96th Cong., 2d sess., February 1980.

12. *New York Times,* November 12, 1978, p. 6, and November 28, 1978, p. 1. See also Barry Wain, "A Proven Way to Help Refugees—Brutality," *Wall Street Journal,* October 1, 1982, p. 30.

13. See Mark J. Miller and Philip L. Martin, *Administering Foreign-Worker Programs* (Lexington, MA: Lexington Books, 1982).

14. *New York Times,* October 22, 1975, p. 16.

15. *Times* (London), July 22, 1982.

16. *Far East Economic Review,* June 15, 1979, pp. 21–27.

17. John McBeth, "A Perilously Short Fuse," *Far Eastern Economic Review,* June 15, 1979, p. 26.

18. Cited in *Far Eastern Economic Review,* June 15, 1979, p. 21.

19. *New York Times,* July 31, 1980; *Christian Science Monitor,* August 6, 1981.

20. Myron Weiner, "Migration and Development in the Gulf," *Population and Development Review* 8 (March 1982), pp. 1–36.

21. Speech at the Republican National Convention, Kansas City, Mo., July 17, 1980.

22. Thomas D. Hoffman, coordinator of "Second Chance" Program, Central American Refugee Center, memorandum on "Salvadoran Refugees 'Second Chance' (Sponsorship) Program" (Washington, D.C., 1982).

23. In the off-the-record words of one participant, "The refugees shine the only spotlight we have on the evils of the Duvalier regime. The American press pay attention to this kind of thing" (Miami, August 21, 1980).

24. H.R.C. v Civiletti, 503 F. Supp. 442 (S. D. Florida 1980) modified, sub. nom. Haitian Refugee Center v Smith, 676 F 2d 1023 (5th Cir. 1982). See also *New York Times,* July 3, 1980.

25. Charles McC. Mathias Jr., "Ethnic Groups and Foreign Policy," *Foreign Affairs 59* (Summer 1981), p. 979.

26. In the case of Israel, it is now conventional political wisdom to explain that country's domestic political shift toward the more aggressive foreign and military policies of the Begin government in terms of the preceding decade's large-scale influx of Oriental Jews, many of whom fled under pressure from predominantly Arab countries.

27. Weiner, "Migration and Development," p. 23.

28. Ibid. See also Allan G. Hill, "Population, Migration and Development in the Gulf States," in Shahram Chubin (ed.) *Security in the Persian Gulf* (London: International Institute for Strategic Studies, 1981), pp. 58–83.

29. For a discussion of the economic consequences over the short and long terms of the European guest-worker programs, see Miller and Martin, *Administering Foreign-Worker Programs.*

30. Philip L. Martin, "Labor-intensive Agriculture," *Scientific American* 249 (October 1983), p. 59.

31. Of the $2.1 billion in U.S. assistance to the world's 10 million refugees in FY 1981, over 75% went toward the resettlement of only several hundred thousand in the United States.

32. For discussion, see Myron Weiner, "International Emigration: A Political and Economic Assessment" (Paper presented to the conference on Population Interactions between Poor and Rich Countries, sponsored by the Harvard University Center for Population Studies and the Draeger Foundation, Cambridge, Mass., October 6–7, 1983), pp. 39ff.

33. According to the World Bank, remittance inflows in 1978–79 accounted for 89% of Egypt's merchandise exports; 77% of Turkey and Pakistan's; 69% of Portugal's; 60% of Upper Volta's; and 51% of Morocco's. The Bank presents no comparable data for Latin America, presumably because much of the remittance flow to countries such as Mexico and Colombia is sent through unofficial

channels by nationals illegally resident in other countries. See International Bank for Reconstruction and Development/World Bank, *World Development Report 1982* (New York: Oxford University Press, 1982), p. 13. The economic significance of such remittances for labor-exporting countries has been greatly increased by the foreign-currency drain and economic dislocations caused by the sharply increased prices for energy imports during the 1970s.

34. The hundreds of thousands who were "encouraged" to leave the Socialist Republic of Vietnam in 1977–79 were heavily of Chinese ethnic origin and were apparently forced to pay departure fees amounting to several thousand dollars (in gold or hard currency) per person. See *Far East Economic Review,* June 15, 1979.

35. Reprinted in *Congressional Record,* December 17, 1982, p. H10256.

U.S. Immigration Policy and the National Interest

By Georges Fauriol

The security of the United States has suffered in the past as a result of the government's impotency in the face of massive illegal immigration, and it will continue to suffer as the situation increasingly worsens. Employment levels, domestic political cohesion, national resources, and the global standing of the United States can all be adversely affected by the current state of U.S. immigration policy. If these concerns are not addressed forthwith, there is a real danger that relative government inaction will be followed by public overreaction.

One of the primary reasons for the lack of attention paid to effective immigration policy in the past is the sensitivity of the subject. After all, the imageries of the United States as a nation of immigrants are both powerful and accurate. The very fabric of American society has been affected by it. However, these imageries most likely refer to a world environment that no longer exists. The extent of annual illegal immigration into the United States—approximately 650,000 in lean years—and the po-

litical, economic, and social ramifications suggest a dangerous anomaly. A gap has developed between the symbols of a "nation of immigrants" and the realities of the "huddled masses yearning to be free."

In focusing on the significance of immigration policy to the national interest of the United States, it is necessary to note two aspects of current U.S. immigration policy that adversely affect the security and development of *other* nations. The "drain" of skilled professionals and proponents of political freedom from many Third World nations, encouraged in large part by U.S. immigration policy, undermines the human pool of political and economic talent of those countries. Conceivably, it enriches our own. The irony is that the economic and political changes required of Third World countries are likely to be delayed if migration to the United States remains an integral aspect of Third World development policy.

Looking over the horizon, the implications of this for the United States are serious though uncer-

tain. As this country speeds toward the twenty-first century, one has to express considerable alarm at the laid-back attitude regarding migration flows to American shores. The linkage with foreign policy and national security is not always a direct one; it is a delicate process, and, above all, one difficult to articulate. To dismiss a relationship between immigration and foreign and security policies suggests ignorance of the interrelationships present in the world today—a world whose future trends will not always be favorable to the United States.

A GLANCE TO THE FUTURE

Few politicians see any political capital in the immigration policy issue. As an editorial writer in *The Journal of Commerce* put it recently, "Immigration policy has little appeal for most politicians. While they are not unaware of the disastrous long-run consequences of doing nothing, they see nothing but grief in taking action now." Current U.S. immigration policy is a national disgrace. The beneficia-

George Fauriol is a scholar with the Center for Strategic and International Studies in Washington.

Source: This article first appeared in *The Humanist* issue of May/June 1984 and is reprinted by permission.

ries of this policy remain politically powerful, unwilling to put aside narrow, special interests for the national good. Those pushing for reform, while enjoying overwhelming public support, do not have sufficient financial or organizational clout to effectively translate this support into action.

The long-run implications of our current "head in the sand" attitude about maintaining de facto open borders are indeed serious. They go to the heart of our security as a nation, our domestic political unity, our economic prosperity, and our role in the international system. Illegal immigration is by its very nature causing pressures beyond those associated with heavy immigration flows in particular and population growth in general.

Opposition to "open borders" or support for immigration reform has for too long been erroneously characterized as representative of a return to "nativism," of an emerging racism. This has led to an unwillingness to examine the more serious and important aspects of U.S. immigration policy.

Though we cannot predict the future, we can, with a certain amount of common sense, glance toward the turn to the twenty-first century and see what the national landscape would look like without modification of U.S. immigration policy. It is from this perspective that immigration policy should probably be shaped. This involves not only an examination of the effects of illegal immigration today but, more importantly, forecasting what the future will bring if the pressures persist.

First, what portion of the 800 to 900 million new job seekers in the developing world between 1980 and 2000 will the United States be forced to accept as a result of porous borders?

Second, will the 15 million Americans earning minimum wages, who compete directly with many illegal aliens for employment, be better or worse off if the system of illegal immigration continues and worsens?

Third, will respect for the laws of the United States, for the integrity of its national sovereignty, be strengthened by perpetuating a weak system of immigration law enforcement?

Fourth, will creation of enclaves of often second-class citizens, speaking only their native tongue, contribute to the political and linguistic cohesion of the country?

Fifth, will the blurring of the distinction between citizen and noncitizen, between lawful and unlawful resident, undermine the integrity of the electoral process and the legal fabric that holds the nation together?

Sixth, will immigration at current levels (nearly 1.5 million annually) contribute to the energy security of the United States, when projections indicate that the growth from legal immigration alone from 1982 to 1992 could consume an amount of energy costing $88 billion annually?

Seventh, will the addition of tens of millions of immigrants to the country over the next few generations improve our chances to conserve our natural resources, reduce our foreign oil dependence, and secure a high standard of living at a sustainable resource use rate?

Finally, will U.S. foreign policy remain coherent and independent and able to best serve the national interest if the decisions concerning who enters this country and uses its resources are strongly influenced by other governments and their populations?

These are serious questions. To dismiss them is shortsighted and would, in fact, suggest that the United States has the luxury of choice and time regarding immigration policy concerns. The new international environment of the 1980s, the recent energy crises, the vulnerable American hold on the global financial system, and the changing structure of the United States domestic economy may imply the opposite. The manner in which immigration and refugee considerations interact in the above mix cannot be underestimated.

Without sovereign control over national borders, the United States can lose control over the size and nature of its labor force, population size, and linguistic and political unity. Furthermore, the size of the nation's population will determine the adequacy of natural resources and the extent to which damages to the environment can be mitigated. This in turn will influence the productivity of the economy and the ability of the United States to compete successfully internationally. Finally, U.S. foreign policy may be greatly undermined by a continuation of the currently fluid nature of immigration policy; foreign powers will increasingly use the emigration threat to induce U.S. concessions or threaten retaliation should the United States move to strengthen its immigration statutes.

The nature of immigration policy can most likely no longer remain the exclusive domain of current dominant special interests. All things considered, immigration policy must be related to broad economic, demographic, and foreign policy themes. As was pointed out in "Illegal Immigration: Challenge to the United States" (a report of the Immigration Policy Panel of the Economic Policy Council of the UNA-USA, December 1981), "Control over entry by noncitizens is one of the two or three universal attributes of nation states."

While much attention has been paid to the domestic economic impacts of immigration, little has been said concerning its relationship with the emerging international economic and political context in which the United States finds itself. In addition, the disruptive effects of uncontrolled immigration on the political unity of the nation has also largely been ignored. The evidence is very strong that the international push factors generating illicit and legal immigration are among the most powerful contemporary factors in international affairs. Thus, the context in which traditional or historical migration to the United States has occurred is no longer relevant to the current global situation. The myths of the past must be discarded for the realities of the present.

U.S. international economic policy and success in competing overseas will depend in large part upon increases in U.S. economic productivity, including a highly trained work force, and increased business investment. Immigration, both legal and illegal, may in the future create a permanent underclass of unskilled workers, many of whom will remain unemployed.

Also, there is a concern that the growing use of racial or ethnic political power blocs in the United States will foster a divisiveness within American society. This issue is not stated here lightly. Since the 1970s, for example, bilingualism has become a highly visible public agenda in schools, governments, and media. Its relationship with present trends of large migration flows of people from Spanish-speaking countries is obvious. Ethnic power group manipulation of U.S. foreign policy is nothing new. Will a nation divided along ethnic or linguistic lines be a united nation, able to carry on a bipartisan and consistent foreign policy?

Finally, uncontrolled immigration is resulting in foreign countries using migration as a foreign policy weapon. Cuba and Vietnam, most notably, have sent their political dissidents, criminals, and espionage agents to the United States in the knowledge that the U.S. government is currently unable to control immigration into this country. Furthermore, hostile governments are patently aware of the destabilizing effects such influxes may have on the "recipient countries," thereby enabling them to create a massive liability for their opposition.

THE NEW MIGRATION: THE POPULATION BOMB REDISCOVERED

Because of the rich folklore surrounding the question of immigration, it is difficult to come to grips with the new realities that confront the United States. As a result, current U.S. immigration policy remains rooted in the convenient mythology of the nineteenth century.

When the United States was empty, with no functional frontiers, it needed immigrants to fill the continent. Those days are gone, yet the myth lingers on. The vast continent is now filled with migrants from every corner of the globe. America's bounty has been replaced by dramatically high unemployment, scarce supplies of natural resources, severe problems of economic productivity, and divisions within the social fabric.

So, too, has the entire world changed. Instead of 1 billion, the world population now exceeds 4.8 billion. The Brandt Commission and the *Global 2000 Report* have warned of the growing incompatibility between increased numbers of people, the supporting natural resource base, and environmental deterioration. Endemic poverty, historically unprecedented levels of unemployment, and related political and civil unrest are emerging as major world forces, with massive international migration a prominent result.

In the developing world, there are over 3.5 billion people. The populations of Panama, Costa Rica, El Salvador, Guatemala, Nicaragua, and Honduras, for example, have grown from 9 million in 1950 to nearly 25 million today; by the year 2000, the numbers will have swelled to 40 million and then to 70 million by the year 2025. The potential migrants to the United States through the rest of the century have already been born; over the next two decades, they will emerge into the labor force of the Third World nations with an explosive power far beyond anything previously experienced by humankind. Those people born between now and the end of the century are simply the tidal wave of the labor force explosion of the twenty-first century.

The annual growth in the populations of the Third World nations

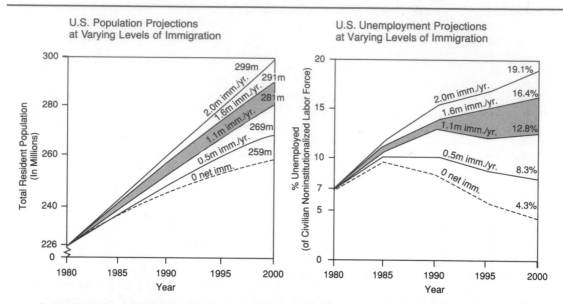

Both of the graphs above show five different immigration scenarios. The upper line represents the case where 2 million immigrants settled in the United States annually. The second and third line represent annual immigration levels of 1.6 to 1.1 million, respectively. The Environmental Fund (TEF) is convinced that the number of immigrants falls within the shaded area. The fourth line represents the case where half a million immigrants stay each year. The bottom line represents the hypothetical case of zero net immigration; though not a realistic scenario, this line shows how natural increase alone affects population growth and unemployment.

Note that these graphs are projections, not predictions. In all likelihood, the pressure for high unemployment would trigger measures to prevent joblessness from rising to the levels shown above.

from which illegal and legal immigrants are coming has not receded—in fact, the annual increase in both overall population and the labor force has continued to increase in gross numbers throughout this period. For example, in 1963 it was projected that Mexico's population by 1980 would grow to 70.6 million; the actual number reached was nearly 72 million, not including the suspected 3 to 4 million Mexicans living in the United States illegally. With respect to the labor force, the region of Central America and the Caribbean as well as South America is adding 4.5 million people to its labor force every year. Though the region has only one-third the overall GNP the United States has, it adds twice as many workers to its working-age population every year.

Even in the face of these increasingly worrisome push factors, important elements of American society continue to press for open borders. For example, Atlantic Richfield's executive vice-president, Ralph Cocks, states that, because Mexico has "all that population growth," they must have an outlet. The United States, says Cocks, "is a natural outlet in that we will have a labor shortage in the next two decades." Similarly, the United Methodist's Council of Bishops has requested that the United States impose no numerical limitations on immigration from Mexico and Canada, make all public services available to illegal residents, and allow employers to continue to hire those unlawfully in the United States. In addition, the Institute for Policy Studies is

organizing what it terms "Third World communities" in the United States around immigration issues, asserting that people have the "right to emigrate" to the United States. In effect, these organizations, and many like them, are threatening the security of the United States.

IMPLICATIONS FOR THE UNITED STATES

There is undisputed evidence that the flow of both legal and illegal immigration, including border crossings and overstays, is increasing dramatically. For example, twenty years ago, the total number of apprehended aliens seeking admission to the United States was under 40,000 per year. By 1970, that number had grown to over

260,000, and by the end of 1983 had grown in excess of 1.3 million. It is indicative of the unfortunate state of current U.S. immigration policy that the number of agents on duty at any one time actively seeking to stop illegal migration has gone up only marginally throughout this same period.

One of the more unfortunate assumptions concerning illicit migration is the view that it is largely a Mexican-United States phenomenon; although apprehensions along the U.S. border are concentrated in the Southwest and predominantly involve Mexico, illegal immigrants come to the United States from at least sixty different countries, according to the 1978 report of the Select Committee on Population and Immigration policy. Although the U.S.-Canadian border is only lightly patrolled, apprehensions of illegal immigrants in this sector are up 70 percent over 1982 levels, with people from China, West Germany, Greece, Haiti, Poland, Nigeria, Canada, and Latin American nations apprehended.

Legal immigration has continued to grow as well, with legal Mexican migration more than doubling from 70,000 in 1973 to 150,000 in 1983. Overall, legal immigration reached the 800,000 mark in 1980 and has since topped 600,000 in each of the following years, a 50 percent increase over the average increase in population attributed to immigration for the decade of the 1970s.

The implications of such growth for the demographic future of the United States is vastly more serious than most observers have acknowledged. The U.S. population, while projected to grow to 250 million by the year 2000 without immigration, will reach nearly 270 million with an annual immigration rate of 600,000. These numbers also assume a continued low U.S. fertility rate (1.8). If U.S. fertility rates climb to 2.0, however, the U.S. population will grow to nearly 270 million even with zero net immigration. Despite the awareness among most Americans of the need to exercise responsible parenthood and the trend toward limiting family size to two children or less, immigration is effectively cancelling the positive impact such a fertility reduction would otherwise have.

The massive impact immigration can have on the ultimate size of the U.S. population can be seen when projected out to the year 2080, a century hence: without immigration exceeding emigration, the U.S. population would be about 250 million *and declining;* but with immigration at 2 million a year, the population would be *558 million and growing rapidly.* (An often overlooked point is that most projections of U.S. population growth made by the U.S. Bureau of Census, and thus viewed as official, assume immigration at 400,000 annually and emigration at 150,000 annually. The emigration numbers are purely speculative; there are no data on emigration from the United States that justify the assumption that such a large number of Americans are migrating abroad, particularly on a permanent basis. The population numbers also assume that recent immigrants will maintain a fertility rate similar to the U.S. native population, an assumption not warranted by the facts.)

NATIONAL POLITICAL COHESION

Much of the debate concerning illegal immigration has centered on the displacement of extant American workers and tax revenues that are foregone. However, there are unique dimensions to the current immigration that have the potential to severely disrupt the political cohesion of the country. Illegal immigration, by virtue of its current size, and because of its concentration among Hispanics, is leading to three fundamental conflicts within American society.

First, the push for bilingual education has centered on the interest and needs of the Hispanic population in the United States. This issue raises a much broader issue. As columnist and political commentator Tom Braden wrote in *The Washington Times* on August 23, 1983:

Do we want a country unified by a common tongue? Or do we want a country made separate but equal by having to deal in two?

I worry about it. Is it prejudice that reminds me that, throughout two hundred odd years, we have been the gainers by having only one?

Second, there is increasing recognition of the potential political clout of the Hispanic population. As a result of high native fertility and large-scale legal and illegal immigration, the U.S. Hispanic population is increasing rapidly. By virtue of the size of the population, attempts can be made to secure political favors. (The National Council of La Raza has claimed that Hispanics will be the largest minority in the country by 1990 and, by virtue of this supposition, should be accorded substantial political benefits.) This can foster a tendency to cater to "Hispanic" interests as somehow distinct from those of other Americans. And to the extent to which the political clout of Hispanics is fueled by open-ended illegal immigration, U.S. sovereignty over its borders can conceivably be influenced by the political expediency of ethnic politics.

Third, a related but perhaps even more profound development flows from the growing numbers of illegal immigrants. Because political representation and the disbursement of substantial amounts of federal funds is based upon population, the 1980 census made major efforts to include illegal immigrants. To the extent that illegal immigrants increase the population of any particular state, their relative political representation is increased, as is their receipt of federal dollars. This suggests a skewed system in which there might be little incentive for states to work *against* the inclusion of illegal immigrants or *for* the reform of immigration statutes, if by the presence of large numbers of illegal immigrants they gain in tax revenues and political clout.

The viability of the nation depends upon an informed electorate and the absence of deep cultural or lingual divisions among its people. Illegal immigration, to the extent that it fosters the establishment of communities of persons unable or unwilling to converse in English, can foster just such divisions. The problem of a large ethnic group, repeatedly fueled by massive immigration—whether legal or illegal—detached from the mainstream U.S. population by language and custom, "could effect the social stability of the nation," says William A. Henry III in *Time* (June 13, 1983). He continues:

The disruptive potential of bilingualism and biculturalism is worrisome: millions of voters cut off from the main sources of information, millions of potential draftees inculcated with dual ethnic loyalties, millions of would-be employees ill at ease in the language of their workmates.

According to a study prepared by the Twentieth Century Fund, bilingual education, on which the U.S. government spends nearly $200 million annually, does not assist in creating a better society but just the opposite. "Anyone living in the United States who is unable to speak English cannot fully participate in our society, its culture, its politics" says the Fund's task force, recommending that funds currently being used for bilingual education be used to assist non-English-speaking children to learn to speak, read, and write in English. Congressman Kiki de la Garza expressed this concern in testimony before the U.S. Supreme Court: "Uncontrolled immigration is threatening the quality of education we can provide our children. . . . Many alien immigrant children have little if any command of the English language and little familiarity with our American customs and traditions, making personalized attention very important," thus placing great burdens on the local school.

Bilingualism fueled by massive immigration flows has unintended consequences as well. In Miami, many of the city's blacks are unable to find work because they do not speak Spanish, a prerequisite for holding a job in many Miami area hotels, stores, and restaurants.

Since its birth, the United States has sought to maintain a linguistic

unity. Our founding fathers were well aware of the conflicts and disunity that were bred by religious and linguistic differences. The United States has been blessed with a common language through which political, social, and economic discourse can be conducted. Illegal immigration is a grave threat to that unity, particularly when it is associated with pressures to provide bilingual education in America's primary school systems. Bilingualism does not strengthen the ability of groups to communicate with each other and build social cohesion. As commentator Eric Sevareid has said, bilingualism could "produce greater strain on this country than black-white relations."

BLURRED CITIZENSHIP AND THE ILLEGAL IMMIGRANT

1980 may be remembered by future historians as a watershed date in American history. For the first time, the U.S. government made a major effort to include illegal immigrants in the National Census. The census not only influences the distribution of federal tax dollars but is fundamental to the apportionment process that determines the number of representatives each state is entitled to have in the U.S. Congress. During the process of a lawsuit brought by the Federation for American Immigration Reform to block this inclusion, it was pointed out that the inclusion of millions of illegal aliens in the census would deprive certain states of representatives to which they otherwise would be entitled, while other states would unfairly gain additional representatives.

Unfortunately, an end to illegal immigration and the curtailment of legal immigration to reasonable levels may be perceived in the future as a threat by the beneficiaries of this growing political clout. Illegal immigration, to the extent that it fuels an increasing number of insular ethnic groups, becomes a tool with which to persuade government policymakers to look favorably upon the demands of ethnic organizations, which could include the maintenance of open borders. This has been most notably demonstrated by the recent action of Tip O'Neill, speaker of the U.S. House of Representatives, in pulling the Immigration Reform Bill off the House calendar. (He has since changed his mind, and the bill is back on the calendar.)

By including illegal immigrants in the census, the U.S. government legitimizes the use of illegal immigration itself as a political tool for the advancement of certain interests in American society. This is certainly not without significant implications for the future of American democracy. The political use of illegal aliens has included attempts by certain states, particularly California, to make major efforts to register illegal aliens to vote. During the Carter administration, the Justice Department informally ruled that it saw no legal reason why illegal aliens could not vote even in federal elections!

It is clear that the right to vote has to be synonymous with the rights of citizenship. Once the distinction becomes blurred between the rights reserved for Americans as opposed to those enjoyed by any newcomer who happens to be lucky enough or careful enough to enter the United States illegally and remain here, the very notion that the United States should have immigration statutes, let alone the right to enforce them, is undermined. The concept of "de facto citizens" implies a legal situation in which the United States has both a political and a moral imperative to grant the rights and privileges enjoyed by the rest of American society to those entering illegally. This is an uncomfortable situation, to say the least.

IMMIGRATION AND EMPLOYMENT: DISQUIETING TRENDS

This country retains a chronically high unemployment rate. To the surprise of many, immigration has become a disquieting factor in American economic life; although 2 million new jobs were created each year during the 1970s, half of them went to legal and illegal immigrants; at the same time, unemployment among Hispanics, blacks, teenagers, and women climbed to between 12 and 22 percent. One has to speculate as to the ways this affects the very foundations of this nation.

Critics contend that Americans have always made good use of its immigrant labor to do its "dirty work." This contention, however, evades the issue: is the United States to perpetuate the working conditions that surround this "dirty work" simply to attract illegal immigrants? What happens when such illegal immigrants wish to move on to better paying positions? Does the United States simply increase the flow of further illegal immigrants to take their place? Should the United States continue to tolerate the impact the presence of such an illicit work force has on U.S. workers and the consequent use of tax-supported services that such toleration entails? Is it in the national interest to perpetuate a situation in which the terms of labor competition are "who will work the longest hours, for the lowest pay, and under the most arbitrary conditions?" These are all serious questions.

In the meantime, the assumption that illegal immigration is predominantly a problem of the agricultural sectors of the U.S. economy stubbornly clings to the national conscience. Most internal enforcement of U.S. immigration statutes takes place in agricultural areas, where legal restrictions have not yet limited the impact the Immigration and Naturalization Service can have. In widespread areas of the U.S. economy, little if any attempt has been made to arrest the employment of illegal immigrants. As a result, the problem fades from public view, is ignored by the media, and only occasionally pierces the national conscience.

While the myth endures, the evidence is markedly to the contrary. A 1979 San Diego County study found that the overwhelming number of working illegal immigrants were in construction, manufacturing, retailing, and service industries, with only 7 to 8 percent in agricultural work. (These data are confirmed by over a decade of INS enforcement efforts at employment sites around the country.) In the same study, it was found that between 60 and 80 percent of the illegal immigrants were holding jobs which Americans would take, with 90 to 93 percent of all construction and manufacturing jobs held by aliens falling into that category.

• In one survey in Chicago, illegal immigrants were found to average $9,000 a year, while in Denver the average wage was over $13,000. These people work in "electronics and plastic companies, foundries, meat-packing plants, rubber products manufacturers, snack food and candy producers, and the like," attests John Crewdson of *The New York Times*.

• One-third of all the workers in commercial construction in Houston have been found to be illegally employed, earning from $4.00 to $9.50 per hour, or up to $20,000 annually, according to a Rice University study in January 1982.

• In Elgin, Illinois, the Illinois Department of Labor had no trouble filling openings left after Immigration and Naturalization Service agents arrested sixty-nine workers earning between $3.50 and $14.00 per hour; within hours, hundreds of local residents applied for these jobs, all of which were filled within three days.

• As a result of "Operation Jobs," conducted during the spring of 1982, important additional information became available on the extent of illegal immigration and its impact on employment. Though the average wage of those immigrants apprehended was $4.81 per hour, in both Denver and Chicago wages reached as high as $10.00 per hour.

There may be a small kernel of truth in the assertion that some unskilled jobs that Americans will not do are those taken or filled by illegal immigrants. The major reason for the poor working conditions and poor wages for these jobs is that these conditions are maintained illegally; the general impression is that illegal immigrants holding these jobs will not complain due to fear that they will be turned over to the U.S. Border Patrol or Immigration and Naturalization Service. For while it is illegal for these individuals to work in the United States, it is not illegal for U.S. employers to hire them. Thus, the very illegality of the immigrants contributes to the maintenance of the very working conditions that cause U.S. workers to shun such employment.

One of the chief problems the United States faces is a work force trained for a number of tasks that are declining in demand, while at the same time new technologies and trading needs require different employment skills and knowledge. As entry-level jobs decrease, particularly as automation increases, the kind of jobs most attractive to immigrants, especially illegal immigrants, will not be available, further exacerbating the competition between and among entry-level job-seekers in American society. The potential cost of such competition is substantial. If but 2 million Americans are displaced, the annual cost (in transfer payments) is estimated to be $14 billion. If indeed up to 3.5 percentage points of our national unemployment rate stems from the presence of illegal immigration, then much of the immigration debate appears shallow and beside the point—if any other single factor in American society could be identified with unemployment of such magnitude, it would be at the top of the national political agenda. Regrettably, immigration policy is not.

FREE LUNCH MYTHOLOGY: TAXES AND IMMIGRATION

It is widely assumed that illegal immigrants seldom use social services and, thus, contribute a greater amount of tax revenues than they receive in benefits. Furthermore, it is asserted that, despite any displacement impact such immigrants may have on U.S. labor force employment, their contributions to the tax base of the society are sufficiently large so as to justify their continued presence within American society.

Evidence is accumulating that points to the conclusion that illegal immigrants may in fact utilize

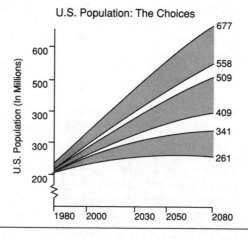

U.S. Population: The Choices

The lowest curve shows what will happen to U.S. population in the next few decades if U.S. fertility (TFR) is 2.0—close to the Census Bureau's best guess—and if immigration and emigration are brought into balance. The middle and upper curves reflect net annual immigration of 1 and 2 million, respectively. The shaded areas show the effect of a 10 percent higher fertility rate.

U.S. Population (In Millions)

677
558
509
409
341
261

600
500
300
300
200

1980   2000   2030   2050   2080

transfer payment services as readily as Americans. Tax-supported services such as sanitation, public transportation, education, environmental cleanup, municipal services—including fire and police protection—and a host of other related services are all utilized by people living in America simply by virtue of their presence here.

In this context, one of the more prevalent myths with respect to illegal immigration is the contention that these workers pay substantial amounts of taxes but receive relatively little in the form of transfer payments such as food stamps, Social Security, or Medicare. However, recent evidence strongly suggests that the extent of the use of transfer payment services is far greater than was previously assumed. First, displaced American workers cost the U.S. treasury substantial amounts of revenue, both in lost taxes and transfer payment benefits. Second, a certain percentage of illegal immigrants work completely off the books and avoid paying taxes altogether. Third, to the extent that illegal immigrant workers are paid below the minimum wage, tax receipts that are collected are reduced. Fourth, a certain percentage of the income of illegal immigrant workers is sent to their native lands, which results in a reduction in purchases and spending in the United States and, consequently, a further reduction in tax revenues. Finally, many illegal immigrant workers have been found to file fraudulent tax returns, claiming dependents in excess of the number allowed and receiving funds when taxes are already underpaid.

Illegal immigrants incur other costs to society as well. In some instances, as with health and educational services, the costs can be particularly heavy due to the low-income characteristics of the illegal alien population. For example:

• A screening of applicants for AFDC food stamps in Los Angeles found 17,000 individuals who withdrew their application when told that the INS would be notified—of those who persisted in applying, 90 percent were found to be illegal immigrants.

• In Illinois, it was found that 45 percent of applicants for unemployment insurance were illegal immigrants.

• Los Angeles County concluded that 1.1 million illegal aliens were costing the county over $629 million annually to educate and provide judicial, health, and other county services.

• Health care costs are escalating as illegal immigrants bear children in U.S. hospitals: in 1981, 81 percent of all children born in just one Denver hospital were to illegal aliens. The resultant health-care costs are enormous.

• For every 1 million Americans that are unemployed, it costs the federal government nearly $25 billion in lost tax revenues, lost economic activity, and increased expenditures for such things as unemployment compensation, food stamps, and welfare. With only 3 million illegal immigrants considered employed in positions that could eventually be opened up to unemployed Americans, the cost to the American taxpayers would be $75 billion. Professor Donald Huddle of Rice University has estimated that, for every one hundred illegal immigrants employed in the United States, seventy U.S. workers are displaced. Every displaced U.S.

worker costs $7,000 in transfer or support payments.

U.S. FOREIGN POLICY, NATIONAL SECURITY, AND THE NEW IMMIGRATION

Already the issues of immigration and refugee policies have acted as substantial destabilizing forces in the already precarious North–South relationship. These issues feed on the larger issues of Third World poverty, population growth, hunger, war, and revolution. For example, the countries of El Salvador, Honduras, and Nicaragua will double their populations in twenty-two years at present rates of growth. The labor force of these three countries alone will double between 1975 and 2000 to 13 million. Poverty, hunger, unemployment, and illiteracy remain serious problems, primarily as a result of an explosive growth in numbers far beyond the capacity of these nations. Add to this archaic political institutions, external ideological influences, and a poor natural resource base, and the ingredients for turmoil and civil conflict are abundant. As General Maxwell Taylor has warned, "If Central America today is an inviting pond to communist fishermen, under the conditions forecast it will offer them a well-stocked lake."

There is a vicious cycle of poor economic and political conditions in the Third World, and a consequent steady stream of migration to the United States. One may argue that present American immigration policy creates this vicious cycle through a lack of enforcement measures, which then encourage and simplify Third World immigration to the United States.

Uncontrolled immigration may be undermining U.S. foreign policy in three further areas: (1) the inability of the United States to control its national borders directly weakens its national security; (2) the failure of the United States to adopt an enforceable immigration policy is leaving it open to international coercion; (3) the traditional ability of the United States to provide a haven for victims of political oppression is impaired by the massive amount of illegal immigration, the majority seeking to improve their economic status, entering the country every year.

Unenforced Borders

It is often said that illegal immigration from the Third World acts as an important safety valve to relieve the population pressures there. Unfortunately, such a view obscures more important issues concerning U.S. national security. For example, while it is undeniably important that the United States maintain productive diplomatic relations with Mexico, in the words of the Economic Policy Council of the UNA-USA, one has to realize that "an unenforced border with Mexico is an unenforced border with the world."

Lacking enforceable immigration statutes, the United States faces pressure from the developing nations that will increase dramatically over the next two decades, just as it has over the past two. As migration increases, its ability to undermine the security of U.S. allies increases significantly as well. Already Somalia, Thailand, and Pakistan have been the recipients of massive movements of those fleeing civil war, political turmoil, and economic difficulty. Such refugee populations are seri-

ously straining the civil and social order of these nations. Engendered as such problems are by the Soviet Union and others, it does not appear likely that these exoduses will be curtailed over the next generation. In fact, hostile countries will continue to find it convenient to expel dissidents and "bad" elements from their own societies, thereby at the same time creating further difficulties for their opposition.

International Coercion

The extent to which U.S. foreign and domestic policy can be manipulated by foreign governments, some openly hostile to U.S. interests, by the use of large-scale illegal immigrant flows, needs to be addressed. Because of its laxity with respect to enforcing the sovereignty of its own borders, the United States finds itself in a vulnerable position. How often will the United States, in the future, find itself reacting to the actions of a foreign power in a manner that is injurious to our society? Would countries threaten to cut off the flow of petroleum should the United States decide to enforce or strengthen its immigration statutes? Would Poland threaten to tighten the grip of martial law unless the United States agrees to accept a greater number of "Polish dissidents"? Would Vietnamese officials continue to exploit the desire of their own people to emigrate, bleeding them of precious life savings, because they know the United States would accept them, no questions asked? Does the United States accept whatever criminals the Cuban government deems it does not want simply because some among the group claim to be political refugees?

Will nations everywhere find in the United States a convenient refuge for their domestic dissidents or political opponents, thus eliminating a potential wellspring of political democracy? Does this country wish to continue to be met with threats from foreign governments wishing to get rid of people they find inconvenient? And how much leverage will this country have with other governments in efforts to have them accept their fair share of refugees and immigrants when they know that the United States itself has no effective means of controlling immigration?

Refugee Policy

Refugees have become one of the more dominant trends in international migration. Along with the traditional element of political refugees have been added those people fleeing civil disturbance, wars, revolutions, coup d'etats, and generally poor economic conditions. Unfortunately, debate about refugee policy usually concerns domestic economic and political impacts with little discussion of the international considerations involved. U.S. refugee policy is in part a foreign policy issue; its importance will increase as the number of refugees in the world, almost 13 million in 1981, continues at present or higher levels.

Ambassador H. Eugene Douglas, U.S. coordinator for refugee affairs, has articulated the need to differentiate between immigrants, both legal and illegal, and refugees. He contends that it is essential that the United States establish a definition by which to determine who is a refugee, and therefore entitled to certain kinds of assistance, and who is an immigrant and therefore not entitled to refugee assistance. There lies a crucial distinction between refugees and immigrants, between the victims of political oppression and the victims or escapees from economic circumstances.

The foreign policy of the United States requires that this country be able to extend to those politically persecuted a safe haven. This is a traditional and humanitarian aspect of U.S. policy, which most Americans associate with the best aspects of American society. In order to preserve this essential aspect, however, there is a need to maintain a foreign policy that has as one of its objectives, according to Douglas, "the protection of its frontiers from excessive illegal immigration." He argues further that the key is a policy that acknowledges the need for restricted entry while preserving the concept of refugee asylum.

CONCLUSION

The national security of this nation depends upon its domestic strength and international stability. This strength requires an ability to control national borders, the maintenance of an independent foreign policy, a prosperous economy, and a cohesive domestic political environment. Uncontrolled migration is undermining this strength. Unchecked immigration, whatever its impact on labor and wage rates, does not just affect the unskilled and marginal job markets. Its impacts, because of its sheer numbers and because of its illegality, affects the very fabric of American society, U.S. national security, cultural, political, and linguistic unity, economic well-being, and international standing.

The question is not whether a change in the foreign policy aspect

of U.S. immigration will come but, rather, when and how it will come. There exist at least three possible scenarios: (1) the immigration policy status quo, slowly overwhelmed by events and forces that have already prompted cries of alarm, results in a radical policy departure in the form of total immigration restriction; (2) a laissez-faire approach to immigration problems results in fundamental alterations of U.S. society—a substratum of illegal aliens grows and an uneasy modus vivendi is found—and the United States is no longer a modern democracy but instead resembles the political order of the Greek city-state democracies; (3) between the extremes of one and two, a constructive response to the global immigration problem is found, resulting in a redirection of U.S. immigration policy as guided by a rational calculation of the national interest.

What is at issue is the need to discriminate among millions of potential immigrants, many equally deserving of consideration for entry into the United States. This implies a foreign policy agenda coupled with a difficult moral one. The demographic revolution of the past generation has delivered the most explosive growth in the labor force the world has seen to date. As this characteristic of the new immigration confronts this country, so must American policy responses be molded from a new appreciation of the times, of the changing global environment.

EPILOGUE: MARCH 1989

Attitudes toward immigration as a national policy issue continue to be divided. Yet, the late 1980s have generated a semblance of consen-

sus: the issue cannot be left unattended. Uncontrolled immigration led to congressional action.

A reevaluation was made in terms of border crime and security management, strains in local social services, job competition, and tensions in interethnic relations. In response to what was perceived as a systemic breakdown, the Simpson/Rodino Immigration Reform and Control Act (IRCA) of 1986 was passed. This effort has attempted to bring undocumented immigration under control while continuing the process of legal immigration. The most visible result of IRCA is, however, characteristic of the challenge at hand: three million illegal aliens have come into the open as a result of the publicity given by the new law; 90 percent of them are Mexican nationals; amnesty has been granted to perhaps as many as 2 million people.

IRCA's origins are symptomatic of the compromises required to push immigration issues to front and center of U.S. national policy concerns. It is the product of a time when many have felt that U.S. borders are too porous, that the U.S. government has lost control, and that the economic climate allows clandestine immigrants to take jobs away from native-born, legal residents.[1] IRCA had the initial result of pushing the issue away from the front page of U.S. public consciousness. Is it likely to last? Probably not.

Although the success of IRCA remains a debatable point, the international features of immigration (and refugee) flows remain uneasily at the crossroads of American concerns for law and order, and a compassionate vision of a "kinder and gentler" world. Although this has a global dimension, in practice immigration/refugee flows have largely become a western hemispheric question for the United States. The fact that INS apprehensions of undocumented workers after IRCA declined in 1988 to 950,000 from 1.2 million in 1983 is not at all encouraging. Los Angeles, for example, is reported to have an estimated illegal population of over one million.

Significantly, the character of the migrant flows are changing. The profile of the Mexican migrant is changing from the temporary agricultural worker to the permanent entrance of entire families. Meanwhile, the flow of Central American migrants (most attempting to claim refugee status) has reached extraordinary proportions, creating in late 1988 and early 1989 entire tent cities at the Texas border. Perhaps more striking than the actual flow to the United States was the indication of future infusion of migrant populations: during the second half of 1988, 71,000 adult Nicaraguans permanently left their country (out of a population of 3.7 million); an early 1989 poll in Nicaragua suggested that 49% of the population would prefer living elsewhere (primarily the United States).

The policy response of the United States therefore remains uneasy. Part of the problem lies in the fact that U.S. foreign and security policy toward Latin America as a whole (and Mexico and the Caribbean Basin in particular) and immigration/refugee concerns are often two sides of the same coin that cannot be easily reconsidered. This has produced bureaucratic compromises—such as the IRCA-moderated Commission for the Study of International Migration and Cooperative Economic Development—each in its own way alluding to the greater good of a cross-border community of shared interests. An object of considerable U.S. political attention in the 1980s, the region has partly as a consequence generated a highly visible immigration agenda for U.S. policy makers. This has triggered legal and humanitarian responses sometimes at cross-purposes with U.S. policy in the region. What constitutes a refugee when U.S. diplomacy is itself deeply committed to a particular course of political action? How does one compare fairly the status of Haitians as opposed to Nicaraguans or Poles? As painful as it may appear to some, the basic fact is that much of Latin America's (or the rest of the world's) exodus to American borders is motivated by deteriorating domestic conditions rather than immediate fears of persecution; the fact that the United States retains such a worldwide appeal, and is relatively easy to enter, are additional powerful factors.

Within the United States, there remain powerful currents that simply appear to muddle any concern regarding immigration. The U.S. national labor pool appears to be shrinking. Ten million fewer people will reportedly enter the work force in the 1990s compared with the 1970s. Whether this affects business or government, or specific sectors such as armed forces recruitment, this could imply a challenge regarding both quality and quantity. This is not unique to the United States; West Germany, where demographic growth rates are near or below replacement levels, has seen its military manpower pool decline to the point of forcing reduction in standing troop force. However, the uncertainty regarding these predictions of shortages relate to the variable impact that continued illegal (or legal) immigration or refugee flows will have in the future.

Much has happened, but as the decade of the 1990s is upon us the immigration policy challenge remains greater than ever. Even if the policy process is able to muddle along and the flexibility of American society remains strong, the inability of relating immigration to other national security concerns is likely to produce some tense moments. The problem is first and foremost conceptual.

Immigration and refugee issues do not operate in a vacuum, however. In fact, they represent a hybrid of domestic and foreign policy concerns. They are the result of favorable socioeconomic and political conditions in the United States coupled with difficulties elsewhere, particularly within the Western Hemisphere. The extrajudicial character of immigration to the United States presents an especially serious challenge. The United States cannot allow external forces or foreign governments to dictate the degree to which the United States should grant citizenship. Meanwhile, large-scale illegal immigration has bred an underground: a cottage industry for false documents, smugglers who trade in human lives, drug traffickers, arms dealers, a flow of contraband, and even intelligence gathering, if not yet terrorism.

With the large number of unconventional issues facing U.S. foreign policy—drugs, economic destabilization, the challenge of democratic governance, environmental and population growth issues, and immigration—the traditional episodic and conceptually compartmentalized approach to immigration and foreign/security policy issues is no longer appropriate. ■

Notes:

1. See Diego Ascencio, "Long-Range U.S. Perspectives on the Immigration Reform and Control Act," in M. Delal Baer (ed.), *Mexico and the United States: Leadership Transitions and the Unfinished Agenda,* (Washington, DC: CSIS, 1988).

Refugee Assistance: Overseas and Domestic

By James N. Purcell, Jr.

I welcome this opportunity to appear before you today as the Department of State's witness to testify on behalf of the Administration's proposed bill, which, upon enactment, would be cited as the "Refugee Assistance Amendments of 1985" and to provide you with the Department of State's views on H.R. 1452, entitled "The Refugee Assistance Extension Act of 1985." Before I address the questions of most immediate concern to this committee, I would like briefly to review recent developments in the world refugee situation and actions by the United States to deal with these developments.

The primary refugee problems facing the world today are concentrated in three general locations: in sub-Saharan Africa, where drought and armed conflict have caused widespread suffering; in Pakistan, where Afghans have sought asylum from the Soviet invasion of their homeland; and in Southeast Asia, where refugees continue to flee the communist-ruled Indochinese states.

REGIONAL REFUGEE PROBLEMS

Africa

By international definition, refugees are those fleeing persecution and oppression in their homelands. In Africa, however, the dividing line has been blurred between those fleeing persecution and those displaced across national boundaries by famine and armed conflict. The UN High Commissioner for Refugees (UNHCR) has declared, for instance, that all those crossing the border from Ethiopia into eastern Sudan and Somalia are "persons of concern to the High Commissioner" and will be given assistance. The first priority of international refugee assistance organizations and of the United States refugee program must be the preservation of human life.

By his personal presence in Sudan, Mali, and Niger this past month, Vice President Bush demonstrated this nation's commitment to aiding refugees and drought victims in this tormented area, where war and famine have combined to create conditions bordering on the catastrophic. Many agencies of the U.S. Government have been working together in support of the international assistance effort. The Bureau for Refugee Programs has worked alongside the Agency for International Development, the Centers for Disease Control, the Department of Defense, the U.S. Public Health Service, and dedicated professionals from private voluntary organizations to mount an emergency relief effort in the Sudan for over 320,000 new refugees.

On the international side, the various UN agencies, after a somewhat slow and disorganized start, have come together under the leadership of the UN Office of Emergency Operations for Africa, headed by Bradford Morse, to concentrate on the longer term needs of the African nations suffering from drought and famine.

The situation in Africa demonstrates quite graphically the fact that the refugee problem in the world today requires that we provide enhanced relief and assis-

James N. Purcell, Jr., is a career member of the Senior Executive Service.

Source: From address before the Subcommittee on Immigration, Refugees, and International Law of the House Judiciary Committee, Washington, DC, April 17, 1985. Reprinted in Department of State, *Current Policy No. 693,* pp. 1–4.

tance, rather than large numbers of admissions. In Africa, the long tradition of providing refuge to persons fleeing famine and war in neighboring countries has been put to a severe test. In the Sudan, approximately 1 million refugees from neighboring countries are being hosted, despite the fact that over 4 million Sudanese are themselves severely threatened by the drought. The rural populations of Africa do not seek resettlement outside their own area and are most in need of relief and assistance, pending a return to their countries of origin.

Southwest Asia

Similarly, over 3 million Afghan refugees in Pakistan and Iran need assistance, not resettlement. This vast refugee population—virtually one-quarter of the pre-1979 population of Afghanistan—poses difficult questions for the long term, which we have only begun to address. With few exceptions, these are tribal peoples who have no desire to resettle outside the area. They want nothing more than to return to their homes in Afghanistan as soon as they can safely do so.

Southeast Asia

Of more immediate relevance to this committee's work is the continuing refugee problem in Southeast Asia, which has been met primarily through third-country resettlement, much of it to the United States. While we are making steady progress on reducing first-asylum populations throughout the region, we should not delude ourselves into imagining that we have within our grasp a simple solution to the continuing outflow from the Indochinese

states. The recent upturn in arrivals from Laos and the influx of 250,000 Khmer from the border have put increased pressure on Thailand. The United States is supporting international efforts to deal with these urgent situations.

Despite these problems, our goal remains—consistent with our humanitarian obligations—the achievement of a continuing reduction in this portion of our worldwide refugee admissions program. We hope to achieve a "steady state" admissions level that is as low as possible. We should recognize, however, that, for the foreseeable future, we will need to continue to admit a reasonable number of Indochinese refugees to the United States, both because it is our humanitarian duty to do so and because it is in our strategic interest to relieve the pressures that refugee populations place on friendly first-asylum states in the region.

U.S. INITIATIVES

Last September, Secretary Shultz announced before this committee the President's initiatives for expanding our portion of the UNHCR's Orderly Departure Program from Vietnam to include additional cases of priority concern to the United States. This expansion is to be accomplished through the inclusion of more Amerasians in the program—we are currently projecting 4,000–5,000 Amerasian departures in FY [fiscal year] 1985—and through the inclusion of 10,000 released reeducation camp inmates and close family members in FY 1985 and FY 1986.

The Amerasian program has brought out over 1,500 Amerasian

children and accompanying family members during the first 6 months of FY 1985—an average of 263 per month, compared to 182 per month in FY 1984—and we are hopeful that this improvement will continue during the second half of the fiscal year. Since its inauguration, the Orderly Departure Program has brought over 5,000 Amerasians and their families to the United States. We can only estimate how many more remain in Vietnam—perhaps 10,000–15,000 —but I wish to reaffirm the President's commitment to take them all over the next 3 years, as announced by Secretary Shultz last September.

Unfortunately, despite our repeated good faith efforts to continue negotiations with the Vietnamese authorities on the release of the political prisoners being held in the so-called reeducation camps in Vietnam, there has been no real progress by the Vietnamese. Since the U.S.-Vietnamese bilateral meeting in Geneva on October 4, 1984, when we formally presented the President's proposal, the United States has proposed twice to the Vietnamese that we resume negotiations on the prisoners' release and resettlement.

In answer to our first proposal to meet in January, the Vietnamese responded that the proposed dates were not considered appropriate but repeated their readiness to continue discussions on this question with the American Government. At the same time, however, they falsely accused the United States of intending to use the resettled prisoners in hostile activities against Vietnam.

In our response to the Vietnamese, we denied categorically their false accusations but noted their stated willingness to continue negotiations and proposed a meeting in February. The Vietnamese have not responded to this most recent U.S. proposal.

Notwithstanding this unresponsive Vietnamese attitude, the United States remains firmly committed to obtaining the release from prison and resettlement to the United States of these prisoners and their families. We will continue to work for the early release of the reeducation camp prisoners, and we continue to hope that Hanoi is serious in its expressed interest in pursuing this matter with us. We will keep the Congress informed of developments in this area.

DOMESTIC RESETTLEMENT EFFORTS

I turn now to the issues of domestic resettlement, which are of particular concern to the committee today.

In the 10 years since the fall of Saigon, over 735,000 refugees from Vietnam, Cambodia, and Laos have found new lives and new hope for the future of their children in the United States. In light of the unusually difficult circumstances of the Indochinese migration—including the sheer numbers involved and the considerable cultural barriers facing groups such as the Hmong, Thai Dam, and Khmer—the results have been remarkable—in some cases, even extraordinary. Among the many success stories one could cite is that of the West Point cadet, Jean Nguyen—introduced to the nation by President Reagan during the State of the Union Address—who will be graduated

from the Academy less than 10 years after her family fled Vietnam. In addition, there are the numerous Indochinese high school valedictorians we read about each graduation season. Indochinese refugee communities across the nation are revitalizing aging inner-city areas through hard work and investment in small commercial enterprises.

A major obstacle to refugee self-sufficiency and the overall success of the resettlement effort has been the high benefit structure of the welfare system in some states. In addition, in the early years of the program, voluntary agencies providing initial reception and placement services to the refugees were not given adequate guidance as to what exactly the Federal Government expected of them.

Since adoption of the legislative amendments of 1982 affecting the reception and placement program, our management of this program has been strengthened considerably. Initiatives by the Bureau for Refugee Programs have included:

• A revised cooperative agreement that provides far greater programmatic and financial specificity;
• Greater oversight by the bureau of initial placement determinations; and
• Establishment of an active, onsite monitoring program.

In addition, recent GAO [General Accounting Office] and Department of State Inspector General recommendations have been incorporated into our management practices.

Since 1982, the Bureau for Refugee Programs has systematically monitored service delivery by voluntary agencies. These in-depth inspections of local affiliates have proven to be of great value in helping the national voluntary agencies to improve the management of their reception and placement programs. I have a statistical summary of the 20 on-site monitoring reviews undertaken to date, which I will be pleased to submit for the record.

One conclusion that emerges from a comparative review of refugee resettlement in different states and regions is that refugees do not have to become dependent on welfare. Demonstration projects in Arizona, Oregon, and Chicago are seeking to break the cycle of welfare dependency through innovative resettlement plans aimed at placing refugees in jobs as soon after their arrival as possible. The "Chicago Project," funded by the Bureau for Refugee Programs, was an initiative of the local voluntary agencies.

All of these projects, however, depend on close cooperation between the public sector and the voluntary agencies. California, which has the nation's highest refugee welfare dependency rate, is about to embark on a 3-year program that alters some basic public assistance program components in an effort to tailor public assistance to the particular needs of refugees. In all cases, locally developed solutions to local problems are proving to be most appropriate—a fact that the Congress recognized in its passage last year of the Wilson-Fish amendment, which authorizes the Office of Refugee Resettlement of the Department of Health and Human Services to fund resettlement demonstration projects tailored to particular states and localities.

LEGISLATIVE INITIATIVES TO ENCOURAGE REFUGEE SELF-SUFFICIENCY

If these developments are a source for optimism in attacking the welfare phenomenon on a state-specific level, there remains the need to address our national mechanism for bringing refugees through the critical transition period of their first months in the United States. The strength of our national system lies in the involvement of private agencies and individuals in the sponsorship and support of refugees seeking to establish new lives as Americans. Consequently, it is the shared view of both the Congress and the Ad-

ministration that we should build on this strength by enhancing and making more explicit the responsibilities of the voluntary agencies and by ensuring an appropriate mix of Federal and private resources to make their resettlement efforts effective.

It is from this general perspective that the Congress and the Administration both are now seeking, through legislation, to address the specific problem of initial high welfare dependency among refugees.

It is apparent that most incoming refugees require support and assistance during the early phases of their assimilation into American society. Once on welfare, many

refugees tend to become dependent on continued public support for long periods of time. Disincentives to early self-sufficiency are created. The voluntary agencies, who assist refugees in the early phases of their introduction to our society, report that the draw of public assistance thwarts their efforts to promote refugee social and cultural assimilation through early entry into the work force. The objective of both the Congress and the Administration has been to provide workable alternatives to early access to public welfare assistance and, instead, to rely as much as possible on the private voluntary agencies to direct refugees to early employment. ∎

Suggested Additional Readings

Brown, Lester. *Population Policies for a New Economic Era* (Washington, DC: Worldwatch Institute, 1983).

Choucri, Nazli (ed.). *Multidisciplinary Perspectives on Population and Conflict* (Syracuse, NY: Syracuse University Press, 1984).

Demerath, Nicholas Jay. *Birth Control and Foreign Policy* (New York: Harper and Row, 1976).

Fauriol, Georges. "Refuge from Reality: The Sanctuary Movement and Central America," *The Humanist* (March/April 1986), pp. 10–14ff.

Glazer, Nathan. *The New Immigration: A Challenge to American Society* (San Diego, CA: San Diego State University Press, 1988).

Gupte, Pranay. *The Crowded Earth: People and the Politics of Population* (New York: Norton, 1984).

Hartmann, Betsy. *Reproductive Rights and Wrongs: The Global Politics of Population Control and Contraceptive Choice* (New York: Harper and Row, 1987).

Marden, Parker *et al. Population in the Global Arena: Actors, Values, Policies, Futures* (New York: Holt Rinehart, 1982).

McCoy, Terry (ed.). *The Dynamics of Population Policy in Latin America* (Cambridge, MA: Ballinger, 1974).

Pastor, Robert. *Migration and Development in the Caribbean* (Boulder, CO: Westview Press, 1985).

Saunders, John (ed.). *Population Growth in Latin America and U.S. National Security* (Boston: Allen and Unwin, 1986).

Teitelbaum, Michael S. *Latin Migration North: The Problem for U.S. Foreign Policy* (New York: Council on Foreign Relations, 1985).

CHAPTER THIRTEEN

Hunger and the Environment

*
*

Population, immigration, hunger, and the environment: All these new and critical issues in U.S. foreign policy are interrelated. Spiraling population increase, however, may be at the root of these other issues.

Excess population, as we saw in the last chapter, and the crowding, lack of job opportunities, and lack of available land (all of which are reflections of unchecked population growth) are among the principle forces pushing people to emigrate. Excess population, along with mismanagement and maldistribution of national resources, is also the cause of hunger and even mass starvation in many parts of the world. Finally, excess population is among the principal causes of environmental pollution and degradation.

To harried foreign policy makers, who often have too many issues to worry about and not enough time to deal with them adequately, hunger and environmental issues often fall at the lower ends of their priorities. It is not that policy makers are not interested or not worried; it is that they have so many other problems to deal with that seem to command greater attention. Moreover, since policy makers are often politicians as well, they tend to respond to the "squeaky wheel" that makes the most noise. And the fact is that since starvation and the environment have small constituencies in the United States (Ethiopians do not vote in the U.S., and hungry street people in our own cities seldom do either), these issues have seldom received the attention they deserve.

Recently, however, this has begun to change. Television, with its gruesome, night-after-night reports of massive starvation in Central Africa and elsewhere, has been the principal agent in focusing attention on the plight of hungry peoples. More than just a reporter of these events, television has also become a participant in the process, helping to mobilize massive campaigns to aid the starving. In the environmental area, Canada, as well as the states of the Northeast, has helped force attention to the issue of acid rain. The so-called greenhouse effect—an apparent (but still controversial) global warming trend caused by the steady increase of carbon dioxide in the air—has recently received considerable attention. Brazil's efforts to develop by chopping down the Amazon rain forest, burning the trees, and converting the land to agricultural use have aroused world concern, pitting Brazil's desires for growth and economic nationalism against environmentalists who worry that the world's oxygen supply may be severely diminished by Brazil's actions.

All these and other trends have focused new-found attention on hunger and environmental issues. Public opinion surveys tell us (as well as policy makers) that the voting public has become increasingly concerned with these "new issues." In some polls, in fact, environmental and

other new issues have replaced the more traditional concerns about the Soviet Union as *the*
most important foreign policy issues.

These are extraordinary difficult issues with
which to deal in a foreign policy sense. For one
thing, the amount of attention these issues receive is highly variable: One day it is acid rain,
the next day it is starving children in the Sudan,
the next it is the snail darter that is about to
become extinct, the next it is the greenhouse
effect. It is hard to have effective policy when the
issues are so diffuse and our attention span for
any one of them so short.

A second problem is that most of these are
international issues (acid rain comes from Canadian and European as well as U.S. factories;
population is a global as well as a local problem;
pollution is worldwide; and so on), and the sad
fact is that there is no global machinery to
effectively deal with these matters. Nor is there a
global consensus on what their causes are or
what should be done about them.

A third problem is that the agencies established to deal with these issues (the Environmental Protection Agency or the State Department's Office of Oceans and International
Environmental and Scientific Affairs) are relatively new and inexperienced in these matters,
and they lack policy-making clout. The EPA now
has an international division, for example, but
few of its representatives speak foreign languages, and it does not know how to operate
abroad effectively—which is essential since so
many of these issues are global.

There is no doubt that public consciousness
about these issues is rising, and the institutional
apparatus to deal with them has begun to be put
in place. But on all of these issues we still have a
very long way to go.

The Foreign Policy Association begins our
considerations with a careful statement of what it
calls "Farmers, Food and the Global Supermar-
ket." Next come three journalistic assessments,
one from *The New York Times* and the others
from *Time,* on how the internal politics and the
maneuvers of the governing elites distort and
corrupt well-meaning food-distribution programs.

On environmental issues we again turn to
the Foreign Policy Association for a nice introductory statement. Then, scholar and environmental activist Lynton Caldwell analyzes the environmental issues in which he believes U.S.
policy should be more strongly engaged. The
final selection shows how the State Department
has begun to respond to environmental issues.

Farmers, Food and the Global Supermarket

Those who till the soil are the chosen people of God.

—*Thomas Jefferson*

The 1980s have brought difficult times to farmers around the globe. Overproduction, especially in the U.S. and Western Europe, has kept world food prices low and aggravated competition for international markets. Cooperation on food trade issues now seems harder than ever to achieve. Governments are reluctant to make concessions that might endanger their share of world markets, their country's perceived food security, or their farmers' incomes. Meanwhile, farmers have become increasingly dependent on price supports and other expensive subsidies for their livelihood.

The paradox in the food-production equation is that as surpluses have grown, so has hunger worldwide. According to the World Bank, as many as 700 million people now suffer from hunger, due largely to poverty, war and revolution, inadequate food distribution systems, inefficient government policies and severe weather conditions in some parts of the world.

Some developing countries that are struggling to feed their populations are themselves exporters of agricultural products. In 11 out of 21 low-income African nations, farm products account for up to 100% of all exports. These countries have often concentrated on producing crops such as peanuts and pineapples for the international market rather than traditional foods such as sorghum and cassava for domestic consumption.

In the U.S., vast resources, state-of-the-art technology and a long-standing commitment by the government to provide reasonably priced and plentiful food have combined to make agriculture (including farming, food processing, distribution and sales) one of the largest and most efficient sectors of the economy. Agriculture is the only industry represented by a Cabinet-level position. Though farming alone accounts for just 3% of the country's gross national product (GNP), agriculture as a whole accounts for nearly 18% of the GNP and employs over 8 million people, more than the steel and automobile industries combined.

Trouble on the Farm

Agriculture—especially farming—has always been a risky business. During the early 1980s, high interest rates and low food prices sparked one of the worst crises in recent history for U.S. farmers. Many farmers who had borrowed heavily to buy more land and equipment in the 1970s were suddenly unable to service their debts. The resulting farm foreclosures, business losses and bank failures sent shock waves through rural America.

Last summer, the worst drought in 50 years parched the crops and baked the soil of farmers in parts of the U.S., Canada and Mexico. For over seven months, large portions of the U.S. received little or no rain, and by August, the mighty Mississippi River had reached its lowest level since record keeping began in the late 1800s. Production

of corn was nearly 40% less than the previous year, and the soybean crop was down by one fourth. In Canada, grain production fell by a third in 1988; in Mexico, one fifth of the wheat crop and nearly half of the soybean crop were lost.

The contrasts of the 1980s—overproduction in some parts of the world, famine in others—have brought into focus such issues as trade, the environment, hunger, and food and development aid. In recent years, the U.S. has struggled to balance the needs of its farmers with the necessity of addressing these domestic and international problems.

Today's farm policies are still largely dominated by legislation drafted more than 50 years ago. The Agricultural Act of 1981 failed to reduce the costly farm subsidy programs, which were originally mandated under the Agricultural Adjustment Act of 1933. The most recent farm bill, the Food Security Act of 1985, which cut price-support levels but boosted cash subsidies, has reduced surpluses and is slowly aiding in regaining export markets. But its costs (over $25 billion in 1986 alone) made it the most expensive farm legislation in U.S. history. As Senator Robert J. Dole (R-Kans.) once noted, during his more than quarter century in the U.S. Congress "there has always been a farm problem."

THE GLOBAL SUPERMARKET

In the U.S., as in most countries, farm programs have traditionally been driven by domestic rather

Source: From *Great Decisions 1989*, Foreign Policy Association, New York, 1989.

than foreign policy needs. Providing affordable and plentiful food for U.S. consumers and adequate incomes for U.S. farmers has generally taken precedence over international concerns such as promoting trade.

Nonetheless, the fate of the American farm has become directly tied to the global economy. In the early 1970s, when worldwide food trade was expanding at the rate of 10% a year and demand for U.S. farm products abroad skyrocketed, Secretary of Agriculture Earl L. Butz is said to have encouraged farmers to "plant fencerow to fencerow" and thus fulfill what was seen to be America's destiny as "breadbasket to the world."

By the early 1980s, one acre out of three was being farmed for the export market; half of the soybeans and three fifths of the wheat grown in the U.S. were sold abroad. Some states became more heavily dependent on exports than others. Kansas, for example, sells up to 80% of its wheat internationally. "Without exports," says Kansas State University economist B. L. Flinchbaugh, "there would be a lot more people out of business."

Despite this country's continuing dominance in agricultural trade, the food-production equation is changing rapidly, for the U.S. World food output has reached levels never before thought possible, making competition for global markets keen. Many previous customers for U.S. farm products are now important exporters themselves.

Following World War II and throughout the 1950s, for example, Western Europe was a major importer of U.S. food and feed grains. Today, the European Economic Community (EEC, or Common Market)—which includes Belgium, Britain, Denmark, France, Greece, Ireland, Italy, Luxembourg, the Netherlands, Portugal, Spain and West Germany—though still a large importer, is the world's second largest producer and exporter of farm goods.

In 1992, the EEC is scheduled to complete the integration of its economies into a single internal market. This may eventually include Eastern Europe and even the U.S.S.R.—a market of over 700 million people. Because of its size, economic integration is certain to make Europe an even more formidable competitor. Other major food exporters among the industrialized countries include Canada (the world's second largest wheat exporter), Australia and New Zealand.

Cash Crops

It is in the Third World that the most startling changes in food production and trade have taken place. During the "boom" years of the 1970s, when the world economy experienced spectacular growth, newfound wealth from oil revenues and bank loans stimulated local economies, creating a demand for more food and a more nutritious diet in many Third World nations.

Most of these countries could not expand agricultural production fast enough to keep up with the growing demand. Governments in Africa, Asia and Latin America looked to the U.S. and other industrialized nations to help satisfy their food needs. From 1970 to 1980, exports to the Third World accounted for more than 30% of all U.S. agricultural trade.

In the early 1980s, however, demand for U.S. farm products in the Third World fell sharply. This was due to the high price of U.S. products compared with those of other producers, the worldwide recession and the heavy indebtedness of many Third World governments, especially in Africa and Latin America. Third World countries simply could no longer afford massive imports of U.S. food.

To improve their balance of trade and earn much-needed foreign exchange, many of these countries turned to growing crops such as soybeans, wheat and other grains exclusively for export. Because they can be sold on the international market, these commodities are known as cash crops, as opposed to food crops, which are generally raised for domestic consumption.

Brazil, for example, already the world's number one producer of soybeans, is preparing an additional 271 million acres (half as much as the total acreage under cultivation in the U.S.) to grow wheat, corn and more soybeans. India, the world's largest food-aid recipient during the 1960s and 1970s, has occasionally been able to export as much as $1 billion worth of wheat in recent years; Thailand is now the world's second largest rice exporter; and even China, with its enormous population of over 1 billion, is managing to produce surpluses of certain crops. In 1988, growing demand led to record levels of global trade in grain. The U.S. alone sold more than 40 million tons, up from 27 million tons in 1987.

Many economists believe that a chief cause of the world's agricultural production and trade problems is the subsidy programs that the industrialized countries have developed to maintain farm incomes and keep their agricultural products competitive on the global market. According to the World Bank, such programs now cost taxpayers and consumers about $150 billion a year worldwide.

Subsidy Wars

Most Third World nations lack the funds necessary to support farm production. Instead, to provide inexpensive food for city workers, many have chosen to subsidize consumers indirectly by requiring farmers to sell their products at below market rates. This in effect "taxes" farmers by limiting their profits and thus discourages farm production. Consumer subsidies are generally seen as a major reason for the lack of food self-sufficiency in the developing world, especially in Africa.

In the industrialized non-Communist world, farm subsidies take on a variety of forms. The most common include price supports and, as in the case of Japan, import restrictions. Regardless of the market value of a certain crop, the government guarantees that farmers will receive a set price for it. Since income is determined by harvest size, farmers are tempted to produce more than the market can bear. In 1987, for example, the U.S. government paid farmers $3.00 a bushel for corn that sold for around $1.50 a bushel on the open market. The more corn a farmer grew, the bigger subsidy check he or she received.

Production-oriented farm subsidies have led to periods of enormous food surpluses. In 1986, according to a report by the United Nations Association of the U.S.A. (UNA-USA), the U.S. had accumulated enough wheat to produce 27 loaves of bread for every man,

woman and child on earth. Since then, production cutbacks and poor harvests have caused surpluses to shrink by more than two thirds.

Because subsidy programs disrupt global prices and production trends and are seen as a hindrance to international trade, the world's principal trading partners are often said to be battling each other in so-called subsidy wars. According to an Organization for Economic Cooperation and Development (OECD) study, Japanese farmers—by far the most protected in the industrialized world—receive an average of 72% of their income from government subsidies; in the EEC, farmers get 33% of their income from the government; those in the U.S., 27%; and those in Canada and New Zealand get about 23%. In Australia, which gives the lowest subsidies of any industrialized nation, only 9% of a farmer's income is provided by the government.

'Farming the Government'

Supporters of government farm programs claim that they are necessary to provide price and supply stability to an inherently unstable sector of the economy, to assure adequate supplies of food at reasonable prices and to slow the decrease in the number of farms. Critics of the programs argue that subsidies not only distort market prices and create large and unnecessary surpluses, but that they also promote inefficiency and are costly to maintain.

Though only about 60% of all U.S. farms produce price-supported crops and many of those with the highest net worth do not receive any government payments, a U.S. Department of

Agriculture (USDA) study has shown that the average U.S. taxpayer, with a net worth of around $33,000, pays to support the average U.S. farmer, with a net worth of nearly $190,000. Economists estimate that the removal of worldwide price supports and other subsidies would increase world farm prices by only 10%, provide $26 billion a year more in farm income for Third World countries, and reduce food prices in the industrialized countries.

Proponents of farm subsidies claim that these government programs should be judged on their social as well as their economic value. In the EEC—where farmers were recently paid 18 cents a pound for sugar that was worth only 5 cents a pound on the world market—fears of trade embargoes and food shortages, such as those suffered during and after both world wars, have made governments protective of their farmers. What's more, Europe's 9 million farmers (more than four times the 2.2 million in the U.S.) constitute important voting blocs in their respective countries. In Japan, pride in local production, the cultural importance of rice and concern for food security cause the government to pay farmers nearly $2,400 a ton to produce rice it could buy from the U.S. for $225 a ton.

Those who favor subsidies concede they are expensive, but they point out that food costs to consumers have nevertheless declined steadily over the last two decades. The percentage of income spent on food by consumers in the industrialized countries is at an all-time low, just 24% in Japan, 20% in the EEC and 16% in the U.S. and Canada.

Government subsidies have become a way of life for many U.S. farmers. When the government supports farm income from corn at twice the market rate, for instance, it is nearly impossible for a farmer to say no to a subsidy payment. Banks, in fact, often require participation in a government program as a prerequisite for granting farm loans. Farmers cynically refer to their addiction to subsidies as farming the government, not the land.

GATT Negotiations

International cooperation in eliminating obstacles and expanding agricultural trade has been difficult to achieve, despite its importance to farmers and consumers everywhere. The U.S. and other governments have traditionally viewed agriculture as a special industry requiring unusual treatment and extraordinary protection. Because of this attitude, agricultural trade is encumbered not only by high farm subsidies but also by numerous other barriers, such as quotas, embargoes, quarantine regulations and health restrictions, largely imposed to protect domestic producers from foreign competition.

In the past, the U.S. and other major food exporters have successfully managed to exclude agricultural trade policy problems from talks under the General Agreement on Tariffs and Trade. GATT, as the agreement is commonly known, was established in 1947 to promote liberalized trade among participating countries. Trade negotiations by GATT's 96 member countries tend to be long and drawn-out affairs. The current round of talks, for which the groundwork was laid in September 1986 at Punta del Este, Uruguay, is not expected to end for several years.

At Punta del Este the U.S. pushed successfully to have agricultural trade issues placed on the agenda. A year later the Reagan Administration startled other GATT members by proposing the elimination of *all* agricultural-trade-distorting policies—such as domestic price supports, export subsidies, tariffs and quotas—by the year 2000. The proposal reflected the general feeling of U.S. economists and policymakers that the high farm subsidies of the 1980s in the U.S. and other industrialized countries had gotten out of hand.

Though the U.S. proposal was withdrawn in November 1988 due to pressure from the EEC and Japan, most GATT members agree that some sort of compromise on agricultural issues is necessary. A coalition of 14 countries (led by Australia, Canada and New Zealand) known as the Cairns Group, after the Australian city where they first met, has long pushed for freer agricultural trade. New Zealand, in fact, has taken the unusual step of unilaterally reducing its trade barriers and price-support subsidies in the hope that other countries will follow its example.

At home, the Reagan Administration's agricultural trade initiative has been "supported" by some farm groups only because they do not believe it will ever be accepted by GATT's other members. According to Harvard University economist Robert L. Paarlberg, if the initiative is rejected, the farmers will be in a position to demand more trade protection from Congress, a move that could only exacerbate tensions between the U.S. and its major trading partners. Senator Patrick Leahy (D-Vt.), chairman of the Senate agriculture committee, has already said that Congress is prepared to pass a highly protectionist farm bill in 1990 if the current GATT talks do not produce a meaningful agreement on agricultural trade.

As economists C. Ford Runge and Steven J. Taff have noted, "Failure to make progress [in agricultural trade negotiations] will result in enormous costs to importers, exporters, producers, and consumers in the North and South alike."

New Markets

In passing the 1985 farm bill, Congress and the Reagan Administration were betting that lower prices for U.S. farm products abroad would increase the U.S. share of the world food market. To a large extent, this gamble has paid off. U.S. farm product exports have made impressive gains since 1986, increasing by 32% over the past two years.

The export market, however, does have its limitations. Most countries produce and process almost all the food they consume. Only 11% of all farm products grown worldwide are traded internationally, and each year competition among food-exporting countries for a share of the market increases. Since food consumption tends to level off at about 3,000 calories a day per person, increasing U.S. exports to countries where food is plentiful will be difficult.

Many analysts believe that the biggest new market for U.S. farm exports lies in the Third World. After recovering from the recession of the early 1980s and as U.S. prices became more competitive,

Third World purchases of U.S. farm products rose sharply, accounting for 58% of total U.S. agricultural exports in 1986 and 1987. Since debt problems continue to plague much of Africa and Latin America, most of this increase has been in sales to Asian countries. According to Luther Tweeten, a farm economist at Ohio State University, by the early 1990s, half or more of U.S. farm exports will be going to Asia.

One of the major potential Asian markets for U.S. farm products is China. Because of phenomenal economic growth, China's per capita consumption of grain has doubled over the past two decades. Although the country is attempting to achieve self-sufficiency in food production, its burgeoning population has all but made that impossible. By the end of the century, China expects to have 190 million more mouths to feed, and its wheat imports, according to International Wheat Council estimates, will be as high as 32 million tons a year—the equivalent of three fourths of the total U.S. exports for 1988.

Sales to the Soviet Union

Another important and growing market for U.S. grain is the U.S.S.R., where disastrous agricultural policies, artificially low food prices and poor weather conditions have caused such severe food shortages that rationing has had to be adopted at times in major cities. With a larger farm population than all the Western nations and Japan combined, the Soviets produce less than a fourth as much food and fiber.

To make up for production shortfalls, the Soviets have turned increasingly to the global market for their food needs. Over the last two decades, the U.S.S.R. has gone from being a net exporter of agricultural products to one of the largest importers of food in the world. Last October, General Secretary Mikhail S. Gorbachev unveiled plans to overhaul the country's 50-year-old farm strategy by dismantling collective farms in the hope of improving agricultural output.

Although the first U.S. grain sales to the Soviet Union occurred in 1963 during the Kennedy Administration, the U.S.S.R. did not become a major market for U.S. grain until 1972. That year, the Soviets bought nearly 15 million tons—more than a fifth of all the U.S. wheat available for sale. In 1975, the U.S. and the U.S.S.R. signed a five-year agreement, which called for the Soviets to purchase a minimum of 6 million tons of U.S. grain annually and for the U.S. to make a minimum of 8 million tons available to them each year.

After extending the original agreement for two years, a new five-year accord was negotiated in 1983, which set the minimum annual purchase at 9 million tons of grain. In eight of the past fifteen years U.S. sales to the Soviets have exceeded the annual minimum requirements.

Grain Embargoes

Selling grain to the Soviets has always sparked controversy. In 1963 (the year after the showdown over Soviet missiles in Cuba), political opposition, led by such notable conservatives as Richard M. Nixon, and the insistence by organized labor that most of the shipping take place in U.S. cargo vessels, held wheat sales to less than half of their originally intended size. In the early 1970s, when the sales were thought to cause wheat shortages in the U.S. and thus higher food prices, consumer groups and labor leaders pressured the Nixon and Ford Administrations to place partial embargoes on exports of certain grains. During the presidential campaign of 1976, Midwestern grain producers supported Jimmy Carter because he made a point of promising there would be "no more grain embargoes."

Ironically, it was President Carter who felt obligated to embargo any grain shipments above the previously agreed 8 million tons to the U.S.S.R. in retaliation for the Soviet invasion of Afghanistan in December 1979. Had he not taken that step, it is estimated that the sales could have reached a record 25 million tons in 1980. The Soviets reacted angrily to the embargo but were easily able to find other sources, mainly Argentina, to satisfy all of their grain needs.

During the 1980 presidential campaign, the embargo cost Carter his Midwestern support and contributed to his losing the election. In the spring of 1981, under pressure from farm groups and believing that it was not having the desired effect of punishing the Soviets, President Ronald Reagan lifted the grain embargo.

POVERTY AND HUNGER

Despite gains in farm production and the accumulation of surplus grains and other basic foods through the 1970s and 1980s, the specter of hunger still hangs menacingly over much of the world. In 1986, Africa faced one of the worst famines in human history. Some

210 million people, nearly half the continent's population, went hungry; of those, 30 million people in 20 countries were at risk of starvation.

Today it is realized that food production is only a small part of the world's hunger problem. Other aspects include poverty, poor distribution systems, war, rapid population growth, the loss of arable land, faulty or genocidal government policies and natural disasters such as drought and flooding.

According to the UN's *1988 State of the World Population* report, two thirds of the world's chronically hungry live in South Asia and one fifth in sub-Saharan Africa, many on land that can no longer support them by subsistence agriculture alone. For these people, the size of world grain supplies is of little importance. The vast majority lack the income to buy even the least expensive and most basic foods on the open market.

Some of the poorest Third World nations have traditionally used agricultural exports as a means for boosting their gross domestic product (GDP). Often, human and natural resources have been diverted from subsistence farming to the production of crops for foreign markets. In Guatemala, a country where 80% of the population suffers from nutritional deficiencies, 90% of the arable land is dedicated to such export crops as coffee, cut flowers and snow peas. In Senegal, one of the poorest of the sub-Saharan African nations, over half the cultivated land is devoted to growing peanuts for the European market.

In recent years, the trend toward growing export crops has slowed. As economist Paarlberg

points out, in many African nations the production of cash crops is actually falling faster than that of food crops. The problem is not what they grow, but the fact that they are not investing enough in any type of agriculture. Also, notes Paarlberg, there is nothing wrong with cash crops if the profits they generate go back to small farmers, enabling them to buy better food. Instead, many governments misuse the profits by diverting them into nonproductive areas.

Even in the more prosperous developing countries absolute poverty prevents much of the population from satisfying its daily nutritional needs. In Brazil, which enjoys one of the highest per capita GDPs in the Third World, nearly 65% of all workers live below the poverty line and, according to some reports, up to two thirds of the population suffers from malnutrition.

Population Growth

One major factor contributing to the conditions of poverty and hunger in many developing countries is their rapidly expanding populations. Between 1950 and 1985, the population of the Third World increased by more than 100%, growing from 1.7 billion to 3.7 billion. In contrast, during the same period the population of the industrialized world grew by 50%, from 800 million to 1.2 billion. According to the U.S. State Department, 90% of all future world population growth will occur in the Third World.

Population control became a major international issue during the late 1960s. A decade later, 66 countries with 91% of the developing world's population had initiated policies or programs to pro-

mote family planning. These programs have met with varied degrees of success. Cuba, Singapore, South Korea and Taiwan, for example, have achieved "replacement-level fertility," with their birth and death rates nearly matching. China, too, has made enormous progress in population control, cutting its fertility rate by more than half over the past two decades. On the other hand, in Kenya—the first sub-Saharan African nation seriously to address family planning issues over 20 years ago—the birthrate is now the globe's highest.

Though once in the forefront in promoting worldwide family planning programs, the U.S. since the early 1970s has given little priority to population control. Under the Reagan Administration, opposition to abortion and the belief by government officials that population growth in itself is not necessarily detrimental to economic development led to a cutoff of U.S. support for such organizations as the International Planned Parenthood Federation.

Today, due to continued high birthrates in some countries, improved health care, reduced infant mortality and increased longevity, world population as a whole is still increasing by approximately 2% per year. This translates into 150 births every minute; or 220,000 every day; 80 million each year; and about 1 billion every 12 years. In Africa, the continent with the least dense population overall but the most alarming growth rate, the population has been growing at a rate of 3% to 4% a year. At those levels of growth, many African countries are expected to double their populations in 25 years or less.

By the year 2000, the earth will be home to some 6 billion people. With most of this increase taking place in the Third World, the primary question is how the developing nations will produce the food or income necessary to feed their growing populations.

Feeding Themselves

Some Third World nations, despite the difficulties they face, have made great strides toward becoming self-sufficient in food production. India's grain harvests, for example, have nearly tripled over the past 30 years, going from 51 million tons in 1950 to 135 million tons in 1988. By the end of this decade, the government of Prime Minister Rajiv Gandhi hopes to raise grain output by an additional 30%.

These impressive gains in India's food supply are the result of the Green Revolution, a multinational effort to intensify agricultural production in the Third World. In 1943, hoping to find a cure for chronic hunger, the Rockefeller Foundation sent a team of U.S. scientists to Mexico to study ways of increasing food production. From this early research came new plant hybrids capable of boosting per acreage yields of such important food grains as wheat and corn. By 1955 Mexico had doubled its wheat harvest, and in 1956 it became self-sufficient in food for the first time in its history as an independent state.

The Green Revolution soon spread throughout Latin America and Asia. In 1960, the Ford and Rockefeller foundations jointly created a research center in the Philippines devoted exclusively to the study of rice. By 1966, scientists at the center began releasing the first of many "superstrains" of rice that were capable of producing higher yields and were more resistant to pests and disease than conventional varieties.

The new varieties of food grains readily adapted to modern methods of agricultural production. Whereas the older strains broke down under modern farming techniques, the new varieties, called semidwarf because of their size, were hardy enough to stand up to intensive chemical fertilization and mechanical harvesting. Because of their shorter growing season, many of the semidwarfs also allowed for two or even three crops a year. Thus, the Green Revolution not only changed what Third World farmers grew but also how they farmed.

The use of semidwarf plants brought dramatic results in global food production. New varieties now account for over half of all the rice and wheat grown in Third World countries. The average yield per harvested acre has climbed from less than half a ton to approximately one ton. Between 1974 and 1985, grain production increased 60% in India, 40% in China and 300% in Thailand. In fact in 1985, India appeared to suffer from too much rather than too little grain, with surplus stocks exceeding storage capacity by 2 million tons.

Output: Losing Momentum

Because of the Green Revolution's emphasis on chemical fertilizers, irrigation, seed hybrids and other expensive inputs, those who have benefited the most have been the larger farmers with access to credit. The revolution has not touched the vast majority of the world's small farmers, according to Edward Wolf, a senior researcher with the Washington, D.C.-based Worldwatch Institute:

"Overall, nearly 100 million people in Latin America, 280 million in Africa, and over 990 million in Asia raise food under difficult conditions at yields little changed since mid-century." These farmers, Wolf notes, often use the same cultivation and harvesting techniques their ancestors employed centuries ago.

There appears to be a loss of momentum in the growth of food production in Africa (where the Green Revolution has not reached) and in South America, the two continents with the fastest growing populations. According to Lester Brown, a former USDA official and president of Worldwatch, Africa—where government policies tend to discourage investment and innovation in agriculture—was the first continent to suffer a decline in per capita food production since 1945. Its per person output has fallen 15% since it peaked in 1967. In South America, the second continent to experience such a decline, per capita food production has dropped by 13% during the 1980s.

Unrenewable Resources

Falling farm output in some parts of the world underscores the fact that many of the globe's resources are already being strained to their limits. As the UN's 1988 population report explains, in rural areas of developing countries the consumption of food, water, fuel and fodder is depleting supplies faster than they are being replenished. In sub-Saharan Africa, overgrazing and unwise cultivation have turned 160 million acres of land back into desert in the past 50 years. In the Sudan, the desert is spreading south at the rate of some 60 miles every 17 years.

The destruction of prime arable land is not confined to less-developed countries. The high growth in world grain output has partly been achieved by plowing land that is now in danger of erosion. Even in the U.S., overproduction damaged millions of acres of farmland during the 1970s, raising fears of a recurrence of the "dust bowl" conditions of the 1930s. According to government estimates, 5 billion tons of topsoil are washed or blown away each year from U.S. fields and farmlands. As mandated under the 1985 farm bill, the USDA is taking 45 million acres (11% of all cropland) out of production because it is too erodible.

Irrigation is also rapidly becoming a major environmental issue. According to a UN study, millions of acres of land are lost each year due to the salt and alkalies that are naturally found in irrigation water. As the water is pumped into the fields for irrigation, residues of the impurities eventually accumulate. Unless they are dissipated through such management practices as "flushing" or deep plowing, they destroy the soil's productivity.

Salinization is believed to be affecting some 10 million acres of cropland in the U.S. alone. Worldwide, it is estimated that from 2 million to 4 million acres of land are lost to salinization each year. Still, the importance of irrigation to the world food supply cannot be overstated: China produces 70% of its food on irrigated land; Pakistan 85%; and India 55%. The alternative, dry-land farming, greatly decreases annual production and the range of crops that can be grown.

Low-Input Farming

Concern over the harmful environmental impacts of agricultural chemicals, including fertilizers and pesticides, as well as the widespread burning of tropical forests to create arable land, has given rise to a worldwide movement toward low-chemical agriculture. Low-chemical agriculture (called "low-input" farming by the USDA) emphasizes traditional farming techniques, such as crop rotation, mulching and organic weed and pest control. For example, certain legumes can be planted in maturing cornfields to hold nutrients and prevent soil erosion. Other plants will choke out weeds and discourage insects.

Advocates of low-chemical farming argue that it can reduce agricultural production costs and environmental risks while preserving and even improving farmland for future generations. Critics claim that its use is infeasible on a large scale, that it would lead to declining yields, higher costs and less food security worldwide.

In 1987, Congress appropriated $3.9 million for the creation of the Low-Input/Sustainable Agriculture (LISA) program for U.S. farmers. Under LISA, funding is provided for research and educational projects to improve low-input farming techniques and to raise public awareness of their long-term benefits.

Though low-chemical farming is considered best-suited for small- and medium-sized farms, LISA funds are also being used to research the program's applicability on a much larger scale. A number of commercial grain producers in the Midwest have for some years managed to maintain profitable farms using few or no chemical herbicides, insecticides or inorganic fertilizers.

The U.S. government is also funding research and pilot projects in sustainable agriculture in the developing world. In Honduras, for example, the U.S. Agency for International Development (AID) is helping to support an experimental farm run by the Vermont chapter of the Partners of the Americas program. Many program participants have been able to double or triple their crop yields while improving their lands.

Food for the Hungry

One traditional way of dealing with chronic and emergency food shortages is through food aid, the actual transfer of surplus food from one country to another. Under the Food for Peace program, the U.S. has been selling food on easy terms to developing nations (or providing it free to the poorest countries or groups of poor people in more-affluent developing nations) since 1954.

During the 1960s and early 1970s, food aid was used primarily as a means of strengthening and rewarding U.S. allies in the developing world. The main recipients were Israel, Turkey, South Korea, Pakistan and South Vietnam. In 1974, Congress decreed that 75% of all food sales under the program had to go to the world's poorest countries, those in Central America and sub-Saharan Africa.

By the late 1970s, the Food for Peace program had shrunk to a relatively small $1 billion a year, where it remains today. Although annual U.S. food aid in the 1980s has averaged less than half the volume registered in 1965, the U.S. remains the single largest food donor in the world.

Critics of food aid programs charge that massive donations of

U.S. agricultural products have undermined the farm economies in recipient countries by flooding the market with low-priced food, prompting many local farmers to stop planting crops and accept food aid instead. Critics also point out that some recipients have used aid as a political tool. In Ethiopia, where famine killed 300,000 people in 1984–85, shipments of donated food were hindered or held up by both government and rebel forces in an attempt to influence the outcome of a bitter civil war.

To many people in the U.S. and other Western nations, providing aid to the world's needy is seen as a moral obligation that transcends politics and economics. As Laura Kullenberg, director of an Oxfam America program in Africa, told *Time* magazine, "This is a life-and-death situation [in Ethiopia], and our choices are limited. Our mission is to make sure food gets to people in need, not to make a political point."

AID officials and private relief organizations around the globe have expressed concern that the drop in grain reserves and the increase in commodity prices brought on by the 1988 drought will limit the amount of food available for shipment to poor developing nations during 1989. Higher prices mean that AID dollars buy less. In 1986, the world grain surplus reached a high of 458 million tons, a 101-day supply. Following the 1988 summer harvest, the surplus was only 250 million tons, a 54-day supply— below the 57-day level that more than doubled world grain prices in 1973. The USDA has forecast that the spring 1989 harvest will bring the surplus back up to a 65-day supply.

Some food policy analysts fear that a continued decline in world output will push borderline countries into dependency, while making relief goals all the more difficult to achieve. These concerns contributed to a USDA decision to cut in half the amount of land to be taken out of production in 1989.

Development Aid

U.S. aid for agricultural research and development in the Third World has also come under criticism in recent years for being potentially too successful. Some U.S. farm groups and policymakers believe that boosting agricultural productivity in developing countries will lead to increased competition for shrinking global markets in years to come. As one U.S. senator has said: "How can we get control of the deficit if we send money overseas which works toward lowering global commodity prices and causes Commodity Credit Corporation [CCC] and price maintenance programs to rise?"

Critics often cite soybean production in Brazil, which was partially developed through an AID grant, as an example of an agricultural aid program backfiring on U.S. farmers. Other such programs that may have affected U.S. exports include grants for rice research in Thailand and cotton production in Paraguay. In 1986, Congress passed an amendment prohibiting the funding abroad of any program that promotes the growth or production of an agricultural commodity for export that would compete with a similar commodity grown or produced in the U.S.

Yet the key to U.S. export growth may lie with improved farming in the Third World. Numerous studies have shown that increased agricul-

tural production in developing nations leads to an increase in income, and hence in their demand for agricultural imports (as has happened in South Korea and Taiwan). One of the first things very poor people do when they become a little better off is improve their diets. Demand for meat, dairy products and processed foods increases, creating an even bigger demand for cereals and feed grains that are readily available on the international market.

According to policy analysts such as Paarlberg, finding solutions to the problems of food production, agricultural trade and hunger may prove difficult, but it should by no means be seen as impossible. Much will depend on the direction that U.S. agricultural policies take in coming years.

U.S. FARM POLICY

Developing an agricultural policy that satisfies the economic, environmental and food security needs of the country is one of the biggest challenges facing U.S. policymakers. Every President since Harry Truman has discovered that reforming the farm program is no easy task.

Government involvement in farming has a long history in the U.S. In 1862, an important year for farmers, Congress passed the Homestead Act, offering free land to those who chose to cultivate it, and created the USDA as a means for providing information on agriculture to farmers throughout the country and for distributing seeds and plants. It also provided Federal aid in the form of land grants to establish an agricultural and mechanical college in each state. In 1887, Congress passed the Hatch Act, granting $15,000 a year for each state and territory to establish agricultural experiment stations.

In the early years of the twentieth century, the Federal government financed a number of farm support programs that provided for education and research, farm credit, and market regulation. By 1914, the USDA had an annual budget of $22 million. But it was legislation passed by Congress during the depression that laid the foundation for today's agricultural policies.

Depression Years

By 1929, when the stock market crash shook the world's financial system, U.S. farmers had already suffered through a decade-long depression of their own. During World War I, grain scarcities in Europe, brought on by the war, created a great demand for U.S. farm products, leading to what is still known today as the golden age of U.S. agriculture. When Europe recovered from the war, demand for U.S. food fell sharply and rural America went into a steep decline.

In 1933, as part of President Franklin D. Roosevelt's New Deal, Congress passed the Agricultural Adjustment Act, creating the CCC, a credit system that allowed financially strapped farmers to borrow operating expenses from the government against their unharvested crops. At harvest time, if a crop's price was less than the amount of the loan, a farmer could clear his debt by simply turning his or her crops over to the government. If prices increased, however, the farmer could sell the crops at the market rate, pay the government back the loan and pocket the difference. In order to reduce yields and stabilize prices, the Agricultural Adjustment Act also permitted the government to pay farmers to cut production of certain commodities, including wheat and corn.

The catch in the CCC program was that loan rates were set by a so-called parity system, with prices pegged to the golden-age highs of 1910–17. Because 1930s market prices were much lower and production costs had fallen so far since 1910, critics of the program claimed that CCC loan rates maintained the market value for farm products at artificially high levels. The program's proponents, on the other hand, argued that the high loan rates guaranteed farmers a decent income by providing a fair market price for their products.

World War II brought another boom to the U.S. farmer, as demand for food at home and abroad caused prices to double between 1939 and 1945. After the war, the U.S. continued to ship farm products to Europe under the Marshall Plan. Between 1948 and 1950, a total of $4 billion worth of food, fertilizer and feed—over half of all U.S. agricultural exports—was purchased with government grants and loans.

Public Law 480

After Europe's recovery in the 1950s, demand abroad for U.S. agricultural products again fell sharply. The Agriculture Act of 1949, however, had not anticipated the decline in demand. The price supports it mandated encouraged farmers to maintain the high levels of production of the Marshall Plan years. As a result, government-owned surpluses soon swelled to unmanageable proportions.

To cope with the surplus and provide food aid to countries in need, Congress in 1954 enacted Public Law (PL) 480. Under PL 480, surplus farm commodities could be given away, bartered or sold for currencies other than dollars. In this way, any country lacking dollars could simply print enough of its own currency to purchase U.S. surplus foods. Thus, the U.S. government unloaded much of its grain surplus on the world market with little or no real cost to the governments of purchasing countries. Due in large part to PL 480, U.S. grain exports quadrupled between 1955 and 1957, with 80% of the sales going to Third World nations.

In many ways, PL 480 created more problems than it solved. Other food exporters, including such important U.S. allies as Canada, Australia and New Zealand, were upset over its effect on world market prices. U.S. hopes of gaining diplomatic leverage from PL 480 sales were often disappointed because recipient countries tended to view their purchases as a favor to the U.S., since they helped reduce the surplus. What's more, U.S. surpluses continued to grow.

During the early 1960s, to address a worrisome trade deficit, President John F. Kennedy instructed the USDA to intensify efforts to expand dollar sales of farm products abroad. The EEC had begun reducing its dependence on grain imports from the U.S. in 1961, after it adopted a Common Agricultural Policy (CAP), a farm program designed to protect West European farmers from U.S. and other competitors. The loss of sales to Western Europe was partially offset by a 70% increase in wheat sales to Japan and the opening of the Soviet market for U.S. grains in 1963. Still, total U.S. farm exports fell in the 1960s, with the U.S. share of worldwide wheat sales down from a high of 20% in 1960 to a low of 12% by mid-decade.

To protect the flagging farm economy, Congress introduced a direct income subsidy program for farmers in the early 1970s. This program determined an annual "target" price for wheat and other grains that was somewhat higher than the CCC loan rates. If market prices fell below target prices, a "deficiency payment" was sent directly from the government to participating farmers to make up the difference.

In the 1970s, the U.S. farm economy witnessed its greatest expansion ever. High population growth worldwide, poor harvests abroad (especially in the Soviet Union), economic growth in the Third World and a devaluation of the U.S. dollar brought sharp increases in demand for U.S. food products.

Government policy was driven by the mistaken belief that demand would continue to outpace supply. It failed to take into account the changing world food market. The commodity boom of the 1970s, created by loose U.S. monetary policies and unsustainable borrowing, would soon turn into a "bust" in the 1980s, when tighter U.S. monetary policies triggered a world recession.

Europe and many Third World countries, such as China and India, were greatly expanding their own agricultural production, which was bound to cut into demand for U.S. farm products. The U.S. government nevertheless encouraged farmers to expand production as rapidly as possible. As a result, U.S. revenues from agricultural exports reached an incredible $44 billion in 1981. But government-held surpluses also continued to grow.

In anticipation of continued high inflation, the Agricultural Act of 1981 set target prices and other price supports at new, unreasonably high rates. The Administration of President Reagan, anxious to please its farm constituency, then set crop loan payments for 1981 and 1982 at higher levels than were required under the new law. Since the amount of a farmer's loan still depended on the size of his or her crop, farmers were indirectly encouraged to plant as much as possible. Consequently, grain surpluses reached record highs.

Growing grain surpluses prompted the Administration to introduce in 1983 a Payment-In-Kind (PIK) program to discourage farmers from producing certain crops, such as wheat and corn, and to promote the using up of surpluses. For every bushel of wheat a farmer didn't grow under the PIK program, for example, he or she received a bushel of government surplus wheat to sell on the open market. In 1983, the average commercial farm received PIK subsidies of nearly $30,000.

The PIK program reduced U.S. wheat and corn acreage by 25%. This, together with the global economic recession of the early 1980s, high dollar exchange rates and high commodity loan rates, caused U.S. food exports to drop by almost 40%. As the U.S. cut back, other countries expanded their output and took over markets previously served by the U.S.

In an attempt to increase the competitiveness of U.S. food products abroad, Congress passed the Food Security Act of 1985. This bill set limitations on the amount of crops that could be produced under government subsidy and lowered loan rates, bringing down both domestic and export prices. It also set into motion the U.S. aggressive Export Enhancement Program, which gave high export subsidies and helped launch a spectacular recovery in U.S. agricultural trade.

The 1985 bill failed, however, to reduce by any significant amount the target prices set in 1981. Since it is the target price that guarantees a farmer's income for each bushel grown, farmers continue planting crops with which the market is already flooded. ■

A Further Lesson in the Politics of Swollen Bellies

By Jane Perlez

It has been eight months since the last train with food arrived in the besieged town of Aweil, [the Sudan], a once-fertile place where tens of thousands of people have been trapped by war and famine.

Its bags of grain were portioned out in meager rations, in what must have seemed like a last rite to about 200,000 starving people, according to a stark letter written by a Roman Catholic priest in the town.

Jane Perlez is a *New York Times* reporter.

"We have 1,500 sacks left," wrote the Rev. Rudolf Deng, referring to a secret cache of grain meant to be a last-ditch supply for the time after the train departed. "This is a drop of water in an ocean of misery and abject poverty."

Since Father Deng's letter was written in March, no food has arrived for civilians in Aweil, a Government-held town 800 miles southwest of Khartoum that is a focus of the brutal Sudanese civil war.

RESCUE PLANS DON'T MATERIALIZE

At least 8,000 people died there between June and September, said a Government official in Khartoum, Dr. Pacifico Lado Lolik.

But even though the Sudanese Government and Western relief officials are aware of the town's plight, numerous rescue plans for Aweil have failed to materialize.

The failure to get aid to Aweil and other population centers in the south illustrates the limitations of Western efforts to ease the famine of the Sudanese civil war.

Western diplomats here say their efforts to help civilians inside the southern war zone are hampered by the fractured Sudanese Government, which is heavily influenced by the National Islamic Front. The Government regards people in the largely Christian and animist south as sympathetic to the forces of the rebels, the Sudan People's Liberation Army.

FOOD AS A WEAPON

Both the Government and the rebel group use food as a weapon. One diplomat said that while the delivery of supplies to children is sometimes acceptable to the Government, food deliveries to keep adults alive are generally considered tantamount to supplying arms.

A major practical obstacle facing the Western donors trying to deliver aid to Aweil, diplomats say, has been the Sudanese Government's refusal to negotiate with the rebel group for safe passage into Aweil. Rebel forces are said to be near the Aweil airstrip.

But several Western diplomats and Sudanese officials said that underlying the practical difficulties is the reluctance of Western governments to sacrifice friendship with the Sudan on the altar of humanitarian aid.

In recent years Western governments have become increasingly concerned about keeping at bay the fundamentalist movement led by the National Islamic Front, which seeks to reimpose the Sharia, or Islamic law. The Sudan, Africa's largest country, is strategically situated between Ethiopia and Libya, with Egypt bordering to the north.

While Western governments have criticized the Marxist Government of neighboring Ethiopia for hindering famine relief efforts there, diplomats here say they fear that pressuring the Sudanese Government, by publicly criticizing it or cutting off aid, could have little positive effect and might strengthen the hand of the front.

"We're stuck in the attitude to relief of trying to keep in with the Sudan Government, of trying to do it within the limits of what the Government will do," said a Western diplomat unhappy with the pace of Western aid to southern Sudanese. "There is the fear that if you confronted the Government you wouldn't be allowed to do anything."

"I think the Western donors can only do so much," said Asma Dallalah, relief coordinator for Sudanaid, a nongovernmental Sudanese relief organization. "There is only so much you can do in someone else's country. It is the Government's responsibility to see the food goes where it should."

PLANS FOR AIRLIFT FAIL

After a team from the United States Agency for International Development successfully airlifted supplies to Abyei, where thousands of starving refugees had trudged from Aweil, several plans were devised to help Aweil itself, a place viewed as much worse off.

The agency asked that a plane be donated to an American aid group in Ethiopia, Air Serv, so that it could fly food to Aweil. The plane arrived here more than three weeks ago, but has not left Khartoum Airport.

The United States won an agreement in principle from the Sudanese military to fly American grain to Aweil on a Sudanese military plane. But the Sudanese then said they could not free the plane they had promised.

The Sudanese Prime Minister, Sadiq el Mahdi, promised Western ambassadors more than two weeks ago that 40 rail cars would be set aside for relief food on a train to Aweil. So far the train has not left.

SKETCHY RADIO REPORTS

The only nonmilitary contact between Aweil and Khartoum is over a radio once used in the town in a rice project financed by the

European Economic Community. Now and then, Ms. Dalallah gets sketchy reports of the harrowing conditions. Her last contact was for a radio transfer of $187,000 for 700 bags of grain (more than $3 a pound) that the local priest contracted to buy from profiteering Aweil merchants four months ago in an act of desperation.

Even though there was no food, no medicine and only one doctor, a bizarre sense of justice appeared to prevail in Aweil. The priest had been taken to court for failure to pay for the grain, and the money was sent to keep him out of jail. ■

Famine

By Michael S. Serrill

The situation in Ethiopia is not yet as bad as it was two years ago, when hundreds died daily of hunger and disease in mass feeding camps. As of last week there was enough food to last for a month and enough promised in the international aid pipeline to nourish the country through April. While thousands of peasants have been temporarily uprooted from their villages, they have learned the lesson of 1984–85 and have gone in search of food before they are too weak to travel. U.N. officials say that for the moment there are no permanent feeding camps, where more died of rampant infectious disease than of hunger the last time around. Those who gather at Wukro go back to their villages after receiving a month's supply of food, then return in a month or so.

But things could rapidly deteriorate if the available food cannot be distributed quickly enough. "The next few weeks are crucial," said Dr. Goran Hanson, a Swedish Red Cross worker in Addis Ababa. "If food and transport do not arrive in time to keep people in their villages and prevent them from gathering in famine camps, it will simply be disaster. We desperately need food, trucks and planes. We are now short of all three."

The response from the West has again been generous. Last week BBC Correspondent Michael Buerk, whose reporting first alerted the world to the scope of the last famine, led an appeal that raised $650,000 in five days. Weeks before the latest drought attracted publicity, the major private food-aid agencies—the Red Cross, Oxfam, Caritas, Care and Catholic Relief Services—were shipping food by sea and air and distributing it to the needy.

Why, after two short years, do hundreds of thousands, even millions, again face starvation? While Western experts primarily blame the lack of rain, many place much of the responsibility on the shoulders of Ethiopian President Mengistu Haile Mariam, whose rigid and secretive Communist regime has done little to avert another tragedy. Not only does the Addis Ababa government seem more concerned with putting down various insurgencies than with feeding the hungry, but it has also continued policies that seem designed to aggravate rather than resolve problems of poverty.

Those policies include a population-resettlement program, the opening of Soviet-style collective farms and a "villagization" effort that moves farmers off their isolated homesteads and into government-built settlements. The collective farms are such a doctrinaire Stalinist scheme that even the Soviet Union has urged officials in Addis Ababa to scale back their ambitious plans.

Geldof, who received an honorary knighthood from Queen Elizabeth II for his Band Aid efforts, was back in Ethiopia last week, and his indictment of Mengistu's role in the new famine was harsh and to the point: "I would say that the cardinal responsibility of any government is to feed its own people, and any government refusing to do that is irresponsible."

In 1984 hundreds of thousands had already starved to death before the government admitted to a famine. And Mengistu, a former army major with a tendency toward the grandiose, was widely denounced for spending an estimated $100 million to commemorate the tenth

Michael S. Serrill is a writer for *Time* magazine.

Source: From *Time,* December 21, 1987, pp. 34–38, 43. Reported by Leonora Dodsworth/Rome, Scott Macleod/Washington, and James Wilde/Wukro. Copyright 1987 Time, Inc. Reprinted by permission.

anniversary of the revolution that deposed Emperor Haile Selassie. There are signs he may be curbing his spendthrift ways: in September, when the country was renamed the People's Democratic Republic of Ethiopia, Mengistu opted for a cocktail party instead of a banquet.

Like much of Africa, Ethiopia has always been subject to ecological disaster. Droughts and famines were reported as early as 253 B.C. In the great drought of 1888, a third of the population is said to have died from malnourishment and disease. This latest calamity is part of a 30-year pattern that has seen the rains repeatedly fail along the Sahel, the wide swath of land that cuts Africa in half just below the Sahara. After the 1984–85 drought, which killed an estimated 2 million people in Africa, there was a brief period of uncommon optimism in Addis Ababa. In 1985 and 1986 the rains were good for the first time since 1981. Though hunger persisted, no one was starving. When the rains came on schedule last June, it looked as if the nation would have a third year of good luck. But July was bone dry—not a drop of water the entire month. Stubbornly hopeful, farmers replanted. In August the rain sputtered, then, late in the month, stopped. The crops withered and died.

Worst hit was the far northern province of Eritrea along the Red Sea, where the crop failure exceeded 80%. More than 40% of the harvest was lost in Tigre, 44% in Wollo and 35% in Harar, the Ogaden desert region that juts into Somalia. Altogether, nine of Ethiopia's 14 provinces are suffering food shortages.

In this age of the green revolution, with crop yields skyrocketing, drought no longer automatically means famine. India, for example, is now in the midst of its worst drought in decades, but because it has a food surplus and a relatively organized system for feeding the hungry, few are expected to starve. Usually it is the combination of drought, mismanagement and civil war that brings famine. Ethiopia is afflicted with all three.

Getting the food to the hungry is made more difficult by inadequate port facilities, poor or nonexistent roads and insufficient planes and trucks to transport food to rural areas. But the biggest block in the pipeline is civil strife. The government is battling 23 rebel groups and factions in every part of the country. The two strongest insurgent armies are in Tigre and Eritrea, the provinces hit hardest by the drought. Eritrea has been in rebellion against the government ever since it was annexed by Ethiopia in 1962, and a guerrilla movement began building in Tigre in 1977.

During the last famine the rebels and international agencies had a policy of live and let live. But in late October, Eritrean People's Liberation Front guerrillas attacked an unguarded convoy of 23 trucks on its way from Asmara, capital of Eritrea, to Mekele, capital of Tigre. One driver was killed, and the trucks—loaded with 674 tons of food, enough to feed 30,000 people for a month—were destroyed by grenades. The E.P.L.F. claimed that some of the trucks contained military equipment, a charge that U.N. officials deny. Since then, the E.P.L.F. has attacked two Ethiopian military-civilian convoys that reportedly included food trucks.

The rebel sabotage brought the entire operation for Tigre and Eritrea to a halt for more than a month. Not only were the convoys under threat from Eritrean and Tigrean rebels, but even those agencies willing to risk assault could not move their trucks because the government closed the roads. "If many people die this year and next, it will not be due to drought but the politico-military situation," said one relief worker.

Convoys are moving again during daylight hours in Eritrea, with agency staffers driving the perilous roads at their own risk. But much of Tigre remains cut off; the Tigrean People's Liberation Front has demanded that the Mengistu government rescind its resettlement policy before it guarantees the safety of the food trucks.

Resettlement is an ambitious government scheme to move 1.5 million peasants from the overcrowded and barren north to the more fertile south. While international agricultural officials acknowledge that the program is a legitimate effort to solve some of the country's long-term social and economic problems, they charge that in past years the Mengistu government carried it out with unnecessary cruelty. According to some Western diplomats, the regime broke up families and forced villagers to move to camps that had no housing, no water, no health facilities and often no food. Of the 600,000 northerners who were resettled during the last famine, 100,000 died, according to Doctors Without Borders, a Paris-based relief group. The government ejected the group from the country at the end of 1985 after labeling its charges "preposterous." Nonetheless, Mengistu suspended the resettlement program in early 1986, only to restart it last month. So far, 7,000 "volunteers" have been moved south, and the government plans to transfer up to 300,000 next year.

The rebels assert that the real motive behind the program is to persecute Eritreans and Tigreans and drain the rebel fronts of potential recruits. Dr. Frederick Machmer, head of the U.S. relief team in Addis Ababa, believes the rebels are disrupting the aid effort so the international community will accept "that they are a force to be reckoned with and that they control areas of the north." Geldof, whose organization owned some of the trucks blown up in October, finds the tactics of both sides despicable. Said he last week: "To attack food trucks and seal off roads in these conditions is tantamount to mass murder."

The convoy attacks are all the more tragic because the international agencies were well prepared to cope with the famine this time around. The U.N. and the Ethiopian government kept abreast of agricultural conditions through an "early warning system" that included satellite surveillance of farming areas. Months ago, at the first sign that the rains might fail, the agencies acted. One of the first nations to dispatch aid was the U.S., whose Agency for International Development is still bitter over charges that it did not do enough during the last crisis.

AID dispatched 10,000 tons of food to Ethiopia on May 7, when crops failed in Harar. When the rains failed in the highlands in July, 10,000 tons were sent to bolster the country's reserves. And when it was certain that a new drought had begun in August, the U.S. approved the delivery of 115,000 tons, valued at $43 million. The first 30,000 tons are scheduled to arrive this month.

In Washington, Reagan Administration officials speak proudly of the U.S. contribution two years ago and now. Said one: "The last time around we got criticized for not doing enough, but we spent half a billion dollars trying to help starving people. What did the Russians do? They gave Ethiopia two planes." The Soviets insist they gave much more, including food, medicine, blankets and tents, and they are pouring in humanitarian aid now. Western experts say these claims are overstated.

Despite a continuing flow of arms from Moscow, Western diplomats suspect that the Soviets are not happy with their ally. When Mengistu visited Moscow in April, Soviet Leader Mikhail Gorbachev cautioned him to "proceed from realities and not outrun stages of development." Politburo Member Lev Zaikov was reportedly blunter when he visited Addis Ababa in September.

Last Saturday the U.N.'s Food and Agriculture Organization (FAO), which has been monitoring the drought situation from the start, issued a new report that increased the projected food need for 1988 from 950,000 tons to 1.3 million tons. So far, 550,000 tons have been promised by aid groups, or 42% of what will be needed. Michael Priestley, the U.N. official who coordinates the overall relief program in Ethiopia, stresses that more aid must be committed immediately. "It will take five months for a food shipment to get here if it is pledged this week," he said. "If we don't get the pledges now, there will be a break in the pipeline."

Forty-two thousand tons of food are currently in Ethiopia, with shipments arriving daily. By the end of this month, an additional 90,000 tons are expected, thus ensuring Ethiopia enough food through Christmas if some of the hungry are put on three-quarter rations. Relief workers are racing to distribute food. Rebel attacks and logistical problems have cost valuable time, however, and in the past few days the pace has quickened. Last week three transport planes left Europe for Ethiopia and are now airlifting food from Asmara, near the Red Sea port of Assab, to Mekele. The European Community, which organized the operation, eventually hopes to deploy ten planes. "The airlift is vital," says Priestley. "But 700,000 people in Tigre need food immediately, and the aircraft must be backed up by trucks. If we don't start widespread distribution, there will be famine camps."

FAO officials are also sounding the alarm. "In terms of organization, we are better equipped this time," says Peter Newhouse, a senior FAO economist. "But if donation decisions are not made immediately, and it's not raining in Ethiopia by March, then we are in trouble. We will move from a disaster to a catastrophe."

The tragedy that afflicts Ethiopia also plagues much of Africa. The belt of privation cuts a ragged T through the continent. The horizontal bar is made up of the famine-prone nations of the Sahel; the vertical bar extends from the Sudan down through Uganda, Tanzania, Malawi, Zambia, Mozambique and into tiny Lesotho. To the west of this scythe of hunger lie Zaïre and Angola.

The worst threat of famine is in war-torn countries and their neighbors. Sudan, for example, is home to about 975,000 refugees, 70%

from Ethiopia and the rest from Uganda, Zaïre, and Chad. While traditionally gracious hosts to those in need, the Sudanese are also enduring a drought and are rapidly losing patience. Earlier this year Ethiopian refugees streaming into the Sudanese border town of Kassala were attacked by mobs. "We have been involved in refugee problems since the Congo crisis of the 1960s," say Al-Amin Abdul Latif, Sudan's Ambassador to Egypt. "Enough is enough."

One of Africa's neediest cases is Mozambique, the former Portuguese colony on the Indian Ocean that is almost as poor as Ethiopia. Mozambique has been embroiled in civil war from the moment it became independent in 1975. Its economic infrastructure has been destroyed by rebels, and the U.N. estimates that 6 million people face starvation in the west and north, where reliefworkers are afraid to go. Says a Mozambican army officer who recently toured some of the worst-hit areas: "I talked to people who had barely enough flesh to cover their skeletons. Their bones made noises under the skin."

In Angola, where the Soviet-backed government is battling South African-supported rebels, the famine is mostly man-made. In some disputed areas, there are acres of ripe grain that cannot be harvested because the fields are laced with finger-size mines. Relief convoys find few passable roads and are in constant danger of attack from rebels. Though statistics are hard to come by, those who suffer most in Angola seem to be the young. The U.N. Office of Emergency Operations reported in 1986 that up to 45% of the children in Huambo province, where guer-

rilla activity is common, suffered from malnutrition.

Another nation in agony is Malawi, which is suffering from both disastrous crop failures and an influx of 300,000 refugees from neighboring Mozambique. "Unless massive food supplies are brought in urgently," says a Western aid official, thousands will die.

Even when the rains come, they can be a cruel gift. Heavy downpours swept over parts of southern Africa two weeks ago, breaking a harsh drought. But they also destroyed some of the more delicate plants that had survived the dry spell, and the soggy ground will hamper distribution of maize meal recently shipped into the area by the U.N.

Will Africa, fabulously rich in natural resources, ever end the cycle of war, disease and overpopulation that helps to keep it poor and famished? Most African governments, including those much less radical than Ethiopia, continue to be wedded to quasi-socialist, postcolonial economic policies that reduce agricultural productivity, even as populations soar and create a voracious demand for more food. "In contemporary Africa, both rural starvation and rising levels of urban employment are the outcome of a set of agricultural policies designed to subsidize the cost of living of urban consumers at the expense of rural producers," says Michael Lofchie, an Africa expert at UCLA. Since 75% of Africa's people still live in rural areas, such a policy is a prescription for deepening poverty."

Only now have some governments, encouraged by the U.S. and Western Europe, acknowledged that farmers have to be given financial incentives to produce more.

With the continent $200 billion in debt to the West, the lending nations have not hesitated to twist arms. The E.C. and the WorldBank are currently withholding $250 million in development aid for Ethiopia until its leaders agree to raise artificially low prices for agricultural products and allow farmers to sell more of their products on the open market. "For humanitarian aid, there are no conditions," says an E.C. spokesman. "For structural aid, there are conditions."

In Ethiopia, says Jay F. Morris, deputy U.S. AID administrator, "the problem is fundamental. They are taking a bad ecological situation and making it worse. By forcing farmers who do grow more than they consume to sell to the state at prices below the cost of production, they are not providing the incentive to produce the maximum that the land, however poor, would yield." Ethiopia's food production now totals 6.8 million tons a year, with little prospect for future growth; Western experts say the country will require an estimated 2 million tons of imported food in 1990. It almost seems, says Morris with a sigh, that the Ethiopians are "determined to render themselves a perpetual beggar nation."

Meanwhile, the people of Ethiopia seem rich only in patience. As the sun climbs in the sky, those awaiting food donations outside Wukro quietly sit on their haunches. One man, Gebre Yohanes Haile, 50, has brought along his chief resource: his ox. His family is sick with hunger, and so only he and the animal made the journey. Thus he will receive just one ration: twelve kilos of wheat, two of beans and two of oil. He will sell his ox for $200, and then pay $150 for 100 kilos of grain, twice the usual cost. "We have food for today," Gebre says. "I don't know about tomorrow."

A dull roar rises from the crowd. Registration is over, and distribution has begun. Men in white shirts decorated with big red crosses dole out the rations. Elders load the 100-lb. bags onto their backs and scurry back to their village groups, shoving people out of the way as they go. As the grain is divided, the people smile. They laugh. Some even sing. They are happy. They have food.

"They won't be laughing in a couple of weeks' time," says an Ethiopian official with tears in his eyes. "Now they smile even on half rations because today they can exist." His gloomy prediction seems true. The road between Mekele and Wukro remains closed most of the time. And nobody knows just when the next food convoy will come. ∎

Does Helping Really Help?

By Otto Friedrich

Am I my brother's keeper? God answered Cain's evasive question by putting him under an eternal curse, and so the traditional answer has been a cautious affirmative. But what if my brother already has a keeper, one who has a gun and who claims the right to decide whether my brother will get any of the food I send him?

That is more or less the question that bedevils Western officials as they face the horrors of another famine in the Ethiopia of Lieut. Colonel Mengistu Haile Mariam. All too clear in the public memory are those televised pictures from 1984–85 of starving children with their matchstick arms, their swollen bellies and their huge, staring eyes. The public may also remember reports of relief shipments being taxed $50 a ton to help finance Mengistu's 225,000-man army, the largest in black Africa, and of sacks of Western grain rotting on the docks or disappearing into the black market.

As if Mengistu's tyranny were not bad enough, the secessionist rebels in famine-threatened Eritrea are now showing that they too can and will interfere with United Nations food shipments. Says Manuel Pietri of the Paris-based International Aid Against Hunger: "There is a perverse game between the government and the rebels to make aid not work, unless, of course, they can turn it to their own advantage." But the stronger of the two parties, Mengistu's government, is the source of most of the trouble. Says an aid official in Washington: "I'll tell you what the government's three priorities are: fighting the rebels, fighting the rebels and fighting the rebels." Comments a colleague: "The Ethiopian government has the worst human rights record in Africa."

This sense of Ethiopia as a bottomless sinkhole for Western aid inspires some skeptical experts to wonder whether such assistance is really wise. Regular international rescue efforts do little to encourage recipients to learn to feed themselves, the skeptics argue, and a tougher approach just might force Ethiopia to mend its ways. "What will aid do?" asked Britain's *Economist* last month. "It will strengthen the dominion of Ethiopia's ignorant rulers. The weather is the only calamity not directly caused by Colonel Mengistu ... and his cronies. Their Russian advisers have taught them to run vast state farms that produce no food. Imitating Stalin's anti-kulak terror, they have shot 'hoarders and saboteurs' prudent enough to store grain ... Help for the starving may make some of them suffer more, and reinforce the grip of the government that caused them to starve. Yet something must be done."

But what? "The aid Ethiopians need is diplomatic pressure, not food," says Rony Brauman of Doctors Without Borders, a French charitable organization that was expelled from Ethiopia two years ago for criticizing Mengistu's brutally handled program to resettle residents of rebel-threatened areas. "If we have a duty, it is to pressure the government to change its policies. Otherwise, in two or three years, we're going to see the same bodies, the same TV footage, the same appeals from humanitarian agencies to come to the rescue." But as a French government official asks, "Who is going to take the responsibility for

Otto Friedrich is a writer for *Time* magazine.

Source: From *Time*, December 21, 1987. Reported by Alastair Matheson/Nairobi and Tala Skari/Paris.

saying 'All right, now we're going to stop all aid. Finished. Not one more sack of flour'? At that point, you've reached the political and moral limits of the debate."

What must be done, according to U.S. Congressmen Toby Roth, a Wisconsin Republican, and William H. Gray III, a Pennsylvania Democrat, is to put economic pressure on the Mengistu regime until it stops violating the basic human and civil rights of its people. Last January they introduced a bill, now cosponsored by 81 other Congressmen, that would prohibit all U.S. loans and new private investments in Ethiopia and would ban all imports of the country's coffee, its main export. "Ethiopia is a stench in the nostrils of humanity," says Roth. "We are not going to stop humanitarian aid. There are people starving, and we want to help those people. But we don't want to help Mengistu. We are in a dilemma. It is like trying to pick up a porcupine."

The Roth-Gray legislation has been introduced several times before, however, and it has not come close to passing. Others in Congress wonder how making Ethiopia even more impoverished would help its starving masses. Nor is there much chance that such pressure would make the authoritarian Mengistu modify his tactics. "If we were simply to fold our hands and say, 'Well, we'll allow 6, 7, 8 million people to die,' I don't know that there is any evidence that that would change their agricultural policy," says Jay F. Morris, deputy administrator of the U.S. Agency for International Development (AID). "For most governments, to lose a million of their citizens would generally force some sort of change in policy, but

it didn't there. So I would argue that the withdrawal of our assistance would probably doom more innocents to a meaningless death . . . Given our American tradition of providing help, it would be barbaric for us to turn our backs."

The idea that governments have a moral obligation to feed the inhabitants of other countries is a relatively recent notion. For centuries, hunger was a major weapon of war. Starvation was taken for granted during the great sieges of the Middle Ages and the religious wars of early modern times. Victims of 19th century famines in Ireland and Russia were encouraged to emigrate elsewhere. Charity was basically a responsibility of the church, or of no one.

When Britain blockaded the German coast during World War I, it was considered somewhat quixotic for a young U.S. official named Herbert Hoover to organize a relief program that fed 10 million civilians in German-occupied Belgium. Early in World War II, when Germany once more occupied Belgium and Britain again blockaded the coast, the then neutral U.S. considered renewing its Belgian relief—until Winston Churchill adamantly forbade it.

In the half-century since then, feeding the world's hungry has become an accepted part of Western foreign policy, sometimes for political gain but often as an end in itself. Many people consider it morally wrong not to give food to poorer countries when the West has so much of it, especially in this year of near record U.S. farm output and a growing West European food glut. "If there is any politics in what we are doing," says Frederick Machmer, U.S. AID chief in Addis Ababa, "it is the fact that the U.S.

public would be very angry if we didn't give food aid to the Ethiopians." To Brother Gus, an Irish missionary who works in Addis Ababa, the matter is simple. "If you can stomach thousands of children dying for lack of food because you don't like the government, that is your problem," he says. "My problem is to try to feed them all, children, the parents, the aged, the young, wherever they may be."

Despite the criticisms of Mengistu's regime, some of his heavy-handed policies appear to have rationales behind them. It is true, of course, that rebellious Eritrea, governed as an Italian colony from 1890 until World War II, has a tribal makeup different from the rest of Ethiopia. Yet the country as a whole contains more than 80 distinct ethnic groups, and poverty-stricken Eritrea could hardly survive as an independent entity. It is also likely that Mengistu's motives for forcibly transporting 600,000 peasants from Eritrea and neighboring Tigre to the less populated southern part of the country were more political than humanitarian. Nonetheless, a number of Western experts have agreed that those parched and eroded northern provinces cannot support their inhabitants as well as the more fertile south.

Similar reasoning applies to Mengistu's much criticized policy of "villagization," which coerces peasants to move from their scattered farms into village collectives. "What makes developing countries really backward is their inability to benefit from modern science and technology," Mengistu told *Time* in an interview last year. "People live in isolation on hilltops . . . It is only when you have peasants together in villages that they can benefit from ... technology to combat difficult conditions."

Though Mengistu is widely blamed for the disaster, the series of famines actually began in 1973, under the inept and autocratic Emperor Haile Selassie. Far from seeking help, the Ethiopian government in the 1970s strenuously denied that any famine existed, and U.N. officials diplomatically remained silent about the tragedy.

Some reputable outside observers think criticism of the Mengistu regime has been exaggerated. One of them is Father Thomas Fitzpatrick, director of Caritas International, the Rome-based Catholic emergency-aid organization. "There was not massive corruption or diversion during the 1984 famine," says Fitzpatrick, an American who supervised Catholic aid in Ethiopia at the time. "There weren't distribution foul-ups to the extent that has been reported. It's true that some ships were backed up in the harbors. True, it rained once unexpectedly, and some grain was exposed and began to rot. But no more than 3% of all the aid that went through our hands went to waste." Even if the complaints about Mengistu were true, Fitzpatrick adds, "to the extent that food given to a country

saves the government of that country the foreign exchange it would have to spend on that food—O.K., food aid helps support that government. But you have to ask, 'Without food aid, would the government spend less on its war effort, or would it let these people starve?' "

To Mengistu's critics, all such defenses are simply evidence that those who want to provide aid become prisoners of the system: anyone who faults the dictator risks being expelled, like France's Doctors Without Borders. "We have to be discreet," concedes Frank Conlon, Africa program director for Lutheran World Relief. "In relief situations, you often don't have a lot of time for dialogue." Says Laura Kullenberg, director of the Horn of Africa program run by Oxfam America: "This is a life-and-death situation, and our choices are limited. Our mission is to make sure food gets to people in need, not to make a political point."

U.S. officials estimate that there is now enough food committed to Ethiopia to last until spring, but whether it gets out of the warehouses and to the hungry depends heavily on the available transportation. Relief officials estimate they need nearly 300 additional trucks

to haul food from distribution centers to rural areas, but the Mengistu regime has thus far provided only 100. So welfare officials are falling back on a vastly expensive airlift. It is notable that the Soviets, who sell Mengistu most of his weapons, have sent very little in the way of either food or transport.

"What will we in the West do?" observes Pietri of International Aid Against Hunger. "We will end by choosing the most costly, screwed-up solution that benefits the least amount of people, and we'll do it in a spectacular way." But just how much real choice is there? "The ethic is an absolute one," says Daniel Callahan, director of the Hastings Center, a New York-based institute that studies moral issues. "The price of not providing aid is a basic denial of humanity, far greater than the possible political damage. It may indeed help a corrupt and totalitarian regime, but you cannot ignore the fundamental necessity of life." So as the West wonders whether it should bail out that infuriating regime once again, the answer appears to be unpleasant but nonetheless unavoidable: yes, because everyone is his brother's keeper when that brother is starving. ■

The Global Environment   *Reassessing the Threat*

If present trends continue, the world in 2000 will be more crowded, more polluted, less stable ecologically, and more vulnerable to disruption than the world we live in now.

—*Lead sentence of* The Global 2000 Report to the President, *published in 1980.*

[I]t is dead wrong.

—*Heritage Foundation scholar Julian L. Simon's assessment of the* Global 2000 *report in* The Resourceful Earth, *1984.*

Everything that Global 2000 *said has come to pass.*

—Worldwatch Institute president, Lester R. Brown, 1987.

A series of environmental accidents in two recent years has jolted public attention. On November 1, 1986, a Swiss chemical plant accidentally released toxic waste into the Rhine, polluting the water up

Source: From *Great Decisions 1988,* Foreign Policy Association, New York, 1988.

to 400 miles away. On April 26, 1986, an accident at a Soviet nuclear power plant in Chernobyl sent a radioactive cloud into the atmosphere; 31 people died. More than 2,300 died in December 1984, when an accident at a pesticide plant in Bhopal, India, released toxic fumes into the air.

Like supernovas, such accidents burst into view suddenly, disappear from the headlines quickly, and leave behind a residue of public concern over the health of the earth's environment—that delicate balance of resources such as air, water, soil and energy upon which human life depends. But the most serious threats to the environment are rarely in the headlines—they are not accidents but day-to-day human actions in a rapidly industrializing world.

Drive a car. Turn on the air-conditioning. Cut down a tree. Put on hair spray. These activities are believed to contribute to acid rain, depletion of the ozone layer and climate change. Each of these actions, multiplied by whatever percentage of the earth's 5 billion people perform them, is gradually changing the earth's environment.

Scientists believe that there are thresholds of damage to the environment, which, once crossed, cannot be undone. But what these thresholds are and when they are crossed is a source of continuing debate that has caused an almost constant reassessment of the nature of the threats to the environment.

On the one hand, the earth appears to be remarkably resilient, responding to proper care. Only a few years after it introduced improved management techniques and reduced its rate of population growth, China achieved food self-sufficiency. Eighteen years after the

U.S. passed clean air and water legislation, both are visibly cleaner. And thanks to energy conservation, among other things, the U.S. is less vulnerable to sharp price hikes of Mideast oil such as those that were so disruptive in the 1970s.

On the other hand, because so much is still unknown, damaging changes can take place much more quickly than anticipated. It has long been known that aerosol spray cans release chemicals into the air that damage the ozone layer, the section of the stratosphere that forms a protective layer around the earth. It had been assumed until recently that the damage would not threaten human health for at least a century. Research has suggested the damage may be imminent.

Foreign Policy Agenda

Environmental decisions frequently involve some trade-offs between protecting the environment and promoting economic growth. But when tacked on to foreign-policy making, the decisions are more difficult because they can mean a trade-off between improving one country's environment and another's economic growth. For example, it is widely accepted that air pollutants from U.S. smelters and power plants fall as acid rain in Canada, damaging that country's lakes and forests. Cleaning up the emissions would cost the U.S. billions of dollars. The cost of not doing so would be a severe strain in relations with an important ally, as well as potential damage to parts of the U.S. What policy should the U.S. follow?

From the perspective of national security, the most serious potential environmental threat to the U.S. is a shortage of natural

resources such as oil or strategic metals. Many believe that dependence on such metals as titanium or platinum has made the U.S. more friendly to their source, South Africa, than it might otherwise be. How can the U.S. best protect itself from resource shortages?

The ecological soundness of other countries is also in the U.S. interest. "U.S. national interests in promoting human freedom and economic growth can be undermined by instability in other countries related to environmental degradation, population, pressures, and resource scarcity," said Richard E. Benedick, State Department environmental affairs director. What policies should the U.S. encourage other countries to follow to achieve ecological soundness?

A Look Backward

The Industrial Revolution of the 19th century ushered in the first major man-made changes in the environment. The use of coal to heat homes and to fuel factories caused severe air pollution. Industrial cities were enveloped in a haze of dirty air, smelling of rotten eggs because of its sulfur content.

Until World War II, most countries considered pollution an acceptable price to pay for progress. In fact, some boasted that it was a sign of progress. But after the war a series of incidents focused attention on the environment. In 1952, a particularly bad London "fog"—in reality polluted air—killed 3,000 people in a few days. In 1962, Rachel Carson's book *Silent Spring* described some of the dangerous side effects of the insecticide DDT. In 1969, the heavily polluted Cuyahoga River near Cleveland, Ohio, caught fire.

The UN-sponsored Stockholm Conference of 1972 was important in drawing world attention to the environment and to the possibility of international cooperation on environmental issues. The delegates from 113 countries agreed that the environment should be protected, although there was a sharp dividing line between the industrialized countries, which were worried about pollution, overpopulation, and resource conservation, and the developing countries, which were worried about hunger, disease, illiteracy and unemployment.

Limits to Growth?

The 1973 oil shortage was a powerful signal that the earth's resources might have limits. Although the crisis was more a result of price manipulation on the part of the members of the Organization of Petroleum Exporting Countries (OPEC) than an actual shortage of oil, the consequences for Americans were the same—high prices, long gas lines. Some believed it heralded the beginning of an "era of limits" in which more people would compete for fewer resources.

In 1977 President Jimmy Carter commissioned a report, known as *Global 2000,* to forecast the state of the world's resources at the end of the century. The report's prognosis for the earth's future—if present trends continued—was a frightening one. Excessive population growth, deforestation, energy depletion, food shortages—these were to be the harvests of progress.

No sooner had the official assessment been published than a reassessment began. One of the most comprehensive attacks on the *Global 2000* report was a book

edited by Julian L. Simon and the late Herman Kahn called *The Resourceful Earth: A Response to Global 2000.* They concluded that there was no reason that the earth could not sustain many more people, and that overall standards of living would probably improve.

The reassessment struck a responsive chord with the Reagan Administration. Government intervention to protect the environment was not high on President Ronald Reagan's list of priorities. Candidate Reagan got off to a rocky start with the environmental movement when he said, during one of his campaign speeches, that trees were a source of pollution. Relations were not improved by the appointment of James G. Watt, an outspoken advocate of turning public land and resources over to private developers, as his first secretary of the interior.

But the downgrading of the environment as an issue was not solely a result of Reagan's presidency. Not long after he took office, OPEC oil prices collapsed, ending the sense of scarcity that had made conservation seem urgent. Also, many of the benefits of the legislation of the past decade, including the 1970 Clean Air and Clean Water acts, had come to fruition. U.S. air was cleaner, U.S. water was cleaner. Faced with pressing economic issues, environmental initiatives were put on a back burner.

A New Report

In April 1987 the UN released its own assessment of the state of the environment. The "Brundtland Report" of the World Commission on Environment and Development, named for its chairwoman, the prime minister of Norway, con-

cludes that in most of the world environmental protection and economic growth are inseparable goals. It therefore recommends that international efforts to improve the environment must also address underlying issues such as poverty and a high population growth rate that cause people to abuse the environment.

THE WORLD'S RESOURCES: AN ASSESSMENT

The *Global 2000* report was controversial when it was released and it remains so. Even seven years into the report's projections, there is no agreement as to whether what it forecast is happening. Atmospheric problems—ozone depletion, climate change and acid rain—appear to be as serious as anticipated. Many resource shortages, on the other hand, appear less critical, giving credence to those who would leave management of such resources to the free market. A roundup of some of the major issues follows.

The State of the Air

In August 1985, a NASA satellite 600 miles from earth confirmed the existence of a hole in the ozone layer above Antarctica. Ozone is a deep-blue gas made up of oxygen atoms that is found throughout the earth's atmosphere, from ground level to some 30 miles above the earth. At ground level, ozone is considered a health hazard as it is one of the components of smog; but from middle levels of the stratosphere on up, which is where the absence of the gas was discovered, it has a protective function, which is to shield the earth from some of the sun's ultraviolet rays.

The hole first appeared as early as 1977, but went unnoticed because the NASA satellite that could have detected it had automatically discarded the unusual results. The hole caught most scientists by surprise because until its discovery the consensus was that ozone depletion would take place at a rate of between 2% and 4% per decade. No sharp falloff had been anticipated.

Scientists hypothesize that the hole has been caused by an increase in a man-made substance called chlorofluorocarbons or CFCs. CFCs have been called the Boy Scouts of industrial chemicals because they are neither poisonous nor flammable. But once released into the atmosphere, they soar upward toward its outer reaches and "eat" the protective ozone. If enough of the ozone layer is depleted, it could mean unacceptably high levels of ultraviolet radiation, which could cause a sharp increase in skin cancer. They could also cause damage to the body's immune system and harm plant and aquatic ecosystems, as well as altering the earth's climate.

The U.S. has been aware for some time that CFCs damaged the outer ozone layer. In 1978, the EPA and the Food and Drug Administration banned the use of those compounds as propellants in aerosol sprays, one of the major sources of CFCs. (Today, substitutes are used as propellants.) But the decline from sprays was offset by an increase in the use of CFCs as coolants in car air-conditioners and refrigerators, as well as for packaging and insulation, the other major sources of CFCs. With increased CFC production by China and Western European countries, worldwide CFC levels have continued to rise.

In 1980, the UN Environment Program (UNEP) convened a meeting of scientists to discuss appropriate action. Although the negotiations got off to a slow start, they came to a dramatic conclusion in September 1987 when 24 nations plus the European Community signed a protocol designed to protect the earth's fragile ozone shield. Under the terms of the agreement, the signatories would freeze use of CFCs at 1986 levels in 1989 and would cut consumption of the chemicals by 20% by 1994. They agreed to cut consumption by an additional 30% by 1999.

The agreement represented a very real attempt at international cooperation. Said Benedick, who represented the U.S. at the talks, "For the first time the international community has initiated controls on production of an economically valuable commodity before there was tangible evidence of damage." Although the protocol was widely supported, some environmentalists wished that it had gone further. David Wirth, a lawyer for the Natural Resources Defense Council, has said that an 85% reduction in CFCs over the next five years is necessary to stabilize the ozone layer.

Climate Change: A Real Threat?

In 1957, scientists at an observatory in Mauna Loa, Hawaii, began to register an increased level of carbon dioxide (CO_2) in the atmosphere. The level has continued to rise each year since then. Many believe that CO_2 lets energy from the sun pass through but prevents the earth's heat from escaping, with the result that the earth's temperature is rising. This is called the greenhouse effect.

Scientists estimate that if industrial countries expand fossil fuel use 4% per year, by the year 2030 the amount of CO_2 in the atmosphere will be double preindustrial levels. The result is expected to be an increase in average temperature of just over 5 degrees Fahrenheit within the next 45 years. By contrast, during the last Ice Age, when sheets of ice covered much of Europe and North America, the earth's average temperature was only about 5 degrees colder than it is today.

There would also be shifts in rainfall patterns associated with a CO_2 rise. The result will be a drastic shift in the world's agriculture. The Sahara Desert could once again be fertile, the Great Plains, a desert. As the temperature rises, the oceans will slowly warm by absorbing heat from the atmosphere and together with melting ice will cause sea levels to rise.

The greenhouse effect remains a controversial theory, however, because of the difficulties in measuring climate change. Climate is not a constant. According to Professor H. E. Landsberg of the University of Maryland, ". . .rhythms of decades and centuries are part of the global climate system." Using data going back to the 16th century, Landsberg said that short-term shifts in climate are not unusual. Other skeptics note that only about 10 years ago the National Center for Atmospheric Research released a report saying the earth was getting colder.

There is agreement, however, that the amount of CO_2 in the atmosphere has increased greatly in this century, and this is attributed mainly to two sources: the combustion of oil, primarily by automobiles, and deforestation.

When trees are burned or left to decompose after forests are cleared, they release carbon. From 1860 to the present, the combustion of fossil fuels has been the source of 185 billion tons of carbon. During that same period, forest clearing caused more than 100 billion tons to be released. The U.S. is the largest generator of carbon today, followed by the Soviet Union.

The U.S. has participated in international conferences on global warming and is active in research on this problem. The Reagan Administration, however, has been skeptical about the likelihood of climate change, but has said that if a global warming is in effect, the best way to stop it would be to substitute nuclear- for oil-produced energy and to discourage deforestation.

Others would like to see more immediate corrective action. Changes advocated include funding research for nonnuclear alternatives to fossil fuels, and international campaigns to stop deforestation and to clean up emissions in Third World countries.

Ironically, the 1979 energy crisis may temporarily have accomplished what negotiations could not. The second oil crisis of that decade boosted oil prices dramatically and forced the major oil-using countries to take a more serious look at conservation. They began conserving fuel and therefore generating less carbon. Since then, carbon emissions have grown at an encouragingly low rate.

Acid Rain

In 1983 West Germany decided to survey the state of its forests. It found that 34% of the trees were suffering from some sort of damage. The next year's survey found 50%, and the 1986 survey found 52%. The Germans have named this problem *Waldsterben*—forest death. The primary culprit is believed to be acid rain.

When certain compounds, specifically nitrogen oxide (NO_x) and sulfur dioxide (SO_2), are released into the atmosphere they are chemically transformed and then fall to earth as acids in rain, snow or fog. Acid rain is believed to harm trees by weakening their resistance to natural events, such as drought, insect attacks and frost. Acid rain is also believed to kill fish. There are no known human side effects.

Acid rain is a particularly contentious environmental issue because the fossil-fuel smelters and power plants that are the source of the offending emissions are oftentimes not in the countries that are suffering. In Europe, winds sweep the acid rain from the major producer, Britain, to the Scandinavian countries, which produce little. Canada claims that one half of the SO_2 that falls on its eastern provinces comes from the U.S.

Since coal is neither expensive nor in short supply, its usage is unlikely to decrease; in fact, many developing countries project increased coal use. Environmentalists argue, therefore, that the best way of reducing acid rain is to establish emission controls. In March 1984, nine European countries and Canada established the "30% club," so called because they committed themselves to reduce 1980 levels of SO_2 by at least 30% over the next decade. The club was later joined by Bulgaria, East Germany and the Soviet Union, whose coal usage, already great, is expected to increase.

The U.S. has not been willing to join. Administration spokesmen argue that while the Europeans are just getting involved in such issues, U.S. legislation passed between 1973 and 1983 brought about a 28% drop in SO_2 emissions. U.S. coal-burning electric power plants have already spent billions on scrubbers—equipment using wet lime or limestone—to remove most of the emissions. Further pollution controls are too expensive, the Reagan Administration has argued, in the absence of a more definitive link between coal and acid rain.

Safe Water

For many, contamination of the water supply is a much more imminent concern than a disaster such as Chernobyl. Particularly worrisome to a lot of environmental activists are the health-threatening effects of toxic waste dumps, which, if not properly handled, seep into towns' water supplies. In 1980, 710 families from the town of Love Canal, outside of Niagara Falls, N.Y., were evacuated from their homes when chemicals from a buried waste dump were found to be seeping into their basements.

The health emergency at Love Canal prompted Congress to create a $1.6 billion Superfund in 1980 to clean up abandoned hazardous waste dumps. The Superfund legislation was renewed in 1986. As of 1985, only 6 hazardous-waste sites had been completely cleaned up; an estimated 1,400 to 2,200 remain to be cleaned up. The costs are estimated at between $10 billion and $100 billion, the range being so wide because there are many abandoned sites about which little is known.

In November 1986, water safety became an international issue when a toxic waste spill by a Swiss chemical plant caused severe damage to the Rhine river, an important source of water and fish for the European countries that share it. In some parts of the Rhine, all living creatures were killed. Although the Swiss firm has said it will pay some reparations, the damage to the Rhine will cost billions to repair and may take anywhere from 2 to 20 years.

Ironically, the European countries that border the Rhine are signatories to a variety of treaties regulating their usage of that river, but not one deals with how to assign responsibility for pollution. In other words, it remains unclear how to determine how much Sandoz should pay and how to force it to pay if it doesn't want to. Negotiations to set in writing arrangements for dealing with further Rhine spills are expected.

Energy Resources

The successful conservation of oil and the small but increasing use of renewable fuels have enhanced national security by cushioning the U.S. from disruptions from hostile sources. Compared with 1977, the peak year of U.S. oil consumption, when 47% was imported and 17% came from Arab members of OPEC, in 1986 the U.S. imported 33% and depended on Arab OPEC for 7%.

The drop in oil imports reflects a combination of free-market and government actions. The OPEC price shocks raised the price of oil, making it profitable for the U.S. drillers to produce. The high prices, as well as congressional legislation, encouraged manufacturers to make cars and other

products more energy-efficient. The recession of 1981–83 caused a sharp drop in economic growth, which meant that oil use declined.

At the same time, renewable energy projects have come to play a more important role than expected, thanks in part to tax incentives. They now provide about 5% of all U.S. energy needs. Sources of renewable energy are wind, water, the sun, and waste materials from which alcohol fuels are derived. They are so-labeled to distinguish them from oil and coal, which, once used, cannot be used again— for any practical time frame.

Does this mean the U.S. is protected from future OPEC shocks? Those who say no argue that over the long term the U.S. will be more vulnerable than ever because it is depleting its own reserves rapidly. At the 1985 rate of consumption, according to Worldwatch Institute analyst Christopher Flavin, the "ultimate depletion of global oil resources is between 50 and 88 years away." This view got some support from an Energy Department report in 1987 that predicted serious overdependence on Mideast oil by the mid-1990s.

Those who say yes believe that there are vastly more oil resources in the earth than have been projected. They note that projections as far back as 1885 have consistently underestimated the amount of oil available. By the time oil really does run out, they argue, the U.S. can turn to coal or nuclear power.

Nuclear Energy

There have been no new nuclear plants ordered for construction in the U.S. since the 1979 Three Mile Island accident in Pennsylvania. However, this could

change. In February 1987, the staff of the U.S. Nuclear Regulatory Commission drafted a proposal that would allow controversial projects at Shoreham, N.Y., and Seabrook, N.H., to go forward.

Worldwide, 15% of electricity is nuclear-generated and the percentage is expected to rise to 20% by 1990. Dr. Hans Blix, director-general of the International Atomic Energy Agency (IAEA), said that to produce with coal the amount of electricity that the world gets today from nuclear energy would require the entire U.S. coal production. "We are dealing with a grown-up industry," Blix observed, "not an infant one. . ."

The accident at Chernobyl was seen by many environmentalists to be evidence of the great threat that nuclear energy poses to the environment. It was caused by human error during the course of a safety check. When the accident took place, a radioactive plume was spewed into the air by a raging fire that lasted for 10 days. The winds carried the waste around the earth, and within days much of Europe was experiencing the highest level of radioactive fallout ever recorded there.

Advocates of nuclear energy, such as Blix, believe that it still poses far less of a threat to the environment than its alternatives. "Nuclear power stations do not emit any SO_2, NO_x, or CO_2," said Blix. "They do not contribute to acid rain, dying forests or a change of the global climate. . ."

Biological Diversity

There are some 1.5 million identified forms of life. Scientists suspect that between 5 million and 10 million additional forms exist, but many evolve and disappear before they are identified. According to the Worldwatch Institute, the coming years may see a loss of tropical species almost equivalent to the mass extinction of the dinosaur period.

One reason for this is the decline of the tropical rain forests. The broadleafed evergreen canopy that is characteristic of many of these forests shelters an amazing variety of different habitats. As a result, although they take up only 7% of the earth's land area, rain forests are the home of a disproportionate number of animal and plant species, perhaps one half of those on earth. In recent years, many rain forests have been cut down to make way for development. In addition, degradation of forests makes them more vulnerable to fire. In 1983, a severe forest fire on the island of Borneo destroyed 3.5 million hectares of tropical rain forest, an area nearly the size of Taiwan.

Worldwatch Institute associate Edward C. Wolf has compared deforestation to Russian roulette. He is concerned that deforestation will lead to a loss of species that will sharply reduce the amount of biological diversity on earth, depriving humans of potentially important, though yet unknown, forms of plant and animal life. Just as research in hybrid grains yielded great results with the Green Revolution, so hybrid animals may provide unknown benefits. The yakow, for example, combines the hardiness of a yak with the higher milk production of a cow.

Conservation biologists favor setting aside "gene parks," large tracts of land reserved for endangered species where scientists could study the species' potential. This would be a more affirmative step than the Endangered Species Act of 1973, which simply requires the government to list those species that are endangered and forbids the hunting of and trade in the most threatened species.

Others believe that the current protection is sufficient. "One should not propose saving all species in their natural habitats, at any cost ... any more than one should propose a policy of saving all human lives at any cost," write Julian Simon and Aaron Wildavsky, professor of political science at the University of California. One way of preventing extinction is through seed banks, which store samples of rare species.

Soil Erosion

Soil erosion is the wearing away of topsoil by wind and rain. Americans faced an extreme example of soil erosion in 1934, when a severe drought hit the overworked farms of the prairie states. The resulting dust storms smothered crops, forcing many small farmers off their land.

Soil erosion is set in motion when increasing numbers of people try to grow more food on existing land or clear forests to expand their cropland or obtain wood for fuel or building material. When land is overworked and when trees disappear, the soil loses its ability to hold on to valuable nutrients, and water and the fertility of the soil begins to decline.

All countries today—developed and less-developed—face the problem of soil erosion. Since the mid-century, most countries have achieved great gains in agriculture, but at a cost: wide tracts of land, much of it marginal, have been overworked. By the late 1970s, soil erosion exceeded new soil formation on one third of U.S. cropland. In the 1985 Food Security Act the U.S. took an important step toward halting soil erosion by encouraging farmers to covert 45 million acres of highly erodible cropland (11% of U.S. land under cultivation) to grassland or trees by 1990.

Soil erosion is particularly damaging in parts of Africa because the rapidly growing population is so dependent on agriculture for food and money, and the decline in that continent's soil fertility has been a major cause of its decline in income. Government policies have been partly to blame. Many Third World governments hold down the price of food for city dwellers in an effort to win their political support. The low prices increase the city's demand for food, while lowering the farmers' profits, forcing them to farm on more and more marginal land. Political and social disruptions, such as civil war or a large influx of refugees, also contribute to soil erosion.

There are various methods to offset soil erosion, such as terracing, planting hedges or contour plowing. But underlying the discussion over the best way to help improve agricultural productivity in the Third World is another deeper and more divisive debate, that over the role of population.

Population Growth

In 1987 the world's population topped the 5 billion mark, a threefold increase since the turn of the century. At about the same time, the two most populous countries in the world, China and India, achieved food self-sufficiency. Two theories as to how this seemingly paradoxical chain of events happened illustrate the basic difference in views on population.

Many environmentalists believe that population is the single most important factor that determines environment. In their view, a fairly simple equation describes the state of the world's environment: resources divided by population. "The more children there are in the average family, the lower the quality of life for society as a whole," said Lester Brown.

In 1950 Western Europe produced only slightly more grain per capita than Africa. By 1985, Western Europe was producing over three times the amount of grain per capita that Africa was. Total grain production over that 35-year period grew by 164% in Western Europe, by 129% in Africa. Both continents succeeded in increasing their food production greatly, yet one has a food surplus, the other hunger. The difference, Brown concludes, is in Africa's high population growth rate versus Western Europe's slower growth rate.

China's radical turnaround, some environmentalists are convinced, is a result of its successful, though draconian, population measures that have brought about a sharp decrease in population growth. They view India, on the other hand, as a more ephemeral success: they believe its food supply will ultimately be overtaken by population growth.

This viewpoint is vigorously contested by critics, among them President Reagan, who argue that from a demographic viewpoint, things are much better now than they ever have been. Economist Mark Perlman writes that "the outstanding demographic fact of our times is the relatively recent continued expansion of life expect-

ancy for virtually all age groups." Supporters of this view believe that the rate of population growth, which has been slowing over the course of the century, will eventually come to a halt when more countries are industrialized. They therefore tend to put priority on policies that will lead to development, rather than policies that will control population.

Proponents of this view attribute China's success in agriculture to its introduction of free-market mechanisms to its farmers, which made them more efficient. Africa's failure to sustain itself, they believe, is not caused by overpopulation, but by the actions of its governments that encourage inefficient policies.

Reflecting this view, the Reagan Administration has reversed the longstanding U.S. leadership of the population control movement. In August 1986, the U.S. announced it was withdrawing all financial support from the UN Fund for Population Activities (UNFPA), the international agency responsible for coordinating family planning programs in 134 countries. The ostensible reason was the reports of forced abortions in China, which receives UNFPA aid.

THE LINK TO FOREIGN POLICY

On February 18, 1987, the U.S. Environmental Protection Agency (EPA) released a reassessment of the problems posing the greatest risk to human health and the environment that suggested the agency may have been emphasizing the wrong ones. It redefined some issues that had loomed large in previous discussions on the environment, such as the management of

hazardous materials and wastes, as "high effort, low risk" issues. It assigned air pollution problems causing ozone depletion, acid rain and climate change a higher priority.

One striking aspect of the EPA's reassessment is that the top-ranked problems are all foreign policy issues. Of course, most environmental issues are international concerns to some degree, since the environment does not respect national boundaries. But air and water pollution issues are unique in that they cannot be resolved by the efforts of one nation alone, the way, for example, Congress could establish a superfund to clean up abandoned toxic waste sites.

Environment vs. Growth

Protecting the environment is expensive. In Japan, which has the strictest laws covering acid rain, pollution control accounts for 25% of the total cost of coal-generated electricity, an enormous sum. Environmental protection may add expenses that make it more difficult for a company to compete internationally. But the cost of not protecting the environment may also be prohibitive, both in terms of money and the quality of human life. Recovery from the accidents on the Rhine and in Chernobyl will take years and cost billions of dollars.

In the U.S., the environment versus economic growth debate is an important part of the discussion of acid rain policy. The Canadians blame U.S. pollution for the destruction of 13 salmon-bearing rivers in Nova Scotia and at least 1,600 lakes in Ontario. Another 1 million lakes are considered vulnerable to acid rain damage. The U.S. has restrictions on some of the emissions that are believed to cause acid rain, but the Canadians argue that these restrictions, passed in the 1970s, are inadequate.

In 1985, in an effort to improve strained relations, Reagan and Canadian Prime Minister Brian Mulroney appointed two special envoys to complete a study on the transboundary acid rain issue and make recommendations. The report concluded that the U.S. was contributing to acid rain in Canada. Instead of proposing expensive emissions controls, the report took a middle ground. It called for a five-year, $5 billion (half financed by government, half by industry) program to develop ways to burn coal cleanly. Reagan endorsed the report and in March 1987 he announced that he would honor the agreement by requesting the full $2.5 billion for that effort.

The National Clean Air Coalition, which favors stronger emission controls, considers the report "a step backward." Critics believe that the Administration is just trying to buy more time before cleaning up the pollution, an action they believe it is going to have to take sooner or later. By focusing on research rather than reducing emissions, the Administration is trying to avoid the problem. Michael McCloskey, executive director of the Sierra Club, said the program was an attempt "to create the illusion that this Administration is willing to control acid rain."

State Department official Benedick says that more research is required. "The U.S. will act when it is reasonably certain that such action will achieve its intended results and that those results will justify the social and economic costs involved," he said. Those costs are high. The companies responsible for the emissions are located in those areas of the country that have already been severely afflicted with layoffs. Adding on costs will only make them less competitive and will cost more jobs.

Confronting Shortages

The earth's bountiful resources are not distributed equally. Up to 90% of the supply of certain scarce strategic metals are located in just two countries, South Africa and the Soviet Union. Sixty percent of all proven oil reserves are located in the Middle Eastern member countries of OPEC. How can the U.S. best protect itself from resource shortages?

The Reagan Administration argues that the free market, over the long term, will end any disruptions of supply. Had the government not intervened to try and lower prices and distribute oil in the crises of the 1970s, the market would have adjusted more quickly and the oil, although scarce, would have wound up in the hands of those who most needed it. They note the successful workings of the market in the 1980s. If there is a shortage of oil in the future, they argue, oil prices will go up, marginal wells and investments in alternative fuels will become profitable.

Critics believe that potential oil disruptions are too dangerous to leave to the free market. They note that today, with oil prices low, there is little incentive to explore or invest in alternative programs, which require long lead times. In the event of a crisis, the U.S. will find itself vulnerable to pressure from oil-producing countries. The U.S. should have a comprehensive energy plan and should be stockpiling oil while it is cheap. Many favor a tax on imported oil.

Degradation's Toll

Ecological degradation outside the U.S. can harm U.S. interests. For example, deforestation elsewhere hurts the U.S. because it leads to climate change. "We will build a fool's paradise here in the U.S. if we focus only on our problems...," says James "Gus" Gustave Speth, president of the World Resources Institute.

Ecological degradation can force development to a halt, as soil erosion has done in Ethiopia and many other countries in Africa. The grim harvest of erosion is vast human misery, which can lead in turn to conflict. In Central America, a variety of problems caused a sharp reduction in food production. Population increased rapidly; ownership of most of the land was concentrated in the hands of a very small percentage of the population, meaning that the land remaining for the peasants was greatly overworked. According to the 1984 report of the "Kissinger Commission on Central America," ecological factors such as the above were important ingredients in the civil war that took place in El Salvador and the overthrow of the Somoza dictatorship in Nicaragua. What policies should the U.S. encourage to get countries on a sound ecological footing?

Many environmentalists argue that the first priority for the U.S. should be to increase aid to population-control efforts. They cite a world fertility survey—the largest social science research project ever undertaken, circa 1980—which reported that of the women it interviewed from the developing world, half said they wanted no more children. This is evidence, they believe, that many women in the Third World want family-planning assistance but do not have access to it.

They want the U.S. to support international family planning, including birth control and research in developing new birth control methods.

The Reagan Administration has favored instead focusing on free markets and the capitalist system. An efficient economy is an environmentally sound economy because resources are less likely to be underpriced or used wastefully. (Many environmentalists share this opinion.) The Administration argues that population growth will decline naturally as a country develops economically and as its citizens are better educated. ■

U.S. Interests and the Global Environment

By Lynton K. Caldwell

Since the mid-1960s public awareness of serious maladjustments between people and their environment has been growing. A worldwide environmental movement has emerged, and apprehensions have been aroused—reinforced by studies, conferences, and reports that investigate threatening environmental developments, analyze their causes, and propose remedial action. Scientists have taken leading roles in these inquiries, many of which have been sponsored by governments as well as by nongovernmental and international organizations. This new environmental awareness has posed difficult policy problems. Scientific evidence and public concern have caused governments to address problems for which they have had little previous experience and for which legal and technical solutions have not been readily available. President John F. Kennedy proposed a new course for US policy when he wrote in the introduction to Stewart Udall's book *The Quiet Crisis* (1963):

The crisis may be quiet, but it is urgent. . . . We must expand the concept of conservation to meet the imperious problems of the new age. We must develop new instruments of foresight and protection and nurture in order to recover the relationship between man and nature and to make sure that the national estate we pass on to our multiplying descendants is green and flourishing.

The perception of an environmental crisis that is global in scope has not been universally shared; the notion of limits to mankind's ability to populate the earth and to exploit the resources of its environment is contrary to general and longstanding assumptions. Critics of the environmental movement have declared its assumptions to be unfounded and its rhetoric alarmist, arguing instead that new resources are being discovered and that technology enlarges human capabilities. In their view the global crisis exists largely in the minds of misguided people. Within a narrow and arbitrary logic this rejection of global environmentalism may appear to make sense, but when compared with the growing findings of the sciences regarding the state of planet Earth, these plausible arguments become half-truths. While the critics are entitled to a respectful hearing, their premises need to be made explicit and their selection and treatment of factual evidence made clear. Whether there is indeed an environmental crisis is better ascertained from the realities of the living world than from the tendentious use of logic and statistics.

The weight of evidence and opinion since the early 1970s has demonstrably grown toward recognition that the world is confronted by an environmental crisis of global proportions. Beginning in the technoscientifically advanced countries and among better informed individuals, awareness of environmental problems has spread throughout the world, gaining an unforseen strength in many developing or Third World countries. The mutual need of nations for cooperation in environmental protection measures has been affirmed through new international arrangements, organizations, and agreements backed by national statutory law. New nongovernmental environmental organizations have emerged in nearly every country where voluntary cit-

Lynton Keith Caldwell, Director of the Advanced Studies in Science, Technology, and Public Policy Program, is the Arthur F. Bentley Professor of Political Science and Professor of Public and Environmental Affairs at Indiana University.

Source: From *Occasional Paper No. 35* by Lynton Caldwell. Copyright © 1985. Published by The Stanley Foundation, 216 Sycamore St., Suite 500, Muscatine, IA. 52761.

izen action is permitted. In the UN General Assembly and in the Governing Council of the United Nations Environment Programme (UNEP), rhetoric often exceeds national commitment to action; nonetheless, rhetorical commitment is a necessary prerequisite to action—the word usually must precede the deed.

The implementation of this new dimension in international affairs has not proceeded smoothly or uniformly in the years since the UN Conference on the Human Environment in June 1972 confirmed the legitimacy and importance of the global environment as an issue for international consideration. Much has been accomplished within a relatively short time, and yet as more has been learned about the human impact upon the earth, the more critical the circumstances appear to be. Collectively the nations have the knowledge and technical capability needed to overcome their environmental problems. The crisis is one of choice—of timely and appropriate action to be taken before environmental losses become irretrievable or environmental damage irremediable. Because this crisis occurs within a world of independent yet interdependent nations, the role played by the stronger among them inevitably impacts upon the effectiveness of the whole. Thus the position taken by the United States in world environmental affairs assumes an importance transcending its political boundaries.

As in other countries, there is a diversity of opinion in the United States regarding the relationship of the nation to the world environment. However, there are US interests in this environment that exist apart from opinion. It is important that US citizens, and other peoples as well, understand these interests because the international cooperation essential to coping with the critical environmental problems now confronting the world cannot be effective without US participation and support. The great scientific, technological, and economic resources of the United States—along with a record of past leadership in international environmental policy—place this nation in a unique position in international environmental affairs. There are many practical reasons why US interests require the government of the United States to play a constructive and leading role among nations in shaping sound and far-sighted policies for the protection of the global environment.

WHAT MAKES THE ISSUES GLOBAL?

In developing its policy position for the 1984 UN Conference on Population, the US delegation queried whether there was a global population crisis or merely problems of overly rapid population growth in particular countries. The latter position was adopted on the reasoning that not all countries were overpopulated and in some birth rates were falling. A similar point of view was taken by a Soviet delegate to an international environmental meeting: oceanic pollution, he said, was not a global or international problem but a responsibility for each country in which pollution originated. In contrast, reports from the International Council of Scientific Unions, the International Union for Conservation of Nature and Natural Resources (IUCN), and the UNEP have identified a series of interrelated issues as global in character including excessive growth of human population, air pollution, and overexploitation of the living resources of the seas.

Population growth is not a problem in every country; some have achieved population stability or in a few cases experienced decline. However, high rates of population increase handicap all efforts to improve economic and environmental conditions in many developing countries. National efforts and international assistance in education, health, housing, and rural development have been unable to keep pace with birthrates. Excessive population growth characteristically increases the number of the very poor whose pressure for survival overtaxes their natural resource base. Around the world from El Salvador to Haiti to the Sahel to the Middle East and South Asia, people pressure contributes to deforestation, soil exhaustion, degradation of water supplies, and loss of resources in plant and animal life. The consequences of this pressure upon the environment are not confined to countries in which they first occur but spread across the globe—affecting the quality of air and water, speeding the loss of genetic diversity, and causing mass migrations of peoples seeking escape from an impoverished environment.

Why do some people regard as local, issues that others see as global? The answer in part lies in whether one's focus on environmental problems is confined to the places where they originate, or whether the problems are seen as interconnected by cause and effect to phenomena in other places. On public issues, important policy differences follow from the perspectives taken. People who do not perceive a global environmental crisis and question its reality tend to focus on discrete, geographically bounded aspects of environmental problems. They might, for example, be concerned with oil spills at sea, but not necessarily with international traffic in petroleum that makes the oil spills probable. A more inclusive perspective would involve world energy needs. This comprehensive perspective, which may be called holistic or ecological, is a systems way of looking at events. Systems thinking is implicit in the perceptions and objectives of the international environmental movement. The systems approach to environmental problems reveals why many, although localized in origin, have nevertheless become international issues—some global in extent.

An issue becomes global not because of where it originates, but because of what it affects. Cause-effect relationships in the environment were not often perceived and less often adequately understood before the advent of modern science. Scientific understanding of environmental relationships is moreover a relatively recent development. Three factors in particular account for the ability of science to explain environmental relationships and to influence public and international policy.

The first factor is the development of the means of environmental surveillance by air, sea, land, and outer space. Only in this generation have men been able to see the earth whole. By airplane and satellite the surface of the earth is now systematically surveyed, and photogrammetric records are made for comparison of change over time. Equipment capable of penetrating

the deep sea and outer space, and drilling equipment capable of probing the mantle of the earth have enabled science to greatly enlarge basic knowledge about the planet and its environment. A large number of instruments and techniques have expanded scientific knowledge regarding the structure of matter, including living matter. From nuclear accelerators to electron microscopes, an unprecedented array of instrumentation has enormously expanded human knowledge of the conditions of life on earth—including the effects of human activities on the planetary environment.

The second factor, following from the first, is the greatly enhanced ability to measure. This ability to detect and to compare down to very minute components of things is today absolutely fundamental to government regulations on behalf of public health and safety; it is the scientific basis of policies regarding toxic substances in consumer goods and the environment. As a consequence of these advances in the sciences, people no longer generally believe that "what they don't know won't hurt them." People now tend to suspect that the opposite is more likely to be true.

These greatly advanced techniques for surveillance and measurement would not by themselves change people's perception of their environmental relationships. A third factor is required—a means of synthesis and trend projection that gives raw data meaning. Data alone are not persuasive. To understand complex environmental relationships, data must be analyzed, compared, and related; its changes projected in time series; and a coherent synthesis of relevant in-

formation formulated as findings. This processing of information was scarcely possible before the development of advanced computer technology. The ability to project into the future the interactions of measured trends has enabled scientists to estimate probable causes of past and present developments and to make informed predictions regarding what may happen if current trends continue unchanged. Thus, the computer can reveal relationships and probabilities that the human mind unaided could not readily conceive. From this new source of insight a series of studies and reports has emerged that provides the conceptual foundation for national and international environmental policy.

Beginning with Jay Forrester's *World Dynamics* (1971), more explicitly in the studies on *The Limits to Growth* (1972) and *Mankind at the Turning Point* (1974) sponsored by the Club of Rome, and followed by at least six additional global systems models leading to the US *Global 2000 Report* (1980), the literate world received a picture of its present ecological circumstances with prognoses of its possible futures. In a letter of transmittal to the president, the *Global 2000 Report* summarized its findings:

Environmental, resource, and population stresses are intensifying and will increasingly determine the quality of human life on our planet. These stresses are already severe enough to deny many millions of people basic needs for food, shelter, health, and jobs, or any hope for betterment. At the same time, the earth's carrying capacity—the ability of biological systems to provide resources for human needs—is eroding. The trends reflected in the Global 2000 Study suggest strongly a progressive degradation and impoverishment of the earth's natural resource base.

If these trends are to be altered and the problems diminished, vigorous, determined new initiatives will be required worldwide to meet human needs while protecting and restoring the earth's capacity to support life. Basic natural resources—farmlands, fisheries, forests, minerals, energy, air, and water—must be conserved and better managed. Changes in public policy are needed around the world before problems worsen and options for effective action are reduced.

These conclusions, and those of comparable studies stirred controversy and stimulated conferences and research efforts. Although widely rejected as prophecies of gloom and doom, they have nonetheless changed the thinking of many people regarding the responsibilities of government in relation to the world's environment.

No less significant have been the reports of scientific investigators regarding specific environmental effects and trends. National and international scientific studies have reported findings regarding sulfur dioxide, carbon dioxide, and particulates (for example, dust) in the atmosphere. Other studies have reported the spread of toxic substances in the environment, especially through water and food chains—ending in humans. Reports on environmental factors in health, disability, and death, especially from the World Health Organization (WHO), have contributed to public apprehension. From these and other publications from

many different sources, a growing consensus has emerged regarding the reality of a global environmental crisis. The concept of the biosphere as the sum total of all planetary systems, almost unknown a generation ago, is now commonplace in environment-related international documents and agreements, and is gaining currency among the general public.

A series of global environmental issues have now been identified as critical to human welfare. They are global because their effects, and often their causes, are not contained by national or even continental boundaries. However localized their immediate consequences may be, their effects ramifying in one form or another —economic and demographic as well as ecologic— are ultimately felt, however indirectly, throughout the biosphere. Not all international issues on superficial examination appear to be global. Yet when fully understood, their global character becomes apparent. The United Nations Regional Seas Programme is obviously bounded in implementation, yet its larger purpose is to end the pollution of the globe-encircling ocean environment. National population growth that outruns food supply, human services, and employment opportunities contributes to social unrest that may lead to uncontrollable migration of people, civil disorder, and even international war. No nation can safely assume immunity from the effects of these developments.

SIX CRITICAL ENVIRONMENTAL ISSUES

There are many ways of categorizing environmental problems and the policy issues that follow

from them. Any list of critical environmental issues would include the following six. They are widely regarded as critical because the trends that have placed them on the agendas of scientific inquiry and public policy threaten human welfare over all or large areas of the earth and, unless reversed in the very near future, may result in irretrievable damage to planetary life-support systems. They are also critical because, although the need for remedial action is urgent, remedial means are presently either not available (that is, carbon dioxide in the atmosphere) or would require complex socioeconomic changes that even willing governments could not readily bring about (for example, tropical deforestation). Yet none of these trends are today beyond remedy if the will to reverse them can be mobilized.

One further characteristic of these issues requires notice— none are compartmentalized; each issue interrelates with two or more of the others and with still more issues—ecologic and economic— not mentioned here. These interrelationships pose difficulties for policymaking because any solution to an issue-creating problem may have implications for other issues. For example, toxic contamination has become a critical issue throughout the world and its effects are found in air, water, soil, and food chains. Direct, short-range policies to eliminate toxicants in any single medium (that is through air pollution control) may merely drive the toxic material into other media (for example, from landfills to ground water).

What follows is a summary of the salient facts regarding six critical issues, including examples of what is being done about the issue and by whom. In each of these cases human behavior has disrupted the natural biogeochemical cycles of the biosphere, thereby generating chain reactions and positive feedback that multiply the problems confronting people and their governments.

Quality of the Atmosphere

The earth's atmosphere is now believed to have evolved from an earlier thermochemical condition in which higher forms of life now present could not have survived. The atmosphere has been changed through natural forces, but is now being altered at an accelerating rate by human action. Four aspects of atmospheric change threaten its quality. Three are by-products of modern industrial society. They are emissions of: (1) sulfur dioxide and nitrous oxides resulting in acid precipitation; (2) carbon dioxide accumulating toward a greenhouse effect, raising the temperature of the earth, melting the polar ice caps, and altering weather patterns; and (3) fluorocarbons concentrating in the ozone layer above the earth and impairing its ability to shield the earth from lethal radiation from outer space. A fourth aspect of harmful atmospheric change has been attributed primarily to unwise agricultural practice: soil erosion and desertification. The resulting increased amount of dust in the atmosphere affects agricultural productivity and the health of plants and animals. The phenomenon is global, as measurable quantities of atmospheric dust are carried from Africa to the east coast of the United States and from China to western North America. During the dry season a dust cloud hundreds of miles in extent hangs over southern and western Asia—an indicator of serious maladjustment of human activities and environmental limitations.

No single government can cope with these problems; the acid rain issue is a more urgent agenda item for governments in Western and Central Europe than it appears to be in North America. The carbon dioxide problem is long range, but its implications are extremely dangerous, involving the permanent flooding of coastal areas throughout the world and a trend toward aridity in now fertile food producing areas, notably the US Midwest. No solution to the problem is now in sight beyond abandoning the burning of coal, oil, and natural gas as energy sources. All nations would need to comply. If China, for example, chose to industrialize through burning massive quantities of coal, the carbon dioxide increase might not be stopped regardless of conservation measures in the United States and Europe. The fluorocarbon problem can be solved provided that all industrialized nations cooperate, and this cooperation is more easily attained than with sulfur dioxide or carbon dioxide because no basic industrial necessity (that is, energy source) is involved.

International action is presently focused on the immediate interest of acid rain. The issue has become acute between Canada and the United States; formal agreements have committed the two countries to cooperate in abating the problem, but domestic economic considerations have caused the United States to delay action, arguing the need for more research. The sulfur dioxide, carbon dioxide, and fluorocarbon problems have been addressed in numerous conferences and seminars and by various intergovernmental organizations, including the European Community, the International Council of Scientific Unions, the World Meteorological Organization (WMO), and the Organization for Economic Cooperation and Development (OECD). One result of these efforts has been the Convention on Long-Range Transboundary Air Pollution, now in effect, which had received 30 ratifications as of January 1984. Acid rain has become an international issue in the United States and there is little reason to doubt that its abatement would be in the national interest. The problem lies primarily in the choice of method.

Depletion of Fresh Water

The demands of modern agriculture and industry and increasing levels of population and affluence have placed unprecedented stress upon fresh water supplies. Although the immediate problems of water supply in large countries such as the United States are superficially national, the long-range issues everywhere transcend national boundaries. In the United States, depleting groundwater in Texas and the High Plains has led to proposals to tap fresh water sources in Northwestern Canada and the Great Lakes. Reaction of Canadians and the governments of the Great Lakes states has been almost uniformly negative. Meanwhile environmental disputes have arisen between Canada and the United States over degradation of rivers crossing their international boundary. Residents of Montana have complained regarding the quality of water in the Poplar River affected by a power plant in Saskatchewan, and Canadians in Manitoba have opposed completion of the Garrison Diversion irrigation project in North Dakota if Missouri River water is to be discharged into the Hudson Bay watershed. The United States government has created difficulties for Mexico by preempting Colorado River water for irrigation and urban water supply. To avoid treaty violations, the United States has commissioned a $243 million desalinization plant on the Lower Colorado to deliver an acceptable supply of fresh water to Mexico.

In Europe the fresh water issue is especially acute in the region of the Lower Rhine. In the Netherlands a coalition of environmental groups organized an International Water Tribunal in 1983 to protest the continued pollution of the Rhine by upstream countries and to ascertain the extent to which international treaties, declarations, and domestic laws were being violated. In African and Asian countries, allocation of riparian water rights among semiarid countries has encountered the inevitable issue of water quality. Water supply deficiencies in regions such as the Sahel in sub-Saharan Africa indirectly affect the United States through demands upon US food supply and technical assistance to offset famine, and through political repercussions from possible conflict among the four states forming the Lake Chad Basin Commission (Cameroon, Chad, Niger, and Nigeria). Soviet proposals to reverse the flow of several great Siberian rivers to irrigate Central Asia have raised questions regarding the consequences for the Arctic Ocean and possible effects upon the climate in the Northern Hemisphere.

The United States has excelled in the engineering of water supplies, but has been prodigal and shortsighted in water use. Prospective water shortages in the western United States have led to proposals to divert water from the Great Lakes and Canadian sources, but the consent of Canada would be required and may not be obtainable. Within the United Nations system, freshwater problems have been addressed by the Food and Agriculture Organization (FAO), WHO, United Nations Educational, Scientific, and Cultural Organization (UNESCO) and UNEP. A major UN Water Conference was held in March 1977 at Mar del Plata, Argentina. As early as 1965, UNESCO took a lead in launching the International Hydrological Decade from which evolved the International Hydrological Programme (IHP), and in 1981 the International Drinking Water Supply and Sanitation Decade was initiated by action of the UN General Assembly. A World Register of Rivers Discharging into the Oceans is jointly maintained by IHP and UNEP, and since 1976 a freshwater monitoring program has been carried on jointly by UNEP, WHO, WMO, and UNESCO within the framework of UNEP's Global Environmental Monitoring System.

Loss of Soil Productivity

Scientific studies and reports by FAO identify soil erosion and degrading quality as a largely unrecognized problem of threatening proportions. Its causes and its effects are numerous and widespread. Causal factors include erosion by wind and water resulting from deforestation, overgrazing, and cultivation of steep slopes. Ef-

fects are losses in productivity, degraded air quality, and siltation of streams, lakes, and impoundments behind dams, with a host of tertiary environmental consequences affecting hydropower, industrial water uses, aquatic biota, flooding, and desertification. Following the UN Conference on Desertification held in Nairobi in 1977, a UNEP effort toward combating the spread of deserts was initiated. A two year assessment of the situation presented to the UNEP Governing Council in May 1984 revealed a problem of global proportions and growing severity. It was estimated that since the 1977 conference, desertification has continued to increase at an approximate rate of six million hectares per year.

Topsoil may remain in place and yet lose much of its productivity through excessive dosage with inorganic fertilizers, herbicides, insecticides, and compression by heavy machinery. The long-range effects of the technology of modern agri-business upon crop production are debatable, but every country, and especially the United States, has a stake in the agricultural future. Air and water quality and plant genetics are also factors in this future. World populations are growing toward unprecedented levels, and a major disruption of food production anywhere could have economic and political consequences everywhere. International cooperation thus far has largely been confined to research—for example, in the mapping of world soil types. Soil loss continues to be regarded as primarily a national problem despite the fact that its international repercussions are becoming ever more evident.

Loss of Genetic Diversity

The miracles of modern agriculture have posed an unanticipated threat to natural and agricultural ecosystems through losses in the variety and diversity of many species of plants indigenous to various countries. Patented hybrid seed stock is seen by some agronomists and plant ecologists as threatening, through displacement, the survival of native genetic strains having long-tested survival capability. The issue was considered sufficiently serious to be addressed at the International Conference on Plant Genetics, which met in Rome in April 1981. This issue among others is now on the agendas of the Consultative Group for International Agricultural Research (CGIAR), which is associated with the World Bank, and of the International Board for Plant Genetic Resources, on which CGIAR, FAO, and UNEP are represented.

Habitat destruction through deforestation, draining, conversion of land to cultivation, and urbanization are major factors in depletion or extinction of species. Poaching for food and the commercial sale of protected species has become a threat to the survival of certain species of plants and animals. International cooperation has proved necessary to obtain national protection from the commercial exploitation of threatened plants and animals. Profitable international markets for rare plants, animals, and animal products greatly increase the difficulty of controlling illegal collecting and poaching.

The 1976 Convention on International Trade in Endangered Species undertook to remedy this difficulty by controlling the market for rare and threatened plants and animals. Another international effort to protect variety and diversity in both cultural and natural environments was the 1975 Convention Concerning the Protection of the World Cultural and Natural Heritage—a concept originating in the United States. Associated with this treaty has been the establishment, under the UNESCO sponsored Man and the Biosphere Programme, of biosphere reserves (226 reserves in 62 countries as of late 1983). These reserves and other areas protected through the World Heritage Convention and the international movement to establish and protect national parks, are some of the measures being taken to safeguard variety and diversity among the living species of the biosphere.

The loss of genetic diversity is bad not only because the world thereby becomes poorer and less interesting, but because opportunities and safeguards are also lost. With genetic losses through extinction of plant and animal species are losses of biochemical and behavioral characteristics poorly understood, perhaps undiscovered. Losses of potential sources of food, pharmaceuticals, and opportunities for insight into physiological and behavioral life processes are occurring and have become increasingly unacceptable in view of scientific evidence suggesting that irreplaceable assets are being needlessly sacrificed. The United States, as the principal agent of the green revolution in agriculture and a major market for natural products, has a special responsibility to preserve genetic diversity. Recognition of this circumstance caused the US Agency for International Development in cooperation with other federal agencies to sponsor a conference in 1981 on the preservation of genetic diversity with special reference to the nation's bilateral aid programs.

Tropical Deforestation

The rapid reduction of the tropical rain forest appears on every list of critical environmental issues. Its effects are global, first because the forests are believed to be major regenerators of atmospheric oxygen; second because loss of the forests is accompanied by loss of habitats and species, with the resulting genetic impoverishments previously noted; and third because resulting damage to tropical soils through erosion, laterization (rocklike hardening), and loss of soil fertility impairs the life support base of people and other living things.

Among the causes of tropical deforestation are the cutting of trees for fuel wood and the clearing of land for agriculture and cattle raising. World Forestry Congresses have repeatedly warned governments about the consequences of the loss of the tropical forests. The International Council for Research in Agroforestry collaborates with UNEP's Ecosystems Task Force in promoting research on combining agriculture with forestry. Encouraged by the World Bank, FAO, and UNEP, tropical countries have begun to cooperate in the development of managed tropical ecosystems. In March 1980, UNEP sponsored a conference in Libreville, Gabon, on the world's tropical forests. In 1980 nine African countries meeting in Yaounde, Cameroon, agreed upon a treaty relating to the improved management of tropical forests and ecosystems. Yaounde is also the location of the regional Centre for Scientific Information and Documentation in Tropical Ecology.

The worldwide importance of these conserving efforts was underscored by Tatsuro Kunugi of Japan, chairman of the 1983 UN Conference on Tropical Timber, which was convened under the auspices of the UN Conference on Trade and Development, when he said that the 37 articles adopted constituted "a global policy in resources management, taking into account the implications of this policy for other important sectors such as energy, agriculture, food supply, and the preservation of ecosystems."

Toxic Contamination/ Hazardous Materials

The enormous ingenuity of the chemical industry has produced an unprecedented number of useful compounds during recent decades. This innovation, although widely beneficial, has created serious ecological problems, sometimes resulting from unforeseen side effects (as with DDT and PCBs), and more often from failure to adequately assess the risks involved in releasing new chemicals into the environment and in neglecting to take effective measures for their harmless disposal. Toxic contamination of air, water, soil, and biota was initially believed to be a problem largely confined to developed countries; but international trade, and the atmospheric and oceanic transport of toxicants, has spread the problem around the world.

Investigation of effects and consideration of control measures has been undertaken by many national governments and scientific bodies, by the European Community, the International Labour Organization, WHO, OECD, and by UNEP which has established the International Register of Potentially Toxic Chemicals and the International Programme on Chemical Safety. Two nongovernmental scientific bodies have also been established to address specific hazards: the International Commission for Radiological Protection and the International Commission against Nitrogens and Carcinogens. Concern over possible harmful effects of hazardous materials in commerce prompted the UN General Assembly on 17 December 1981 to adopt by a vote of 146 to 1 a resolution on protection against products harmful to health and environment. The United States cast the sole dissenting vote.

Disposal of radioactive materials is a special concern of the International Atomic Energy Agency, based in Vienna. Each government, however, appears to follow its own preferences in dealing with nuclear wastes. Global contamination by nuclear war is the ultimate hazard, but serious threats to living things are present in peacetime uses of atomic energy.

The foregoing discussion provides a selective sample of the environmental issues that have aroused worldwide concern and have caused governments to institute new forms of international cooperation in defense of their environments and of the biosphere. The hazards of overpopulation and war have not been included in this listing, partly because their threat to the global environment is widely (but not universally) understood. Their potential effects are more inclusive than environmental, and even a cursory treatment of their potential environmental impacts could exceed the limits of this paper. There are few environmental problems that are not somehow related to excessive population growth. The rapidly expanding cities of the Third World—in Africa, Asia, and Latin America—pose very serious social, political, and economic problems for the future. These problems are being addressed through various components of the UN system, but thus far results have been disproportionately small in relation to the dangers inherent in the problems.

HOW THE UNITED STATES IS INVOLVED

Regardless of the policy positions of the government on international environmental issues, US citizens are involved in all of the aforementioned global issues and many more. Although since 1981 the government appears to have retreated from it earlier position of leadership, nongovernmental organizations (NGOs) based in the United States have increased their participation in international environmental affairs. At international conferences on environment and population, contradictory positions have become commonplace between official and unofficial US representatives. This division weakens the influence of each group and raises doubts as to the representative character of official US policies.

For example, at the Session of a Special Character held by the Governing Council of UNEP in 1982 to commemorate the 1972 UN Conference on the Human Environment and to assess its results, the official recommendation of the US delegation was that nations should rely on market forces in preference to regulations to cope with environmental problems. This advice was widely regarded as simplistic by NGO representatives, especially in relation to developing countries in which market economies were weak. Similarly, at the United Nations Conference on Population held in Mexico City in mid-1984, officials of the United States took the position that adverse effects of overpopulation were being exaggerated and that economic growth could overcome the alleged adversities. The NGO population and family planning groups in the United States generally dissented from the government's position, as did many representatives, both official and unofficial, from developing countries with serious population-environment problems.

Responding to charges that the government has abandoned its earlier commitment to global environmental protection, spokesmen for the Reagan administration have denied the charge that the United States no longer leads in world environmental affairs. Their position has been that controls and regulations by governments and through binding international agreements are not the best way to preserve environmental quality. The United States position on the Governing Council of UNEP and in the UN General Assembly has been that greater reliance should be placed on free market forces to correct environmental abuses. In the official view, responsibility for environmental policy should rest with each country, which should adopt its own protective measures without interposition by other countries or by intergovernmental bureaucracies. For example, President Ronald

Reagan in early 1981 withdrew President Jimmy Carter's Executive Order 12264 restricting US export of hazardous materials on grounds that the United States should not try to write rules for the rest of the world and should not impose its standards on other countries.

Although the US position has been that market forces provide a better way to achieve environmental policy objectives, this viewpoint has not won acceptance abroad. Claims that the United States is still leading in issues of international environmental policy are hardly credible when no other nations are following. Because the United States has stood alone on issue after issue since 1981 does not mean that its official position is wrong. But the fact remains that in votes on environmental issues in the UN General Assembly, the division on the hazardous materials resolution was 146 to 1, on the World Charter for Nature 111 to 1 (8 technical abstentions), and in the World Health Organization Assembly the vote on control over export of artificial infant formula for bottle feeding was 118 to 1 (4 abstentions). Risk to infant health arose from the inadequate provisions in many tropical countries for sterilizing bottles, especially in rural areas in which contaminated water added a danger not encountered in breast feeding.

On other issues the United States has been less isolated yet still very much in a negative minority. After having led in drafting the UN Law of the Sea Treaty, which includes numerous environmental provisions, the United States reversed its position, declined to join 125 signatory states, and undertook, mostly unsuccessfully, to persuade its closer allies to abstain. In

addition, the Reagan administration attempted to reduce or eliminate US funding for international environmental programs, notably appropriations for UNEP and the UNESCO sponsored Man and the Biosphere Programme, and the World Heritage Convention. At the 1984 UN Conferences on Population, the official US delegation, as previously noted, took a policy line unacceptable to many other countries and to many US nongovernmental participants. In each of these instances, however, the United States did not oppose the environmental principle involved but rather gave higher priority to economic values or, in the case of the population issue, to a particular view of morality.

For all that, the US government is inescapably involved in international environmental issues in which US interests are at stake. These interests, moreover, are shared with other nations—some with all nations—and are not exclusively US problems. Three issues illustrate the point: acid rain, environment and development in the Caribbean, and the future of Antarctica.

Acid rain has become a high priority issue through Western and Central Europe and in Eastern North America. Its incidence and effects are even wider, but appear to be most acute in the Northeastern United States, Eastern Canada, and in Scandinavia, Germany, Czechoslovakia, and Poland. The issue in the United States is both domestic and international. The official position of the federal government has been ambiguous. President Reagan has declared the issue to be of highest priority for the   Environmental   Protection Agency, but, following strong protests from high-sulfur coal-producing states, the administration appears to have taken a course of delay, calling for more study before action. Nevertheless, the issue will not go away, and action taken by governments in Europe will have effects upon policy in the United States. Meanwhile, the issue tends to corrode not only Canadian-US diplomatic relations, but also buildings, bridges, machinery, and cultural monuments in both countries, and progressively diminishes the viability of streams, lakes, forests, and agricultural lands.

In the Caribbean area the US government has shown great concern for social, economic, and political stability, but its role in international efforts to integrate environmental protection and sustainable development has ranged from negative to ambiguous. Since 1979, when a major Conference in Environmental Management and Economic Growth in the Smaller Caribbean Islands was held in Barbados, a number of cooperative action programs have been adopted. In April 1981, a UNEP-sponsored regional conference met in Jamaica and adopted a Caribbean Action Plan comprising 66 environmental projects, of which 25 were designated as of high priority and 33 for immediate action. In August 1981, a meeting of Non-Governmental Caribbean Conservation Organizations was held in the Dominican Republic and adopted a complementary strategy with assistance from nongovernmental US sources including the Rockefeller Brothers Fund, the University of Michigan, and the Caribbean Conservation Foundation. A Caribbean Trust Fund has been established with regional and external funding, and in March 1983, 13 of the 27 Caribbean nations signed the Treaty of Cartagena for the Protection and Development of the Marine Environment of the Wider Caribbean Region.

Throughout these efforts the role of the US government has been ambivalent. Administration policy has been slow to link environmental protection with economic development and has preferred bilateral aid to financial assistance through multilateral efforts such as the UNEP-sponsored Wider Caribbean Regional Seas Programme. Unwillingness to participate in programs in association with Cuba may also have deterred US involvement. There are substantial indications that many of the roots of poverty and unrest in the region are environmental—a documented example is the ecological impoverishment of El Salvador preceding its social disorders. Nearly two decades before the outbreak of civil war, a Fellow of the Tropical Science Center in San José, Costa Rica, traveling in El Salvador reported massive deforestation, soil erosion, fuelwood crisis, and environmental pollution. He foresaw a social explosion based on poverty attributed largely to "human ecologic problems caused by overpopulation." Similar evidence of man-induced ecological disaster, especially affecting food production, has been documented in many other countries and reported by UN agencies and independent investigations. Massive illegal immigration to the United States has been as much a consequence of the inability of people to subsist on worn-out land as of a desire to escape from political oppression.

The case of Antarctica involves a different set of US interests. The United States has taken a lead in the scientific exploration of the Antarctic continent and in its protection from damaging development and from political conflict. Unlike other nations, the United States, despite its presence and preeminent investment in Antarctic research has made no territorial claims on Antarctica. In 1959 the Antarctic Treaty was signed by 12 nations, including 7 that agreed to suspend their territorial claims for the duration of the treaty. This treaty and subsequent agreements are administered by the Consultative Parties, which do not include UN agencies or most Third World countries. The possibility of mineral wealth in the continent has become a two-way source of contention—first, between the Consultative Parties and those Third World states demanding a share in any material benefits and second, between the forces for resource development and those urging the preservation of undeveloped Antarctica as a natural reserve for science.

Here again US opinion appears to be divided between the administration, together with some private groups, willing to consider controlled development, and most scientific and environmental groups that are strongly opposed. There is also international concern among environmental organizations over the exploitation of Antarctic marine life, especially by Soviet-bloc nations and Japan. The effect on marine food chains of reducing the number of the shrimp-like krill has been questioned by marine scientists. Through all of these and other controversies, the preeminence of the United States in Antarctic affairs gives it a key position in any decision affecting the region. After 1990, a new regime for Antarctica will become necessary unless the present treaty is extended. The United States cannot avoid involvement in Antarctic decisions, and it would appear to be clearly in the national interest for the government and scientific community to cooperate in formulating a policy position that would protect the area from political conflict and from despoliation for resources available elsewhere.

US INTERESTS AND NATIONAL POLICY

In none of the issues previously described have US interests, broadly defined, been injured by policies protective of the global environment. The immediate interests of some US citizens might have been adversely affected by some measures that the overwhelming majority of nations have found to be in the general interest. Even the closest US allies favored controls over export of toxic or otherwise hazardous materials, voted for restrictions on promotion of artificial infant formula in tropical countries, and supported the Law of the Sea Treaty. No national interest whatever appears to have been in jeopardy in the UN Charter for Nature or in appropriations to assist UNEP, international scientific environmental investigations, the World Heritage Convention, or the Wider Caribbean Action Plan. The dollar cost of US contributions to international environmental protection efforts becomes relatively insignificant when compared with the aggregate expenditures of the US government.

It would be unfair to suggest that the position of the United States in international environmental affairs has been wholly negative. Individual federal agencies, notably the National Park Service, the Fish and Wildlife Service, and the Agency for International Development have continued to provide assistance upon request to other countries. In effect, US policy on international environmental affairs has tended toward inconsistency, explained perhaps by a statement attributed to a State Department official quoted in *The New York Times* (28 March 1983) to the effect that "the Reagan administration still does not have an international environmental policy."

It appears that the United States has given up its leadership in global environmental affairs and has unnecessarily prejudiced some of its long-term interest abroad without any significant benefits at home. Its government has been unable to persuade other nations, including its best friends, to adopt its uncertain approach to environmental issues. While environmental policy has not yet become an issue for partisan division in the United States or in most other countries, the rise of "green parties" in several European nations suggests that such division is possible. For the present, however, scientific analyses of public attitudes in the United States, the United Kingdom, the Netherlands, and West Germany show no polarization and reveal similar opinion profiles—a high public concern for environmental quality cutting across social, economic, and political boundaries. A strongly marked increase in environmental concern has become evident in many Third World countries. Paradoxically much of the world that resisted US leadership at the time of the 1972 UN Conference in Stockholm is now receptive to policies and programs that the US supported then but declines to support now.

It seems safe to say that no national interests have been served by the ambiguous positions on international environmental cooperation taken since 1981 by the US government. Where official policy has been calculated to protect the special interests of manufacturers, exporters, or resource developers, it has been generally unsuccessful. Other countries have declined to follow the US' attempted lead, and policies regarded as objectionable in Washington (for example, the infant formula resolution) have been implemented internationally without US participation. An unfortunate instance occurred when a representative of the US Environmental Protection Agency lobbied, unsuccessfully, against proposals in the OECD to adopt international controls over the transboundary transport of hazardous chemicals. Low budgets for international environmental programs may indeed result in higher future costs to US taxpayers. El Salvador and Haiti are cases in point wherein effective US assistance years ago to reverse socio-ecological deterioration would have cost the taxpayer much less than is now being exacted merely to prevent bad situations from becoming worse. The government in Washington—and even the Kissinger Commission in its report on Central America—has not seemed to understand the difficulty of building a productive economy on a ruined ecologic resource base.

The budget cuts and negative votes in international assemblies are symbolic—they have had no significant effect on gross federal expenditures, but they have sent a message to other countries on the apparent indifference of the United States to world environmental affairs. It would be to the national advantage for the president and Congress to reverse this negative impression. International cooperation in the Agency for International Development, the Department of the Interior, and the Environmental Protection Agency could be officially encouraged and financially strengthened. The agency intended for the initiation and review of US environmental policy has been the Council on Environmental Quality (CEQ) created by Title II of the National Environmental Policy Act of 1969 (NEPA). Under the Reagan administration the budget of the CEQ was cut by 75 percent, its professional staff largely disbanded, and the appointment of council members often delayed. Restoration of the CEQ to its former status could be a major step toward regaining national leadership and credibility abroad. The international and domestic role of the CEQ could be enhanced to the national advantage by an expanded implementation of Title II of NEPA, which authorizes and directs the council to sponsor and assist studies relating to environmental trends. No administration thus far has begun to realize the potential of NEPA, best known for its relatively secondary requirement of environmental impact statements.

Maintenance of a continuing dialogue between the large nongovernmental environmental organizations and the federal government could be helpful. It could help to reach mutual understanding that might avoid the spectacle in international gatherings of official US representatives and organizations of US citizens taking opposing positions. Such divisions may demonstrate freedom of citizen action in the United States, but they also weaken the credibility of the United States among other nations.

What policy options would serve US interests in relation to international environmental issues? A more positive role in UN organizations is indicated inasmuch as, despite its defects, the UN system is the only structure approaching universality among nations. Regardless of political differences, all nations share a concern for protection of the biosphere. Hostile governments historically have been known to work together on matters of mutual self-interest, so US participation in "politics of antagonistic cooperation" would not be exceptional. Especially in view of the consequences of environmental deterioration in many Third World countries, US support for UN environmental programs could ward off the much greater costs that the United States might have to bear alone should remedial efforts fail. The United States and the Soviet Union have cooperated in scientific and technical aspects of environmental protection. Joint efforts toward common purposes help to build better relationships among otherwise suspicious and unfriendly nations. The Wider Caribbean Regional Seas Programme would seem to be a logical place for positive rather than reluctant US participation.

The US government might also find ways to encourage and assist nongovernmental international environmental efforts such as the World Conservation Strategy, developed largely through the IUCN. Our country has traditionally drawn a much harder line between official

GLOSSARY OF ACRONYMS

CEQ	Council on Environmental Quality
CGIAR	Consultative Group for International Agricultural Research
FAO	Food and Agriculture Organization
IHP	International Hydrological Programme
IUCN	International Union for Conservation of Nature and Natural Resources
NEPA	National Environmental Policy Act
NGO	nongovernmental organization
OECD	Organization for Economic Cooperation and Development
UNEP	United Nations Environmental Programme
UNESCO	United Nations Educational, Scientific and Cultural Organization
WHO	World Health Organization
WMO	World Meterological Organization

and nongovernmental relationships than have many other countries—France and Japan, for example. US government agencies have assisted the IUCN, but the United States is not one of the 58 nations officially affiliated. Proposals to privatize and commercialize environmental surveillance capabilities, such as Landsat, could have an adverse effect upon environmental science unless protective measures were taken to assure access to the satellite system by other governments and nonprofit organizations.

In summary, the costs of regaining credibility and leadership in international environmental affairs could be much less than the ultimate cost of failure to do so. The position of the US government since 1980 has been sufficiently ambiguous on international environmental issues to permit a progressive movement toward a positive position without making a formal reversal of policy. The United States cannot escape sharing in the consequences of environmental disasters that fall upon the rest of the world. To understand this is also to understand why vigorous positive leadership in international environmental policy is in the national interest as well as in the interest of people everywhere. ∎

State Department Perspectives on Environmental Issues

By John D. Negroponte

STATE'S ROLE IN ENVIRONMENTAL ISSUES

Let me start by outlining for a moment the State Department's role in science and technology generally and environmental issues in particular. To begin with, the Department of State has been charged by the Congress with managing U.S. international science and technology activities as a fundamental element of our foreign relations and in accord with our foreign policy. Of course, the Department carries out its responsibilities in close consultation and cooperation with the President's Office of Science and Technology Policy, the National Security Counsil, the Office of Management and Budget, the National Science Foundation, and other relevant technical agencies including, especially so far as the environment is concerned, the Council on Environmental Quality and the Environmental Protection Agency (EPA). And appropriate, concerned committees and subcommittees of the Congress are consulted.

THE ORGANIZATION OF OES

Within the Department, the bureau that I head, the Bureau of Oceans and International Environmental and Scientific Affairs, is directly responsible for assuring that oceans, nonproliferation, scientific, technological, population, environmental, and health concerns are taken into account as foreign policy decisions are made. Bureau personnel, together with representatives of concerned agencies, represent the United States in international organizations on oceans, environment, science, and technology matters. The bureau, also in coordination with other elements of the Department and relevant agencies, develops overall U.S. Government positions, negotiating strategies, and texts for government-to-government science and technology agreements on such matters; represents the United States in multilateral and bilateral negotiations; and—very important—acts as the link on environmental science and technol-

ogy issues between the Department, private industry, and concerned private sector organizations and institutions.

To carry out its responsibilities, the bureau is organized into four divisions plus a Coordinator for Population Affairs and an Executive Director. Specifically:

The Environment Division is the focal point for international environmental issues, including environmental pollution and natural resources conservation, and international health matters. The division is currently focusing on international negotiations leading to an agreement to protect the ozone layer; acid rain negotiations with Canada; boundary air and water pollution problems with Mexico; an international response to the spread of AIDS [Acquired Immune Deficiency Syndrome]; biotechnology developments with OECD [Organization for Economic Cooperation and Development] countries; prospects for global climate damage; transboundary shipment of hazardous wastes and substances; and harmonization of

John D. Negroponte is a Foreign Service Official, who in 1987 was Assistant Secretary of State for Oceans and International Environmental and Scientific Affairs.

Source: From an address before the International Environment Forum, Washington, D.C., September 18, 1987. Reprinted in Department of State, Bureau of Public Affairs, *Current Policy* No. 1008, pp. 1–4.

international chemical controls and substances. The division also is concerned with environmental policies of the multilateral development banks; the UN Environment Program; biological diversity and tropical forests; enforcement of U.S. and international wildlife trade regulations and agreements; the U.S. Man and the Biosphere Program; and participation by private industry and environmental interest groups in our international environmental programs.

The **Division of Oceans and Fisheries Affairs** has responsibility for ocean-related conservation and resource management issues. This division supports U.S. participation in the Antarctic Treaty, the International Whaling Commission, the North Atlantic Salmon Conservation Organization, and the International Maritime Organization, to name a few examples. It also works on an entire range of issues related to the law of the sea, including, of course, protection of the marine environment.

The **Division of Nuclear Energy and Energy Technology Affairs** deals with issues of nonproliferation, nuclear safeguards, and nuclear energy cooperation. It was very much involved in the Department of State's response to the accident at Chernobyl and also participated in the International Atomic Energy Agency deliberations that led to the adoption last fall of agreements on notification and emergency assistance in case of nuclear accidents. We continue to be interested in this issue.

The **Division of Science and Technology Affairs** is principally concerned with oversight and coordination of international scientific cooperation. There are dozens of government-to-government sci-

ence cooperation agreements between this country and others, reinforced by literally hundreds of direct agency-to-agency cooperative arrangements. These relationships are valuable not only for the science they promote but also for the good will they can create and the access they can develop to important segments of other societies. Science and technology agreements have proven to be particularly beneficial with such diverse nations as China, India, Yugoslavia, and Israel. An effort is underway to bolster our science relations with Brazil, particularly with respect to environmental science. Another important function of the science division is to provide support to the 42 full-time science officers at embassies abroad who, among other things, serve as our eyes and ears on science-related developments in other countries.

Finally, **the Coordinator of Population Affairs** provides foreign policy guidance in the formulation and implementation of U.S. policy on population. There is a clear relationship between population growth, sustainable development, and environmental problems such as destruction of tropical forests or the pollution and health problems caused by urban overcrowding.

KEY ENVIRONMENTAL ISSUES IN THE FORESEEABLE FUTURE

Let me identify some environmental issues that will be with us for the next 5–10 years and more, and our approach to these issues, bearing in mind that much of what we do is strongly influenced by external forces; the Chernobyl re-

actor accident is a good case in point.

I think it is useful to distinguish between environmental issues driven by bilateral or regional considerations, on the one hand, and global environmental questions, on the other. Sometimes the distinctions become difficult to make, and, on occasion, the local and global issues can become intertwined. But I am sure you will agree that the environmental impact of Tijuana's sewage, as destructive to the local environment as it may be, is a qualitatively different issue from the destruction of the planet's stratospheric ozone layer—unless, of course, you happen to live in San Diego. However, an environmental policy official disregards localized problems at his own peril. And, indeed, issues of water and air quality have been high on our bilateral agenda with Mexico and Canada going back many decades.

REGIONAL BILATERAL CONCERNS

So I would suggest to you that, in many respects, the most politically sensitive set of international environmental concerns this country has is with its immediate neighbors to the north and south. I won't elaborate extensively on them at this point. Perhaps we can go into some during the question period. But a partial listing would serve to illustrate my point.

Acid Rain

First, there is the issue of acid rain with Canada. In January 1986, two specially appointed envoys—one Canadian and one American—issued a report detailing recommendations designed to foster a long-term solution to this serious environmental and political problem. President Reagan fully endorsed the envoys' recommendations shortly thereafter and reaffirmed this commitment at his most recent summit meeting with Prime Minister Mulroney in Ottawa. The two governments are now working to implement the report's recommendations, including:

• A 5-year program in the United States for commercial demonstration of clean-coal technologies;
• A commitment to ongoing cooperative activities, including bilateral consultations and information exchange; and
• A greater emphasis on carrying out research on transboundary air pollution issues.

The President also agreed to consider Canadian proposals for an acid rain accord, and our review of these proposals will be concluded fairly soon.

Niagara River Pollution

EPA, Environment Canada, the New York Department of Environmental Conservation, and the Ontario Ministry of the Environment addressed pollution in the Niagara River by reaching an agreement in principle on a four-part management plan to clean up toxic chemicals in the river. The plan, still under negotiation, would include increased monitoring, point and nonpoint source control, and improved communications and management. The two governments also worked together closely 2 years ago in monitoring and cleaning up a mysterious "blob" of toxic chemicals on the Canadian side of the St. Clair River.

Hazardous Waste Shipment

As some of you are aware, the United States and Canada have negotiated a bilateral agreement on the transboundary movement of hazardous waste. By eliminating the need for prior written consent for each shipment of hazardous waste across the border, the agreement will ensure no interruption in legitimate trade of hazardous waste between the two countries.

Caribou Migration

And, in a completely different area of concern, the United States and Canada recently completed a successful negotiation on principles for the management of the porcupine caribou herds whose migratory range extends across both of our territories.

Transboundary Environmental Quality

Turning south of the border, the U.S.-Mexico Border Environment Agreement of 1983 has successfully addressed serious problems of transboundary environmental quality between our two countries, such as air pollution from copper smelters and transboundary shipment of hazardous waste. It has been cited by both sides as a model for cooperation between us which can be extended to other worrisome border issues such as treatment and disposal of municipal sludge.

I could cite numerous other endeavors. But the thought I wish to leave with you today is the commonsensical notion that these transboundary environmental questions are very important ones, which we are seeking to resolve both effectively and pragmatically. What is more, our success in coping with these more immediate and frequently more politically urgent, environmental matters affects our credibility when dealing with global issues.

GLOBAL ISSUES AND COOPERATION

UNEP Efforts

On the global scene, I would like particularly to cite the fine work of the UN Environmental Program (UNEP) in dealing with environmental issues.

In June, I had the pleasure of coheading the U.S. delegation to the biennial meeting of UNEP's Governing Council in Nairobi. I was delighted to confirm at firsthand that UNEP's environmental priorities track closely with those of the United States. In my view, UNEP is providing a unique forum—involving developed and developing countries, the East and the West—for the United States to pursue international action on global environmental problems.

A major UNEP initiative that has just come to fruition is the international negotiation of an agreement on controls for the protection of the ozone layer. The 1985 Vienna Convention for the Protection of the Ozone Layer called for further study before making a decision as to a control mechanism for chlorofluorocarbon (CFC) emissions. After a period of intense activity, a major scientific assessment of the chemical and physical processes affecting the ozone layer was released in January 1986. Then negotiation of a protocol to control CFC emissions was undertaken—and I am pleased to be able to say they were successfully completed just last week with the signature by 24 countries of a new protocol in Montreal. I think we have achieved significant protection for future generations, and at a reasonable cost to ourselves today.

The UN Environment Program has also done very useful work in a wide range of other environmental program activities. We attach importance to the following, in particular:

• The Global Environmental Monitoring System (GEMS), which assembles, analyzes, and disseminates data on global conditions and trends in major environmental media. Additional progress was achieved in developing the Global Resource Information Database, a GEMS component receiving substantial U.S. (i.e., National Aeronautics and Space Administration) support through expert personnel and advanced technology, including space applications.

• The Oceans and Coastal Areas (formerly Regional Seas) Program, which promotes environmental protection and natural resource management agreements among countries bordering specified ocean regions. Principal U.S. attention is being devoted to further implementation of the action plan for the wider Caribbean region (defined to include Puerto Rico, the U.S. Virgin Islands, and the U.S. gulf coast), along with the associated Cartagena convention.

• Current activities of the Environmental Law Program include the protocol to the 1985 ozone layer convention in controlling emissions of ozone-depleting chlorofluorocarbons just signed in Montreal, providing guidelines for notification of international hazardous substances, and instituting international principles and guidelines on environmental impact assessment.

• I am especially pleased to report that, as a result of a U.S. initiative at the June Governing Council meeting, UNEP has agreed to explore the possibility of creating an umbrella convention on biological diversity conservation. Such a convention, by rationalizing the numerous extant international agreements that protect various wildlife and habitats, could ensure that the world's most pressing biodiversity conservation needs are identified as early as possible. UNEP will be establishing a working group in the near future to begin looking into the feasibility of an umbrella biodiversity convention.

Tropical Deforestation

Of particular concern, of course, is the critical issue of tropical deforestation. In this connection, I recently attended the International Strategy Meeting on Tropical Forests convened in Bellagio, Italy, July 1–2, under the auspices of UNEP, the UN Food and Agriculture Organization, the World Resources Institute, the World Bank, and the Rockefeller Foundation. The conference statement sets forth 10 major recommendations for government and private sector efforts to deal with the world's tropical forest crisis and calls for an international task force to develop implementation strategies for review at a second Bellagio conference to be held next year.

The International Tropical Timber Organization, established under the International Tropical Tim-

ber Agreement (ITTA) of 1985, is another international cooperative initiative in tropical forestry. The ITTA is the first international commodity agreement to have conservation among its stated purposes, thereby recognizing the importance and benefits of sustainable development to agriculture, food and water supply, energy, and other sectors. The ITTA provides a system of consultation and cooperation among 41 consumer and producer countries representing 95% of the world's tropical timber trade.

Still another approach to conserving tropical forests now being tested is the "debt-for-nature" concept of swapping modest amounts of written-down private Third World debt for commitments to protect forests. Under this scheme, nongovernmental organizations or other donors purchase international equity notes at their current market value and subsequently "swap" the debt purchased with the debtor nation in return for conservation measures. While their effectiveness remains to be seen, debt swaps may become a useful approach to tropical forest conservation.

An initial debt swap effort has taken place in Bolivia. In July, Conservation International entered into an agreement with the Bolivian Government to retire $650,000 of the country's privately held external public sector debt (purchased at 15¢ on the dollar) in exchange for a pledge to set aside and maintain 4 million acres of tropical forest adjacent to the Beni Biosphere Reserve in the Amazon region. As this agreement is put into effect, we hope to gain a better understanding of the actual on-the-ground benefits that might be achieved through debt swaps.

Promoting Sound Environmental Policies

My bureau is involved in efforts to encourage the multilateral development banks and other aid donors to promote environmentally sound development policies in less developed countries, a task whose enormity I suspect people from as fortunate circumstances as ourselves can only begin to appreciate. But increased environmental understanding in Third World countries will be essential if we are to address successfully such critical concerns of our day as the global climate, biological diversity, and tropical forests. Let me emphasize this point: sustainable development is a complex, difficult process, and it will behoove all of us—not just the official aid agencies—to urge sound environmental and natural resource management practices in all our endeavors abroad. In this latter regard, I would be remiss if I did not mention the good work being done by the World Environment Center, aimed at assisting less developed countries to solve their industrial environmental problems.

The global response to environmental issues, moreover, goes further. There is a growing tendency among countries to move to comparable levels of environmental protection by harmonizing control measures. I think this is all to the good. "Harmonization" is something less than standardization, for it allows flexibility in attaining defined goals; but it is more than just coordination. This trend is clearest among developed countries but can also be seen in the developing countries. Emission standards for cars are a good example of the phenomenon. Canada has adopted U.S. standards, effective September 1, 1987, and the European Community is moving toward U.S. standards in the late 1980s and early 1990s.

Managing Hazardous Substances

But I can better illustrate this point by reference to our response to fears about the management of chemicals and hazardous wastes. The largest environmental program at the OECD concerns chemicals, and the program's goals of the program are fourfold:

• To improve protection of health and the environment from the harmful effects of chemicals;
• To avoid distortions of trade in chemicals;
• To reduce the economic and administrative burden on member countries associated with chemicals control; and
• To foster international exchange of information on chemicals.

We have already seen numerous OECD recommendations and decisions in these areas. One, for example, deals with information exchange related to the export of banned or severely restricted chemicals. Its aim is to ensure that when a chemical is banned or severely restricted in an exporting country, then information is provided from that country to the importing country to enable the latter to make timely and informed decisions concerning that chemical.

More recently, a meeting at the OECD of senior environmental officials committed the organization to a lead role in strengthening international supervision of, and preparedness for, accidents involving significant releases of hazardous substances. It was also agreed at the meeting that the OECD should initiate a major cooperative effort on existing chemicals, the details of which are being worked out.

IMPLICATIONS FOR U.S. INDUSTRY

But what about the implications of all this for U.S. business? Perhaps most important, you should know that we fully appreciate that American business must strive to reconcile environmental responsibility with balance sheets and employment. And the fact that we can negotiate successful international agreements means that we can translate concerns about a level playing field—on which you will not be disadvantaged relative to your competitors by inequitably shared regulatory burdens, for example—into specific international agreements requiring parallel measures by concerned countries. Once again, the protocol on protection of the ozone layer is a case in point. It will come into force only when 11 countries representing at least two-thirds of global consumption have ratified it—making it impossible for a major player to sit out while others bear the burden of restraint.

Another implication of what I have been saying is that industry must help in shaping our environmental policies. We in OES appreciate the opportunity to hear industry perspectives on environmental issues through meetings with trade associations such as the Chemical Manufacturers Association or with individual companies. Industry can have an important impact only to the extent it remains informed and engaged. Recognizing that environmental concerns are certain to be among the important issues not only of the next 5–10 years but well beyond, businessmen and industrialists—directly and through their industry associations—must inform themselves about the facts and make use of the U.S. Government as a resource. In short, do not be shy about making your views known; believe me, other nongovernmental organizations are not. You can also, of course, do more to include environmental concerns in your own longer-term planning and decisions, including factoring costs of likely environmental impacts into your product-pricing decisions from the beginning. I suspect there may be a payoff to being leaders in this area.

Industry also needs to make full use of the various mechanisms for influencing policy. For example, you can benefit by participating fully in the U.S. business/industry advisory group of the OECD; it has an important role in shaping that organization's programs and priorities. Industry should also work with the World Environment Center in providing information and assistance to enhance worldwide environmental management practices.

As most of you probably know, the World Environment Center cooperates with and utilizes the expertise of governments, industries, academics, and nongovernmental organizations. One of its most promising programs is the International Environment and Development Service, funded in part by AID [Agency for International Development], which offers no-cost or low-cost assistance to rapidly developing countries to enhance their environmental protection and safety efforts. Services ranging from industrial pollution control audits to environmental management fellowships are available. Such efforts could be especially valuable in increasing environmental understanding in the Third World because expertise is provided to needy governments or businesses. But I suggest that you not wait for Third World governments to call for help—they may well wait too long.

CONCLUSION

In conclusion, I expect few of you will dispute that environmental issues are serious and are going to be with us for a long time. I hope you will also agree that your active participation in shaping policies is crucial. The State Department is a key point of contact for you—but so are the concerned program agencies, public institutions like the United Nations and OECD, and private groups such as the World Environment Center. I again urge you not to hesitate to use all the available mechanisms to make your views known, at home and abroad.

As a final word, let me add a personal view. The environmental issues I have reviewed today pose serious challenges for you. But they also offer opportunities for a better understanding of the world we live in, for developing useful technologies, and for sales at home and abroad of new goods and services. I hope we can work together to make the most of these opportunities. ∎

Suggested Additional Readings

Caldwell, Lynton. *In Defense of the Earth* (Bloomington, IN: Indiana University Press, 1972).

Ehrlich, Paul R. *Human Ecology* (San Francisco: Freeman, 1973).

Enloe, Cynthia. *The Politics of Pollution in a Comparative Perspective: Ecology and Power in Four Nations* (New York: McKay, 1975).

Falk, Richard A. *This Endangered Planet* (New York: Random House, 1971).

Griffin, Keith B. *World Hunger and the World Economy* (New York: Holmes and Meier, 1987).

Jones, Charles O. *Clean Air: The Policies and Politics of Pollution Control* (Pittsburgh, PA: University of Pittsburgh Press, 1977).

Linowitz, Sol. *World Hunger: A Challenge to American Policy* (New York: Foreign Policy Association, 1980).

Maguire, Andres, and Janet Welsh Brown. *Bordering on Trouble: Resources and Politics in Latin America* (Bethesda, MD: Adler and Adler, 1986).

Meadows, Donella H. *The Limits to Growth: A Report for the Club of Rome's Project on the Predicament of Mankind* (New York: Universe Books, 1974).

Ophuls, William. *Ecology and the Politics of Scarcity* (San Francisco: Freeman, 1977).

"Planet of the Year," *Time* special issue, January 2, 1989.

Quigg, Philip W. *Environment: The Global Issues* (New York: Foreign Policy Association, 1973).

Regens, James L. *The Acid Rain Controversy* (Pittsburgh, PA: University of Pittsburgh Press, 1988).

Shue, Henry. *Basic Rights: Subsistence, Affluence, and U.S. Foreign Policy* (Princeton, NJ: Princeton University Press, 1980).

Warnock, John W. *The Politics of Hunger: The Global Food System* (New York: Methuen, 1987).

CHAPTER FOURTEEN

Terrorism

*
*

Terrorism is a scourge, abhorrent to all Americans; but it has also been enormously effective for those groups who practice it.

To begin with, Americans do not understand terrorism very well. Our own history has been generally characterized by the absence of terrorism. As heirs of the Judeo-Christian tradition, we are repelled by terrorism, the sacrificing of innocent victims for some supposedly higher cause. The fact that most victims of international terrorism in recent years have been Americans has led to increasing national bitterness toward those individuals, groups, and nations that practice terrorism.

Because our own political processes have been relatively free from terrorist activities, we have come to believe that peaceful change is normal and the violence of terrorism abnormal. But that is not true for many countries of the world, where *coups d'etat,* terrorism, revolution, and the planned, orchestrated, calibrated use of violence in the political process is normal, recurrent, and to be expected. Although the U.S. has had little terrorism internally and it is strongly condemned by American public opinion, other groups and countries do not always operate on that same peaceful basis. For terrorists, violence and terrorism are ways to get attention for their cause, to mobilize support, to secure new recruits for the movement, and to garner national or international headlines.

In this pursuit, terrorist groups have often been dramatically successful. Were it not for the seizure of the American embassy hostages—which traumatized our political process for over a year, led to the electoral defeat of President Jimmy Carter, and went on to traumatize us in the Iran-Contra affair—the Iranian government would be just another Third World regime. Terrorism brought it attention. Guerrilla groups in Latin America have long used terror, sabotage, and violence to dramatize their cause and to gain sympathy for it. In the Middle East, of course, Palestinian extremist elements have used terrorism to gain global attention for themselves and gradually to shift world public opinion toward greater sympathy for the notion of a Palestinian homeland. In both of these goals, one would have to say, the terrorists have been remarkably successful.

Not only do Americans not understand this use of purposeful violence very well, we are not well equipped to deal with it, either. First, television dramatizes the terrorists' acts and, by its coverage, gives them the publicity they seek and also puts enormous pressures on the U.S. government to accede to their demands. After all, who can resist the images of weeping mothers and grieving family members who wonder why the U.S. government is doing "nothing" to secure the release of their loved ones? The proper response to a terrorist act is to ignore it at the public level, while quietly and privately going after the terrorists. But in America we cannot do that. The media coverage means that the terrorist act cannot be ignored, and, unlike the French or the Israelis, our political culture prevents us from sending out a "hit squad" to eliminate the terrorists. My guess is that my even mentioning such a possibility in the previous sentence causes most Americans to recoil and say, "We do not do that." But if that is our response, then we must also know that there is not much we as a nation can do about terrorism.

Television, our own abhorrence of and lack of understanding about the use of violent means, and our reluctance to use forceful means against terrorists—all these elements enable terrorists to continue winning victories for their causes and to hamstring American policy responses. Fortunately, the United States has so far remained remarkably free of terrorist activities; but with the success of terrorist activities abroad, our porous borders and almost total lack of security at major installations, and the political culture of Americans that forces us to give in to terrorists in order to release our loved ones and never to take retaliatory actions ourselves, one wonders how long we as a nation can escape the terrorist scourge.

This section of readings begins with a statement on Latin America by political scientist Merle Kling, in which he shows how violence, revolution, and terrorism are recurrent and regular parts of the political process in many countries—in contrast to the United States, where we view such violence as abnormal and pathological. As to what can be done about terrorism, former Secretary of State George Shultz has a calm, reasoned, and careful response. Also included in this section is a spirited discussion of terrorism and what the U.S. should do about it by scholars and public officials Yonah Alexander, Ramsey Clark, John Charles Daly, the late Senator John P. East, and Frank H. Perez. In addition, the Washington Post's David Ignatius offers some suggestion as to the proper U.S. response to terrorism.

Violence and Politics in Latin America

By Merle Kling

At times it seems to me that the absence of bloodshed and death drives us desperate, as if we feel ourselves alive only when surrounded by firing squads and destruction

Don Gamiel Bernal, a character in a novel by Carlos Fuentes, The Death of Artemio Cruz *(New York: Farrar, Straus & Co., 1964), pp. 37–38.*

Force or violence, as Marx observed, may be 'the midwife of every old society which is pregnant with the new,'[1] but neither Marx nor less paternal students of the ontogeny of revolutions recognize the capacity of political midwives to affect the heredity of the political offspring that they deliver. Modal studies of revolution, drawing upon the French and Russian Revolutions for illustrative data, specify the causes of major revolutions, describe patterns in the rhythms of revolutionary movements, assess the durable consequences of revolutionary upheavals. But possible links between varieties of violence and revolutionary outcomes are left unexplored, for well-known studies of revolution, written by authors who wear the conceptual spectacles provided by the political cultures of the United States and Great Britain, treat violence with literary and analytical economy. After all, their political cultures evaluate violence as aberrant, exceptional behavior.

Yet, just as elections may be regarded as manifest aspects of political systems in Western Europe and the United States, revolutions, with their accompanying violence, may be regarded as an aspect of the political culture of many Latin American political systems. Thus elections (in some political systems) and revolutions (in other political systems) become related to distinctive political expectations, demands and norms; to distinctive standards of recruitment of political elites; to alternative definitions of political skill within political systems; and to divergent strategies for the pursuit of power.

ELECTIONS AND NONVIOLENT POLITICAL SYSTEMS

Elections constitute integral elements of nonviolent political systems in contemporary British and North American societies. Socialized into acceptance of nonviolent methods of political competition, virtually all relevant parties to political conflict in these societies expect elections to take place and consider it right that they should take place. The political culture— the prevailing, widely-distributed beliefs, values, cognitions and affective responses—sanctions the resolution of contests for public office by election, by vote, and condemns the intrusion of violence within the arena of internal political conflict. The advocate of violence in these societies, consequently, not only defies the formal juridical rules of the political system; he attacks the

psychological supports of the juridical system, since he threatens highly salient norms.

Violent behavior is not absent from British and North American societies, but it is *predominantly* oriented toward nonpolitical objects. Violence does not significantly affect the choice of governmental leaders, the articulation and aggregation of group interests, the patterns of authority for the entire society, the content of domestic and foreign policies, or the allocation of large, tangible resources. Experts in the employment of organized violence, military personnel, compete for rewards but do not fire their weapons, or threaten to fire their weapons, in order to assist one group of political competitors as against another, to force the adoption of one public policy as opposed to another.

Means become linked with ends. Acceptance of the discipline and restraint of means (elections) is accompanied by contraction of the scope of change envisioned as ends (goals). Advocacy of violence in a political system that has assimilated the norms of elections can be justified only on behalf of drastic changes, on behalf of millennial goals. Since violence represents a deviant means by the standards of such a political culture, it can be embraced only on behalf of deviant ends. A group that acquiesces in the election norms of a nonviolent political culture, accordingly, exposes its goals to subtle forces of attrition. For it proves difficult si-

Merle Kling was Professor of Political Science at Washington University.

Source: From *Latin American Sociological Studies,* Paul Halwas (ed.), University of Keele, Keele, England, 1967, pp. 119–32. Reprinted by permission of Routledge.

Successful Revolutions in Latin America, 1950–65

May 1950	Haiti	August 1954	Brazil
May 1951	Bolivia	December 1954	Honduras
May 1951	Panama	January 1955	Panama
March 1952	Cuba	September 1955	Argentina
April 1952	Bolivia	November 1955	Argentina
December 1952	Venezuela	November 1955	Brazil
June 1953	Colombia	September 1956	Nicaragua
May 1954	Paraguay	October 1956	Honduras
June 1954	Guatemala	December 1956	Haiti
February 1957	Haiti	August 1961	Brazil
April 1957	Haiti	November 1961	Ecuador
May 1957	Haiti	March 1962	Argentina
May 1957	Colombia	July 1962	Peru
June 1957	Haiti	March 1963	Peru
July 1957	Guatemala	March 1963	Guatemala
October 1957	Guatemala	July 1963	Ecuador
January 1958	Venezuela	September 1963	Dominican Rep.
January 1959	Cuba	October 1963	Honduras
October 1960	El Salvador	April 1964	Brazil
May 1961—Jan. 1962	Dominican Rep.	November 1964	Bolivia

multaneously to maintain loyalty to apocalyptic visions and prosaic rules of electoral competition. In a culture of political nonviolence, revolutions, rather than elections, mark rapid and profound transitions in public policies and the massive restructuring of a political system.

The United States and Great Britain, therefore, exemplify political systems in which (1) elections take place regularly and frequently; (2) violence is oriented predominantly toward nonpolitical objects; (3) experts in the manipulation of violence do not utilize their expertise in order to determine public policies and to designate leading governmental personnel; (4) the process of political socialization discourages the selection of violence as an appropriate method for political participation; (5) advocacy of, or resort to, violence is widely perceived as a deviant means associated with the pursuit of deviant ends relative to prevailing norms; and (6) elections are compatible with divergent, but circumscribed, policy outcomes.

REVOLUTIONS AND A CULTURE OF POLITICAL VIOLENCE

In contrast with the United States and Great Britain, many Latin American political systems are characterized by manifestly violent political behavior and acceptance of violence as a 'legitimate' means for the pursuit of power.

1. Frequency of Revolution

The popular image of Latin America as an area of endemic revolution is warranted. The resolution of succession problems by methods not authorised by constitutional prescription is a recurring phenomenon, and the replacement of leading personnel, notably presidents, by acts of violence is common. 'Between independence and World War I,' Edwin Lieuwen notes, 'the Spanish-American republics experienced 115 successful revolutions and many times that number of abortive revolts.'[2] In the two decades 1931–1950, there were 58 successful revolutions.[3] During the period between 1940

and 1955, the office of president in Latin American countries was occupied by 121 men, forty-two of whom managed to remain in office less than one year, and there were 136 successions to the presidency.[4] Between January 1, 1950 and January 1, 1965, as the above list indicates, at least forty successful revolutions occurred. If all the changes in the office of president or the leadership of juntas or the composition of executive councils in Haiti (May 1957) and the Dominican Republic (January 1962 and December 1963) were included, the number would be even larger (see table above).

During the period 1950–1965, consequently, revolutions took place in sixteen of the twenty Latin American republics. Only in Mexico, Uruguay, Chile and Costa Rica was the period marked by the absence of revolution.

2. Pervasive Political Violence

Every election campaign does not culminate in victory. Every outburst of political violence does not culminate in revolution. While displays of politically oriented violence are not confined to successful campaigns for control of the presidency in Latin America, the political systems are permeated by acts of violence. If each violent action does not result in revolution—and it doesn't—the frequency of acts of political violence, nevertheless, encourages the perception of violence as a highly visible means for pursuing political ends.

Although fragmentary reporting and dissimilar criteria for the inclusion and exclusion of evidence prevent the compilation of uniform and complete inventories of violence in Latin America, data on the pervasiveness of political violence in the area are impressive and relatively abundant. One study noted 'some 3,500 Latin American insurgency and insurgency-related events' for the period 1946–1963.[5] The same study comments upon the historical continuity of violence in the area:

> Historians have grown haggard in the task of counting up all the insurgencies and civil wars to which the 'Age of the Caudillos' gave rise. Venezuela, for example, had suffered 52 important revolts by 1912. Bolivia had more than 60 'revolutions' by 1898 and had assassinated six presidents. Colombia had experienced 27 civil wars, one of which claimed 80,000 and another 100,000 lives. These are among the more extreme examples but many of the other republics did not lag far behind.[6]

And a statistical summary of the incidence of internal wars, 1946–1959, compiled by Harry Eckstein from the *New York Times Index,* illustrates the ubiquity of political violence in Latin America. In his

Incidence of Internal Wars, 1946–1959

	Unequivocal	Unequivocal and Equivocal
Argentina	35	57
Bolivia	34	53
Brazil	36	49
Chile	9	21
Colombia	42	47
Costa Rica	16	19
Cuba	80	100
Dominican Republic	2	6
Ecuador	26	41
Guatemala	32	45
Haiti	32	40
Honduras	10	11
Mexico	27	28
Nicaragua	13	16
Panama	23	29
Paraguay	19	29
Peru	20	23
El Salvado	4	9
Uruguay		1
Venezuela	26	36

summary, unequivocal cases include warfare, turmoil, rioting, terrorism, mutiny and coups, and equivocal cases include plots, administrative action and two quasi-private cases that may not be politically oriented (see table above).[7]

In the light of the evidence, political violence cannot be regarded as aberrant behavior in Latin America. It is recurring, chronic and rule-conforming rather than heteroclite. If participants in a political culture of nonviolence expect periodic elections, then politically orientated members of Latin American societies should expect unscheduled but regular manifestations of political violence. For violence, as Harry Eckstein strikingly points out in a series of generalized propositions, is capable of becoming a self-perpetuating style of political behavior:

> In some societies, the most manifest cause of internal war seems to be internal war itself,

> one instance following another, often without a recurrence of the conditions that led to the original event. This means that political disorientations may be followed by the formation of a new set of orientations, establishing a predisposition toward violence that is inculcated by the experience of violence itself. In such cases, internal wars result not from specifiable objective conditions, and not even from the loss of legitimacy by a particular regime, but from a general lack of receptivity to legitimacy of any kind. Violence becomes a political style that is self-perpetuating....[8]

3. The Roles of Experts in Violence

Although military personnel in the United States and Great Britain are not political eunuchs, their roles are relatively restricted. They are likely to articulate interests of limited scope, particularly the competing interests of armed services for budgetary allocations, but they are not likely to perform functions of interest aggregation, general political socialization and recruitment, authoritative rule-making and rule-interpretation. Typically, they do not announce their support for, or opposition to, programmes of medical care for the aged, plans for the nationalization of railroads, or alternative schemes for financing education. Since their doctrinal training tends to identify the symbolism of 'politics' with prohibited activity, military personnel in the United States, in the process of acquiring professional standards of behavior, are encouraged to develop little preoccupation with a large variety of policy outcomes.

One element in Latin American systems of political violence is the *diffuseness,* rather than the specialization, of the roles of experts in violence. They do not merely promote interests of various segments of the armed forces and administer, actively or latently, severe sanctions in order to enforce policies formulated by authoritative decision makers. They conspicuously engage in the selection of governing personnel, the promulgation of public policies, the resolution of succession crises, the competition for office, and the allocation of budgetary resources. Among Latin American military personnel, technical competence in the employment of violence merges with a concern for the diverse policy outputs of the political system.

The low demands for combat duty by Latin American military units against foreign enemies, moreover, mean that military personnel and material can be mobilized for participation in revolutionary maneuvers and interservice rivalries, and that a trained military bureaucracy is available, and possibly eager, to discharge administrative duties that are carried on ineptly (at least in the eyes of some) by civilian officials. Obviously, military personnel are equipped and trained to participate effectively in Latin American revolutions. Thus a study of twenty-nine successful revolutions during 1941–1950 concludes: 'The military played a significant role in the 29 revolutions.'[9] Another study of Latin American presidents between 1940 and 1955 notes that 'national military contingents account for thirty-nine of fifty-seven forcefully attained shifts of presidential personnel.'[10]

The ability of military personnel to occupy the office of president in Latin American societies provides an additional measure of their political influence and power, and the evidence of the recruitment of Latin American presidents from the ranks of military officers is revealing. 'To take a single year,' according to Edwin Lieuwen, 'in 1954 thirteen of the twenty republics were ruled by military presidents.' Moreover, between 1930 and 1957, 'fifty-six military men ... held the presidential office in the twenty Latin American republics for as long as a year.'[11]

Examination of the professional backgrounds of the 121 men who held the office of president in a Latin American country at some time during the period 1940–1955 yields particularly striking results. Relevant data on occupational background were secured for 116 presidents. They were classified into professional categories and, since many presidents (25 per cent of the military group and more than 75 per cent of the civilian group) qualified for more than one category, the total number is greater than the number of men who held office. The number of presidents, classified according to professional background, follows (see table below).

As the study that collected these data points out:

... the military grouping is larger by far than any single ... grouping in the civilian segment of the sample. Furthermore, the members of the military are one of the most homogeneous occupational groups ... Multiple occupational classifications appear much more frequently among the civilian presidents than they do in the military category.

In fact, every state in Latin America had at least one president with a background of professional military service between 1940 and 1955.[12]

Not only do military personnel often secure presidential office in

Military	51
Legal profession	33
Educators	31
'Communications media'—writers, journalists, owners of newspapers, etc.	18
Medical doctors	10
Bankers and financiers	9
Landowners, agriculturalists	8
Other (businessmen, managers, engineers, architects, etc.)	19

Latin America, but they tend to maintain themselves in office for prolonged periods. *Continuismo,* extension of the term of office of an incumbent by a variety of legalistic and manipulative devices, not uncommonly is associated with the tenure of a military president. Hence, men of military background, while constituting only 42.1 per cent of the total number of presidents during the period 1940–1955, held office for almost two-thirds of the time during which the 121 presidents included in the analysis occupied the position; 'nonmilitary' presidents, accounting for 57.9 per cent of the presidents, held the position for only 36.6 per cent of the time.[13]

In the culture of political violence that prevails in Latin American societies, skill in the provocation and organization of violence is not concentrated exclusively in the hands of professional soldiers. Other competitors for power and influence, too, learn to rely upon techniques of violence—however arcane and private the motivations for violence—to pursue their public goals. Thus students engage in frequent riots, sometimes store and fire weapons from inside the legal sanctuary of the universities, and manifest considerable militancy and belligerency in advocating public policies. The 'professional student' of the Latin American university may not qualify as a 'professional revolutionary,' since he lacks the stable party commitment and ideological sophistication (or rigidity) that Lenin set down as requisites for the role; but his preoccupation with public affairs and experience in combatting organized police and military forces often make him approximate the role of 'professional rev-

olutionary' in the sense of one who maintains a sustained interest in the pursuit of governmental authority by means of violence. The culture of political violence, consequently, accommodates both the expert and counter-expert, or amateur, in violence. And when some of the 'amateurs' secure training in guerrilla tactics and terrorism, the line dividing the expert from the amateur becomes fluid. In any case, where expectations of peaceful governmental transitions are low, individuals and groups not integrated into regular military formations also seek to acquire expertise in the techniques of violence. The revolutionary, whether the appellation professional is attached to him or not, like the military man of diffuse political functions, serves to differentiate a culture of political violence and to emphasize the role of experts in violence in such a culture.

4. Legal and Formal Concomitants of Violence

Not surprisingly, there are legal and formal corollaries of the patterns of violence in Latin America: (1) frequent replacement and revision of written constitutional documents; (2) conspicuous departures from prescribed constitutional norms in political behavior; (3) recurrent suspensions of constitutional guarantees, declarations of states of seige, and the conduct of government by decree; and (4) the institutionalization of procedures for exile, including the right of asylum.

In many Latin American countries, constitutions are rather casually discarded when a revolution takes place, the convening of a constituent assembly for the draft-

ing of a fresh document is not a rare event, and the proclamation of a new constitution does not presage an era of documentary continuity. Constitutions, in brief, come and go. During a period of 100 years, Bolivia had ten constitutions, Ecuador thirteen, and Venezuela fifteen. Under these conditions, the transiency of constitutional documents makes it difficult to elevate them to the level of symbols of legitimacy.

Glaring discrepancies between relatively unambiguous written legal prescriptions and political practice are common in Latin America. Despite constitutional requirements, legislatures may not be convened, elections may be indefinitely postponed, the independence of the judiciary may remain unrecognized, principles of federalism or decentralization may be circumvented, the power of the executive may be exercised without constraint, and elaborate statements of civil liberties and social welfare allowed to stand as rhetorical ideals uncontaminated by observance. In the Latin American political culture of violence, only the politically naive search constitutional documents for significant clues to the operation of political systems, and only scholars with vested interests in legalistic studies can rationalize meticulous explications of constitutional texts.

Since constitutions are not sacrosanct, the suspension of constitutional guarantees, the promulgation of a state of siege, and the conduct of government by means of presidential decrees is a recurrent phenomenon. Nomenclature varies, but every constitution in Latin America authorizes these practices. Governing personnel, especially presidents, therefore, can invoke a formal clause to curb speech, press, petition and assembly, to threaten property rights at least temporarily, and to restrict the activities of opposition groups. And the subsequent ritualistic approval of presidential decrees by a legislative body may prove perfunctory.

In an environment of constitutional uncertainty and violent competition for governmental office, the treatment of political opponents, obviously, presents a special problem to an incumbent regime. Some measures at the disposal of Latin American governments are relatively conventional: surveillance, confinement, imprisonment. But exile and rights of asylum have become uniquely stylized aspects of the political systems of Latin America. Like the sequence of movements in a bullfight, the ritual of asylum and exile of political leaders in Latin America is enacted in conformity with relatively inflexible precedents. The political figure who threatens a regime but is vulnerable to punitive action by coercive organs of the government escapes to a foreign embassy; the incumbent regime expresses doubt that the 'escaped' politician qualifies for asylum, since he has committed 'common crimes' (including, if a deposed president, the theft of public funds); after the elapse of a suitable period, the government quietly permits the refugee in a foreign embassy to depart from the country. Persistent efforts at extradition or the denial of safe conduct into exile are rare.

The legal and formal aspects of Latin American political systems thus serve to maintain and perpetuate violence. For overt acts of violence yield an output of consti-

tutional instability, disregard for prescribed legal norms, the conduct of government through executive orders, and the institutionalization of procedures for exile and asylum. In turn, these legal and formal concomitants feed back into the system and contribute to the perpetuation of violence, since constitutions do not inspire respect, prescribed legal rules do not impose effective restraints, decision making by the executive is customary, and the rule of asylum, by protecting the loser in a violent political struggle, does not discourage revolutionary conspiracies.

5. Convergence of Proximate and Early Socialization

Contemporary social scientists seek the sources of political attitudes and modes of political behavior in the nonpolitical, as well as political, experiences of members of a political system. Politically relevant responses, it now is explicitly acknowledged, are learned in families, religious organizations, and schools, as well as in political parties and governmental bureaucracies. Harry Eckstein, accordingly, has pointed out that congruent socializing experiences may serve as a support for stable, democratic political systems. On the other hand, the cues emanating from the various institutions of a society may undermine the stability of a system: authoritarian family structures and officially promulgated democratic norms during the period of the Weimar Republic in Germany often cited as an illustration of incongruence in a political system. Moreover, as Almond and Verba point out, the effects of nonpolitical patterns of authority may be 'culminative.' In their words: 'If one finds

one's self consistently in social situations where one has a voice over decisions, this is more likely to result in a general sense of competence than if the experience with participation in one area is not matched by similar experiences in other areas.'[14]

There is a consensus among observers, both participant and disengaged, regarding the models of behavior and attitudes encouraged by nonpolitical agencies of socialization (the family, the Church and less formally organized institutions) in Latin America. These sensitive reporters of impressions, who lean toward the interpretive essay as a congenial form of expression, emphasize the compatibility between the values and styles imparted by nonpolitical institutions and the perpetuation of patterns of political violence and revolution in Latin American political behavior.

The theme of *machismo* dominates the literature of psychological insight devoted to Latin America. The political world preponderantly is a man's world, and the male learns to value qualities of masculinity: 'Men especially are expected to be men. One takes pride in being *"muy hombre"*.'[15] By means of vocabulary, dress, grooming, posture and promiscuity, the man seeks to demonstrate his virility. He acquires a sensitive shell to protect personal dignity and is expected to respond aggressively to threats to *dignidad*: 'Response [to an affront] must be immediate, direct and normally violent.'[16] And *machismo,* a consequence of socializing experiences within the family, is linked to an adult predisposition for acts of violence. In the words of Octavio Paz: '... the essential attribute of the *macho*—power—almost always reveals itself as a capacity for wounding, humiliating, annihilating.'[17] To put it in psychological jargon: aggression and violence often are externalized, rather than internalized, by members of Latin American societies.

While acts of violence may be motivated by feelings of inferiority and resentment and encouraged by the cult of *machismo,* orientations toward death in Latin America facilitate the acceptance of the fatal consequences of acts of violence. Whereas death is banished from daily, familiar and 'normal' activities (and thus fears of it relegated to the unconscious) in Anglo-Saxon cultures, awareness of death is maintained at a high level of consciousness in Latin American societies. Religious rituals, often representing a blend of Roman Catholicism and autochthonous beliefs, accord frequent and visible recognition to the reality of death. The death-motif is incorporated into toys and pastries. Death masks and representations of skeletons figure prominently in religious processions. Funeral rites are elaborate and, in Mexico, the Day of the Dead is enthusiastically celebrated. The language employed by Octavio Paz suggests virtually a *mystique* of death: 'To die and to kill are ideas that rarely leave us. We are seduced by death.'[18]

Much of the psychological capability for violence may be drained off by nonpolitical activities. A good deal of the energy available for violent behavior may be siphoned off directly into acts of homicide and fights between individuals; or indirectly, by exhibitions of verbal aggression; or vicariously, by attendance at bullfights. But for a minority, politics, especially revolutionary politics, can provide a significant outlet. Early socialization produces tensions that seek resolution in violence, approved social styles for males encourage belligerent behaviour, participation in political violence may provide reassurance for those who boast of a masculinity that is suspect, and prevailing values condone acts of violence, including political violence. Hence an active minority engaged in acts of political violence is inhibited neither by a political system that brands such acts as illegitimate nor by internalized values that censure the resort to violent methods. Since the standards of neither society nor conscience are wrenched by outbreaks of political violence, individuals may mobilize their psychic resources of aggression to take part in student riots, demonstrations, political terrorism and— revolution. Their induction into politics, in the phrase of Verba and Almond, takes place 'through experience with violent revolution.'[19] And thus there is a congruence between early socialization and later modes of political action: nonpolitical agencies of socialization have laid the foundations for a culture of political violence.

6. Compatibility of Revolutionary Means with Diverse Ends

The sequel to elections in a culture of political nonviolence may include limited changes in public policies, but is not likely to be marked by a radical rearrangement of the political system or drastic changes in a wide variety of public policies. In contrast, the range of possible outcomes accompanying a revolution, in a culture of political violence, is extremely broad: the greater the degree of compatibility between violence and the prevailing norms of a political system, the greater the range of policy outputs that may accompany the employment of violence. In such a culture, since millennial aspirations need not be invoked to justify violence, a revolution, like an election in other cultures, may merely rotate personnel. Also like an election, it may serve as a prelude to the introduction of relatively limited changes in public policies. But unlike an election, a revolution may shift personnel, eliminate certain social classes, radically modify the capabilities of various interests to exert influence and power, and transform the system for absorbing and resolving public conflicts. The spectrum of changes engendered by elections in a culture of political nonviolence form a rather small arc. A much larger arc, however, is required to accommodate the range of changes generated by revolution in a culture of political violence. Revolutionary means are compatible with highly diverse ends.

Thus some revolutions in Latin America substitute one military officer for another as president, and leave the political system intact and public policies unaffected. The goal of such revolutions appears as a variant of the familiar slogan of an election campaign: 'Throw the rascals out!' Other revolutions tamper little with the political system, but modify the proportion of royalties on mineral exploitation claimed by the local government. Yet other revolutions (the Cuban and the Mexican are conspicuous examples) reorder the political structure, change the symbol environment and drastically transform public policies. Significantly, the introduction of these far-reaching changes is preceded by relatively prolonged periods of violence. And the politically socializing effects of participation in a particular form of violence are suggested by Fidel Castro himself: 'Had I understood the imperialist phenomenon, I would then [at an early stage in the conflict with Batista] have truly become a Marxist-Leninist. But to reach that point I had to have two years of armed conflict . . .'[20]

Despite certain functional similarities between elections and revolutions, consequently, the potential scope of the changes stimulated by elections and revolutions differs. In a culture of political nonviolence, a revolution signals drastic changes; in a culture of political violence, a revolution *per se* may or may not be a harbinger of drastic change. For a culture of political violence authorizes means that may yield widely divergent ends, whereas a culture of political non-

violence imposes rather severe restrictions on the scope of change that may be pursued by means sanctioned by that culture. Since politically relevant violence neither occurs rarely nor produces uniform outcomes in Latin America, social scientists with good cause have become preoccupied with the study of violence—under such rubrics as internal war, revolution and instability—in its varied manifestations in Latin America.[21] ∎

Notes

1. Cited in Frederick Engels, *Herr Eugen Dühring's Revolution in Science (Anti-Dühring)* (New York: International Publishers, 1939), p. 203.
2. *Arms and Politics in Latin America,* Revised Edition (New York: Praeger, 1961), p. 21.
3. Lee Benson Valentine, *A Comparative Study of Successful Revolutions in Latin America, 1941–1950* (Stanford University: Ph.D. dissertation, 1952), pp. 246–247.
4. Huey Carl Camp, *Presidential Politics in Latin America: The Dynamics of Power* (Washington University (St. Louis): Ph.D. dissertation, 1965), pp. 442–443, Table XXXVI.
5. Atlantic Research Corporation, Georgetown Research Project, *A Historical Survey of Patterns and Techniques of Insurgency Conflicts in Post-1900 Latin America* (Arpa Project 4860) (1964), pp. ii–iii.
6. Ibid., p. 51.
7. *Internal War: The Problem of Anticipation* (January 15, 1962, mimeographed), Appendix I, p. 3.
8. "On the Etiology of Internal Wars," *History and Theory,* Volume IV, Number 2 (1965), pp. 150–151.
9. Lee Benson Valentine, op. cit., p. 261.
10. Huey Carl Camp, *op. cit.,* p. 164.
11. *Op. cit.,* pp. 122, 129.
12. Huey Carl Camp, *Caudillismo: An Empirical Approach* (Washington University (St. Louis): M.A. dissertation, 1960), *passim.*
13. Ibid., p. 431.
14. Gabriel A. Almond and Sidney Verba, *The Civic Culture* (Princeton, NJ: Princeton University Press, 1963), pp. 369–370.
15. Norman Daymond Humphrey, "Ethnic Images and Stereotypes of Mexicans and Americans," *The American Journal of Economics and Sociology,* Vol. 14, No. 3 (April 1955), p. 309.
16. Ibid., p. 310.
17. *The Labyrinth of Solitude* (New York: Grove Press, 1961), p. 82.
18. Ibid., pp. 57–58.
19. Sidney Verba and Gabriel A. Almond, "National Revolutions and Political Commitment," in Harry Eckstein, (ed.), *Internal War: Problems and Approaches* (New York: The Free Press of Glencoe, 1964), p. 206.
20. Quoted in interview with C. L. Sulzberger, *New York Times,* November 7, 1964.
21. For a critical analysis of recent approaches to the study of political violence, see Lawrence Stone, "Theories of Revolution," *World Politics,* Vol. XVIII, No. 2 (January 1966), pp. 159–176.

Terrorism: The Challenge to the Democracies

By George P. Shultz

Five years have passed since the Jonathan Institute held its first conference on terrorism, and in that time the world has seen two major

developments: one a cause for great distress; the other a reason for hope.

The distressing fact is that over these past 5 years terrorism has

increased. More people were killed or injured by international terrorists last year than in any year since governments began keeping

Source: From an address before the Jonathan Institute Conference on International Terrorism, Washington, D.C., June 24, 1984. Reprinted in Department of State, Bureau of Public Affairs, *Current Policy No. 589,* June 24, 1984, pp. 1–4.

records. In 1983 there were more than 500 such attacks, of which more than 200 were against the United States. For Americans the worst tragedies were the destruction of our Embassy and then the Marine barracks in Beirut. But around the world, many of our close friends and allies were also victims. The bombing of Harrods in London, the bombing at Orly Airport in Paris, the destruction of a Gulf Air flight in the United Arab Emirates, and the Rangoon bombing of South Korean officials are just a few examples—not to mention the brutal attack on a West Jerusalem shopping mall this past April.

Even more alarming has been the rise of state-sponsored terrorism. In the past 5 years more states have joined the ranks of what we might call the "League of Terror," as full-fledged sponsors and supporters of indiscriminate—and not so indiscriminate—murder. Terrorist attacks supported by what Qadhafi calls the "holy alliance" of Libya, Syria, and Iran, and attacks sponsored by North Korea and others, have taken a heavy toll of innocent lives. Seventy or more such attacks in 1983 probably involved significant state support or participation.

As a result, more of the world's people must today live in fear of sudden and unprovoked violence at the hands of terrorists. After 5 years, the epidemic is spreading, and the civilized world is still groping for remedies.

Nevertheless, these past 5 years have also given us cause for hope. Thanks in large measure to the efforts of concerned governments, citizens, and groups like the Jonathan Institute, the peoples of the free world have finally begun

to grapple with the problem of terrorism in intellectual and in practical terms. I say intellectual because the first step toward a solution to any problem is to understand that there is a problem and then to understand its nature. In recent years we have learned a great deal about terrorism, though our education has been painful and costly. We know what kind of threat international terrorism poses to our free society. We have learned much about the terrorists themselves, their supporters, their targets, their diverse methods, their underlying motives, and their eventual goals.

Armed with this knowledge we can focus our energies on the practical means for reducing and eventually eliminating the threat. We can all share the hope that, when the next conference of this institute is convened, we will look back and say that 1984 was the turning point in our struggle against terrorism, that having come to grips with the problem we were able to deal with it effectively and responsibly.

THE ANATOMY OF TERRORISM

Let me speak briefly about the anatomy of terrorism. What we have learned about terrorism, first of all, is that it is not random, undirected, purposeless violence. It is not, like an earthquake or a hurricane, an act of nature before which we are helpless. Terrorists and those who support them have definite goals; terrorist violence is the means of attaining those goals. Our response must be twofold: we must deny them the means but above all we must deny them their goals.

But what are the goals of terrorism? We know that the phenome-

non of terrorism is actually a matrix that covers a diverse array of methods, resources, instruments, and immediate aims. It appears in many shapes and sizes—from the lone individual who plants a homemade explosive in a shopping center, to the small clandestine group that plans kidnapings and assassinations of public figures, to the well-equipped and well-financed organization that uses force to terrorize an entire population. Its stated objectives may range from separatist causes to revenge for ethnic grievances to social and political revolution. International drug smugglers use terrorism to blackmail and intimidate government officials. It is clear that our responses will have to fit the precise character and circumstances of the specific threats.

But we must understand that the overarching goal of all terrorists is the same: with rare exceptions, they are attempting to impose their will by force—a special kind of force designed to create an atmosphere of fear. And their efforts are directed at destroying what all of us here are seeking to build. They're a threat to the democracies.

THE THREAT TO THE DEMOCRACIES

The United States and its democratic allies are morally committed to certain ideals and to a humane vision of the future. In our foreign politics, we try to foster the kind of world that promotes peaceful settlement of disputes, one that welcomes change without violent conflict. We seek a world in which human rights are respected by all governments, a world based on the rule of law. We know that in a world community where all nations share these blessings, our own democracy will flourish, our own nation will prosper, and our own people will continue to enjoy freedom.

Nor has ours been a fruitless search. In our lifetime, we have seen the world progress, though perhaps too slowly, toward this goal. Civilized norms of conduct have evolved, even governing relations between adversaries. Conflict persists; but, with some notorious exceptions, even wars have been conducted with certain restraints —indiscriminate slaughter of innocents is widely condemned; the use of certain kinds of weapons has been proscribed; and most, but not all, nations have heeded those proscriptions.

We all know that the world as it exists is still far from our ideal vision. But today, even the progress that mankind has already made is endangered by those who do not share that vision—who, indeed, violently oppose it.

For we must understand, above all, that terrorism is a form of political violence. Wherever it takes place, it is directed in an important sense against us, the democracies—against our most basic values and often our fundamental strategic interests. The values upon which democracy is based—individual rights, equality under the law, freedom of thought and expression, and freedom of religion—all stand in the way of those who seek to impose their will, their ideologies, or their religious beliefs by force. A terrorist has no patience and no respect for the orderly processes of democratic society, and, therefore, he considers himself its enemy.

And it is an unfortunate irony that the very qualities that make democracies so hateful to the terrorists also make them so vulnerable. Precisely because we maintain the most open societies, terrorists have unparalleled opportunity to strike against us.

TERRORISTS AND FREEDOM FIGHTERS

The antagonism between democracy and terrorism seems so basic that it is hard to understand why so much intellectual confusion still exists on the subject. We have all heard the insidious claim that "one man's terrorist is another man's freedom fighter." Let me read to you the powerful rebuttal that was stated before your 1979 conference by a great American, Senator Henry Jackson, who, Mr. Chairman, as you observed, is very much with us.

The idea that one person's "terrorist" is another's "freedom fighter" cannot be sanctioned. Freedom fighters or revolutionaries don't blow up buses containing non-combatants; terrorist murderers do. Freedom fighters don't set out to capture and slaughter school children; terrorist murderers do. Freedom fighters don't assassinate innocent businessmen, or hijack and hold hostage innocent men, women, and children; terrorist murderers do. It is a disgrace that democracies would allow the treasured word "freedom" to be associated with acts of terrorists.

Where democracy is struggling to take root, the terrorist is, again, its enemy. He seeks to spread chaos and disorder, to paralyze a society. In doing so he wins no converts to his cause; his deeds inspire hatred and fear, not allegiance. The terrorist seeks to undermine institutions, to destroy popular faith in moderate government, and to shake the people's belief in the very idea of democracy. In Lebanon, for example, state-sponsored terrorism has exploited existing tensions and attempted to prevent that nation from rebuilding its democratic institutions.

Where the terrorist cannot bring about anarchy, he may try to force the government to overreact, or impose tyrannical measures of control, and hence lose the allegiance of the people. Turkey faced such a challenge but succeeded in overcoming it. Martial law was imposed; the terrorist threat was drastically reduced, and today we see democracy returning to that country. In Argentina, the widely and properly deplored "disappearances" of the 1970s were, in fact, part of a response—a deliberately provoked response—to a massive campaign of terrorism. We are pleased that Argentina, too, has returned to the path of democracy. Other countries around the world face similar challenges, and they, too, must steer their course carefully between anarchy and tyranny. The lesson for civilized nations is that we must respond to the terrorist threat within the rule of law, lest we become unwitting accomplices in the terrorist's scheme to undermine civilized society.

Once we understand terrorism's goals and methods, it is not too hard to tell, as we look around the world, who are the terrorists and who are the freedom fighters. The resistance fighters in Afghanistan do not destroy villages or kill the helpless. The *contras* in Nicaragua do not blow up school buses or hold mass executions of civilians.

How tragic it would be if democratic societies so lost confidence in their own moral legitimacy that they lost sight of the obvious: that violence directed against democracy or the hopes for democracy lacks fundamental justification. Democracy offers mechanisms for peaceful change, legitimate political competition, and redress of grievances. But resort to arms in behalf of democracy against repressive regimes or movements is, indeed, a fight for freedom, since there may be no other way that freedom can be achieved.

The free nations cannot afford to let the Orwellian corruption of language hamper our efforts to defend ourselves, our interests, or our friends. We know the difference between terrorists and freedom fighters, and our policies reflect that distinction. Those who strive for freedom and democracy will always have the sympathy and, when possible, the support of the American people. We will oppose guerrilla wars where they threaten to spread totalitarian rule or deny the rights of national independence and self-determination. But we will oppose terrorists no matter what banner they may fly. For terrorism in any cause is the enemy of freedom.

THE SUPPORTERS OF TERRORISM

If freedom and democracy are the targets of terrorism, it is clear that totalitarianism is its ally. The number of terrorist incidents in or against totalitarian states is negligible. States that support and sponsor terrorist actions have managed in recent years to co-opt and ma-nipulate the phenomenon in pursuit of their own strategic goals.

It is not a coincidence that most acts of terrorism occur in areas of importance to the West. More than 80% of the world's terrorist attacks in 1983 occurred in Western Europe, Latin America, and the Middle East. The recent posture statement of the Joint Chiefs of Staff put it this way:

Terrorists may or may not be centrally controlled by their patrons. Regardless, the instability they create in the industrialized West and Third World nations undermines the security interests of the United States and its allies.

States that sponsor terrorism are using it as another weapon of warfare, to gain strategic advantage where they cannot use conventional means. When Iran and its allies sent terrorists to bomb Western personnel in Beirut, they hoped to weaken the West's commitment to defending its interests in the Middle East. When North Korea sponsored the murder of South Korean Government officials, it hoped to weaken the noncommunist stronghold on the mainland of East Asia. The terrorists who assault Israel are also enemies of the United States. When Libya and the Palestine Liberation Organization provide arms and training to the communists in Central America, they are aiding Soviet efforts to undermine our security in that vital region. When the Soviet Union and its clients provide financial, logistic, and training support for terrorists worldwide; when the Red Brigades in Italy and the Red Army Faction in Germany assault free countries in the name of communist ideology— they hope to shake the West's self-confidence and sap its will to resist aggression and intimidation. And we are now watching the Italian authorities unravel the answer to one of the great questions of our time: was there Soviet-bloc involvement in the attempt to assassinate the Pope?

We should understand the Soviet role in international terrorism without exaggeration or distortion: the Soviet Union officially denounces the use of terrorism as an instrument of state policy. Yet there is a wide gap between Soviet words and Soviet actions. One does not have to believe that the Soviets are puppeteers and the terrorists marionettes; violent or fanatic individuals and groups are indigenous to every society. But in many countries, terrorism would long since have passed away had it not been for significant support from outside. The international links among terrorist groups are now clearly understood; and the Soviet link, direct or indirect, is also clearly understood. The Soviets use terrorist groups for their own purposes, and their goal is always the same—to weaken liberal democracy and undermine world stability.

A COUNTERSTRATEGY AGAINST TERRORISM

Having identified the challenge, we must now consider the best strategy to counter it. We must keep in mind, as we devise our strategy, that our ultimate aim is to preserve what the terrorists seek to destroy: democracy, freedom, and the hope for a world at peace.

The battle against terrorism must begin at home. Terrorism has no place in our society, and we have taken vigorous steps to see that it is not imported from abroad.

We are now working with the Congress on law enforcement legislation that would help us obtain more information about terrorists through the payment of rewards to informants and would permit prosecution of those who support states that use or sponsor terrorism. Our FBI is improving our ability to detect and prevent terrorist acts within our own borders.

We must also ensure that our people and facilities in other countries are better protected against terrorist attacks. So we are strengthening security at our Embassies around the world to prevent a recurrence of the Beirut and Kuwait Embassy bombings.

While we take these measures to protect our own citizens, we know that terrorism is an international problem that requires the concerted efforts of all free nations. Just as there is collaboration among those who engage in terrorism, so there must be cooperation among those who are its actual and potential targets.

An essential component of our strategy, therefore, has been greater cooperation among the democratic nations and all others who share our hopes for the future. The world community has achieved some successes. But, too often, countries are inhibited by fear of losing commercial opportunities or fear of provoking the bully. The time has come for the nations that truly seek an end to terrorism to join together, in whatever forums, to take the necessary steps. The declaration on terrorism that was agreed upon at the London economic summit 2 weeks ago was a welcome sign that the industrial democracies share a common view of the terrorist threat. And let me say that I trust

and I hope that that statement and the specific things referred to in it will be the tip and only the visible part of the iceberg. We must build on that foundation.

Greater international cooperation offers many advantages. If we can collectively improve our gathering and sharing of intelligence, we can better detect the movements of terrorists, anticipate their actions, and bring them to justice. We can also help provide training and share knowledge of terrorist tactics. To that end, the Reagan Administration has acted promptly on the program that Congress approved last year to train foreign law enforcement officers in antiterrorist techniques. And the President has sent Congress two bills to implement two international conventions to which the United States is a signatory: the International Convention Against the Taking of Hostages and the Montreal convention to protect against sabotage of civilian aircraft.

We must also make a collective effort to address the special problem of state-sponsored terrorism. States that support terror offer safehavens, funds, training, and logistical support. We must do some hard thinking about how to pressure members of the "League of Terror" to cease their support. Such pressure will have to be international, for no one country can exert sufficient influence alone. Economic sanctions and other forms of pressure impose costs on the nations that apply them, but some sacrifices will be necessary if we are to solve the problem. In the long run, I believe, it will have been a small price to pay.

We must also discourage nations from paying blackmail to terrorist organizations. Although we recognize that some nations are

particularly vulnerable to the terrorist threat, we must convince them that paying blackmail is counterproductive and inimical to the interests of all.

Finally, the nations of the free world must stand together against terrorism to demonstrate our enduring commitment to our shared vision. The terrorists may be looking for signs of weakness, for evidence of disunity. We must show them that we are unbending. Let the terrorists despair of ever achieving their goals.

ACTIVE DEFENSE

All the measures I have described so far, domestic and international, are important elements in a comprehensive strategy. But are they enough? Is the purely passive defense that these measures entail sufficient to cope with the problem? Can we as a country—can the community of free nations—stand in a solely defensive posture and absorb the blows dealt by terrorists?

I think not. From a practical standpoint, a purely passive defense does not provide enough of a deterrent to terrorism and the states that sponsor it. It is time to think long, hard, and seriously about more active means of defense—about defense through appropriate preventive or preemptive actions against terrorist groups before they strike.

We will need to strengthen our capabilities in the area of intelligence and quick reaction. Human intelligence will be particularly important, since our societies demand that we know with reasonable clarity just what we are doing. Experience has taught us over the years that one of the best deterrents to terrorism is the certainty that swift and sure measures will be taken against those who engage in it. As President Reagan has stated:

We must make it clear to any country that is tempted to use violence to undermine democratic governments, destabilize our friends, thwart efforts to promote democratic governments, or disrupt our lives, that it has nothing to gain, and much to lose.

Clearly there are complicated moral issues here. But there should be no doubt of the democracies' moral right, indeed duty, to defend themselves.

And there should be no doubt of the profound issue at stake. The democracies seek a world order that is based on justice. When innocents are victimized and the guilty go unpunished, the terrorists have succeeded in undermining the very foundation of civilized society, for they have created a world where there is no justice. This is a blow to our most fundamental moral values and a dark

cloud over the future of humanity. We can do better than this.

No matter what strategy we pursue, the terrorist threat will not disappear overnight. This is not the last conference that will be held on this subject. We must understand this and be prepared to live with the fact that despite all our best efforts the world is still a dangerous place. Further sacrifices, as in the past, may be the price for preserving our freedom.

It is essential, therefore, that we not allow the actions of terrorists to affect our policies or deflect us from our goals. When terrorism succeeds in intimidating governments into altering their foreign policies, it only opens the door to more terrorism. It shows that terrorism works; it emboldens those who resort to it; and it encourages others to join their ranks.

THE FUTURE

If we remain firm, we can look ahead to a time when terrorism will

cease to be a major factor in world affairs. But we must face the challenge with realism, determination, and strength of will. Not so long ago we faced a rash of political kidnapings and embassy takeovers. These problems seemed insurmountable. Yet, through increased security and the willingness of governments to resist terrorist demands and to use force when appropriate, such incidents have become rare. In recent years, we have also seen a decline in the number of airline hijackings—once a problem that seemed to fill our newspapers daily. Tougher security measures and closer international cooperation have clearly had their effect.

I have great faith that we do have the will, and the capability, to act decisively against this threat. It is really up to us, the nations of the free world. We must apply ourselves to the task of ensuring our future and consigning terrorism to its own dismal past. ∎

Terrorism   *What Should Be Our Response?*

John Charles Daly, moderator; Yonah Alexander, Ramsey Clark, John P. East, and Frank H. Perez

JOHN CHARLES DALY, former ABC News chief: This policy forum, part of a series presented by the American Enterprise Institute, is concerned with the treatment of a cancer upon the global body politic—savage, ruthless, brutal violence. Our subject: Terrorism: What Should Be Our Response?

The use of terror is the quintessential expression of "the end jus-

tifies the means." Since the beginning of civilization, international order has been a fragile thing ravaged again and again by the reach for freedom or power, the two great motivators of organized society, and by the often psychotic savagery of individuals striking out at the societies that gave them birth, to satisfy their egos or to vent their frustrations.

Rarely in human history has terror been used but with the justification that the goals sought would prove good and just. Accordingly, the most vicious acts of man, even to the present day, are too often cloaked in the idealistic rhetoric of political revolution while the underlying motive is revenge against society or a savage appetite for power and recogni-

Source: Reprinted with permission from *Terrorism: What Should Be Our Response?* by John Charles Daly, Yonah Alexander, Ramsey Clark, John P. East, and Frank H. Perez, published in 1981 by the American Enterprise Institute for Public Policy Research, Washington, D.C.

tion. At the same time, history is replete with violent action accompanying legitimate goals. Where does violent action end and naked terror begin?

Dumping British tea in Boston Harbor is a far cry from the casual murder of thirty-two innocent people during the 1973 Black September incident of passenger lounge mayhem and airplane hijacking in Rome and Athens by extremists of the Palestine Liberation Organization (PLO). This savagery was used to demand that Greece release to the movement two Arabs, also Black September guerrillas, who had murdered three people and wounded fifty with machine guns in a lounge in the Athens airport.

The justification for the Black September incident was that anyone traveling to Israel, no matter what his nationality or whether abroad an American airliner—the United States had airlifted weapons and supplies to Israel in the 1973 war—was automatically an enemy of Palestine and therefore a legitimate target. Even the Palestine Liberation Organization condemned this attack as harmful to the Palestinian interest.

In 1973 here at home, two policemen, one white and one black, were casually murdered on a New York City street by the Black Liberation Army, a remnant of the Black Panthers of earlier notoriety. Their justification in the political rhetoric of terror was that the system had destroyed them.

Also in 1973 the Symbionese Liberation Army (SLA), a group of whites and blacks from American universities, prisons, and streets, casually murdered the Oakland, California, superintendent of schools in what the SLA described as a war against the fascist capitalist class and all its agents of murder,

oppression, and exploitation. The SLA's leader, Cinque, who the following year engineered the kidnapping of Patricia Hearst, said: "We are savage killers and madmen willing to give our lives to free the people at any cost."

The people are the focus of the examination we are going to conduct tonight—an examination of terrorism. What should be our collective response to terrorism, here and abroad?

To examine this issue we have an expert panel. Frank H. Perez—a career Foreign Service officer with service as a political adviser to the U.S. mission at the North Atlantic Treaty Organization (NATO) and as alternate U.S. representative to the strategic arms talks in Geneva—is the acting director of the Office of Combating Terrorism in the State Department.

Senator John P. East, a Republican from North Carolina and a former professor of political science, is a member of the U.S. Senate Subcommittee on Security and Terrorism.

Ramsey Clark, the author of *Crime in America,* has served as adjunct professor of law at Howard University and the Brooklyn Law School and as attorney general of the United States.

Yonah Alexander is professor of international studies and director of the Institute for Studies in International Terrorism at the State University of New York, a research associate of the Center for Strategic and International Studies at Georgetown University, editor in chief of *Terrorism,* an international journal, and the author or editor of publications on the theory, practice, control, and rationalization of terrorism.

Even in the atmosphere of violence in the early 1970s, the United

Nations was unable to agree on a satisfactory definition of terrorism. So that we may better understand our subject—What should be the response to terrorism?—I would pose the same question to each of the panelists in turn: How would you define terrorism?

JOHN P. EAST, U.S. senator (Republican, North Carolina): Terrorism is not new in our time; what is new is the degree and the quality of it. I would define terrorism as the use of violence, either random or selective, to further ideological and national aims. Its purpose is to intimidate, to traumatize, and to force the society or group being terrorized in the direction that the terrorists obviously want it to go. It is an instrument of goading.

RAMSEY CLARK, former U.S. attorney general: Terrorism is the use of physical or psychological violence to force people through fear to act as one wants them to act. Originally, in the political context, it meant terror by agents of government, specifically the Reign of Terror in France.

It is important to remember that the definition should include all its forms. If governments can engage in terror—the strafing of little villages by heavy jets is a form of terror—then it can be the police, the SAVAK, DINA, the BOSS terrorizing the people to force them to act as they would have them act. It can be engaged in by extremists of the left or the right. The United States has known no greater terrorism than that inflicted on large segments of our population over many decades by the Ku Klux Klan: How many lynchings? How many cross burnings? Today we see terror from the left and the right; widespread, it has no regard for life or for human beings.

FRANK H. PEREZ, acting director of the Office of Combating Terrorism: My definition of terrorism is straightforward: it is a criminal act to bring about political change. In this country we have no laws against terrorism. We do have laws against criminal acts, and we view a political act that involves murder, kidnapping, or bombing as a criminal act. That is my basic definition.

YONAH ALEXANDER, director, Institute for Studies in International Terrorism: I would like to start with the inability of the United Nations to reach a consensus on who the terrorists are. Some nations perceive terrorists as national liberation movements. So we have a problem from a universal point of view, but, from the point of view of law enforcement, there is no problem. If someone breaks the law, that is a crime, whatever the motive.

Mr. Clark referred to the Reign of Terror, government by intimidation. Obviously, governments also use terror to intimidate their own citizens and others; for example, Idi Amin's Uganda, Libya, and some other states. But I hope we are going to focus on substate terrorism, terrorism from below, because I think we see changes when we compare contemporary terrorists with older precedents—changes in technology, in targets, and in toleration.

As a starting point, perhaps we can agree that we are dealing in a broad sense with both governmental and nongovernmental, threatened and actual use of psychological and physical force to achieve certain goals—political, economic, social, whatever. Sometimes they are imaginary; sometimes they are real. This is a very broad definition, and I hope we will focus specifically on nonstate violence.

MR. DALY: We have, in your definitions, a broad understanding of what terrorism is. Our task tonight is to determine what responses should be made to it. Most governments have responded to terrorism with conventional means. In effect, they have strengthened security—metal detectors at airports, identity cards on entering office buildings—and then have hoped for the best. Attempts at multinational programs have been largely ineffective.

Let me ask, first, does the international community take the threat of terrorism seriously?

MR. PEREZ: That is a very difficult question to answer. Certainly, many parts of the world take the problem seriously and are prepared to do something about it. But to deal with international terrorism, which is a universal problem, you have to have all nations in agreement. We now have a number of nations, such as Libya, that support and engage in terrorism.

There are a number of resolutions agreed to by many countries but no enforcing mechanisms exist. The only international agreement that includes any enforcement mechanism is the Bonn Declaration on aircraft hijacking, which the seven Economic Summit countries have subscribed to.

MR. ALEXANDER: The problem is, first, the absence of a definition that is recognized by the international community. If we cannot agree on what terrorism is, how can we deal with cures? The Soviet Union, for example, and the United States perceive national liberation movements differently.

We have to start with the contributing factors and then deal with the responses, because if we find that a number of nations support this type of violence, it is very difficult to control it. We must examine the various factors that contribute, and the major one in my judgment is the role of states.

MR. CLARK: I think that dealing with terrorism must be an international process. We hammered out a Universal Declaration of Human Rights. It implies some world consensus about what is essential to human dignity. We have international covenants on political, social, economic, and cultural rights. I believe that rather than trying to come together on some definition, with all our cultural and political and economic and social differences, we ought to begin to develop a process.

The Universal Declaration of Human Rights tells us that we agree on many things. We may not act in accordance with our words, but that is always a problem of law. We have the international covenants. Now people must work for the creation of an international court of criminal justice, an international court of habeas corpus, and begin to identify acts, offenses, on which they can agree.

It is bad for children to skyjack airplanes: all countries should agree on that. Skyjacking should be an international crime, and people who engage in it should be brought before that court.

It is wrong to torture prisoners or to eliminate people in Guatemala, wrong for the government and wrong for its opposition. Those offenses should be addressed.

It is unconscionable to take hostages in the U.S. embassy in Tehran, and a writ of habeas corpus should reach in there. I think if we begin that process, we can begin to reach an agreement. At least, those who will not agree will identify themselves as the outlaws.

SENATOR EAST: I am not sure that we take terrorism seriously in the sense that we understand the motives for it. I think Mr. Clark makes some excellent points, but I might disagree with his implication that through the right kind of legal arrangements, the right kind of international contracts, we might be able to cut through the Gordian knot of terrorism.

What I feel that position fails to take into account is the deep theoretical and ideological character of terrorism in our time. The twentieth century has been plagued by fanatical totalitarian systems. One thinks of Nazi terrorism in the 1930s or of communist terrorism in our own time. People are motivated by ideas. And until we fully understand the ideological character of terrorism and what it is that drives these people to their fanaticism, we are only treating the symptom; we are not really in a position to get to the underlying motives.

We have a tendency, perhaps, in the United States to look upon the struggle against terrorism as simply another form of law enforcement, for which we need some form of habeas corpus to release hostages, and so on and so forth. What that loses sight of is that terrorism, by definition, is going to violate every tenet of accepted legal standard and practice. It is driven by powerful furies. Until one understands the furies, one is not going to be equipped to deal with terrorism practically, strategically, or tactically.

There, I fear, we may not be taking it sufficiently seriously. We are looking for a simple, legalistic answer.

MR. DALY: To go back to what you said, Mr. Perez, in 1963 there was a Tokyo convention, in 1970 a Hague draft convention, in 1971 a Montreal convention on aviation sabotage, and in 1973 two joint air security conferences in Rome. Would you agree that all have produced very little coordinated international effort to handle the question of terrorism, to find a response to it?

MR. PEREZ: This year we have had two hijackings in which the hijackers have not been brought to justice. The two countries they wound up in are adherents of the Hague Declaration. At the Ottawa summit in July, a statement on terrorism was issued that called for sanctions against Afghanistan for its failure to live up to its international obligations.

The point is that we have these pieces of paper but we need the resolve on the part of the international community to make them stand up.

MR. ALEXANDER: The problem, it seems to me, is the confusion over the definition: Who are the terrorists, and who are the freedom fighters?

Therefore, I do not think we can expect a universal consensus and response. We must look at various unilateral responses. The United States, for example, when it decided that Libya was violating U.S. domestic law or diplomatic conventions, expelled Libyan diplomats.

Then there are bilateral arrangements between the United States and, even, Cuba in regard to hijacking and international arrangements—the European Convention on Terrorism and agreements on certain types of terrorism. The United Nations, for

example, was able to prepare a convention on hostages in December 1979.

I do not think you can have a comprehensive international convention. You have to deal with specific, technical aspects or, as Mr. Clark indicated, with specific victims. I would like to see a convention that would protect, let us say, children, or women, or the innocent.

We have to move on the international level step by step. But I would suggest that a practical approach is, first, the unilateral—and it is a question of perception of the threat—and, second, cooperation with like-minded nations. We can achieve more that way.

MR. CLARK: I would like to get back to Senator East's statements about the furies. This is the hardest part. What motivates people to do these things?

It is very dangerous to generalize. We read Jane Alpert's new book, *Growing Up in the Underground.* She set off a bomb in Foley Square. She said she felt as if she were riding down Broadway in her wedding dress; she had a bundle of sticks of dynamite in her lap, and she was going down to Foley Square to set this bomb off. You find, finally, in reading her book no ideology, but absolute capriciousness. It's sex, it's trying to please Sam, it's drugs, and all the rest.

Consider Bobby Sands. We do not solve problems by accusing people of being terrorists. We have to talk about what motivates a man to be willing to die by slowly, deliberately starving himself to death? What could be more painful? Do we have the capacity to wonder?

Sometimes it is a long conditioning of injustice. What can you expect from the people of Guatemala, of Chile, of other countries, if their friends and relatives have been systematically exterminated by the government? Those are things we have to examine. As we examine them, to try to work with only like-minded countries will polarize and divide. What we want to do is to communicate with everybody.

I do not know what we accomplished when we threw Libya's representatives out of the United States. Libya exists, for better or for worse. And so did China when we would not recognize it. And so does Cuba today when we will not recognize it.

We live on this planet together. Dialogue is essential to understanding, and we have to work for universal dialogue and universal standards. They can be achieved because, finally, all humanity knows it is wrong to take life—innocent life if there are innocent and guilty lives—it is wrong to take life.

SENATOR EAST: Although I think Mr. Clark has made a number of excellent points, we may have the tendency of our time to yield to sentimentality about the character of these acts and the motives for them. During the 1930s, for example, one could rationalize the Nazi storm trooper mentality and the use of violence and terror in Germany by saying that Hitler and his entourage had some legitimate grievances arising from inflation or the imperfections of the Treaty of Versailles. One has to be careful of falling too easily into sentimentalism, in which terrorism is rationalized as simply a matter of the need for therapy.

To probe to a little deeper level of theoretical understanding, there are movements in our time, people's ideologies and furies, that take on the character, if you will, of evil. I would say that Nazi storm trooperism is simply not understandable, cannot be rationalized away, as a response to grievances. And neither, I feel, can the Qaddafi regime, or the Khomeini regime, or the terror that kills a Sadat—and the national figures, such as Arafat, Khomeini, or Qaddafi, who approve this sort of thing.

I am not willing to pass that off easily by saying, "Well, these good chaps are upset, and they have grievances, and until we get behind their grievances. ..." If we allow that kind of explanation to creep into law enforcement in any country or as a standard by which we attempt to evaluate and deal with international terrorism, ultimately we will simply yield to it, because we will not be in a position to appreciate that there is a fanaticsim here—frequently, I would contend, an evil—that seeks to destroy and bring about tormented and perverse ends. Let us not be naive about it.

MR. ALEXANDER: On a philosophical level, I fully agree with Mr. Clark. I like to be idealistic, but we have to look at reality. We are talking about terrorism as an instrument of both the weak and the strong. I wanted to discuss nonstate groups, but if we talk about states or the use of terror by states to achieve foreign policy objectives, then, of course, it's a different ball game.

In general, the question is, In what context are we discussing terrorism? In a democratic society, in a democratic context, there are other options, other alternatives; there is no need to resort to violence to achieve ends. There is a process, whether it is in Ireland or in the United States or in Western Europe.

When we examine the profiles of the terrorists, we see that they come from a privileged class, from the middle and upper middle class; those who rebelled against the Caviar society, for example, in Germany.

If we generalize, then, we are not dealing specifically with the problem. The problem is this: In certain circumstances, particularly in democratic societies, we do have options, and there is no need to resort to violence. In other areas, such as Central America or the Middle East, there are also alternatives.

You mentioned Sadat. He believed that there is a way, there is an option of peace. There is no need to confront one another on the battlefield. There is no need to resort to terrorism and violence if there is another option. Unfortunately, there are those who do not accept that.

The question is, In what context are we discussing terrorism? If we discuss it in democratic societies, there are options. And even in third world countries or in the Middle East or Central America, there are different avenues. You yourself have tried in Iran to find a *modus vivendi*. If there is a willingness, there is a way to resolve the problem.

MR. PEREZ: I would like to respond to the point Mr. Clark made. My concern is that while these terrorists feel very strongly about their cause, most of the terrorist groups are small and elitist. They are trying to bring about radical changes, but they do not really represent the people.

Moreover, they use strictly criminal acts. In Northern Ireland there have been over 2,000 people killed in the violence, a lot of them innocent people who have had nothing to do with it. In Spain there is a fragile democracy, which the Basques are threatening to overthrow by forcing a military takeover. In Italy, certainly, and in Germany, small minorities have nihilistic or anarchistic objectives.

So I do not think we can look upon terrorists from the standpoint Mr. Clark described. We have to look on them as criminals. I have dealt with many members of the families of victims of terrorism, I have gone through this with them day by day, and I know what they have suffered.

MR. DALY: Mr. Perez, the army, the FBI, the Secret Service, customs officials, the Post Office, the Department of Transportation, in response to the administration's concern over the spectacular terrorism of the early 1970s, have given high priority to coordinating a response to terrorism and to improving the collection and dissemination of intelligence on terrorism. Has this been effective either internationally or domestically, in your experience?

MR. PEREZ: I think we have a very good working relationship within the government. There are thirty agencies that deal with this subject. We have the interdepartmental group on terrorism, which contains the key agencies concerned with the problem, and they are working well together. This administration has given a greatly increased emphasis both to the collection and to the analysis of intelligence. I can assure you that intelligence is very important. We regularly receive reports of impending attacks against our people overseas, which allow us to take precautionary measures.

MR. DALY: Senator East, you favor easing restrictions on the FBI and the CIA in their intelligence gathering on domestic terrorism. What do you propose?

SENATOR EAST: Well, one specific thing I have proposed is modification of the so-called Levy guidelines that were issued in 1976, which, in my judgment, have greatly impaired the ability of the FBI to investigate and to determine whether particular individuals or groups have the potential for evolving into terrorist-prone and violence-prone groups.

Now, to investigate groups of this kind, the FBI must show that the individual or group has either committed or is about to commit violence; it is imminent. And that, to me, is a Catch 22 situation. The FBI has to prove at the outset the very thing the investigation is designed to prove.

I appreciate the need to see that the FBI and the CIA are under legitimate and prudent control. But we need to look carefully at them and give them the investigatory instruments they need to track carefully and to be able to anticipate and even to prevent this sort of thing in this country. Now they are playing the role of fireman, as they did, for example, with the events in New York involving Kathy Boudin; they simply respond to acts of violence that have already been created and then begin to investigate.

That is treating terrorism simply as another problem of law enforcement, of simple criminal law. But terrorism takes on a wholly different quantity and quality. It is the qualitative difference—the power of ideology and ideas behind it—that I feel we are losing sight of in this country, and perhaps elsewhere.

MR. DALY: Mr. Clark, as a former attorney general of the United States, how do you look upon easing the present restrictions on the FBI and the CIA?

MR. CLARK: It would be a terrible mistake. They should be strengthened, and they should be incorporated into positive legislative law, not executive law. Executive Order 12036 can be changed by a president. It can be ignored with impunity. We ought to remember who we are. We are Americans. We believe in freedom. The worst thing we could possibly do, and tragically out of proportion to the threat, is to abandon our freedom because of the fear of terrorism.

Let us look at the real world. In the United States in 1980, we had 654,000 aggravated assaults; we had 548,000 robberies; we had 23,000 murders. This is crime in America. It is something of enormous and immediate concern to us. It reflects our character.

Yet what do we talk about? We talk about terrorism. According to the FBI, there were twenty-nine acts of terrorism in the United States in 1980. Think of Italy, West Germany, other countries. We have not had that sort of terrorism. We will not have that sort of terrorism unless we engage in a general repression, denying the very foundation of the country. We were born on principle and the idea of freedom.

This is why I think it meaningless to try to talk about individual terrorism and not government terrorism. It is like talking about the tides and not mentioning the moon.

SENATOR EAST: The attorney general is a man of great repute and great experience in this area, and he is concerned about threats to civil liberties; so I dissent reluctantly. But on the question of whether we have given too much power to the CIA or the FBI or too little, I would argue that civil liberties form a mosaic and that the most fundamental civil liberties are to be protected in one's person and to a degree in one's property. At a minimum, government ought to be able to do that. To me those are fundamental civil liberties, civil rights, as much as freedom to speak and to carry on.

If a government cannot protect those most fundamental of civil rights, a very serious theoretical question is raised about the efficacy of that government. All I ask is that we make sure that the CIA or the FBI—I focus particularly on the FBI in an internal domestic context—has tools adequate to protect us in those fundamental civil liberties.

I think it was former Supreme Court Justice Jackson who said that the First Amendment is not a suicide pact, and what we are saying is that we must give government the tools to protect us in basic and fundamental rights. I do not see anything inconsistent with civil liberties. In fact, I contend we would be strengthening the civil liberties of individual Americans and others.

MR. CLARK: I do not see how a government can protect civil liberties if it violates them. I think we have to believe in these things. The Bill of rights is not a suicide pact, and we are going to live by it because we believe in it.

When we look at what we get for all this, we get Frank Terpil, don't we? We get Edwin Wilson, don't we? And who gets wiretapped? Martin Luther King, the prophet of nonviolent social change, and the president's brother. That is what we get by violating civil liberties. You call that freedom?

MR. ALEXANDER: I think we ought to bridge these two positions. I do not see inconsistencies if we analyze the situation. First, terrorism is an attack against democracy. Terrorism is totalitarianism, a denial of basic human rights. And I agree that this is fundamental. If we do not have principles, why do we exist? But there is a result, there is an effect on misguided groups, indigenous groups as well as foreign groups in the United States and across the continents.

I agree also that we have to be careful in a democracy not to overreact, but we have to work on different levels. There is no question about the need for intelligence at the law enforcement level, but we have to be cautious not to break the law; therefore, Congress is looking closely into the issue of charters for the CIA and the FBI. But simultaneously we have to work on the political level—for fair government, fair laws, help to minorities—and try to balance the situation.

At the same time, when we have small terrorist groups emerging once again, the New World Liberation movement in California attacking utilities, anti-Castro groups, various foreign groups operating in the United States, and terrorism in other democracies, what are we to do in terms of law enforcement?

I think we have to monitor this, we have to watch it. We have to work also on the political level to provide alternatives so that people can express their grievances and find a solution, a political solution, rather than use the deed for propaganda. In modern times it is very dangerous to allow the situation to deteriorate. Today we talk about throwing the bomb, but in the future, terrorist groups might resort to biological, chemical, and nuclear devices, and that would spell the destruction of civilization itself.

MR. PEREZ: One of the great concerns about terrorism is that it forces governments in trying to deal with it to do things that affect their citizens' civil liberties and human rights. Fortunately, in the most enlightened countries, the Western European countries, for example, the governments have been able to tighten up their laws in a constitutional and lawful manner to deal with the situation. In many other countries, however, governments have gone too far, and we have seen the situations that have developed, say, in the southern cone of South America. This is a very serious problem that terrorism raises, and it is one that governments have to consider carefully.

MR. DALY: Technology was mentioned earlier, and I wonder what opinion all of you have of technology as an element in a program to hold off terrorism or inhibit it greatly. Computerized thumbprint identification to catch the altered passport, aircraft cabins equipped to fill with instant incapacitating gas, and so forth—are these any real hope for the future?

MR. PEREZ: I do not see any technology on the horizon that would allow us to cope with the problem. On aircraft hijackings, for example, there is talk about a gas that could be used, but such gases have side effects; if there were old people or sick people, the gas might kill them instead of incapacitating the terrorists.

The only way to deal with terrorism is to have experienced people who know how to handle it. The first thing to do is to try to prevent it. We must tighten security, as we have done at airports. Since we instituted the enhanced security measures at airports, over 20,000 weapons have been picked up in routine screening.

We also need experienced people who know how to handle hostage negotiations and to resolve them peacefully. We have seen special forces used around the world—Entebbe, Mogadishu, last year in London at the Iranian embassy. The United States now has a much improved ability to assault if that becomes necessary in a terrorist situation, but I do not see any magic solution on the horizon through technology.

MR. ALEXANDER: The problem of technology has to be seen on two levels: the technology used by terrorist groups against their adversaries and the technology used by governments.

Because of the development and accessibility of sophisticated weapons, this becomes a very serious problem. I am not talking about biological, chemical, or nuclear devices: even using missiles to bring down an aircraft with hundreds of people is a terrible tragedy. Basically, we have to do what we can. Technology also has a positive aspect in identifying and tagging explosives, for example.

It is a question of whether the government perceives that there is a threat. Once the government agrees or decides that there is a real danger to its very survival, probably it would forego various civil liberties.

For those who live in a country like Israel where they face terror-ism by PLO squads, it is a different issue than for the American people. It is a question of how the public would perceive the threat and whether the public and the media would support appropriate action by the government.

MR. CLARK: My experience with technology in this field has been long and unhappy. I think it endangers both safety and liberty. It escalates research and development on both sides.

It is like the arms race. We watched wiretapping, which has proved, in my judgment, clearly ineffective in domestic law enforcement. Then we saw jamming devices from the other side in organized crime and elsewhere. We saw their technology improving on ours. We saw the erosion of liberty as we began to put wiretaps on the wrong people.

We establish the National Crime Information Center, and the first thing we know we have computer data on millions of people that cannot really be screened and that endangers their liberty and enrages people.

We must work with the causes, and technology can only work with the symptoms, with the active outer crust and edge. We have to get down to the causes and recognize that it is very often injustice, as much as it hurts us to say it, that drives people to the wildness we see manifested in terrorism.

SENATOR EAST: I would like to pick up on the point that Mr. Alexander made. I am a bit more troubled by the technology that can be developed and applied by the terrorists themselves. He mentioned the kinds of things they might possibly use to hold an entire society or segments of it hostage. We must obviously be sensitive to that. To get back to the point I was making earlier, we need to be able to track that and investigate it and anticipate it and prevent it, because once the acts are done, it does not do much good to treat it as simply another matter of law enforcement.

With all due respect to the distinguished former attorney general, it strikes me that he is suggesting we might unilaterally give up the development of our own technology for investigation and anticipation. I think that would be a fatal error given the ideological character of much of terrorism in our time.

It is a force that cannot simply be explained away by a list of grievances. If we applied that reasoning to domestic law enforcement, we would not enforce law. We would simply assume that crimes were committed because somehow someone had been deprived or had grievances.

I am troubled by that as applied to domestic law enforcement, and if it is applied to international terrorism, I think it is a potential blueprint for enormous disaster.

MR. CLARK: I did not hear anyone suggest that domestic laws not be enforced because there are causes of crime. It is simply that we must address the causes, too. It is more than a game. We care about children and society. If we do not address the causes, we will continue to have this trouble.

We have not had real problems in this society until recently with the capacity of people to exist underground, because people have loved the government. Until 1969, when I left the Department of Justice, in the whole history of the Federal Bureau of Prisons, there were not twenty people who had escaped, remained underground, and been unaccounted for. Now it is becoming easy.

The best enforcement, the only real enforcement, is the people. When the people are watching out and believe in freedom and in their country and when the police are deeply integrated into them and people love and respect them, you do not have a problem.

But when you alienate them, when you saturate with technology, when you engage in constant surveillance, then you are slowly dividing the country. The greatest tragedy would be if the fear of terrorism caused us to abandon freedom and to believe that we could find safety that way; we would lose both.

MR. DALY: There is one more area of response we could usefully examine. Should the United States unilaterally, in the absence of international agreement on an antiterroristic program, use economic weapons against clearly identified exporters of terrorism such as Libya?

MR. PEREZ: We do have a number of laws that deal with this subject, and we are required by the Senate to provide a list of those countries that support terrorist acts. This is the Fenwick amendment to the Export Administration Act. The countries designated now are Libya, Syria, South Yemen, and Iraq, and we will reexamine the list at the end of this year.

We do not sell these countries any military equipment or material that could support terrorist operations. We have denied sales of commercial aircraft to Libya to indicate our displeasure with their support of international terrorist acts.

SENATOR EAST: I support the idea that we ought to take effective and prudent action against exporters of international terrorism, and probably the leading exporter today is Qaddafi in Libya.

I certainly agree that it is a matter of judgment precisely what kind of action to take. In the case of a man like Qaddafi, unless the actions taken are effective in curtailing the exportation of terrorism, they may simply give dignity to the man and a cause by public grandstanding that is not particularly effective. I would support effective means to curtail their exportation of terrorism as much as I would support effective efforts to anticipate it, prevent it, and curtail it in the United States.

MR. CLARK: Of course, we should use economic sanctions against countries that engage in internal or external terrorism. You cannot make the world safe for hypocrisy, and for the United States to buy oil from Qaddafi and then call him bad names has a certain element of hypocrisy about it.

But we cannot be selective. The terrorism of South Africa must not be ignored. They are using Mirage jets, they are using Huey helicopters, and they are bombing the hell out of southern Angola and other places. That is terrorism of the most violent sort, and some of it is not direct, such as their support for Jonas Savimbi and others like him.

It is interesting: even when we talk domestically, our talk about terrorism is selective. I believe and I think I can demonstrate to anybody who wants to listen that within the United States the most violent terrorist organization is the Omega 7, but nobody ever mentions Omega 7. They will kill you quick.

MR. PEREZ: I talk about them all the time.

MR. CLARK: You have not mentioned them tonight, and they are very rarely mentioned and compared with the Provisional Irish Republican Army or the Palestine Liberation Organization.

MR. PEREZ: I can assure you that the FBI is conducting a very vigorous investigation into this group.

MR. CLARK: I have been to Washington several times urging them to do it, and I have not seen any results.

MR. PEREZ: I can guarantee you that they are.

MR. ALEXANDER: I think we must approach problems on the diplomatic, economic, and military levels and also on the level of communications.

First, I would like to see the media draw a line between commandos and guerrilla fighters and terrorists. There is so much confusion. That is one thing. Second, we have to defuse what I would call the religionization of politics or the politicization of religion, the Khomeinis or the Islamic fundamentalists or waving the flag of religion to achieve certain political secular ends.

I think the church can play a role. I think the media can play a role. I think education can play a role. I think families can play a role. It is like crime. We have to operate on different levels: there is no one solution to the problem; there are many approaches. Unless we mobilize all our forces, we will remain hostages forever.

MR. DALY: We have painted a very broad canvas, and it is time for the question-and-answer session.

RUSSELL CHAPIN, American Enterprise Institute: One of the troublesome aspects of terrorism is the taking of hostages. I wonder if Mr. Perez would tell us what the policy would be about the taking of hostages. Would we pay ransom to free hostages? Or is that the cornerstone of our policy?

MR. PEREZ: Our policy on this issue is very clear: we will not give in to terrorist demands or blackmail. We will not pay ransom. We will not release prisoners. And as Under Secretary Kennedy said recently before the Senate Foreign Relations Committee, we will not bargain for the release of hostages.

Ours is strictly a no-negotiations policy. I think the reason for it is obvious, that if we give in to terrorist demands, we will be faced with more of the same and will endanger more innocent people.

MR. CLARK: The first point always is saving life. Both Attica prison and the Tabas raid in Iran illustrate the issue. No one analyzing the situation believed you could save the hostages at Attica prison by force. The real issue was the dignity and authority of the state as against the lives of the hostages. The police went in and killed thirty-nine people, including nine hostages. No hostage had been killed by the prisoners.

As for the Tabas raid, the idea that a military operation could move into the heart of an urban population of 4 million people in Tehran, work through the labyrinth and tunnels under the U.S. Embassy, and get those people out alive is ridiculous. To try it was to risk their lives.

Lives should come first, and lives can be saved. I was attorney general when the first airplane hijacking, at least of recent times, occurred. The FBI had rifles trained on the tires, and they asked, "May we shoot them out? We can keep that plane from taking off." I said, "Suppose you shoot—you make that noise. Someone inside is half crazy, and he fires a gun and kills somebody, hits a gas tank, and the whole plane ..." The first thing is to try to save lives. You engage in dialogue; you talk to people. There is always the possibility of effective communication. You do not pay ransom.

SENATOR EAST: How do we, in the long run, prevent the occurrence of a constant cycle of the use of terrorism and the taking of hostages? By not acting in a more decisive way initially, we may encourage this sort of thing. Under your own standard of preserving life, you may in the long run lose more lives because you encourage terrorists to play the game of taking hostages, knowing that it is not a high-risk game for them. That is the problem we must confront in setting long-term policy.

MR. CLARK: The idea that trying to save lives encourages terrorism is unsubstantiated in experience and is invalid. It takes a certain amount of conditioning over a long period of time for people to get themselves up to do something that wild, because they know how dangerous it is for them as well.

It is that sort of fear, that we have to take a few lives now or destroy the village to save it, that has caused us to engage in hostility and in violence and finally in war. We wage war to seek peace. We have said that all through history, and it does not work.

MR. PEREZ: Our view is that everything should be done to resolve the situation peacefully but that if we give in to the terrorists' demands, we will just invite more of the same.

MR. CLARK: Suppose the demands are just?

MR. PEREZ: How do you determine whether the demands are just?

MR. CLARK: By using your reason, by examining the facts. Can't we determine what is just? I thought we could.

MR. PEREZ: I think it would depend on the situation. At Princess Gate last year in London, for example, terrorists took over a building and threatened to kill people. Negotiations were attempted, but finally the terrorists started to kill people. After they killed the second hostage the SAS counterterrorist force stormed the building and rescued the rest of the hostages. We have to be prepared to do that. The important thing is to apprehend or bring to justice the terrorist or hijacker.

Last year there were thirteen hijackings to Cuba. On the last hijacking, in September, the Cubans finally agreed to return the hijackers to the United States. We brought them here and gave them forty years. We have had only one more hijacking so far this year, in July. In that instance, the Cubans said they would take jurisdiction and announced that they mete out harsh punishment for this crime.

I think that is what you need. You need international cooperation to deal with this problem. Cuba and the United States are at opposite ends on political views but found it convenient to cooperate in this situation.

FATHER HINTON, executive director of the National Catholic Conference for Interracial Justice: Is it possible to differentiate between common criminality, in which class I would put terrorist acts either individual or collective in Western Europe or even in the United

States, and acts of terror, however reprehensible, in pursuit of political goals for which there are broad community constituencies or at least sympathies, as in Northern Ireland? Mustn't we differentiate between those two in order to understand what we are talking about?

SENATOR EAST: That is an excellent point. One distinguishing characteristic of terrorism, at least as I would define it and use it, is that it is used against the innocent and those understood to be innocent, people who have no direct involvement at all, who are not a legitimate military threat to what these people are attempting to do or what they are attempting to defend. In other words, they terrorize the innocent in order to traumatize, to intimidate, to begin to move the whole society or group in the direction they want to go.

The killing of the innocent, I submit, is a distinctive characteristic of terrorism. I am not suggesting it cannot occur as an aberration in general military operations, but a policy that cannot distinguish between the innocent and those who are legitimate military objects is a distinguishing characteristic of terrorism.

MR. PEREZ: I would like to reenforce that. When Lord Mountbatten was killed, for example, a nephew was killed, a boat boy was killed, and I think the mother-in-law of his daughter was killed. A lot of innocent people are killed. This is not just or right whatever the political cause.

The Provisional Irish Republican Army is not really an army; it is a small terrorist organization with perhaps a hundred hardcore members and several hundred supporters. They engage in hit-and-run tactics, not in a military formation. I do not consider insurgency or guerrilla warfare, in which military units engage military units, terrorism. But when innocent people are killed and injured, I consider this terrorism.

MR. ALEXANDER: I would like to mention again the role of states. What did Iran try to do in resorting to this kind of activity against the innocent—humiliate the United States?

If I may paraphrase Clausewitz, it is continuation of war by other means. We are talking about (a) substate groups and (b) state entities resorting to terrorism because they feel that they cannot face their adversaries on the battlefield. We have to look at both of them.

MR. CLARK: The idea of the innocent has little meaning. If we talked about the innocent we would have to outlaw nuclear weapons, as we should. We have to ask the meaning of Hiroshima, the meaning of Dresden, the meaning of strafing in South Lebanon, where the guilty cannot really be distinguished from the innocent. You cannot even see them when you are flying 600 miles an hour.

There are situations where there is deep emotional commitment to an end, and it has to do overwhelmingly with freedom. The people of Iran engaged in one of the most remarkable revolutions of our time, and it taught us many lessons. It was essentially nonviolent. In 1978 the shah's forces, one of the most sophisticated and violent forces over such a population in history, with more tanks than the British army, more jet aircraft of the United States than any country except the United States, killed 40,000 or 50,000 Iranian people.

Not twenty Iranian soldiers were killed. It was a nonviolent revolution. The people took to the streets. They closed the factories. They closed the shops. They closed the fields. They closed the schools. They closed the bazaars, everything.

Finally the shah had to leave. That the revolution went to pieces and came to a reign of terror should not surprise us because history shows how desperately hard it is to move from a long history of tyranny to social justice. How many good illustrations do we have?

When we look at Ireland, we have to recognize that we are dealing with a widespread emotional phenomenon and that there are true believers who would starve themselves to death slowly and painfully.

When we look at southern Africa, we see the black people say, "We are going to be free of this racist system of apartheid." What we need to do in such situations is not simply to condemn, because I oppose all violence. I oppose violence against the military as well as violence against the nonmilitary. I do not like to see young soldiers or anybody else get shot. But we have to ask how we can address the injustice that drives these people to this degree. If we begin to do that and then begin to work on South Africa and on Margaret Thatcher and people like her, we can hope to solve problems.

SENATOR EAST: I feel, with all due respect, that Mr. Clark has a very bad double standard. He explains the terrorism of the shah's regime. But certainly the Khomeini regime is engaging in terrorism of an unspeakable sort, and it ought to be said publicly.

MR. CLARK: I agree absolutely. I never said it was not.

SENATOR EAST: As for the Viet Cong, who were frequently looked upon as good humanitarians, certainly the bloodbath that has occurred in Indochina. . . .

MR. CLARK: We killed a million there.

SENATOR EAST: The genocide in Cambodia . . . I find a double standard in what you are saying. There seem to be no enemies to the left in this matter of judging international terrorism.

The great threats of terrorism in our time have come from the great totalitarianisms, primarily of the right and the left, Nazism and communism. I think one can start there. We can look at Dachau and at the Gulag as examples of it, and we can see other manifestations of it.

But the notion that, for example, the shah alone or South Africa alone is the culprit and we do not mention the Viet Cong or Khomeini and the Qaddafis and the PLOs and the fanaticism of the Soviet Union and the Viet Cong and the terrorist activity of Cuba—certainly no one with a sensitivity to civil liberties and an appreciation of the use of terrorism in our time could let those examples pass by without commenting on them.

MR. CLARK: I imagine I have spent a lot more time in those countries fighting for individual liberties than you have, Senator. And I believe in them deeply there.

SENATOR EAST: I served with the army during the Korean War, and I am simply suggesting that no one has a monopoly on virtue or wisdom in their concern.

MR. CLARK: I do not think so either. I am against those who use violence. I am against having the United States support tyrannical governments, as it has done generously over the years.

SENATOR EAST: I am simply fleshing out your picture by stating that there are other tyrannical governments, the Khomeini government, the Viet Cong government, which also would have to fit into the categories you have defined.

MR. CLARK: I agree with that.

MR. PEREZ: It is strange that there are oppressed people in the Soviet Union and Eastern Europe but there is no significant terrorism there, while there are fewer oppressed peoples in the West and a big terrorism problem exists.

It is also useful to think about the Soviet role in all of this. The Soviets support violence around the world. They support the so-called freedom movements and the national liberation fronts, all of which resort to violence and terrorism. They support countries like Libya and Cuba. Cuba has clearly been a prime supporter of terrorism in Central America and in Colombia. In the most recent incident, the M-19 terrorists who took over the Dominican embassy early last year were given a hero's welcome in Cuba. We found out later that they and other M-19 terrorists were trained by the Cubans. They were then reinfiltrated into Colombia to conduct terrorist operations. As a result, the Colombian government broke relations with Cuba.

The point is that governments support this violence that leads to terrorism, and that is one of the problems we have to deal with.

MR. CLARK: It's a dirty business, Mr. Perez. And we have done our share. We still have to ask how Patrice Lumumba died, how Diem died. We know what William O. Douglas said: he said we killed him. How did Salvadore Allende die? How did Henri Curiel die?

Because we are the United States, because we care about life, and because we care about freedom, we should never adopt other standards. We should resist all forms of violence, but we have been supporting totalitarian governments.

BILL WICKERSHAM, executive director of the World Federalists: In 1978 the House of Delegates of the American Bar Association adopted a resolution favoring negotiations toward a convention establishing an international criminal court with jurisdiction expressly limited to three criminal acts: international aircraft hijacking, violence aboard international aircraft, and crimes against diplomats and internationally protected persons. Supporters of this measure believe that if such an international court were in existence, problems of extradition would be considerably lessened.

I want to direct my question to Senator East: When Mr. Clark referred to a criminal court, an international criminal court, you noted that we would have to understand the furies of various governments and ideologies before the establishment of the rule of law. My question is, Do we do that same thing in domestic affairs? Isn't there an analogy here? In other words, if we want to fashion a rule of law, don't we try to get as many people as we can to agree with it before we can understand the furies or make anyone a saint?

SENATOR EAST: In trying to develop any overarching governmental entity coming out of some conception of federalism, initially there has to be a cultural identity and a cultural tradition and history that give some degree of homogeneity. In building the American federal system, for example, we enjoyed a common heritage. We had a common language, a common religion, common institutions from England, and so on—a common culture in which we could build a federal system.

When we talk about an international community, we begin to appreciate the impossible ideological divisions. That is the great flaw in world federalist thinking, and it underscores the enormous difficulties we face in establishing international tribunals that can resolve issues in the same way we would expect the Federal District Court of Eastern North Carolina or the Court of Appeals in Richmond or even the United States Supreme Court to resolve them.

At least there is a certain cultural identity, but that is not true internationally, and problems are infinitely more intractable on the international scene than they are in the domestic context. So I am concerned that progress would come very slowly, if at all.

MR. ALEXANDER: I do not think the problem is the lack of legislation or international conventions or the process or organization and structure. We have a fairly large body of international law dealing with terrorism directed against the diplomatic community, and we have seen that Iran broke the law; in spite of the fact that the International Court of Justice supported the United States, the Iranians refused to abide by it.

If we talk about political exceptions to the extradition law, we find situations where nations have violated their extradition commitments. One good example is France's release of Abu Daod in spite of the fact that Germany and Israel wanted to extradite him.

It is not the lack of law or the lack of a system. It is a question of the willingness of nations to stand by their obligations. I would like to see a court dealing with hijacking or with attacks against innocent people, but we have to be realistic about the system.

To return to my original point about like-minded states, the European community or democratic nations in the world would have to get together and say, "Okay. We are ready to deal with the specific crimes. We are going to set up our own human rights court, the same model dealing with terrorism." But at the international level, I do not think we can have a comprehensive system to deal with the problem.

MR. CLARK: Western Europe does have a court at Strasbourg. It has, in civil rights cases among others, told West Germany it cannot deprive Baader-Meinhof gang members of counsel because the European Covenant on Individual Rights and Liberties accords them that.

I do not see how you can say we have the laws and the courts when there is no international court that has jurisdiction over the criminal conduct we have been talking about. The world court does not have that jurisdiction; so we should create a court that does. Then we will see who will abide by the law; we will see who the lawless ones are. We need that court, and we need it to have sanctions. If we cannot believe in that, we are condemned to a violent future.

MR. DALY: This concludes another public policy forum presented by the American Enterprise Institute for Public Policy Research. On behalf of AEI, our heartfelt thanks to the distinguished and expert panelists, Mr. Frank H. Perez, Senator John P. East, Mr. Ramsey Clark, and Mr. Yonah Alexander, and to our guests and experts in the audience for their participation. ■

After Iran-Contra: Let's Get Smart About Terrorism

By David Ignatius

This week's report on the Iran-contra affair was a reminder of the ability of terrorists to drive America crazy. For nearly a decade, the hostage-takers have been winning. They have kidnaped our citizens, driven our presidents to acts of desperation and folly and paralyzed our political system in a seemingly endless cycle of bungling, cover-ups and recriminations.

More than a year of investigating the Iran-contra affair has taught us all something about how *not* to

David Ignatius, an associate editor of *The Washington Post,* is editor of the Outlook section.

fight terrorism. Next time, our leaders undoubtedly will be wise enough to refrain from trading arms for hostages. But what other lessons does this fiasco teach? If we decide as a nation to say "Never Again!" to our past disorderly approach to terrorism, what policies should we adopt instead?

We should begin by avoiding the erratic swings of the past few years. The Reagan administration got into trouble as it lurched from one ill-considered policy to another: It declared war on Iranian-sponsored terrorism in 1984, then shipped weapons to Tehran in 1985 and '86, and then lurched back toward war this year by sending an armada to the Persian Gulf. Somehow, there ought to be a balanced and sustainable policy that avoids these extremes.

The outlines of a sensible antiterrorism strategy emerged last week at a symposium hosted by the Center for Strategic and International Studies. The leadoff speaker was Terrell Arnold, a terrorism consultant and former head of the State Department's counter terrorism program. Here's a sampling of some of the advice offered by Arnold and the other speakers:

• Treat terrorism as a crime, rather than as a political problem. We should try, to the extent possible, to handle international hostage-taking the same way we do domestic kidnaping—with a combination of quiet negotiation and tough law enforcement. The same rules that our police apply in domestic kidnaping cases should prevail abroad. That means dialogue with the kidnapers, especially initially. But if the hostages aren't released quickly, we should be prepared to use force to free them. Since normal police tactics probably won't work in places like Lebanon, we should be ready to use stealth and trickery to lure terrorists out of their sanctuaries to jurisdictions where they can be apprehended and prosecuted. Finally, we should try in Beirut—as in Boston—to put kidnapers in the crosshairs of a sharpshooter's rifle. If they threaten to harm their captives, we should shoot to kill. This isn't assassination, but simply the application of standard law-enforcement techniques. It won't be easy to apply this approach in Lebanon, but it's worth a try.

• Tone down the rhetoric. The antiterrorism tirades by President Reagan and Secretary of State George Shultz in 1984 and 1985 only inflamed the problem and added to the atmosphere of political crisis. We could have done without Reagan's 1985 attack on Iran and Libya as "outlaw states run by the strangest collection of misfits, looney tunes and squalid criminals since the advent of the Third Reich." Ditto for Shultz's bellicose 1984 warning that we were becoming the "the Hamlet of nations . . . wallowing in self-flagellation." Explains Terrell Arnold: "Exaggerated rhetoric pushed us to pay too much to get our people back. . . . It excited the kidnapers to raise the ante."

• Recognize that military force has its uses. The American raid on Libya last year worked. It frightened Col. Gadhafi and probably deterred Libyan attacks against American targets. Perhaps more important, the American air raid prodded European nations to take action themselves against Libyan terrorist networks in Europe (if only to forestall further air raids by the crazy Americans). The F-111 turned out to be a surprisingly effective antiterrorism weapon, and the next time we're provoked, we should be ready to use it.

Don't be afraid to talk with terrorists. Negotiation is a tactic used by most police departments in domestic hostage incidents, and it should be used abroad as well—but quietly, by trained intelligence officers, rather than by hamfisted NSC staffers. Terrorists can even become good sources of intelligence. During the 1970s, for example, the United States maintained a security-cooperation relationship with Yasser Arafat's chief of intelligence. The PLO man provided timely information that helped save many American lives. That sort of relationship makes sense today—provided it's done discreetly. Says Arnold: "It doesn't make sense to say that you won't talk."

• Never say "never." "A rigid anticoncessions policy is at odds with common sense," says Arnold, and he's right. Just because we've learned the folly of trading arms for hostages doesn't mean that we should reject, out of hand, the sort of modest concessions that may allow kidnapers to release their hostages without losing face. Instead of maintaining an inflexible no-concessions policy (one that we will probably have to abandon eventually), we should say "no concessions of substance," argues Arnold. And we shouldn't specify —ever—what concessions we might or might not be prepared to offer.

• Keep the president away from hostage politics. Our chief executive shouldn't meet hostage families, and he shouldn't welcome the hostages home when they're freed. That may sound heartless, but the

Iran affair shows how vulnerable presidents and their advisers are to the human tragedy of kidnaping and the pleas of hostage families for help. The cold fact is that we probably help our hostages most when we appear to be helping them least. Public attention only enhances the hostages' value to their captors. To reinforce this harsh lesson of the Iran-contra affair, Congress should enact a law banning any public celebrations at the White House when hostages are released. Such occasions provide terrorists with an incentive to grab the next American and begin the psychodrama all over again.

• No more yellow ribbons. The American public should act with the same dignity and restraint as the president. We shouldn't allow terrorists to exploit our compassion. Television networks may continue to broadcast interviews with grieving widows and tearful relatives, but the rest of us should resolve not to watch. The image of "America Held Hostage" that emerged during the 1979 seizure of our embassy in Tehran and the 1985 TWA hijacking should never be repeated.

• Maintain a dialogue with Iran and other states that support terrorism. The Reagan administration was right in trying to make contact with political moderates in Iran and repair relations between the two countries. The mistake was that we did so clumsily—piggy backing on an ongoing Israel arms-trading operation and using dubious characters like the Iranian "prevaricator" Manucher Ghorbanifar and Saudi tycoon Adnan Khashoggi. Selling arms to the Iranians was a monumentally bad idea. But continuing the political dialogue makes sense. It would be

disastrous if the Soviets were the only superpower talking to both sides in the Iran-Iraq war. Terrorism expert Robin Wright of the Carnegie Endowment explains: "America must come to grips with militant Islam, for which Iran has become a leading symbol. The time for rapprochement with Iran was almost ripe when the Reagan administration began the folly of the arms-for-hostages swap."

• Curb our obsession with the Middle East. Americans show little interest in terrorist incidents in most parts of the world; but when they happen in the Middle East, they drive us crazy—in ways that make it harder to deal with the problem. American hostages have been released quietly this year in Mozambique, Sudan and the South Pacific. In these instances, says Arnold, "negotiators could work quietly to get the hostages out."

Because of our focus on the Middle East, we often forget that terrorism is a worldwide problem. State Department statistics [see accompanying chart] show that terrorism is actually declining, and that the recent growth areas have been Asia and Latin America, rather than the Middle East. Between 1985 and 1986, the number of international terrorist incidents increased 83 percent in Asia and 33 percent in Latin America—but not at all in the Middle East. In Europe, terrorist incidents of Middle East origin declined 47 percent from 1985 to 1986 and were down 71 percent during the first half of 1987 compared to a year earlier.

Depoliticizing terrorism in the way Arnold recommends may be impossible in our democracy. When the U.S. government wants to stay cool during a terrorist inci-

dent, the news media will often be working overtime to keep the story hot. That tension is inescapable in a democratic nation, and it probably means that we'll never be as disciplined or efficient as a closed society in dealing with problems like terrorism.

Bringing terrorists to justice will also be easier said than done. The Iran-contra report offers depressing evidence of how few intelligence resources we have available in Beirut. If it's too dangerous to try to rescue the hostages now, it may also be too dangerous to try to apprehend their captors. But the terrorists can't hide behind their hostages forever.

We also have some new legal tools that can help achieve Arnold's goal of handling terrorism as a criminal problem, rather than a political one. Congress passed an antiterrorism act last year that extends U.S. legal jurisdiction to terrorist crimes that are committed against Americans overseas. That means that when terrorists attack Americans, they may be extradited to face prosecution in the United States. In areas like Lebanon where the machinery of law enforcement has collapsed, the United States should look for creative ways to capture terrorists and bring them to justice.

The Reagan administration, alas, violated nearly every one of Arnold's simple rules during the Iran-contra affair. Starting in 1984, when Lt. Col. Oliver North was briefing reporters on his plans for gung-ho "pro-active" tactics against terrorism, administration policy began to jump the tracks. North and CIA Director William Casey tried everything in their increasingly frantic efforts to deal with the captors of the Beirut hostages:

International Terrorist Incidents

Total Incidents in 1985, 1986

1985	1986	% change
785	774	-01%

Incidents of Middle East Origin in Western Europe

| 74 | 39 | -47% |

Total Incidents, 1st Half of Year (Preliminary Figures)

1986	1987	% Change
439	396	-10%

Incidents of Middle East Origin in Western Europe (Preliminary)

| 28 | 89 | -71% |

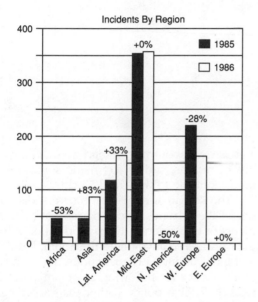

Incidents By Region

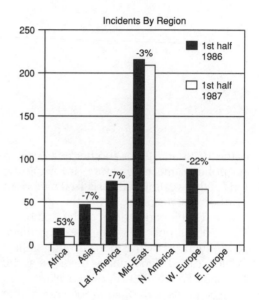

Incidents By Region

from an alleged assassination attempt against a Moslem sheik in West Beirut to the shipment of weapons to Iran. None of it worked. As the congressional report on the Iran-contra affair states bluntly, they were "taken to the cleaners."

Never again. ■

Suggested Additional Readings

Arnold, Terrell. *The Violence Formula: Why People Lend Sympathy and Support to Terrorism* (Lexington, MA: Lexington Books, 1988).

Cline, Ray, and Yonah Alexander. *Terrorism: The Soviet Connection* (New York: Crane Russak, 1984).

Evans, Ernest. *Calling a Truce to Terror: The American Response to International Terrorism* (Westport, CT: Greenwood Press, 1979).

Freedman, Lawrence Z., and Yonah Alexander. *Perspectives on Terrorism* (Wilmington, DE: Scholarly Resources, 1983).

Grosscup, Beau. *The Explosion of Terrorism* (New York: MacMillan, 1987).

Laqueur, Walter. *Terrorism* (Boston: Little Brown, 1977).

Miller, Abraham. *Terrorism and Hostage Negotiations* (Boulder, CO: Westview Press, 1980).

Rivers, Gayle. *The War Against the Terrorists* (New York: Stein and Day, 1986).

Stohl, Michael, and George A. Lopez. *Terrible Beyond Endurance: The Foreign Policy of State Terrorism* (New York: Greenwood Press, 1988).

Wardlaw, Grant. *Political Terrorism: Theory, Tactics, and Counter-Measures* (New York: Cambridge University Press, 1982).

Wilkinson, Paul. *Terrorism and the Liberal State* (London: MacMillan, 1986).

CHAPTER FIFTEEN

North-South Relations

*
*

In the 1970s and 1980s another new issue in foreign policy came to the fore, involving the relations of the wealthy, industrialized nations of the northern hemisphere with the generally poor, underdeveloped nations of the South.

The South put forward the argument, strongly influenced by the then-current intellectual fashion called dependency theory, that the development and affluence of the North had come through its exploitation of and at the expense of the South. The South, which corresponds more or less to what we also call the Third World or the developing nations, therefore demanded that the North make up for this history of exploitation by reparations and through the massive transfer of resources from North to South. The South also had other demands (greater voting power in the UN, larger representation in the international lending agencies, and so on) that it pressed on the North.

Many European governments, as well as the administration of Jimmy Carter, were sympathetic to the South's demands. One does not know if this sympathy came out of guilt over the North's prosperity and the South's poverty, out of a sense of justice concerning the plight of the poor, or whether the North (or at least some of its intellectuals and government leaders) actually accepted the arguments of dependency theory. Doubtless all three motives were involved. In any case, the North did respond partially, talked

a great deal about increasing foreign aid, wrote lots of reports, and in fact made some greater funds available to the Third World.

The Reagan Administration reversed a number of these trends. It did not accept the arguments of dependency theory, it did not believe the North *owed* anything to the South, it did not feel guilty about past U.S. actions, and it faulted Jimmy Carter for following a romantic and unrealistic foreign policy. Rather than acceding to the South's demands, the Reagan Administration determined to confront the often corrupt and abusive regimes present in the Third World—and their Soviet backers—and not to accept but to respond forcefully to the criticism leveled against us. The U.S. let it be known that it would not agree to any massive transfers of resources from North to South and that such giveaways should not be thought of as a substitute for a sound, market-oriented strategy of development. The rhetoric heated up at the UN and elsewhere as the U.S. let it be known that it did not consider itself responsible for all the world's poverty and problems. The U.S. criticized Third World nations as strongly as they had criticized it.

It is likely that both approaches were too extreme. The Carter Administration *was* consumed by guilt (over Vietnam, Watergate, and other ills), was far too willing simply to turn the other cheek in the face of unwarranted Third World criticism, *did* have a romantic foreign policy, and did not advance a sound development strategy. On the other hand, it was probably self-defeating for the U.S. under Reagan to be so strongly critical of the Third World, to cut itself off from dialogue with it. The Reagan administration should have understood that the rhetorical criticism of the U.S. by the Third World came in large part out of their own feelings of inferiority, and the administration should not have been unwilling to even appear to sympathize with the plight of the Third World or to meet it part way. In the time since then, it might be said that the massive transfer of resources from North to South has already *de facto* taken place, in the form of the massive unpaid and unpayable Third World debt.

The United States needs a strong, positive policy toward the Third World. It need not be based on guilt and romanticism nor on confrontation. Rather, it needs to be prudent, constructive, empathetic, and helpful. The fact is that after three decades of experience with development in the Third World (as distinct from the theoretical debates that prevailed at the beginning), we now have a solider grasp of what works in development and what does not. We know that Marxism-Leninism doesn't work very well (except as a formula for power, but not for economic development), that excessive state control doesn't work very well, and that authoritarianism

and totalitarianism don't work very well. What does work is democracy, freedom, open markets as well as open political systems, a regime of law and of legal protections, and a government that functions honestly and efficiently—one that both provides for social justice for a nation's unfortunates and opens up possibilities for the people's natural talents and ambitions to express themselves.

Long experience indicates that these are among the major ingredients of a sound development strategy. On that basis it would seem that both U.S. policy interests and the developmental aspirations of the Third World could go forward together, in tandem rather than in confrontation.

This selection begins with a statement by the editor of this volume on the political, economic, and social science agenda involved in the North-South dialogue. Next comes an essay by Indian scholar Jagdish Bhagwati suggesting that confrontation with the North is unlikely to pay off for the South and that a calmer, more reasoned, and more specific bargaining position is now in the South's best interests. Finally, *The Wall Street Journal's* Karen Elliott House shows that even with all the economic changes of recent decades both in the developed and the developing world, the United States is likely to remain overwhelmingly the world's dominant power long into the twenty-first century.

Cancún and After: The United States and the Developing World

By Howard J. Wiarda

The meetings of heads of state and foreign ministers of the eight already industrialized and the fourteen developing nations[1] held at Mexico's lush island resort of Cancún raised high hopes and expectations among some, consternation and frustration among others. The real meaning and substance of the meeting were often obscured by the media's forced reliance on the official press briefings and, in the absence of other information, the emphasis on the food eaten, the elaborate security precautions, and the luxury of the surroundings. By now Cancún has faded from the headlines, but the issues and agendas raised are likely to be with us for a long time.

The Cancún meeting may have been a watershed. It is not that the place is so important or even that this particular gathering was so crucial. The issues have been building for years. But what Cancún did was to provide a prestigious forum and sounding board for the Third World ideas, and to bring some of these home to the American public for the first time. Among other things Cancún served to illustrate how isolated the United States is internationally not just from the developing nations but often from its allies as well; how much we have become dependent on many Third World nations for raw materials, commodities, and markets; the degree to which future agendas of international agencies and conferences will be dominated by Third World demands that the U.S. lower its protective tariff walls (with all the potential

for disruptions of the domestic economy that implies) and that ways be found for major transfers of wealth from North to South; and last but perhaps not least, whether the United States may not have so alienated itself from the Third World that it will be very difficult to restore good relations again.

THE ECONOMIC AGENDA

Both Cancún and the unsatisfactorily incomplete North-South dialogue have pitted the "have" nations against the "have-nots." Within both these camps there exist further divisions. Many of the poorest-of-the-poor nations, the less developed countries, or LDCs, would like to focus on the issues of a debt moratorium; others such as Brazil (among the Newly Industrialized Countries or NICs) are currently seeking new financing and do not want to make the lenders nervous by such talk. The "have-nots" are also divided into oil-rich and oil-scarce nations; into those who are "making it" (such as Brazil, Mexico, Venezuela, South Korea) and those, the vast majority, who are not (the correlations between these two sets of categories are not one-to-one: Venezuela is oil-rich, Brazil is not). The industrialized nations are often divided between the currently more conservatively governed Anglo-American nations and the socialist and social-democratic nations of the Continent, many of whom side in varying degrees with Third World aims. The divisions ex-

ist and they make for dramatic headlines, but it is equally clear that the United States has become increasingly isolated in such forums.

While the Third World is divided on some issues, it has remained remarkably unified for almost two decades now on the basic demand for a fundamental reallocation of the world's wealth. The agenda includes more and easier credit terms, better access to Northern markets for goods manufactured in the Third World, higher and stabler prices for the primary goods the Third World exports, and easier terms for the purchase of oil. These are clearly negotiable and not unreasonable goals, but they have often been obscured by the rhetoric of "massive transfers of wealth," which the major Northern countries find unacceptable.

The locus of such discussions is of course critical to their outcome, and here again trouble is brewing. The developing nations have pressed to hold discussions on the major issues above in the United Nations General Assembly, a forum in which they hold not only an enormous majority but which is perilously close to being dominated by the Communist nations, their clientele, and the more radical of the Third World bloc (such as Libya or Cuba).[2] The United States prefers to hold discussions in agencies or forums such as the World Bank, General Agreements on Tariffs and Trade (GATT), or the International Monetary Fund (IMF), which it has in the past been able to dominate. But it should be

Source: From *PS*, Vol. XV, No. 1 (Winter 1982), pp. 40–48. Reprinted with permission of the American Political Science Association.

emphasized that these latter agencies have also been under intense pressure in recent years to provide greater Third World representation and to accommodate its demands; the trend has clearly been in that direction.

The United States, while providing limited public assistance (the measurement of which is open to diverse interpretations), has recently urged a strategy of private initiative and free-enterprise capitalism as a means of development for the Third World; and a new office has been created within the Agency for International Development (AID) to promote the strategy. Privately, some administration officials admit that will not work in societies where there is no or only a weak entrepreneurial class; and one suspects the administration's position is actually based on the following considerations: the president's own strongly-held beliefs, the need to satisfy a significant *United States* constituency, and the interest of some U.S. industries such as oil. But in a world in which in virtually every other country except the United States, and especially in the developing nations, greater statism rather than less seems to be both the preferred way and the almost inevitable result of increasing global economic complexity and interdependence, expanded social pressures and services, and the perceived need for state guidance and control of turbulent economic pressures—such a policy is unlikely to prove realistic. Fortunately, Mr. Reagan appears to be a good listener; and if the right voices get to him, the administration may yet be persuaded that conditions in Santo Domingo or Sri Lanka are different from those in Iowa or Illinois.

While the United States' advocacy of *laissez faire* capitalism is not likely to find great receptivity in the Third World, the Third World's own prescription of immediate and massive transfers of wealth from North to South is equally unrealistic. In the long run, however, one suspects that a good part of its program is likely to be realized. The Third World feels that time, morality, and worldwide public opinion will eventually work in its favor. And if one recognizes the degree of vulnerability and dependence the United States and the rest of the industrialized world have or soon will have on Third World resources (the U.S. sells more goods to developing countries than to Japan and Western Europe combined; markets in the Third World are growing faster than those of any other area), the strength and solidarity of new OPEC-like cartels (the demand for bananas is, admittedly, less inelastic than that for oil, but wait until we see what happens to the price of such essentials as copper, manganese, or bauxite), and the trends in the international forums where many of these issues will be decided (increasingly away from the United States), the prospects seems to favor the Third World. Each American administration, of course, hopes it will be out of office when the real crunch comes.

Cancún provided an opening for such changes and, with Mr. Reagan present, a legitimacy heretofore lacking for the Third World's demands. The United States may choose not to go any further than it already has in responding to the Third World agenda; but if it selects that option it will not only be further isolated but also runs the risk, now that the impetus to alter

the international system has begun, that it may eventually find itself with no other choice than to go along.

The situation is roughly analogous to that governing the Law of the Sea Treaty (LOS) negotiations. The United States does not like various provisions in the proposed treaty and may well choose to continue acting unilaterally with regard to certain sea and seabed activities; but if the Treaty is then adopted anyway by the rest of the world as now seems possible, the U.S. may be forced to accept in one form or another its major precepts. That is in any case the strategy the Third World will adopt with regard to the LOS treaty if the U.S. rejects it, and it is undoubtedly what the Third World will do with regard to the transfer-of-wealth issue should the United States stand entirely against any further negotiations.

At Cancún Mr. Reagan was cordial but noncommittal, and the U.S. statement was crafted carefully so as to be purposely ambiguous, to make it appear the U.S. would not stonewall on all future discussions, to say "no" (or perhaps "maybe") in a cooperative way. The statement emphasized that Third World nations should first improve their domestic economic policies, which could be translated as meaning they should expect no increases in U.S. aid, and that future talks should take place in a forum where there is a "cooperative spirit," which means not the General Assembly. The statement meant to give the impression of progress while also implying a U.S. holding action.

In the meantime there remains room for bargaining over more concrete, less grandiose issues. That is undoubtedly a further aspect of the U.S. strategy. These include such issues as foreign assistance and loans in their many forms, the lowering of U.S. tariff walls on select Third World products, some easing of credit restrictions, assistance to help finance discovery and production of oil and other fuels in the Third World. Negotiations over these issues will be protracted, enabling the U.S. to adjust and compromise and play for time; but the other and larger issues will remain.

THE POLITICAL AGENDA

From the beginning the Cancún conference involved politics at least as much as economics. The decision to exclude Cuba's Fidel Castro from the proceedings, the condition under which President Reagan agreed to attend, and the decision of Mr. Reagan himself to go to Cancún given the potential pitfalls and the avoidance by American presidents of such forums in the past, served as preludes to the actual discussions at the conference itself and were all preeminently political matters. The issues *at* Cancún were also political, involving the willingness of the Northern nations to negotiate, where such negotiations should take place, and the power such chosen bodies should have. Cancún did not involve discussions over the appropriate prices for tomatoes or cucumbers.

The differences within and between the blocs represented are also primarily political. Both blocs are misnamed, although the issues dividing them are fairly clear-cut. The less-industrialized nations, referred to as the "South" but whose ranks include India, Yugoslavia, and others north of the equator,

saw Cancún as a means to reinvigorate the global negotiations that have been largely stalled for the past three years. And it is largely for political reasons that the "South" hopes to vest ultimate decision making on such negotiations in a body, the General Assembly, where the voting is in terms of one-nation-one-vote, thus guaranteeing the "South" will prevail at least at the formal ballot level. The fact must also be faced realistically that conducting further negotiations in the UN agencies is certain to involve political efforts by the Soviet Union and its clients in the Third World at further isolating the U.S. internationally, using the discussions as a propaganda forum and embarrassing the U.S. by trying to wrench unacceptable concessions from it.

The "North" is no less a misnomer. Conspicuous by its absence is the Soviet Union, a northern and a comparatively developed nation, that refused to attend the Cancún meeting and spurns all such "North-South" dialogues on the grounds that only the "colonialist" and "imperialist" Western countries bear responsibility for the world's poverty. However, should the discussion move to the UN, the Soviet Union and its now numerous bloc would surely side with the South. Nor, as indicated, are the Western allies themselves united: Britain under Mrs. Thatcher has generally supported the U.S., while France and Germany have increasingly followed more independent policies, and Holland, Sweden, and others are inclined to side with the Third World.

The Northern nations, primarily the United States as we have seen, have heretofore resisted any global

bargaining in a forum where small nations like Grenada would have a voice equal to that of the largest and richest countries. The U.S. had preferred those agencies (GATT, World Bank, IMF) where voting is weighted toward those who make the largest financial contribution or have the largest global interests. It is generally agreed that in the international economic order there are four main means, in descending order of importance, by which the Northern nations have maintained their preeminence;[3] (1) the structure of the world market economy through which the industrial nations dominate most major markets; (2) the framework of rules designed to maintain order and stability in world markets; (3) national rules geared to promote and protect domestic markets, industry, and trade, rules which affect the Third World not least by the sheer size of the rich economies in comparison with the weaker ones; and (4) at the operational level through buying and selling in which the largest countries and their firms have numerous advantages. If this categorization is valid, then institutions like GATT and the IMF can be considered a part of category (2) above in which, by design and by definition, the economically strong are favored.

The idea that one might or ought to reform the international economic order is not new. In the contemporary setting Nkrumah, Tito, Nyere, Castro, and, most recently, Willy Brandt have been important spokesmen. Raúl Prebisch and the Economic Commission for Latin America (ECLA) had earlier provided much of the intellectual justification by emphasizing the widening gaps in the present international economic system between those countries that are chiefly exporters of primary goods and those that export manufactured products. Rather than narrowing, the gap between the developed and the (often hopefully) developing nations was bound to widen; hence the demand for a redress of such imbalances. It is important to emphasize the degree of unanimity among the Southern nations on the fundamental flaws in the existing international system and the reasons for them.

The "Southern" nations, moreover, were skillful in presenting their case.[4] The UN resolution calling for the establishment of a "new international economic order" and for the "elimination" of the "widening gap between the developed and the developing countries" was passed at the Sixth Special Session of the General Assembly in April, 1974. The timing was not accidental. It came on the heels of the malfunctioning of the Bretton Woods system, the first round of major hikes in oil prices, an unsettled period in commodity prices, and at the onset of a worldwide economic slump. These events both revealed the vulnerability of the industrialized countries as never before, and the divisions among them as they all scrambled individually to secure their oil supplies. Not only was the economic insecurity of the "North" thus revealed but the international political framework of its dominance also seemed wobbly.

Doubtlessly, in presenting their demands the Southern nations overemphasized the Northerners' vulnerability and the opportunity for advantage it afforded. Nonetheless, the Southerners did see a chance to press ahead on the redistributional agenda, which they had long advocated but lacked the strength and opportunity to implement. They gained some success via the Brandt Commission report and in other forums, but it was precisely the stalling and frustration of their further efforts that led to the call for the Cancún meeting.

Essentially what Cancún was all about was the Southerners' efforts to present their case to an American president who was initially opposed but whom they hoped would be open-minded, and to attempt to persuade Mr. Reagan to moderate however slightly the U.S. opposition to global negotiations within a forum such as the UN. In this overarching task they feel they achieved success, although the language of the communiques emanating from Cancún remained vague and future steps are still undecided. The U.S. will doubtless go along with the idea of some limited "global" negotiations, but the degree to which these will be diluted is still not certain. One low-ranking U.S. official has said of such negotiations that "we support them as long as they don't get results."

More constructively, others are exploring whether it is possible that a UN agency might review but not veto decisions taken at GATT or the IMF, or whether small negotiating groups representing member states' interests and composed mainly of experts from the nations affected and not members of the UN missions might be established for discussing particular issues. In the absence of agreement by the key parties no obligations would be involved. Conditions might also be imposed, by others as well as by the U.S., on the outcome of such negotiations or the nature of the negotiations themselves.[5]

The General Assembly might still vote on these matters, but its actions would be, as on other issues, more hortatory than substantive. Having committed itself to negotiations, however, it would likely prove very difficult for the United States to resist any concessions whatsoever. In this sense Cancún and Mr. Reagan's presence there was a major victory and opening wedge for the Third World's redistributional program.

THE SOCIAL SCIENCE AGENDA

The methodologies and prevailing developmental approaches of the social sciences were not on the formal agenda at Cancún; nor at a meeting of heads of state would one expect them to be. Nevertheless, such concerns are lurking strongly in the background among the intellectual elites that help advise heads of state in the Third World and among some of the state leaders themselves. Certainly such concerns are prominent as underlying influences in the international forums in which the economic and political agendas mentioned above are and will be discussed. The matter should be of particular interest to political scientists.

The issue is this: not only have many Third World leaders and intellectuals rejected the presumption of economic and political hegemony long held by the Northern nations, but they have come to reject as well many of the social science notions underlying such assumptions which also condemn them to a status of inferiority and "underdevelopment." The emerging nations no longer believe or accept that they are but pale and retarded imitations of the West fated to follow its same developmental stages, that the West offers both lessons and a model from which they can learn or that they must imitate, or that the Western experience of a small group of countries in the north of Europe and America in the nineteenth century provides *the* developmental formula that they both ought to imitate in an ethical sense and *must* follow in accord with the unfolding of an inevitable historical process.[6]

Third World leaders tend to see the development literature of the 1960s, that once enjoyed so much popularity as the dominant interpretive paradigm, as biased, ethnocentric, and prejudicial, insensitive to their own distinct histories and cultures and often running roughshod over them, inimical to and sometimes mocking of their often revered traditional institutions, helping to perpetuate myths about Third World backwardness and Western superiority (not just in an economic sense but politically, socially, and often morally as well), hostile and damaging to indigenous ways and institutions, and wrought with, to them, irrelevant Cold War overtones. As the United States primarily and Western Europe secondarily have lost both will and strength to serve as policemen of the world, and as their economies have proved vulnerable, the social science concepts that often undergirded the Western sense of dominance and superiority have come increasingly under attack as well.

Along with the attack on the presumed superiority and univer-sality of the social science models derived from the West has come a new concern and search for indigenous concepts of development. In part this lies behind the resurgence of Islamic fundamentalism and the notion of an Islamic state, law, and society; behind the reexamination by Third World leaders of such institutions as India's caste associations and African tribalism, which Western developmental political sociology had largely confined to the dustbins of "tradition" and discarded history but which numerous Third World leaders are now reconsidering as possible bases for new and indigenous societal forms; and behind the resurgence of corporate and organic-statist models (in a variety of types) throughout Latin America. Within the Third World, hence, and as a reflection of these trends, efforts are being made to formulate an Islamic social science of development, an Indian social science of development, a sub-Saharan African social science of development, a Latin American social science of development, and so on.[7]

Some perspective is necessary. The comments above are not meant to minimize the wrenching conflicts within the Third World over such issues, the divisions and sheer confusion *à la* Naipaul that exist, the pull that the West still has. The dilemma for many Third World leaders is thus not whether to turn their backs on the West but how to modernize without necessarily Westernizing, how to use the capital and technology of the West without accepting the social and political concomitants that often accompany such changes, how to achieve, in novelist Carlos Fuentes's words, the health, wealth, and efficiency of the West without sacrificing deep ethical and cultural roots or the viability of historic and often preferred institutions.

This is a fundamental dilemma that corresponds with another: how to reconcile the rising expectations of Third World peoples as well as their growing consciousness of their own identity and interests *with* the traditional power and high living standards of the industrialized North. This growing awareness of cultural and political diversity in the Third World and the need for a different balance between their own and imported institutions, between what is distinctive and what is universal in each nation's or culture area's development process, is not unrelated to the growing assertiveness of the Third World and its demands in the economic and political spheres, at Cancún and elsewhere.

CONCLUSION

Cancún provided new-found momentum for Third World concerns while also interjecting some realism into the debate. There will be no wholesale or immediate transfer of wealth from North to South but there is abundant room for compromise over such issues as lower tariff barriers for Third World products; a greater Third World voice at GATT, the IMF, or the World Bank; bilateral tax and investment treaties; energy; multilateral coverage to encourage investment; and so forth. Compromise is also possible on the respective forums for such discussion, involving studies, hearings and exhortations at the UN combined with hard bargaining in agencies like the World Bank. It is also possible that the hortatory advocacy of massive transfers of wealth may in part be replaced by mutually beneficial collaboration that seeks to create new wealth and jobs in *both* North and South.

At Cancún the United States demonstrated its willingness to listen, bend somewhat, and perhaps compromise. At present a renewed search is underway in the U.S. government for the appropriate forums (perhaps not the General Assembly but a modified Cancún of "select" countries) and mechanisms to deal with the ensuing discussions. That is a hopeful sign, but there are major limiting factors as well. The domestic mood would not appear propitious for either much greater foreign assistance or the lowering of tariff barriers that cost U.S. jobs; nor would Congress or the White House be likely to initiate such steps, certainly not in an election year.

The U.S. has said that it will listen to Third World grievances, but the context of increasing U.S. isolation internationally, waning patience with both the Third World demands and the UN agencies from which they ensue, coupled with shaky and in some cases near-bankrupt economies in the Third World and mounting social and political pressures both at home and abroad, must be kept in mind. And even if the U.S. does listen, the gaps of empathy and understanding are so great as to lead in all likelihood to greater disjunction and conflict rather than any mutual understanding. As a rich, powerful, and comparatively conservative nation, the United States may be willing to provide some economic and technical aid, but a true understanding of Third World cultures, problems, aspirations, and special needs—and from the Third World's own point of view—seems remote. Political and social scientists could help bridge these gaps, but the models of development they have espoused in the past are often part and parcel of the same ethnocentric assumptions underlying our assistance programs.

The Third World requests have a powerful logic and legitimacy behind them from the point of view of both international social justice and the requirement of contemporary economic interdependence between North and South. In our present circumstances of economic recession, political isolation, and growing dependence on Third World resources, we may come to recognize that we may need the Third World almost as much as it needs us. Hence, the discussions that follow Cancún will depend on both the different national and bloc interests represented *and* the attitudes that all parties assume.

Cancún may be seen as one of the initial stepping stones in what will surely be a long passage. But the journey will certainly not be made easier, even if the will and favorable U.S. political circumstances are present, by the conditions of global economic downturns, recession, and stagnant or contracting economic pies with fewer new pieces to hand out in which both North and South now find themselves. ∎

Notes

1. Why these nations were invited and not others remains something of a mystery to those not invited.
2. An amusing but also discouraging account of one such, not unrepresentative, UN forum is Walter Berns, "Where the Majority Rules: A UN Diary," *The American Spectator,* 14 (November 1981) 7–12.
3. Susan Strange, *Sterling and British Policy* (London: Oxford University Press, 1971); and Peter C. J. Vale, "North-South Relations and the Lomé Conventions: Treating the Symptoms and Not the Causes" (Braamfontein: The South African Institute of International Affairs, July 1981).
4. The analysis follows that of Vale, "North-South Relations."
5. Some reasonable suggestions for such negotiations have been set forth in an Op-Ed statement by former Ambassador Richard N. Gardner, "Beyond Cancún," *New York Times* (November 8, 1981).
6. These ideas have been elaborated and analyzed in considerably greater detail by the author in two papers: Howard J. Wiarda, "The Ethnocentrism of the Social Sciences: Implications for Research and Policy," *The Review of Politics,* 42 (April 1981), 163–97; and "Toward a Non-Ethnocentric Theory of Development: Alternative Conceptions from the Third World." Paper presented at the 1981 Annual Meeting of the American Political Science Association, New York, September 3–6, 1981.
7. See, on this theme, Edward Said, *Orientalism* (New York: Pantheon, 1978); G. H. Jansen, *Militant Islam* (New York: Harper and Row, 1980); Vrajenda Raj Mehta, *Beyond Marxism: Toward an Alternative Perspective* (New Delhi: Manohar Publications, 1978); Howard J. Wiarda, *Corporatism and National Development in Latin America* (Boulder, CO: Westview Press, 1981); Howard J. Wiarda (ed.), *Politics and Social Change in Latin America: The Distinct Tradition* (Amherst: University of Massachusetts Press, rev. ed., 1982). Additional literature and sources on these themes are cited in the two articles in note 6 above.

Rethinking Global Negotiations

By Jagdish N. Bhagwati

The Global Negotiations at the United Nations have been stalemated ever since the UN General Assembly resolved at the 34th Session in 1979 to launch them in 1980 at a special session. The continued frustration of the South over this stalled situation and the bitterness generated by the sense that the North has been intransigent inject a sorry note into the ongoing North-South dialogue that traces back at least to the 1964 UNCTAD Conference. As attempts are currently being made to seek yet again a successful launching of the Global Negotiations during 1983, it is important to assess the underlying objectives that the South aspires to, and indeed to ask whether the Global Negotiations are the ideal, or possibly even a feasible, way to achieve these objectives.

A HISTORICAL OVERVIEW: OIL AND ALL THAT

The story of North-South relations, and the dialogue concerning them, could be written in oil. In fact, the present state of Global Negotiations and the constraints and prospects that it presents in the evolving North-South situation cannot be meaningfully understood unless the key role played by oil is appreciated. Before oil entered the picture, North-South issues were already on the international scene, but they were to be transformed with the triumph of OPEC. A backward glance at that transformation is most illuminating.

Phase I: LIEO, Pax Americana, and the pre-OPEC Era

The postwar period was indeed the era of the Liberal International Economic Order (LIEO) par excellence. Under US leadership, which was tantamount to *Pax Americana,* the international institutions founded at the end of the war (IMF, IBRD, and GATT) provided the institutional umbrella under which trade, investments, and growth prospered. Unprecedented growth rates characterized the 1950s and 1960s, a Golden Age that has sadly vanished. But already the seeds of Southern unhappiness were sprouting during this period. Two, in particular, need to be noted.

First, the process of decolonization created many of the new nations of the South. In consequence, they played no role in shaping the specialized international agencies that defined the LIEO: Many of these nations simply did not exist at the time of this creation! This meant that they had little weight in the voting patterns; they were skeptical that their interests would be properly accounted for in the deliberations of these agencies; and even if they stood to gain from the workings of these agencies, perhaps the division of the gains was skewed against them. Politically, therefore, this translated into the familiar position that divides the South from the North: a preference for the one-nation one-vote approach, which in turn implies a preference for negotiations at the United Nations rather than at the international agencies with their traditionally weighted voting procedures.

Second, the dominant ideological position embodied in the LIEO was not fully shared by the new countries. And it could not be, especially in matters dealing with the classical choice between protection and freer trade. Historically, few countries have embraced free trade when they were behind. Moreover, export pessimism was fairly rampant in various guises during the 1950s, when several developing countries opted for import-substituting (IS) industrialization. But if views diverged on this fundamental issue, they were to grow apart on several others too. The LIEO reflects the traditional, mutual-gain approach under which benign neglect, with the right Benthamite framework, leads to the improvement of all. But as developing countries struggled with their problems and the early optimism about aid-assisted take-offs gave way, and aid programs withered with the decline of the Cold War, rival philosophies appeared, accentuating the differences in perceptions, prejudices, and principles. In particular, the benign neglect school had now to compete with the malign neglect

Jagdish N. Bhagwati is professor of economics and director of the International Economics Research Center at Columbia University.

Source: From Jagdish Bhagwati and John Gerard Ruggie (ed.), *Power, Passions, and Purpose: Prospects for North-South Negotiations,* MIT Press, Cambridge, MA, 1984.

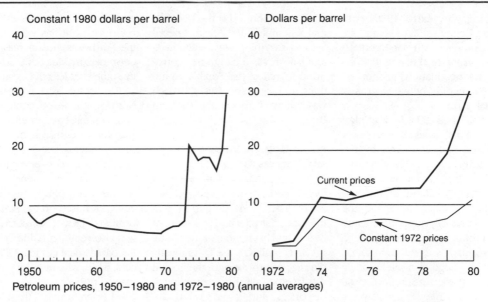

Constant 1980 dollars per barrel

Dollars per barrel

Current prices

Constant 1972 prices

Petroleum prices, 1950–1980 and 1972–1980 (annual averages)

school—recall the famous aphorism: "Integration into the world economy leads to disintegration of the national economy"—and, in certain influential radical critiques, with the malign intent school as typified by the view that aid was an extension of the imperialist arm that sought to suffocate the new countries in a neocolonial embrace.[1] *Rashomon* is rooted in reality; and only an ideologue would deny these harsh possibilities altogether. So the ideological picture became increasingly blurred, with the South often not quite in harmony with the dominant ideological position of the North on the LIEO.

The period up to 1973 was therefore characterized by a growing, but still manageable, ideological and political disharmony between the politically influential countries of the South and the North. The postwar institutional structure, and its basic underlying rationale, were not yet subject to any radical onslaught. In fact, the developed countries had already made some accommodating responses by modifying the specialized agencies to reflect the Southern desires and concerns—introducing Part IV in GATT in 1964 and clearing the grant of GSP through waiver of Article 1 of GATT for ten years in the area of trade; instituting new low-conditionality facilities at the IMF to benefit Southern nations, the Compensatory Financing Facility in 1963 and the Buffer Stock Facility in 1969;[2] and creating at the IBRD the International Finance Corporation in 1956 and the International Development Association in 1960. Even the creation of UNCTAD in 1964 to oversee the manifold developmental problems of the developing countries, although a result of their aspirations and efforts at the UN, must also be viewed in this light, despite UNCTAD's later identification with Southern positions and the resulting tensions with specialized agencies such as GATT, and hence the disfavor it has subsequently incurred in the North.

Phase II: The Rise of OPEC and NIEO

The mildly accommodationist status quo of the postwar international regime was sharply interrupted by the success of OPEC, beginning in 1971. Four aspects of the resulting shift in the tone and content of the North-South dialogue must be emphasized.

First, the example of OPEC suggested to the developing countries that other commodities could be cartelized to extract resources unilaterally from the North. Hence reliance on commodity exports, which had always been thought of as a sign of dependence and the necessity for industrialization, was now considered a source of strength! The economic concept of "commodity power" was born. The use of the 1973 oil embargo also suggested the political concept of commodity power: the North might be dependent on the South for commodities if the South could take unified positions and threaten interrupted supplies of commodities.

Hence, the early 1970s witnessed a definite shift of gears. The South entered, with a perception of new strength, the negotiations phase, for negotiations cannot occur meaningfully between grossly unequal partners.

Second, and this is a critical point, the South's perception of new power was largely shared by the North at the time. OPEC's demonstrated strength made commodity power seem credible; and it was also directly pitted alongside the South in mutually supportive legitimation roles. Western Europe, feeling particularly vulnerable to OPEC and by and large also intellectually less antipathetic to Southern positions than the United States, played a major role in the conciliatory Northern response, which also led to the Conference on International Economic Cooperation (CIEC) at Paris during 1975–77.

Third, the key role of OPEC and commodity power in this equation made emphasis on commodities in the new situation inevitable. Just as GSP had become the symbol of the New Delhi UNCTAD II in 1968, commodity schemes were the symbol of the early 1970s and indeed at the Nairobi UNCTAD IV in 1976 where the negotiations on the integrated Program for Commodities were agreed upon.

Fourth, this key focus on commodities went hand in hand with the stance that the entire range of international economic issues—trade, money, aid, energy, raw materials, etc.—be negotiated together. This was partly a negotiating ploy, to prevent energy being negotiated in isolation to the North's advantage. But it also reflected the view, embodied in the New International Economic Order proclaimed at the 1973 Algiers Non-Aligned Confer-

ence and embraced at the UN General Assembly's 1974 Sixth Special Session, that the postwar LIEO institutional structure had to be reorganized to reflect the South's aspirations and interests. This approach was followed also at the CIEC in Paris.

Phase III: Déjà Vu and Regress

The euphoria that attended OPEC's success, however, soon vanished. The 1976–79 period was therefore characterized by a sense of déjà vu and frustration for the South.

First, OPEC itself gradually dimmed as a threat once the first oil shock (especially the quadrupling of oil prices during 1973) was absorbed, oil prices stabilized in subsequent years and conservation programs got hesitantly under way.

Second, commodity power was soon realized to be illusory; oil was seen to have been a special case. The desired commodity schemes were therefore de facto transformed from unilateral OPEC-type producer cartels into joint arrangements between producers and consumers, thus destroying their original *raison d'être* for superstellar status in North-South negotiations. Therefore, the Northern sense of vulnerability diminished during this period, and the urgency of reaching an accommodation with the South in a global negotiation, either at CIEC or elsewhere in the UN, vanished quickly from the scene.

Third, from the South itself, this tendency was reinforced in a paradoxical fashion. The successful recycling of petrodollars to several of the more developed of the developing countries meant that these were now being integrated into the current international regime. Their ca-

pacity to adopt militant, radical-reformist positions with respect to the North was thus increasingly undermined, making Southern solidarity somewhat less of a reality.

The result was regress in the North-South negotiations, with the South unable to exert effective pressure for its demands but still wedded to them. The North basically played along, conversing but making no real concessions. While the Northern lack of response was generally premised on the belated perception of lack of Southern power, it was also reinforced, in my view, by the paradoxical fact that OPEC's success, while whetting the South's demands politically, had also weakened significantly the Northern leaders' macroeconomic situation and hence their political and financial capacity to respond constructively, especially in regard to redistributive measures such as foreign aid flows. Thus, even the Carter Administration, despite its early professions of commitment to Third World causes, failed to deliver. A *Guardian* cartoon at the time captured this latter point rather well by showing Carter, Schmidt, et al. on the beach, busy reading a book on how to swim, while the Third World is drowning in the ocean. The caption read: "Hang in there; we will come out and get you as soon as we have learnt how to swim."

Phase IV: Return to Strong Posture: The Global Negotiations

During 1978–80, the 6 percent cut in world supply triggered by the Iranian Revolution led to the second set of sharp increases in the real price of oil: this time by 80 percent. This turn of events was the catalyst for a new lease of life for the notion of negotiating from strength.

At the Manila UNCTAD Conference in 1979, several developing countries had raised afresh the question of a special energy deal for the South. This was taken up at other Southern meetings throughout the succeeding months. The dramatic rise in oil prices that preceded the 1979 Havana Conference of the Non-Aligned Nations seems to have prompted Algeria to resurrect in Havana the NIEO approach it had launched in 1973 and to move these nations into resolving that comprehensive, global negotiations should be launched on North-South issues. This approach again found favor both with OPEC, which sought to defuse the Southern demands by linking energy to nonenergy issues, and with the North that again was reacting to the energy situation with renewed concern. As with Algiers, the Havana consensus was followed up at the UN General Assembly in its 34th Session, where it was resolved that, at its 1980 special session, a round of global negotiations on international economic cooperation for development would be launched. These Global Negotiations, as a legacy from the unsuccessful CIEC attempt during 1975–77, would simultaneously embrace a whole range of issues: trade, finance, aid, energy, raw materials, etc. And the venue would be the UN, with the Committee of the Whole of the General Assembly acting as the preparatory body for these negotiations.

Phase V: The World Recession and Its Aftermath

But the consensus for launching Global Negotiations has been followed by inaction. Why?

The most compelling reason is that the oil card is currently played out. The success of conservation played a minor role. But ultimately the world recession, following on the tight-money policies of the Federal Reserve combined with the expansionary budget deficits and the resulting phenomenal rise in US interest rates, delivered the *coup de grâce*. In a sagging world oil market, as OPEC is increasingly in public view as a cartel in distress, the Global Negotiations have lost their political rationale once again. OPEC has nothing to offer, nothing to threaten: no quid pro quo therefore can be demanded from the North. Negotiations from strength, therefore, are simply unrealistic once again. And, hanging over the entire issue is the ideological orientation of the Reagan administration which has shifted the United States from the traditional, sympathetic, and accommodating role to a rather unabashed "rejectionist" one, as evidenced most dramatically in the refusal to sign the Law of the Sea treaty in Jamaica.[3] We are therefore back to regress on the Global Negotiations. Where should we then turn?

WHAT SHOULD WE DO?

If the current capacity of the South to negotiate from strength, to extract concessions from the North, is virtually negligible, it is imperative that the Global Negotiations be reexamined realistically.

A principal lesson seems to be the futility of persisting with the Global Negotiations at this juncture, if at all. The most attractive option from the viewpoint of the South seems therefore to be an adjournment—at least until further notice. Or, if this sounds too drastic, a time limit for formally returning to efforts at launching them could be negotiated: a period of one year might be best, since it would broadly coincide with the beginning of a new presidential term in the United States and also with the anticipated recovery of the world economy. Given the South's political investment in the Global Negotiations, this step, in either of the two forms suggested, would naturally be preferable to abandonment of the talks altogether.

But this step, while disappointing to those wedded to the Global Negotiations, can be combined with simultaneous positive initiatives that seem presently to be negotiable and also consonant with some of the key objectives of the South. In particular, the fears over the international debt situation, in the midst of a profoundly disturbing world slump, have opened up a genuine area of mutual concern that draws into its ambit a number of influential countries of the North and the South.[4] The resulting recent exploratory thoughts by Mr. Regan, and in response by several Europeans, suggesting that an international monetary conference might be organized outside the IMF framework, and evidently with wider participation, represent an opportunity for the South to enter the scene actively. The South's spokesmen ought to move in on the ground floor of this idea, ensure that they participate constructively in its agenda, and thereby promote both their interests and their desire for more effective participation in the design of the resulting changes in the international monetary regime. Such an initiative would require both political action (e.g., active mobilization of the political leadership of the South, to get the US administration to support the conference proposal) and economic preparation (which would mean that the South provides the expertise to itself and assurance to the North that its participation at the conference would be mutually rewarding).[5]

I must emphasize the need for a thorough and careful preparation for entering and performing at such a conference. It is important that the Southern interests be realistically defined, and interests that do not concern us directly be dealt with at arm's length. In my view, the South ought to urge steps by the North for a quick recovery of the world economy. However, it should leave the matter of macroeconomic coordination and management, including the disharmony on exchange rate stability, as a debate between the Europeans and the United States. Nor should the South get involved in OPEC concerns (which were yesterday's Northern concerns) about stabilizing oil prices. The Southern interests lie, of course, in world recovery but the methods ultimately settled upon to institute it are for the most part not ones where we have special expertise or immediate interests.

I stress this last point particularly since the South, especially India and Colombia, attracted unnecessary irritation from the United States at the November 1982 GATT ministerial meeting in Geneva by opposing the proposal to extend the GATT to services. This matter was of special concern to the United States, which sees its comparative advantage shifting to services, and since the threat was greater to the Europeans and Japanese, who were nevertheless willing to go along with the studies of this proposal, the appropriate response of the developing countries should have been simply to say: "If

you wish to open up this can of worms, fine; but we assert our right to protect our infant service sectors and therefore any extension of GATT to services will have to exempt the developing-country members through suitable clarification of Part IV et al."[6] I might also add that the South missed a fine opportunity at the GATT ministerial meeting in Geneva of putting UNCTAD into the services picture by reminding the developed countries that UNCTAD already had been studying the services for many years and that the proposed studies could be organized jointly under UNCTAD and GATT auspices.

Furthermore, the South should not attempt to resurrect the grandiose notions that have no bearing on the present crisis: a world central bank or the SDR-link are proposals that, no matter how attractive in certain circles and meritorious perhaps in the classroom, have simply no place in the South's current repertoire if it is planning to play a constructive, self-helping role at such a conference.

In my view, the South ought to concentrate instead on two interrelated items. First, the question of appropriate institutional structure and governing principles for debt management for the lucky few "middle-income" developing countries who borrowed heavily during the 1970s and who now have the Northern banks in their embrace: and second, the question of how to assist the unlucky low-income developing countries, many in Africa, but also including Bangladesh, which need official assistance, official debt relief and the like, especially in view of the collapse of their primary earnings.[7]

While the monetary conference, if it transpires, can provide

an instructive departure from the specialized agencies in favor of a wider participation, it would also bring into play a possible role model for a compromise between the South's and the North's positions on the specialized agencies versus the UN as forums for negotiating on North-South issues. The monetary conference would discuss the substance of what ought to be done, trying to reach a consensus. But it does not rule out, in its present conception, the possibility that the ultimate negotiations would be conducted at the IMF itself (unless of course new institutions outside of the IMF were to emerge from these deliberations, as seems unlikely). A way of breaking the impasse at the Global Negotiations would be precisely to explore this possibility: that the UN Global Negotiations become, in effect, a discussion forum where the different issues are addressed within a comprehensive view of the problems facing the world economy and the North-South relations therein; whereas the actual negotiations are conducted at the specialized agencies. A possible enlargement of the UN role could then also be to bring the negotiated agreements at the specialized agencies back to the UN for a wider ratification. Attention would then have to be paid also to strengthening the specialized agencies in the direction of a greater Southern voice and Southern interests, a phenomenon that has certainly occurred, albeit slowly, in the preceding two decades. But this overall shift in focus and conception of what Global Negotiations ought to aim at and accomplish is something that we need to discuss seriously at this conference. ■

Notes

1. These diverse schools of thought were delineated and discussed at some length in my introductory essay in a book that I edited, *The New International Economic Order* (Cambridge, MA: MIT Press, 1977).

2. For an illuminating discussion of several of these changes, see John Ruggie "Political Structure and Change in the International Economic Order: The North-South Dimension," paper presented to the conference "Rethinking Global Negotiations," International Economics Research Center, Columbia University and Indian Council for Research in International Economic Relations, New Delhi, 6–8, January 1983.

3. The increasing influence of Secretary of State Shultz, however, may blunt the cutting edge of this reversal of the US role.

4. In this context, it is relevant to note that where genuine mutual interests obtain, North-South cooperation seems to emerge without our urging. The problem with the Brandt Commission's eloquent plea for more aid for the South, among other things, was simply that it appealed to mutuality of economic interests that simply were implausible except to those who wished to assist the South anyway. In this, the Commission was of course playing the same game, and with even less success, as the early aid advocates who proposed enlightened self-interest as an argument in favor of aid, but who invoked it in a political form (i.e., that aid would make the world safer for democracy).

5. The serious handicap under which the South operates in international negotiations owing to inadequate technical preparation has been documented by several observers. A particularly frank appraisal is to be found in *The North-South Dialogue: Making It Work* (London: Commonwealth Secretariat, 1982).

6. I should add that the United States also erred in trying to open up GATT to services while simultaneously trying to raise the graduation issue, thus arousing the fears of the SOUTH NICs that they would be under pressure to sign a service protocol without necessary exemptions eventually.

7. There is enough mutuality of interests in the case of the middle-income countries, between Northern banks and Southern borrowers, for such a dialogue to be rewarding. The question of the low-income countries has, rather, to be put on the moral plane, much like famine relief.

The Nineties and Beyond   *For All Its Difficulties, U.S. Stands to Retain Its Global Leadership*

By Karen Elliott House

Imagine a great-power race, spanning the course of the next generation. There are five entrants.

In lane one is the Soviet Union, dazzling the crowd with displays of political gymnastics, but actually running at such a slow pace it risks being lapped by the competition.

Next is the People's Republic of China, a more highly motivated competitor, but sadly saddled with an enormous burden—one billion people—that slows its stride to a crawl.

In lane three is Europe, preening for the crowd in its new uniform of unity, but still all too prone to run in many directions at once and probably better suited to be a sports commentator than a race entrant.

Then there is Japan, the world-record sprinter of recent years and a heavy betting favorite. There is a real question, however, whether Japan has the legs or the lungs to go the distance.

Finally comes the U.S., the defending champion and by far the most complete and naturally gifted athlete in the race. Yet, doubts abound about its will to win.

Everywhere these days, there is head-shaking and hand-wringing over the decline of America. Doomsayers are busily handicapping entrants in the race to replace America as world leader.

"Kiss No. 1 Goodbye, Folks," blares a headline in the Washington Post.

"America, Europe Is Coming," warns another in the International Herald Tribune.

"Emergence of Superrich Japan as Major Superpower" is the title of yet another gloom-and-doom article, in Time.

And Yale historian Paul Kennedy's book *The Rise and Fall of Great Powers,* the bible of American doomsayers, topped the best-seller list in the U.S. for 24 weeks.

Karen Elliott House writes on international affairs for *The Wall Street Journal.*

TOPSY-TURVY

Clearly, pessimism about America is in vogue. The sudden emergence of America as the world's largest debtor, Japan as the globe's richest creditor and the Soviet Union as its most ardent preacher of pacifism seems to many Americans to have turned the world upside down, raising doubts about whether America any longer can or should lead.

But as with many fashionable ideas, this one doesn't bear up well on closer scrutiny. In an effort to draw a reliable picture of the world that will develop in the next century, the Journal undertook an exhaustive survey: talks with several hundred leaders and laymen in America, Japan, Europe, China and the Soviet Union, involving 100,000 miles of travel. The picture that emerges is clear, if surprising: whether America relishes the role or not, it is the preeminent power in the world today and will remain so for at least the next generation —and probably longer.

This will not be the America of the immediate postwar era, the lone Western power dictating a global agenda, but rather the America of this generation, a team captain cajoling and corralling others in the interests of global peace and prosperity.

CAN DO

"America is the most vital nation in the West and will remain so," says Helmut Schmidt, the former West German chancellor. "It is a nation of vitality and optimism, and that helps a lot even if it sometimes blinds wisdom."

Most of those interviewed expect the world to be both politically and economically a far better place—with reduced chances of superpower war and increased prospects for prosperity—than anyone dreamed possible even a decade ago. The coming era, most predict, will be one of competition, not confrontation. To the extent that is so, it is largely because America has matched the Soviets militarily, bested them ideologically and buried them economically, forcing Moscow to focus on internal overhaul if it is even to remain in the great-power race.

But negativism about America's chances dies hard. Many of the same post-Vietnam pessimists who a decade ago doubted America's ability to compete with the Soviets politically and militarily now have decided that the real global contest is simply economic, and that in this arena Americans can't compete with the Japanese—even though America's economy in 1988 was nearly twice the size of Japan's.

Paradoxically, many foreigners, like Mr. Schmidt or former French President Valery Giscard d'Estaing, are more upbeat about America's prospects than are many members of America's own financial and foreign-policy establishment. Here in America, a fair generalization would be that politicians are more pessimistic than financiers, the money men are more gloomy than businessmen, and businessmen more downbeat than men on the street.

Notably, America's most enthusiastic cheerleaders are the emerging nations of the Pacific, often cited as the new center of global gravity and sometimes simplistically seen as Japan's economic vassals. There, America remains the preferred leader and Japan the distrusted and often detested neighbor.

"If Japan doesn't play an international role equal to its economic power, it's a problem," says Lee Hun Jo, president of South Korea's Lucky Gold Star. "If it does play a big role, that's a problem too, because they will dominate us."

In the contest for global power and influence, each of the contenders for power has some ardent boosters. Many cite Japan's huge trade surpluses and its increasing technological prowess as proof Japan will lead in the 21st century. Others look at Europe's effort to create by the end of 1992 a unified market—one that would exceed in size even that of the U.S.—and predict Europe's rapid emergence. Still others hail Mikhail Gorbachev's public-relations coups and Moscow's continuing military clout as evidence of an eventual Soviet resurgence. And a few predict the unstoppable triumph of the unleashed entrepreneurial instincts of one billion Chinese.

But there are fundamental flaws in all these forecasts. Power is not simply money, market size, might or masses. Power—the elements that enable a nation to influence events in a fashion favorable to its own interests—derives from a combination of military, political, economic and cultural clout, including the intangibles that make a nation admired and respected.

A close look at America's mix of strengths compared with those of other pretenders to power indicates why America should have little competition for preeminence in the 1990s and beyond. "We have a winning hand," says former Secretary of State George Shultz. "We just have to play it."

ARMS AND ECONOMICS

Militarily, the U.S. is certainly a leader. Few Western experts any longer talk of Soviet superiority, even though Moscow boasts greater numbers of troops, tanks and missiles. This isn't just because of Ronald Reagan's military buildup; it is basically because as military might becomes more reliant on modern technology, the natural advantage tips toward America's technological society. Also, for all the talk about budget pressures in the U.S., America remains infinitely richer and more capable than the Soviets of funding defense.

Economically, America remains the world's largest producer, and no one interviewed for this series, even the pessimists, believes it won't still have the largest economy 20 years hence. Indeed, a recent study by American wise men projected that America's share of total global output will rise by 2010 to nearly 30% and then, as now, be twice Japan's share.

Some skeptics insist America's economy is shrinking relative to others in the world. And it is true that for a time in the 1950s America accounted for nearly half of the world's gross national product, a far larger proportion than now. But that period was a historical aberration when Japan and Europe were still devastated by World War II. By the mid-1960s, with the world fully recovered, America's share of global GNP stood at 25%, and it has held steady at around that level ever since. In short, nothing in these numbers supports any handwringing over American decline.

Others say Japan is growing much faster than the U.S. But again, recent trends show otherwise.

During the 1960s Japan's economy grew at a blistering 11% a year, compared with America's average growth rate of 3% a year. Through much of the '80s, however, the Japanese and American economies have both grown in the range of 3% to 4% a year.

THE CAPITALIST MODEL

But there is much more to its strength than size. America is the world's free-enterprise model. And the free-enterprise system, with its incentives to grow and prosper, is demonstrably far more robust than statist systems, whether socialist or merely bureaucratic. Free enterprise is catching on worldwide among the booming nations of East Asia, in the rapidly deregulating economies of Western Europe, in the recent experiments of Eastern Europe and most notably in the bastions of socialism, China and the Soviet Union.

Paradoxically, some American pessimists, such as economist Lester Thurow, see the need for America to "manage" its economy to become more globally competitive. Yet it is precisely the open, freewheeling nature of American free enterprise that its practitioners consider its greatest source of strength. "I have a flexibility a Japanese or Germany company can only dream of," says John Welch, chairman of General Electric Co., a company that earns 25% of its $40 billion in annual revenues from exports and overseas production. "I can make a deal to put a plant in Spain without asking my government, my banker or even my shareholders. A Japanese company must consult its government. A German company consults its bank. I act." To try to mimic German or Japanese "economic management" is to "play to our weaknesses, not our strengths," Mr. Welch adds.

In fact, Japanese companies increasingly are trying to emulate America's emphasis on individual initiative and creativity rather than simply marching in state-orchestrated step. "The easy path of following America's lead is over," says Jiro Tokuyama, head of Mitsui's research center. "Now Japan must find its own way. We can produce capable technocrats but not yet creative visionaries because we emphasize lifetime security, not individual leadership here."

SECRET WEAPON

Economic strength, of course, ultimately rests on human resources. Here, too, America has the advantage. While Japan, despite a rapidly aging population, works hard to maintain its racial purity by closing its doors to outsiders, America's human resources continually are replenished by waves of immigrants. Some 600,000 legal immigrants arrive each year, far more than go anywhere else in the world. And many more arrive illegally.

These people restore national energy and enthusiasm and bring new talents. They live and thus keep alive the American dream. In this sense, America isn't doing immigrants a favor by letting them in; it is the immigrants who strengthen and thus favor America by coming. Moreover, while Japan largely excludes women from its work force, America has led the industrial world in recognizing and using the talents of its women.

It is certainly true that America has its economic problems. Chief among them is that its people consume more than they produce and save very little of what they earn. As a result, America in 1988 recorded a $130 billion trade deficit and a $150 billion budget deficit. These deficits are cause for concern but hardly for despair.

"It's a little like having a kid who has a tough flu," says John Reed, the chairman of Citicorp. "You worry about the kid; you are solicitous. But probably in this day and age, you don't view it as life-threatening. America has a tough flu, that's all."

The budget deficit is twice as large as it ever was in the Ford or Carter years. Yet the U.S. economy has grown so much that as a percentage of GNP, the deficit now is roughly equivalent to the 2.8% in Mr. Carter's last year, and it is half the 1983 peak. A nation, like an individual, can afford more debt if its wealth is growing.

SOLUTIONS AT HAND

More important, the deficit could be slashed rather quickly if Americans were, for example, ready to pay for gasoline even what they paid at its 1981 price peak. Then, with crude oil at about twice its current price, gasoline cost roughly $1.35 a gallon, compared with around 95 cents now. If the U.S. chose to pay that difference in a gasoline tax, the federal Treasury—collecting about $1 billion for each penny of tax—would reap some $40 billion a year, and the budget deficit could be slashed by nearly one-third. That is more than even the most pessimistic economists say is necessary to restore investor confidence.

While politicians call a higher gasoline tax regressive and unrealistic—and while any deficit-closing move carries economic risks—the point is that if politicians can convince Americans that the deficit is truly a problem, solutions are available. "It's hard to take seriously that a nation has deep problems if they can be fixed with a 50-cent-a-gallon gasoline tax," says former French Foreign Minister Jean Francois-Poncet.

The trade deficit, the other bugaboo in America's future, appears to be on the way to fixing itself. With the dollar weak against other currencies, American goods are cheaper and thus easier to sell abroad, and the trade gap is gradually shrinking. "The U.S. already has become competitive again," says Alain Chevalier, former chairman of LVHM Moet Hennessy Louis Vuitton of Paris. "America's isn't a problem of productivity but of consumption."

Nevertheless, economists such as Fred Bergsten of the International Institute of Economics in Washington and Mr. Thurow, dean of the Sloan School of Management at MIT in Cambridge, Mass., decry America's dependence on foreign money to finance its deficits. The U.S., they warn, is borrowing some $15 billion a month, largely from Japanese and West German investors. Much of this, of course, finances imports from those countries.

PRESSURE TO LEND

While this borrowing does make America vulnerable to the decisions of Germans and Japanese, those countries and their investors know that if the lending stops, America stops consuming their goods. Because America is such a major market for the entire world, a halt in purchases here would mean that not just America, but along with it the world, would plunge into recession. Citicorp's Mr. Reed recalls that in the late 1970s the global economy was booming and some abroad were beginning to believe they could continue to do so irrespective of America. But Paul Volcker, then chairman of the Federal Reserve, imposed his anti-inflation measures, throwing the U.S. into an economic slump.

"We put on the brakes, and the result was a global recession," says Mr. Reed. "Global trade didn't return to 1980 levels for another six years."

So Japan and West Germany seem unlikely to stop financing U.S. deficits. In short, economic interdependence is a two-way street, and America is still living in the biggest house.

America's major strength, however, isn't its military or even its economic might, but rather its democratic ideal. To countless millions around the world, America really is, in the phrase Ronald Reagan so often has used, "a shining city on a hill." The big question for America isn't whether others want her to lead—most still do—or whether she has the ability to lead. The question is does America have the will to lead.

"If you decide the U.S. is the natural world leader, and act like it, you would be, of course," says Alfred Herrhausen, the chairman of Deutsche Bank, in a comment paraphrased by businessmen and politicians from Bonn to Beijing.

National will is no small issue. Yet the other contenders for global leadership—Europe, Japan, China and the Soviet Union—by and large face greater liabilities and have fewer innate advantages.

JAPAN'S CHANCES

Japan is, at best, a major commercial and economic power. It is a physically small country all but devoid of natural resources. It has an aging population of modest size (120 million) that it chooses not to invigorate with immigrant infusions. Above all, it is an insular nation, in Asia but not part of Asia, superficially westernized but not Western. For all of its international economic clout, it remains a cultural and political island.

While America isn't always loved as a leader, at least since the end of the Vietnam War, it rarely has been hated. While some Americans and Europeans talk nervously of an Asian trading bloc with Japan as its leader, Asians do not. To them, the idea is something between a myth and a nightmare.

First of all, Japan still is widely resented in Asia for its World War II brutalities in Korea, China, the Philippines and elsewhere. No Asian neighbor looks forward to another era with Japan, the region's preeminent power.

Secondly, the differences among Asian economies are so great that a trading bloc similar to the one European nations envision after 1992 is simply impossible, Asians say. Japan and China are the East's largest economies, but Japan's per capita income is over $13,000 while China's is $280. The conditions for trade among equals simply don't exist.

LEVERAGE FOR AMERICA

So, while Asia is a major market for Japan, it isn't likely to be a self-sufficient trading zone. The Asian market isn't large enough to satisfy Japan's export goals, even though Japan now enjoys a trade surplus with every other Asian nation. Japan is eager to import its neighbors natural resources, but it shows no interest in becoming the market of last resort for the manufactured goods of all the developing economies of the area.

Those countries thus continue to rely on the American market, a dependence that gives Uncle Sam both economic and political leverage in Asia. "Economically, Asians want the U.S. in North Asia to counterbalance Japan, and politically Japan and all Asia want the U.S. presence to counterbalance the Soviet Union and China," says Park Ung-suh, a South Korean economist.

Besides its other handicaps, Japan lacks military might. While it spends more on arms than all but the two superpowers, its military is defensive in nature. And all the world, especially its Asian neighbors, hopes fervently to keep it that way.

Finally, to the rest of the world, Japan stands for no political ideal beyond its own economic self-interest. It can export Mazdas, microchips and even management techniques, but none of this amounts to leadership. "The Japanese haven't shown any inclination to lead," says Mr. Volcker.

Europe has greater possibilities to emerge a global leader than Japan, but it is unlikely to realize that potential. If European nations were truly united, their economic power would dwarf Japan's and at least equal that of America. Their combined GNP and educated populations would be larger than America's. If truly unified, a "United States of Europe" could also have enormous political and military clout. But 1992, even to the most optimistic Europeans, is not about a united political entity. It's about commerce.

"Unhappily, in Europe there is no leadership," says Mr. Giscard d'Estaing. "Only Mrs. Thatcher has the guts and the goals, but her goals are wrong. She is trying to recreate a Victorian empire. The others are wimp Europeans. They say they are for unity but can't do it."

THE BEAR'S MARKET

Then there is the Soviet Union, a military superpower that surely will remain at least the second-strongest on the globe. But missiles and tanks don't make it the equal of America any more than Hondas and VCRs bring Japan such status. Mr. Gorbachev acknowledges he has a failing economy; even many of his supporters doubt he can turn it around, at least anytime soon.

Nearly all the Soviet Union's economic vital signs have declined in the past two decades. GNP growth, 5% a year in the late 1960s, has run about 2% a year so far in Mr. Gorbachev's rule. Industrial growth has slowed over the same period from 6.3% a year to 2.1%, while the gains in agricultural output have shrunk from an average of 3.5% a year in the late 1960s to 1% a year recently, according to the Central Intelligence Agency.

"If they aren't successful [economically], then the Soviet Union just plain isn't going to be as powerful in the future as they are today," says Admiral William J. Crowe, chairman of the Joint Chiefs of Staff.

Beyond this Herculean task, Mr. Gorbachev must contend with nationalist centrifugal forces spinning out of control from the Baltic states to Armenia. Outside the national borders, he faces an Eastern

The Superpower Contenders Compared

	UNITED STATES	SOVIET UNION	JAPAN	EUROPEAN COMMUNITY	CHINA
Population (in millions)	243.8	284.0	122.0	323.6	1,074.0
Gross National Product (in billions of 1987 U.S. dollars*)	$4,436.1	$2,375.0	$1,607.7	$3,782.0	$293.5
Per capita GNP (1987 U.S. dollars*)	$18,200	$8,360	$13,180	$11,690	$270
GNP Growth Rate					
1966–70 (annual average)	2.8%	5.1%	11.0%	4.6%	N.A.
1971–75 (annual average)	2.3%	3.1%	4.3%	3.0%	5.5%
1976–80 (annual average)	3.3%	2.2%	5.0%	3.0%	6.1%
1981–85 (annual average)	3.0%	1.8%	3.9%	1.5%	9.2%
1987	2.9%	0.5%	4.2%	2.9%	9.4%
Inflation (change in consumer prices)	3.7%	−0.9%	0.1%	3.1%	9.2%
Total Labor Force (in millions)	121.6	154.8	60.3	143.0	512.8
Agricultural	3.4	33.9	4.6	11.9	313.1
Nonagricultural	118.2	120.9	55.7	131.1	199.7
Unemployment Rate	6.1%	N.A.	2.8%	11.0%	N.A.
Foreign Trade					
Exports (in millions of U.S. dollars)	$250.4	$107.7	$231.2	$953.5**	$44.9
Imports (in millions of U.S. dollars)	$424.1	$96.0	$150.8	$955.1**	$40.2
Balance (in millions of U.S. dollars)	−$173.7	$11.7	$80.4	−$1.6	$4.7
Energy					
Consumption (in bbl. of oil equiv. per capita)	55.6	37.3	22.7	24.4	4.8
Oil Reserves (in billions of barrels)	33.4	59.0	0.1	7.6	18.4
Oil Production (in millions of bbl. a day)	9.9	12.7	Negligible	3.1	2.7
Natural Gas Reserves (in trillions of cu. ft.)	186.7	1,450.0	1.0	112.9	30.7
Coal Reserves (in billions of metric tons)	263.8	244.7	1.0	90.5	170.0
Agriculture					
Grain Production (in kilograms per capita)	1,150	740	130	480	402
Meat Production (in kilograms per capita)	109	65	31	82	18
Military					
Active Armed Forces	2,163,200	5,096,000	245,000	2,483,400	3,200,000
Ready Reserves	1,637,900	6,217,000	46,000	4,565,800	1,200,000
Defense Expenditures Share of GNP	6.5%	15%–25%	1.6%	3.3%	4%–5%
Living Standard					
Life Expectancy (years)	75	69	78	76	68
Automobiles (registrations per thousand)	570	42	235	347	Negligible

*Data were converted at U.S. purchasing power equivalents
The data presented here—with a few exceptions—are for 1987, the latest year for which comparable data are available for all countries.

Europe many believe is irretrievably moving beyond Soviet control. That process will only accelerate if Mr. Gorbachev carries out his United Nations pledge late last year to pull some troops out of Eastern Europe and transform those that remain into strictly a defensive force.

Furthermore, communism has lost its ideological appeal even in most of the Third World. The Soviet Union increasingly is being viewed as a spent revolution—and a model of how not to run one's economy. So Mr. Gorbachev and his successors will have to spend the next decade or more grappling with almost insoluble internal problems—or, from failure or frustration, resort to military expansionism.

THE LONG MARCH

China, for its part, is a second-rate nuclear power with a massive but ill-equipped army. Its economy probably has more promise than the Soviet Union's, if only because the Chinese have a long tradition as entrepreneurs. Parts of China, particularly its coastal provinces, are booming, raising the possibility that this ocean of poverty could throw up several islands of prosperity a generation from now. Most of China remains a backward and overcrowded Third World nation, however, and even Sinophiles agree it will take several generations for the country as a whole to painfully claw its way to modernity.

China-watchers and Chinese officials do believe, though, that the country is irreversibly on that route. "At the moment the planned economy still dominates, but the market economy has proved its strength and can't be put in the bottle again," says Li Shenzhi, vice president of the Academy of Social Sciences in Beijing. But he, too, speaks in terms of generations, not years, before China can achieve parity with other global powers.

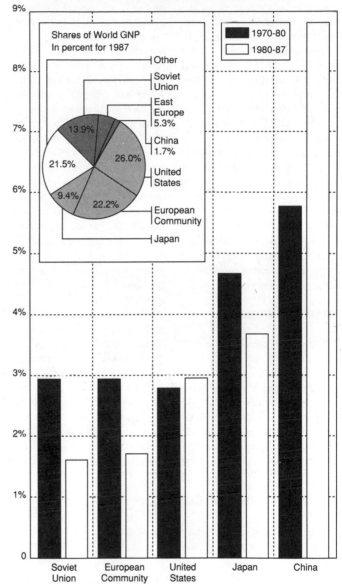

How Fast the Superpowers Are Growing
Average annual growth rate of real gross national product, in percent

Legend: ■ 1970-80 □ 1980-87

Shares of World GNP
In percent for 1987

- Other
- Soviet Union
- East Europe 5.3%
- China 1.7%
- United States 26.0%
- European Community 22.2%
- Japan

Pie values: 13.9%, 21.5%, 9.4%, 22.2%, 26.0%

Bar categories: Soviet Union, European Community, United States, Japan, China

Note: Growth rates are based on data translated into U.S. purchasing power equivalents.
Source: CIA Handbook of Economic Statistics

In terms of America's status, all this is basically favorable news. It means that the U.S. now faces a future with the Soviet threat—both military and ideological—sharply reduced, though still potentially destabilizing. It is a world in which a growing number of nations are seeking to experiment with democracy and free enterprise in direct emulation of America. And America, of course, can take a good deal of credit even for the success of its competitors, having helped reconstruct postwar Japan and Western Europe as dynamic forces in a global economy.

It might seem all this should be cause for self-congratulation, not self-flagellation. Most of the world doesn't see America declining. One German strategist, Josef Joffe, opened a speech to an American conference on the topic of decline by mockingly saying, "Oh Lord, if I have to live in a declining country, please let it be America."

A PARADE OF WORRIES

But America's establishment often tends toward self-doubt, even as Americans are fond of proving the experts wrong. When the Soviets launched Sputnik in the late 1950s many of the leading minds of America deplored its decline and hailed the inevitable preeminence of the Soviets. A presidential commission warned that the Soviet Union had a growth rate 50% higher than America's and was probably spending twice as much on arms. It was said then of the Soviets, as it is now said of the Japanese, that they were producing tens of thousands of scientists while U.S. education was producing football players.

In the late 1960s, Richard Nixon and Henry Kissinger began to prepare Americans for a multipolar world in which American decline was inevitable. The superpowers' military might would take a back seat to the economic power of Europe and Japan. Since then, Mr. Kissinger and others have successively written off Europe as plagued by Eurosclerosis, only to proclaim it now an Olympic sprinter.

By the mid-1970s, it was the Arabs who were seen as invincible. Saudi Arabia was a super "petropower." Its hard-currency reserves of at least $200 billion in 1980 dwarfed those Japan has now. Yet few talk today of Saudi power, or even influence.

In the late 1970s, the establishment moved on to worrying about American political and military decline. The Soviets had invaded Afghanistan. Iran had grabbed 52 American hostages. Jimmy Carter proclaimed malaise. A humiliated nation tossed him out to bring in Ronald Reagan, with his simple promise to restore American power and prestige.

Now eight years later, with the U.S. having spent $1.8 trillion on defense, having stood down the Soviets in Afghanistan, the micromarxists in Grenada, Col. Gadhafi in Libya and the Iranians in the Strait of Hormuz, many of these same American officials and experts have decided military power is virtually useless, that money is what matters and America doesn't have enough of it.

The syndrome amuses many America-watchers. "I do not believe at all in American decline," says Hubert Vedrine, national security adviser to French President Francois Mitterrand. "Americans adore frightening themselves."

Seizaburo Sato, a Japanese political scientist and adviser to former Prime Minister Nakasone, is even more emphatic. "The 20th century was the American century," he argues. "And the 21st century will be the American century." ■

Suggested Additional Readings

Commission (Pearson) on International Development. *Partners in Development* (New York: Praeger, 1969).

Doran, Charles F. *et al. North/South Relations: Studies of Dependency Reversal* (New York: Praeger, 1983).

Girling, John L. S. *America and the Third World* (London: Routledge and Kegan Paul, 1980).

Hansen, Roger. *Beyond the North-South Stalemate* (New York: McGraw-Hill, 1979).

Harris, Nigel. *The End of the Third World: Newly Industrializing Countries and the Decline of an Ideology* (Middlesex, England: Penguin Books, 1987).

Independent (Brandt) Commission on International Development Issues. *North-South: A Program for Survival* (Cambridge, MA: MIT Press, 1980).

Mortimer, Robert A. *The Third World Coalition in International Politics* (Boulder, CO: Westview Press, 1984).

Rostow, W. W. *Rich Countries and Poor Countries* (Boulder, CO: Westview Press, 1987).

Shulman, Marshall D. *East-West Tensions in the Third World* (New York: Norton, 1986).

Train, Adm. Harry D. *et al. The Relations between Democracy, Development and Security: Implications for Policy* (New York: Global Economic Action Institute, 1989).